THE FRENCH PACIFIC ISLANDS

French Polynesia and New Caledonia

The French Pacific Islands

French Polynesia and New Caledonia

VIRGINIA THOMPSON and RICHARD ADLOFF

1971
Berkeley   Los Angeles   London
UNIVERSITY OF CALIFORNIA PRESS

University of California Press
Berkeley and Los Angeles, California
University of California Press, Ltd.
London, England
Copyright © 1971, by
The Regents of the University of California
Library of Congress Catalog Card Number: 71–138634
International Standard Book Number: 0–520–01843–5
Printed in the United States of America

To
René Gauze

Contents

vii

Introduction

Of the 173 million square kilometers covered by the Pacific Ocean, the land area represented by French Polynesia and New Caledonia together amounts to little more than 23,100 square kilometers, and both territories consist of island groups scattered over a huge region. French Polynesia's five archipelagoes and one hundred and twenty or more islands, with a total surface of 4,000 square kilometers, are dispersed over 4 million square kilometers. New Caledonia, on the other hand, is far larger (19,100 square kilometers) and more compact. Its core, the Grande Terre (16,750 square kilometers), is the second-largest island in the Pacific after New Zealand, and clustered nearby are some 200 islets and one fairly sizeable archipelago, the three Loyalty Islands (barely 2,300 square kilometers). In both territories, one island and its principal town are clearly dominant, not only in size and population but also politically, economically, and culturally. In French Polynesia this outstanding island is Tahiti (1,042 square kilometers), where the capital city of Papeete contains more than half the territory's population. In New Caledonia, an analogous role is played by the Grande Terre and its administrative center, Nouméa.

French Polynesia and New Caledonia comprise high islands and atolls, and both territories are situated slightly north of the Tropic of Capricorn, but they exhibit certain marked physical differences. In the former territory, the high islands are volcanoes composed of basaltic rock and are deeply eroded, and its atolls are coral formations covered by enough soil to permit the growth of coconut palms and shrubs. Their typically tropical hot and humid climate is tempered by the wind and by differences in altitude, and their rainfall is generally heavy despite appreciable regional variations. In contrast to the infertile laterite of the high islands' mountain slopes, the coastal zone and valleys have rich volcanic soil where the vegetation is varied and exuberant and tropical crops can be cultivated. However, the fauna, both indigenous and introduced, are comparatively limited, whereas in the surrounding ocean many species of fish abound. For centuries these islands have been inhabited by the seafaring Maoris, and the Leeward-group island of Raiatea is believed to be the ancient Polynesian religious and cultural center of Havaiki, from which migrations to Hawaii, the Cook Islands, and New Zealand set out.

New Caledonia's Grande Terre, like the high islands of French Polynesia, is very mountainous, heavily eroded, and cut by watercourses which bring alluvial soil to the deep valleys and plains, but its geology, climate, and vegetation are more varied. The salient physical characteristics of the Grande Terre are the contrast between its eastern and western portions and the difficulties of intercommunication between its regions. Nevertheless, all of that island's coasts are accessible from a navigable lagoon inside a surrounding barrier reef, and the Grande Terre as a whole is highly mineral-bearing. Aside from the Isle of Pines and the Belêp archipelago, which are respectively the southern and northern prolongations of the Grande Terre, its other island satellites—of which the Loyaltys are by far the most important—are either small atolls or calcareous plateaus. The climate of New Caledonia is less typically tropical than that of Polynesia, being more tempered by the prevailing trade winds and, on the Grande Terre, by its mountainous configuration. Its seasonal changes are clearer-cut and its rainfall less regular and abundant than is the case in Polynesia, and the whole group is periodically ravaged by cyclones.

The topographic and climatic variations between the two coasts of the Grande Terre are chiefly responsible for their contrasting vegetation. Largely through destructive cultivation practices, forests have been reduced to a small area, mainly on the east coast and on the mountain tops, but the vegetation of the Grande Terre is more varied than that of French Polynesia. Some of its flora consists of ancient and rare plants and trees, and New Caledonia is unique in that 83 percent of its species are not found anywhere else in the world. There are more than thirty species of conifers, three times the number to be found in any other part of the Pacific region. Among these are eight species of araucarias, and the archaic character of much of the indigenous flora is typified by these and by the tough bushes and thorny grasses of the western mountain slopes. Throughout the Grande Terre one finds the niaouli, a variety of gum tree that has become the tree-symbol of New Caledonia. In the forests that still exist on some mountainsides and in part of the east-coast region, there are banyans, acacias, tamanous, kaoris, tree ferns (some 15 meters tall), and many creepers, or lianes. Sandalwood, formerly abundant, is now almost extinct, but the tall columnar pine is still found in the south, especially on the Isle of Pines.

New Caledonia's indigenous fauna, on the other hand, include few useful animals, but among them are species that are archaic and that comprise so many rare specimens that New Caledonia has been called a "museum of living fossils." These include the large snail called *bulime,* which is the main food of another rare species, the *cagou,* a bird that has wings but does not fly. The survival of such creatures is perhaps the most interesting consequence of New Caledonia's isolation, which also has profoundly affected both its native Melanesian population and its European immigrants. No snakes exist on the Grande Terre, the only indigenous mammals are seven varieties of bats, and most of the animals now in the island—cattle, sheep, deer, and dogs—were introduced by the Europeans.

In modern times, the remoteness of New Caledonia and Polynesia from France, as well as from other islands and continental land masses of the Pacific area, has greatly influenced their history and their political and economic development. Because their inhabitants, both indigenous and European, were so long cut off from most contacts with the outside world, their sense of isolation has been only slightly attenuated by recent improvements in the means of communication. New Caledonia's nearest sizeable neighbors are Australia and New Zealand, 1,500 and 1,700 kilometers away; it is 7,000 kilometers from Japan, 10,000 from the west coast of the United States, and 20,000 from France. Tahiti, naturally, is nearer than the Grande Terre to Los Angeles (6,400 kilometers) and Honolulu (4,474 kilometers), but farther from Paris (25,000 kilometers), Sydney (6,000 kilometers), and Tokyo (9,500 kilometers).

Not only are the constituent areas of the two French island territories fragmented by vast stretches of ocean, but they are separated from each other by 5,000 kilometers. Indeed, they belong to two different ethnic and geographic worlds. New Caledonia is situated in the southwest Pacific and its indigenous population are Melanesians, whereas French Polynesia lies in the central-eastern part of that ocean and, as its name suggests, is peopled by another ethnic group. The interest of a comparative study of two such divergent areas is further enhanced by the differences in their political, social, and economic evolution, despite a certain uniformity in the type of government given them by France over approximately the same period of time.

Although they became colonies during the nineteenth-century period of intense rivalry between French and British imperialisms, and were subjected to the same contradictory French policies of centralized authoritarianism, strict economic controls, and universal human brotherhood, French Polynesia and New Caledonia show marked divergencies. In the former territory, a more cohesive and self-conscious native society has retained—despite intensive crossbreeding with Europeans—greater cultural vigor and a sharper political focus than have the Melanesians of New Caledonia. Because the latter island first served as a French penal colony and then attracted free white immigrants by its mineral wealth, the indigenous Melanesians have been retarded in their development by years of geographical and cultural segregation from the dominant French settlers. The Grande Terre's nickel has now made it the most industrialized island in the Pacific and has brought its inhabitants the highest living standards in the area, whereas Tahiti's economic resources are limited almost wholly to its attraction for tourists.

Despite such striking disparities, both island groups have significant common features. Both are administered as Overseas Territories by a governor appointed by the Paris government, whose powers are shared to a very limited degree with a locally elected assembly. The governor of New Caledonia is also high commissioner for the western Pacific, and in that capacity he is responsible for French interests in the New Hebrides condominium and the territory of Wallis and Futuna. Numerically, the populations of New Caledonia and French Polynesia are roughly equal, and both have a strong sense of their own individuality, yet they are also aware of their dependence on France for military defense, cultural guidance, and overall economic support. The tightening of French controls, due to their growing importance to the Gaullist government in recent years, has been resented in both territories, though for different reasons. Nevertheless, because Polynesia has become the site for France's nuclear-weapons tests and New Caledonia's nickel has assumed international importance, the two island groups are experiencing an unprecedented prosperity at the same time as a curtailment of such political privileges as they previously enjoyed.

This situation is not only anomalous but also anachronistic, in view of the rapidity with which many other Pacific islands with far smaller resources and European populations are moving toward autonomy, if not independence. France clearly intends to keep New Caledonia and French Polynesia, the most distant remnants of its once far-flung empire, as Gallic outposts in an area dominated by Great Britain and the United States. Although in those territories the autonomy movement is fast gathering strength, their inhabitants are conscious of their weakness and still deeply attached to France emotionally and culturally, hence their demand for self-government has stopped short of insisting on independence.

As yet, no full account of current political, economic, and social developments in either territory exists, although the abundance of literature about their other aspects is impressive, considering their remoteness and the small size of their area and populations. Of the two island groups, French Polynesia has provided the greater stimulus to anthropologists, archeologists, and writers of fiction and travel narratives. New Caledonia, on the other hand, has been the object of research by a few geologists and sociologists and the theme of reminiscent accounts by veterans of the Pacific war who saw service there. The neglect of the two territories' contemporary evolution by historians can be explained to some extent by the slight importance of these islands when they are viewed in a global context. Nevertheless, they merit study as microcosms of heterogeneous and long-isolated peoples who only recently have been compelled to participate in world events. The French islands' isolation from their neighbors in all but small-scale commercial exchanges has thus far largely immunized them from the contagion of extreme nationalism, but it is unlikely that New Caledonia and French Polynesia can much longer remain aloof from the mainstream of events elsewhere in the Pacific Ocean.

The aim of this book is to examine the phenomena responsible for the French islands' present transitional situation and to indicate the problems that their inhabitants will inevitably face when and if the islands' status is changed from a quasi-colonial to a sovereign one. In the course of their research preparatory to such an analysis, the writers interviewed a considerable number of Polynesians, Melanesians, and Europeans during a field trip to the islands in 1965. To many officials, politicians, businessmen, scholars, and religious leaders, only a few of whom have been mentioned by name, we are deeply indebted for much helpful information and generous hospitality.

DECEMBER 1970.

Part I
FRENCH POLYNESIA

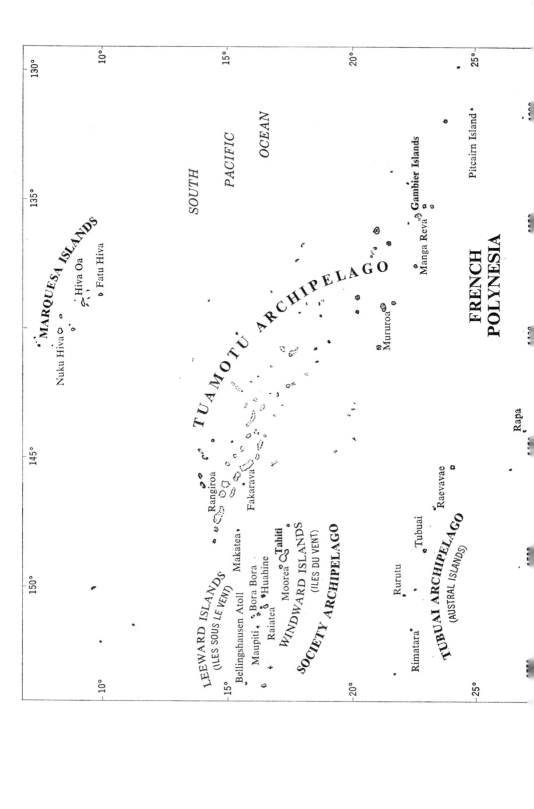

1

Land and History

French Polynesia comprises some one hundred and twenty islands, of which slightly over half are inhabited, situated in the south Pacific Ocean about midway between Australia and the west coast of South America. Although the islands are scattered over an immense region, 2,500 by 3,000 kilometers in extent, the land area totals only about 4,000 square kilometers and is made up of islands varying widely in topography and dimensions. Of these, Tahiti—the most important in every respect—covers approximately one-quarter of the total land area.

On the basis of its physical features, the territory may be divided into two main groups. One of these consists of the volcanic archipelagoes of the Society Islands (the Windward and Leeward groups), the Marquesas, almost all the Gambiers or Mangarevas, and the Austral or Tubuai Islands. In the other group are the atolls of the Tuamotu-Gambier group and Clipperton. The volcanoes are extinct, erosion has cut deep valleys among the rocky plateaus and peaks of the mountainous islands, and the population is concentrated on a narrow coastal band. Most of the volcanic islands and atolls are encircled by a coral reef, through which, in some cases, narrow passes lead into the lagoons. There are no rivers or streams on the atolls, and though watercourses are numerous on the volcanic islands, they normally flow there only after heavy rains.

Because French Polynesia extends over so immense an area, the climate varies widely from one archipelago to another. The Marquesas have a typically equatorial climate, whereas the Gambiers and Australs enjoy almost a temperate one. Variations on the same island are due largely to differences in exposure to winds and in altitude. The cyclone season extends from December through March, and it is during those months that 72 percent of the annual rainfall occurs.

French Polynesia's geographical configuration has greatly influenced the territory's economy and has also affected its political evolution. The dispersion and isolation of the islands, as well as their great distance from France, have accentuated the importance of the means of communication and made difficult both their economic planning and their governance. This handicap, however, also allowed French Polynesia to evolve largely in its own fashion and thus to preserve its cultural and social characteristics to a greater degree than other more accessible places in the Pacific, such as Hawaii.

Scholars and scientists have long and inconclusively debated the origins of the Polynesians. On the basis of indigenous flora and fauna, introduced cultivated plants, local oral traditions, and physical, linguistic, and cultural characteristics, some have concluded that the Polynesians originated in southeast Asia, whereas others believe they came from the Americas. There is general agreement, however, that their migrations began centuries ago, and that one main Pacific center from which they radiated was Raiatea Island in what is now French Polynesia.[1] Overpopulation, food shortages, and internal conflicts probably caused the successive displacements of these venturesome seafaring people. Whatever their origin, their physical characteristics were similar and they gradually evolved into a group having closely related languages and religious practices. Virtually isolated from the rest of the world, they developed highly hierarchized societies and their economies were based on agriculture and fishing.

Although Europeans began visiting what is now French Polynesia in the late sixteenth century, only fragmentary and unreliable information about the numbers and distribution of its indigenous population was recorded until some years after France established its protectorate over them. Successive censuses taken by the French administration showed a marked decline in the number of Polynesians living there during the late nineteenth and early twentieth centuries. The sharp reversal of that trend during the period between the First and Second World Wars is certainly the outstanding phenomenon of French Polynesia's contemporary history. Furthermore, since World War II the population has been increasing even more rapidly in all the archipelagoes except the Tuamotu-Gambiers. This has been due to a decline in the mortality rate rather than to an increase in the number of live births, and the shift in the population's distribution can be attributed almost wholly to internal migrations rather than to large-scale

---

[1] For basic information in this chapter, the authors are indebted to works by H. Deschamps, J.-P. Faivre, J. C. Furnas, J. Guiart, A. Huetz de Lemps, C. A. Julien, G. Kling, P. O'Reilly, C. Robequain, R. L. Stevenson, R. Teissier, C. Vernier, and F. J. West. See bibliography.

immigration. Tahiti, and especially Papeete, have grown to the point where they contain more than half the total population of French Polynesia. In all the islands, the recent spectacular rise in population has been characterized by an increase in the proportion of women to men, of children to adults, and of half-castes or *demis* to the pure-blooded Polynesian component.

For many years, Western observers and the Polynesians themselves assumed that the native population of the islands was doomed, sooner rather than later, to extinction. Its numerical decline was unmistakable over a period of about seventy-five years, but was probably somewhat misleading because the population estimates of the early European navigators were too often taken at their face value. At the end of the eighteenth century, Captain Cook surmised that Tahiti then had 240,000 inhabitants and the Marquesas 70,000, but neither he nor other explorers of that era visited all the islands, and they saw little beyond the coastal villages of those that they discovered. The early English missionaries, who stayed longer and came to know the islands far better, were more realistic in their appraisals. In 1828 they concluded that the Polynesian population of Tahiti was 8,658, a figure almost exactly confirmed by the first French census in 1848. Although the censuses sporadically taken during the latter half of the nineteenth century were both incomplete and unreliable, there is little doubt but that the number of Polynesians, and especially of Marquesans, was shrinking.

This fall in population was attributed to the decimation wrought by new diseases brought to the islanders by foreigners, such as measles, tuberculosis, influenza, and syphilis, as well as to the introduction of opium and of alcoholic beverages. A less tangible but deeper-rooted cause of the demographic decrease was probably the psychological reactions to the social and economic innovations introduced by the newcomers. Robert Louis Stevenson, who spent some months in the Marquesas during the 1880s, graphically described the resigned acceptance by its inhabitants of their imminent extinction and wrote of their proneness to suicide, infanticide, abortion, and cannibalism. He felt that they suffered from a "disease of the will rather than of the body," and that this was caused by their inability to withstand the cultural shock to their traditions and socioeconomic order.

Where there have been fewest changes, important or unimportant, salutary or hurtful, there the race survives. Where there have been most . . . there it perishes. Each change, however small, augments the sum of new conditions to which the race has to become inured. There may seem, *a priori*, no comparison between the change from "sour toddy" to bad gin, and that from the island kilt to a pair of European trousers. Yet I am far from persuaded that the one is any more hurtful than the other; and the unaccustomed race will sometimes die of pin-pricks.[2]

On the other hand, Stevenson found the Tuamotuans less attractive than the Marquesans but better equipped physically and psychologically by the harsh conditions of life in the "Dangerous Archipelago" to cope with change. During the next half-century, his prediction proved to be accurate, for the number of Marquesans continued to dwindle while that of the other islanders slowly began to increase. It was not until 1926, when there were only 2,255 Marquesan survivors, that the trend in that archipelago was reversed. Gradually, everywhere throughout the islands, improvements in the health service and the means of communication, as well as the injection of new blood strains by European and Chinese immigrants, resulted in an upward demographic trend. Indeed, the islanders have even acquired a marked taste for the new conditions of life which they formerly rejected.

According to tradition, the ancient Polynesians were divided into four main social groups: princes and chiefs (*arii*) held to be of divine origin, nobles and bourgeois (*iliaotai* and *raatiraa*), commoners (*manahune*), and slaves and servitors (*ofeofe* and *teuteu*). Of great political and religious significance were the genealogies of the clan and its chiefs, whose perpetuation was entrusted to priests. Rites were celebrated at open-air temples (*marae*), where the main cult was that of the god Oro. Tabus proclaimed by the priests and hereditary chiefs became the main instruments of their power, which rested only secondarily on physical force.

Some of the islands were united under a single chief and were divided into districts, each headed by a sub-chief. Certain chiefs gained control over neighboring islands, which thus became minor fiefs administered by appointees of lesser rank. Commoners formed the largest element of the population of Tahiti and the other Windward Islands (Moorea, Makatea, and Maio), and they were governed by princes or high-ranking chiefs. Much the same pattern of rule prevailed on the nearby Leeward Islands (Huahine, Raiatea, Tahaa, Bora Bora, and Maupiti), and together they formed what became known as the Society Islands, a name given them by Captain James Cook in honor of the Royal Society of London, which sponsored his voyages.

[2] Stevenson, R. L., *In the South Seas*, p. 46.

The visible exercise of a chief's power lay in his distribution of the produce from agriculture and fishing to which his rank entitled him. Yet his authority, which rested on a religious and hereditary base, was more paternalistic than absolute. Specifically, it was tempered by a council composed of sub-chiefs, whose consent was required for important policy decisions.

The European penetration began in the late eighteenth century. The Polynesians had been psychologically prepared for this event by a legendary prophecy of the arrival by sea of foreigners who would conquer the islands and destroy their idols. Spanish, Dutch, English, French, and American navigators visited Polynesia in increasing numbers over a period of three centuries. Among those who contributed most to the Western world's knowledge of these islands were Wallis, Bougainville, and, above all, Cook in the late eighteenth century. During three successive voyages (1769–1777), Cook discovered the Leeward Islands, two of the Australs, explored the Marquesas, and anchored at Moorea, where an exceptionally beautiful bay still bears his name. He mapped the area and described at length Tahiti, where he made friends with many of the chiefs, notably Tu, prince of Papeete, who later took the name of King Pomaré I. Ambitious, clever, and persevering, Pomaré succeeded in dominating the other Tahitian chiefs, making Moorea a vassal island, and annexing Mahetia. In this he was aided by some Europeans, among them the famous mutineers of the ship *Bounty*, who brought in firearms and taught his people to use them. It was the English Protestant missionaries, however, who most aided Pomaré to consolidate his power.

On March 7, 1796, the first eighteen pastors sent by the London Missionary Society (L.M.S.) landed on Tahiti and were welcomed by Pomaré with a gift of land. Their arrival coincided with the victories that gave Pomaré control over Tahiti and some neighboring islands. Despite, and perhaps in part because of, the support given them by Pomaré, the English missionaries had so much difficulty in converting the islanders that it took twenty years to complete their Christianization. The greatest handicaps encountered by the missionaries were the indifference of the Polynesians to their preaching, the disorderly and amoral behavior of many of the European residents or transients, a recrudescence of paganism, and the coming of French Catholic missionaries.

Because of their prestige, their disconcerting behavior, and the foreign merchandise that they imported, the European adventurers and traders modified the economy and undermined the traditional order based on hereditary rank and religious sanction. Yet it was the missionaries who, by their determined efforts to "reform" the Polynesians, were most responsible for the disintegration of native society and who aroused the determined opposition of the traditionalists. The first Europeans who came to the islands were both charmed and repelled by what they saw there. Bougainville was so delighted by these insular Gardens of Eden and their easy-going and attractive inhabitants that he called their archipelago the New Cytherea. The early explorers also admired the seamanship of the Polynesians, the extensive irrigation work they had carried out on some islands, and the stone bridges they had built in certain places. Nevertheless, they noted with distaste the seamy side of native life—human sacrifices, slaughtering of war prisoners, cannibalism, and infanticide. Most shocking of all to the missionary pioneers was the "amorality" of the Polynesians, and the men of God felt that they must take drastic steps to eradicate sin from this "seat of Satan." Through the establishing of schools, but far more through the cooperation and finally the conversion of King Pomaré II in 1818, the English Protestants ultimately triumphed, though not without violence and setbacks.

Pomaré II's despotic ways, as well as his protection of the missionaries, aroused the hostility of rival chiefs. They were decisively defeated in battle in 1815, and after the king was baptized four years later, all Tahiti came under the sway of Christianity. In the same year that he was formally converted, the king promulgated a missionary-inspired law code that forbade polygamy, adultery, human sacrifice, and infanticide, and also compelled observance of the Sabbath. The Leeward Islands were likewise Christianized after the conversion of the prince of Raiatea, and Pomaré extended his suzerainty over them. The western Tuamotus, which had been conquered by Pomaré I, accepted Christianity after missionaries went there, and in 1825 the same pattern was repeated in the Austral Islands. Only the cannibalistic Marquesans resisted mass conversion. The politico-religious triumph of the king and the missionaries reached its apogee in 1821, at which time, ironically, the king died as the result of alcoholism.

Because the Christianization of the Society Islanders stemmed from the conversion of their chiefs, a radical change in the attitude of the reigning sovereigns could and did jeopardize the missionaries' authority. Thanks to the influence they acquired over Queen Pomaré IV, two of the most aggressive English missionaries—Pritchard and Ellis—

in 1836 succeeded in preventing two French Catholic missionaries from gaining a foothold in Tahiti and stopped a traditionalist sect, the Mamaia, from revolting against their domination. They were unsuccessful, however, in their attempt, by stirring up public opinion in Britain against French encroachments in the island, to persuade the British government to establish a protectorate there. By a show of armed force, France was able to assert its ascendancy over the queen, and then quelled a rebellion by her subjects in 1844–1846. The next year, the French government negotiated Great Britain's recognition of a French protectorate over Tahiti, Moorea, the Tuamotus, and two of the Austral Islands. The L.M.S., now realizing the futility of further resisting the determination of France to eliminate the influence of British missionaries in Tahiti, turned over its work there to the French Société des Missions Evangéliques in 1862.

The death of Queen Pomaré IV in 1877 ended a half-century reign that had brought momentous developments in her realm. Two years later her childless son, Pomaré V, ceded his kingdom to France in return for the retention of his title, the right to grant amnesty, a pension, and a French pledge to respect Tahitian laws and customs. Soon afterwards, French citizenship was conferred on all his former subjects. This status was not extended to the Marquesas, which had been taken over by France in 1842, nor to the other islands that eventually became part of the new colony called the Etablissements Français de l'Océanie (E.F.O.). As independent units for some years, the Leeward Islands underwent many internal struggles, and their annexation by France in 1888 was the result of German infiltration there from Samoa. Beginning in 1878, German overtures to the Leeward Islands chiefs so alarmed both the British and French governments that they decided to reconcile their differences in the area. In exchange for France's renunciation of a military occupation of the New Hebrides, Britain agreed to let the French take possession of the Leeward Islands. Once more, however, a settlement reached by these two Western powers was not wholeheartedly accepted by the local chiefs, and a revolt by the prince of Raiatea was dealt with by a short punitive military expedition.

Again it was the threat of German influence in the Austral Islands, only two of which had passed under French control along with Tahiti, that led first to a protectorate over them and then to their annexation by France in 1900. Similarly, the protectorates established over the Gambiers and Rapa were followed by outright annexation, respectively in 1881 and 1901. Clipperton Island, taken over by France in 1858, had been forgotten from the time its guano deposit was exhausted until Mexico laid claim to it in 1908. The dispute over this claim was submitted to the King of Italy for arbitration, but it was not until 1931 that he finally awarded Clipperton to France.

In this piecemeal fashion the islands were assembled as a colony. The conflicts about their ownership were chiefly the result of persistent hostility between Protestant and Catholic missionaries bent not only on converting the islanders to their respective creeds but also on establishing theocratic states, by force if necessary. Pritchard in Tahiti and Father Laval in the Gambiers succeeded in permanently converting the local chiefs to Christianity and in temporarily imposing a strict puritanical regime on them and their subjects. When the missionaries' control was later threatened by revolts or by rivals, they did not hesitate to demand the support of their respective governments, whose imperialistic ambitions were beginning to clash in much of Asia and Africa. In Madagascar, notably, the same scenario as in the E.F.O. was reenacted with, curiously enough, one of the same leading protagonists—the English missionary, William Ellis. In both Madagascar and Polynesia, it was the traditionalist leaders who instigated the few ineffective revolts against foreign rule, for their subjects docilely followed their customary chiefs in both religious and political changes.

Despite the islands' lack of economic resources and the small land area involved, acquisition of the E.F.O. was pursued with a remarkable degree of perseverance on the part of successive French governments. Winning the islanders to Catholicism played a more important role in the motivation of the Second Empire than it did, perhaps, in that of the July monarchy and certainly that of the Third Republic. The French in Polynesia and elsewhere used missionaries as the precursors and instruments of empire-building far more than did the British, but the conflict over possession of the Pacific islands antedated by some years the major struggle between them for colonies. In the mid-nineteenth century, France had far smaller trading interests in the E.F.O. than either Great Britain or the United States, and the colony's economic potential was limited. Furthermore, France failed to acquire control of the Polynesian-inhabited Cook and Easter islands, which ethnically belonged to the E.F.O. group. Yet the natural beauty of Tahiti and its dependencies attracted artists and writers who created there a legendary paradise which to this day brings to those islands many Western visitors and residents. The glamor that has grown around Tahiti has created a tourist "industry" which may serve to compensate in part for the lack of more basic economic assets.

During the latter half of the nineteenth century, especially after France established an orderly unitary government in the E.F.O., Westerners and Chinese came in increasing numbers to live and trade there. These factors accelerated the dissolution of the traditional political, social, and economic order. The chieftaincies and tabus founded on indigenous custom and religion, already undermined by the wholesale Christianization of the population, soon vanished, leaving few traces, and they were largely replaced by French political and economic institutions and cultural values. Extensive intermarriage between the newcomers and the Polynesians created a growing class of half-castes, locally called *demis*, who became predominant in the administration and the economy of the E.F.O.

Although the French had taken possession of the E.F.O. in order to acquire ports in the Pacific, they considered the colony's value for mercantile shipping greater than its strategic importance for the few French naval ships maintained in that ocean. When World War I began, therefore, the garrison stationed in Tahiti numbered only 300 men, the great majority of whom were reservists.

On September 22, 1914, two German warships commanded by Admiral von Spee steamed into Papeete's harbor and bombarded the town. This attack killed one Polynesian and one Chinese and caused material damage estimated at one million francs. The consequences for Tahiti might have been far worse if the local commander had not previously destroyed the buoys marking the pass into the harbor and its stocks of coal, and if he had not also threatened to execute the 40 German crewmen from a freighter captured by the French a few days before, who were being held as hostages.[3] Soon the German ships departed and went to the Marquesas to procure meat supplies, for which they thoughtfully paid the francs they seized from the treasury there.

This short but dramatic episode was followed by two more far-reaching wartime developments, of which the first was the military conscription of all eligible local French citizens. Together with 1,200 volunteers they made up the Tahitian contingent of a Pacific Battalion that fought in France and Salonika and suffered 262 casualties. Rejoicing over the armistice of November 11, 1918, was cut short by an

[3] *L'Océanie Française,* August 1916.

epidemic of Spanish influenza which was far more devastating to the islanders.[4] More than 500 of Papeete's 3,000 inhabitants died, and the districts were also decimated. The colony's very small health service could not cope adequately with the crisis. The governor, Gustave Julien, was severely criticized in the local press for indifference to the people's suffering, although in the preceding years he had done much for their social development. Senator Coppenrath has pointed out that the impression left by this disaster was so deep that for many years thereafter, Tahitians referred to the major events of their lives as having occurred before, during, or after the great epidemic.

[4] Coppenrath, G., "Evolution Politique de la Polynésie Française depuis la Première Guerre Mondiale."

2

The Colonial Administration and the Settlers

The perennial conflict between the local administration and the settlers, which continues to this day, began soon after the naval government of the islands was replaced by a civilian regime in 1883. Two years later, the organic decree of December 28, 1885, gave the E.F.O. a legal framework which was the nearest thing to a constitution that it ever received. However, the way in which this decree was interpreted by the French authorities in Paris and Papeete only served to increase the tension between the two opposing local forces.

As the representative of the President of the French Republic, the governor of the E.F.O. was commander of its armed forces and undisputed head of the local administration. Assisting him were the five officials in charge of the services of the interior, the judiciary, the military, health, and finances, who formed his privy council. The instability characterizing the tenure of office of those officials, as well as their steadily growing authority, were the main causes of the settlers' frequently expressed discontent with the local administration. During the thirty-two years preceding World War I, the colony had no fewer than twenty-four titular or acting governors, and the top civil servants were replaced with equal frequency. Appeals from the French settlers for a greater continuity of policy and for a minimal five-year assignment for the men charged with its execution went unheeded by Paris [1] until the interwar period brought a somewhat greater gubernatorial stability.

Initially the governor's wide powers were slightly held in check by those of an eighteen-member elected general council, set up by the 1885 decree. He was required to consult the council on specific subjects, and its members had a limited control over budgetary revenues and expenditures. Briefly, during the Protectorate, Tahiti had had an assembly elected by the landowners; its president was Tati, the great chief of Papara, whose support for the French and opposition to the

[1] *L'Océanie Française,* March 1913.

Mamaia and other anarchic elements of that period had been of considerable importance.

Under the French civilian administration, six of the councilors were elected from Tahiti and Moorea, four from Papeete, four from the Tuamotus, and two each from the Gambiers and the Australs. Theoretically, the native French citizens of the Society Islands were eligible as councilors, but in practice the language requirement—ability to speak French—eliminated them. Furthermore, the lack of qualified candidates in the outer islands and the difficulties of transportation meant that their representatives were chosen from among Papeete's residents, thus further weighting the council in favor of Tahiti. Soon the councilors were criticized for representing only a very restricted electorate and for voting funds almost wholly to the benefit of the Tahiti settlers and to the detriment of the outer-islanders, who nevertheless contributed about half of the revenues. The airing of personal feuds among the councilors and their running up of a sizeable public debt, as well as their vociferous demands for greater financial autonomy, provided the governor—who was resentful of the restrictions they imposed on his authority—with an excuse to solicit Paris for suppression of the council. A first step in that direction was taken in two decrees of August 10, 1899. These eliminated from the council representatives from the Marquesas, Tuamotus, Gambiers, Tubuai and Rapa, which were made separate administrative units each with its own budget and council. Within four years this half-measure came to be regarded as insufficient, and on March 19, 1903, the general council was totally eliminated and was replaced by a *conseil d'administration consultatif*. At about the same time, the governor extended his powers over the district administration.

Being a purely administrative body able only to advise the governor on the budget, the new council enjoyed none of the powers of its predecessor. For the twenty-seven years of its existence, it was composed of only seven members: the governor as chairman, the secretary-general, the heads of two administrative services, the mayor of Papeete, and the presidents of the Chambers of Commerce and of Agriculture. Obviously it was almost wholly unrepresentative of the 10,000 French citizens, not to mention the 20,000 French subjects, living in the E.F.O. at the time it was constituted. The only opportunity open to the colony's 4,500 registered electors to make their voice heard in Paris was to choose a representative to the advisory Conseil Supérieur des Colonies. Moreover, thanks to the pressure applied by the local administration to a large portion of the electorate —the civil servants and the military—that representative was always a politician with influential connections in Paris and invariably one who had never set foot in the E.F.O.

During the years immediately after World War I, the demand for changes in the local administration and for a more effective representation of the settlers' interests was aggravated by the depression of the early 1920s. Governor Auguste Guédès, who arrived at Papeete in April 1921, was disagreeably surprised to find a public debt amounting to 951,000 francs and a population actively hostile to his proposal to meet the deficit by retroactive taxes on business transactions and imports. The Chamber of Commerce opposed the measure, a mass demonstration of protest was organized, and a Committee for the Defense of Taxpayers was formed under the leadership of Constant Deflesselle, owner of the virulently antiadministration newspaper, *L'Echo de Tahiti*.[2] The demonstrators of August 31, 1921, were restrained by the army, but the governor agreed to receive a delegation to express their grievances. While he satisfied the traders by immediately suppressing the proposed taxes, he so angered the civil servants by also agreeing to the demonstrators' demand for reducing the bureaucracy's emoluments and numbers that the civil servants protested effectively to Paris. Guédès' recall a few months later for "weakness in the exercise of his authority" was a victory for both the French residents and the bureaucracy, and it laid the foundation for troubles in the years that followed. It convinced the residents that mass demonstrations were an effective technique of protest, and the bureaucrats learned that they could appeal to the Paris authorities over the head of the governor.

From that period dated the local insistence that the E.F.O. be represented, as the *anciennes colonies* had long been, by a deputy in Paris, but it was not until 1946 that this demand was satisfied. Throughout the interwar period, the French government continued to claim that a strong administration was necessary in a colony so distant from the Metropole and so vulnerable to alien influences. As to the civil service of the E.F.O., it was true that most of the technical departments were inadequately staffed. The Education Service had no director at all, the Judicial Service included no career magistrates, the expert sent to head the Survey Department could not operate for lack

[2] Coppenrath, G., "Evolution Politique de la Polynésie Française depuis la Première Guerre Mondiale"; see also p. 225.

of personnel, and an Agriculture Service was yet to be organized.[3] Paris claimed, however, that these were simply transitory conditions, resulting from the decimation of qualified French manpower resources during World War I. The net result of these charges and counter-charges was an increase in the number of French officials in the E.F.O. during the interwar years and no real decrease in the powers of its governor. The Minister of Colonies opposed a reconstitution of the general council, and he concurred in the view expressed in December 1922 by Governor Louis Rivet that as yet there was only a handful of persons in the colony qualified to grasp the questions of vital concern to it.[4] Although Rivet did much for the socioeconomic development of the E.F.O., the overall administrative system under which he operated remained unpopular with the local French residents. Nevertheless, the middle and late 1920s were years of relative prosperity for the colony, and it was only the presence of an increasing number of Asian residents that agitated public opinion during that period.

THE ADMINISTRATIVE STRUCTURE OF THE DISTRICTS AND OUTER ISLANDS

Traditionally, district chiefs and councilors were chosen from among certain noble families, but a decree of December 21, 1897, gave the governor authority to confirm them in office and to dismiss them at will. This law transformed them into unsalaried functionaries responsible for tax collection and the execution of public works. Even before this practice was formalized, R. L. Stevenson, who visited the Marquesas in 1888, noted that the chiefs there had lost their prestige among the people and as agents of the central government were fast "revolting public sentiment." [5]

This process was accelerated by a law of 1900 which permitted the presidents of district councils, who functioned as mayors of rural communes, to be chosen from outside the council's membership. District councils were made up of seven members elected for a four-year term from lists of candidates drawn up by the local administrator. The great majority of the councils operated ineffectively because few of their members understood French and even fewer were competent to handle the small funds placed at their disposal. Furthermore,

---

[3] *L'Océanie Française,* January–March 1920.
[4] Coppenrath, "Evolution Politique."
[5] Stevenson, R. L., *In the South Seas,* p. 51.

"there were conflicts of authority between the appointed chiefs, who were presidents of the district councils, the gendarmes, and the pastors of the Tahitian church," [6] the last-mentioned of whom enjoyed great influence as the repositories of Polynesian culture. The only genuine local government institution in all the E.F.O. at that time was the municipal council of Papeete, created in 1890 when the capital had only 1,500 inhabitants. The mayor, his two deputies, and the council's twelve other members were freely elected, had real authority over urban affairs, and possessed some financial autonomy. It was not until December 1931 that a second municipal commission, with a partly elected membership, was created for Uturoa, capital of the Leeward Islands.

In the outer islands, many of the functions that had been performed by district councils under the Protectorate were handed over to the *gendarmerie* in 1877. Thereafter the gendarme, assisted by native policemen (*mutoi*), was called upon to supervise road maintenance, tax collection, and the registration of vital statistics and land transfers, without having received any specialized training. In some areas, the gendarme was also expected to act as notary, clerk of the court, and agent of the post and telegraph service. Some performed such multiple administrative tasks with competence, but most of the gendarmes lived in isolated places and worked without adequate supervision, and thus were tempted to assume dictatorial powers. Theoretically they were responsible to the chief administrator of their island group, but he too was weighed down by many and varied duties. To economize personnel and money, medical doctors were appointed to administer the outer-island archipelagoes and to preside over their advisory councils, except on the Leeward Islands, where the health and administrative services were separated. A timid move toward decentralization was made in 1930–1931, when advisory councils were appointed in the Marquesas and Tuamotus. This did not, however, alter the overall situation, and the outer islands continued to be woefully understaffed and infrequently controlled by the central government, whereas there was a plethora of civil servants concentrated in Papeete.

In June 1929 the mayor of Papeete and the presidents of the two Chambers there presented a memorandum to M. Moretti, Inspector of Colonies, then visiting Tahiti, in which they urged a revision of the administrative structure. The thesis of this memorandum was that the existing malaise between the people and the government could be dis-

[6] West, F. J., *Political Advancement in the South Pacific*, p. 84.

sipated only by giving the French citizens the right to decide the rate, assessment, and division of taxation. Naturally the governor, whom Moretti consulted about these proposals, reacted adversely to sharing his powers, claiming that such an electorate would use any financial autonomy to stir up further public hostility to the administration. Undiscouraged by this setback, the same petitioners submitted an identical plea to another visiting Inspector of Colonies, and this time their efforts bore fruit.

On October 1, 1932, after a vain attempt to satisfy public opinion by slightly expanding the membership and attributes of the Administrative Council, the government created a wholly new body, the Délégations Economiques et Financières. The Délégations were composed of ten officials—seven elected members and three appointed native Notables—and the subjects on which they must be consulted were increased. The delegates' main task, like that of the now defunct Administrative Council, was to advise on the budget, whose revenues had been seriously reduced by the economic depression. But because the elected delegates insisted that the deficit could be met only by reducing the number of Metropolitan officials serving in the E.F.O., whose number had tripled since World War I, and because they sought the elimination of civil servants from the Délégations and more than advisory powers, the new organization was no more successful than its predecessor in enlisting public cooperation with the administration. The governor was accused of acting like a petty tyrant after he had had a Polynesian arrested for failing to salute him and had forbidden the Tahitians to sing in the streets of Papeete after 9 p.m.[7] In the wake of a series of incidents during the Délégations' meeting of September 1934, the elected members withdrew and the budget was voted by the civil servants.

Throughout the rest of the decade, the Délégations, with their official majority, continued to function, and power remained wholly in the hands of the administration. The governor still combined executive with legislative powers, and a decree of August 22, 1928, also gave him control over the colony's magistrates. He was aided only by his privy council, and it was the governor who drafted decrees, assessed taxes, and ignored the rights of the 25,000 French citizens under his jurisdiction.

The popularity of the administration was not enhanced by the in-

---

[7] *L'Océanie Française,* November–December 1934.

volvement of high officials in the Kong Ah bankruptcy of 1933,[8] and in a local scandal known as the Affaire Rougier.[9] The bankruptcy affected prominent members of the Chinese community and a struggle for control of the copra trade, and the Rougier Affair was complicated by widespread resentment against freemasonry and the Popular Front government in France. An appeal to the Minister of Colonies by some civil servants, after Governor Montagne had dismissed the head of the judicial service for insubordination, led to the governor's recall in May 1935. He was replaced as governor by Chastenet de Géry, sent from Paris to apply oil to the troubled waters of Tahiti. Actually, however, the waters of the E.F.O. were troubled during the interwar period by only a very small segment of its population, largely by the French citizens living in Papeete. Their main grievance, especially during the world economic depression, was the numbers, salaries, and fringe benefits of the Metropolitan civil servants—often the friends or relatives of the incumbent governor. It was claimed specifically that they constituted an unduly heavy financial burden for the taxpayers, who numbered only about one-fourth of the colony's 40,000 inhabitants. The latter's vociferous demands over many years were reinforced in the minds of the French-reading public by criticisms made during the interwar years about the Metropolitan civil servants in books written by such famous Frenchmen as Paul Gauguin and Alain Gerbault. Thus by 1939 the ground had been prepared both in France and in the colony for significant changes, but it took the impact of World War II to bring greater administrative and financial autonomy to the E.F.O.

[8] See pp. 100–101, 146, 186n.
[9] For details, see Coppenrath, "Evolution Politique."

3

World War II and the Postwar Reforms

The impact of World War II on the E.F.O. was quite different from that of World War I. The reaction there to the French defeat and the Franco-German armistice of June 1940 was one of shocked bewilderment. By and large, the native inhabitants, to whom the war seemed remote, remained indifferent, although some chiefs and Notables expressed their sympathy and their desire to continue fighting on the side of the British. The French residents who heard the appeal of June 18 by Charles de Gaulle were divided in their reactions. That officer was unknown to them, whereas Marshal Pétain was a famous and respected figure. Their attitudes were dictated by the differences, both personal and political, that had long divided them. Cut off from direct communication with the Metropole, they listened avidly both to Radio Saigon, which preached allegiance to the Vichy regime, and to the B.B.C., which urged the French of the Pacific to join forces with Britain. Governor Chastenet de Géry, torn by conflicting emotions, resorted to *attentisme,* as did many of his compatriots.

In July 1940, however, a group led by Dr. Emile de Curton, administrator of the Leeward Islands, M. Senac, his counterpart in the Tuamotus, Georges Bambridge, mayor of Papeete, and Edouard Ahne, principal of the Tahiti Protestant School, formed a *Comité de Gaulle.* They persuaded the hesitant governor to hold a referendum on September 2, on the issue of whether or not the E.F.O. should rally to Free France. According to Dr. de Curton,[1] 5,564 votes were cast in favor of joining the Gaullist forces, and only 18 against it. Fortified by this overwhelming mandate and the cooperation of the Délégations Economiques et Financières, as well as that of the crew of a French ship then anchored at Papeete, the committee compelled the governor to resign the next day. A proclamation of loyalty to Free France was drawn up, and about a thousand volunteers declared themselves ready to create a new Pacific battalion and to fight alongside the

[1] Curton, E. de, *Tahiti: Terre Française Combattante,* pp. 70–94.

British.[2] A week later an English warship appeared at Papeete, bringing an offer of support to the local Free French from neighboring British territories, but its presence there caused the Vichy radio to claim that the E.F.O. French had been forced into siding with De Gaulle. In fact, the colony's French community continued to be divided as to its loyalties, with many officers and some high officials opting for Marshal Pétain. On September 18 the pro-Pétain element tried to stage a coup d'état, but it failed, and a few weeks later, on November 3, 1940, General de Gaulle named Dr. de Curton governor of the E.F.O.

The energetic doctor was now able to give free rein to his personal and political animosities, and he did not hesitate to carry out a wholesale purge of his adversaries. A few native Notables were arrested, but it was mainly on the local French doctors and magistrates that the new governor's wrath fell. According to one authority, the Papeete prison became so overcrowded with argumentative Frenchmen that it was the liveliest place in town.[3] This spectacle is said to have delighted the Polynesians, who are easily amused. Deprivation of the services of the doctors, in whom they had never had much faith, left them indifferent, but the dearth of judges and lawyers checked, at least temporarily, their propensities for litigation. Some of the prisoners had to be transferred to the islands of Motuuta and Maupiti, where they "seceded" from the E.F.O. and prepared for the arrival of Vichy warships.[4] Then, suddenly, another administrative shake-up took place, and the prisoners were released and returned to their homes.

This new situation was due to the unheralded arrival in Papeete of Inspector-general Brunot, sent by De Gaulle to report on the confused state of things in Tahiti. Dr. de Curton resented Brunot's presence and activities, and on the first anniversary of De Gaulle's appeal cabled a protest to the general in London. Brunot, however, like De Curton before him, assumed a dictatorial attitude, declared himself to be governor of the colony, and conducted his own purge, not only of the pro-Vichy elements but also of the leaders of the Gaullist committee. These developments, which included a quarrel with the local British consul, were duly reported to De Gaulle, who then took action. On July 9, 1941, he named as High Commissioner for the

---

[2] Grandchamp, R., "Les Etablissements Français de l'Océanie," *Revue Militaire d'Information*, Paris, October 1956.

[3] Reverzy, J., *Le Passage*, Paris, 1954, p. 26.

[4] Loursin, J.–M., *Tahiti*, p. 57.

French Pacific islands Thierry d'Argenlieu, a naval officer and former Carmelite monk, who arrived in the E.F.O. two months later. D'Argenlieu stayed only long enough to appoint a member of his entourage, Georges Orselli, governor of the colony on October 1. Orselli deported all the troublemakers, including Brunot, De Curton, and Senac, and by governing with an iron hand succeeded in restoring order in Tahiti.

Under Orselli's governorship, which lasted until 1945, Tahiti regained its stability and even made contributions to the war effort. Not only did the E.F.O. raise money for the Free French, but by increasing the production of copra and phosphates it helped to offset the Allies' shortage of these commodities that had resulted from the Japanese conquests of other sources of supply in the Pacific. In 1942 the Free French government acceded to the United States government's request for permission to set up an air and naval base on the island of Bora Bora. About 5,000 American troops were stationed there for almost five years, and they provided the island with a well-built airfield, as well as many half-caste children despite Governor Orselli's efforts to reduce American contacts with the Polynesians to a minimum.[5]

Although the indigenous population, in general, played a passive role throughout World War II, three hundred volunteers, mainly Polynesians and *demis,* formed the Tahitian company of the Pacific battalion that distinguished itself in the fighting in North Africa, Italy, and Provence. Of these, ninety-six were war casualties, and the survivors, under the command of Captain Robert Hervé, did not return to the colony until a year after V-J Day. This long delay in their repatriation, the unsettling effect of their wartime experiences, and above all the preemption by French expatriates of the jobs they had expected to find on their return created a resentment that was to have far-reaching political consequences in the early postwar years.

Within the French community of Papeete, the long-standing antipathies between political liberals and conservatives and between expatriates and the local-born had been aggravated by the wartime split between Gaullists and Pétainists. Years of virtual isolation had resulted in shortages of all kinds, the government services were fast deteriorating, the city's streets were neglected, and the housing situation was critical. Discontent was also rife in the outer islands, where the planters resented Governor Orselli's imposition of a low price for

[5] Oliver, D. L., *The Pacific Islands,* p. 383.

copra and where he had severely rationed even the locally produced sugar.[6] Inevitably the demand for more autonomy grew apace, and only the spark provided by the returned war veterans was needed to transform it into something closely akin to nationalism.

Within three weeks after the Japanese surrender, a representative assembly was instituted in the E.F.O. by the Provisional Free French government at Algiers, probably as a reward for the colony's early support of General de Gaulle. Modeled after the General Councils of provincial France, the representative assembly was to be elected by adult suffrage of all the islanders, declared to be now full-fledged French citizens and justiciable under French penal law. Voting as a single college, the newly enfranchised citizens were to elect ten representatives from Tahiti and its dependencies and ten from the other islands—five to represent the Leeward Islands, two each from the Tuamotus, Marquesas, and Gambiers, and one from the Australs.

As was the case with the new assemblies created in French tropical Africa, the powers of the E.F.O. representative assembly were confined largely to economic affairs, the most important being its right to vote the local budget. This budget, however, was to be drafted by the governor-in-council, and it still included obligatory expenditures over which the new assembly had no control. Debates on political matters were forbidden, but the assembly had to be consulted on specific subjects and it could pass resolutions on matters of general administration. Its members were also authorized to elect their own officers and a permanent commission, admit the public to their sessions, and publish the minutes of their debates. No changes of any importance were made at this time in the local-government institutions. Consequently the reform as a whole, although liberal in the light of the past, did not appreciably diminish the governor's authority or the control exercised by the Paris government.

Not until the constitution for the Fourth French Republic had been voted in the fall of 1946 were further changes made in the E.F.O.'s governmental structure. Thenceforth the E.F.O. was no longer to be a colony but an Overseas Territory, and was to be represented in the Paris parliament by a deputy and a senator and in the French Union Assembly by a councilor. A decree of October 24, 1946, also prolonged

---

[6] According to a letter of protest (printed in the *Pacific Islands Monthly* for February 1946) from a Raiatea planter, the colony had more raw liquor at its disposal during the war than at any time since Captain Cook visited the islands, because the governor required that 80 percent of the cane crop be made into rum.

the term of office of the local assemblymen from four to five years, raised the age of eligibility for candidates from twenty-one to twenty-three years, and permitted the assemblymen to share with the governor the right to initiate budgetary expenditures.[7] No further changes were made until a law of 1952 liberalized the composition of the assembly after the expiration of its first mandate. Its name was then changed from representative assembly to territorial assembly, and the residence and linguistic requirements were reduced, respectively, from three years to two and from the ability to read and write French to a fluent speaking knowledge of the language. An even more significant concession was an increase in the number of assemblymen by the addition of five members from the outer islands, so as to offset the predominance of Tahiti's representation in the assembly. These changes did not take into account the islanders' perennial demands for a reduction of the governor's powers, of the number of Metropolitan officials serving in the territory, and of the over-all control exercised by Paris.

When the elections to the first assembly took place in December 1945, there had been no time to organize political parties throughout the islands, the only experienced electorate being that of Papeete's municipality. Consequently it was the men who had long been prominent in the capital's business and political life who dominated the assembly, and they were mostly conservative in their views. Alfred Poroi, a Protestant *demi* businessman and municipal councilor, was elected not only assemblyman but also mayor of Papeete, an office that he was to hold until defeated in October 1966. Two other Protestant leaders also won election: the Reverend Charles Vernier, who was elected to the first French constituent assembly in 1945, and Georges Ahne, son of a charter member of the Comité de Gaulle, who became the E.F.O.'s first deputy in the French National Assembly in 1946. For some years after the war, membership in the Protestant church and an honorable record in the Resistance were prerequisites for holding public office in the E.F.O., and they also played a part in the meteoric rise to fame of the first prominent Polynesian politician Pouvanaa A Oopa.

Pouvanaa's blue eyes and fair complexion testified to his part-Danish origin. He was born on May 10, 1895, at Huahine, one of the Leeward

---

[7] West, F. J., "Local Government in French Polynesia and American Samoa," *Journal of Local Administration Overseas*, July 1963, p. 88; Bourgeau, J., *La France du Pacifique*, p. 210.

Islands which had longest held out against the imposition of French rule. A carpenter by trade, a fundamentalist by religious conviction, and a veteran of World War I, he first came to the administration's attention in 1940, when he circulated a petition asking that all shops selling alcoholic beverages in the islands be closed, that the general council be revived, and that the distribution of textiles and fuel be made more equitably. For reasons that remain obscure, Pouvanaa had developed a xenophobic view of the resident foreign community. In February 1941 he founded various agricultural organizations, among them Les Amis de Tahiti, to defend indigenous economic interests against the encroachments of the *popaas* (Europeans) and the Chinese. Suspected of soliciting Anglo-American support to attain his ends, Pouvanaa was exiled on August 12, 1942, to his native island, from which he later escaped in a dugout canoe, and after a journey of some nine hundred kilometers he reached Bora Bora. There he asked the American commanding officer to forward a letter to General de Gaulle, but instead he was turned over to the French authorities, who again exiled him, this time to Bellingshausen Island, one of the Leewards.

In an open letter printed in *Te Aratai* on February 25, 1948, Pouvanaa attributed his deportation to his having persuaded "1,000 people to sign a good document, which was then sent to the American and British consuls, asking only for what is just and necessary for the people to live on . . . and since then I have been alternately free and in prison." [8] During one of his many detentions in the course of the remaining war years, a prison doctor described him in a report as "vain, ambitious, and obsessed by delusions of grandeur." Be that as it may, Pouvanaa rapidly acquired prestige in the eyes of the islanders by his persistent opposition to the administration. Released and permitted to return to Papeete in the summer of 1945, he opened a waterfront cafe. There he continued to advocate resistance to the authorities, although on July 10 he had signed a pledge "to serve only the cause of France and under no circumstances to ask the aid and protection of foreign nations." [9]

By appealing to the traditions of the Polynesians and voicing their grievances, Pouvanaa shook them out of their political apathy. He spoke eloquently in the Tahitian language and his speeches were liberally sprinkled with Biblical allusions. He was called the *metua* (father), and some attributed magical powers to him. Yet his first at-

[8] Gauze, R., "Panorama Politique de l'Après-Guerre (1945–1965)," p. 2.
[9] *Ibid.*, p. 7.

tempts to win elected office were unsuccessful. In the elections to the first French constituent assembly, he received only 44 votes, and this probably discouraged him from becoming a candidate for the first postwar representative assembly. In the elections to the second constituent assembly, he won 3,766 votes, but was declared ineligible by the administration because he was then once more in prison. Six months later, he supported the candidacy of his wife for the post of deputy in the National Assembly, and though she received about one-third of the 14,402 votes cast, Georges Ahne won the election.

Pouvanaa's followers, realizing that his popularity required organizational backing and his vague ideas a more explicit program, formed a Comité Pouvanaa on February 28, 1947. Among its organizers was Jean-Baptiste Céran-Jérusalemy (usually referred to as Céran), a young *demi* employee of the government printing office. He became the committee's secretary and its brains, although Pouvanaa remained its spiritual leader and titular head. Restricted initially to Papeete, the committee soon expanded its activities to the islands by organizing popular meetings and by distributing tracts and a newspaper, *Te Aratai*. In its first issue, on May 6, 1947, this party organ asked for a modification of the organic law of 1885 in "a Tahitian spirit on behalf of the Tahitians, and for a freely consented membership in the French Union." It contained no demand for independence or for the dismissal of all Metropolitan officials, but its program embodied many of the other desiderata long expressed by the local-born. It was far less radical in its demands than a petition bearing 2,000 signatures that was sent at about the same time to the assembly by the veterans' Union des Volontaires. That document asked for the suppression of the privy council, the expulsion of certain officials and war profiteers, an enlargement of the powers of the assembly, the recruitment of only indigenous personnel for the local administrative cadres, and the promulgation in the E.F.O. of French laws guaranteeing freedom of the press and of assembly. It was clear that the veterans and the Comité Pouvanaa would soon make common cause, and their relations with the administration grew correspondingly tense.

Within a short time, the two organizations gave evidence of their strength. In May 1947 they were able to arouse popular indignation against the territory's secretary-general, when it was learned that he was planning to return to France by way of the United States. This official had been in control of the E.F.O.'s scant supply of hard currency, and it was widely rumored that he and his wife intended to use some of the territory's dollars to buy American luxury goods for their personal use. The Pouvannists picketed the ship but were unable to prevent the secretary-general's departure. Nevertheless, their mass protest created an atmosphere of resistance to the government that was to be manifested more effectively a few weeks later.

On the morning of June 22, a French liner docked at Papeete, and among its passengers were three Metropolitan officials who had been assigned to serve in the local administration. An angry crowd, most of whom were veterans, gathered at the wharf and threatened to prevent the officials from disembarking. The inflammatory speeches by its leaders—among them Pouvanaa—perched on the gangplank, were greeted by shouts of approval, and the passengers were unable to land. They and the ship's captain, exasperated by the delay, urged the governor to take strong action. He hesitated, but eventually declared a state of emergency, had the officials disembarked under protection of the armed forces, and arrested Pouvanaa and the other main ringleaders, Céran, Jean Florissan, and Noel Ilari. The following November, Pouvanaa and his companions were tried on the charge of harming the security of the state, but because there had been no bloodshed and the testimony of witnesses was contradictory, they were acquitted and were released amid popular rejoicing. Moreover, Pouvanaa emerged from this episode with a new luster that added to the halo of martyrdom he had already gained from his wartime escapades. Yet in the Papeete municipal elections of December 14, 1947, the candidates supported by the Pouvanaa Committee and the Union des Volontaires were defeated by those of the Union de Défense des Intérêts Tahitiens, headed by the outgoing mayor, Alfred Poroi. His group demanded greater local autonomy, a reduction in the number of Metropolitan functionaries, and the pegging of the C.F.P. franc to the American dollar. Indicative of the predominance of local interests in E.F.O. politics was the inability of two branches of Metropolitan parties to make any political headway in the territory. These were the S.F.I.O. (Section Française de l'Internationale Ouvrière), installed at Papeete on May 15, 1947, and the R.P.F. (Rassemblement du Peuple Français), on August 17, 1950.

In comparative terms, 1948 was a year of political calm in the territory. The Pouvanaa Committee shifted its main activities to the economic sphere, and on January 31, 1948, Céran formed the Coopérative des Travailleurs Tahitiens. (For the next two years, however, this cooperative vegetated, and it showed little vitality until it received a loan of 250,000 C.F.P. francs granted by the representative assembly in 1950.) Interest in politics was suddenly revived in mid-1949 by the death of both the deputy and the senator of the E.F.O. In the by-election for the National Assembly post, on October 23, 1949, Pouvanaa was a candidate. Besides the support naturally given by his committee, he received that of a member of the French Communist Party who came to the territory to campaign for him. To the surprise and displeasure of the European community, he was elected, receiving 9,800 votes—twice as many as went to Charles Vernier, his nearest rival.

Pouvanaa's success led to two far-reaching local political developments. Poroi's party, which took the name of Union Populaire Océanienne on November 18, 1949, added anticommunism to its platform. More important was the transformation of the Pouvanaa Committee, early in 1950, into a political party called the Rassemblement Démocratique du Peuple Tahitien (R.D.P.T.). It began to advocate that Tahitians replace all expatriate officials, take over local banking and trading firms from the Metropolitan French and the Chinese, make Tahitian the official language of the territory, and adopt the flag given by the British to Queen Pomaré in place of the French *tricolore*. By 1950 the new party claimed a membership of 7,500, and its first congress, held that year, was attended by 81 delegates from the sixty sections it had formed throughout the islands.[10]

Such a program, as well as the support given Pouvanaa by the French Communist Party, inevitably aroused the fears and opposition of the conservatives. On October 18, 1949, a few days before his election, Pouvanaa, in an open letter published in the *Courrier de l'E.F.O.*, refuted the charge that he was a communist:

I, the undersigned Pouvanaa A Oopa, declare myself to be a Christian. I offer myself to my constituents as a Tahitian, [with] concern for their interests and for those of Christianity. I deny and declare to be lies all the words attributed to me as a communist. I am not on the side of the communists, and if elected I will not join their party. I swear before God and on my faith and honor to remain independent . . . and I am willing to take this oath before a notary and in the presence of rival candidates.

True to his word, Pouvanaa joined no political party in the National Assembly until September 2, 1951, when he became a member of a center group, Action Paysanne et Sociale, and he never made a speech in the Parliament during the decade that he was a deputy there. Pouvanaa's nonparticipation in the Assembly debates was usually

[10] Minutes of the French Union Assembly, June 6, 1950.

ascribed to an inadequate knowledge of French, but a journalist who talked with him often during his years at the Palais Bourbon claimed that he was more proficient in the language than he ever admitted.[11]

Despite his failure to defend the interests of his constituents in the National Assembly, Pouvanaa's popularity remained undiminished in the E.F.O. His extraordinary personality appealed to something deeply ingrained in the Polynesians, symbolizing and expressing their vaguely felt dissatisfaction with the status quo. Yet his support came not from the traditional Polynesian aristocracy but from members of the Protestant church, the trade unions, and the veterans' organization. Popular as he was among the Polynesians and well-organized as was his party throughout the islands, the R.D.P.T. was for some years unable to control the representative assembly or to get its candidate elected to the Council of the Republic.

There could hardly have been a greater contrast to Pouvanaa than Senator Robert Lassalle-Séré, who was elected to the Council of the Republic shortly before Pouvanaa became a deputy. Lassalle-Séré had had a distinguished career with the colonial troops and had gained a knowledge of the islands as inspector of the E.F.O. administrative and technical services, and he owed his election on May 20, 1949, to the twenty members of the conservative representative assembly. During his term as senator, Lassalle-Séré obtained tariff concessions from the French government for imports from Tahiti, and also proposed three laws that should have ingratiated him with the territory's inhabitants.[12] These law projects envisaged making Tahitian, equally with French, the territory's official language; suppressing the local sale of alcoholic beverages; and abolishing the Privy Council, long considered by the local inhabitants to be a Star Chamber wholly subservient to the governor's wishes. In a letter to the president of the representative assembly on May 5, 1950, Lassalle-Séré listed the services he had rendered the territory and wistfully asked why he was nevertheless unpopular in the E.F.O. The assembly tried to reassure him by a prompt vote of confidence, but this could not alter the fact that as an expatriate official and as France's representative on the South Pacific Commission,[13] he had little appeal for the local electorate, and when his term expired in 1952 he did not seek reelection.

[11] Mazellier, P., *Tahiti*, p. 104.
[12] Minutes of the permanent commission of the representative assembly, June 14, 1950.
[13] See pp. 346–356.

Two years before the elections in which overwhelming support was demonstrated for Pouvanaa's program, the revolts of 1947 in Madagascar and Indochina had made the French government realize that drastic changes in the E.F.O.'s political structure were imperative. On June 24 and July 31, 1948, the French Union Assembly inconclusively debated a government proposal to change the qualifications, number, and method of voting for members of the representative assembly. Nothing came of this proposal, however, until the question was revived by the R.D.P.T. at its first congress. Among the resolutions it then passed were denunciations of the presence of increasing numbers of expatriate officials and of the "provocative and repressive" policies advocated by Senator Lassalle-Séré. The R.D.P.T. again pledged its support for Pouvanaa, and he was reelected as deputy the following year, receiving 70 percent of the votes cast.

This reaffirmation of the popularity of Pouvanaa and of the R.D.P.T. platform impelled the representative assembly to ask the French government to send a mission to study changes in the territory's administrative structure.[14] Yet the slow-moving National Assembly continued to procrastinate, and for nearly a year after the representative assembly's mandate had expired it even failed to set a date for new elections. Because that body was the electoral college for the territory's representative on the Council of the Republic, this also meant that the post of senator remained vacant. For many months, therefore, the E.F.O.'s only elected representatives were Pouvanaa and the municipal councilors of Papeete and Uturoa. Finally, late in 1952, a four-man parliamentary mission was sent to the E.F.O. (as well as to New Caledonia). After consultations with local leaders, it submitted recommendations that led to the reorganization of the assembly [15] and also to some changes in the local-government institutions.

As early as 1949, the representative assembly had been asked by Paris to give its views on reforming the district councils. The assembly's resolutions on this subject called for a diminution of their control by the governor and for greater financial autonomy. They were pigeonholed by the Minister of Overseas France until they reached the floor of the French Union Assembly in revised form on July 10, 1952. What caused the French government to move at long last was the prospect that the R.D.P.T. would control the next assembly, and the realization that to offset this it must create some effective counter-

[14] *Marchés Coloniaux,* Aug. 18, 1951, p. 2289.
[15] See p. 42.

poise. This could have been done by strengthening the district councils and transforming them into full communes, each with an independent budget. Because of the small size of the territory's rural settlements, however—they averaged only some four hundred inhabitants each—such a move was considered impractical at the time, and no changes of any consequence were made in them until 1953. The eventual reinforcement of the powers of the two full communes of Papeete and Uturoa proved wise, for their councils distinguished themselves by never falling under the control of the R.D.P.T.

No proposal for a reform of the civil service in the E.F.O. was made at the time by the French government, although the local population's resentment of the presence of the expatriate officials had grown with the rise in their number in the postwar years. Many officials who had been deported to Indochina by the Free French regime had been reassigned to the islands, with no loss of seniority or pay. In consequence, the local-born functionaries continued to be at a disadvantage with respect to promotion and salaries and were, moreover, under the authority of expatriates well-known for their pro-Vichy sentiments.[16] When the administration proposed that incomes be taxed to meet the rising expenditures for personnel,[17] the assembly refused its assent. Poroi, its vice-president, who led the revolt, was warmly applauded by his colleagues when he asserted that of the two major disasters from which the territory had suffered—the epidemic of 1918 and the postwar plague of functionaries—the latter was far worse. To support the assembly's stand, the Tahitian civil servants formed a union, late in 1951, which called a strike—in part successful—for an increase in their cost-of-living allowances. Not until 1956, however, did the territory receive some satisfaction of its demands for a decrease in the number and pay of Metropolitan officials and in the powers of the local administration and the Paris government, and also for greater control over the resident Chinese community.

[16] *Pacific Islands Monthly,* February 1951.
[17] Minutes of the representative assembly, April 25, 1950.

4

The Evolution of the R.D.P.T.

Although the Rassemblement Démocratique du Peuple Tahitien (R.D.P.T.) displayed unity during its early years, that unity did not long endure, in part because Pouvanaa's leadership was largely negative and sometimes contradictory. The rank and file of the islanders continued to support him because he symbolized resistance to the government and to foreigners, but his program and his primacy in the party were increasingly challenged by its officers.

When it came to carrying out his simple general ideas, Pouvanaa soon showed that he had neither training nor liking for technical questions or for day-to-day administration. In his desire to enjoy life unhampered by alien controls and to shun the obligations imposed on citizens of a modern state, he was typically Polynesian. However, he did understand and sympathize with the Polynesians' primary concern—to obtain good prices for their copra and fish—and with their desire to buy certain luxury goods. In proposing to reduce the tariff on imported foodstuffs, however, he failed to foresee that this would lessen the territory's revenues, derived largely from customs duties. Moreover, he proposed no substitute for the French subsidies on which the territory had come to depend. Worse still, by advocating a redistribution of the land he antagonized the rural property owners, who were his main supporters.[1] Not only was Pouvanaa's policy somewhat incoherent and unrealistic, but he had no confidence in the advice of experts and mistrusted some of his closest collaborators in the R.D.P.T., notably Céran-Jérusalemy.[2]

Céran—comparatively well educated, and hypersensitive like so many talented individuals of mixed blood—was also very ambitious. He had done military service during World War II, and held a modest post in the administration when chance brought him into con-

[1] Robson, N., "French Oceania Takes Stock."
[2] Mazellier, P., *Tahiti*, p. 106.

tact with Pouvanaa.[3] Soon the two men found that they saw eye to eye in many respects, and Céran became a charter member of the R.D.P.T. and its main organizer, modeling it after the French Communist Party. Dissatisfied with the number-two position in the party, yet unable to challenge Pouvanaa's leadership directly, Céran set himself to shape the R.D.P.T.'s evolution. He exerted his influence through the labor organizations, and he was either the founder or secretary of the unions of Christian longshoremen, the building and public-workers unions, and various organizations of farmers and fishermen. He had direct control over the Coopérative des Travailleurs Tahitiens, and was instrumental in the rise of a young Metropolitan labor leader, Frantz Vanisette, who had married his sister. (Vanisette was a sailor who had served in Indochina and was demobilized at Papeete in 1947. After an unsuccessful effort to earn a living as a peddler in France, he returned to the islands in 1952, where he joined the R.D.P.T. and became first an employee of his brother-in-law's cooperative, and then secretary of the Syndicat des Gens de Mer.) Céran's only setback at this time was his inability to infiltrate the local organization of veterans.

On January 26 and 27, 1952, the R.D.P.T. held a congress at Papeete to prepare for the next elections to the representative assembly. These did not take place until January 23, 1953, when the R.D.P.T. won 18 of the 25 seats at stake, and their distribution showed that its strength lay in the rural areas. None of its members was elected in Papeete, where the municipal elections three months later confirmed the strength of Alfred Poroi and his followers.[4] The Leeward and Marquesas Islands sent two independents to the assembly, but the R.D.P.T. had such a comfortable majority that it was able to elect all the assembly officers, including Céran as president, and to monopolize all the committees.[5]

From the time of the assembly's opening meeting on March 16, 1953, it was evident that the session would be stormy. As was customary, the governor, René Petitbon, made the inaugural speech, although he had been informed the previous day by the R.D.P.T. leaders that his presence was not indispensable. Then the secretary-general, Th. Diffre, who was the administration's spokesman at assembly ses-

[3] See p. 32.

[4] *Pacific Islands Monthly,* February, May, 1953.

[5] These were the Permanent, Finance and Economic Affairs, Plan, Outer Islands, and Social and Administrative Affairs Committees.

sions, was chided by the majority party for arriving late, and a few days later the party asked for his recall. Next a quarrel broke out between Mayor Poroi and Noel Ilari, the assembly's first vice-president, which would have culminated in a duel had the governor not intervened. Despite these flurries and the members' preoccupation with trivia, the assembly managed to get down to work on two items of its agenda. It elected to the Council of the Republic the controversial Dr. Jean Florisson, who had been a royalist in French politics but locally an early militant of the R.D.P.T. Then it voted to change the name of the territory from the E.F.O., considered a "colonialist" survival, to that of Tahiti and Dependencies. Subsequently the assembly changed its mind several times about this nomenclature, and ultimately it accepted the Parliament's proposal of the name French Polynesia in 1956.

The first session of the new assembly contained the germ of a conflict that was soon to create a rift in the ranks of the R.D.P.T. This developed over Céran's surprising proposal that the territory be "departmentized," i.e. be transformed into an Overseas Department of France. The cause of this *volte-face* on the part of so staunch an opponent of Metropolitan officialdom is not clear, unless he made the proposal at the behest of the Compagnie des Phosphates de l'Océanie, to which he owed his seat in the assembly. In any case, his move impelled Poroi, who wanted local autonomy but not integration with France, to go to Paris to express his disapproval of "departmentization" in particular and of the R.D.P.T.'s aggressive tactics in general.[6] Further evidencing his hostility to the author of the "departmentization" proposal, Poroi challenged the validity of the vote taken in the October 13 session of the assembly which elected Céran to the French Union Assembly.[7] More seriously, the rejection of "departmentization" at this same session, by a vote of 15 to 10, split the R.D.P.T. and placed the party in a minority position in that body.

The conflict between the supporters and adversaries of Céran added one more issue to what had now become standard dissensions—those between the R.D.P.T. and the opposition and between the assembly as a whole and the administration. Quarrel as they did among themselves, the assemblymen nevertheless stood together when it came to criticizing the activities of the Chinese in the territory, the government's neglect of the outer islands, and above all, the number and pay

[6] *Pacific Islands Monthly*, June, July, 1953.
[7] For details, see minutes of the French Union Assembly, March 11, 1954.

of Metropolitan officials. A head-on collision over the respective rights and obligations of the administration and the assembly was barely averted in late 1954.[8] The assemblymen complained that the government was refusing the cooperation they required to carry out their legitimate tasks. To emphasize their resentment, they refused to vote the 1955 budget, and the R.D.P.T. at its fourth congress on October 28 called again for the resignation of Diffre. A reconciliation was effected with the secretary-general, however, the budget was finally voted, and the addition of two new recruits to the R.D.P.T. in June 1955 made it once more the majority party in the assembly—a position that it retained until after the elections of November 1957.

In Paris, too, all the posts available to the territory were held by the R.D.P.T., and the French government's attempts to lift the parliamentary immunity of Pouvanaa and Céran were defeated. Dr. Florisson was senator for the E.F.O., Céran was its French Union Assemblyman, and Pouvanaa was reelected deputy on January 25, 1956. Yet Florisson's ambivalent political views undermined his influence, Céran did not have his party's full support, and even Pouvanaa's electoral strength was steadily declining. In the 1951 elections the R.D.P.T. won 69.8 percent of the territory's votes, but its percentage had fallen to 58.1 in 1956. Nevertheless, the R.D.P.T. still felt strong enough to advocate a radical policy—the transformation of the territory into an autonomous Tahitian Republic. In alarm, the opposition forces closed ranks, for they now realized that they could never defeat the R.D.P.T. if they remained disunited. In 1956, therefore, a new party called the Union Tahitienne was formed, with a platform that called for maintaining the "French presence" in the territory. Its president was Alfred Poroi, and its secretary Rudolf Bambridge, a young *demi* lawyer who had made a surprisingly good showing against Pouvanaa in the legislative elections of 1956.

A new orientation and impetus were given to local political life by the *loi-cadre,* an enabling act passed by the French Parliament on June 23, 1956. It brought drastic changes to all of France's overseas dependencies, mainly by creating a government council in each territory, whose members would be elected by the local assembly and would share executive powers with the French administration. While the governor appointed by Paris would preside over the new council and could veto its decisions, the territorial assemblymen were to elect the councilors. The candidate receiving the largest number of votes

[8] Minutes of the representative assembly, Nov. 23, 24, 1954.

would become the council's vice-president, exercising many of the powers of a premier. His six fellow-councilors were to be called ministers, each of whom was given responsibility for the functioning of an administrative service. Civil servants were to be divided into state and local cadres, and responsibility for the latter was to be invested in the government council.

Among the other important reforms effected by the *loi-cadre* was an increase in the number of assemblymen to thirty, and they were to be elected from 5 newly constituted circumscriptions—16 from Tahiti and its dependencies, 6 from the Leeward Islands, 4 from the Tuamotu-Gambiers, and 2 each from the Marquesas and the Australs. Proportional representation was instituted and voting was to be according to party lists, each of which must be elected or rejected as a whole. These innovations were not welcomed wholeheartedly in the territory, because they spelled greater political influence for the conservatives, who were preponderant in Papeete, and reduced that of the rural voters, who were the R.D.P.T.'s mainstay. Nevertheless, as a whole the *loi-cadre* certainly opened the way for the territory to move toward self-government, although the governor retained his veto power and was still responsible for execution of the laws voted by the assembly. In addition to the dissatisfaction caused by that proviso, discontent was aroused by the Parliament's long delay in voting the decree that made the *loi-cadre* applicable to French Polynesia, for this meant that elections to the new assembly could not take place before November 3, 1957.

Although in those elections the R.D.P.T. captured 17 of the 30 seats, it won only 45 percent of the total votes cast, and the opposition forces showed greater strength than ever before. In the Leeward and Austral Islands the R.D.P.T. held its own, winning respectively 53 and 65 percent of the votes, but its popularity had declined in the Windward Islands and Gambiers (38 percent in both circumscriptions), and in the Marquesas (36 percent).[9] Three independents were elected and the Union Tahitienne won 10 seats, but the anti-R.D.P.T. forces might have done better had they not dispersed their votes among rival lists of candidates.

The R.D.P.T.'s electoral victory did not serve to unify the party,

[9] At that time, the Windward Islands had a population of 42,336, and 14,679 registered voters. The corresponding figures for the Leeward Islands were 14,000 and 4,974; for the Marquesas 3,902 and 1,351; for the Australs 4,247 and 1,571; and for the Tuamotu-Gambiers 4,205 and 3,982. See minutes of the French Union Assembly, April 4, 1957; Gauze, R., "Panorama Politique, p. 31.

for at once it gave rise to a conflict for the top posts in the government council. The struggle for the vice-presidency lay between Pouvanaa and Céran, whose latent antagonism now came into the open. Céran had recently offended Pouvanaa by demoting him to the honorary presidency of the R.D.P.T., and he had also alienated some of his erstwhile supporters, including Senator Florisson, by his generally autocratic behavior and obvious thirst for power. With the help of the party *militants de base,* Pouvanaa wrested the government council vice-presidency from his rival, and Céran perforce had to be content with the presidency of the assembly and of its permanent commission.

Pouvanaa took over the Interior portfolio, and named as Minister of Economic Affairs Jacques Tauraa, a trader and planter from the Windward Islands; as Minister of Public Works, Agriculture and Fisheries, Pierre Hunter, a schoolteacher from the Leeward Islands; as Minister of Education and Youth, Walter Grand, president of the previous assembly; as Minister of Health and Social Affairs, René Lagarde, a Metropolitan journalist; and as Minister of Finance and the Plan, Henri Bodin, a European merchant and scholar. (Grand then appointed as his *chef de cabinet* Jacques Drollet, a *demi* schoolteacher who was later to become the R.D.P.T.'s leading theorist.) The inclusion in his cabinet of two supporters of Céran—Grand and Lagarde—showed that Pouvanaa was not in full control of his party. Perhaps because he realized this weakness, Pouvanaa without demur accepted the French government's appointees as heads of the administrative services and its separating of the state cadres from the local civil service.

The forces opposing the R.D.P.T. soon showed that they had learned a lesson from their electoral defeat. They united to form the Union Tahitienne Démocratique (U.T.D.) under the banner of Mayor Poroi, Rudolf Bambridge, and the latter's cousin, Gérald Coppenrath. The 13 members of the new party then tried to widen the breach inside the R.D.P.T. by throwing their influence on the side of Pouvanaa. Far from succeeding, however, this attempt had the effect of increasing Céran's influence in the government and municipal councils, where he managed to serve both his own interests and those of his sponsor. the phosphate company.[10] Notwithstanding these successes, or per-

---

[10] By adroit bargaining, Céran obtained a reduction in the export duty on phosphates in return for an increase in Papeete's communal revenues. See Gauze, "Panorama Politique," p. 34.

haps because they made him too self-confident, Céran soon over-reached himself and brought about the R.D.P.T.'s downfall.

Using his position as president of the assembly, Céran tried next to undermine the powers of the governor as well as those of Pouvanaa. His efforts reached a climax in the budgetary session of April 22, 1958, when he induced the R.D.P.T. majority to pass a law instituting income tax in the territory. Although Céran, in a talk with the authors seven years later, stated that the initiative for this law was not his, its authorship was widely attributed to him at the time. In any case, publication of the new law in the *Journal Officiel* produced no overt reaction from the newly installed governor, Camille Bailly, but it aroused immediate and strong opposition from the Papeete business community. The latter formed a Groupement des Petits et Moyens Con-tribuables, distributed a tract vehemently opposing the R.D.P.T. on this issue, and organized a mass demonstration in front of the assembly hall.

Early in the morning of April 29, a crowd estimated to number from several hundred to 1,000 laid siege to the seventeen R.D.P.T. assembly-men who were meeting in the hall, and booed and threw stones at Pouvanaa when he attempted to address them from a window. It was not until three hours later, under the protection of a military detach-ment, that the assemblymen could leave the hall. That same after-noon the demonstrators assembled at the governor's residence, but he refused to act under such pressure and the day ended in a draw. The next day, however, he yielded and reconvened the assembly, which then abrogated the income-tax law after the R.D.P.T. members decided to abstain from voting. Thus a protest which began over a purely eco-nomic measure ended by assuming a political coloration. Apparently the demonstrators were agitating not only against the imposition of an income tax but also against the R.D.P.T.'s policy of severing the territory's ties with France. The immediate effect, thanks to a per-manent split in the R.D.P.T's top leadership, was to terminate that party's long domination of local politics.

The R.D.P.T.'s resounding defeat at the hands of the demonstrators led to mutual recriminations between Céran and Pouvanaa, and then to the former's resignation from all his assembly posts. The virtual elimination of Céran's influence opened the way for the U.T.D. at long last to be represented both in the assembly committees and in the French Parliament, and on June 8, 1958, its candidate, Gerald Coppen-rath, was elected to succeed Dr. Florisson in the Council of the Republic. Now the assemblymen were divided into what were in effect three parties—the pro- and anti-Pouvanaa groups and the U.T.D. For some time thereafter the U.T.D. was the strongest of the three, and its members were united behind a policy of maintaining close ties with France.

The question of the territory's relations with France were suddenly and dramatically highlighted as the result of a major event in the Metropole, which had even greater local repercussions than those that followed application of the *loi-cadre*. This event was the return of General de Gaulle as head of the French government, following the Algiers coup of May 13, 1958. He had been warmly welcomed when he came to the islands on a private visit in 1956, although clearly he had been acclaimed as leader of the Resistance rather than as head of the R.P.F. His decision to hold a referendum, in which the overseas dependencies were to choose between independence without further French aid and membership in a new French Community, cast the R.D.P.T. into disarray. On July 14, Pouvanaa convened a party congress to discuss the referendum, but its only known accomplishment was the expulsion of Céran from membership in the R.D.P.T. A few days later Céran retaliated by calling together his own congress, which pronounced his expulsion illegal and, after some hesitation, decided to vote against independence in the referendum set for September 28. On August 25, Pouvanaa and his supporters reacted by opting for a negative vote on membership in the French Community.[11] Probably neither Pouvanaa nor Céran wanted an independence that would end French subsidies to the territory, but their personal rivalry had become so intense that it compelled them to adopt divergent attitudes.

As the date of the referendum drew near, Pouvanaa campaigned fervently in favor of independence, allegedly saying that he would say no to General de Gaulle as Jesus had said no to Satan.[12] Meanwhile, Céran and his followers joined the U.T.D. and the administration in advocating an affirmative vote. So evenly did the opposing forces seem matched that the outcome was in doubt until the last ballots were counted.[13] The final tally showed that 14,818, or 64.4 percent of the votes registered, favored joining the Community. Most of the 8,467

[11] Pouvanaa was said to have asked General de Gaulle to dissolve the assembly and to come in person to the territory to "restore order," and that when that request was refused he decided that the vote in the referendum should be negative.

[12] *Le Monde,* May 31, 1963.

[13] *Ibid.,* Sept. 5, 1958.

negative ballots were cast in the Leeward Islands, Pouvanaa's strong-hold and the traditional area of anti-French sentiment. On the ground that this vote showed that Pouvanaa had forfeited the confidence of the electorate, Governor Bailly dissolved the government council on Octo-ber 8.

Two nights later, fires broke out in Papeete, for which Pouvanaa was held responsible. In an effort to explain such an irrational act, it was said that Pouvanaa had been made vengeful and violent by this first defeat at the hands of the electorate in 10 years. He was arrested along with six of his followers, who were apprehended while carrying Molotov cocktails. Although the evidence against Pouvanaa was wholly circum-stantial, his parliamentary immunity to arrest was lifted, and he re-mained in prison until he was tried, almost exactly one year later. On October 28, 1959, after a surprisingly quiet five-day trial, the verdict was rendered in the presence of barely five hundred persons. On the charges of attempted murder and arson and the illegal possession of firearms, the Criminal Court of Papeete sentenced Pouvanaa to 8 years in prison and to 15 years of banishment from the territory. At the same time, thirteen of his alleged accomplices received prison sentences ranging from 18 months to 6 years, and they accepted the verdict with-out appealing. Pouvanaa's appeal was rejected in January 1960, in March of that year he was secretly shipped to serve out his sentence in France, and two months later he was deprived of his seat in the Na-tional Assembly.

On the eve of Pouvanaa's trial, Céran tried unsuccessfully to organ-ize a demonstration in his favor. After the sentence was pronounced, public prayers on behalf of Pouvanaa were offered, but outside the churches and without the participation of the Protestant clergy. Neither the clergy's apparent aloofness, however, nor the public's calm accep-tance of the verdict meant that Pouvanaa had been discredited in the eyes of his compatriots. Probably at least one-third of the population thought that he had been framed and still venerated him as their leader. Moreover, neither the mistakes that he had made nor the errors of his adversaries (including those of the administration) succeeded in de-stroying his party or causing it to lose its seat in the National Assembly.

In his excellent analysis of French Polynesia's political history, F. J. West argues that Pouvanaa's strength derived from his party's organiza-tion on the basis of traditional attitudes and kinship ties and from his appeal to the wellsprings of Polynesian sentiment.[14] Nevertheless, as

14 West, F. J., *Political Advancement in the South Pacific,* pp. 108–118.

Dr. West points out, Pouvanaa operated within the context of imported alien institutions. In the vacuum created by the disappearance of the old order long before World War II, the framework of a modern society with its church, labor, and administrative organization had been solidly laid, albeit on a genuinely indigenous foundation. The result has been an original Franco-Polynesian admixture, to which the Tahitian coloration was given by Pouvanaa and his party. Although Pouvanaa became largely a nostalgic symbol after 1958, the Tahitian character with which he imbued local politics has been perpetuated, not only by the reconstituted R.D.P.T. but also by the *demis,* who are the territory's elite.

5

The Parties and the Centre d'Expérimentation du Pacifique

Because of French Polynesia's affirmative vote in the referendum, the assembly had to choose a new statute for the territory in the fall of 1958. Surprisingly enough, the pro-Pouvanaa faction in the R.D.P.T., without asking the advice of its imprisoned leader, opted for "departmentization." Equally surprising was Céran's reversal of position, for he came out in favor of a territorial status as the first step toward creating an autonomous Tahitian republic. Naturally the U.T.D. also preferred that French Polynesia remain an overseas territory, but it desired that fundamental changes be made in the role of the government council. To calm political passions, its spokesman, Gérald Coppenrath, proposed on November 14 that the councilors abandon their individual attributes and their title of minister and exercise only collegial powers. His proposal included returning to the governor authority over the territorial civil services.

Owing to the imprisonment of Pouvanaa and his most intransigent followers, as well as to Céran's reluctant consent, the U.T.D. proposal was accepted by the assembly, with only two members abstaining. It became law on December 23, 1958, and two months later a new five-man government council was elected, on which the newly allied U.T.D. and Pouvanist R.D.P.T. members won all but one seat. In the March 8, 1959, municipal elections, control of the councils of Papeete and Uturoa once again went to the U.T.D., which had now become affiliated with the Metropolitan Gaullist party, the Union de la Nouvelle République (U.N.R.).

With the support of Dr. Florisson, Céran had been trying during the interim to reunite the R.D.P.T. under his leadership by proposing that Pouvanaa be elected president of the assembly. This strategy failed, however, and on May 20 Jacques Tauraa was chosen for that post through the combined votes of the U.T.D. and the R.D.P.T. opponents of Céran. By his frequent and opportunistic changes of front, Céran had lost the confidence of his former supporters and also that of

Pouvanaa, who, from his prison, sent his blessing to the R.D.P.T. group headed by Tauraa and Drollet. A year later Pouvanaa again rejected Céran's overtures and promoted the candidacy of his son, Marcel, to succeed him as deputy in the National Assembly. Temporarily discouraged by this setback, Céran, preceded by Dr. Florisson, left the territory for France just before Pouvanaa was sentenced.

Céran's absence and Pouvanaa's imprisonment definitely cooled the political atmosphere, but they also created a void which neither the new leaders of the R.D.P.T. nor those of the U.T.D. were able to fill. Although in the elections of July 1960 to the National Assembly, the R.D.P.T. rallied behind Pouvanaa's son, a veteran of World War II with an outstanding military record, it had difficulty in choosing his running mate. Eventually John Teariki and not Jacques Tauraa won the party's endorsement, and Céran's candidacy was once more rejected.[1]

In opposition to Marcel A Oopa, the U.T.D. ran as its candidate Rudolf Bambridge, who had been Pouvanaa's unsuccessful opponent in the last legislative elections. Bambridge, a Protestant, chose as his running mate a Catholic, Georges Leboucher, so as to eliminate from his ticket a rivalry between those two faiths which had often influenced the choice of voters. Bambridge, preoccupied with his legal profession and farming interests, had been reluctant to enter politics in 1956,[2] but he had done so to strengthen the ties between his country and France. By 1960, however, his party had been weakened by the internal conflict between himself and Coppenrath, on the one side, and Mayor Poroi on the other, and this handicapped the U.T.D. in trying to profit by the R.D.P.T.'s concurrent disunity. Bambridge's prospects were brightened on the eve of the elections by the sudden departure of Marcel A Oopa to undergo surgery in France. Although Bambridge was defeated by the narrow margin of 1,183 votes, he polled more than any of the other unsuccessful candidates.[3] Marcel A Oopa owed his victory to his father, and not to any real difference between his platform and that of the U.T.D. In the National Assembly, he advocated no change in the existing relationship between France and French Polynesia, and joined the center Catholic party, the Mouvement Républicain

---

[1] Contributing to Céran's defeat was his open opposition to a proposed increase in the export tax on phosphates, for it exposed him as the defender of big business and undermined his claim of championing the "little people."

[2] Interview with the authors, April 20, 1965.

[3] For details of this election, see *Marchés Tropicaux*, July 2, 1960, p. 1519.

Populaire (M.R.P.). A year after his election he died in Paris of cancer of the throat, and was succeeded by John Teariki.

In the territory, the game of musical chairs inside the U.T.D. and the R.D.P.T. was resumed after a brief lull following the election of Marcel A Oopa. Dissatisfaction in the assembly with the weak leadership of both parties created a political malaise. Toward the end of 1960, it was intensified by an economic depression resulting from the sharp fall in prices for the territory's exports. On December 17, the assembly's vote of no-confidence led to the resignation of the government councilors, but the men who replaced them initiated no radical changes in the territory's policy.

The U.T.D. suffered perhaps even more from internal dissensions than did the R.D.P.T., which remained faithful to Pouvanaa and demanded his return to Polynesia. In April 1961, Pouvanaa was reelected president of the party, and in October his daughter-in-law, Céline, was chosen to take his seat in the territorial assembly. Yet throughout 1961 the R.D.P.T. was beset with quarrels, especially between the old guard and the Young Turks who wanted to take over the leadership. Jacques Drollet underwent one of his periodic political eclipses; Frantz Vanisette staged a comeback and was elected president of the assembly,[4] but this time with the support of the U.T.D.; Dr. Florisson, the last Metropolitan member on the R.D.P.T. executive committee, was excluded from its membership; and Céran in vain maneuvered to regain his preeminence among the party leaders. In April 1962, however, success crowned Céran's efforts when he replaced Drollet on the permanent commission and the assembly accepted his proposal to censure the government council. These successive reversals of the council showed clearly that the return to its pre-*loi-cadre* status had not brought political stability to the territory.

Céran finally succeeded in his strategy, less because of an increase in his personal following than because the long-standing rift between the U.T.D. leaders had reached the point of no return. The imminence of the territorial-assembly elections, scheduled for October 14, 1962, precipitated important changes in the old parties and the formation of new ones. In the preceding July, Céran and his followers formed a group distinct from the R.D.P.T., called the Pupu Tiama Maoho (P.T.M.), but of more immediate significance was the breakup of the

---

[4] An interesting sidelight on this election was provided by the first ballot, which gave 17 votes to Pouvanaa and 9 to the long-deceased Queen Pomaré. See *Pacific Islands Monthly*, April 1961.

U.T.D. While Poroi and Vanisette headed what was still called the U.T.D., Bambridge and Coppenrath broke away to organize a new party called the Union Tahitienne, allied with the U.N.R. (U.T.-U.N.R.). At about the same time a host of new political groups were born, and this proliferation of parties reflected the population's growing interest in politics as well as increasing divergencies in their views. For the thirty seats to be filled in the assembly, 346 candidates on 52 party lists competed for the votes of a registered electorate now numbering 34,010 persons.[5] Of these, however, ten thousand abstained from voting, and the great majority of the new parties died still-born.

As a result of this election the R.D.P.T. took fourteen assembly seats, the largest number filled by any party, but for the first time it failed to win an absolute majority. The U.T.D. won five seats and the U.T.-U.N.R. eight, thus reversing the trend shown in the senatorial elections held the previous month. On that occasion Poroi had defeated Coppenrath to become a Councilor of the Republic, and Jacques Drollet had won a third of the votes. In the assembly, two of the remaining seats went to independents and Céran was the only member of the P.T.M. elected. Both of these elections showed that Céran had a very limited personal following, and that, of the two conservative parties, the U.T.D.'s strength was still strategically located in the territory's two main cities.

Although the R.D.P.T. declared itself satisfied with the results of the assembly elections, they foreshadowed a government council to be formed by a coalition between the pro-Pouvanaa R.D.P.T. and the U.T.D. Moreover, they encouraged the R.D.P.T. to intensify the agitation for Pouvanaa's return. Pouvanaa, however, insisted that he would be able to return only if Tahiti won its independence, although clearly the territory was not yet ready to take such a radical step. Le Peuple Polynésien, the first local party to demand independence for French Polynesia after the 1958 referendum, had been formed shortly before the October 1962 elections, but it then received no support at the polls. Moreover, in December the assembly voted unanimously a resolution "solemnly" stating that French Polynesia wanted to "remain an integral part of the French Republic, while admitting an evolution in the statute of the territory."

In part this stand reflected the worsening economic situation in the territory, which made continuing ties with France more imperative and a soft-pedalling of controversial matters judicious. Yet the R.D.P.T.

[5] Gauze, R., "Panorama Politique," p. 73.

was now so deeply committed to Pouvanaa's return that it could not afford to ignore that issue. On November 7, the assembly accepted a resolution proposed by Drollet asking the French government to abrogate Pouvanaa's sentence of banishment, although all the U.T.D. members except Poroi had abstained in the vote.[6] The governor promptly told the assembly that it had exceeded its prerogatives; nevertheless, Pouvanaa's return became a factor in the legislative elections held on December 2. Although the outgoing deputy, John Teariki, was again returned to the National Assembly, defeating the perennial runner-up, Rudolf Bambridge, by 2,373 votes,[7] the R.D.P.T. candidate was elected by only 32.8 percent of the ballots cast, and this new evidence of the party's declining popularity indicated no overwhelming support for its program. It is quite possible that the R.D.P.T. might have lost the election had it not been for the split among the conservatives.

The parlous state of the territory's budget, revealed in the session which began on December 13, temporarily pushed political questions into the background. It was clear that new taxes would have to be imposed, with disastrous effects on the economic situation, unless France increased its financial aid to the territory. Governor Grimald's speech at the new assembly's first meeting had contained the assurance that "France would not leave French Polynesia to its fate." So it was decided to send a mission representative of all parties to Paris to ask the French government for a special subsidy of 100 million C.F.P. francs to balance the territorial budget. As Drollet and Tauraa were included in this mission, it was a foregone conclusion that they would use the opportunity to press for Pouvanaa's return. The financial but not the political aspect of their mission was successful. What is more, they learned of a new development in French policy that was to alter drastically French Polynesia's political, economic, and social situation.

Georges Chaffard [8] graphically described the interview between the members of the mission and the French President. After De Gaulle had thanked them for the resolution expressing the assembly's fidelity to France, he announced his government's decision to create a Centre d'Expérimentation du Pacifique (C.E.P.), to be

---

[6] Reportedly, Poroi had bargained his affirmative vote against a seat for his son on the government council. This so outraged some members of his party that eight of them, including Vanisette, resigned, and Poroi and the 19 municipal councilors faithful to him felt impelled to cable General de Gaulle affirming their attachment to him and to France.

[7] Céran received 2,635 votes, but once again more than 12,000 of the electorate failed to exercise their franchise.

[8] *L'Express*, Aug. 6, 1964.

bolstered by an aeronaval base there. Tauraa and Teariki looked at each other, a little frightened. After a short hesitation they dared to formulate some timid objections. With a wave of his hand, De Gaulle said: "Go tell that to Messrs. Kennedy and Khrushchev. If they decide to give up their nuclear armament I will do the same. There will be no danger, all the necessary precautions will be taken. We shall make tests only when the wind blows in the right direction.

The reaction in French Polynesia to the report of the mission was one of hostility. Its members were bitterly attacked in the assembly for failing to secure a pledge for Pouvanaa's return, and their success in getting the 100-million C.F.P. franc subsidy was all but forgotten. Initially the assemblymen apparently failed to grasp the full implications of the C.E.P. project, and it was Teariki who was the first to express openly his opposition to any nuclear testing in the islands. In his maiden speech to the National Assembly on January 22, 1963—the first speech ever made there by a Polynesian—he wasted no time on expressions of loyalty to France and sharply criticized the government for its decision. To Teariki the price asked by France for easing the territory's financial plight was far too heavy. More than any other of his compatriots, Teariki expressed in clear terms their fear of becoming, like the Japanese, victims of radioactivity.

Of the three major French policies affecting the evolution of French Polynesia during the postwar period—the institution of elective representative government, the referendum vote on its statute, and the creation of the C.E.P.—the last-mentioned had by far the greatest local impact. To some degree this was the natural result of installing the C.E.P. in the islands, but its repercussions went far beyond its immediately visible effects. Aside from apprehensions about the population's survival and the socioeconomic changes that the C.E.P.'s implantation would make in Polynesian life, it awakened and reinforced the old grievances against French domination. Specifically, it deepened existing divisions in the population and in the parties, and also created new ones. The consternation caused by the prospects opened up by the C.E.P. increased with that project's materialization. Because of the emotions thus aroused. France moved progressively to increase the economic compensations offered in return for the population's acceptance of the role that had been arbitrarily assigned to the territory.

By and large, the Polynesians remained passive, fatalistic, and ill-informed as to the possible deleterious effects of nuclear testing. Many of them, in fact, obviously enjoyed the immediate improvement in their living standards that came with the full employment engendered by the C.E.P.'s operations. Among the elite, the conservatives in the U.T.D. and the U.T.-U.N.R. refused to consider any loosening of the ties with France, which was the only alternative to accepting the C.E.P. In their view, the best tactic was to use the C.E.P. as a bargaining counter to increase French funds for the territory's development. The more radical leaders tended to see the issue largely in political terms. They were concerned, in particular, lest the thousands of French nationals brought in to work in the C.E.P. swell the conservative vote in local elections and thus cause the R.D.P.T.'s political eclipse. They also saw in the project an opportunity to revive agitation for Pouvanaa's return and for an increase in the territory's autonomy. Pouvanaa, who naturally was consulted by his followers, at once asserted that the only possible response to the C.E.P. was to demand independence for the territory.

Local reactions to the C.E.P. project, although generally adverse, were so diverse and so subject to change that at first none of the parties was able to take a definite stand on the issue. The conservatives arrived at a consensus earlier than did the R.D.P.T., for the latter party was torn by disagreements stemming in part from personality and tactical conflicts. For example, the enthusiasm of those who saw in the C.E.P. an issue that might be exploited to bring about Pouvanaa's return was dampened by the possibility that it might revive Céran's influence, for he had once more become the *metua*'s most vocal champion. All of the R.D.P.T. leaders wanted a more liberal statute for the territory, but the moderates stopped short of advocating independence. They did not believe that French Polynesia could survive being cast adrift financially, and to press for independence would cost the party its alliance with the U.T.D., on which it depended for control of the assembly.

The moderates' dilemma was not solved by the successive visits in the spring of 1963 of French ministers and generals, who came both to inspect the progress made in setting up the C.E.P. and to reassure the population as to its effects on their welfare. Far from succeeding in the latter objective, these visitors awakened new fears that served to increase local antagonism to the C.E.P. project. The French Overseas Minister, Louis Jacquinot, stirred up a hornet's nest when he announced that two companies of the Foreign Legion, well known for its ruthless behavior, would be stationed in the islands. Then he let it be known that Paris, although it might modify the territory's administrative structure, would neither permit Pouvanaa to return nor grant the islands greater autonomy. In sum, all that he had to offer in return for the sacrifices entailed by the C.E.P. was a notable improvement of the territory's infrastructure. Obviously the choice of French Polynesia as France's new base for developing its *force de frappe,* far from promoting more self-government there, meant that the screws would be tightened by Paris.

This clarification of France's intentions both intensified local opposition to the C.E.P. and hardened the lines between the die-hards and the moderates in the R.D.P.T. As to the C.E.P., the French government made the conciliatory gesture of inviting the assembly to send a mission to its Sahara testing base so that its members could see for themselves that all possible precautions were being taken to obviate the dangers of radioactivity. Céran succeeded in being selected as a member of this mission and also in visiting Pouvanaa in France on his way back home to the islands.[9] He brought back word that Pouvanaa insisted that the R.D.P.T. no longer equivocate, and this dispelled any doubt that the party would commit itself to independence at its next congress, now scheduled for December 2.

The imminence of this decisive vote, in addition to a petition circulated by the R.D.P.T. on the eve of the congress asking that no more French troops be sent to Polynesia, impelled the administration to take action. On November 6 it dissolved both the R.D.P.T. and P.T.M. parties, had their headquarters searched, and seized their archives. None of the party members, however, was arrested, and indeed they all continued to sit in the assembly. Some observers believed that the R.D.P.T. moderates were actually relieved by their party's dissolution because it eliminated the traumatic pressure that had been exerted on them by the extremists. As for the U.T.D., its leaders' first and natural reaction was one of pleasure at the discomfiture of their rivals, but this was succeeded by concern lest they undergo the same fate. Furthermore, they began to see the highhanded action of the administration in suppressing an indigenous party as still another evidence of the expatriate officials' determination to assert complete control over the territory. This fear was enhanced by rumors to the effect that five hundred Réunion Islanders would be brought in to work on the C.E.P. installations, and this caused the assembly to pass a unanimous vote of protest. Then in February 1964, the French government ob-

[9] Upon his return he tried to have printed in a special issue of *Te Aratai* a photograph of himself taken with Pouvanaa, but the administration refused its permission.

tained the territory's consent to its request for sovereign rights over the two atolls of Mururoa and Fangataufa, where the C.E.P. tests were to be conducted, only by the ruse of referring the decision to the more malleable permanent commission.

In the National Assembly, Teariki continued to hammer away at the dangers to the islanders' health from nuclear testing, and in this campaign he received some support from the government's opponents and from the Metropolitan and foreign press.[10] Each of the seven French ministers who came to the territory was presented with a *cahier de doléances* by the local opponents of the C.E.P., who would not be mollified by the promise of French price supports for the territory's copra or by the assurances given by French scientists that their fears of dangerous radioactivity were unfounded. The influx of thousands of foreign troops and technicians was causing appalling inflation and creating social disturbances, not to mention a severe housing shortage and traffic jams. The cumulative effect of all these developments reawakened the Polynesians' latent xenophobia and the fears of Metropolitan competition long nursed by the *demi* leadership. Toward the end of the year, the administration's project for fiscal reform, including new taxes, was the final straw, and now the business community joined the clamor of the politicians against the C.E.P.

In its income-tax proposal, the administration had the general support of the R.D.P.T., which, despite the 1958 debacle,[11] had never renounced this facet of its ideology. This led to a sharp break between Poroi, the U.T.D. leader of the business community, and Tauraa, the moderate R.D.P.T. president of the assembly. By extension it ended the alliance between the fourteen R.D.P.T. assemblymen and the five U.T.D. members, and soon brought about a surprising alignment of the former with the U.T.-U.N.R. Observers, noting the diametrically opposed policies of those two parties and the incompatibility of their respective leaders, called this a marriage between the carp and the rabbit. Yet the new coalition was solid enough to overthrow the government council in January 1965 and replace it with one comprising three R.D.P.T. and two U.T.-U.N.R. councilors.

Hard on the heels of this political upset, which itself had followed closely upon the public opposition to income tax, came a strike by the local-born civil servants. The strike lasted a week and the local civil

10 See Capet, H., "Death for Tahiti," *The Atlantic Monthly*, July 1963; *Aux Ecoutes*, Aug. 2, 1963.

11 See p. 44.

servants won an appreciable pay rise, but it fell short of their demands for parity with Metropolitan functionaries. Thus socioeconomic agitation, attributable directly and indirectly to the C.E.P., was compounded with the uneasy party realignment, and together they further weakened the territory's fragile political and economic structure.

6

The Political Scene

The incoherence characteristic of French Polynesia's history and the lack of unity among its elite have been faithfully reflected in the composition and activities of its territorial assembly. By their working procedures and because of the weakness of party leadership and discipline, the assemblymen have accentuated the basic disunity of that body. Only on their two general objectives—greater freedom from administrative control and promotion of the territorial civil service—were they in accord, but they could not agree on the strategy they should and could use to attain them. During the decade 1958–1968, fundamental disagreements came to a head over four interrelated issues—Pouvanaa's return to the islands, the naturalization of the resident Chinese,[1] the installation of the C.E.P., and a new statute for the territory.

Superficially, the assembly's day-to-day procedures were modeled after those of the French Parliament. The government council, elected by and from the assembly membership, was not fully responsible to it, and the council's executive power was slight compared with that of the French administration. Although the ultimate authority rested with the French legislature, it was in practice the territorial governor who kept a tight rein on the essentials of power. In late 1958 his powers were further reinforced at the expense of the government council, after a brief period of experimentation with a more liberal regime.

The extent to which this hybrid system worked depended on the degree of cooperation between the administration and the assembly, between the latter and the government council, and between the parties in the assembly. As for the first-mentioned of these relationships, much depended on the personality of the governor and even more on that of the secretary-general, who was the administration's liaison officer with the assembly. Except in crises, notably those associated with mass demonstrations, popular referendums, or prolonged labor unrest, the governor did not intervene directly and, in any case,

1 See pp. 104–106.

he rarely remained in the territory for more than a year or so. It was the secretary-general, the second-highest-ranking Metropolitan official in the local hierarchy, who bore the brunt of the assemblymen's resentment of the Paris government's general indifference to, or slowness in satisfying, their demands for greater freedom of action.

To some degree the territory's increasingly straitened finances accounted for the accretion of the government's authority. As expenditures grew far beyond the capacity of the territorial revenues to meet them, the French government successively took over the cost and therefore the control of vital local services, such as communications, secondary education, and tourism. In part, however, the assembly itself was responsible for the deterioration of its authority, for in November 1958 it voted to demote the government councilors from their ministerial posts and grant them only collegial powers. This was done on the probably justifiable ground that the ministers had been prone to corruption, nepotism, and playing party politics.

It was true that the dearth of qualified men and the political apathy of the Polynesian masses hampered the development of elective representative institutions, as could clearly be seen in the functioning of the district councils and even that of Papeete's municipal commission. (Many of the Papeete municipal councilors were also territorial assemblymen.) Yet the confusion that existed between executive and legislative powers could have been minimized if more care had been taken by the assembly in choosing the government councilors. Usually the leaders of the majority parties in the assembly waited until the eve of an election before drawing up their lists of candidates, and then made a few telephone calls to obtain the latter's consent. Moreover, the assembly tended to trespass on the powers of the council it had elected by sending, for example, missions to inspect projects for which the government councilors were theoretically responsible.[2]

Jealous as it was of its prerogatives vis-à-vis the administration and the government council, the assembly followed procedures that were hardly models of parliamentary behavior. Many members appeared at sessions only long enough to pick up their pay checks.[3] Often meetings had to be adjourned for lack of a quorum, and the work of assembly committees was usually done by the same few conscientious members. If in this respect the territory's deputy and senator were among the

[2] Minutes of the territorial assembly, June 29, 1967.
[3] In December 1964, the assemblymen voted to increase their monthly emoluments of 43,000 C.F.P. francs by 20,000 a year.

most chronic offenders, they had at least the excuse of additional duties that took time and frequent trips to Paris. The administration was legitimately charged with railroading controversial measures through the closing days of a session, with presenting its proposals without sufficient preliminary study, and with sometimes bypassing the assembly by submitting projects for decision to the five-man permanent commission,[4] but the assemblymen themselves were not above reproach in procedural matters. With respect to revising the code of civil law, for example, the assemblymen failed for fully a year to vote on a report that had been given them, because only a handful of them had taken the trouble to study the document.[5] Furthermore, the assemblymen fell increasingly into the unfortunate habit of discussing what were called *questions préalables* [6] before taking up the established agenda. On the pretext that such questions required immediate debate, their authors were able to air their own partisan views, and the government councilor concerned, caught short, was unprepared to deal with them.

Sometimes the assemblymen admitted that their working methods needed reform, but they refused to curb the party partisanship that was the basic weakness of the assembly's activities. When, in May 1965, the time came to elect new assembly officers, the recently formed R.D.P.T.-U.T.-U.N.R. majority insisted on a monopoly of all the elective posts. This evoked a strong protest from the U.T.D. although it, too, had pursued the same policy of excluding the opposition when it had formed part of the assembly majority. Led by Poroi and Vanisette, the opposition members left the hall after vainly demanding the dissolution of the assembly on the ground that it no longer represented the electorate. Walkouts by a disgruntled minority, no-confidence motions in the government council, and over-frequent consultations of the electorate had by now become standard practices. It is doubtful whether French Polynesia's successive assemblies have ever truly represented the population's wishes, which have always been more of an economic and social than of a political nature.

How far the political parties themselves reflected public opinion is a matter for doubt, because accurate figures of relative party strength are simply not available. In the spring of 1965 the authors were in-

---

[4] See p. 56.

[5] Minutes of the territorial assembly, June 24, 1966.

[6] This term has no exact English equivalent. "Preliminary questions" are those posed by members for debate prior to taking up the regular agenda.

formed, at Papeete, that the R.D.P.T. then supposedly had 9,000 dues-paying members,[7] the U.T.-U.N.R. 8,000, and the U.T.D. 4,000. These unreliable data must be regarded in relation to such factors as the high percentage of abstentions, which characterized all local elections, and the locus of party strength. There is no doubt but that the U.T.D. and U.T.-U.N.R. were stronger than the number of their members suggests, for they comprised most of the moneyed and educated citizens and were concentrated in the two towns that dominated the territory. Yet the electoral impact of the conservatives had been weakened by their split into two parties under competitive leadership.

The strength of the R.D.P.T., on the other hand, still lay in the rural Protestant communities, where it continued to make effective use of its widespread organization and its control of the district councils as means of influencing the outcome of elections. Nevertheless, the election returns showed a steady ebbing of the R.D.P.T.'s popularity, partly because it failed to carry out its pledges to bring back Pouvanaa and to tackle the land problem, and partly because it lacked dynamic leadership. The inability of contemporary French Polynesia to produce inspiring and valid leaders is undoubtedly a main cause of its disunity and weakness. Many of the men who have come to prominence since World War II are now middle-aged and have used up much of their political credit, and there are no replacements in sight. To the question repeatedly put by the writers to a wide range of local personalities as to who among the younger generation would be tomorrow's leaders, no specific answers were forthcoming in respect to either the R.D.P.T. or the conservative parties.

Among the old-time R.D.P.T leaders, Céran, Frantz Vanisette, Jacques Drollet, Jacques Tauraa, and John Teariki are outstanding. For many years, Céran held the number-two spot in the party through his organizational abilities and talent for intrigue, but he has recently lost much of his following because he has failed to inspire confidence in his political integrity. Similarly, Vanisette, by his flunctuations in party loyalty and policies, has seemed to be mainly motivated by personal ambition. His turbulent temperament as well as his European origin have further militated against the effective control of the labor movement to which he has aspired. Of very different caliber is Jacques Drollet, a man of high principles, intelligence, and culture, who has often been called the brains of the R.D.P.T. He early staked his politi-

[7] Annual dues were 50 C.F.P. francs, but important party members were expected to (and did) contribute more.

cal fortunes on the leadership of the local civil servants, but he is too much the intellectual to have mass appeal. Moreover, his recent defense of the C.E.P. and of maintaining close ties with France has not endeared him to the youthful radicals. His brother-in-law, Jacques Tauraa, is also considered to be a moderating influence in the highest R.D.P.T. councils, and from May 1959 until October 1967 he was regularly reelected president of the assembly, but he has been noncommittal on vital issues and has no popular following. John Teariki, like some others of his colleagues who rose to prominence in the post-Pouvanaa period, is a landowner and shrewd businessman, but unlike many of them he has taken an unequivocal stand in opposition to the C.E.P. and in favor of local autonomy. When he ran for reelection to the National Assembly on March 19, 1967, he was barely defeated by Francis Sanford, but thereafter he cooperated with the new deputy to strive for their common goals in all but one instance.[8]

A scrutiny of the voting record of the R.D.P.T. elected representatives shows that its leaders have not respected party discipline or pursued consistent policies, except perhaps in regard to pressing for Pouvanaa's return, and even there they were only superficially united. During the decade 1958–1968, the political history of French Polynesia resembles a nineteenth-century romantic drama in which the principal character, who dominates the play, never appears on stage. Pouvanaa, the central figure, remained in the wings and exercised his influence through directives given to the party emissaries who visited him in his place of exile. In terms of practical results, these directives had less effect than the prestige conferred on such visitors merely by having been in his presence and, if possible, being photographed with him. Actually there was nothing oracular about Pouvanaa's pronouncements, especially after he became increasingly determined to have the legal case against him reopened as a preliminary to his returning to Polynesia. Failing this, he instructed his followers to demand independence even though it would mean an end to France's aid to the territory.

Cogency was given to Pouvanaa's demands by the opposition stirred up in the territory by France's arbitrary decision to conduct nuclear tests in the islands, but the conservative and the moderate R.D.P.T. leaders recoiled before the responsibilities and dangers that independence would bring. They were not convinced, as were Pouvanaa and his most ardent followers, that a more powerful and generous United States would provide the territory with as many advantages as did

8 See p. 121.

France, and they were, moreover, deeply imbued with French culture. Step by step, the French government eased the terms of Pouvanaa's imprisonment and exile, but stopped short of abrogating his sentence of banishment. This was not done until he became seriously ill, which made the risk of adverse local repercussions should he die in exile greater than the danger of agitation should he return to the islands. It could be said that the prospect of Pouvanaa's return was wholeheartedly welcomed only by the older generation of Polynesians, for whom he was still a traditionalist symbol. Needless to say, the conservatives had no wish to see the advocate of secessionism return, and even the old guard R.D.P.T. leaders were more embarrassed than satisfied by the materialization of what had long been nominally their party's chief objective. They had been managing the R.D.P.T. without Pouvanaa for almost a decade, and realized that his views were unrealistic and anachronistic and that his imperious temperament had not been mellowed by time. As for the younger generation, they wanted the good life with all its material advantages, and were little disposed to listen to an Old Testament prophet preaching a return to their cultural sources.

On the other main issue facing the territory in the years 1958 to 1968—the role of the government council, the dissolution of the R.D.P.T. and P.T.M., the naturalization of the Chinese, the installation of the C.E.P., and, above all, the revision of French Polynesia's statute —the R.D.P.T. assemblymen either frequently changed their minds or abstained from voting. Although most of the R.D.P.T. leaders opposed the C.E.P. as constituting a danger for their country, some of the most prominent of them refused to take a formal stand on this matter, largely because the party could come to no agreement on the wider issue involved—that of the territory's future relationship with France. Only the small hard-core group of Pouvanaa's followers, led by Félix Tefaauta and other Leeward Islanders, consistently demanded independence. For the most part they were assemblymen from the outer islands, sectarian Protestants, and without formal education above the primary level, who had little grasp of the political and economic implications for their territory of an independent status.

As for the conservatives, they were ideologically more consistent, economically more prosperous, and socially more homogeneous than were their opponents. They were united by their desire both for greater administrative autonomy for the territory and for close ties with France. They represented local vested interests and the best-educated and most deeply Gallicized elements in the country, but they were split by loyalties to the triumvirate who provided their leadership. Alfred Poroi is a successful businessman, many times mayor of Papeete, a strong opponent of income tax, and an equally fervent advocate of the "French presence" in Polynesia. Like Poroi, Rudolf Bambridge is a well-to-do Protestant, a staunch Gaullist, and a defender of close ties with France, where he studied law. Member of a prominent family— in whose veins flows the royal Pomaré blood—Bambridge has an attractive personality. His political ambitions stemmed from his opposition to Pouvanaa's secessionism. His outlook is that of the landed squire with a genuine concern for the welfare of his country. Gérald Coppenrath, his cousin, is also a cultured lawyer trained in France, where he took an active part in the Resistance. Although Coppenrath is a practicing Catholic and is somewhat overshadowed politically by Bambridge, these cousins share a common interest in promoting local youth organizations and hold the same general political views. By and large, what seems to separate the two U.T.-U.N.R. leaders from the U.T.D. is not ideological differences but the antipathy they feel toward Poroi, whose maneuvers to defeat Coppenrath in the 1962 senatorial election they cannot forgive.

French Polynesia's politicians may be divided by ideological, religious and educational differences and, especially, by personality conflicts, but their disunity cannot be attributed to diversity in their ethnic origins. Some Metropolitan Frenchmen, after a brief foray into local politics soon after World War II, found themselves unwelcome, and they soon withdrew to materially more rewarding positions in the administration or in business enterprises. The resident Chinese have not participated directly in domestic politics, using their influence only in cases where their economic interests are involved. Consequently, it has been the *demis* who control both the R.D.P.T. and the conservative parties and who fill all the elective posts and the territorial civil service.

Father O'Reilly's remarkable biographical studies [9] of Tahitian personalities show how prolific were the Western pioneers—missionaries, merchants, and adventurers—who came to settle in Oceania in the nineteenth and early twentieth centuries. From their unions with Polynesian women has come a sizeable *demi* population, who have usually intermarried among themselves, and as a result, a large per-

[9] See bibliography.

centage of the *demis* are related to each other by blood or by marriage.

Not surprisingly, such close kinship ties and unavoidable intimacy have not always made for harmonious relationships. Especially has this been true in so competitive a domain as that of politics, and not infrequently members of the same family find themselves in opposing camps. Among the "radicals," Vanisette and Céran, although brothers-in-law, soon broke up their political partnership, and in the ranks of the conservatives, two of the Bambridge brothers founded rival parties.[10] Superficially, the *demis* might seem divided into competitive political organizations, but basically they are united by their common frustrations, and this also accounts largely for the transformation of the R.D.P.T. from a "radical" into a "bourgeois" group. The assembly and parliamentary posts are now controlled by the *demis,* but the highest political authority still lies with the Paris government, and the real economic power with the Metropolitan firms and the Chinese merchants. The *demis* are insulated from the Polynesian population not by any racist feeling, as is often the case with half-castes in Asia, but by unavowed sentiments of cultural and economic superiority.[11] As for the Polynesian peasants and seamen, they are at the bottom of the power scale, cut off from both the Metropolitan French and the *demis* by their poverty, as well as by inertia since they lost the leadership of Pouvanaa. The feelings of both Polynesians and *demis* toward French sovereignty are ambivalent, for different reasons, and this is reflected by their respective and changing views about the territory's statute and its relationship with France.

[10] In March 1965 Rudolf's brother, Tony, founded a small party with the grandiose name of Mouvement pour le Renouveau et le Salut de la Polynésie Française.

[11] According to M. Panoff, the *demis* called the rural masses "natives," or, more commonly, "têtes de chevrette" ("shrimp-heads"). Although the *demis* claim that those terms are not derogatory, the latter was the name applied to slaves and commoners by the old Polynesian aristocracy. See Panoff, M., "Tahiti et le Mythe de l'Indépendance," *Les Temps Modernes,* February 1965.

7

Autonomy or Independence?

So controversial did the question of revising French Polynesia's statute become that for many years the assembly avoided taking a firm stand in favor of any of the solutions proposed. The assemblymen were extremely reluctant to delegate any of their limited authority to the executive branch, and were increasingly unable to satisfy the growing financial demands of the local civil servants, hence they could never bring themselves to vote any resolutions on the subject. The possibility of opting for "departmentization" [1] became a hardy perennial on the assembly agenda, but here the opposition to such a transformation was more clear-cut. "Departmentization" would bring a prefect to replace the governor, and a host of new Metropolitan officials to the territory. Worst of all, in the eyes of local businessmen, it would lead to the imposition of French income-tax laws, a burden which they had strongly and effectively resisted since World War I.

Nevertheless, French Polynesia was surely if reluctantly moving toward "departmentization," a process accelerated by the changing status of the territorial civil servants. Application of the *loi-cadre* had reduced the civil-servant cadres in the territory from three to two, but both were still open to Metropolitan candidates recruited either locally or in France, and the latter still occupied the top echelons. The inability of the local-born functionaries to attain parity with Metropolitan officials was due largely to their lack of comparable educational qualifications. This did not, however, lessen their sense of grievance, for they held France responsible for such discrimination because it had failed to provide higher educational facilities in the territory. To be sure, a law of October 29, 1958, had made it possible for territorial civil servants to enter the Metropolitan cadre, which had a more privileged status, and thenceforth the civil service had been progressively *"océanisé"* (staffed by indigenous personnel). Indeed, by the mid-1960s considerable progress had been accomplished in this re-

[1] See p. 40.

spect in the lower and middle echelons, and a beginning had been made in appointing local-born officials to a few top posts.[2] As of early 1963, only 137 of the 1,858 functionaries serving in the territory were Metropolitan Frenchmen, and several hundred members of the local service had been integrated into the Metropolitan cadre. Yet, despite the obvious advantages in regard to pay and security, many others still hesitated to ask for such a transfer because they risked being posted outside of French Polynesia.[3]

In January 1965, the authorities exerted pressure on all local-born functionaries to ask for their transfer to the Metropolitan cadre, as this would mean that their status would be improved and also that France would pay the total cost of the civil service in the territory. The assemblymen yielded to this pressure for practical reasons, although it meant the loss of their control over still another area of domestic affairs, and by 1969, all of the local functionaries had become members of the state cadre. The process was carried a step further when the assembly concurred in France's proposal to incorporate the local development plan in that of the Metropole.

A feeling of helplessness to arrest this creeping "departmentization" began to pervade the territorial assemblymen. All they had been able to do was to suggest ways in which the territory's statute could be advantageously revised. The committee was never able to submit a report, however, and in 1965 Drollet told his colleagues that they should admit frankly that an impasse had been reached:

We never have been and never will be able to move toward autonomy without being taxed with wanting independence, and this would make us liable to imprisonment or to being called communists. But neither will we ever accept "departmentization" . . . and only the disappearance of the Rue Oudinot (the French Ministry for the Overseas Departments and Territories) will bring about a change. If that should happen, our local capitalists will invest their money elsewhere, and it is they who determine our fate. In the meantime, let us continue to call on the French taxpayer, who already pays for so many things, including the stupidity of the government.[4]

Drollet's counsel of despair was not heeded by the more intransigent members of the R.D.P.T. Under the leadership of Teariki they broke away from such moderates as Drollet and Tauraa to form in 1965 a party with, significantly, a Tahitian name, the Te Ora.[5] Although the

[2] In 1961, a Tahitian had been named administrator of the Austral Islands.
[3] Minutes of the territorial assembly, July 8, 1965.
[4] *Ibid.*
[5] Its full title was Pupu Here Aia Te Nunea Te Ora, or Movement of Patriots.

Te Ora stopped short of demanding independence, Teariki did try to use his position in the National Assembly to force the French government to free Pouvanaa and to refrain from nuclear testing in the islands. In the French presidential elections of December 1965, Teariki voted for François Mitterand because the latter promised, if elected, to permit Pouvanaa to return to Polynesia and to suppress the C.E.P.[6] Naturally this undermined his influence with the Gaullist members of the National Assembly and consequently his usefulness to the territory, and it certainly contributed to his defeat when he ran for reelection as deputy in March 1967. In the meantime, however, Teariki and his party gave expression to the population's resentment against the C.E.P. and the rapid rise in the cost of living for which its presence was responsible.[7]

In September 1966 General de Gaulle came to Tahiti to inspect the C.E.P. installations, and his visit gave Teariki a golden opportunity to voice forcefully his opposition to nuclear testing to the arbiter of French Polynesia's destiny. He submitted a memorandum to the French president charging France with exploiting the territory's financial difficulties and growing economic dependence on the C.E.P. operations so as to increase its grip on territorial affairs. In an interview with De Gaulle on September 7 he did not mince his words, asking the general why he did not

apply to Tahiti the excellent principles which you urged on our American friends at Phnom-Penh—to leave with your troops, planes and bombs. Then all Polynesia would be proud to be French and we would again become your faithful friends.[8]

Although, a few days before this, the general had been subjected to a turbulent anti-French demonstration at Djibouti, he did not heed this plea, but neither did he convince Teariki that the C.E.P. tests were necessary for the islands' defense or were serving the cause of world peace.

That Teariki was voicing the growing political malaise of his compatriots, in which opposition to the C.E.P. was merging with the demand for greater local autonomy, was shown by the elections held during the following 12 months. In October 1966, a newly formed party, the Union Communale, which opposed nuclear testing, won control of Papeete's municipal council. This put an end to the 24-year

6 Minutes of the territorial assembly, May 16, 1966.
7 See pp. 136–138.
8 *Le Figaro*, Oct. 6, 1966.

reign of Alfred Poroi, who had campaigned under the slogan of "a vote for Poroi is a vote for the French presence." [9] Papeete's new mayor was Georges Pambrun, a sixty-year-old pharmacist, who had joined the Te Ora and whose campaign was supported by both Teariki and Céran. Yet his election could not be interpreted as a wholehearted endorsement of the Te Ora's program, let alone a demand for independence, for the personal animosities which Poroi had aroused were a potent factor. However, this election and the two others held in 1967 did indicate that the forces favoring Pouvanaa's return and opposing the C.E.P. were coalescing with those demanding a revision of the territory's statute.

In the March 19, 1967, elections for the National Assembly, the much larger participation by the electorate and the multiplicity of parties and candidates reflected a greater interest in policy questions, which had theretofore been the concern of only a small segment of the elite. As might be expected, Céran was a candidate, but the only two serious contenders for the post of deputy were John Teariki and Francis Sanford. The latter was a fifty-five-year-old *demi* civil servant with a distinguished wartime record, who had been elected mayor of Faaa in 1965. Like Teariki he advocated more local autonomy, but because his was a less colorful personality and his political position less well known, it was widely expected that Teariki would be reelected.[10] Indeed, the vote was very close, and Sanford did not win until the run-off election, in which he received only 13,633 votes of the 27,254 cast by an electorate then numbering 37,552 persons.[11] While Sanford formed his own party, the New Path or Te Ea Api,[12] to contest the election, his victory was due mainly to the support given him by the U.T.D. and by the administration, both of which preferred him to Teariki as the lesser evil.

The French Gaullist parties, which had thrown their influence behind the candidate of their affiliate, the U.T.-U.N.R., had such a slender majority in the National Assembly at that time that Sanford's adherence became of vital importance to the French government. Sanford lost no time in profiting by the uncertainty as to his party affiliation in the Parliament to win support for his demands that the

[9] *Pacific Islands Monthly,* November 1966.

[10] *Le Monde,* March 3, 1967.

[11] The votes cast by members of the armed forces working at the C.E.P. were said to have tipped the balance in Sanford's favor.

[12] Sanford's opponents derisively called this party Te Ea Ati, or Path of Misfortune.

territorial assembly be dissolved and a referendum held in Tahiti to
ascertain the population's wishes concerning autonomy. In this he was
supported by Teariki, who, in turn, tried to persuade Sanford to include formal opposition to the C.E.P. in his program. In the assembly
meetings of May and July 1967, the two men, joined by Céran, urged
its members to take a firm stand in favor of autonomy, arguing that
the time was propitious because France had just granted a liberal
statute to French Somaliland. The assemblymen again refused to commit themselves, however, claiming that they had no moral right to
mortgage the territory's future in view of the imminence of elections
for a new assembly, and that, in any case, voting such a resolution
would exceed their legal powers.[13]

In preparation for this election, to be held on September 10, 1967,
the established leaders rallied their forces and three small parties were
formed.[14] The election gave Sanford's Te Ea Api ten seats in the
new assembly, the U.T.-U.N.R. and Te Ora seven seats apiece, and
the U.T.D. three seats, and three others went to independents. Inasmuch as Teariki's party had supported Sanford's policy, the autonomists claimed that they had won a victory, but the French government
refused to admit that the vote had been conclusive and to take under
consideration a revision of the territory's statute.

The new assembly, however, soon showed a very different orientation from that of its predecessor. In 1967 it supported the views of its
autonomy majority by expressing, albeit indirectly, its opposition to
the C.E.P. On November 16, 1967, it passed a resolution asking that
six scientists of international standing be witnesses of the next nuclear
tests and submit their report to the assembly. The French government
took this as an adverse reflection on the competence of the French
scholars who claimed that the tests represented no danger to the population. Considering this stand to be a "flouting of Polynesian opinion,"
Sanford resigned from the Independent Republican Party in the National Assembly, which he had joined in the hope that it would support
his demands.[15] His resignation from that party in January 1968 did

[13] Minutes of the territorial assembly, July 6, 1967.
[14] These were Charles Taufa's Tahoera U Api No Polynesia Farani, which
took no clear stand on the autonomy question; Gérald Coppenrath's Ora O Tahiti,
which opposed autonomy but advocated greater decentralization; and Adrien
Tuarau's Mouvement Démocratique Polynésien, which favored maintaining the
status quo. None of these received significant support at the polls.
[15] Sanford, like Teariki before him, joined the center group, Progrès et Démo-
cratie Moderne, in February 1968.

not alter the French government's position, although it deprived the Gaullists of an absolute majority in the National Assembly. In March 1968, General P. Billotte, Minister for the Overseas Territories, even refused to receive a joint delegation sent by the assemblies of New Caledonia and Polynesia to ask for a revision of their territories' statutes.

A stalemate seemed to have been reached—for neither New Caledonia nor Tahiti was ready to struggle for independence—when the "events" of April and May 1968 in France profoundly affected the situation. Encouraged by the revolutionary movement of French students and workers, the Polynesian assembly passed a resolution on June 8 over the opposition of the U.T.D. members, asking for an autonomous status in the French Community, and later that month Sanford was reelected to the National Assembly.[16] Once again the French government might have turned a deaf ear even to this clear expression of the territory's wishes, had it not been for the financial crisis in France, which came to a head there during the autumn months. This led not only to an amnesty for Pouvanaa on November 11 but also to the government's decision, announced on November 24, to desist from further nuclear testing throughout 1969. As before, it was the turn of events in France, rather than developments in the territory itself, that changed the latter's destiny.

Neither the amnesty for Pouvanaa nor the French government's *volte-face* in regard to nuclear testing—probably because the latter involved only a suspension of the experiments and a small reduction in the C.E.P. personnel—have failed to quell or even to curb the autonomy movement. On February 19, 1969, the Te Ea Api and the Pupu Here Aie banded together to pass a resolution in the territorial assembly in favor of a new statute that would give French Polynesia self-government, leaving to France responsibility only for the territory's foreign relations, defense, currency, and the administration of justice. To draft the new statute, the majority proposed a committee to which the assembly and the Paris government would each name six members. Furthermore, they advocated a statute that would be subject to future amendment but irrevocable unilaterally by France, and in the meantime they insisted on a return to the type of government council that had existed under the *loi-cadre* of 1956.

[16] According to Georges Chaffard, Teariki did not run in this election and supported the outgoing deputy's reelection in return for Sanford's agreement to openly oppose nuclear testing in the islands. See *L'Express*, Oct. 20, 1968.

Needless to say, the Paris government gave no sign of having taken official note of this resolution. The situation might have remained on dead center indefinitely had not still another dramatic development in France given French Polynesia two more occasions to express its views as to its future relations with France. These were the referendum of April 27, 1969, and the presidential election of the following June. Although the issue of regional councils in the referendum interested the local electorate only insofar as they believed that such councils in the territory might aggravate the trend toward "departmentization," the majority who cast an affirmative vote were mainly voicing their continued personal confidence in General de Gaulle. As for the presidential election, the 51 percent of the voters who favored Alain Poher over Georges Pompidou were showing their desire for a change in the territory's status rather than any preference for either candidate. Comparing these two votes, it is noteworthy that abstentionism increased from 27.3 percent in the referendum to 34.4 percent in the June election, and that Pompidou received less support at the polls than his predecessor. Evidently Gaullism was less popular in the territory than was De Gaulle, but it is not certain whether the increased abstention reflected the electorate's indifference or hesitation on the part of the business community, especially the Chinese, who were concerned by the trading slump that had followed a reduction in the C.E.P.'s operations.

The announcement by President Pompidou in August 1969 that nuclear testing in the atolls would be resumed in 1970 naturally strengthened the local drive for autonomy. That that movement should not be equated with the demand for independence was indicated by the population's reaction to Pouvanaa's return on November 30, 1968. A stroke which the *metua* had suffered the preceding January had at long last decided the French government to take the calculated risk of ending his long exile. Pouvanaa, accompanied by Sanford, was greeted at the Faaa airport by a crowd of more than two thousand, including most of the territory's leading politicians, but he was too tired and ailing even to respond to his welcomers. Before leaving Paris, however, he had held a press conference, in which he had stated in his usual Biblical manner, "I asked for bread but they gave me a stone. . . . I have been pardoned . . . but the matter is not yet ended." [17] Since his return, Pouvanaa's presence has caused not even a ripple of excitement among the islanders, and there has been no question of reopening the case against him, as he wished. The French government

[17] *Pacific Islands Monthly,* January 1969.

had accurately judged that Pouvanaa was a spent force and that his return would be anticlimactic. If Pouvanaa's exile is no longer a political issue useful to the autonomists, however, they still find leverage in the C.E.P.

The new series of nuclear-weapons tests, begun in May 1970 at Mururoa, comprised eight explosions, one of which was witnessed by Sanford and Teariki and another by the French minister of defense, Michel Debré. The two local leaders reportedly have been favorably impressed by the precautions taken by the C.E.P. personnel, and their comments were more courteous than recriminatory. Debré and his entourage went swimming in the lagoon six hours after a thermonuclear bomb was exploded to prove that the dangers of resultant radioactivity were negligible. These developments, combined with Debré's concurrent announcement that although nuclear testing would be continued until 1975 the number of explosions would be reduced to one series each year, seem to have weakened the adverse local reactions to the C.E.P. Even the protests formally registered by European peace organizations and by Japan and Peru were less vehement than their former ones.

Nevertheless, the Polynesians' apparent acceptance of, or resignation to, the continuation of nuclear testing has not entailed any diminution of their demand for greater autonomy. This demand has simply shifted its focus from the C.E.P. back to the French government's policy in general and that of the local administration in particular. The polemics exchanged between the autonomists and Pierre Angeli, who succeeded Sicurani as governor in January 1969, reached a climax in mid-May 1970 when he postponed indefinitely the opening of the territorial assembly session because of a disagreement with Teariki over an "interpretation" of that body's internal regulations. In August 1970, the visit made to the French Pacific islands by Henry Rey, the new French minister for the overseas territories, provided the occasion for more serious dissension. The autonomists had expected Rey to initiate a "dialogue" with them in regard to reforming the territory's statute, but they learned to their consternation that the minister would spend most of his time in Polynesia visiting the Marquesas, the archipelago most remote from Tahiti.

In a strongly worded letter printed in *Le Monde* on August 21, 1970, Sanford wrote:

I accuse the French government of despising the Tahitians and of ridiculing their representatives. For 3 years I have voted in support of the government (while) I and my friends have struggled to gain internal autonomy for the territory. We have asked for no more than . . . an executive elected wholly by the assembly and regional competence for internal affairs. . . . Can it be reasonably assumed that our problems can be regulated in Paris? . . . For 3 years we have met with a refusal on the part of the central government to carry on a dialogue . . . Patience has its limits and today these limits have been reached.

To show their displeasure at the minister's ignoring of this appeal, his adherence to his original schedule, and his failure to address a session of the territorial assembly, its members refused to attend the official ceremonies of welcome to Rey.[18] When the minister was about to leave Papeete, there occurred a demonstration of protest by about a hundred persons led by Sanford and Teariki. Suddenly the Polynesian flag they were carrying was torn from their hands by an irate gendarme and thrown to the ground, whereupon a Tahitian did the same to the tricolor brandished by a contingent of progovernment supporters.

Fortunately this incident created no immediate serious disorders, but it did reflect a growing politicosocial malaise in Tahiti.[19] The minister's visit also showed France's determination to maintain the status quo, apparently in the belief that it could safely dismiss the autonomists' agitation as simply that of a vociferous and unrepresentative minority, albeit one that controlled the territorial assembly. To be sure, the autonomists have reiterated their intention of remaining French, have restricted their desiderata to self-government, and also have displayed an ambivalent attitude toward the C.E.P. Yet France's assumption that any concessions made in regard to autonomy would only reinforce the small-scale movement for independence initiated by Pouvanaa may be based on a false premise. It is possible that France's refusal to compromise may eventually impel the autonomists to raise their sights and opt for total sovereignty.

Certainly the autonomists' present mood is one of exasperation with the French government, and it was most recently exacerbated by Governor Angeli's high-handed expulsion on September 8, 1970, of Maître Marcel Lejeune, a Metropolitan notary whose strong autonomist views had been publicized in *Le Journal de Tahiti*. No explanation was given of this measure, which was taken under a law dating from World War II that empowered the governor to deny residence privileges to any person not born in the territory. It was probably due to his conviction that Lejeune was the master-mind responsible for

[18] *Le Monde,* Sept. 23, 1970.
[19] *La Dépêche,* Sept. 1, 1970.

organizing the protest demonstrations during Rey's visit. Sanford at once denied the allegation and forthrightly denounced this arbitrary action, which he described as a "political expulsion" and "a return to the era of *lettres de cachet.*" [20]

By reviving the practices of authoritarian colonialism and by ignoring the Polynesians' most elementary political rights, the French authorities are running the grave danger of transforming what is now a moderate opposition into an extremist movement. Obviously they are counting, perhaps over-much, on the Polynesians' traditional loyalty to France and on their willingness to pay almost any political price for the continuance of France's protection and of its financial support. An axiom accepted for many years in France and the territory alike is that Polynesia's isolation and lack of economic resources make it unviable as an independent territory and necessitate its continued dependence on outside aid.

Alternatives to France as sources of such aid which have sometimes been suggested are the United States or a union with New Caledonia. America's opulence and way of life have undeniable attractions for the Polynesians, as was seen during World War II, when "the local population was fascinated by the bulldozers, huge planes and great ships, and also by the clothes, food, cokes and cigarettes that flooded ashore, and every night free movies." [21] Pouvanaa's bid for American intervention vis-à-vis the local administration enhanced the French government's chronic suspicions of "foreign influences" in general and of the "Anglo-Saxons" in particular. More recently, France's determination to keep Polynesia as a *chasse gardée* was evidenced by De Gaulle's negative response in 1964 to the request by the United States that it be permitted to reopen its consulate in Papette, build a NASA tracking station in the islands, and send a scientific mission to study coral reefs. Even American tourists, on whom French Polynesia increasingly depends for its revenues, are sometimes suspected of being military spies reconnoitering C.E.P. installations.

As for joining forces with comparatively rich New Caledonia, the Polynesians' parochialism has made them oppose the creation of a single High Commissariat for the French Pacific islands on the several occasions when this has been proposed by economy-minded Paris of-

[20] *Le Monde*, Sept. 12, 1970. The "Affaire Lejeune" is complex, for it involved a dispute between Air Tahiti, in which Lejeune was a substantial shareholder, and Air Polynésie, a subsidiary of U.T.A., which held a monopoly of the air service between Papeete and Moorea.

[21] Furnas, J. C., *Anatomy of Paradise*, p. 148.

ficials. In 1949 they even refused to align themselves in the French Parliament with the Caledonians in protesting against the devaluation of the C.F.P. franc. Obviously they are afraid of being dominated by New Caledonia, which is four times the size of Tahiti and has a totally different economic base. (By extension, their fear for some years extended to the S.P.C.[22] because its headquarters were in Nouméa, and only after that organization established a coconut-research station in the Tuamotus and assisted medical research in Tahiti did this hostile attitude change to one of active cooperation.) Beginning in the early 1960s, however, New Caledonia was viewed in a more favorable light when it became a source of remunerative employment for emigrant Tahitians and a mission sent there to study their working and living conditions submitted an enthusiastic report to the territorial assembly. Maurice Lenormand, when he was New Caledonia's deputy, endeared himself to the R.D.P.T. leaders by protesting in the National Assembly against the installation of the C.E.P. in Polynesia. Then in the spring of 1968, members of the Polynesian mission in Paris joined with Lenormand's successor, Rock Pidjot, in presenting their case for revision of the statutes of their respective territories.

Although the bases for a fruitful collaboration between the two island groups seem to have been laid at the parliamentary level, the great distance between them, as well as their ethnic and economic divergencies, make a closer and more formal union unlikely. Indeed, French Polynesia has a romantic appeal and a certain strategic value, but it is an economic liability which no outside country would lightly assume. For the present, the islands' elite seem to feel that their best chances lie in bargaining directly with France for greater autonomy, and for some years to come their contacts with other areas will probably be determined by their relations with Paris. The question then arises as to whether the majority of islanders truly want independence. A clue to their attitude toward France might be found in their voting record, although the changes in the R.D.P.T. leadership and the fragmentation of the conservative parties somewhat impair the usefulness of elections as a political barometer. The elections, however, do show that attitudes differ markedly from one archipelago to another, and sometimes even on the same island.[23] Moreover, an imponderable of

[22] See pp. 346–356.
[23] The Marquesas and the Tuamotu-Gambiers group have always voted solidly in favor of the Gaullist government, whereas nearly two-thirds of the population of the Australs, aside from Rapa, have been opposed to it. The Leeward Islands have a strong anti-French tradition, except in the municipality of Uturoa. As

the near future is the effect on the economy of the possible phasing-out of the C.E.P., which inevitably will cause unemployment and diminishing revenues. This may appease the autonomist politicians, but it will increase the islands' dependence on French subsidies.

The remarkable analysis of the independence factor in the territory's evolution made in 1965 by Michel Panoff (an expert sent from France to study the land problem in Tahiti) still seems valid.[24] It was Panoff's conviction that no significant segment of French Polynesia's population wanted independence, because both the *demis* and the masses needed France as a convenient whipping boy and the French presence as a buffer between them. Although France's sovereignty prevented the *demis* from gaining total political power in the territory, it also enabled them to avoid assuming financial responsibility for running French Polynesia and moral responsibility for any troubles that arose there. Furthermore, the threat of a popular demand for independence provided useful leverage in wresting greater autonomy from France. At the same time the *demis* realized that the word "independence," like the nuclear bomb, would lose its magical properties if actually put to use. Thoroughly French in their outlook and manner of living, the *demis* have sprung to the defense of the tricolor whenever secessionism has threatened to raise its ugly head.

As for the Polynesian population, their xenophobic tendencies had not yet been transformed into nationalism and they took refuge in passive nostalgia for a glamorized past. For them, too, France has become a bulwark—in their case, against total domination by the *demis* and the Chinese. In the 19th century, the Polynesian chiefs looked upon the European missionaries and traders as useful adjuncts in perpetuating their sway, but soon found that the Westerners had become the real masters of the islands. Gradually both the chiefs and the masses accepted the inevitability of alien control, and strove to make the best bargain possible with their foreign masters as the price of their submission. At first they played off the British against the French, then Metropolitan Frenchmen against the *demis*, and more recently they have used obliquely the attraction exerted by the United States as a means of asserting themselves against both. Independence now seems to be regarded by its inhabitants as a mirage for a territory so small, dispersed, defenseless, and economically weak as French Polynesia, but their attitude may well change.

to the Windward Islands, Moorea and Makatea have been R.D.P.T. strongholds, and this is also true of the districts of Tahiti, but not of Papeete.
[24] *Les Temps Modernes,* February 1965.

8

The Evolution of the Economy

At the turn of the century, the replacement of sailing ships by steamers caused profound changes in the economy of the E.F.O., which was inhabited at that time by 30,000 Polynesians and a handful of French planters, officials, and troops. Papeete became a port of call for steamers plying the south Pacific, notably for ships operating between the United States and Australia and New Zealand. Paradoxically enough, the opening of the Panama Canal on the eve of World War I diminished rather than enhanced Papeete's role as an international shipping center.[1]

The discovery of rich phosphate deposits on Makatea Island in 1906 led to an expansion of the economic base of the E.F.O., which until then had rested solely on agriculture and fishing. Although it brought to the colony the first sizeable French capital investments and group of technicians, it did not herald any further industrial development. Nevertheless, the growing world demand for vegetable oils at about the same time attracted the attention of Western capitalists to the French islands' copra potential, particularly in the Tuamotu, Marquesa, and Leeward Islands. Concurrently vanilla was first cultivated commercially on some of the volcanic islands. With the development of those two products, tariff barriers were instituted to protect the colony's output and the rural economy began to be modernized.

The introduction of a money economy was accompanied by the advent and growth of a fiscal system based on the imposition of customs duties and of a head tax on the population. Since the colony's meager revenues were almost wholly derived from import and export duties, which fluctuated with the variations in its foreign trade, the French government frequently made grants to cover its operating expenses. On the whole, France regarded the colony's financial situation as generally satisfactory, for its revenues usually exceeded its expenditures,

[1] See pp. 162–163.

although the former were unstable because they depended upon the sale of only four products—copra, phosphates, vanilla, and shell (nacre).

THE INTERWAR PERIOD

World War I hampered the E.F.O.'s development less by curtailing its external trade—which depended essentially on the United States and neighboring Pacific countries—than by other repercussions there of the hostilities in Europe. The mobilization of many French residents to fight on the Western front, the German bombardment of Papeete's port, and the scarcity and irregularity of shipping during four years created obvious difficulties. Worse still, the influenza epidemic that occurred at about the time of the 1918 armistice decimated close to one-fifth of the islands' population.

The prosperity engendered immediately after the war by the high prices paid for the E.F.O.'s exports was soon dissipated by a depression that began in 1921. When prices for the colony's exports fell sharply in 1922, the ensuing budgetary deficit and drain on the reserve fund caused the government to propose new taxes and an increase in the rates of existing ones. At once the Chamber of Commerce voiced loud protests, and these were echoed by the citizens of Papeete, who proceeded to form a Comité de Défense des Interêts Politiques et Economiques. That committee sent a delegation to present a petition to the governor, which was escorted by most of the town's population. The mission was successful, for the new taxes were annulled and expenditures for administrative personnel were reduced.

Throughout most of the 1920s the E.F.O. enjoyed financial ease. By 1925 the budget had a surplus of more than 5 million francs and a reserve fund amounting to almost 10 millions. Consequently France reduced its annual subsidy by nearly half (to 86,000 francs) and informed the colony that thenceforth it would have to pay for salary increases to high-ranking officials, improvements in the port, and the damage caused by the cyclone of 1926. This led to an increase in customs duties and the charge for merchants' licenses, which provoked a fresh wave of protests. Papeete's citizens criticized the fiscal system in general, and in particular denounced the tax on business transactions that had been introduced immediately after World War I. Unmoved, the French government was preparing to eliminate all of its subsidy in 1929 when the world depression dealt a disastrous blow to the E.F.O.'s external trade, which was closely tied to the dollar and sterling blocs.

An upward revision of the tax rates in 1930 inevitably produced another outcry against the administration and heated debates in the General Council, whose members claimed that it unjustly penalized the small segment of the population which paid almost all the taxes. Rather than always propose an increase in taxation, it was said, the administration should first reduce its own expenditures, which were then absorbing nearly three-fourths of the colony's revenues. Thanks to these attacks by the councilors, the pay of functionaries was reduced in 1932 by 1.3 million francs, as compared with the previous year. The attacks were also responsible for an increase in the export duties paid by the phosphate company, which was a perennial target of the councilors because it repatriated its profits to Europe and employed only foreign labor.

Between 1932 and 1934 the economy of the E.F.O. hit bottom. Within one year its external trade had declined by nearly half in value, and its budgetary deficit came to nearly 8 million francs. Local indignation against the administration's "inertia and immobilism" reached such a pitch, and the colony's financial position became so precarious, that France was moved to take some constructive action. On July 3, 1931, the Chamber of Deputies voted to lend 15 million francs to the E.F.O., to increase its annual subsidy to the colony to 5.5 millions in 1933, and to establish procedures for granting agricultural loans, and it sent an Inspector of Finance there to recommend revisions in its fiscal system. As matters worked out, the loan was never made, the agricultural-credit system was a fiasco, and the recommendations for changes in the tax system were never implemented.

Until the world depression, the E.F.O.'s resources had been considered by Paris as sufficient for undertaking such public-works projects as the colony needed. To be sure, the *mise-en-valeur* plan launched by Minister Albert Sarraut in 1921 for all the French Empire had allotted a modest place to the E.F.O., notably for improvement of Papeete's port and for augmenting the health and education services, which then received the smallest allocations from the E.F.O.'s revenues. Late in 1930, the territorial administration submitted to the Paris authorities a program whose execution would require a loan of 23 million francs. Of this sum, 5 millions were to go to repairing the wartime damage done to Papeete's port, 3 millions each to road construction and to administrative buildings, and 1.5 millions each to new water-distribution systems, interisland shipping, and the medical service, and the balance was to be distributed among various smaller public works.

The French authorities approved the first four items and increased the sum allotted to the health and education services, but they eliminated the other items and reduced the amount of the loan requested by 8 million francs. Moreover, the Senate delayed for 2 years endorsing even that sum, and then made its approval contingent upon the colony's balancing its operating budget from local resources. By this time, however, the E.F.O.'s economy had somewhat revived, so the administration decided not to accept the loan and to finance a more modest public-works program from indigenous resources. In 1938, 2 million francs were withdrawn from the reserve fund to buy some modern equipment, and Governor Chastenet de Géry drew up another plan for economic and social development that included expenditures for the Marquesas and the Tuamotus. It was approved by the Financial and Economic Delegations, but World War II broke out before this first attempt at planning for the E.F.O. could be executed.

The signs of economic recovery noted late in 1934 were confirmed the following year, which ended with a budgetary surplus for the first time in 6 years. Nevertheless, the administration refused to be carried away by this welcome affluence and pared expenditures from 15.3 million francs in 1934 to 12.9 millions in 1935. Several of the government's services were merged, but no changes were made in the fiscal system. When the government proposed instituting a tax on gasoline to undertake urgently needed repairs of Tahiti's roads, the general council promptly rejected it. More pleasing to its members was the governor's whittling down of expenditures for administrative personnel by 50 percent and increasing those for improving the health and education of a population that had grown by nearly 10,000 persons since World War I. Surpluses also occurred in 1936 and 1937, hence the budget was allowed to expand gradually, and in the latter year it came to 18 million francs in revenues and 15 millions in expenditures.

On the eve of World War II, therefore, the colony's position could again be considered satisfactory from a strictly financial viewpoint, but the basic weaknesses in its economy had not been remedied. Less than one-fifth (17.2 percent) of the colony's revenues came from direct taxes, whereas a very large proportion (82.8 percent) derived from indirect taxes, mainly customs duties, which depended very largely on the low and fluctuating prices paid for the exports of only four commodities. Taxation was certainly not excessive, but the burden was not equitably distributed, for three-fourths of the population was believed to pay virtually no imposts at all. The sole local sources of loans were still the Banque de l'Indochine and individual Chinese traders acting unofficially as bankers.

THE POST-WORLD WAR II PERIOD

For almost a century, the islands' economy was little affected by the small-scale efforts made by foreign settlers and merchants to develop crops and exports. Economic development through planning, in the modern sense of the term, did not penetrate the E.F.O. until some years after World War II. Given the islands' poverty, their distance from France, and the Polynesians' indifference to "progress," it is not surprising that the territory lagged far behind other French dependencies in utilizing the opportunities for development offered by the overseas plan of April 30, 1946.

Within 6 months after the plan had been approved by the Parliament, a 10-year program was drawn up that would include specific plans for the various territories, to be drafted in consultation with the local authorities. To implement the overseas plan, the Fonds d'Investissement pour le Développement Economique et Social (F.I.D.E.S.) was created, to which France would supply funds in the form of outright subsidies from the Metropolitan budget. Another source of financial aid for the same objectives was the Caisse Centrale pour la Coopération Economique (C.C.C.E), also financed by French taxpayers, which would grant long-term, low-interest loans to both territorial administrations and private enterprises. The territorial revenues were to supply the money needed to maintain and operate the projects constructed with the funds provided by the F.I.D.E.S. and the C.C.C.E.

Although its economic equipment was antiquated and had become even more dilapidated during the war and the early postwar years, the E.F.O. did not prepare its 10-year plan until the spring of 1949. Another year passed before the F.I.D.E.S. sent an engineer to the territory to study the situation at first hand. He was disconcerted to find that only two of the projects submitted by the local planners had been adequately prepared, and that the others were either incomplete or so poorly drafted as to be unusable. The territorial assemblymen readily admitted the validity of this criticism, but not surprisingly they blamed the plan's defects on France's failure to staff the local public-works service with competent technicians. There was still another delay, during which the 10-year plan, for whose execution the F.I.D.E.S. allocated 1,278 million C.F.P. francs, was divided into several 4-to-5-year instalments. A very large proportion of this sum was to be devoted to improvements in the means of communication, mainly the port, roads, and bridges, but considerable amounts were also allocated to building schools, dispensaries, and water-distribution systems.[2]

To correct what some considered to be an undue emphasis on the economic infrastructure, and also to meet the needs of a rapidly growing population, the authors of the second plan (1955–1958) gave greater encouragement to agricultural production and to projects that promised immediate monetary returns. Even before this plan could be put into operation, the F.I.D.E.S. announced a sharp cut in its overall allocation of funds, but perhaps of greater significance was the reorientation given the second plan by the E.F.O. The proportion allotted to social development was reduced from 42 percent to 40 percent, the share provided for economic equipment was cut from 50 percent to 39 percent, and that assigned to production was raised from 6 to 19 percent.[3] So depleted had the E.F.O.'s resources become by that time that the assemblymen in November 1934 asked France to grant the territory a delay in repaying the 9 million C.F.P. francs it owed for the maintenance of works already constructed by the F.I.D.E.S.[4]

Their experience with planning throughout the 1950s made both France and the territory realize for the first time just how fragile was the islands' economy and how dependent it had become on French support. After 1959 there were no further illusions as to the country's ability to finance any appreciable part of its own development program. The funds from France became outright subsidies, and not until after 1964 were they supplemented by far smaller contributions from the European Common Market's investment program. Prices for French Polynesia's few exports fell sharply during the early 1950s, and the prospect of a further decline in its revenues loomed on the horizon with the imminent exhaustion of Makatea's phosphate deposits. The

---

[2] Deschamps, H., and J. Guiart, *Tahiti—Nouvelle-Calédonie—Nouvelles-Hébrides,* p. 69.

[3] Minutes of the representative assembly, Dec. 7, 1953, March 22, 1954.

[4] *Ibid.,* Nov. 14, 1954.

rapid growth in the population and the emigration of outer-islanders to Papeete mainly accounted for the increased importation of consumer goods and the decrease in agricultural output. Clearly the territory was living ever more beyond its means, and for some years to come no appreciable expansion in its productivity and exports could be expected to result from the new orientation of the development plan. Although France in 1957 had finally agreed to build the Faaa airport, this would not lead to any influx of tourists in the near future.

Consequently, in 1959, when the time came to draft French Polynesia's third plan, a more serious effort was made to take an inventory of its resources and needs and to devise a long-term program that would increase and diversify its production, check the rural exodus by increasing facilities and amenities in the villages, and create employment opportunities for Papeete's expanding population. The detailed program that resulted from this stock-taking[5] has remained French Polynesia's basic blueprint, though it has undergone modifications in relation to the rising cost of living and to the resources available.

By 1961, when the third plan went into operation, its total cost was found to have been gravely underestimated, for building costs had risen in the interval by nearly 30 percent and wages by 25 percent. Obviously the territory would have to ask France for more aid, and in 1962 a group of senators came from Paris to study its needs and the territorial assembly sent a mission to request the French government for additional funds. It was to the startled and apprehensive members of that mission that General de Gaulle made known his decision to install the C.E.P. in the islands.[6] To make the C.E.P. more acceptable to the islanders, the general agreed not only to meet the budgetary deficit and take over the cost of the territory's secondary schools and communications services, but also to finance the expanded public-works programs. Consequently the 1961–1963 plan was extended through 1965, and its prospective annual expenditures were estimated at 6.5 million Metro. francs.

In a speech to the National Assembly on January 22, 1963, John Teariki did not deny that France had come to the aid of the territory substantially, but he held French policy responsible for the budgetary deficit which made such aid necessary. If the Paris government had listened to the assembly's pleas and reduced the number of Metropolitan officials serving there, he said, the islands could have financed

[5] *La Polynésie Française* (La Documentation Française), p. 35.
[6] See pp. 52–53.

their own equipment. And if the F.I.D.E.S. had not dispersed the 120 million or more C.F.P. francs it had been spending annually in the territory upon so many uneconomic projects, French Polynesia would have had sufficient resources of its own to meet the rising cost of its health and education services. To a slight degree, such criticism may have been responsible for the marked increase in French financial aid to the territory during the 1960s. In any case, French public funds for the execution of the 1961–1965 plan totaled 43,409,000 Metro. francs.

The C.E.P. brought vast improvements in French Polynesia's infrastructure. A new port, hospital, and radio station; airfields in the outer islands; roads; urbanization projects, including water-distribution systems; and a host of new buildings for the use of the administration and the general public were among the most important permanent assets of the C.E.P. legacy. Furthermore, almost all the machinery and equipment used for the C.E.P.'s construction projects was eventually to be bequeathed to the territory's public-works service to carry out future projects. To meet the cost of maintaining and operating its newly acquired facilities, and to enable the local authorities to plan a program for the next 5 years that would take up the slack in employment which would inevitably follow completion of the C.E.P. installations, French Polynesia's fourth plan (1966–1970) was incorporated into that of France. Total expenditures for the fourth plan were anticipated to amount to 13 to 14 billion C.F.P. francs, to which it was hoped that the European Common Market fund would contribute some 600 millions annually, the territorial budget and private investors supplying smaller amounts and France paying for the balance.[7]

This massive and rapid injection of French public funds, as well as a concurrent growth in private investments, were responsible for the territory's undeniable prosperity in the 1960s. Governor Jean Sicurani told the territorial assembly on October 11, 1966, that the C.E.P. had directly and indirectly provided French Polynesia with 38 percent of its revenues in 1964 and 57 percent in 1965, and in 1966 it accounted for half of the territory's total economic activity. He added that the gross national product, which had been growing by 9 percent a year from 1960 through 1962, had risen from 5 billion C.F.P. francs to 10

[7] To carry out this program, various state-sponsored organizations and companies were set up. Among the more important of these were the Société d'Equipement de Tahiti et des Iles to develop land for agriculture, animal husbandry, and tourism, and the Société de Tahiti et des Iles to undertake research and to advise on the investment of funds to finance housing and industrial projects.

billion between 1963 and 1966. During 1965 and 1966 the C.E.P.'s expenditures had totaled about three times the territory's local revenues and twice the amount spent by the F.I.D.E.S. in the islands. Commercial firms had multiplied and prospered as never before from the sale of imported goods as the result of full employment and the presence of thousands of new consumers. By early 1966, the money in circulation in the territory had risen to 1,300 million C.F.P. francs from 550 million in 1960.

Inevitably the medal has had its reverse. Owing to the vast increase in imported equipment and consumer goods and the decline in exports, the trade deficit grew phenomenally.[8] Prices for merchandise, housing, and services had also risen vertiginously, and the high wages paid by the C.E.P. made it so difficult for the public-works service to recruit laborers that it was unable to carry out some of the projects for which it had the funds. Tourism declined both because of the fears inspired by the C.E.P.'s nuclear testing and because of the inconveniences resulting from the presence of its personnel and equipment. Opponents of the C.E.P. were quick to point out that the territory's current prosperity was not only artificial but transient, and that it risked doing permanent injury to the island's basic economy. The Polynesians' increasing abandonment of the traditional occupations was a bad augury for the future, and the discontent engendered among a population which had become accustomed to high wages and living standards that could not be maintained might be transformed into political and social agitation.

Foreign capital and enterprise have been responsible for French Polynesia's economic evolution to a greater degree than in many former colonial areas. This is particularly striking because the islands, except for Makatea's phosphates, possess none of the resources that normally attract aliens to make such investments of time, money, and energy. In positive terms, the Polynesians have done nothing to promote such a development. On the contrary, they long resisted—passively rather than actively—any changes in their way of life, and only in very recent years have they been willing to hire out their labor in order to buy consumer goods. This newfound desire for the "good life," best illustrated by the ever-growing attraction of Papeete for the outer-islanders, may well persist, but it does not necessarily indicate a profound transformation in their refusal to play a dynamic role in the modern world. There is a striking discrepancy between the

8 See p. 136.

modernization of the territory's economy sought by the *demi* elite and the reluctance of the Polynesians to make the effort required to achieve it. Thus their lack of interest in producing beyond the satisfaction of their immediate needs, and in expanding French secular educational and Western medical facilities, makes them generally indifferent to projects for increasing exports and for building more schools and hospitals. They would, however, like greater ease of living and more facilities for travel and diversion.

This insouciant and pleasure-loving attitude has been one of the islanders' main attractions for foreigners, and therein lies the crux of the problem. The development of tourism, in which so many current hopes are placed, depends largely on maintaining the traditional Polynesian ambiance. To Westerners weary of an industrial civilization, the islanders personify something intangible that draws them to French Polynesia. Yet the Polynesians are now succumbing to some of the material aspects of that civilization which they have come to enjoy as a by-product of the activities of the C.E.P. Although the C.E.P. may have simply accelerated a change in their attitude that was already in the making, and although the utility of the islands as a base for nuclear testing is probably drawing to a close (along with the swollen French subsidies of the last few years), that center has already left a psychological fall-out that is likely to have permanent effects. After years of being forced along the road to modernization by Christian missionaries, the French administration, and foreign traders, the Polynesians are now moving voluntarily in that direction. It is ironical that in so doing they are jeopardizing the very asset that has drawn tourists to the islands, and thus risk drying up the source of funds most likely to provide them with the means of acquiring the material things that they have come to want.

9

The Demographic Picture

The evolution of French Polynesia's economy has both influenced and been affected by the structural and numerical changes in its population. Between 1911 and 1962, the population of the islands tripled, albeit unevenly from one archipelago to another, and there was a marked shift in its center of gravity, as can be seen in table 1. (The over-all population-density figure of approximately thirteen persons to the square kilometer is meaningless for the volcanic islands, where the interior is uninhabited.) In 1926, 40 percent of the total population lived in Tahiti and 60 percent in the outer islands, whereas in 1962 these proportions were almost exactly reversed. All the archipelagoes experienced an increase in the size of their populations, but the rates of growth were not identical, and Tahiti's grew far more rapidly than did that of the other islands. During the decade 1946–1956 the over-all population increase of 38 percent for the E.F.O. was led by the Windward Islands (51 percent), followed by the Marquesas (40 percent), the Tuamotu-Gambier group (25 percent), the Leeward Islands (24 percent), and the Australs (5 percent). Then between 1956 and 1962, the tempo of migration to Tahiti accelerated rapidly with the arrival of 1,500 from the Leeward Islands, 3,000 from the Tuamotu-Gambier archipelagoes, and 500 from the Australs. It is noteworthy that comparatively few immigrants came to Tahiti from the Marquesas.[1]

1962 is the last year for which statistics may be taken to indicate permanent population trends, for the sudden influx of transient foreigners who came to work for the C.E.P. began in 1963. Throughout the post-World War II period, the immigration of aliens has counted for little in the population's growth, and indeed that of Asians had virtually ceased after 1928. As of 1956, only 5 percent of all the in-

[1] *Recensement Général de la Population* (*Décembre 1956*), Service de Statistique, Ministère de la Coopération, Paris, 1960. See also *Europe-France-Outre-Mer*, no. 423, 1965.

TABLE 1

COMPOSITION AND DISTRIBUTION OF FRENCH POLYNESIA'S POPULATION, 1911–1962 (SELECTED YEARS)

	Ethnic composition		
Year [a]	Non-native	Metropolitan French	Total, including native
1911	2,700	. . .	26,500
1931	6,300	. . .	40,400
1946	10,700	3,200	55,400
1951	9,100	2,200	62,700
1956	9,535	2,300	73,200
1962	10,455	2,790	84,550

			Distribution				
				By island groups			
Year [b]	Tahiti (all)	Town of Papeete	Windwards	Leewards	Australs	Marquesas	Tuamotu-Gambiers
1946	24,700	12,430	29,340	12,460	3,910	2,975	6,690
1951	30,500	15,220	35,385	12,900	3,975	3,260	7,155
1956	36,325	17,250	42,400	14,600	4,030	3,935	8,240
1962	45,430	19,900	52,070	16,180	4,370	4,840	7,100

[a] Complete data for 1911 and 1931 are unavailable.
[b] Data for 1911 and 1931 are unavailable.

habitants had been born outside the islands, and between 1956 and 1962 the number of alien Chinese had actually declined from 6,901 to 5,685. The Metropolitan French contingent has remained remarkably stable numerically, between 2,000 and 3,000 persons, although its composition has changed over the years. In 1848 the Metropolitan French comprised 76 settlers and traders and 400 functionaries and troops; by 1951 the civil servants numbered only 355 and the trader-settler element had grown to 1,069.

In evaluating the number of European residents, it should be remembered that the registers of vital statistics, more often than not, are incomplete, inaccurate or illegible, and that many of those listed in them as Europeans are actually of mixed blood. No caste lines or racist sentiments divide the *demis* from the Polynesians and Europeans. Intermarriage has in fact become so common that the pure-blooded

Polynesians are now probably a minority in the total population, although the Polynesian strain predominates in the outer islands and in the districts of Tahiti. In the capital itself, with its concentration of Westerners, *demis,* and Asians, the Polynesians are a minority. This situation, however, may be in the process of changing because of the large-scale migration of outer islanders to Papeete, the rise there in the proportion of women to men, and the rapid growth in the number of adolescents—all of which are modifying the composition of that town as well as swelling its size.

Although Papeete is said to be the oldest township in the south Pacific, it was not until early in the 19th century that it acquired importance. The early European navigators anchored in the bay of Matavai, but their successors were increasingly attracted to Papeete because of its sheltered roadstead and access to abundant fresh water.[2] With the increasing ship traffic at Papeete, a small settlement of Polynesians grew up there, and in 1827 Queen Pomaré made Papeete her principal residence. Sixteen years later it became the capital of the newly established French Protectorate, although it then had a population of only some 1,500 persons. Papeete had to wait another 50 years to acquire a municipal government, and its population numbered no more than about 5,000 when World War I broke out.

During the interwar period, the influx of Asians and Polynesian outer-islanders spurred Papeete's growth, and in 1946 it had 12,417 residents. Its spectacular expansion, however, dates from the early 1960s, when the construction of the Faaa airport was followed by development of the tourist industry and by implantation of the C.E.P. Papeete has overflowed into the suburbs, its growth has been haphazard and anarchic, and its population—of whom fewer than half were born there—is highly cosmopolitan and unstable. In other respects, too, Papeete is differentiated from other settlements in the territory. Agriculture and fishing have lost much of their importance and tourism has become its most important economic activity. Papeete's lack of primary products, sources of energy, and sizeable local market deny it an industrial future, and its greatest assets remain its location at the crossroads of the south Pacific, its excellent airport, and its modern harbor, not to mention the natural beauty of its hinterland and its reputation for glamor.

[2] Doumenge, F., "Development of Papeete—Capital of French Polynesia," *South Pacific Bulletin,* July 1967.

THE CHINESE MINORITY: IMMIGRATION [3]

The first Chinese to reach Tahiti were a handful of troublesome coolies landed at Papeete in 1856 from a steamer en route from Australia to San Francisco, but not until eight years later did a large number of Chinese come to the island. An Englishman, William Stewart, who had acquired a plantation at Atimaono, 40 kilometers from Papeete, was given permission to bring in 1,000 Chinese laborers to grow cotton there. In 1864–1865, the 993 Chinese he had recruited arrived in the colony under a seven-year contract. His company, however, went bankrupt before their contract expired, and the great majority of the laborers were rounded up and forcibly repatriated to China. A few managed to stay in Tahiti, where they found work as agricultural laborers or domestic servants, and gradually they were joined by new immigrants from China. Although the Chinese totaled fewer than 400 in the 1880s, they were already regarded with apprehension by the resident French merchants because they deserted farming as soon as they had accumulated enough money to set themselves up as shop-keepers. When John Hart, an American settler, asked permission in 1889 to import 200 Chinese coolies for another cotton-growing venture, the general council objected strongly. The councilors asserted that the Chinese would spread disease and the habits of gambling and opium-smoking among the Polynesians, but their real objection was that the Chinese would soon transform themselves from agricultural laborers into competitive traders.

Because of the chronic shortage of farm labor, the Chamber of Agriculture and the local administration—unlike the European merchants—favored Chinese immigration under certain conditions. Generally speaking, the controls imposed on Chinese immigration and residence until the end of the 19th century were the same as those applied to all foreigners. The Paris government repeatedly turned down requests from the general council and Chamber of Commerce that restrictions be placed on the number of Chinese immigrants, of licenses granted to Chinese merchants, and of the areas where the Chinese would be permitted to live and to work, on the ground that such restrictions would contravene the Franco-Chinese treaty of 1885.

[3] For the basic data used in this section, the authors are greatly indebted to the authoritative monographs on the Chinese minority by René Gauze and Gérald Coppenrath, as well as to the studies of Richard Moench.

Consequently the flow of Chinese immigrants continued to increase after the turn of the century, and they soon spread from Tahiti to the outer islands. Because living conditions were primitive and profits small, the Chinese encountered little or no opposition from other traders, and they soon gained a virtual monopoly of the export-import commerce, local trade, and interisland shipping.

The administration finally yielded to mounting pressure in Tahiti, beginning in 1902, and Chinese immigrants were required to carry passports visaed by the French consul at their port of embarkation in China and to register with the police upon arrival at Papeete. In 1908 a regulation was imposed exacting a money deposit against the eventual repatriation of all Chinese immigrants other than agricultural workers. These restrictive measures, however, did little to check the Chinese influx, which, in 1907, for the first time included women immigrants and which, after 1911, was accelerated by the revolution of that year in China. Between 1907 and 1914, 2,512 Chinese (of whom about 200 were women and children) arrived in the colony, and it was they who laid the foundation for the sizeable minority community that developed there after World War I. The second large wave of Chinese immigrants occurred between 1921 and 1928, partly as a result of the opening of a direct shipping service between Hong Kong and Papeete, but even more because of the recruiting of laborers in China to work the phosphate deposits of Makatea.

That it was the colony's economic situation that determined the flow of Chinese between the mainland and the E.F.O. was demonstrated in the early 1930s when the world depression so undermined the islands' economy that many Chinese workers returned home. This emigration tapered off by the mid-1930s, when the economy began to improve, yet in that decade as a whole the departures of Chinese largely offset their arrivals, and for the first time in the colony's history the number of locally born Chinese children exceeded that of adult immigrants. In the years just preceding World War II, the unsettled conditions in China, the Japanese invasion of the mainland, and the increase in the number of Chinese attending local French schools all contributed to reducing Chinese mobility and to rooting the Chinese community more firmly in the E.F.O. When World War II broke out, the resident Chinese minority numbered 5,469, almost none of whom had immigrated within the preceding few years.

When shipping services with China, interrupted during the war, were reestablished some time after V-J Day, there occurred a large-scale exodus of Chinese from the E.F.O. In 1947–1948, two chartered steamers carried back to China 757 members of the local Chinese community, of whom 496 had been locally born. After the communist take-over of the mainland in October 1949, many of these emigrants tried to return to Tahiti. The local administration, however, turned a deaf ear to their pleas, only too happy that the local Chinese problem had been eased and also that communist propaganda which might have been brought in by some of the returnees had been excluded. Thanks to the collusion of a venal official, 63 of the emigrants managed to be readmitted to the islands, and their clandestine reentry revived anti-Chinese sentiments which had lain largely dormant since the cessation of large-scale Chinese immigration during the interwar period.

Twice in 1950 the representative assembly heatedly debated the question of Chinese immigration and naturalization. It was now clear that curtailment of immigration was the only effective means at the authorities' disposal in their dealings with the Chinese. So adept were the Chinese at resisting all external efforts to penetrate their community and to organize them that little control could be asserted over them once they acquired a foothold in the territory. Yet the assembly-men agreed that it would be inhumane under current circumstances to shut the door completely to Chinese immigration, so they voted to ask the administration to screen applicants for immigration with the utmost care and to submit to the assembly for approval the names of those acceptable to the government. Since then, Chinese seeking admittance to French Polynesia have been granted only tourist visas, with the result that both Chinese immigration and emigration have been reduced to negligible proportions. Between 1941 and 1962, only 100 immigrants were enumerated among the 5,000 or more resident Chinese who retained their legal status as aliens.

THE CHINESE MINORITY: OFFICIAL CONTROLS AND TAXES

The *congrégation*—an organizational form used by France in all her colonies having sizeable Chinese minorities—was established in Tahiti in 1871. On November 16, of that year, the governor appointed No Foo Sii, a former Atimaono laborer called John Smith for reasons unknown, as its chief. Smith was expected to keep his compatriots informed of all relevant official regulations, to be their spokesman to the authorities, and to report to the administration on the activities and whereabouts of all members of the Chinese community. Not surprisingly, Smith was unable to play this multiple role to the governor's satisfaction, and in 1875 a second *congrégation* chief was appointed. He, too, soon proved to be an ineffectual intermediary, and a few years later the *congrégation* organization was abandoned, not to be revived until a new chief was appointed in 1913.

Irritated by the administration's inability or unwillingness to check Chinese immigration and activities, the general council—supported by a virulently anti-Chinese local press—voted a series of discriminatory measures between 1895 and 1908. The most significant of them was a residence tax (*taxe de séjour*) to be paid by all Chinese not engaged in agriculture or domestic service. The Paris government, however, refused to approve either this measure or one establishing a head tax, and so the general council proposed a fee of 2,500 francs to be exacted of all immigrants arriving in the colony. Paris vetoed this proposal as well, but did suggest in its place a registration fee that would be added to the license paid by Chinese merchants and that ranged between 100 and 1,200 francs a year. Papeete's Chinese traders did not accept this docilely, and they hired a French lawyer to defend their interests. This he effectively did by stressing the treaty rights of the local Chinese and the vital role they played in the colony's economy. Far from being a danger to the health, morality, or trade of the population, he argued, the Chinese were an asset, and the Conseil d'Etat in Paris, to which the question was referred, endorsed his view in 1899. Consequently, for the next few years the local administration followed a more liberal policy in respect to granting trading licenses to the Chinese, the *congrégation* organization remained in abeyance, and the number of Chinese immigrants increased.

The anti-Chinese forces were not long discouraged by this setback, and they returned to the attack during the first years of the twentieth century. To some degree the local administration yielded to their pressure and Chinese immigrants had to submit to a medical examination before disembarking and to being fingerprinted by the police. But it was the imposition of an annual tax on all male Asian and African immigrants on December 28, 1908, that again aroused the local Chinese community to action. Once more they appealed successfully over the head of the local authorities to the Paris government. On the eve of World War I, the Conseil d'Etat not only annulled the tax as illegal but compelled the Papeete treasury to reimburse the Chinese who had paid the tax during the preceding 5 years. This decision on the part of the highest French constitutional authority put an end to the efforts by

the local anti-Chinese forces to impose specifically discriminatory legislation. Although the registration and residence taxes were maintained
and even increased during the succeeding years, they were applied
uniformly to all aliens and not exclusively to the Chinese. Moreover,
when the *congrégation* organization was revived for the Chinese minority in the 1920s, the authorities gave it a more liberal and elastic
form than before. The three *congrégations* then formed followed the
existing organizational divisions in the Chinese community, and their
chiefs were elected by the membership and no longer appointed by
the administration.

Although the world depression reduced the size of the Chinese minority in the colony, it also reawakened anti-Chinese feeling among
the European residents. A series of spectacular Chinese bankruptcies,
with far-reaching repercussions on the islands' economy, touched off
renewed demands for imposing stronger controls on Chinese activities,
notably by requiring traders to keep their accounts in French and according to European methods, and to employ French citizens up to a
minimum of half their personnel. More far-reaching were the laws
passed in this period with respect to land ownership and taxes. Before
1905, only 17 Chinese had acquired real property in the colony, but
by the early 1930s the foreclosure of debts during the depression had
brought considerable areas of land under Chinese ownership. The land
laws of 1932 and 1934 were therefore carefully drafted so as to prevent
further Chinese inroads in that domain.[4] Two decrees in 1931—which
in reality were fiscal reprisals—imposed a supplementary duty to be
paid by licensed Asian traders and industrialists, as well as a higher
residence fee, to which all immigrants arriving in the colony after January 1, 1932, were made liable. Once more the Chinese used the
strategy that had been so successful before World War I, but this time
the Conseil d'Etat rejected their plea. The Chinese, however, protested
effectively against another measure, also dating from 1931, that had
been inspired by the government's difficulties in collecting taxes from
the Chinese. This measure held the *congrégation* collectively responsible for the payment of its members' taxes and obliged all Chinese
residents to belong to one of the three existing *congrégations*. This was
so patently unfair, in that a *congrégation* was compelled to accept as
members men known to be poor credit risks, that the measure was
rescinded in 1933. At the same time, all foreign residents except
laborers were placed under the direct supervision of the police.

[4] See p. 110.

After World War II the situation of the Chinese minority changed radically as a result of developments in the territory and in China. Taxation, however, remained the principal bone of contention between the Chinese residents and the local authorities. With fair success the Chinese continued to resist paying what were, in all but name, heavily discriminatory taxes, while the newly elected local politicians—like their predecessors in the general council—tried to use the fiscal weapon both to protect local economic interests against the Chinese and to swell the territory's revenues. In the early postwar years, the new factor in this situation was the intervention by the official representatives of Nationalist China in Paris and in Papeete to obtain a reduction in the steadily rising taxation to which their compatriots in the E.F.O. were subject. The government of the Kuomintang was too weak to exert effective pressure, and its diplomats succeeded only in intensifying anti-Chinese sentiment in the territory. During 1954, the time-worn proposals to restrict the number of Chinese permitted to live in the E.F.O. and to expel all those who failed to pay their taxes were again voiced in the assembly. Though these threats were obviously unrealistic, they did frighten many Chinese delinquents into paying their back taxes.

Gradually a more cooperative attitude developed on both sides. The assemblymen more or less tacitly agreed to treat the Chinese as stateless foreigners and slowly to ease official controls over them and to diminish discriminatory taxation. Indeed by the early 1960s, neither the authorities nor the Chinese were any longer thinking in those terms but were debating the advisability of liberalizing the laws regulating naturalization of the Chinese. The issues involved were so complex and the attitudes of the various communities concerned so divided that the territorial assembly for some years preferred not to debate the question at all. "Assimilation" became the key word and touchstone in any discussion of the naturalization question, but the term was so imprecise that it lent itself to various interpretations. It was the French government, which had the final say in such matters, that decided whether or not each Chinese applicant was sufficiently "assimilated" to be granted citizenship, but this decision was colored by many considerations. Among these were the candidate's ability to speak and write French, which largely depended on his having attended a French school; whether his manner of living was based on Occidental or traditional Chinese standards; and above all his political affiliations and economic activities. To understand the complexities involved one must take into consideration the Chinese role in the territory's economy, the status of the Chinese associations, and the evolution of the traditional Chinese schools which they founded.

THE CHINESE ROLE IN THE ECONOMY

There is no branch of the economy of French Polynesia in which the Chinese have not participated, and in some they have won control. Directly or indirectly, half of the territory's economic activities are in the hands of the Chinese, if that term is used to include the local-born and naturalized elements of that community. By and large, the Chinese are strongest in the role of middleman and weakest in that of producer.

Brought in originally as agricultural laborers, the Chinese have largely forsaken farming for trade, but it is still the Chinese who, as tenant farmers and sharecroppers, grow most of the territory's European vegetables and some of its vanilla. Despite the Polynesian land-tenure system and the French laws perpetuating it, the Chinese are owners of real property variously and vaguely estimated at 3 percent or 15 percent of the known arable area. They have been able to rent land on short-term leases, but farming is only marginally profitable, and for the Chinese it has been generally far easier and more remunerative to lease a shop or market stall. By their thrift, industry, adaptability, communal solidarity, and keen money sense, as well as because of the Polynesians' indolence, insouciance, lack of discipline, and indifference to profit, the Chinese in the territory—as in many other parts of the world—have had their most conspicuous success in trade. Although their biggest enterprises are centered in Papeete, they have expanded throughout the archipelagoes comprised in French Polynesia.

Traditionally the family has been the basic unit of Chinese economic activity. By extension, the dialect spoken and the village of origin in China have also determined the distinctively Chinese mercantile relationships and complex credit system known in French Polynesia as *tung ka*. In the traditional pattern, the head of a Chinese trading family has preferred to associate his sons closely with his business by training them as children in its practices. They are lodged, fed and clothed, and they work hard as unpaid clerks in the expectation that some day they will inherit the business. This situation is slowly being modified by the higher education which a growing number of Chinese youths are receiving in French and American schools. Because French

Polynesia trades far more with the West than with Asia, the older
Chinese merchants want their sons to be grounded early in Occidental
business methods which they themselves have had to learn in hard and
long years of experience.

The *tung ka* system has grown out of the particular situation of the
territory's Chinese minority and of their geographic and economic set-
up. It regulates almost wholly the dealings between Chinese merchants
in Papeete and the outer islands, although on rare occasions it includes
European and *demi* traders. The import-export wholesalers established
in the capital lend merchandise to young men, usually their relatives or
regional compatriots, who are starting out to do business in rural areas.
This merchandise is used either to stock shops in the outer islands or as
advances to Polynesian producers of copra, shell, and vanilla, who in
return pledge their prospective output as security. This is obviously a
risky business, for not only may the borrower fail to honor his debt,
but the prices for shell and vanilla are particularly subject to sudden
fluctuations. Some Chinese merchants have made large profits whereas
others have undergone crippling losses, but the speculative aspect of
this trade appeals to the deep-rooted Chinese gambling instinct. Moreover, for the rural retailer who lacks capital to start a business, the
tung ka system has the advantage of providing him with merchandise
without his having to borrow money, and for the urban wholesaler that
of being assured a regular supply of the territory's main exports. The
practical side of this relationship is paralleled by a social and sometimes highly personal one. Often there develops a bond of personal
loyalty between the patron-merchant and his retailer client, which may
be reinforced by the exchange of gifts on appropriate occasions and
even by ties of marriage. Although the *tung ka* relationship is still
widespread in French Polynesia, its paternalistic and personalized
features are beginning to give way before the growth of formal credit
institutions, specialization in various commercial domains, and, to a
limited extent, cooperative societies.

Official statistics give no clue to the proportion of wholesale to retail
merchants in the Chinese community or to the amount and area of
capital investments by the Chinese. Nor do the successive censuses
taken in French Polynesia provide data as to the occupations of the
naturalized Chinese, for they comprise only those classified as aliens.
The greater educational opportunities now open to young Chinese have
provided them with a wider choice of occupations, and they are
notably acquiring a virtual monopoly of clerical jobs in the private

sector, Alien Chinese cannot enter the civil service, however, and in practice the exercise of the liberal professons is sharply limited by the small size of the paying clientele.

Although banking as a legitimate occupation has been barred to the Chinese since the disastrous bankruptcies of the 1930s, the Chinese indirectly finance many of the territory's productive activities, notably shell-diving and the preparation of copra and vanilla. Only briefly and as laborers did they play a role in producing what was for many years the territory's third major export, phosphates. As industrialists, their activities were confined to the manufacture of soft drinks and carbonated water until 1968, when the territory's first industrial coconut oil-mill was built and managed by a Chinese firm of Papeete.[5]

It seems paradoxical that the jealousy and fears inspired by Chinese competition for many years among the French and *demi* trading communities should be diminishing at a time when the economic role played by the Chinese appears to be stronger than ever. The number of licensed Chinese merchants, however, should perhaps not be taken as an indication of their relative strength, for often several licenses are issued to the same merchant, and their total has remained proportionately much the same in relation to the growth of the population and of the economy.[6] With the cessation of shipments of phosphate, the one major export that had always escaped Chinese control, and the replacement of copra exports by those of coconut oil milled by a Chinese firm, the grip of the Chinese on the export trade as a whole has certainly become firmer. As for the territory's imports, the situation will become clearer after the cessation of the C.E.P. activities, which have distorted the whole import picture, but it appears that until 1969 the French trading firms had enlarged their hold on that aspect of French Polynesia's foreign trade. Consequently a modus vivendi may now have been reached between the big French and Chinese merchants in the delimitation of their respective economic strongholds, and this may account for the present lack of complaints about Chinese parasitism, formerly a standard feature of the debates in the assembly and the Chamber of Commerce. It seems unlikely that objections to more liberal naturalization qualifications for the Chinese would now come from this quarter.

[5] See pp. 120–121.

[6] R. Gauze notes that in 1899 there were 77 licensed Chinese merchants, of whom 64 were in Papeete; in 1962, 547 licenses were issued to Chinese, and 251 of these went to Papeete traders. See his *La Minorité Ethnique Chinoise,* p. 138.

CHINESE ASSOCIATIONS

After the administration's abortive attempt to form a Chinese *congré-gation* in 1871, the local Chinese were left to organize themselves so long as they did not trouble the public order. Yet for more than 25 years the only association they founded was a mutual-aid society at Mamao on land donated by some Chinese who had worked on the Atimaono plantation. As time went on, the purely social activities of that society failed to meet the needs of the growing Chinese community. In 1911 a Papeete businessman, Chin Foo, founded an alternative association, the Société Immobilière Sin Ni Tong, which soon took over the management of the Mamao property and of the Chinese cemetery at Arue. During World War I, trouble broke out not only between the new association and the government but also among the members of the Sin Ni Tong. The administration took stern steps after discovering that the Sin Ni Tong's proclaimed philanthropic activities were largely a cover for an illegal gambling establishment. The disagreement that troubled the Sin Ni Tong's membership was over whether or not to support Sun Yat Sen's revolutionary activities. The conservative members, led by Chin Foo, broke away on May 20, 1921, to found the Chung Fa Fui Kon, or Chinese Philanthropic Association. The younger and more radical elements, numbering 131, formed the Chinese National League of Papeete, which later took the name of Kuomintang of Tahiti. Among the leaders of the latter group was Yune Seng, manager of the important local banking firm, the Kong Ah Company.

The Sin Ni Tong, with which Chin Foo remained associated and which included some of the wealthiest members of the Chinese community, survived as a politically neutral association and still nominally a philanthropic organization. It continued to operate gambling and opium dens, however, and consequently it was closed down several times by the authorities. The other two associations were more politically oriented, and when violent quarrels broke out between their members they, too, fell afoul of the local police. Yet when the administration decided in 1922 to organize the Chinese community into three *congrégations,* it adhered to the existing division into associations which the Chinese had worked out for themselves.

After 1923 the Chinese became more discreet and adopted a policy of avoiding clashes with the authorities. They also endeavored to avoid activities that might arouse adverse reactions from the French business community. During the 1920s, five new Chinese associations were formed.[7] Except for two purely sports groups, all the new associations formed during the interwar period were nominally charitable or professional in their orientation, and the three oldest of them each organized its own Chinese school. In reality these associations functioned more and more as social clubs devoted to gambling and opium smoking. Of the older ones, only the Kuomintang continued to operate as a political group, whose leaders maintained close contacts with the parent organization in China. By 1930 it claimed to have 1,600 members, of whom 250 were women. But in the mid-1930s the Kuomintang suffered from repercussions of the Kong Ah bankruptcy because of its close relations with Yune Seng. Moreover, political differences and personality conflicts added other rifts, and during World War II one dissident element broke away to form the Koo Men Tong, also known as the Association Amicale de la Chine Libre de Tahiti. The Koo Men Tong grew rapidly and succeeded in winning official recognition from the local administration, but its position became somewhat anomalous after the arrival at Papeete in 1944 of the first Chinese consul sent by the Chungking government, who supported both it and the orthodox Kuomintang association.

In the post-World War II period, the Chinese association receded into the background and became inconspicuous social and philanthropic clubs, and increasingly they reflected the evolution of the whole Chinese community. The Koo Men Tong, still under the presidency of Yune Seng, had about 450 members, and the Kuomintang was reduced to a membership of 425 but remained the most active politically and culturally of the three long-established Chinese associations.[8] The 400 or so members of the Philanthropic Association, headed by two sons-in-law of Chin Foo, tried to maintain the traditional Chinese customs cherished by the older generation of the community.

The two first-mentioned organizations stressed their loyalty to Nationalist China, but all of them were mainly engaged in a wide range or social and cultural activities that included maintaining hostels for aged and indigent Chinese and operating schools. They were financed in part by annual membership dues of about 120 C.F.P. francs, but far

[7] These were the Cercle de Commerce Chinois, the Association de Bienfaisance Nam Hoi, La Fraternité, Kioun Fou, and the Cercle Céleste.

[8] The Papeete Kuomintang had an annex at Uturoa, whose membership took in 170 of the 466 Chinese living there.

more by contributions from their wealthy members and the income from illicit lotteries and gambling. Their older members continued to celebrate traditional Chinese holidays, but the younger ones turned increasingly to modern social diversions and were decreasingly political-minded as ties between the local Chinese and China became more tenuous. To some degree these associations still expressed the deep-rooted Chinese sense of cultural unity and nationalist sentiments, but their members' growing identification with the French and Polynesian elements in the territory was undermining their solidarity as a community. An indication of this changing outlook was the immediate success achieved by an Association pour le Devenir de la Polynésie Française. As its name suggests, it advocated assimilation to the territory, and within 3 years after its founding in 1963 it had a membership of over 700 young Chinese.

CHINESE SCHOOLS

The transformation of the Chinese associations from pseudo-political organizations and bastions of Chinese "apartness" into social clubs has been paralleled by the decline and disappearance of the association-founded Chinese traditional schools.

In view of the size of the Chinese community in the E.F.O. before World War I, it is surprising that the first Chinese schools there were not opened until 1922. The explanation is that the early Chinese imgrants were predominantly adult males and the few children in the Chinese minority were either sent to local mission schools or to China for their education. When the first Chinese school was officially inaugurated on December 15, 1922, at the request and on the initiative of the president of the Kuomintang association, it offered night classes for adults. As time went on, courses for children were added to the curriculum, and by 1928 it had 70 pupils. Eventually two other Chinese associations established schools for their members' children, and a fourth was founded at Uturoa. At their peak, the combined attendance at these schools was approximately 1,000, some of whom had already received instruction in the French schools.

The principal linguistic vehicle in the Chinese schools was Hakka until 1950, when it was replaced by Mandarin. In 1946 so many of the Chinese-school students failed their examination in French that all the Chinese schools were closed until more drastic reforms could be made. At that time the Kuomintang school had 219 pupils, the Koo

Men Tong school 339, the Philanthropic Association school 237, and the Uturoa school 80. Dissatisfaction with the functioning of the Chinese schools was not confined to the French administration. Parents and the more enterprising Chinese students themselves complained of the poor quality of teaching, despite attempts to improve it by bringing in two professors from Taiwan and, after 1957, by the requirement that instructors in the Chinese schools possess the *brevet élémentaire*. The basic difficulty, however, was that in the territory the traditional Chinese education was a dead end professionally, for the curriculum comprised such irrelevant subjects as literary Chinese, letter-writing, and Chinese history, geography, and music. Only the diplomas issued by the state and the officially recognized mission schools gave their holders access to institutions of higher learning and to jobs in the private (and public) sector. As of 1951, only 310 children were in Chinese schools, compared with the 875 Chinese pupils then attending mission schools, and when the Chinese schools were finally required to close down on June 1, 1964, their combined attendance totaled only about 200 students. Moreover, most of these were younger people who were attending primary state or mission schools and who were sent by their parents to the Chinese schools so that they should not lose contact with their traditional culture.

The census taken 2 years before the Chinese schools were suppressed showed clearly that the traditional culture had already lost considerable ground. Of the 9,527 members of the Chinese community enumerated in 1962, 3,372 stated that they could read and speak Chinese but most of them admitted to knowing only a few hundred characters, and 1,581 could speak and read only Chinese. The fact that 354 spoke and read Chinese and Tahitian, 568 Chinese and French, and 801 Chinese, French, and Tahitian may not seem impressive in relation to the size of the Chinese community, but these numbers did represent a greater proportion of those linguistically assimilated than in any previous census. The fact that members of the Chinese community voiced no objections to the closing of their traditional schools reflected their practicality rather than any lessening of their well-known enthusiasm for education. As of 1962, 2,572 Chinese children were attending French schools in the territory, and of these, 602 were at the secondary or technical level, 1,292 in mission schools, and 429 in state schools. In addition there were 20 local-born Chinese in French universities, 34 in those of the United States, and 4 in mainland China.

NATURALIZATIONS

For nearly a hundred years after they first came to the islands, the Chinese showed almost no interest in being naturalized, and this indifference conformed to official French policy and to European public opinion. Despite the obvious advantages in respect to taxation, access to the civil service, and acquisition of landed property, citizenship was not sought by the Chinese minority, partly because of their loyalty to China and partly because they objected to performing the military service that French citizenship entailed.

This attitude prevailed so long as it was possible to maintain close contacts between the E.F.O. and mainland China. Beginning in the 1930s, however, these contacts were interrupted or diminished by the Japanese invasion of China and then by World War II, and when the communists took over the government of China in October 1949, ties with the mainland were severed. To be sure, both official and informal contacts were maintained with the Nationalist Chinese government at Taipeh, but these did not have the same emotional impact for the E.F.O. Chinese as did those with China proper. Moreover, the consul sent by Taipeh to Papeete was staunchly pro-French, and though he strove to maintain cultural links between Taiwan and the overseas Chinese he also encouraged the latter to identify themselves more with the life around them than with obsolete Chinese traditions. Thus indirectly the attitude of Taiwan's emissary became a factor impelling the Chinese minority to seek naturalization.

The establishment of the communist government at Peking was also decisive in changing the attitude of the French authorities toward the naturalization of the Chinese minority. The French came around to believing that the surest way of immunizing the Chinese residents against communist propaganda was to give them more of a stake in the territory. They had also come to realize that one reason why the Chinese lived in such a crowded and disorderly fashion, behind or above their shops, was because they had no incentive to improve property which, as aliens, they could never own. Moreover, it was obvious that the younger Chinese who had been educated in French schools were insisting on more privacy, comfort, and space than their elders, and were conforming more to Western living standards. Thus the answer to the problem of the Chinese minority seemed to be in more rather than less integration with European society. In 1960, the Paris government ordered the local administration to facilitate the naturalization of Chinese applicants, and by 1964 about 40 percent of the resident Chinese had acquired French citizenship.

Objections to the enfranchisement of the local Chinese have never been raised by rural Polynesians. Before the immigration of Chinese women there had been considerable intermarriage between the two ethnic groups, and today there are some 3,000 Sino-Polynesian half-castes. Although there is a xenophobic strain in the Polynesians and they resent the Chinese feeling of superiority to them, relations on the whole have been good, especially in the outer islands, where the Polynesians regard the Chinese as indispensable to the economy, notably as a source of credit.

The Tahitians tend to ignore Chinese profits from the sale of merchandise to them, and they think only that the Chinese will grant them loans and not be too rigid about demanding repayment. The Chinese merchant doesn't seem to mind if the Tahitians use his store for interminable conversations without buying anything, and he may even join in their talk. His customers treat the Chinese either with arrogance or familiarity.[9]

Relations between the Chinese and the *demis* are not so cordial. In 1950 Pouvanaa protested strongly to the Minister of Overseas France against further naturalizations of the Chinese, and he urged their forcible repatriation—a rather surprising attitude in view of the considerable strain of Chinese blood in his own family. Since then, the *demis* have been fighting a rearguard action to prevent the Chinese, even those naturalized, from infiltrating the administration and the liberal professions, not to mention elective offices. They have, however, been somewhat reassured by the lack of interest shown by the Chinese in local politics and by the fact that many local-born Chinese who have had higher education abroad have preferred not to return to Polynesia because the opportunities for gainful employment there in the liberal professions are scarce.

Thus more of a consensus than ever before had been realized in respect to liberalizing the naturalization laws for the Chinese minority, when General de Gaulle's sudden recognition of the Peking government on January 24, 1964, added a new dimension to the question. This move precipitated, for the first time in a decade, a large-scale debate on the Chinese problem in the territorial assembly, which in recent years had been inclined to sweep the whole issue under the rug. Many of the outstanding *demi* politicians, led by Teariki, claimed

[9] Coppenrath, G., *Les Chinois de Tahiti*, p. 85.

that they favored assimilation in principle, but they sought to make the acquisition of French citizenship subject to so many conditions and delays that a Chinese applicant could not but be discouraged. Nevertheless, more unanimity than ever before was achieved, notably in opposing the assignment of a Chinese communist consul to Papeete. Obviously he would have far greater means at his disposal than the Taiwanese consul, and would be far more dangerous in that he could easily create serious divisions in the resident Chinese community. The assembly finally approved a cable to General de Gaulle stating that

the territorial assembly, concerned by the local repercussions following recognition of the Peking government, respectfully insists that diplomatic steps be taken to prevent communist infiltration and urges a more liberal procedure for naturalizing the Chinese as well as the maintenance of the Taiwan consul in French Polynesia.

The assembly's plea was heeded, and although Taiwan's consul had to leave a year and a half later as the result of pressure from Peking, he was not replaced by a communist diplomat. The French government was anxious above all to prevent dissension as well as espionage in the territory that had been chosen as the site for its nuclear-weapons experiments.

10

The Rural Economy

LAND TENURE

In ancient Polynesia, land might not be sold, and only usufruct rights could be inherited by a family or clan. A law voted by the Tahitian legislature on March 28, 1851, stated that Tahitians had never given away their land, and never would. When Queen Pomaré accepted the French protectorate on September 9, 1842, she stipulated that her landed property and the lands belonging to her people should remain in the hands of their present holders, and that all disputes involving land must fall within the competence of the courts of the country.[1] Beginning in 1845, however, land transfers were permitted. Eleven years later the islands were placed under the jurisdiction of the protectorate and made subject to French civil law, but on condition that the existing land-tenure system be respected. Although at the time of King Pomaré's abdication he asked that "all matters relating to the land be left in the hands of the native courts," those courts were abolished in 1887 when Tahiti was annexed by France.[2] Thus, from the outset, the French breached the traditional land-tenure system.

Since the islands became a colony, the French administration has repeatedly and ineffectually tried to institute the legal registration and delimitation of private property. A law of August 24, 1887, calling upon landowners to register their property met with no response. No greater success attended the application of a decree of March 22, 1925, designed to simplify the registration procedures and make them less onerous. To this day there are some islands where not a single land title has been registered.

For these successive failures there are many reasons. The most important is that the Western concept of private property conflicts with Polynesian tradition of collective—usually family—ownership of land.

[1] Minutes of the French Union Assembly, May 27, 1952.
[2] The Tahitian High Court, however, was reestablished in 1892.

Even small areas sometimes have as many as 100 to 200 owners, all with equal rights and many of them unknown to one another. In some archipelagoes, notably the Tuamotus, the population not only is semi-nomadic but owns shares in land dispersed over a dozen atolls. Stevenson, who visited one of the Tuamotus in the 1880s, found the island deserted, and observed:

the Governor in Papeete issued a decree: All land in the Paumotus (Tuamotus) must be defined and registered by a certain date . . . the inhabitants of Rotoava, in particular . . . owned—I was going to say land—owned at least coral blocks and growing coco-palms in some adjacent isle. Thither—from the gendarme to the babe in arms . . . they had taken ship some two days previous to our arrival, and were all now engaged in disputing boundaries.[3]

Aside from the obstacles inherent in the Polynesian social order, the French administration has not undertaken the land survey required by law as preliminary to the registration and sale of land. As yet only Papeete and its suburbs have been properly surveyed,[4] because urban land has acquired a considerable money value. There are no privately employed surveyors in the islands and the government has few at its disposal, for the pay is poor and the work entails living in the outer islands.[5] In 1962 the government created a Land Bureau, one of whose sections was assigned the task of collecting genealogical data on all the land-owning families in Tahiti so as to ascertain exactly who were the co-owners. This bureau's work has been slow and full of errors, for it has had to depend upon deficient registers of vital statistics. In the outer islands, such registers are usually kept by barely literate Notables,[6] who have not taken into account the Polynesian propensity for frequently changing names and for adopting children without legal formalities.

SETTLERS AND AGRICULTURAL COMPANIES

Despite the handicaps described above, the administration took over certain areas as state land, and conceded some of them to a few early

[3] Stevenson, R. L., *In the South Seas*, p. 178.

[4] Even this survey was long delayed, a cyclone in 1906 having destroyed all existing records.

[5] See minutes of the territorial assembly, Jan. 7, Nov. 15, 1965; Nov. 28, 1966.

[6] On July 8, 1965, the assembly voted to increase the pay of those who kept the registers of vital statistics. As evidence of the need to improve their caliber, one member cited a birth certificate to which had been appended the comment, "Avis favorable."

French settlers. In some cases, too, concessions were acquired by foreigners, either by fraud or by force. In the nineteenth century, Western smallholders were usually men who had jumped ship in the islands, or former functionaries, soldiers, or sailors who retired to the E.F.O. after completing their tours of duty. Most of them failed after a few years, for they had no capital to invest and were therefore forced to borrow money to clear the land, plant their crops, and live until they could reap the first harvest. Agricultural labor was not available to them even if they had had the funds to hire it. Those who tried to cultivate the soil themselves found the climate too enervating and often had to give up for reasons of health. The more robust and tenacious exhausted themselves in fighting plant pests, insects, and the pervasive vegetation, and were barely able to feed their families, much less to sell their output at remunerative prices. In the mid-nineteenth century, some settlers tried vainly to grow sugarcane and, during the American civil war, cotton, but they were soon forced to give up.

With one partial exception, no kinder fate attended the operations of the few agricultural companies which tried to farm in the E.F.O. on an industrial scale. This exception is the Compagnie Française de Tahiti, which leased the islands of Mopelia, Scilly, and Bellingshausen, and has there been producing about 1,000 tons of copra annually.[7] It is often claimed in Tahiti that in the nineteenth century, hundreds of hectares in its valleys were bartered by the Polynesians for a few gallons of rum, but with poetic justice these large properties proved worthless to the unscrupulous interlopers. There were no access roads to the hinterland, and no laborers willing to work the land, and the problem was not resolved by an attempted introduction of Chinese coolies.[8] After the Panama Canal was opened, more Europeans came to the islands and acquired a few long-term leases. In this way, during the interwar period, four large concessions were leased in the Marquesas and one on the Leeward Islands. After unsuccessful attempts to grow cotton, coffee, tobacco, sugarcane, and European vegetables, the surviving companies turned to coconuts, vanilla, and shell, which are the only products that have been—at times—remunerative in French Polynesia. The most prosperous periods for copra-producers and vanilla-growers have occurred either after wars or when climatic

[7] For the history of this company and its relations with the local inhabitants and administration, see Chadourne, M., *Vasco*, New York, 1927, pp. 188–204; minutes of the representative assembly, March 24, 1954.

[8] See p. 91.

conditions in competing countries have created world shortages in such output.

Because the history of European agriculture in French Polynesia, whether undertaken by individuals or by companies, has been one of unmitigated failure, such enterprises are no longer considered to be a threat to the indigenous landholders. Not only is farming, even on a large scale, rarely a paying proposition, but it has become virtually impossible to acquire arable land either by sale or by lease. In the interwar period, an increase in land ownership by the resident Chinese was regarded as a serious threat. Yet with the exception of a few dozen market gardeners, the Chinese had no wish to farm the land themselves. They acquired it for speculative purposes through the fore-closure of debts owed them by the Polynesians. This situation, which became acute during the depression of the early 1930s, impelled the administration to issue two decrees, on July 4, 1932, and June 23, 1934, forbidding the sale of land belonging to Polynesians to foreigners except with the specific permission of the governor-in-council.[9] These safeguards of the Polynesians' land heritage were reinforced by an-other decree, of June 18, 1940, which extended this prohibition to land rentals for a period of ten years or more.

When elected institutions were introduced after World War II, the representative assembly acquired some control over local land ques-tions. Although its members concurred with the administration's main objective of keeping the land in native hands, they felt that the mea-sures already adopted gave too much power to the governor and were also unfair to Polynesians who wanted to obtain money for their land. The assembly therefore rejected an administration proposal to forbid the sale of any undivided land, even if such property were duly regis-tered with the authorities.[10] The assemblymen were primarily con-cerned to prevent speculation in land, not only by the Chinese but also by Metropolitan Frenchmen, and especially by local *demi* capitalists who were reportedly then in the process of acquiring considerable real property. To force landowners to relinquish properties which they were simply holding in anticipation of a rise in land values, the assembly accepted a government proposal to tax undeveloped urban and arable rural land covering 50 hectares or more. In 1951, however, it asked that this measure be rescinded with respect to urban property,

[9] *L'Océanie Française,* July–August, November–December 1932; May–June 1934.

[10] Minutes of the representative assembly, April 26, 1950.

because it was causing hardship to Polynesian landowners in Papeete, who were unable to build for lack of capital.

AGRICULTURAL PRODUCTION

While the land-tenure regulations were effective insofar as they prevented the Polynesians from losing control of their land, they were largely negative in that they did not bring about any increase in agricultural production, which continued to be hampered because of the perpetuation of the traditional land-tenure system. As for its positive aspect, the system has certainly given the Polynesians a sense of security, and it is said that there is not a single Tahitian who is not at least a part-owner of some land. Yet because there are so many co-owners of even small plots of ground, there is no incentive to develop jointly held property. Each proprietor wants to obtain the maximum from his share, but is unwilling to develop the land because any improvements that he makes will automatically benefit the other owners, who may not have shared in the work or invested any money in it. Moreover, co-ownership has given rise to endless and expensive litigation over land, and such disputes, particularly in the Tuamotus, clutter up the calendars of the lawcourts. In the early 1950s, the administration eased this aspect of the problem to some extent by empowering the outer-island magistrates and justices of the peace to settle local land disputes so that litigants should be spared the time and expense involved in coming to Papeete for a judgment. Nevertheless, more constructive reforms were required to solve the problem of the continuing indivision of property, and it was proposed that owners be encouraged by fiscal concessions to register individual titles to their land.[11]

Nothing came of this proposal, and as of 1960 it was calculated that about 70 percent of all the arable land in French Polynesia was still held in undivided ownership. Moreover, a large proportion of this collectively held land, varying from one island group to another, was left uncultivated.[12] On Tahiti, not more than 17 percent of the cultivable area was actually farmed; in the Leeward Islands 39 percent; in the Tuamotus 36 percent; in the Australs 26 percent; and in the Marquesas 6 percent. Most of these collectively owned properties were small. Furthermore, on Tahiti, not more than 3 percent of all the culti-

[11] Speech by Governor Toby to the representative assembly, Nov. 14, 1954.
[12] *La Polynésie Française* (La Documentation Française), p. 20.

vated land was planted to food crops. Strictly speaking, agriculture was confined to the volcanic islands, for only coconut palms could grow on the atolls.[13] Even on the high islands, only the flat coastal land was farmed, for there was no means of access to the mountainous and fog-bound interior. Certainly more land could have been cultivated along the littoral if the swamps had been drained and planted to wet rice, but the Tahitians were willing to grow only their traditional crops of taro and fruit trees, whose output they themselves consumed, or such cash and food crops as coconuts, that require little regular care. Indeed, to the Polynesians the ideal form of vegetation is the coconut palm, which continues to yield food and many other useful items for half a century, and without much effort on their part.

Before World War II, the local administration displayed a defeatist attitude about increasing locally grown foodstuffs, even though the prices for imported rice, milk, flour, and beef doubled at Papeete between 1936 and 1939. The situation was regarded as hopeless because the Tahitians disliked growing food crops beyond the satisfaction of their immediate needs and because importing foreign labor was considered too expensive and socially inadvisable. It was not until the war, when food production declined in relation to the rapid growth of the population, especially in the towns to which the outer islanders were flocking, that this attitude changed. In April 1950 the representative assembly decided to encourage Polynesians holding long-term leases on arable land to acquire title to them by interest-free instalment buying over a ten-year period.[14] As urban unemployment continued to increase, it was realized by 1954 that a greater effort must be put forth to make farming attractive by improving agricultural techniques, extending more credit to farmers, and assuring a better price for their output. Only by making cultivation of the land profitable could the emigrants be persuaded to return to their islands to farm. As to the much debated problem of collective land ownership, it appears that the authorities have now abandoned any idea of forcing the population to accept the Western concept of private property, and are now seeking some formula of cooperative farming that could produce an increase in agricultural production within the context of Polynesian socioeconomic traditions.[15]

[13] Before World War II, schooners serving the atolls were required to carry soil to them from Tahiti, which the atoll-dwellers could purchase at a low price.

[14] Minutes of the representative assembly, April 4, 1950.

[15] Panoff, M., *Les Structures Agraires en Polynésie Française.*

OFFICIAL POLICY AND GOVERNMENT SERVICES

Early in the 20th century a Chamber of Agriculture was formed at Papeete to advise the administration concerning crops, credit facilities, and agricultural techniques. Over the years it has published a bulletin in French and Tahitian, which is distributed without charge to district councils, schools, and any individuals who ask for it. As a semipublic institution, the Chamber has received annual subsidies from the territorial budget, but in 1954 there was so much dissatisfaction with its operations that the assembly reduced the subsidy.[16] A few years later, the Chamber underwent one of its frequent reorganizations, and it was then promised more generous government aid if it would draw up a comprehensive and realistic agricultural program for the islands.

The Chamber's deficiencies made it imperative to create a more technically oriented organization, but it was not until November 23, 1946, that a service for agriculture, animal husbandry, and forestry was formed, and not until 1954 was it separated from the public-works department. The long delay in creating a specialized service was due to the assemblymen's perennial fear that it would bring more Metropolitan officials to the territory. In 1953, however, the Fonds d'Investissement pour le Développement Economique et Social (F.I.D.E.S.) had made a grant that enabled the E.F.O. to be divided into five distinct agricultural sectors, each with its own *chef de service*. This left the territorial budget responsible only for the salaries of the subordinate employes and those of the central administrative staff.[17] Even with an enlarged personnel, the agricultural service could do little for the E.F.O.'s ten thousand farmers dispersed over 120 islands, and it continued to be the target of criticism for neglecting food production and concentrating on export crops. To show their dissatisfaction, the assemblymen refused to allocate more money to the service's experimental station for high-altitude crops at Taravao. However, they did agree to finance an enlargement of the Pirae station so that it could train more agricultural monitors specifically for the outer islands.

Until 1965, the Pirae station provided the only formal instruction in agriculture in French Polynesia. Candidates for admission to its school were required to have a primary-school certificate and to pass a com-

[16] Minutes of the representative assembly, Dec. 8, 1954.

[17] As of 1960, the salaries of 24 agricultural *conducteurs* and monitors cost the budget 11,761,000 C.F.P. francs.

petitive entrance examination. Even after enlargement, however, the school's capacity was restricted to 20 pupils, and of these only 6 or 7 finished its two-year course. Moreover, 85 percent of its graduates entered the civil service rather than became practical farmers. To remedy this deficiency, the agricultural service proposed that a distinctively agricultural orientation be given in the final year of the territory's primary schools, and the assembly agreed to underwrite the experiment.

In 1965 the French government agency, the Bureau pour le Développement de la Production Agricole (B.D.P.A.), was asked to send a mission to the territory to recommend appropriate changes in the school curriculum. The B.D.P.A. expert, Jean Dourthe, stayed in the islands for two years, during which he wrote four textbooks (one manual for each of the four island groups) and trained a few instructors to teach five new classes for boys from thirteen to fifteen years of age in the outer islands' public schools.[18] From the outset Dourthe ran into opposition from the head of the territorial education service, and he failed to enlist the cooperation of the assemblymen. The president of the permanent commission characterized his efforts as a "total fiasco," [19] largely because the Polynesians would undergo agricultural training only if it led to a post in the civil service. Moreover, so long as the C.E.P. offered plenty of well-paid jobs, it was useless to try to interest youths in such a dubiously remunerative occupation as farming. To make farming profitable posed almost insuperable problems, among them a reform of the irregular and costly interisland shipping service.[20]

The efforts made by the administration and the assembly to provide farmers with credit facilities and to organize a cooperative movement were not much more successful than their attempt to teach modern techniques. As long ago as 1932, a Crédit Agricole Mutuel had been established, financed by the territorial budget and the Banque de l'Indochine. Its purpose was to grant medium- and short-term loans to the members of 9 agricultural cooperative societies, 15 "organizations of agricultural interest," and 18 agricultural associations formed at about the same time.[21] In two years the Mutuel's funds were exhausted without its having appreciably increased agricultural production.[22]

[18] See Dourthe, J., "Agricultural Education in French Polynesia."
[19] Minutes of the permanent commission, Jan. 31, 1967.
[20] See pp. 158–161.
[21] *L'Océanie Française,* September–October 1934.
[22] *Ibid.,* November–December 1936.

In 1948 the representative assembly, with some misgivings, agreed to the government's proposal to set up both producers' and consumers' cooperatives. Again, however, the movement failed to take root except in two of the outer islands, in part because of the opposition of Papeete's merchants. In 1954, however, the first successful local credit organization, the Crédit de l'Océanie, was founded, and ten years later it was able to report that it had granted loans to the rural sector amounting to over 91 million C.F.P. francs.[23] In the meantime, the cooperative movement continued to languish. Expert advice was sought from the B.D.P.A., but with no greater success than for the agricultural-education program. The two advisers who came to French Polynesia stayed only a few weeks and disagreed as to their recommendations. Again the assemblymen felt frustrated by their inability to get from the expensive services of Metropolitan experts practical results in terms of expanded agricultural output. Of the handful of cooperative societies that have survived, the only one that has succeeded in increasing food-crop production is that of market gardeners in the Austral Islands.

FOOD AND EXPORT CROPS

On islands of such luxuriant spontaneous vegetation as grows on French Polynesia's volcanic soil, the paucity of crops is striking. In 1920 it was noted that no new crops had been introduced in the islands during the previous decade, and that the colony was becoming overly dependent on two export crops—vanilla and coconuts.[24]

It was thought at the time that this could be remedied by instituting an agricultural service, but this trend continued even after such a service was created subsequent to World War II. Indeed, in the 1960s the tendency to neglect both food and export crops has been accentuated, although a rapid increase in the population and the addition of thousands of employes of the C.E.P. have swelled the number of consumers. Despite much greater efforts by the administration and the relevant technical services, the place of agriculture in the local economy has declined dramatically and imports of foodstuffs have greatly increased. There seems little hope of any substantial increase in production in the foreseeable future unless some means of making farming more remunerative can be devised.

Tubers are the most important single element of the Polynesian diet,

[23] Minutes of the territorial assembly, Nov. 10, 1964.
[24] *L'Océanie Française,* January–March 1920.

supplemented by some corn and beans and by the produce of bread-fruit trees, banana plants, and citrus trees, all of which grow abundantly on the high islands. The taro, most widely cultivated of the tubers, is grown both on the coastal plains and in the mountain valleys wide enough to permit a primitive form of irrigation. Breadfruit trees are almost as popular with the Polynesians as coconut palms, for they begin producing at the age of five years and their enormous fruit has high nutritive value. Its fermented white pulp, along with taro and wild bananas, is a main ingredient of *popoi* (similar to the Hawaiian *poi*.)

In the volcanic islands, nature is so bountiful in supplying what Polynesians consider to be their essential foods that they feel no need to cultivate vegetable crops for sale. It has been the Chinese who, for many years, have provided Papeete with European vegetables from the slopes of nearby hills. During recent years the Polynesians have acquired some taste for such vegetables, but as local production cannot meet the demand, they are being imported from the United States, New Zealand, and Australia in increasing quantities. Far more vegetables could be grown in Tahiti, but production there is stagnant, if not actually decreasing. A 1959 census of Papeete's market gardeners showed that 76 of the 78 then cultivating Western vegetables were Chinese, not one of whom—even those who had been so occupied for 25 to 30 years—owned the land he farmed.[25] Because of the land-tenure system, the Chinese could obtain only short-term, renewable leases, and almost exclusively for areas located on steep mountain slopes that were much harder to cultivate than the flat coastal land. Furthermore, because the income they receive is not proportionate to the effort expended, neither the Polynesians nor the younger Chinese have been attracted to that occupation. The 1959 inquiry showed that only 11 of the 76 Chinese market gardeners had taken up that type of farming during the previous decade.

The results of that census convinced the authorities that drastic steps must soon be taken if locally grown European vegetables were not to disappear with the retirement or demise of the present generation of Chinese market gardeners. It was felt that the rapid growth of the tourist trade had made it imperative to grow more fresh vegetables locally. Since the only Polynesians who might be termed authentic peasants were the Austral Islanders, it was decided to encourage the farmers of Tubuai to become market gardeners. The assembly

[25] Gauze, R., *La Minorité Ethnique Chinoise*, p. 172.

voted large sums and the agricultural service devoted much time and effort to forming them into a cooperative society and training them to grow European vegetables in quantity by modern techniques. By 1966, 70 Tubuai farmers, of whom 15 were young men, had been trained to use fertilizers and grow vegetables by intensive cultivation methods. That year they produced over 300 tons of vegetables.[26]

While the Tubuai experiment proved to be a technical success, there remained the unsolved problem of transporting the output to market and of persuading the Papeete merchants to sell it, for it brought them smaller profits than did imported foodstuffs. Eventually the transport problem was solved at the cost of granting a monopoly to one shipping company, but enlisting the cooperation of Papeete traders proved much more difficult. Nevertheless, the Tubuai experiment was considered successful enough to be extended to the Gambier Islands. The sacrifices entailed by this encouragement of the local production of vegetables might well never have been made had it not been considered necessary to provision the troops and technicians of the C.E.P. who began to flood the territory in 1963. It seems doubtful that these efforts will continue, at least on the present scale, after the C.E.P. personnel leaves the islands, and even with a smaller population the territory will probably not reduce its food imports, which now supply over half its requirements.

Polynesians have lyrically described the coconut palm as an object of beauty which also provides shade and lends itself to multiple domestic uses. Its trunk serves as pillars for their houses and its fiber as cord, its milk makes a refreshing drink as well as a fermented one, and its oil is used as fuel, cosmetic, and medicine. The coconut palm requires little care and grows almost everywhere on both the high and low islands. But it is copra—the dried coconut—which is the mainstay of the territory's economy.

Coconut-palm groves cover a total of 48,325 hectares, of which over half are to be found in the Tuamotu-Gambiers.[27] Yields vary from island to island but are generally small, averaging less than one ton of copra to the hectare. Copra has remained the main source of the Polynesians' cash income despite wide variations in exports, a steady growth in domestic consumption—currently estimated at one-half to

[26] Minutes of the territorial assembly, Oct. 11, 1966.

[27] In the Windward Islands 6,425 hectares are planted to coconuts, in the Leeward Islands 8,000 or so, in the Marquesas over 4,200, and in the Australs approximately 1,500. See *La Polynésie Française* (La Documentation Française), p. 21.

one-third as much as the quantity exported—and numerous obstacles to its production and sale. Among the handicaps to production are the extensive damage done to the crop by rats, the obsolescence of the great majority of palm trees, soil deficiencies in the atolls, the rudimentary care given to plantations and to the processing of nuts, and the long delay in undertaking scientific research on coconut culture.

Improving the care given to coconut plantations and to the preparation of copra is related to the problems, not yet solved, that derive from the collective ownership of land.[28] Rat damage, however, has been minimized in the atolls and Leeward Islands by ringing the palms with zinc bands to prevent the rodents from climbing up the trunks to eat the nuts. In the 1920s, when rats were responsible for a decline in copra exports by as much as one-third on some of the islands, the government proposed reviving the export tax on copra which had existed prior to World War I. The proceeds from such a tax were to be used to finance a large-scale banding operation.[29] This measure, however, was opposed by the Chamber of Agriculture and also by the producers, whose copra was fetching high prices during most of the interwar period. When the export tax was finally reimposed in 1955, the revenues it brought in were used not for protection against rat damage but to finance a price-stabilization fund.

Polynesians have been reluctant to expend the energy and money needed to band their trees, especially as the metal must be replaced after 7 years, but they have gradually been convinced of its value by a marked increase in the productivity of groves where that operation has been undertaken. It has been even more difficult to persuade them to cut down aged palms and to replant with selected species. Only the stagnation in copra production convinced the territorial assemblymen in 1961 that they must offer cash bonuses to growers who would band their trees and replant their groves. At that time only 250 hectares in all the islands had been replanted, and it was then calculated that within the next 15 years, 85 percent of the palms on the atolls must be regenerated if copra production was to be maintained at even the existing level.

In part, the long delay in replanting and in remedying soil deficiencies was traceable to the lack of any scientific research on coconut-palm culture in French Polynesia. It was not until 1959 that such a station was installed at Rangiroa, the largest of the Tuamotu atolls,

[28] See pp. 107–108.
[29] *L'Océanie Française*, May–June 1927.

financed by the F.I.D.E.S. and the S.P.C., and placed under the technical management of the Institut de Recherches pour les Huiles et les Oléagineux (I.R.H.O.), a specialized French government agency.[30] The Rangiroa station has devoted itself to increasing the productivity of coconut palms grown on coral atolls, and has concentrated on getting prompt and practical results, rather than on conducting pure research. After 4 years of experimentation, it was able to popularize the results of its work on soil deficiencies and on the proper spacing of planted trees—results which are applicable to all the Pacific atolls.

The territorial assembly has been willing to contribute toward this station's operations about a million C.F.P. francs a year, because coconut culture is vital for the survival of the Tuamotuans, who have no alternative means of livelihood except diving for shell.[31] Obviously the territory's expenditures for coconut-palm research can be considered as an investment not in the economic but in the social sense. Labor shortage for this crop is not crucial because normally it is supplied by the landowners' families, and the task requires neither much time nor skill. It has been calculated that by present methods the upkeep of groves and the gathering of nuts, as well as the preparation of copra, require, on the average, only 35 working days a year per hectare. Often, however, when the price for copra is low, even this minimal effort is not made and the nuts are simply not gathered.

In 1955 it was decided to create a stabilization fund that would pay bonuses to Polynesian producers when the world price fell below a certain level. This fund was managed by a committee made up of officials and the representatives of producers and exporters, and it was financed by the latter group, the French Fonds National de Régularisation des Cours des Produits d'Outre-Mer, and the territorial budget.[32] Under the second territorial-development plan, the government has undertaken to standardize and improve the quality of copra exports, mainly by introducing modern drying techniques and also by clearing several hundred kilometers of *pistes* (tracks) to provide access to groves located in the mountainous interior of the high islands. Trans-

[30] In 1966 the S.P.C., which had been contributing 500,000 C.F.P. francs a year to this project, ceased its grant.

[31] The fact that many Tuamotuan employes of the C.E.P. are using their savings to build houses on their home islands is regarded as a hopeful indication of their intention to return there.

[32] The grants made by the two last-mentioned sources each amounted to about 70 million C.F.P. francs annually. See *La Polynésie Française* (La Documentation Française), p. 22.

port is a big factor in production costs because of the great distances between the islands, and here again, France and the local budget have had to provide subsidies to the shipping firms.[33]

Considering the territory's dependence on French supports, it is not surprising that the full application of the European Common Market agreements has been anticipated there with great uneasiness, and it was a decisive factor in the assembly's decision to build a coconut oil-mill in French Polynesia. The project was first launched in 1963 by a local businessman, Ronald Patton, who was exasperated by the obstacles put in his way by the two local organizations of producers and exporters. Although he soon left the territory, his project was accepted 2 years later by the government council, the assembly, and Governor Sicurani. A committee was formed to study the problem and missions were sent to France where the aid of various experts was enlisted. Work on the oilmill project was carried on in considerable secrecy because of the strong opposition to it both in France and locally. In France its opponents were mainly the industrialists, who had been processing the islands' copra, and the Messageries Maritimes, which received a subsidy to transport it. In the territory the groups opposing the project were the exporters and some of the producers who stood to lose by the elimination of copra exports. They directed their propaganda principally to potential investors in the oilmill, warning them that the territory's copra production was declining to the point where an oilmill could not fail to lose money.

Soon after the assembly accepted the principle of building an oilmill, the two firms, the Société Sin Thung Hing (S.S.T.H.) and the Société Commerciale Française (SOCOFRA), submitted bids for construction and operation of the mill, both offering to invest approximately equal funds and to buy French Polynesia's total output. Because the S.S.T.H. was a local Chinese firm associated with the American Pacific Vegetable Oil Company, and the SOCOFRA a Marseille-based company with influential support in Paris and Papeete, political considerations entered into what should normally have been a purely economic question. Furthermore, the S.S.T.H. already supplied most of the territory's fuel imports and building materials, and because it obviously intended to use its tankers to transport the copra it would purchase for milling, it might acquire a monopoly of interisland shipping, which depended largely on copra

[33] Each ship carrying copra to France received a subsidy of about 10 million C.F.P. francs from the territorial budget.

cargoes. A further complication arose from the hostility felt in the assembly toward the decision of its permanent commission to accept the S.S.T.H.'s offer without awaiting the plenary body's consent. Despite the eagerness of all concerned to stop the financial losses caused by the heavy subsidies to producers, exporters, and shippers, the wrangling entailed a 6-month delay while a compromise was worked out with the S.S.T.H. regarding ownership of the shares in the future oilmill. It was not until September 1967 that agreement was finally reached. The mill began operating 7 months later, and in May 1968 the first oil was shipped out of Papeete.

The decision to build the oilmill was of the greatest importance to the territory's economy, but it has created new controversies and brought into the open existing conflicts between persons, ideologies, and vested-interest groups. Probably the Polynesian producers and the territory's budget will benefit by the oilmill's operations, but the whole issue has accentuated the disunity of the elite and has underscored the artificiality of the existing political organizations. The final vote in the assembly cut across party lines, placing Sanford in opposition to Teariki and lining up as the latter's supporters not only Céran and Vanisette, as might be expected, but also the conservative Coppenrath.

French Polynesia is the only island group in the Pacific where vanilla is cultivated on a commercial scale. Vanilla is one of the oldest export crops in the islands, the first plants having been introduced there as early as 1846. It grows well in limited areas in the humid valleys of the volcanic islands, particularly on Moorea and the Leeward group, and its quality is reputed to be good. Generally speaking, vanilla is grown by the Polynesian landowners and some Chinese sharecroppers, pollinated by Chinese specialists and a few Polynesian women, and sold by Chinese traders to Chinese exporters.[34]

Polynesia's vanilla production is very responsive to price fluctuations, and production also depends upon the care taken of the plants and of the soil, which vanilla-growing rapidly exhausts. Because the pollination and preparation of the pods require time, skill, and patience, those operations are very largely in the hands of the Chinese. It is also the Chinese who are willing to run the risks involved in trading in the highly speculative and irregular vanilla market. Whenever prices are high, as they were in the 1920s and again in the late 1960s, plantations

[34] *L'Océanie Française*, April–June 1931, January–February 1939; *La Polynésie Française*, p. 22; *South Pacific Bulletin*, January 1961.

have been enlarged. But as it takes 4 to 5 years for the vines to come into production, growers who have increased their planted area are sometimes left with large stocks on their hands if the market has fallen in the interval. During periods of low prices, the plantations are neglected and the vanilla poorly prepared. At various times the administration has tried to improve and standardize the quality of exports and to curtail thefts of beans, and in July 1965 the assembly lowered the duty on vanilla shipments in an effort to check speculative sales.[35] Vanilla remains a crop important to the territory's economy, but Polynesia is a very small producer compared with Madagascar, and the whole trade has been adversely affected by the development of synthetic substitutes in the major consuming markets.

Coffee plays a role somewhat similar to that of vanilla in the local economy, for it also helps to cushion French Polynesia against the dangers of coconut monoculture. It grows only in the high islands, and its production—far less renumerative to producers than that of vanilla and amounting annually to only a few hundred tons—is closely tied to the sales price. Only the arabica variety is grown in French Polynesia, and its quality is good. Nevertheless, because harvesting the berries requires abundant labor and coffee prices are generally low in the world market, the territorial authorities do not intend to develop it as an export crop. Its cultivation is, however, being encouraged as a family crop for domestic consumption, which is steadily increasing.[36]

FISHERIES

Fishing has always been regarded by the Polynesians as a congenial occupation to provide food for themselves, rather than as a sport or as a commercial enterprise. Many varieties of fresh- and salt-water fish are available to them, and fish supply almost all the protein consumed by the islanders. Although edible fish are still abundant enough to meet their food needs and even to provide a surplus for foreign canneries, the Polynesians complain that their waters are not so productive as formerly. In part this is because the fish caught near certain coral reefs are periodically poisonous, but more because the great majority of Polynesians fish for their own immediate needs and almost wholly in the lagoons. Only in the Leeward Islands is collective fishing still

[35] Minutes of the territorial assembly, July 8, 1965.
[36] *Ibid.*

practised, especially in the Maupiti lagoon, where the heavy tides carry fish inside the barrier reef.

Production is impossible to estimate because almost all the catch is consumed by the fishermen and their families. Probably less than 1,000 tons of fresh fish are sold each year in the Papeete market by Tahitian, Moorean, and Tuamotuan fishermen. Commercial fishing could be greatly increased if they ventured more into the open sea, as shown by the large catches of tuna and bonito made by Japanese and American companies in nearby waters. To enable the Polynesians to buy the type of boat and equipment required for deep-sea fishing, a few fishermen's cooperative societies were formed in the late 1950s and financed by loans granted by the Crédit de l'Océanie. By 1962, the Crédit had granted 28 such loans, totalling 5.2 million C.F.P. francs.[37]

The advent of the C.E.P. has affected both favorably and unfavorably the evolution of French Polynesia's fisheries. On the negative side, the fear of eating fish poisoned by radioactivity has been a main argument used by the C.E.P.'s opponents, and the suspicion that Japanese ostensibly fishing near the islands might be military observers in disguise has lurked behind the government's refusal to grant permission for them to do so. On the positive side, the C.E.P. personnel has been a fast-growing market for the local catch, and the port—built largely for the C.E.P.'s use—includes facilities for a fishing industry. Certainly the implantation of the C.E.P. was in part responsible for the authorities' final decision to establish a local fishing industry, and in the early 1960s missions were dispatched to Hawaii and Japan to study relevant techniques, fishing equipment and types of craft.

The first materialization of the new industry took the form of a cold-storage and freezing plant built at Rangiroa in April 1964. The following month, a boat equipped to carry 12 tons of frozen fish was put into operation.[38] But when the proposal to build a second refrigerated plant was debated in the assembly, no decision could be reached on the site because of the competing claims of the outer-island assemblymen.[39] Similarly the government's initiative in making the fisheries service separate from that of agriculture and animal husbandry encountered opposition from the assemblymen, who, as always, suspected that it would involve the budget in paying the salaries of additional

[37] Fourcade, F., in B. Covit, ed., *Official Directory and Guide Book for Tahiti,* p. 91; speech by Y. Attali at the S.P.C. meeting on economic development, March 14, 1962.

[38] Devambez, L., "Fisheries Development in French Polynesia."

[39] Minutes of the territorial assembly, Nov. 28, 1965.

Metropolitan officials. Eventually these obstacles were overcome by France's willingness to finance the new fisheries service and the training of Polynesian fishermen by Japanese experts, and in 1967 the long-mooted plan to develop a local fishing industry got under way.

Despite this late start and the probable departure of many C.E.P. personnel in the near future, the outlook for a small local fishing industry is hopeful. The islands' fish resources are abundant and the market prospects are good. The number of potential Polynesian consumers is growing rapidly, and the surplus catch could doubtless be sold abroad or to a local cannery.

PEARLS AND SHELL

For nearly a century, diving for pearls and shell (nacre) has been practised in the Leeward, the Gambier, and above all, the Tuamotu Islands. Indeed, even by 1885, diving was so intensive that the French government sent the first of a series of experts to see what could be done to replenish the lagoons, whose resources were fast being depleted. It was not until 1901, however, that an attempt was made to check excessive production, and then only by restricting the concessions to gather shell granted to foreign companies. Gradually, restrictions on diving were also imposed, but they soon proved to be inadequate, although the productivity of some lagoons had been appreciably reduced by cyclones that sanded them up. In 1931 the colony had so large an accumulation of unsalable shell stocks that diving was suspended during certain months of the year, and minimal dimensions for shell to be exported were established. A few years later, a research laboratory for oyster culture was created.

In practice, the new regulations were not rigorously enforced, and it was the price factor that has actually determined production. When the price for shell falls below a certain level, divers do not feel it worth their while to risk their health and lives in so hazardous an occupation. When shell exports were resumed after World War II, production became so lucrative that there was a large-scale increase in diving, so in 1951 still another expert was sent from France to see what could be done to check the abusive exploitation of the E.F.O.'s resources. He recommended not only a strict application of the existing regulations but also a regeneration of the lagoons with species imported from the New Hebrides.[40] His suggestions were carried out, but inevitably no

---

[40] Deschamps, H., and J. Guiart, *Tahiti—Nouvelle-Calédonie—Nouvelles-Hébrides*, p. 64.

marked increase in shell productivity could be expected for some years. In the meantime, the government decided to concentrate the activities of divers at certain specified times and places where their operations could be effectively policed and medical care provided. The chief center was at Hikueru, one of the richest of the Tuamotu lagoons, about 700 kilometers east of Tahiti. Every year, 500 to 600 divers and their families come to Hikueru. Temporary shelters are erected for them, Chinese traders set up shops, and they are even provided with entertainment by mobile movie units and traveling circuses.[41]

Virtually all the shell now produced comes from some 40 lagoons, and output averages from 600 to 800 tons a year. All of it is exported to Europe for button manufacture, but since the early 1960s the demand has slackened because of increasing competition from plastics. A supplementary source of income for the divers is being sought through the development, possibly in cooperation with a Japanese company, of black-culture-pearl production, of which French Polynesia would have a potential monopoly. In 1967 the government began research on this project at Rangiroa atoll and also formed a company for its exploitation. The outcome of this experiment is still uncertain and, in any case, black culture pearls could be sold in only a very limited luxury market.[42]

ANIMAL HUSBANDRY

When the first European navigators discovered Tahiti, the only animals they found there were pigs, chickens, dogs, and rats, and to them they added, over the years, sheep, turkeys, ducks, geese, cats, and horses. Cattle, the most useful of all the livestock they introduced in the eighteenth century, were sufficiently abundant by 1858 to provision passing ships with beef.[43] Later in the century the government gave some financial encouragement to animal husbandry, but not enough to enable owners to fence their properties. Consequently, vagrant animals did some damage to crops, although most of the cattle were pastured in coconut-palm groves and were few in number. As of 1908, there were no more than 1,400 head on the two islands of Tahiti and Moorea, where they were the most numerous, and with the aim of developing the herds there, breeding stock was imported from New Caledonia, New Zealand, Australia, and the United States.

[41] Robequain, C., *Madagascar et les Bases Dispersées de l'Union Française,* p. 497.
[42] *Industries et Travaux d'Outre–Mer,* August 1967.
[43] *L'Océanie Française,* October 1911.

Although pigs and cattle flourish on the high islands and although pork is the favorite Polynesian dish, the growth in the number of edible animals has not kept pace with that of the population, especially since World War II. In 1960, the territory's cattle were officially estimated at 11,000 head, pigs at 10,000, horses and sheep at a few hundreds, while the number of chickens and goats defied tabulation.[44] Most of these animals roam the islands in a semi-wild state and even their numbers in Tahiti and Moorea, where over half the herds live and for which the official figures are more accurate, are probably underestimated. In any case, the herds yield not much more than 175 tons of meat a year, and the territory has to import some 500 tons of tinned or frozen meat annually. At Taravao and Pirae, the two stud farms maintained by the animal-husbandry service and financed by the F.I.D.E.S. and the local budget have tried to improve the local cattle stock by crossbreeding with imported bulls. The Taravao station provides about half the milk consumed in Papeete.

The domestic demand for meat and milk, not to mention butter, eggs, and cheese, is far from satisfied by local production. Theoretically, livestock could become a source of wealth for the islanders, but its increase is hampered by the lack of sufficient and suitable pastureland and by the Polynesians' indifference to rearing animals with care. In March 1970, the Chamber of Commerce accepted proposals by the government to reduce meat imports by subsidizing local animal husbandry, on condition that they involved no increase in taxation.

[44] *La Polynésie Française* (La Documentation Française), p. 25.

11

External Trade and Local Industry

From the depth of the depression in the early 1930s, the years before World War I were looked back upon as a period when the islands' foreign trade flourished. Actually, from 1903 to 1906 the colony experienced a slump due to the low prices paid for its shell and vanilla and to the interruption of interisland shipping during those years.[1] Furthermore, considerable damage was done by the cyclones of 1903 and 1906, and in the latter year the disaster of the San Francisco earthquake and fire adversely affected the E.F.O.'s trade with the United States. Beginning late in 1906, however, the islands' economy revived, and this improvement was maintained fairly steadily until the war broke out in 1914.

During this period, the E.F.O.'s exports comprised phosphates (after 1908), vanilla, shell, coconuts, oranges, and especially copra, which by 1911 had become by far the most remunerative item. Trade in copra was resumed after interisland shipping had been restored. Vanilla shipments also increased in value following the administration's efforts to improve the preparation of beans and to standardize exports. This was also the era when the government made its first moves to regulate diving for shell. Although cotton had disappeared from the list of exports, phosphate had just been added to it.[2] Imports came mostly from the west coast of the United States, which was only 12 days by ship from Papeete, and for the same reason Americans had also become the principal buyers of the E.F.O.'s major exports. Germany, France, and Great Britain lagged far behind, though the French share was growing slowly each year. Between 1906 and 1910, the volume of the E.F.O.'s external trade almost tripled, and the plan to cut a canal across the Panama isthmus gave rise to expectations of further large increases.

[1] See pp. 158–159.
[2] *L'Océanie Française*, July 1911.

THE INTERWAR PERIOD

Because the United States had become the E.F.O.'s main trading partner, the colony's external trade did not suffer greatly during World War I. The widespread boom in the sale of tropical produce that immediately followed the 1918 armistice was briefly interrupted by a depression in the early 1920s. In 1924, however, the upward surge was resumed, and it continued until late 1929, when the prices for copra and especially vanilla tumbled sharply. During the next few years, the colony's trade declined much further, reaching a low point in 1933 of 34.2 million francs for a volume of 120,000 tons of commodities traded. Not all the E.F.O.'s exports reacted in the same way: shell and vanilla proved to be the most responsive to the downward pressure on prices, and shrank both in volume and value. Copra and phosphate shipments, on the other hand, increased in tonnage despite the steadily falling prices paid for both. Similarly, imports grew in volume though they decreased in value.

A slight improvement in the trade picture was noted in 1934, and it became much more pronounced in 1935. In that year the E.F.O.'s external trade, totaling 170,000 tons, included 50.1 million francs' worth of exports, thus reversing the unfavorable trade balance of the preceding years. The year 1937, with a value of 107 million francs for the colony's external trade, marked its high point during the last pre-World War II years, but the devaluation of the franc in 1936 distorted the true value of its earnings. What is noteworthy about the trade situation in 1937, however, is that it was the last year in which exports balanced imports, for in 1938 the E.F.O.'s imports rose by 75 percent in value whereas its exports increased by only 16 percent, and the colony once more was faced with a trade deficit.

Although the colony's external trade had resumed respectable proportions by the time World War II was declared, nothing had been done to remedy its basic weaknesses and deficiencies. There had been no appreciable improvement in interisland shipping, the scale of production had not been enlarged nor its scope diversified, nor had the colony succeeded in acquiring an adequate labor supply. To be sure, the colony lacked rich resources, a large and enterprising body of native consumers and wage-earners, and sufficient capital investments, but it had not done all it could to develop what it had and its economic prospects remained very limited.

Some of the main weaknesses in the E.F.O.'s economy were clearly indicated by the type and volume of its imports. During the late 1930s, imports annually totaled about 22,000 tons, headed by foodstuffs and beverages (nearly 42 percent), household articles (17.6 percent), fuel (13.3 percent), textiles (approximately 7 percent), construction materials (4.8 percent), and miscellaneous items (15.5 percent).[3] Their cost, however, rose between 1936 and 1938 from 36.7 million francs to 63.2 millions, nearly doubling the cost of living for the segment of the population that maintained Western standards. The world depression naturally had awakened interest in producing in the colony some of the items it had been importing, and as early as October 9, 1929, the administration announced that financial encouragement would be given to local industries processing indigenous agricultural and maritime products. Two years later, however, an inventory of existing industries other than that of phosphate extraction showed that little had been accomplished.[4] Rum was still made by the Société Atimaono, which had a fine plantation but antiquated machinery that had never worked to capacity. A brewery, established at Papeete in 1920, met some of the local demand for beer and ice, and on Raiatea, 20,000 oranges were processed daily for their juice. Two large and two small shipyards built a few schooners of 200 tons maximum and also had repair facilities for boats. Power-generating plants provided current for lighting the towns of Papeete and Uturoa, using coconut fibers and petroleum for fuel. A few furniture-making shops and soft-drink factories in Tahiti completed the extremely limited range of the colony's industrial production, whose history had been marked by successive failures to develop other industries.

If the range of local industries as well as the colony's imports varied little during the interwar period, this could not be said of the places of origin of imports. Much of the administration's zeal, which might better have been put into developing local production during that period, was devoted to reorienting the colony's trade to and from France. It was not until 1923 that the French steamship line, the Messageries Maritimes, began using the Panama Canal for a new service between France and the Pacific islands via the Antilles. As a result, France rose to second place as the colony's provisioner the following year. In 1933 the E.F.O.'s tariff system was revised so as to favor French merchandise, although goods imported from all countries still

---

[3] *Ibid.,* January–February 1939.
[4] *Ibid.,* September–October 1931.

had to pay a duty of 6 percent ad valorem. In 1936 the devaluation of the franc further strengthened trading ties between France and her colonies.

Although its geographic situation still impelled the E.F.O. to buy considerable merchandise from the United States and British Pacific territories—especially after the pound was devalued in 1931—the most noteworthy trend of the interwar years was the growing role of France as the E.F.O.'s main provisioner and purchaser. From ranking a poor second to the United States among the colony's clients throughout the 1920s, France attained the top place in 1933 after Americans ceased buying the E.F.O.'s copra. Between 1931 and 1938, France increased its purchases of the islands' output from 31.7 percent of the total to 47 percent. Over the same span of years, the United States' share fell from 25.7 percent to 7 percent, though the percentage varied from one year to another. On the eve of World War II, Japan held second place among the islands' clients, buying 16 percent of their total exports. Since such exports still comprised only the four traditional products, the relative positions of the colony's customers depended on the amounts they bought of copra (47 percent of the value of total exports in 1938), vanilla (26 percent), phosphates (19 percent), and shell (2.4 percent).

Copra shipments, which amounted to only about 8,000 tons before World War I, have been consistently the colony's most valuable export since the turn of the century, despite great irregularities. Export tonnages rose rapidly after the war, and then tapered off to the present average of some 20,000 tons a year. Throughout the prewar decade, France bought all of the islands' exported copra, and French ships carried that bulky and cheap commodity half way around the world although no comparable tonnages of return freight could be found. Much less voluminous and valuable were vanilla shipments, the E.F.O.'s second-ranking export. In quantitative terms, they reached their apex in 1911 with the sale of 256 tons. In the 1920s the price declined, and with it the volume and value of the colony's output. Beginning in 1934, an improvement in the price stimulated exports, which topped 100 tons for the first time in 20 years. During each of the three years preceding World War II, the price for vanilla rose rapidly, with the result that exports increased by 20 percent in volume and quintupled in value.[5]

During the interwar period, phosphates became the colony's third

[5] *Ibid.,* May–July 1939.

most valuable export and certainly its most voluminous one. Phosphate mining has been the territory's sole important modern industry, for aside from limited deposits of mediocre-quality coal and chromite on Rapa Islands, phosphates are the only mineral resource of commercial importance. Makatea's exceptionally rich deposits were found by chance in 1906 by an agent of the public-works service, who forthwith acquired a lease on the island and permission to carry on mining operations. Two years later he founded the Compagnie Française des Phosphates de l'Océanie (C.F.P.O.). Labor difficulties and, even more, the vast distances separating Makatea from its main pre-World War I markets raised production and shipping costs to such a level that the C.F.P.O.'s product could not compete in Europe with North Africa's output. World War I gave a big impetus to the industry, however, by providing it with new markets in the Pacific. Throughout the 1930s, production increased because Japan was buying most of Makatea's phosphates, and in 1937 a record was established with the sale of 160,000 tons, almost all of it to Japan. More irregular and far less important clients were Australia and New Zealand, and by 1939 the only European countries still buying Makatea's phosphates were the Scandinavian ones.[6]

Unlike phosphate exports, which grew steadily throughout the first half of the twentieth century, those of shell declined to the lowest rank in the colony's foreign trade. From the pre-World War I high point of annual shipments, totaling more than 1,350 tons worth 3.4 million francs, they dwindled to their lowest point in 1934 with 60 tons, valued at 91,000 francs. Thanks to the franc's devaluation, they rose to 365 tons (value 763,000 francs) on the eve of World War II, but the ineffectiveness of the administration's efforts to regulate diving and to replenish the lagoon beds,[7] as well as the saturation of Western markets, were responsible for the collapse of this unusual industry.

THE SECOND WORLD WAR AND ITS AFTERMATH

The E.F.O.'s isolation from France during World War II did not affect its economy so adversely as was the case with French tropical Africa, whose trade had been far more closely linked with the Metropole. Because the great majority of Polynesians continued to live largely by a subsistence economy, and because the E.F.O. had always

[6] *Marchés Coloniaux*, Oct. 24, 1953, pp. 2982–2983.
[7] See pp. 124–125.

traded heavily with the United States and its British Pacific neighbors (with whose war effort it aligned itself in 1940), the islanders suffered comparatively few privations.

It was in the first postwar years that the islanders felt the pinch as a result of the reorientation of their foreign trade to France and the imposition of French trade and currency controls. The system of rationing imported foodstuffs and textiles, begun during the war, was retained for some years thereafter. Although this locally instituted system was criticized by merchants and the general public for its inefficiency, cumbersome formalities, and favoritism, it was the Paris government that was held responsible for the inappropriate type of commodities—such as perfumes and liqueurs—sent to the islands by France, and for the infrequency and irregularity with which French ships arrived there.

Given the foregoing situation, it was inevitable that a black market should develop in commodities that were in short supply, such as flour, cloth, and sugar. Because no building and few repairs had been done during the war years, housing was scarce, and the cost of living rose rapidly. Yet foreign visitors in 1947 reported that the population was suffering no great hardships. By the end of 1950, trade had returned almost to normal, and all the official restrictions had been lifted except those imposed by the price-control commission, on which the representative assembly had members. Papeete's businessmen were mollified by being able again to sell copra in any market and to dispose freely of all the foreign currency earned by the territory's exports.

THE MID-CENTURY DECADES

The basic pattern of the islands' foreign trade as established before World War I did not change fundamentally until 1963 (for imports) and 1966 (for exports). Between 1963 and 1968, the vast increase in imports, not only of equipment but of consumer goods (including foodstuffs), due to the C.E.P.'s installation, may be regarded as a transient phenomenon. In the reverse direction, exports have declined both in tonnage and in variety, because of the elimination of phosphates, the substitution of oil for copra, and the rural exodus, which has reduced the production and shipment of agricultural commodities. (See table 2.) The consequent growing aggravation of the trade deficit, characteristic of almost all the postwar years, seems likely to be a permanent feature of French Polynesia's external trade, though it may be partly offset by the better balance of payments resulting from a probable development of the tourist industry. Another constant element in the territory's trade picture has been the ranking position held by France as the islands' main provisioner, but in the years to come, France's preeminence may not be so overwhelming as it has been in the heyday of the C.E.P.

During the 1950s and 1960s, there was no significant modification in the territory's four major exports or their destination.[8] The islands' economy continued to depend on copra, vanilla, shell, and (until 1966) phosphates for its locally earned revenues. Exports reached a maximum of 354,000 tons valued at 902 million C.F.P. francs in 1962, but declined 4 years later to some 200,000 tons (61 million C.F.P. francs). Their value is harder to estimate than their volume because of successive devaluations of the franc during the post-World War II period. There is no doubt, however, but that the income from agricultural exports declined steadily and also disproportionately to the decrease in their tonnages. The territory's markets, on the other hand, have remained fairly stable, with France increasing its purchases of copra, shell, and vanilla; Japan, Australia, and New Zealand taking all its phosphates; and the United States remaining a negligible purchaser. France and the franc zone have been regularly its most important customers and provisioners, and supplied about two-thirds of the territory's imports while taking some three-fourths of its exports in 1967–1968.

TABLE 2

FRENCH POLYNESIA: EXPORT TRADE, 1966–1968

Commodity	Volume (tons)			Value (millions of C.F.P. francs)		
	1966	1967	1968	1966	1967	1968
Copra	20,223	15,830	7,500	229.4	202.4	145.3
Copra oil	0	0	6,844	0	0	163.2
Copra cake	0	0	2,720	0	0	12.6
Vanilla	115	59	68	115.6	72.3	74.9
Shell	151	130	184	20.0	15.9	22.7
Phosphate	200,113	0	0	245.6	0	0

Source: *Marchés Tropicaux*, Aug. 2, 1969.

[8] French Polynesia began exporting small tonnages of shredded coconuts in 1952, cowhides in 1959, and coffee in 1948, but without exception these exports have since all but ceased because they could not support the freight costs.

France has subsidized all stages of copra production, transport, and sales, but its policy has sometimes run counter to the territory's interests. Between 1946 and 1949, the French government required all producers of vegetable fats in its overseas dependencies to sell their total exports to an official agency at a price below that then prevailing in world markets. Suddenly and without warning, in June 1949, France ceased buying because the French market was then saturated with vegetable oils, and only through joint intervention by the overseas parliamentarians (supported by the C.G.T. labor federation) was it persuaded to reverse this decision. Not only did France resume its purchases but it offered a guaranteed market and higher-than-world prices to its overseas suppliers. For the ensuing 19 years French Polynesia supplied about 25 percent of the French market's needs in vegetable oils, until, in 1967, France ceased giving the islands' copra a guaranteed market and a high price.

In world markets, copra prices remained high for a few years after World War II, reaching their peak in 1951, after which they fluctuated widely. In Polynesia, production and exports were subject to annual variations that were related to the price paid to growers, the wages in alternative occupations, and climatic conditions, in that order of importance. For the islanders, the overall decline in world prices has been cushioned by the Copra Stabilization Fund, created on September 30, 1955; by the subsidies paid to French ships carrying their copra; by the devaluations of the franc; and, more recently, by the exportation of locally manufactured coconut oil rather than crude copra. Yet copra has supplied a varying percentage of the territory's total exports, ranging from 62 percent in 1921 to 28.8 percent in 1958.

Vanilla has alternated between second and third rank among the territory's exports. To a far greater extent than in the case of copra, its production and sale have suffered from the generally steady decline in world prices owing to competition from more important producing countries and from synthetic substitutes, and to the lack of artificial supports. Probably the failure to grant bonuses for the production of vanilla is due to its relatively low value compared with copra exports and, above all, to the virtual monopoly of its preparation and export by the Chinese. Moreover, vanilla enjoys no preferential treatment in the French market, although France takes almost all of the territory's exports of that commodity. The volume of vanilla exports has ranged between 150 tons in 1962 and 222 tons in 1961, and their value has come to some 200 million C.F.P. francs a year.

Phosphate shipments, which amounted to only about 100,000 tons in 1925, increased very rapidly during World War II. After a pause between 1945 and 1949, they attained an annual average in the 1960s of 550,000 tons or so, worth approximately 420 million C.F.P. francs. During the last years of its operation in Makatea, the C.F.P.O. sold its entire output in the Pacific area, including small shipments to the western United States.

Shell has always been a poor fourth in the quartet of French Polynesia's major exports. It has been hard to find buyers for all the shell produced in the territory, so the government has consistently tried to curtail production. Exports have ranged widely between 400 and 850 tons a year, worth on the average 50 to 60 million C.F.P. francs annually, until 1965 when a sharp fall in prices caused sales to drop to their lowest point since 1955. France has exempted the islands' shell from import duties in the French market, and in recent years has been buying somewhat less than 30 percent of the territory's total shell exports.

If French Polynesia's exports have shown almost no diversification in their composition and little in their clientele, quite the contrary is true of its imports. Although France's role as provisioner has grown appreciably, especially since 1963, the territory's imports are varied and come from many sources. Generally speaking, they can be divided into the two categories of consumer and equipment goods: in the former, foodstuffs, textiles, and fuel head the list, and in the latter, machinery and motor vehicles. French Polynesia now imports more than two-thirds of its food and beverage requirements, and the increase in this sector reflects not only the growth in the population but also the Westernization of Polynesian dietary tastes. In 1966, the value of such imports equalled that of the territory's total imports in 1962 (or about 2 billion C.F.P. francs). Flour, edible oils, and wine have come mainly from France and Algeria; rice from Vietnam, Cambodia, Madagascar, and the United States; dairy products from Australia and New Zealand; sugar from Guadeloupe; and tinned meat from Australia, New Zealand, and the United States. As to other consumer goods, cotton cloth has been imported from the United States, France, and Hong Kong; fuel from the United States and, very recently, from Iran; and automobiles and building materials mainly from France.

For many years France and the United States together accounted for 85 percent of the total imports in terms of value, but the equipment materials brought in for the C.E.P. rapidly increased the former's share. The French percentage rose from 30 percent in 1940 to 63 percent 10 years later, and then to 71 percent in 1965, while that of the United States declined between 1963 and 1965 from 21 percent to 12.2 percent. The vertiginous growth of imports beginning in 1963, in conjunction with the persistent retrogression of exports, caused the long-chronic trade deficit to grow by leaps and bounds. The outstanding increase occurred between 1963 and 1964, when imports grew by 120.8 percent. This trend persisted, although not on such a spectacular scale, until 1967, when, after completion of the major C.E.P. construction works, they tapered off, only to increase again markedly in 1968.

What sums were directly added to the territory's revenues from duties on the imports brought in specifically for the C.E.P. and for work on Papeete's port is the subject of various estimates. The figure of 5,699 million C.F.P. francs, cited in the assembly debate of July 6, 1967, may well have been an underestimate. Certainly the territory would have received more from the former source had not many of the supplies used by the C.E.P. been transported in navy ships and either exempted from or given preferential rates in respect to import duties. This was a grievance voiced by Papeete's merchants and some assemblymen,[9] who swelled the local ranks of those opposed to the C.E.P. Yet, thanks to the C.E.P., never before had French Polynesia experienced so rapid and large an expansion of its economy, had so much money in circulation, or counted so many importers in business.

THE PATTERN OF TRADE AND INFLATION

External trade has been centralized at Papeete, where the main export-import firms and the Chamber of Commerce have their headquarters. From Papeete, imports are distributed, for the most part, by Chinese-owned schooners to the outer islands. There Chinese retailers sell or exchange them for the islanders' produce, which is carried back by the same schooners to the capital for export. Both the wholesalers and retailers, as well as the producers, have resisted any official attempts to curb or even regulate free trading, with the result that price controls in Tahiti and the administration's efforts to curtail the merchants' profit margins in the outer islands (instituted on January 1, 1953) have been ineffectual. In any case, price controls have

[9] Minutes of the permanent commission, Feb. 14, 1967.

been applicable only to certain categories of imports and not to locally grown foodstuffs, prices for which have risen steadily.

Although Tahiti early acquired the reputation of being one of the most expensive and formality-ridden islands in the Pacific, it was the filming there of the American motion-picture, "Mutiny on the Bounty," in 1961 that gave the territory its first taste of serious inflation. Because Metro-Goldwyn-Mayer was willing to pay exorbitant sums for housing and services, rents and wages shot up, and with them the cost of living for residents who lived in Western style. Some 100 actors and technicians remained in Tahiti for about a year; comfortable houses rented for 500,000 Metro. francs a month; laborers were paid four times the going rate; and a large share of the 27 million dollars which the film reportedly cost was spent in the islands. The bubble burst with completion of the film, but prices never returned to their pre-M.G.M. level, nor was the Tahitians' attitude toward money or toward work ever again quite the same. The large increase in the number of tourists visiting Polynesia during the early 1960s to some degree perpetuated these phenomena. But it was not until the 15,000 or so military and technical personnel for the C.E.P. began to arrive in 1963 that inflation assumed fantastic proportions.

With the great upsurge in the number of consumers and the quantity and price of imports, the number of business firms in Papeete grew from 56 in 1961 to 359 in 1964 and to 559 by early 1967.[10] Already in 1963, the assemblymen had become so alarmed by the inflationary trend that they asked France to send experts to study and recommend measures to counter it. However, the mission never came and, in any case, the assemblymen remained basically opposed to any extension of official controls. Consequently, no changes were made in price controls, the most recent of which dated back to May 18, 1951. Only reluctantly did the assembly accept the government's proposal to freeze prices as of August 1, 1966, on certain commodities. Governor Sicurani described such a measure as only a palliative, and he indicated his intention of proposing basic structural reforms in the anarchic commercial system so as to bring supply and demand into better balance.[11] A survey of the evolution of prices for 70 basic commodities, early in 1966,[12] showed that between 1959 and 1965 the cost

[10] Minutes of the territorial assembly, May 9, 1967.
[11] Speech to the territorial assembly, Oct. 11, 1966.
[12] *Le Monde,* July 16, 1966.

of living had risen 39 percent. The prices of foodstuffs, particularly those locally grown, showed an overall rise of 80 percent, rents had increased 60 percent, and prices of urban land had at least doubled.

The prospect of governmental intervention in trading that might result in the elimination of small merchants to the benefit of big business aroused the assembly's opposition, despite its members' insistence that something should be done to protect both the producer and consumer. In their resistance to an enlarged role for the administration in the regulation of trade, they were joined by the Chamber of Commerce as well as by the producers, and together they petitioned the government to rescind the price freeze. The only alternative they could suggest, however, was simply that the C.E.P. leave the islands, for they held it responsible for all the territory's current social and economic perturbations and for none of its prevailing prosperity.

For the first time, French Polynesia was enjoying full employment, while wages were at an all-time high and the budgets had revenues of unprecedented amounts that permitted the financing of public works long desired by the electorate. The assemblymen's fears lest the C.E.P.-induced inflation was cancelling out many of these benefits and that the economy's growing dependence on France was sapping their last vestiges of autonomy were echoed and amplified by some foreign journalists. These critics claimed that the territory was living dangerously beyond its means, that only the owners of hotels, restaurants, and taxis were profiting by the boom, that the rural exodus was harming agricultural production and creating disastrous housing and social problems for Papeete, and that the presence of so many Metropolitan troops and technicians was fanning anti-French feeling to the point where there would soon be an explosion.[13] In brief, they contended that the current prosperity was both artificial and transient, and that it would soon be followed by unemployment and a depression of colossal dimensions. By February 1967, there were signs that the tide was slowly ebbing, for the cost of living had declined by 2.5 percent as compared with the preceding 6 months, and there was hope that prices might be moving toward greater stability. The suspension of nuclear testing in 1969 and the consequent revival of tourism gave rise to hopes for a better-balanced territorial economy, but in August 1969 these were dashed by the 12.5-percent devaluation of the franc, which increased the cost of imports, and by the announcement that nuclear experiments would be resumed in 1970.

[13] *Ibid.;* see also Farwell, G., *Last Days in Paradise.*

LOCAL CRAFTS AND INDUSTRIES

Under the stimulus of tourism, handicrafts are being revived to a limited extent in French Polynesia. They have long been declining, in part because of the islanders' fondness for novelties and, especially, for imported Western merchandise. In the late 18th century, Captain Cook, returning to Tahiti after an absence of 8 years, noted that the traditional stone hatchets had already been almost wholly replaced by metal ones. In modern times, this trend has been accelerated by the great increase in imports, which are rapidly Occidentalizing the islanders' clothing, food, and housing.

To revive the traditional crafts, the first public exhibition of indigenous wooden sculpture (*tiki*), locally woven cloth, and objects made of shell was organized at Papeete in 1955, but it was not until 1963 that such crafts received greater official encouragement. In October 1964, a group representing Tahiti's 200-odd craftsmen met at the Chamber of Commerce to plan for the formation of a Centre des Métiers, and later the F.I.D.E.S. agreed to pay the salary of a French expert to organize it. Unfortunately the expert arrived before the funds necessary to build a center for crafts had been made available, and after a year in the islands he had been able to promote the production of only a few of them and the sale of none.

Tourists were indeed buying more and more locally manufactured curios, but the proceeds, it was said, were not going to the craftsmen but to the shopkeepers who sold their work.[14] The 1,500 or so artisans then estimated to be working throughout the archipelagoes were isolated, and except for those making musical instruments in the Marquesas under the sponsorship of the local Catholic mission, they were totally unorganized.[15] Consequently the assembly dismissed the Metropolitan expert, but expressed its willingness to vote funds for building a series of artisanry centers on the islands where craftsmanship still survived, and for the organization of craftsmen into cooperative societies. Some programs of this type have been carried out by the S.I.T.O.,[16] but the future of Polynesian handicrafts depends on a better organization of their output and sale and this, in turn, will be very largely determined by the development of tourism.

[14] Minutes of the territorial assembly, Feb. 4, 25, 1965.
[15] *Ibid.*, Dec. 1, 1966.
[16] See p. 141.

TOURISM

Although tourism is not an industry in the normal sense of the term, it has been so described since 1964, when it became the territory's chief revenue-earner. For many tourists, Tahiti's greatest asset is the reputation for exoticism and glamor that it gratuitously acquired in the nineteenth century through the writings of Pierre Loti and the paintings of Paul Gauguin. The Tahitian image they created has been partly offset, however, by the local tendency to rest on unearned laurels, the ambivalent policy of the administration toward tourism, the high prices and inadequate facilities of the islands, and the lack of distractions for visitors staying for more than a short time. In recent years, the activities of the C.E.P. have aggravated local liabilities by adding to the physical encumbrances fears of radioactivity as well as an unpropitious psychological atmosphere. Since the mid-1960s, however, the steady decline in agricultural productivity, the elimination of phosphate exports, and the suspension in 1969 of nuclear testing have all impelled the authorities to redouble their efforts to promote tourism.

For many years, Tahiti's idyllic reputation remained an unexploited form of capital, and only a scattering of rich middle-aged Westerners or indigent youthful adventurers visited it as tourists. Although the authorities welcomed the former for the money they brought in, they were more concerned to keep out the latter because of what was feared to be their deleterious influence on the islanders' traditional way of life and on the territory's resources. This was particularly true of the years following World War II, when food and housing were in short supply and beachcombers were numerous. Many crewmen jumped ship and, after exhausting the proceeds from the sale of radios, typewriters, and other items they had smuggled ashore, often became public charges.[17] To discourage such unwanted arrivals, the administration required visitors to bring in a certain amount of foreign currency and to convert it into C.F.P. francs. Furthermore, they entangled would-be foreign residents in meters of red tape, the while proclaiming that tourists, but not "undesirable aliens," would be welcomed. As recently as 1955, an American steamship company was said to have given up its project to build and operate a hotel in Tahiti because of the local requirement to staff it wholly with native per-

[17] *Pacific Islands Monthly,* April 1950.

sonnel, whom they found charming but not adapted to such work.[18]

With the improvement in transportation between French Polynesia and the outside world, the pattern of tourism began to change, and with it the attitude of the local administration and assembly towards it. Between 1959 and the end of 1960, the income derived by the territory from tourism rose from 129 million C.F.P. francs to more than 252 millions, and in 1964 it increased to 420 millions.[19] Over the 1960–1964 period, the number of tourists in the islands grew from 4,000 a year to nearly 14,000, not counting the thousands of passengers on cruise ships touching at French Polynesia.

Naturally this enormous monetary return for the minimal effort involved encouraged the government and the local business community to go all-out for tourism. In 1961–1962, France supplied the funds to form a Société d'Industrie Touristique d'Outre-Mer (S.I.T.O.), whose tasks were to build accommodations for tourists, promote handicrafts for the tourist trade, set up a school to train Tahitian hotel and restaurant staff, and facilitate the installation of a holiday colony by the Club Mediterranée on Bora Bora. At about the same time, the assembly amended the territory's fiscal and tariff regimes so as to encourage capitalists to invest in improving and enlarging Tahiti's hotels. Tourism duly increased until late 1964, when it declined by 9 percent compared with the preceding year, owing in part to a suspension of the air service with Australia and New Zealand and in part to the advent of the C.E.P. The upward trend, however, resumed in 1965 and increased during each of the succeeding years, reaching a record total in 1968 of 28,400, two-thirds of whom came from the United States.[20] Encouraged by this revival, and taking into account the rapid drying up of other sources of income from local production, the government pressed ahead with plans for an expansion that could enable the islands to handle 70,000 tourists a year by 1970.[21]

This policy was not accepted and carried out without some misgivings and setbacks. Although foreigners were still legally barred from buying real property, the prices for land and rentals had risen sharply, especially in Papeete and its environs. The impact on a small, long-isolated population of the influx of thousands of foreign tourists, some reportedly of "dubious morality," was regarded with apprehen-

[18] *Ibid.*, June 1956.
[19] *Marchés Tropicaux*, Oct. 21, 1961, p. 2524.
[20] *Ibid.*, Aug. 2, 1969, pp. 2153–2154.
[21] Speech of General P. Billotte to the territorial assembly, Feb. 24, 1966.

sion by both the Protestant and Catholic clergy, as well as by some Polynesians whose traditions of hospitality were beginning to wear thin under the strain. The French administration, always sensitive to any threat of increased "Anglo-Saxon" financial and cultural influence in the islands, was not reassured by reports to the effect that 60 percent of the tourists were Americans and 15 percent British, whereas only 3 percent were French.[22] It was clear that foreign investments and visitors were indispensable, however, and steps were taken to remedy the defects in the organization of tourism that had been revealed by time and experience. Loopholes in the investment code were successively eliminated, new building of tourist accommodations was undertaken, and the rates of taxis and hotel rooms were regulated.[23] Still reluctantly but more realistically and competently, the authorities and population—French, *demis*, and Polynesians—have accepted the necessity of encouraging tourist visits as the territory's only viable economic resource.

PHOSPHATE-MINING

For more than half a century, the C.F.P.O. extracted phosphate of 82.8 percent mineral content from the rocky island of Makatea, which occupies an area of about 25 square kilometers in the Tuamotu archipelago. In 1908, when the company started mining there, Makatea lacked water and had no inhabitants except a few fishermen and coconut-growers living along the coast at Momou. They were neither numerous enough nor willing to provide the C.F.P.O. with the labor it needed, and in addition, their ownership rights over the island presented complications concerning its lease.[24] Consequently, the company had to bring water to the island, as well as some hundreds of laborers, to build housing for them, and to import machinery and other equipment. In order to load the freighters riding in the open sea in depths of as much as 400 meters, the C.F.P.O. built a strong jetty, as well as a railroad from the mining area to the drying plant. Costly and complex as was this enterprise, it proved profitable for all concerned in terms of dividends to its shareholders, duties on exports levied by the territory,[25] and the salaries paid to the officials, tech-

[22] Minutes of the territorial assembly, April 9, 1965.

[23] *Ibid.*, Oct. 15, 1965.

[24] Robequain, C., *Madagascar et les Bases Dispersées de l'Union Française*, p. 498.

[25] These brought in 700 million C.F.P. francs between 1956 and 1966.

nicians, employes, and laborers directly or indirectly involved in the C.F.P.O.'s operations.

Communal life on Makatea, as it evolved under the auspices of the C.F.P.O., was a unique experiment in the south Pacific, and as such was studied by scholars for its social and economic implications.[26] After the C.F.P.O. ceased its operations there in 1966, many of the laborers returned to their home islands with their savings, new skills, and prestige, while a minority swelled the population of Papeete. As to the future of Makatea itself, it has been proposed to reforest the plateau with sandalwood trees, improve the coconut groves of Momou, and develop the island as a base for industrial fishing.

OTHER INDUSTRIES

With the exception of phosphate mining, there has been very little industrial development in French Polynesia, owing to the lack of primary materials, electric power, skilled laborers, and a sufficient number of local consumers. An inventory of existing industries made in 1931 [27] is virtually the same as that of today, except for the new coconut oilmill [28] that is producing solely for export. A number of other industries have occasionally turned out for export a few hundred tons of sugar and rum, tinned fruit, shredded coconut, soap, and perfume, but they have now either disappeared or process only for the domestic market. A few of the latter, such as those making furni-, ture, building schooners, and milling coconut oil, have always pro- duced exclusively for local consumers, but with only one exception they have not met all the indigenous demand. This exception is the recently enlarged and modernized Hinano brewery, which turns out some 50,000 hectoliters of good-quality beer a year for local con- sumption and export, as well as soft drinks and ice.

Three electric-power plants exist in the islands, and since World War II the demand for power has greatly increased. The output of current doubled between 1958 and 1961 to reach 8,300,000 kwh, and 2 years later it grew to 12,200,000 kwh.[29] A private company, the Etablissements Martin, has long held the concession to generate and

[26] See bibliography, works by L. Molet and F. Doumenge.

[27] *L'Océanie Française,* September–October 1931.

[28] See pp. 120–121.

[29] Le Goyot, Lt.-Col., "Le Bataillon d'Infantérie de Marine et du Pacifique"; Conseil de la République, *Rapport d'Information, annexe au procès-verbal de la séance du 28 juin 1962.*

distribute electricity under a contract it negotiated with the territory, which regulates the price it can charge for its current. Between 1960 and 1965, the concessionnaire invested 211.5 million C.F.P. francs, or twice the amount called for in its contract, in improving its service, but it refused to increase its network further unless the assembly permitted it to raise its rates. The assemblymen were eager to have electricity extended to areas beyond the main urban centers, but because the Etablissements Martin was a monopolistic private company and because the demand for a vast increase in its facilities came mainly from the C.E.P., they hesitated to authorize the price increase asked.[30] At the end of 1965 the C.E.P., impatient at the long delay, decided to import the machinery required to generate its own current. Although the expansion thus effected does not now benefit other consumers, it is expected that eventually the territory will inherit the C.E.P.'s generating plant.

[30] Minutes of the permanent commission, Sept. 15, 1966; minutes of the territorial assembly, Nov. 15, 1965, June 24, 1966.

12

Finances

CURRENCY AND BANKING

The terms still sometimes used by Polynesians to designate certain modern currencies show how widely varying were the nationalities of those who traded in the islands during the nineteenth century. *Tara,* the Polynesian deformation of dollar or piastre, was the name given to the Chilean currency that was commonly used in the islands until its circulation was prohibited by a decree of November 7, 1911. Yet even after World War II, the smallest denomination of the banknotes issued by the Banque de l'Indochine (B.I.C.) continued to be called *tara.* Of similar origin are the terms *rera* for the Spanish *réal,* and *pene* for the English penny.[1]

The French franc was the colony's sole legal tender until the decree of December 25, 1945, created the C.F.P. (Colonies Françaises du Pacifique) franc for both the E.F.O. and New Caledonia. As it was officially explained, this step was taken to bar the inflation then prevailing in France from spreading to its dependencies, whose geographical location required them to trade heavily with the dollar and sterling blocs. It evoked local resentment primarily because at that time the E.F.O. had a large reserve in dollars and sterling which it was obliged to convert into C.F.P. francs, and secondarily because in issuing the decree the French government had not consulted the territory's elected representatives. Theoretically the C.F.P. franc was convertible into foreign currencies, but in practice the controls imposed by the Office des Changes in Paris forced the E.F.O. to trade almost wholly with the franc zone.[2] In 1950 these restrictions were lifted, but meanwhile the territory had suffered further from the franc's devaluation two years before. Subsequently there were several local panics arising from reports of another sudden devaluation of

[1] Atea, J.-P., *Sous le Vent de Tahiti,* p. 28.
[2] See p. 132.

the franc, but since December 1958 the value of the C.F.P. franc in relation to the Metro. franc has not changed.

Another even longer-standing grievance of the islanders relates to the note-issue privilege held for many years by the B.I.C., which opened a branch at Papeete during World War I. On many occasions the territorial assemblymen have urged the French government to transfer the note-issue privilege from that "soulless monopoly" to an *institut d'émission* that would be created specifically for the territory. Nevertheless, the B.I.C.'s privilege was renewed after World War II, albeit on condition that it invest a considerable volume of its capital in local-development enterprises under the territory's control. Accordingly, the B.I.C. has made appreciably larger local investments than in the past, but the territorial assemblymen have never succeeded in obtaining a full accounting of such operations, in particular as to the size of the profit that the B.I.C. has realized from its speculative land purchases. It is known, however, that during the 1960s the B.I.C. put many millions of C.F.P. francs into the territory's new brewery, refrigerated plant, pearl-culture industry, and hotels, and that it has financed studies related to the new port, the copra oilmill, and the general development of tourism. Complaints are still made about the B.I.C., which remains the principal bank for European mercantile interests, but they are less vociferous and less frequently heard than before because of the postwar creation of other sources of credit.

Since the Kong Ah bankruptcy in the mid-1930s,[3] Chinese financiers have been restricted to lending their money informally to trusted clients. Other private capitalists have used notaries as intermediaries for making loans to individuals at interest rates of around 8 percent.[4] Before World War II, the only legally recognized banking institution in the colony other than the B.I.C. was the Caisse Centrale de Crédit Agriculturel Mutuel (C.C.C.A.M.), which was founded December 9, 1944, so as to lend money on short, medium, and long terms for inexpensive housing construction, and later its capital was increased from 10 to 12 million C.F.P. francs. Despite such modest means and the limitation of 100,000 C.F.P. francs that was placed on single loans, the C.C.C.A.M. was popular with the Polynesian peasantry. During the first postwar decade, the representative assembly, supported by

[3] See pp. 100–101, 186n.
[4] Minutes of the territorial assembly, Feb. 17, 1965; Coppenrath, G., *Les Chinois de Tahiti*, p. 76.

the French Union Assembly,[5] asked the government to raise the C.C.C.A.M.'s loan ceiling to 500,000 C.F.P. francs and to extend its services to include credit for fishermen and artisans. The government ignored such pleas because it was then planning to create another banking institution, which it expected would eventually absorb the C.C.C.A.M.

Because of the C.C.C.A.M.'s limited scope and because the B.I.C. was permitted under its statute to grant only short-term loans, the French government in 1950 proposed the launching of a public organization adapted to local-development needs, to be called the Crédit de l'Océanie (C.O.). At first the representative assemblymen opposed its taking over the assets and personnel of the C.C.C.A.M., "which has been well managed and has given satisfaction," [6] but their reluctance derived mainly from a fear lest the C.O. be taken over by traders to the detriment of Polynesian peasants. Finally, on December 20, 1954, they did accept the proposal after receiving the government's pledge that the C.O. would give priority to the needs of farmers, include artisans and fishermen and members of the liberal professions among its clients, and be made a public institution on whose board of directors the assembly would be represented by two members. Two and a half years passed before the C.O. was actually inaugurated on August 16, 1957, with half of its capital of 40 million C.F.P. francs subscribed by the territory and the other half provided by a loan at an interest rate of 2.5 percent from the C.C.C.E.[7] The scope of the C.O.'s activities was appreciably widened by the permission it received to accept bank deposits, and as of 1962 it had 3,300 deposit accounts aggregating 51 million C.F.P. francs. It was not until the following year, however, that the C.O. could balance its books and begin actively to fulfil the role assigned to it of meeting the credit needs of a clientele for which other sources of loans were unavailable. The persistence of undivided land ownership made it difficult for the majority of Polynesians to offer the needed guaranty.

Between September 30, 1963, and January 31, 1965, the C.O. granted 3,192 loans totaling 630,426,370 C.F.P. francs at interest rates which varied with the type of enterprises involved. Loans for development of the rural economy paid a rate of 4.5 percent; housing, 5 percent; transport, 6 percent; and trade, 7 percent.[8] As regards the amount of

[5] Minutes of the French Union Assembly, Aug. 10, 1954, June 7, 1956.
[6] Minutes of the permanent commission, July 24, 1950.
[7] See p. 82.
[8] See minutes of the territorial assembly, March 18, 1965,

money loaned, the sums granted for house-building were about three times larger than those for agricultural production.[9] Although the C.O. has had a fair record as regards the repayment of loans, 41 percent of those outstanding in 1965 were in the agricultural sector. Bad weather conditions, poor sales prices, and the handicap of providing negotiable collateral (given the common ownership of landed property) were in part responsible for this defection, but many of the defaulters were reportedly solvent and simply felt that their social position or political influence enabled them to ignore the terms of repayment.[10] These were the same phenomena that had handicapped development of the cooperative societies for many years. Nevertheless, the C.O.'s operations were regarded as a success, and it opened a branch at Uturoa, where the B.I.C. also had an agency. In 1966 the change in its name to the Société de Crédit et de Développement de l'Océanie heralded an expansion of its activities and an increase in its capital to 70 million C.F.P. francs.[11]

In 1967, galloping inflation in French Polynesia alarmed the government into finally acceding to the assembly's long-expressed desire to have a savings bank in the territory. Its even longer-standing plea, however, that a commercial bank competitive to the B.I.C. should be opened in the islands was not met until August 1969, when the Bank of Hawaii, encouraged by the increase of tourism in the territory, opened a branch in Papeete. Jacques Drollet had asserted in the assembly in 1964 that too many vested interests opposed such a breach in the monopoly held by the B.I.C.[12] To be sure, the B.I.C.'s resources and its experience in the course of a half-century in the islands gave it a great advantage over any potential competitor. In 1966, it had granted loans aggregating 2,277 million C.F.P. francs, about half of them to trading firms and the other half to the building industry, housing, individuals, transport, fishing, and agriculture, in that order of importance.[13]

BUDGETS AND TAXES

Until the advent of the C.E.P., French Polynesia's export trade was the key to its budgetary position, for the volume of exports was closely

[9] Between September 1959 and February 1965, the C.O. granted a total of 387,497,000 C.F.P. francs for housing and only 77,813,000 for farming.

[10] Minutes of the territorial assembly, March 18, 1965.

[11] *Ibid.*, May 9, 1967.

[12] *Ibid.*, Nov. 26, 1964.

[13] *Ibid.*, May 9, 1967.

related to that of imports, on which the duties were the largest single element of the territory's budgetary revenues. Even though exports had already begun to shrink before the C.E.P.'s activities aggravated their decline, those activities involved a huge increase in imports as well as in employment, beginning in 1963, that provided the territory with revenues and the islanders with ready money on an unprecedented scale. These developments, however, did not alter French Polynesia's budgetary dependence on indirect taxation, but simply enhanced the proportionate contribution made by import duties to its income.

In view of the growing difficulty of balancing the budget during the post-World War II period, the territorial assembly cast about for ways of increasing revenues. The big profits made by foreign mercantile firms during the years of high prices for exports, as well as the flight of their capital, noted particularly in 1953,[14] made aliens an obvious target for heavier taxation. The fact that it was the Chinese who were regularly in arrears for their tax payments reawakened the assemblymen's latent hostility to that ethnic minority, and they proceeded to raise the charge for merchants' licenses.

To a much more limited degree, firms doing business in the E.F.O. whose headquarters were in France were also considered fair game, but they were not so vulnerable because they wielded a political influence that the Chinese lacked. In 1957, a special tax on foreign firms which failed to employ local-born workers to the extent of at least half their personnel was voted by the assembly. Yet the phosphate company, regarded as the chief offender in this respect, was able to prevent any appreciable increase in the duty paid on its exports. Similarly, 3 years later, when the tax on the profits made by industrial and commercial firms was raised from 8 percent to 10 percent, most of them succeeded in avoiding compliance. Generally speaking, those possessing wealth in one form or another, regardless of nationality, have been able to escape heavy taxation. When the assembly, hard pressed in 1954 to increase revenues, voted to impose a tax on undeveloped land, such a storm of protests arose from urban Tahitian property owners that the measure was repealed the following year. Only on luxury imports, such as alcoholic beverages, cigarettes, automobiles, and the like were the assemblymen able to create or raise tax rates during the 1950s. By and large, taxes in the territory could not be

---

[14] The representative assembly that year was told that four merchants of Papeete had just transferred outside the territory the equivalent of 74.5 million Metro. francs. See minutes of the representative assembly, Nov. 25, 1953.

considered excessive, but their burden fell most heavily on the consumer.[15]

The basis of the territory's fiscal system had been laid during the
interwar period, and was supplemented by a few laws passed in 1946
and 1948. Subsequent modifications amounted more to tinkering with
the existing structure than to making fundamental changes in the
whole system. In reality, the assemblymen feared any move that
might lead to the application locally of French fiscal laws, including
the long-opposed income tax. Clearly any leader who favored income
tax for the territory was committing political suicide. With some
reason, opponents of income tax have been able to argue that its
imposition would aggravate the already inequitable incidence of taxation locally and would produce few tangible results. Surely the
Chinese would find some way, they said, of circumventing the law,
and since the very great majority of the population were farmers and
fishermen who produced almost all of what they consumed, and sold
little of it, such income taxes as they could pay would not be worth
the cost of collecting them. Yet although income tax was ruled out for
the time being, all those concerned with the territory's governance
realized that some source of additional revenues must be found to
meet the growing budgetary deficit.

During the mid-1950s, the territory's expenditures increased at the
rate of some 30 millon C.F.P. francs a year, largely as the result of
budgetary contributions to its economic equipment and the expanding
health and educational services. Despite its financial stringency, the
territory throughout that decade continued to allocate some 40 million C.F.P. francs a year to economic investment and about one-fourth
of its revenues to the social-development services. Public-debt payments were small, amounting to only 3 percent of the total expenditures annually, but the cost of the administrative personnel still absorbed 47 percent of the locally raised revenues. Although, under pressure, the public-works and agriculture services had been streamlined,
and only in exceptional cases were more officials for the islands recruited in France, the number of locally born civil servants was growing, as were their demands for higher pay and greater perquisites.

Nevertheless, the assemblymen refused both to alter their policy of
increasing indirect rather than direct taxation and to ask France to

[15] As of 1963, taxes paid by the 70,000 inhabitants of French Polynesia
amounted to 460 Metro. francs per capita annually. See *Marchés Tropicaux*, April
20, 1963, p. 938.

subsidize the territory's operating budget. When faced with a deficit of 69.4 millon C.F.P. francs in the 1960 budget, however, they swallowed their pride and requested Paris to give the territory more time to pay back the debt it owed to the F.I.D.E.S. and the C.C.C.E. The word "subsidy" grated on their ears, yet they gladly accepted France's "contributions" to the islands' economic equipment, which annually amounted to more than was raised locally from taxation. Between 1948 and 1960, France's aid, by whatever name it was called, totaled over 5 billion Metro. francs, of which 1,227 millions went to promoting production, 1,761 millions to social development, and 3,613 millions to the infrastructure.[16]

Finding alternative or supplementary sources of revenue presented almost insuperable difficulties because the tax ceiling under the existing system had apparently been reached, agricultural exports were declining, and the phosphate company was scheduled to terminate its shipments in 1966. As matters worked out, however, the 1966 budget proved to be the easiest to balance since that of 1949, although it had grown to the record total of 1,782 million C.F.P. francs and included 441 millions for economic investments. In 1965 France had taken over some of the largest expenditures and also agreed to assume the cost of the pay increase for the territorial civil servants, amounting to 40 million C.F.P. francs. Import duties on the equipment and matériel brought in by the C.E.P. were raised, so that the budget acquired additional funds amounting to 45 percent of the total revenues. Despite the loss of some 400 millions in revenues from the cessation of phosphate exports, the budget for 1967 declined only slightly, to 1,756 million C.F.P. francs. Although expenditures that year included 870 millions for the health and education services (40 percent of the total), 35 millions for the Copra Price Stabilization Fund, and 62 millions for the municipal treasuries of the four communes, the deficit came to no more than 160 million C.F.P. francs, a comparatively modest amount.[17]

When the budget proposed for 1969 amounted to 4,135 million C.F.P. francs—a record figure—the administration insisted that new taxation was indispensable to meet the anticipated deficit of 60 millions. Reluctantly the assemblymen agreed to impose a 10-percent

[16] *La Polynésie Française* (La Documentation Française), p. 34. Moreover, in the years 1958 to 1963 the territory received credits from the European Common Market Development Fund totaling $4,216,000, and during the 1964–1969 period a total of $951,000 from the same source. See *Marchés Tropicaux,* January 17, 1970, p. 118.

[17] Minutes of the territorial assembly, May 9, 1967.

sales tax, but, as before, an island-wide strike of shopkeepers, followed by a mass demonstration at Papeete on February 19, 1969, forced them to rescind the measure. The great majority of the territory's business community firmly oppose any drastic changes in the archaic fiscal system, and apparently believe that future budgetary deficits can be met by expanding the tourist industry. The most farsighted among them realize that this will require substantial improvements in the territory's means of communication and hotel accommodations, not to mention more local production of Western-style foodstuffs.

Because French taxpayers cannot reasonably be expected to foot the bill, the only alternative is an appreciable increase of investments by private capitalists. Early in 1965, the governor had broached the subject of attracting more private capital to the islands, but more than 2 years passed before he submitted to the assembly on May 12, 1967, a draft investment code providing long-term fiscal advantages to both large and small private investors, along with a proposal to reduce the duty on matériel imported for the construction of their enterprises. Whether or not this code will attract more private capitalists to French Polynesia remains to be seen. But it was certainly the investments made by the C.E.P. that accounted for the sizeable increases during 1965–1966 in the funds placed by American enterprises,[18] as well as by the B.I.C. and other sources of capital, in the territory's industries.[19] These investments, however, came from foreign and *demi* sources and not from Polynesians. The Polynesians' failure to put their money into the new coconut oilmill was very disappointing to the assemblymen, who had insisted on reserving a block of stock for them in that enterprise, but it should have caused no surprise in view of the longstanding lack of indigenous support for the cooperative societies. Polynesian peasants obviously distrusted joint stock companies, which they felt were too large and impersonal and gave too small returns on their capital. They preferred to invest such small sums as they had at their disposal in buildings, on which they could get 25 to 30 percent interest, or in lending money to individuals at rates that permitted them to realize a 36-percent return on their money in 3 years.[20] In terms of money, the contributions from Polynesian sources would in

[18] By the end of 1968, American capital investment in hotels in the islands amounted to $12 million.

[19] See pp. 141–144.

[20] Minutes of the territorial assembly, June 8, 1967.

any case do little to promote the territory's economic development. Psychologically, however, it was unfortunate for the country's evolution that the Polynesians remained indifferent to, or unconscious of, the value of playing an active role in their islands' development.

13

Transportation

French Polynesia's isolated position in the mid-Pacific has had both favorable and unfavorable effects on its evolution. It has permitted the islanders to retain their own special character, but their lack of communications with the modern world has certainly been detrimental to their economic development. The territory has no railroads, a very limited road network, fitful shipping services, and—until very recently —only sporadic air communications with Europe, the Americas, and even other regions of the Pacific.

ROADS AND MOTOR VEHICLES

French Polynesia has made little progress in extending its road system over the past half-century, but the quality of its roads has improved and they are used by many more motor vehicles. The territory's total network consists of roads along the coastal belts of Tahiti (175 kilometers), Moorea (60 kilometers), and Raiatea (37 kilometers), as well as a dozen or so kilometers on Bora Bora. On the other islands there exist simply tracks, or *pistes*, of which only a few are motorable. Nowhere do the roads lead into the interior, which is accessible only by trails, of which the majority date back to precolonial times. As the Polynesian chiefs of those days were frequently engaged in warfare, they were concerned more to block than to increase such means of communication.

As might be expected, Tahiti is the island that has benefited most by such improvements as have been made in the territory's system, and now all the settlements there are connected by road with Papeete. In addition to the macadamized highway that encircles Tahiti-Nui, there are two branch roads that penetrate the Taiarapu peninsula. Moorea and Raiatea also have circular routes with antennae leading for varying distances into their hinterlands, but it was not until the mid-1960s that they were made motorable throughout the year. Since 1964 the public-works service has made a big effort to improve the existing network, mainly by surfacing roads and constructing permanent bridges. Such work has been carried out as part of French Polynesia's development plan and financed by the F.I.D.E.S., as well as by loans from the C.C.C.E. that are guaranteed by a local road fund (Fonds Routier). A tax on gasoline provisions this fund, but it is sufficient to undertake only improvements and not any new road construction.

The activities of the C.E.P. and the rapid expansion of tourism have contributed to the roads' deterioration by vastly increasing the number of cars, especially on Tahiti. As of 1928, there were in all the E.F.O. only 422 privately-owned automobiles, 33 buses, and 27 trucks.[1] By 1967, there were altogether 12,172 motor cars, trucks, and buses in the islands, as well as the 500 or so military vehicles belonging to the C.E.P., most of which circulated in Tahiti.[2] In recent years, also, there has been a threefold increase—from 8,000 in 1963 to nearly 24,000 in 1967—in the number of motorcycles, a form of transport that was almost unknown before World War II.[3] Little use has been made of animal traction and the bicycle remains, as it has been for many years, the normal form of native transport. Indeed, it is believed that even today about one-third of the total population lives isolated from the road system.

AIR TRANSPORT

Until World War II, the E.F.O. had no airfield, although there was a base for military hydroplanes at Papeete. In 1942, the American armed forces built an airdrome with two runways at Bora Bora, but owing to what was euphemistically called "a regrettable misunderstanding with the French administration, the American military destroyed the numerous and remarkable installations they had built, which would have been of great use to us."[4] A request made in 1947 by a newly constituted private company, the Trapas, for 4 million C.F.P. francs to put the Bora Bora airfield into usable condition was granted by the assembly, but work on it stopped in 1950 at about the same time as the Trapas company ceased its activities.

It is not surprising that in its 2 years of operation with a single hy-

[1] *L'Océanie Française,* July–August 1928.
[2] In 1968, there were 534 traffic accidents in Tahiti, in which 11 persons died.
[3] *Marchés Tropicaux,* Feb. 24, 1968, p. 480.
[4] Minutes of the French Union Assembly, March 24, 1953.

droplane the Trapas was unable to provide a regular and adequate service for mail and passengers between Papeete and Nouméa.[5] In voting a monthly subsidy of 100,000 C.F.P. francs to the Trapas company, the assemblymen had expected it soon to become a subsidiary of Air France, which would assume its operating expenses. They were disappointed in this, as well as in its anticipated extension beyond New Caledonia, "which has no commercial or touristic ties with us." [6] Consequently, the assembly refused further support to the Trapas, whose subsidy and solitary plane were transferred to another equally unsatisfactory local company. This was Air Tahiti, formed to provide an interisland service and managed by the Régie Aérien Interinsulaire (R.A.I.). Both the R.A.I. and the Trapas company incurred large deficits, furnished poor and irregular service, and failed to provide the E.F.O. with adequate communications with the outside world.

For two years Senator Robert Lassalle-Séré endeavored zealously and unsuccessfully to induce the French government to add Bora Bora to the airfields served by Air France on its Paris-Saigon-Nouméa run, and to replace the territory's old hydroplane with land planes that would enable the territory to increase its tourist trade. France did send a military officer to study the situation in 1950, but there the matter rested and for some years no further move was made to remedy the E.F.O.'s isolation by air. The Paris authorities, while recognizing in principle the strategic value of Tahiti's geographical position, continued in practice to give it a low priority in their overall plans to develop the French Union's means of communication. In view of what were then considered to be the "dubious returns" from developing tourism in the islands, the cost of building an airfield in such difficult terrain was considered by them to be prohibitive. Few Frenchmen, they believed, could or would afford a round-trip air fare to the E.F.O., and at that time the encouragement of "Anglo-American" tourism was considered undesirable. Dr. Jean Florisson, who succeeded Lassalle-Séré as senator for the E.F.O., supported this view, claiming that the Polynesians themselves were opposed to large-scale tourism because they feared that it would raise their cost of living and alter their way of life. Therefore, the consensus was that it would be better and more economical to improve the existing infrastructure, subsidize the local Aero Club to provide emergency air transport and train a few Tahitian

[5] *Pacific Islands Monthly,* April 1950.
[6] Minutes of the permanent commission, Feb. 28, 1949.

pilots, and continue using hydroplanes which could utilize the lagoons and did not require the construction of airfields.

As a result of this policy there was almost no development of air service in the E.F.O. throughout the 1950s. Until the middle of that decade, the only foreign planes calling at Tahiti were those of New Zealand's Tasmania Empire Airways Ltd (T.E.A.L.) on their route to and from Auckland via Suva, Samoa, and the Cook Islands. In 1955, a French company, the Transports Aériens Internationaux (T.A.I.) began a service between France and the E.F.O., and 3 years later it took over the R.A.I., which was still operating irregularly with a single hydroplane and a solitary pilot. In 1959 the assembly increased the subsidy for the interisland air service to 5,300,000 C.F.P. francs, and this enabled still another local company, Air Polynésie, to buy a few small amphibious aircraft and to include in its itinerary 33 island lagoons.

No important change in the situation occurred until 1957, when the French government, after years of indecision, finally agreed to build an airfield capable of handling four-engine jet planes, in the lagoon of Faaa, a suburb of Papeete.[7] Arguments in favor of building such an airfield were the vast increase that had recently occurred in Pacific air traffic, the desire to maintain French prestige and reinforce the military base in this distant outpost, and, above all, the need to aid the territory's faltering economy by developing tourism. Although the Faaa airfield was estimated to cost some 2 billion Metro. francs, it was preferred to Bora Bora, whose improvement would require nearly one-third of that amount and which was, moreover, 140 kilometers distant from Papeete.

The Faaa airport, completed in October 1960, was officially inaugurated 7 months later with the arrival of a T.A.I. DC-8 jet plane from France, and the following month that company began service also between Tahiti, Nouméa, and Wallis Island. Bora Bora continued to be served by the same old hydroplane, but in 1962 an airfield was built at Uturoa, on Raiatea. In the late 1960s, a limited interisland service was still being provided by R.A.I., and in 1967–1968 two new local companies began offering charter flights to the few islands that had small airfields. France withdrew landing rights at Tahiti for the T.E.A.L. company in late 1963, but 2 years later, Pan American Air-

---

[7] For an analysis of the issues involved in this decision, see minutes of the French Union Assembly, July 5, 14, 1956; *Marchés Coloniaux,* April 20, 1957, p. 1000.

ways began a weekly jet service between San Francisco and Auckland, with stops at both Honolulu and Faaa. Thus French Polynesia finally acquired regular air services linking it not only with Europe and North America but also with Hawaii, New Caledonia, and New Zealand.

A project has been drawn up under the current 5-year plan to build three airstrips in the Tuamotu archipelago and one each in the Austral, Marquesa, and Gambier Islands. The 90 million C.F.P. francs allotted to this construction by the F.I.D.E.S., however, were clearly inadequate, and there has been difficulty in finding the necessary funds. The delay has been compounded by disagreements among the territorial assemblymen about the sites of the proposed airstrips. In the meantime, the C.E.P. has built some airfields for its own use on a few of the atolls. Inevitably these are not related to the territory's need for better and more regular means of interisland transportation, a need which is particularly crucial in view of the failure of local shipping companies to provide a satisfactory alternative service.

SHIPPING: INTERISLAND

Complaints by traders, administrators, doctors, and the general public regarding the inadequacy of interisland shipping have been perennial throughout the territory's economic history. The basic difficulty has been and still is that interisland shipping depends almost wholly on trade, particularly that of copra, and that it is controlled by individual merchants or trading companies, most of which are Chinese. The transport of passengers on their schooners is incidental, and the schedules and itineraries of interisland shipping are determined by trade profits. Imported merchandise is carried to the islands producing copra, vanilla, and shell, where it is bartered for those products. The result is that the most distant and least productive of the islands sometimes go for a whole year without being visited by any trading schooner, and their inhabitants continue to depend on locally built sailboats as their very limited means of transportation.

From time to time the adminstration has tried to supplement this defective service with its own vessels. Before World War II, it operated a few motor boats, mainly for the use of its doctor-administrators in the outer islands. For a short time, too, the ships of the Messageries Maritimes stopped at one or two of the islands on their voyages between France and Papeete. Beginning in 1898, a government-owned steamer, the *Croix du Sud*, made trips to some of the islands, but after it was shipwrecked in 1903 the service was suspended for some years. Shortly before World War I, the same itinerary was taken up successively by another steamer and a schooner until 1921, but such voyages were "capricious" to the point where there were no such ships at all during long periods of time.[8] The administration was naturally criticized for its failure to subsidize and organize properly an interisland shipping service, and also for its choice of vessels that were invariably over-age, costly to operate, and generally inappropriate for the tasks assigned them.[9]

Even though the government added two more schooners to the interisland run during the interwar period, this did not break the vicious circle that has long been detrimental to the territory's interisland shipping. Trading schooners continued to call at islands only when and where there was a profitable cargo to pick up. Because their schedules and itinerary were irregular, producers had no incentive to increase output, for produce often deteriorated while waiting long months for a vessel to arrive and carry it to Papeete for export. Chinese merchants remained effectively in control of interisland shipping, although by law shipowners and captains were required to be French citizens. These shipowners also ignored the legal requirement to carry minimal navigational (and safety) equipment, and their nautical almanacs were usually outdated and their sextants inaccurate. The few hardy passengers who sailed to the outer islands had to put up with the schooners' erratic schedules, traveled in great discomfort and at considerable expense, and risked their lives on unseaworthy vessels sailing among unmarked reefs and passes into the lagoons.

Shipping shortages during and after World War II worsened an already bad situation. It was not until March 24, 1953, however, that the representative assembly gave its assent to making contracts on an experimental basis with some shipowners so as to end the "prevailing anarchy." [10] In return for a monopoly of the trade of specific islands, the concessionaires agreed to make regular weekly or monthly trips to them. By 1957, shipping monopolies had been established for all the archipelagoes except the Leeward Islands, which alone of all the island groups had always enjoyed fairly regular service by private enterprise. Yet the results of this experiment proved so immediately unsatisfactory

[8] *L'Océanie Française*, August 1911, January–February 1934.

[9] See report of a French naval officer, J. Mercier, in *L'Océanie Française*, March–April 1934.

[10] Minutes of the representative assembly, September 24, 1953.

that the monopolistic contracts were rescinded the following year. The shipowners were therefore moved to get together for the first time and to form a group under the leadership of the Société Sopéda, which proceeded to divide the servicing of the islands among its members.

In the late 1950s, the French navy eliminated or reduced navigational hazards, and the number and quality of schooners serving the outer islands also improved. At the close of the decade, French Polynesia had a fleet comprising 26 schooners aggregating 2,086 tons, 75 fishing boats averaging 65 tons apiece, and 9 tenders. Annually the schooners transported between Papeete and the outer islands some 75,000 tons of products and merchandise, as well as several thousand passengers.[11] The rates charged for both cargo and passengers were set each year by local decree.

Because of the development of tourism, the steady decline in the outer islands' productivity, and the growing emigration of their inhabitants to Papeete, further improvements became imperative. Even though the shipowners had been forbidden to carry any more live animals because they arrived at Papeete half dead from hunger and thirst, no progress had been made in ameliorating the conditions for human transport. Men, women, and children still slept on deck on heaps of copra sacks in "dreadful promiscuity." [12] Some of the islands had no ports, and the most distant and impoverished among them remained as isolated as before, while the more productive ones were often visited simultaneously by competitive trading schooners. There continued to be an uneconomic imbalance between the small quantity of the expensive merchandise they carried on the outgoing voyage and the volume of the far less valuable copra transported on the return trip.

In 1962 the bankruptcy of the Société Sopéda, which had managed the shipowners' pool, forced the government to take action, and it commissioned four experts to study the situation, in 1965–1966, and to propose remedies. Of their reports, that of the Naval Inspector, Percier, was the most complete, but all the experts agreed as to the major causes of the islands' poor shipping service, confirmed its domination by Chinese merchants,[13] and submitted generally analogous recom-

---

[11] *Situation Economique et Perspectives d'Avenir, 1959–60*, Papeete, 1960.

[12] *Les Débats*, July 9, 1961.

[13] Forty percent of the tonnage was in the hands of European firms, 30 percent was wholly Chinese-owned, and the Chinese also predominated in the ownership of the remaining 30 percent. As to the ships' crews, there were no Chinese

mendations. They stressed the disparities in the age, size, and equipment of the territory's fleet, which ranged from a few modern and capacious schooners to small, decrepit sailing junks; the lack of ports, quays, and repair facilities in the outer islands; the drawbacks of combining import and export trading on the same "floating bazaars"; the failure to grant loans to shipowners on any rational basis; and, above all, the disorderly and anarchic competition among the shipowners for the trade of the productive islands and their total neglect of others.[14] The experts recommended that the safety regulations be made more effective and that the periods of time that schooners remained tied up at Papeete while waiting for profitable freight to accumulate be reduced.

The situation was somewhat eased in the early 1960s by the C.E.P.'s agreement to provision some of the most remote islands, such as Rapa, in essentials, but this was obviously only a stop-gap solution. In the middle of the decade, a new crisis arose when a strike was called by both sailors and owners of the interisland service. The former demanded a pay raise, which the latter claimed they could not grant unless the territory authorized an increase in the rates they were permitted to charge for the transport of freight and passengers. Although the assemblymen resented the shipowners' refusal to submit detailed figures to substantiate their claim that operating costs had doubled between 1959 and 1966, they increased by 30 percent the subsidy granted for carrying copra and passengers between Papeete, the Tuamotus, the Gambiers, and the Marquesas. Subsequently the owners reached a compromise agreement with their sailors in respect to wages. All elements involved, however, realized that some fundamental reform in interisland shipping must take place.

The authorities now seem to have accepted the necessity for subsidizing interisland shipping where it is unprofitable, granting monopolies to shipping firms for certain islands, and even financing the purchase of some new schooners. In return, however, they are determined to control the profits made by private shipping and the conditions of transport so as to assure the regularity and inclusiveness of interisland services.

---

skippers or sailors but only cabin boys, cooks, and supercargoes. See G. Coppenrath, *Les Chinois de Tahiti*, p. 75.

[14] Minutes of the permanent commission, March 28, July 22, 1966.

SHIPPING: OCEAN

During the second half of the 19th century, many of the sailing ships plying the Pacific—some of which were locally owned—called at Tahiti, which thus had regular, if slow, sea communications with North and South America as well as with Australia. The French government itself maintained five schooners in the colony for the use of its administrative and military staffs.[15]

Successively, the development of steam navigation, the separation of the French Ministry of Colonies from that of the Navy, and the opening of the Panama Canal drastically altered the islands' shipping picture and, paradoxically, diminished the E.F.O.'s maritime communications with the outside world. The local shipowners were unable to meet the competition from foreign steamers and had to abandon their trade with Australia and the Americas, concentrating on the only commerce that was still profitable to them—that between Papeete and the Tuamotu archipelago. The navy, no longer responsible for the administration of the colony, reduced the number of its ships sent or stationed there. Although the Messageries Maritimes, subsidized by the French government to include the E.F.O. in its Far Eastern service, provided a link between the colony and France, 24,000 kilometers away, the territory became progressively isolated from the world, and Tahiti from all the outer islands except those nearest to it.

Hopes for a revival of the E.F.O.'s foreign trade rose with the announcement of plans to build a canal across the Panama isthmus. Tahiti's "brilliant future" as a strategic and commercial center in the Pacific was the subject of several books, notably those written by the deputy and journalist, Paul Deschanel.[16] For some years the authorities debated the respective merits of Rapa, the Marquesa archipelago, and Tahiti as the best site for a new port that would be capable of berthing and fueling the largest trans-Pacific ships, but it was not until two missions had been sent from France to study the possibilities between 1911 and 1912 that Papeete was chosen.

Soon World War I broke out and the project remained in abeyance until it was revived by Albert Sarraut, who gave top priority to Papeete's port in his *mise-en-valeur* blueprint for all the French Empire.[17]

---

[15] Auzelle, R., *Plan Directeur d'Aménagement de l'Agglomération de Papeete, Rapport d'Enquête Monographique*, p. 4.

[16] See especially his *La Politique Française en Océanie*.

[17] See pp. 80–81.

Under his plan, some work was done on the port and a drydock was built at Papeete. By the time they were finished, however, trans-Pacific shipping had acquired the habit of by-passing the E.F.O. and, in any case, the economic depression which began in 1929 had sharply curtailed world trade. In 1936, ships of the Union Steamship Company ceased to call at Papeete on their route from San Francisco to Wellington and Sydney, thus gravely hampering the E.F.O.'s trade with the United States and British territories in the Pacific.[18] Chartered freighters continued to carry Makatea's phosphate directly to its markets in Japan, but the colony's sole maritime link for general world trade was the monthly service provided by the Messageries Maritimes, which connected it with the French ports of Marseille and Le Havre by way either of the Suez or the Panama Canal.

The cessation of communications with France in mid-1940 again drastically altered the E.F.O.'s shipping pattern. To provision the isolated colony and move its copra exports, British and American ships again came to Papeete, with the blessing of the Free French authorities. After the war, however, the French government tried to revive what amounted to a virtual monopoly by the Messageries Maritimes of the transport of the E.F.O.'s foreign trade. Since that company had lost many of its ships during the war, its service to the territory was infrequent and irregular, with the result that the islanders complained bitterly of isolation and shortages. In the early 1950s, however, Papeete acquired a new drydock and the Messageries Maritimes a few new freighters, and gradually its cargo—though not passenger—service to the E.F.O. improved, but at the same time its rates rose.

The early 1960s saw additional improvements to Papeete's port. On January 1, 1962, in order to make it independent of the fluctuating grants allotted to it on a year-to-year basis from the territory's budget, its management was made autonomous and placed under a board of directors which comprised representatives of the territorial assembly, the Chamber of Commerce, Papeete's municipal council, and various technicians. In mid-1963, the French government announced that it would build a new and larger port at Papeete because the old one could no longer handle the traffic, which had doubled during the preceding 4 years.[19] In reality, the decision was motivated by the need to have a port for the C.E.P. in Tahiti. Inasmuch as the existing port was not accessible to large ships through any of its three passes in the coral

[18] See pp. 128–131.
[19] *Marchés Tropicaux,* Oct. 26, 1963, p. 2570.

reef, and as it was impossible to appreciably enlarge its facilities, a wholly new port was to be built on the island of Motu-Uta in the center of Papeete's lagoon.

Work on the new port began in April 1964 and was completed in June 1966, and almost all its cost of 60 million Metro. francs was borne by the French government. At the time the port was inaugurated, its breakwater measured 800 meters, its quays 2,000 meters, and its warehouses 18,000 square meters. Completion of the project included the construction of buildings for the merchant marine, the customs service, and the Ecole Maritime, as well as the purchase of a 1,000-h.p. tugboat that would enable 30,000-ton vessels to dock alongside.[20]

[20] Secretary-general Langlois' speech to the territorial assembly, May 9, 1967.

14

Labor

From the earliest days of colonization, the territory's labor shortage was regarded by the French as the greatest handicap to its economic development. Because of the small and decreasing number of Polynesians, as well as their avoidance of regular and hard work, the government made no attempt to introduce the system of forced labor, as it did in other French colonies. Only prisoners and, occasionally, villagers on some of the islands were required to maintain roads and public buildings.

The first French administrators soon lost all hope of interesting the Polynesians in increasing their production and in hiring out their services as laborers for the settlers. All Polynesians were to some degree landowners, and under the traditional communal way of life, relatives were entitled to any surplus food crops that might be raised by the family. Nature provided the islanders, almost without effort on their part, with many of their essentials, such as heat, fuel, and housing, for which Westerners worked hard. The Polynesians were willing to exert themselves briefly for desirable objectives not otherwise attainable, to oblige their guests, or to perform tasks requiring the use of their traditional skills. As for wage-earning, the problem was not that they they found accepting money for their services humiliating, but that they considered the surrender of their independence over a long period the ultimate degradation.

French officials therefore came to believe that the solution of the problem of economic development lay, first, in inducing more French settlers to come to the colony and, secondly, in importing foreigners—usually Asians—to do the manual work. But these policies, too, were doomed to failure. The few French settlers who came to the islands soon gave up farming,[1] because the climate was unfavorable for their crops and debilitating to their physique, and their efforts were poorly remunerated. Some of the French emigrants to Tahiti undoubtedly

[1] See pp. 108–109.

had been misinformed as to the real living and working conditions there, and left after becoming disillusioned. Those who had come with romantic expectations but no material resources had to be repatriated at government expense. On more than one occasion, the French governor remonstrated with the Paris authorities, urging them to screen emigrants more carefully and to inform applicants that would-be settlers coming to a colony with such limited economic opportunities must bring with them the capital and skills that would enable them to be self-supporting. Westerners other than French also felt the lure of the South Seas, and on the eve of World War II, they numbered 325 in Polynesia. Of this floating foreign population, the government expelled 20 to 30 each year as "undesirable."

The foreign laborers also, whom the administration began importing in the late 19th century, soon proved to be unsatisfactory, but they were easier to dispose of than were the nationals of Western countries. As early as May 16, 1884, a dispatch from the Minister of Colonies forbade the local authorities to recruit any more aliens to work on the settlers' plantations. The foreign Oceanians who had been brought into the colony a few years before were to be repatriated because they were "given to strong drink, unruly and hard to supervise." As for the Chinese, they gave satisfaction so long as they remained farm workers but not after they left agriculture for trade.[2] After World War I, an immigration service was formed to bring in and deal with workers from nearby areas, but little came of its activities. Only the phosphate company persisted in recruiting and employing laborers from the Antilles, China, Japan, and Indochina, but almost all of them were repatriated during the depression of the early 1930s. Only 85 Tonkinese and 28 Japanese were still in the colony when World War II began.

Not only were the experiments with immigrant labor a failure but the war made it impossible to recruit alien workers, so employers were forced to turn once again to Polynesians. The phosphate company—the C.F.P.O.—which had the greatest need of labor of any enterprise in the territory, adopted an astute policy. By providing its Polynesian workers with care, comforts, training, diversions, and higher pay than they had ever before known, it built up a stable and efficient labor force.[3] Initially the C.F.P.O. recruited Cook Islanders, to whom it offered wages three times higher than they received at

[2] See pp. 91–92.
[3] See pp. 142–143.

home. At first the New Zealand government was bitterly criticized in the Cook Islands for permitting a French company—albeit one with considerable British capital—to lure away workers who could develop their home islands.[4] Later, however, the remittances regularly sent back to the laborers' families quieted the opposition, and the Cook Islanders soon took such a liking to life on Makatea that more volunteered to work there (or to renew their contracts) than were needed. The C.F.P.O. was even able to become selective in its choice of employes. By a rigorous medical examination it weeded out the physically unfit, and by requiring "character" references it was able to eliminate those likely to cause trouble. At the peak of their employment on Makatea, Cook Islanders numbered 351, the great majority of whom were repatriated in 1956.[5]

In the mid-1950s, there were so many outer-islanders without work in Papeete that the administration asked the C.F.P.O. to give preference, in taking on workers, to local-born Polynesians. The most likely candidates for such labor were the Tuamotuans, whose atolls had very meager resources and who were harder-working, more thrifty, and more disposed to emigrate than other islanders. The C.F.P.O. was as successful in handling the French islanders as those from the Cook Islands, and its policy proved that, contrary to the prevailing view, they could be technically trained and became interested in regular disciplined work under the proper conditions. By the time the C.F.P.O. ceased operations in 1966, it had trained some hundreds of Polynesians as mechanics, carpenters, masons, and electricians, and its wages had enabled them to save enough money to build houses and buy imported luxuries when they returned home. In a press interview in 1961, the head of the C.F.P.O. paid this tribute to his Polynesian employes:[6]

When [Tahitian] workers are well fed and have confidence in their employers, they show exceptional qualities—physical in respect to endurance, agility, and skill, and also intellectual and moral. After long experience I can state that they have no equals in all the Pacific. Our company uses them in all branches with success. Our electrical service is wholly staffed by Tahitians, from the post of engineer to the humblest laborer. We have a head nurse, almost a doctor, who is a Tahitian; our sailors, all Tahitians, are without peers.

[4] *Pacific Islands Monthly,* December 1954.
[5] *Ibid.,* July 1947, February 1951, December 1954; *Journal de la Société des Océanistes,* December 1959.
[6] *Marchés Tropicaux,* Nov. 11, 1961, p. 2645.

Similar testimonials have been given by the employers of Tahitians working in the New Hebrides and, above all, in New Caledonia. It could be argued, of course, that the labor shortages in those islands made employers exaggerate the capacities of whatever workers they could lay their hands on, and also that only the most enterprising young Tahitians emigrated. Yet the C.E.P. and its related enterprises in the territory have also been able to train a satisfactory labor force from among the indigenous farmers and fishermen. The answer to the question as to why for so many years the French islanders were regarded as unstable and indifferent wage-earners seems to lie not only in the persistence of the traditional communal practices of Polynesian society but also in the lack of incentives and opportunities for gainful employment in the territory itself.

The only two areas where there have long been concentrations of wage-earners are Makatea and the port of Papeete. Far smaller numbers have been employed as sailors on interisland boats and as farm laborers by a few planters in Tahiti and the outer islands. As to industrial, commercial, and administrative employment, such as existed has been centered at Papeete. There the top posts were held by Frenchmen, Chinese, or *demis,* and the largest number of Polynesians have been employed as domestic servants or in subordinate positions in the administration and in the building industry. Since World

TABLE 3

FRENCH POLYNESIA: PRINCIPAL OCCUPATIONS OF THE
ACTIVE POPULATION, BY GENERAL CATEGORIES,
1956 AND 1962

Occupation	1956	1962
Agriculture, forestry, and fishing	10,408	10,482
Mining	819	710
Government employment	490	2,472
Construction	902	2,199
Trade	885	1,667
Army, police, customs	527	553
Domestic service	259	1,644
TOTAL	14,300	19,727

Source: Mimeographed sheet dated May 1965, probably based on 1962 census; La Documentation Française, Service de Documentation, Paris.

War II, the census reports for 1956 and 1962 [7] show an increase between those two years in the number of persons gainfully employed, but to some extent this simply reflects the demographic increase. Unfortunately, the 1962 figures draw no distinction between the ethnic groups concerned, and they also distort the current picture by including the workers at Makatea, now closed down, and those who labored briefly on the construction of the Faaa airport. Table 4 is more meaningful in that it provides a breakdown for some of the categories of employment and for the sex ratio.

TABLE 4

FRENCH POLYNESIA: WAGE-EARNERS IN CERTAIN
CATEGORIES OF EMPLOYMENT, BY SEX, 1962

Category	Men	Women
Commercial and industrial employees	348	118
Independent commercial and industrial workers	894	405
Liberal professions	79	10
Higher cadres, private sector	114	8
Middle cadres, private sector	159	90
Higher cadres, public sector	126	9
Middle cadres, public sector	474	540
Employees, public sector	318	269
Other workers, public sector	331	19
Foremen	35	1
Manual laborers	2,587	285
TOTAL	5,465	1,754

Source: Analysis of 1962 census report by Prof. M. Desroches; cited by J. Guiart, "L'Emploi en Polynésie Française," *Outre-Mer Français*, 1er trimestre, 1968.

Both the census of 1956 and that of 1962 show that a still overwhelming but stationary number of islanders are engaged in the traditional occupations of farming, fishing, and forestry, but they provide no clue as to what money the Polynesians may earn in their leisure time. Nor do those reports throw light on the duration of the jobs listed or the exact work involved in the occupations classi-

[7] See table 3.

fied. The category called *personnes isolées* (14,275) in the first post-World War II census seems to lump together all self-employed individuals, such as artisans and traders, along with those supporting themselves in the primary sector. Furthermore, the number listed as wage-earners (5,508) suggests that a far larger proportion of the total population than seems likely were then working full time to earn their living. Clearly evidenced, however, by all the analyses is the overwhelming predominance of manual laborers among the wage-earners, the small number of women gainfully employed, and the relative importance of "independent" workers of both sexes in government service, trade, and industry. In the course of the past decade, the number of persons engaged in the mining industry dwindled to the vanishing point, whereas that of those employed as domestic servants and in government, trade, and industry has vastly increased.

The overall increase in wage-earning employment between 1956 and 1962 is trifling in comparison with the upsurge that followed the installation of the C.E.P. and its associated enterprises. The ranks of wage-earners grew from 7,250 in 1960 to 14,300 in mid-1966, and this growth was accomplished at the expense of the primary-sector labor force.[8] In the latter year, the C.E.P. was directly or indirectly responsible for employing 4,384 persons, of whom 3,841 were Polynesians. This meant that nearly one-third of the territory's active population was working for the C.E.P., or about four times as many as were employed at Makatea and at Papeete port. It also should be noted that the C.E.P. and the private companies associated with it drew two-thirds of their labor force from islands other than the Windward group. Specifically, the majority of them came from the Tuamotu-Gambier and Marquesa archipelagoes, which thus lost one-third of the young men who were engaged in farming and fishing in those islands.

UNEMPLOYMENT

In general terms, it is as misleading to speak of "unemployment" in French Polynesia as it is to apply the term "wage-earner" to the many islanders who only sporadically take paid jobs. "Unemployed" can be appropriately applied only to the 300-odd wage-earners of the public-works service and Papeete municipality who were dismissed from regular jobs in 1954, and to the approximately 500 employes

[8] Gov. Sicurani's speech to the territorial assembly, Oct. 11, 1966.

of the C.F.P.O. who had to leave Makatea when mining operations ended there in 1966. The great majority of Polynesians have never been wage-earners in the Western sense of the term, and the growing number of outer-islanders living in Papeete without regular sources of earned income cannot properly be called *chomeurs*. These islanders have come to the town for various reasons, among them the lack of diversions and of opportunities for secondary or technical education, as well as of gainful employment, in their home islands. A study made early in the 1960s of the immigrants from Rurutu and Rimatara who have "colonized" a suburb northeast of Papeete showed that the men were occasionally employed at the port or in the building industry, while their wives earned a little money by stringing shell necklaces.[9] Although most of these immigrants cannot even make ends meet, they continue to dream of someday owning a motorcycle, a radio set, and new clothes. As yet they cannot properly be called an urban proletariat, for they can always return to their home islands, where they are landowners.

"Full employment" is another misleading term that is often used by apologists for the C.E.P. in pointing out the benefits which that center has brought to the territory. In reality, it simply means that many men who have never before hired out their services now work regularly for money. Taking into consideration the unemployment caused by the withdrawal of the C.F.P.O. from Makatea, the C.E.P.'s activities have been responsible for perhaps only 2,000 new jobs in the territory.[10] It is true that the C.E.P. has created far more opportunities for gainful employment than ever before existed in French Polynesia, and at record wages. Perhaps, however, its most worthwhile contribution to the territory's development has been its job-training program, which has enabled some of its employes to gain skills that should qualify them for better-paid jobs than they could otherwise have aspired to.

VOCATIONAL EDUCATION

During the depression of the 1930s, a short-lived effort was made by the administration to institute vocational training in the colony's public schools.[11] When the project was revived after World War II, it

---

[9] Mazellier, P., *Tahiti*, p. 68.
[10] Guiart, J., "L'Emploi en Polynésie Française."
[11] *L'Océanie Française*, February–March 1930.

was again placed within the framework of the school system. In 1950 an apprenticeship center to train carpenters, metalworkers, and electricians was installed as an annex to the *collège* of Papeete, and applicants for admission were required to hold a *certificat d'études primaires*. No training was offered, however, in accountancy, stenography, commercial English, or radio repair—fields in which the demand exceeded the supply. It was not undertaken until the late 1950s, when the Chamber of Commerce began offering courses in those subjects. Under the auspices of the Catholic church, the Collège Javouhey taught household economics to girls. As of 1960, there were 157 students enrolled at the apprenticeship center, 72 in the *cours ménager*, and several hundred in short courses at the Chamber of Commerce.[12] By no means all of the students were Polynesians or completed their training, and perhaps 20 graduates a year were awarded the *certificat d'aptitude professionelle*. At the time, the small scale of this instruction was considered appropriate to the apathetic attitude of the Polynesians toward vocational training and to the local demand for skilled workers. The sole enterprise that turned out mechanics, masons, electricians, and the like in comparatively large numbers was the C.F.P.O., but they were trained exclusively for that company's needs.

The development of tourism in the early 1960s led to the creation of a center specifically to train hotel personnel. After the territory had contributed the land and a subsidy of 1 million C.F.P. francs a year, and France had donated twice that sum, the center was opened in October 1962. Its pupils received instruction without charge, free midday meals, and a promise from the Syndicat de l'Hôtellerie to employ all its graduates.[13] This center could not be termed an unqualified success, for the cost of training each of its 20 pupils came to 180,000 C.F.P. francs, many of them dropped out, and some of its few graduates left the territory for employment elsewhere. Undiscouraged, the assemblymen in 1966 decided to levy an "apprenticeship tax" to help finance an enlargement of this center. The local authorities remained convinced that it was the lack of skills that accounted for the high cost and poor quality of French Polynesia's labor, and this belief was reinforced by the difficulties encountered by the C.E.P. in recruiting skilled workers.

One of the inducements held out to the assemblymen by promoters

---

12 *La Polynésie Française* (La Documentation Française), p. 38.
13 Minutes of the territorial assembly, Nov. 25, 1964; June 20, 1965.

of the C.E.P. was that that center would give training to 1,000 Polynesian workers. Although the number actually trained by the C.E.P. by 1967 came to only half that figure, the results were so satisfactory that when the C.E.P. began laying off personnel in 1967 it replaced some of the Europeans by its own Polynesian trainees. Between January 1, 1966, and January 1, 1967, the C.E.P.'s force of unskilled employes declined from 1,829 to 1,162 but that of its skilled Polynesian workers rose from 1,357 to 1,520.[14] In fact, the C.E.P. training program was such a success that in 1966 the apprenticeship center was transformed into a technical *lycée,* four Polynesians were sent to France on scholarships for additional instruction, and the following year, a "rapid-training center" was installed at Tipuerai, offering a series of 6-month courses in vocational skills.

So large and sudden an increase in the ranks of local skilled workers naturally poses the problem of their future employment. Even before the suspension of nuclear testing was announced in November 1968, local leaders had begun to discuss what could be done to maintain a high level of employment after the C.E.P. ceased to function. It was calculated that this eventually would leave some 3,000 Polynesians without jobs, and that by no means all of them could be absorbed by the new public-works and hotel-building projects. In any case, they could not hope to receive the same wages as those that the C.E.P. had been paying, and, if forced to return to farming and fishing in their home islands, would find readjustment difficult. One of the tasks of the social-welfare service founded in 1967 was to help the returnees adapt themselves to their old way of life, but such a readjustment would be exceptionally hard for the hundreds of workers who had acquired skills in recent years. Probably many of them would remain to swell the number of immigrants eking out a precarious living in Papeete, and pessimists foresaw that this might well lead to social and political agitation discouraging to capital investment in the territory.[15] Even the most optimistic forecasters felt that it was most unlikely that the territory's economy, even under highly propitious circumstances, could expand sufficiently to offer large-scale employment. The alternative solution open to surplus wage-earners, both skilled and unskilled, was emigration to France, the United States, or other Pacific islands.

[14] Guiart, "L'Emploi en Polynésie Française."
[15] *Ibid.*

EMIGRANT WORKERS

Soon after World War II, a trickle of Tahitians began emigrating to the New Hebrides, where the labor shortage was acute and wages therefore were exceptionally high. This movement was not large, in part because of Pouvanaa's opposition to emigration on principle and in part because of the "divided responsibility" that was inherent in the condominium structure of those islands' government.[16] The latter difficulty did not exist in New Caledonia, where the repatriation of Tonkinese and Javanese immigrants coincided with the start of a development program that required laborers far in excess of those locally available. Early in 1954, an emissary of the New Caledonia administration came to the E.F.O. to seek the local authorities' approval for the recruitment of laborers there. He arrived in Papeete at a propitious moment, when local employment was at a very low ebb. Consequently, approval of his proposal was soon given by the administration, the Chamber of Commerce, and the representative assembly, on condition that the emigrants' work contracts be drawn up by the two governments concerned and include a repatriation clause. As of 1960, French Polynesians working in New Caledonia numbered 1,000, and 3 years later there were twice as many. In 1964 the assembly sent a mission to Nouméa to study the conditions under which Tahitian laborers were living and working there, and its members returned very satisfied. The consensus among French Polynesia's leaders now seems to be that, given the local population's rapid growth, the future of many of the territory's young men lies not in its home islands but in emigration to lands of greater economic opportunity.

LABOR LEGISLATION, WAGES, AND THE COST OF LIVING

For the period before World War II, almost the only available data on wages and working conditions relate to French citizens who were wage-earners in Tahiti. At Papeete's port and in its few factories, an eight-and-a-half-hour working day generally prevailed, skilled laborers earned a maximum of 40 to 50 francs a day and unskilled labor 10 francs, and higher wages were paid for overtime work. An immi-

[16] *Pacific Islands Monthly,* February 1952.

gration service created in 1920 dealt exclusively with the recruitment and conditions of employment of alien laborers, and a decree of March 24, 1924, regulated those of indigenous agricultural, commercial, and industrial workers.

After the war, many of the new, liberal labor laws of France, as well as the machinery for enforcing them, were made applicable to the E.F.O. with some modifications. The post of labor inspector was created and an advisory committee on labor questions, composed of an equal number of employers and employes as well as government officials and members of the representative assembly, was formed. As might be expected, many assemblymen objected to the appointment of a labor inspector, not only because he was a Metropolitan official but also because the cost of his housing, automobile, and servants—though not his salary—was borne by the territorial budget.[17] They objected that it was ridiculous to hire a labor inspector for so small and overwhelmingly agricultural a country as the E.F.O., and that a local administrator could easily do the job at less expense. Opposition was again voiced when the newly arrived inspector submitted to the assembly a 24-article draft law laying down the conditions for laborers working under contract. In many respects this law anticipated some of the main provisions of the Overseas Labor Code later passed by the Parliament, in 1952, in regard to the duration of the working day and safeguards for workers. To allay the assemblymen's anxiety, the inspector argued that it contained no important innovations but simply updated the 1924 regulations.[18]

The Overseas Labor Code was made applicable to the E.F.O. by a decree of January 24, 1953. This brought the territory into line with other French dependencies in providing for a 40-hour working week, collective labor agreements, overtime pay, family allowances, and a minimum wage (the *salaire minimum interprofessionel garanti,* or S.M.I.G.). As elsewhere, the S.M.I.G. was related to the cost-of-living index. Gradually, compulsory compensation for work accidents, maternity and prenatal bonuses, and pensions for disabled and over-age workers were added to the code, placing Polynesian workers on a par with their counterparts in France and making French Polynesia one of the most advanced areas in the Pacific in the matter of labor legislation. Consequently, since 1953 virtually all the labor problems

[17] Minutes of the representative assembly, Jan. 24, 1949.
[18] *Ibid.,* April 28, 1950.

that have given rise to debate and in some cases to conflict concerned the rates of the S.M.I.G., which regularly lagged behind the rising cost of living, and those of family allowances and pensions.

The sharp rise in living costs after World War II made Tahiti one of the most expensive islands in the Pacific, and the automatic wage-scale increase had not yet been introduced to cushion its effects on wage-earners. In 1949 it was estimated that wages in Papeete ranged between 3,000 and 6,000 C.F.P. francs a month, whereas an unmarried wage-earner had to pay 3,000 monthly for his rent, another 3,000 for food, and 1,500 for incidental expenditures.[19] His situation was greatly improved a few years later by the automatic wage scale tied to the cost-of-living index, which was based not only on essentials but also included such items as tobacco, fuel, and cinema tickets. A foreign observer commented that by the end of 1951, the E.F.O. had the highest wages of any of the Pacific islands, approximating those of Australia and New Zealand.[20] Nevertheless, the territory's wage-earners demanded a more comprehensive base for the cost-of-living index, an end to wage discrimination among different categories of workers, and a uniform wage zone for all the islands. Agricultural wage-earners were allotted a S.M.I.G. lower than that for other workers, and the E.F.O. was divided into four wage zones delimited according to the estimated differences in living costs in various areas of the islands.[21] For the year 1957, French Polynesia's wage bill totaled 494 million C.F.P. francs, 411 millions of which were paid to Polynesians, 30 millions to Metropolitan Frenchmen, and 53 millions to other foreigners.[22]

The advent of the C.E.P. not only led to an upsurge in living costs and consequently of the S.M.I.G., but created such a labor shortage that many workers received higher pay than the officially guaranteed minimum wage. Successive increases in the S.M.I.G. in November 1963, May and November 1964, and June and November 1966 reflected the tempo at which the cost of living in the territory was climbing. Between 1957 and mid-1966, the S.M.I.G. more than doubled, rising from 20.7 C.F.P. francs an hour to 42.5. Family allowances followed a similar trend, increasing from 400 C.F.P. francs a month

[19] *Marchés Coloniaux,* July 16, 1949, pp. 1566–1567.

[20] *Pacific Islands Monthly,* December 1951.

[21] Zone A, the highest-wage zone, comprised Papeete and its immediate environs; zone B, Uturoa, Taravao, Taiohae, Aturoa, and Punaauia; zone C, the remaining districts of Tahiti and Moorea; and zone D, the rest of the territory.

[22] *La Polynésie Française* (La Documentation Française), p. 23.

in December 1964 to 500 in September 1965 and to 800 in May 1967 for the 24,000-odd children of wage-earners eligible for such benefits under the code. The last-mentioned increase clearly overtaxed the resources of the Family Allowance Fund, which out of its 410 million C.F.P. franc budget was already paying half the cost of free lunches in rural schools, providing clothing and vacation camps for needy children, and improving the housing for poor families.[23] To meet this new expenditure, as well as a concurrent increase in the monthly pensions of retired wage-earners, the contributions of the territory's 800 or more employers to the fund were raised, despite the latter's protests.

Unquestionably it was the revenues derived from the C.E.P.'s activities that made possible this "riot of spending" for social-welfare causes. The actual wages directly paid out by that center to Polynesian workers, however, accounted for only 200 to 300 million C.F.P. francs of the territory's total wage bill of 1,500 millions in 1965. Between 1960 and 1962, the salary increases granted to civil servants and military officers in the territory totaled another 300 million C.F.P. francs. The rapid rise in the S.M.I.G., which benefited perhaps some 6,000 to 7,000 other wage-earners, was attributable to the fast-mounting living costs, for which the C.E.P. was ultimately responsible, but many of the recent budgetary expenditures have been due to the assemblymen's desire to assure a more equitable sharing of the new prosperity. In 1965 they succeeded finally in persuading the administration to reduce the four wage zones to one, but the S.M.I.G. for agricultural wage-earners has continued to be 10 C.F.P. francs an hour lower than that for other workers. The inequitable distribution of wealth has been somewhat mitigated by the remittances sent home by the outer-islanders employed by the C.E.P., but the concentration of wealth in Tahiti has become even more pronounced than in the past. The disparity between the resources of the rural Polynesians and those of the growing middle class of *demis* and Chinese in Papeete has widened, and it may eventually cause social and political unrest.

LABOR ORGANIZATIONS AND DISPUTES

Civil servants, stenographers, mechanics, dockers, and a host of other wage-earners rapidly organized their own unions after World War II,

[23] Minutes of the territorial assembly, Nov. 28, 1965; Map 5, 1967.

so that by 1946 there were 26 such organizations registered with the authorities. Early in 1947, 11 of these unions, with a reported membership of 2,000, formed a Union des Syndicats Tahitiens (U.S.T.), which sought representation on the newly created advisory labor committee. The U.S.T. was affiliated with the French communist federation, the Confédération Générale du Travail (C.G.T.), which not only helped it with organizational techniques but also provided it with enough funds to print a bulletin that claimed a circulation of 1,800 subscribers.[24] Two other French labor *centrales,* the socialist Force Ouvrière (F.O.) and the Catholic Confédération des Travailleurs Chrétiens (C.F.T.C.), quickly followed the C.G.T.'s lead and organized unions of their own in the territory.

Although the U.S.T. was the first in the field and the F.O. gained a certain following among the civil servants, the Christian unions soon outdistanced them both. The U.S.T. acknowledged that many of its member unions had been "unrealistically and over-hastily organized in the wave of enthusiasm for trade unionism that swept over the islands," [25] but two other handicaps accounted for its failure to dominate the whole labor movement. One of these was its leadership by Frenchmen or *demis,* and it is noteworthy that among the U.S.T.'s member unions only one—the Syndicat des Gens de Mer—had a Polynesian executive secretary. The U.S.T.'s second handicap was its communistic orientation, which was regarded with antipathy by a population strongly Christianized and submissive to the directives of its clergy.

The dockers of Papeete, because of their number and their concentration in the capital, formed the strongest union in the territory, but they were split between rival Christian and communist leaders. Numerically the second-most-important union, that of the C.F.P.O.'s workers, was more effective than the dockers in achieving their objectives, but it was so isolated on Makatea that its successes benefited only its own members. That trade unionism had taken root among those two groups of wage-earners was shown by the occurrence of strikes in 1947, but the strikes also betrayed its weakness. That year, the U.S.T. leader, Alexis Bernast, campaigned against the high cost of living for workers, and on that issue he was elected to the representative assembly. Bernast was a World War II veteran and an energetic trade unionist, whose somewhat checkered career included an

---

[24] *Bulletin de Presse des E.F.O.,* March 1947.
[25] *Bulletin des Syndicats Tahitiens,* Dec. 10, 1947.

unsuccessful venture as a cotton planter in the New Hebrides, followed by 9 years on Wallis Island as an administrative agent of the New Caledonia government. After moving to Tahiti, he became secretary of the building workers' union, and in the assembly he claimed to speak in the name of a majority of the territory's organized workers. Because he championed the Papeete dockers, among whom there had recently been some agitation, Bernast became a main target for attack by the conservative assemblymen. In particular they resented his proposal to limit the number of permanent dockers to 200, for it would have given the dockers' union a stronger bargaining position in pressing for better working conditions.[26] It was not until the economic recession in 1954 awakened the administration's concern over the growing influx of outer-islanders to Papeete that the Labor Inspector successfully revived Bernast's proposal. In the meantime, union membership had fallen from about 1,800 to 1,500 for the whole territory, and in 1951 Bernast was not reelected to the assembly.[27] His defeat marked the eclipse of the U.S.T. as a political force and also its disintegration as a labor federation.

The Makatea workers were more successful than the dockers in the two strikes that they launched in 1947. The French administration's refusal to permit alien Raratongans to join the local union, followed by the C.F.P.O.'s dismissal of a prominent labor organizer from an important post in the company, touched off the first strike.[28] Soon afterward, 10 Tahitians who had been hired on an experimental basis were also dismissed, as "incompetent workers," and their fellow unionists struck again. In both cases the strikers succeeded not only in bringing about the reinstatement of the dismissed workers but in winning an improvement in their own lodging, food, and vacation leaves. As working conditions on Makatea were already superior to those prevailing elsewhere in the territory, the C.F.P.O. employes thus attained a markedly favored position. This emphasized the disparity between them and the dockers, whose strikes in 1951 and 1955 were again failures. The intervention of Pouvanaa in the 1951 strike was not only unsuccessful but convinced the administration that the strikers were politically motivated, with the result that troops and militiamen were called in to unload ships.[29] Nevertheless, Pouvanaa's

[26] Minutes of the permanent commission, July 28, 1948.
[27] *Marchés Coloniaux*, July 16, 1949, p. 1567.
[28] Robson, N., "French Oceania Takes Stock."
[29] *Pacific Islands Monthly*, June 1951.

intervention proved to be an exceptional episode. To be sure, Céran and Vanisette used their leadership of unions as a springboard for election to the assembly and often spoke there on behalf of their constituents, yet trade unionism as such has played almost no political role in French Polynesia.

The small number and the dispersion of organized workers, as well as their isolation from labor federations in France, have militated against their effectiveness. Although the C.F.T.C. organized a Confédération des Travailleurs Chrétiens du Pacifique, most of whose 4,000 members were in Tahiti, that *centrale* did not include the Protestant unions. Moreover, the policy of the C.F.T.C. was to shun politics and to concentrate on pursuing wholly economic and social objectives for its members. In any case, many of its goals were realized through legislation introduced by the government, and the territory's labor inspector was active in negotiating collective agreements that incorporated a large proportion of the C.F.T.C.'s demands and in settling labor disputes. Furthermore, the other big French labor confederations, which were more militant politically than the C.F.T.C., soon lost interest in their small branches in the islands and failed to provide them with either funds or moral support. For example, the territorial teachers' union, which had agreed to back the F.O.'s strike in France, was alienated by that *centrale*'s refusal to reciprocate when the Polynesian teachers submitted demands for an improvement of their own status. Consequently the territorial union broke away and declared its autonomy, and this example was followed by other organized laborers in the islands.

A logical consequence of this growth in the number of autonomous unions was that when their members needed political support they turned not to the French federations but to the territorial assembly, which was usually more sympathetic to their pleas. It was at the request of the wage-earners on Hao and Mururoa that the assembly, in 1965, sent a mission to those islands which succeeded in persuading the companies engaged in C.E.P. projects to improve working and living conditions there.[30] Likewise, the following year it was thanks to an arrangement negotiated by the assembly with the shipowners that the sailors on the interisland services received partial satisfaction of their demands for higher pay.[31] Although not even a majority of the territory's wage-earners have benefited by the collective

[30] Minutes of the territorial assembly, Jan. 23, 1965.
[31] Minutes of the permanent commission, July 22, 1966.

agreements made between the unions and the employers' organization,[32] labor legislation and its enforcement have, generally speaking, moved ahead of the unions' demands. French Polynesia's wage-earners have shown themselves to be too few in number, too seasonal, and too divided into small, dispersed groups to act effectively on their own behalf.

[32] In 1957 there were believed to be 748 employers in the territory, of whom only the most important were organized into a Union Patronale.

15

Religion

Christian missionaries, first Protestant and later Catholic, worked so efficaciously in French Polynesia that within about half a century they had converted the entire population of the islands. Traditional beliefs, which sometimes reflected old tribal antagonisms, did not, however, disappear without a trace or a struggle. The most aggressive form assumed by resurgent paganism was the Mamaia cult,[1] whose followers in Tahiti and the Leeward Islands almost succeeded in overthrowing the Pomaré monarchy and ousting the English missionaries. Teau, its grass-roots prophet, was said to be a mad deacon who proclaimed himself a reincarnation of Jesus Christ. He read the Bible and prayed frequently with his disciples, but he also preached a seductive doctrine which gave assurance to every believer that he would go to a heaven filled with "beautiful women who never aged and who never said no." [2] The aid of local chiefs was enlisted by the missionaries in a bloody suppression of the cult. In any case, the Mamaia cult was already losing ground because its leaders' rash prophecies of the imminence of the Second Coming and Judgment Day were not fulfilled.

The Mamaia cult was but the outstanding manifestation of more widespread efforts by the Polynesians to preserve traditions and customs that were crumbling under frontal assaults by the missionaries and the colonial administration. As in certain regions of tropical Africa, the native population tried to reaffirm its personality and cohesion by launching new cults that were unorthodox variations of Christian doctrines and form of worship. In reality, they were movements of social protest, which by assuming a pseudo-Christian guise were perforce tolerated by the authorities, who professed to believe in religious freedom. They further resembled the Messianic African

[1] See pp. 14–15.
[2] See Furnas, J. C., *Anatomy of Paradise*, pp. 280–81, for an amusing and instructive account of this cult.

sects in that they developed almost exclusively among the native Protestants, who thus practised what they had been taught in regard to the individual's right to interpret the Bible according to his conscience. Among the islanders converted by the L.M.S. missionaries, not only did various Protestant denominations find followers, but also such divergent sects as Jehovah's Witnesses, Seventh Day Adventists, and, above all, Mormonism, took root. The unorthodox character of those sects, and their fragmentation, permitted their indigenous adherents to express both their individuality and their dissidences.

MORMONISM

Within 20 years after the arrival of Mormon missionaries in the islands, their converts had divided into two groups, one of which followed Brigham Young and the other Joseph Smith. Soon after this schism occurred, an American Mormon missionary who visited the islands introduced innovations into the church service, and this added still another element of discord. His partisans split away to form a third group variously called Kanitu and Sanitos, with whom the Josephites quickly made common cause. Such divisions, however, did not detract from the overall appeal of Mormon doctrine for the Polynesians, despite its strict disciplinary aspects. Among its congenial features were the acceptance of polygamy, the possibility for backsliders of being cleansed of their sin by rebaptism, and the opportunity for all members to hold some church office. R. L. Stevenson felt that Mormonism was a religion admirably suited to the austere and frugal Tuamotuans, to whom its "mysterious" practices appealed because it gave them a sense of exhilaration and adventure.[3] More recently, the fact that the Mormon church was of American origin and under American control played a part in its acquiring new members, who could thus indirectly and with impunity express anti-French sentiments.

THE PROTESTANT AND CATHOLIC MISSIONS

The London Missionary Society missionaries arrived in the islands on March 5, 1797, but it was not until 1813 that their first converts embraced Protestantism. The influence of the L.M.S. grew with the

[3] Stevenson, R. L., *In the South Seas*, pp. 195–196.

founding of mission schools, which trained native pastors and promoted literacy in the Tahitian tongue. Through their conversion of the Pomaré monarchs and the principal chiefs, the influence of the English Protestants received strong backing, and the support they gave to and received from the traditional authorities proved to be of mutual benefit. Specifically, such local support enabled the L.M.S. missionaries, for some years, to prevent the French Catholics from gaining a foothold in those islands where Protestantism had already become entrenched. In many areas the semiautonomous native ecclesiastical hierarchy installed by the L.M.S. mission was identical with that of traditional society. By this device, the loyalty of rural Polynesians was easily transferred to the pastor and deacons of the parish, who were often none other than the local chiefs. In this way the village church came to "enshrine Polynesian customs" which serve as "a focus for kinship groups, social life, and social ambition." [4] The local-government institutions later created by the colonial administration never were able to wield authority to as great a degree, but conflicts usually did not arise between them, because the rural councilors and the parish officers in a given locality often were one and the same.

Not content with integrating traditional authority into the new ecclesiastical organization, the L.M.S. missionaries undertook—with equal success—to bring native customs into line with the prejudices and social behavior then characteristic of English Protestantism. They exacted from their converts an absolute respect for the Sabbath rest, church-going twice on Sundays, "decent" clothing, and attendance at semiweekly hymn-singing and Bible classes. Monogamous marriages were insisted upon and the use of tobacco and alcoholic beverages forbidden, and the missionaries' regulations had the force of law in the small, virtually theocratic domains under their control. Only the tradition of obedience to authority, now incarnated in the pastor-chief, can explain the acceptance of so rigorous a regime by the easygoing and undisciplined Polynesians. Not only did they acquiesce in its imposition with astonishing rapidity, but in recent years they have even shown a nostalgic regret for the good old days. In 1945, for example, when the inhabitants of Rurutu became French citizens automatically, 60 percent of them asked that the missionary-inspired rules of the nineteenth century be retained. Later, in the 1958 referendum, the large percentage of negative votes cast in the Leeward

4 West, F. J., *Political Advancement in the South Pacific*, p. 120.

and Austral islands was interpreted as an indication of those islanders' preference for living under the regime instituted by the L.M.S.[5]

So much has been written about the puritanism and provincialism of the early Protestant missionaries in the South Seas that the equally bigoted behavior of some of the Catholic missionaries has been largely overlooked. At first, the Picpus Congregation [6] was instructed to begin its mission work only in the islands not preempted by the Protestants, and with some difficulty its missionaries installed themselves in the Gambiers. Thanks to their good fortune in curing a local chief of his ailments, they gained a foothold on Mangareva, where they became firmly established within two years.[7] With the support of the traditional authorities there, Fathers Laval and Caret compelled the islanders to burn their idols, attend mass regularly, and strictly observe all Catholic practices, under penalty of severe physical punishment. The population was obliged not only to build churches and convents, but also to gather shell (nacre) which the missionaries sold in Tahiti to supply funds for the cause. As a result, agriculture and fishing were neglected and the islanders' living standards deteriorated rapidly. So isolated were these clerics from supervision by the Papeete administration that their harsh rule continued unchecked for 30 years. Not until they tried to impose the same regulations on a visiting French sea captain, whom they jailed for eating meat on Friday, was the attention of the Paris government drawn to their tiny theocracy. Eventually, civil administrators took over the Gambiers, but that archipelago was not the only one in the South Pacific to suffer from such arbitrary priestly rule.

Although the Picpus Congregation remained the premier Catholic order in the E.F.O., the Marist Fathers, the Ploërmel Friars, and the nuns of St. Joseph de Cluny also sent missionaries to the French islands. Thanks to their zeal, Catholicism took firm root in the Marquesas and the eastern and central Tuamotus, where Protestantism had not forestalled them, but the Catholic missionaries began to yield increasingly to the temptation of attacking heresy in its established strongholds. They made little headway in the Leeward and Austral islands, but did succeed in building churches and, above all, schools

[5] Vérin, P., "La Conversion des Iles Australes et ses Conséquences."

[6] The name of this Congregation was derived from that of the Paris street, the rue de Picpus, in which the Order of the Sacred Hearts of Jesus and Mary and of the Perpetual Adoration of the Blessed Sacrament had its headquarters.

[7] Furnas, *Anatomy of Paradise*, p. 286.

in the Windward group, notably in Raiatea and Tahiti. Because in the early days all the Catholic missionaries were French and the Protestants British, the perennial antagonism between the adherents of those two faiths was reinforced by the concurrent, widespread rivalry in empire-building between France and England.

London and Paris, especially the latter, supported the activities of their missionary nationals, but the rivalry between Protestants and Catholics did not cease with the islands' annexation by France. Indeed, so deep-rooted was this doubly motivated antagonism that it persisted even after the L.M.S. missionaries were replaced by French pastors sent to the colony in 1863 by the Société des Missions Evangéliques of Paris. Even in the second decade of the twentieth century, there still prevailed a belief among the native Protestants that the Catholic missionaries kept mistresses and that the Pope's daily diet consisted of Protestant babies.[8] The Catholics, for their part, perpetuated the old saying that to be Protestant was tantamount to being anti-French. In such propaganda, however, they did not receive the same support from the civilian administrators as they had had from the naval officers who first governed the islands. Although anticlericalism was never so virulent in the colony as in France itself and was confined mainly to the resident Metropolitan French community, it did lead to some friction between the mission and the civil servants.[9] Some Catholics in the E.F.O. believed that anticlerical officials were responsible for giving permission to such sects as the Seventh Day Adventists, Jehovah's Witnesses, and Christian Scientists to proselytize in the colony. This allegation could not, of course, be made in connection with the Mormons, who had established themselves in the islands at about the same time as the first Catholic missionaries.

The fact that, beginning in 1863, the Protestant missionaries in the islands were French certainly eased the relations between them and the Papeete government. Furthermore, the choice of pastors sent by the Paris Evangelical Society to take over the work of the L.M.S. was most fortunate. Charles Viénot, Thomas Arbousset, François Atger, and, especially, Frédéric Vernier were not only patriots of outstand-

---

[8] Calderon, G., *Tahiti by Tahiti*, p. 242.

[9] Even though the Freemasons in the E.F.O. were divided into two groups— those who owed their allegiance to the Grand Orient and those who adhered to the Veritas lodges in France—they were collectively accused by the strongly Catholic elements in the French community of using their influence with fellow-Masons in the administration in regard to business deals in general and to the Kong Ah bankruptcy in particular.

ing piety and character but also able organizers. They immediately recognized the need to establish cordial relations with the administration by proving that they were even more loyal to France than were their Catholic competitors. It was largely because of their intervention that the Rurutu and Rimatara islanders agreed to accept French rule in the late nineteenth century, and it was not for lack of trying that Frédéric Vernier was unable to persuade Teraupoo, the rebel chief of Raiatea, to lay down his arms.[10]

Frédéric Vernier was mainly responsible for the revival and reorganization of the Protestant church in the E.F.O., and he also drafted a new statute for it which, after difficult negotiations, was accepted by the French government in 1884. By the terms of this concordat, the government accepted the internal autonomy of the church and paid its pastors' salaries in return for the right to veto decisions taken by the church authorities.[11] The ecclesiastical organization formed under the concordat was modeled after that of the Reformed Church of France, modified by some of the regulations imposed by the L.M.S. mission. Parish councils, composed of the pastor and deacons, elected representatives to the six *arrondissement* councils, whose members in turn chose 26 delegates to the Conseil Supérieur, the highest local authority of the Polynesian Protestant Church. The parish councils, by the early 1960s, numbered about 70.

For many years, all the top officials of the church were white missionaries, but in 1953 a Tahitian was elected vice-president of the Conseil Supérieur, and in 1963 Pastor Rapoto became its first Polynesian president. His rise to that post coincided with the granting of full autonomy to the Polynesian Protestant church by the Paris Evangelical Society on the centenary of its installation in the islands. Although white missionaries continued to be sent to French Polynesia, they came as advisers to the native pastors who asked for their assistance.[12] The willingness of the indigenous pastors to accept missionary counsel may be ascribed to the fact that they are no longer drawn from the Tahitian intellectual elite, for whom other paths to

[10] The Vernier family, in 78 years of unbroken service in the territory, is an outstanding example of Protestant loyalty to both church and state. Frédéric's grandson, Charles—author, teacher, preacher, and long-time president of the Protestant Conseil Supérieur—received nearly 90 percent of the votes when he was elected the E.F.O.'s first deputy after World War II, and two of his sons were killed while active in the Resistance.

[11] See Preiss, G., "The Church in Tahiti."

[12] Comments by Pastor Rapoto to the authors, April 22, 1965.

influence and power are now open. Today the great majority of pastors are outer islanders, as are most of the small group of about 12 students attending the Hermon theological seminary at Papeete. Polynesian Protestants are proud of their church's autonomy, yet they seem to shrink from assuming full responsibility for its management, especially in the financial domain.

Relations between the Protestant church and the administration have been good ever since the concordat of 1884 and, paradoxically, became even closer after the pastors' salaries ceased, in 1927, to be paid from the colonial budget. The introduction of elected representative government after World War II, however, has had both beneficial and harmful effects on the evolution of the Protestant church. The assembly has been increasingly generous in granting subsidies to mission schools, but on the other hand the development of party politics has created divisions among the Protestants and has not improved their relations with the Catholic community.

During the interwar period, the old hostility between Protestants and Catholics tapered off, for by then the population had been wholly Christianized—at least nominally. The two major faiths carried on their work in fairly well-defined geographical areas, their church organizations followed much the same pattern, and their efforts were concentrated in the fields of education and medical care. Catholicism continued to be the dominant religion in the Marquesas, Gambiers, and eastern and central Tuamotus, whereas Protestantism prevailed in the Leeward and Austral islands. Although there were more Protestants than Catholics in the Windward group, it was in Moorea and Papeete that the old rivalry persisted most strongly, especially between their respective mission schools. To some extent the birth of political parties in 1945 reawakened the old antagonisms, for it was among the Protestant islanders that Pouvanaa's propaganda found its strongest response. Even after Pouvanaa's exile had brought greater calm to the political scene, his R.D.P.T. party continued to find most of its followers in the old Protestant strongholds. Generally speaking, however, contacts were minimal between the two church hierarchies until the "ecumenical spirit" promoted by Pope John XXIII began to make itself felt locally in the 1950s.

The submissiveness to authority generally characteristic of Third World Catholic converts has been particularly marked in French Polynesia, where it has been the least evolved islanders who have been the most receptive to Catholicism. There has never been any question of granting to Polynesian Catholics the autonomy that has been conferred on native Protestants. Although the Vatican has gradually raised the territory's three Apostolic Vicariates to the rank of bishoprics, they are still controlled by the European ecclesiastical hierarchy. As of 1960, French Polynesia had only four local-born priests, of whom one was a *demi* and the other a Chinese, whereas there were 61 European priests, monks, and nuns.[13] In 1964, after 120 years of Catholic proselytism in the islands, the first two native nuns took their vows, and no more than 15 indigenous candidates were studying for the priesthood in the local seminary. It was not until 4 years later that the comparatively high post of coadjutor to the archbishop of Tahiti was assigned to a local-born priest.[14] This failure to develop a strong native clergy was defended by the head of the Catholic mission to the writers on the ground that few Polynesians had the vocation required of the priesthood because they would not accept the "high level of sacrifice" demanded by that calling.[15]

The perpetuation of European control over Polynesian Catholics has unquestionably influenced the relations between the Catholic mission and the local administration, especially in recent years. Until the referendum of 1958, Catholic priests in the territory were as reticent as the Protestant pastors in regard to telling their flocks how to vote in elections, although both groups of clergy let it be clearly known how they themselves stood on various issues. In 1958, however, the Catholic mission openly took a stand in favor of an affirmative vote, and how closely its directive was followed was shown by the nearly 100 percent of "yes" votes registered in the islands where Catholics were in a clear majority. The Protestant community was divided in voting on that referendum, but later its leaders came out strongly in opposition to the installation of the C.E.P.[16] It is noteworthy that a Protestant layman, John Teariki, has been the most outspoken opponent of nuclear testing in the territory. Although individual Catholics have expressed disapproval of the C.E.P., their position has not been formally supported by the mission hierarchy. The Catholic mission's usually cooperative attitude with the government may well

[13] *La Polynésie Française* (La Documentation Française), p. 17.
[14] *Le Monde*, March 27, 1968.
[15] Talk with Father Patrice, April 23, 1965.
[16] The Protestant journal, *Notre Lien*, was the first to publish the report that the C.E.P. would be located in the islands, several weeks before this was officially announced by General de Gaulle.

explain why its schools have consistently received larger subsidies than their Protestant counterparts, despite claims by the local administration that their respective allocations are determined solely by academic criteria.

POLYNESIAN CHRISTIANS

During the past century and a half, the number of Christians of all denominations has steadily increased in French Polynesia. Inevitably, this largely reflects the growth in the population, for which the clergy's insistence on the sacrament of marriage has been at least partly responsible.[17] The Christian community's numerical increase, especially in the early years, was due also, in part, to the undeniable improvement in the material well-being of its converts. It was the missionaries who taught villagers how to plant crops, rear animals, and improve their water supply; tried to inculcate a sense of hygiene among them; treated them for diseases; and cared for lepers. To be sure, they exacted a "tithe" in return, which might take the form of lottery games or "contributions" but was nonetheless a church-imposed tax.

Since World War II, the state has taken over, to a large extent, the mission's former role in education, health, and development of the rural economy. Although the missions continue to maintain good schools and hospitals, the material incentives to become church members have decreased, and it is now almost wholly among the Chinese that converts may still be won. Of course, it is always possible to increase the membership of a church by luring away members of another religious group, and in this the Mormons have been notably successful. Their disgruntled Catholic and Protestant competitors attribute their losses to the Mormon church as being due to the greater financial resources placed at the disposal of both Mormon sects by their respective mother churches in the United States.[18] Certainly all the sects that have American backing are able to provide their mem-

---

[17] In the Marquesas, for example, tradition associated marriage with pregnancy, and infanticide and emigration were expected to take care of the surplus population. Catholic missionaries frowned on infanticide and exerted pressure on lovers to enter into early marriage, with a resultant increase in the Marquesan birthrate. See Furnas, *Anatomy of Paradise*, p. 295.

[18] The Mormons proper are attached to the Salt Lake City organization, whereas the Sanitos' support comes from the Reorganized Church of the Latter Day Saints in Missouri.

bers with greater facilities, but they also perpetuate the fervor and extremism which the Protestant and Catholic missions have lost with the passage of the years and which have been replaced by a more tepid and tolerant form of Christianity.

TABLE 5

FRENCH POLYNESIA: RELIGIOUS AFFILIATIONS OF THE
POPULATION, IN SELECTED YEARS, 1946–1963

Year	Protestants	Catholics	Sanitos	Mormons	Adventists	Other cults [a]
1946	31,577	13,381	1,912	1,019	616	725
1951	34,441	15,096	2,073	1,218	794	867
1963	45,812	25,227	2,768	2,327	1,682	1,132

[a] Mainly Jehovah's Witnesses, Christian Scientists, and Buddhists.
Source: Census reports.

Table 5 indicates the relative size of the various religious communities and their growth, but these data do not reflect the instability of the population's church allegiances. Not only do church members sometimes suddenly switch from one faith or denomination to another, but there is a growing element—not represented in the table—of persons classified in the censuses as *non-déclarés*. Some of these described themselves as freethinkers, and others stated that they were without any formal religious affiliation. This group is variously estimated to constitute between 6 percent and 15 percent of the population, but it is apparent that their overall number is growing and that the majority of *non-déclarés* live in Tahiti.

From the earliest days, both the Protestant and Catholic missionaries have recognized the superficial nature of their converts' Christianity. The Polynesians' "lack of discipline" and their "self-indulgence" have been frequently bemoaned, and these tendencies are mainly responsible for the missionaries' insistence on frequent and regular attendance at church services and the observance of a strictly ethical code of behavior. In this respect, many of the native clergy have proved to be more bigoted and puritanical than even their white missionary mentors. Yet despite all such efforts to impose a rigid discipline on the native Christians, the Polynesians' fondness for alcohol, their sexual promiscuity, and their general inconstancy apparently have not diminished appreciably. Indeed, all observers have noted an increase in their "materialism," particularly since the C.E.P.

brought sudden prosperity to the islands. There has been a conspicuous decline in the number of candidates for the ministry and the priesthood, and the concurrent slackening in church attendance is ascribed to the increase in the number of sports events, dance halls, and movie houses.

For many years, Christianity provided the main force of social constraint in a society which had rapidly sloughed off its traditional beliefs. The fear of hell, which had replaced that of the pagan gods, and the authority of the clergy, which had succeeded to that of the chiefs, held the people in check by substituting new taboos for the old ones, but they are no longer as effective as they once were. Church membership is still a "social necessity", but in many cases it has become largely a formality. New opportunities for material gain and power have come into existence outside the framework of the Protestant and Catholic religious organizations, but they have not been accompanied by any substitute for the Christian code of morality.

16

Education and Cultural Activities

Western missionaries pioneered education in the Pacific islands as they did elsewhere in the early stages of empire-building by the European powers. Curiously enough, it was in two areas which later became French colonies that the London Missionary Society (L.M.S.) established the first schools. In both Madagascar and French Polynesia, the early association of English Protestantism with formal education influenced the evolution of their school systems, as well as that of their church organization and even of their political development.

It was in Moorea that the L.M.S. mission set up two schools at the turn of the century. Among the Polynesians who began attending them in increasing numbers was young King Pomaré III. Because the main purpose of the mission schools was to train Polynesians for the ministry, teaching was done in the vernacular. The L.M.S. schools continued to flourish until the English missionaries were superseded by those of the Société des Missions Evangéliques de Paris, who had not embarked on their educational work in the islands until 1842.[1]

Catholic mission education in the islands began in 1834 with the arrival of the first French missionaries, but it lagged behind that of the Protestants for some years. Because the Society Islands had been largely preempted by Protestant schools, the nuns of St. Joseph de Cluny and the missionaries of the Frères de Ploërmel concentrated their educational work in the peripheral archipelagoes. Besides the difficulties caused by their belated arrival and by entrenched Protestant competition, the Catholic schools suffered from repercussions of France's anticlericalism early in the twentieth century. For a few years the Catholic mission schools in the Marquesas were closed by the administration, so the Ploërmel missionaries left those islands and transferred their operations to Papeete. The Cluny nuns, however, stayed on in the Marquesas, where eventually they were able to reopen schools.

[1] *Journal de la Société des Océanistes,* December 1960.

Although many prewar colonial administrators harbored anticlerical sentiments, the practical advantages of leaving the school system almost wholly in the hands of the missionaries proved irresistible to the economy-minded Paris authorities. The missionaries could hardly be said to have maintained excellent schools in the main islands, however, except in comparison with the few and deficient ones that existed in the outer islands. R. L. Stevenson, who visited the schools of the Catholic missionaries in the late nineteenth century, graphically described the dreary instruction they provided, their discouragement at the results, and the life of their pupils:

The youth, from six to fifteen, are taken from their homes by Government, centralized at Hatiteu (Marquesas), where they are supported by a weekly tax of food; and, with the exception of one month in every year, surrendered wholly to the discretion of the priests . . . the holiday occurs at a different period for the girls and for the boys; so that a Marquesan brother and sister meet again, after their education is complete, a pair of strangers . . . a harsh law, and highly unpopular; but what a power it places in the hands of the instructors, and how languidly and dully that power is employed by the mission! Too much concern to make the natives pious, a design in which they all confess defeat, is, I suppose, the explanation of their miserable system.[2]

Judging by contemporary reports from French officials and journalists in the early 20th century, the instruction provided in the state schools was almost as little related to the needs and life of the outer islanders. In 1921, therefore, Albert Sarraut included in his *mise-en-valeur* program [3] a project to improve the islands' education service, which had been receiving the smallest allocations of any in the territorial budget, Subsequently the number of state schools operating in the outer islands was greatly increased and their curricula were given a more practical orientation, but in Tahiti the mission schools reinforced their already strong position vis-à-vis the public institutions.[4]

How important was the missions' role in the colony's education system was suddenly borne in on the administration when, in the early 1930s, it appeared that the depression might force them to close their schools. Although by that time the public-school system for the whole territory was far more extensive than that of the missions, it would have cost the local budget at least 500,000 francs simply to

2 Stevenson, R. L., *In the South Seas*, p. 63.

3 See pp. 80–81.

4 *L'Océanie Française*, November–December 1933; January–February 1934.

pay the salaries of the missions' 30 lay teachers. To ward off such an eventuality, the administration made a small effort. Although the term "subsidy" was never used—and in any case would have been inapposite—to describe the small grants made by the colony and Papeete municipality, ranging from 3,500 to 30,000 francs, to the mission schools according to their enrolment, such aid nevertheless enabled the mission schools not only to remain open but even to increase their staff and enrolment during the next few years.

As of 1935, there were 50 teachers instructing the 1,837 pupils then attending the eight mission schools throughout the E.F.O.,[5] compared with 130 teachers and 5,395 pupils in the seventy-eight state schools. The ranking state school was the Ecole Centrale of Papeete, which was the only one in the whole colony authorized to award primary-school certificates and *brevet élémentaire* (B.E.) diplomas equivalent to those of France. Its principal was also head of the education service, which included in its jurisdiction the Ecole Principale des Tuamotus at Fakarava, district schools scattered along the littorals of the main islands, and the preparatory "native schools" which it was planned to transform eventually into district or regional schools. Only 3 of the teachers in the state service were Metropolitan *instituteurs,* 67 were "instructors of the local cadres," and the rest were either monitors or auxiliaries. Quantitatively the school network at that time was considered satisfactory, but its quality and distribution left much to be desired. Twenty fairly large settlements in the colony were without either a mission or a state school, and teaching standards everywhere except perhaps in Papeete were deplorably low. To raise their level, Governor Chastenet de Géry, by a regulation of February 8, 1938, aligned the legal status of the colony's teachers with that of their Metropolitan counterparts, revived the *cours normal* (which had been discontinued during the depression) to improve their training, and eliminated the local diplomas whose validity was not recognized outside the E.F.O.

Since World War II, the principles laid down and the practices evolved during the interwar period have not changed in respect to the emphasis on primary education and to the cooperation between state and mission schools. Today all the school-age children in the territory attend primary schools, and the collaboration between the

[5] Together the two systems provided instruction of sorts at the primary level for nearly three-fourths of the school-age population. See *L'Océanie Française,* January–February 1935.

public and mission educational authorities has become closer. State schools have not been established where mission schools already operate, even in Uturoa, the second-largest town in the territory, and subsidies from public funds to mission schools have been greatly increased, as has the state's supervision over them. Rural education, with all the heavy expenditures and the difficulties of building, staffing, and maintaining many small, widely dispersed schools is still almost wholly the territory's responsibility, whereas urban education continues to be mainly in the hands of the missions.

Even more than before the war, Papeete's schools, both religious and lay, offer the most advanced instruction available in the territory. Tahiti's primacy has been further enhanced by the establishing there of the first secondary schools to be created in the islands. Its Ecole Centrale has risen from the rank of a higher primary school to the status of a state *lycée,* and a second *lycée* was opened in 1967 on Tahiti. French has now become the linguistic medium for the territory's education; the curriculum in all schools, except for history and geography, has been more closely modeled on that of France; and the diplomas and certificates issued by the local schools are identical with those of the Metropole. Although the territory now has far more ample funds than formerly for building and staffing its schools and for awarding scholarships to promising students at home and in France, and has augmented the facilities for technical and secondary education, it faces even greater problems than before in improving the quality of instruction, particularly in the outer islands. In brief, the pattern is much the same as before, for the changes made during the postwar years have been those of scope and degree, rather than of kind.

PRIMARY SCHOOLING

When World War II ended, the E.F.O. had 71 state primary schools, with 6,432 pupils, or about 70 percent of all the children then receiving instruction at that level.[6] This numerical preponderance of state over mission schools became even more marked during the governorship of René Petitbon (1950–52), an *agrégé* and former *lycée* profes-

[6] Of these schools, 21 were situated in Tahiti, 20 in the Leeward Islands, 8 in the Tuamotus, 5 in the Marquesas, and the balance here and there in the other islands. "Carnets de Documentation sur l'Enseignement dans la France d'Outre-Mer," No. 20 (pamphlet), Papeete, 1946.

sor, who zealously promoted lay education in the territory. In any case, the mission schools, which were then educating 30 percent of all the primary-school children, had nearly reached the limit of their capacities. Financially they were in a less favored position than were the state schools, and consequently were unable either to increase the number of their pupils or to widen their geographical base, which remained almost wholly confined to the Windward and Leeward Islands. The state system, on the other hand, was able to enlarge its role because of a vast increase in the French government's support for overseas education after World War II.

The pressure on both systems mounted considerably after primary education for all the territory's children between the ages of 6 and 14 was made obligatory in 1947. To cope with this, the mission schools had to enlarge their facilities, and the ecclesiastical authorities reluctantly decided that, in order to do so, they must charge all but indigent parents a monthly fee of 50 C.F.P. francs (later raised to 160 francs) for each child in their primary schools. State schools, however, continued to provide instruction free of charge. Although the F.I.D.E.S. aided mission as well as public schools with grants for the construction and equipment of buildings, and a few missionaries still taught school, the missions nevertheless had to pay for their schools' maintenance and provide the salaries of their lay instructors.

The territorial assemblymen as well as the municipal councilors, many of whom had been educated in mission schools, realized that substantial grants to the missions must now be made if their schools were to continue to function. Subsidies from the territorial budget, which in 1945 had averaged about 80,000 C.F.P. francs per mission school each month (supplemented by 12,000 C.F.P. francs from the municipality for Papeete's schools), were rapidly increased, particularly after the missions began to follow the state's lead by providing education at the secondary level. Since the missions used these subsidies to enlarge and improve existing facilities rather than to expand into new areas, their predominance over state schools in the urban settlements of Tahiti, in Raiatea, and in the Marquesas became even more marked than before the war. Between 1945 and 1960, not one public primary school was built in Papeete, although the number of school-age children in that town had grown from less than 10,000 to nearly 16,000 during those years.[7]

If the missions provided schooling for three times as many of

[7] *La Polynésie Française* (La Documentation Française), p. 36.

Papeete's children as did the state primary schools, the burden of financing rural education at that level was borne almost entirely by the territorial budget. With the help of the F.I.D.E.S., the territory was able to provide schools for all the island settlements where mission education did not exist, including remote Rapa, which had a total population of 287, but it could not enlarge or even repair many of the older buildings. Classes were not only over-large but also incomplete scholastically. Only 81 of the state primary schools in the territory in 1960 offered the complete cycle of studies (six grades) that prepared pupils for the *certificat d'études primaires* examination, yet even that situation was an improvement over previous years. It was not until 1938 that the first such certificate was awarded in the Leeward Islands, 1947 in Moorea, 1951 in Makatea, and 1957 in the Australs, and in 1960 none at all was given in the Tuamotus.[8]

Primary-teaching personnel

To fulfil the territory's commitment to provide primary schooling for a population growing at the rate of 3 percent a year, in which the number of school-age children was estimated at 15,800 in 1960, the authorities faced an ever-more-acute problem of recruiting more and better-trained teachers for the outer islands. At that time there were approximately three times as many teachers in the state schools as in those of the missions, but only half of the former, or 158, had a *brevet d'études du premier cycle* (B.E.P.C.), which was considered the minimum qualification for teaching the primary grades. Moreover, not all the monitors and auxiliaries who made up the rest of the teaching staff had a *certificat d'études primaires*, and it was difficult to persuade even such unqualified teachers to accept posts in the outer islands because of the poor pay, the isolation, and the primitive living conditions there. Mission teachers were certainly no better equipped academically and were less well paid than their state colleagues, but at least the great majority of them lived in the main towns. It was not until 1965 that fully qualified teachers in the outer-island state schools were given an allowance for housing in an effort to forestall their frequent demands for transfer to an urban post. This, of course, did not solve the problem for the majority of them, whose credentials did not entitle them to civil-service status and whose proportion in the state primary service was growing rapidly with the

[8] Service des Affaires Economiques et du Plan, Polynésie Française, *Situation Economique et Perspectives d'Avenir, 1959–1960.*

need to provide instruction for an ever-larger school-age population. Perforce, the territory had to employ more and more teachers on short-term contracts, and this rapid turnover in personnel led to a further deterioration in the quality of outer-island education.

To compound the territory's difficulties in this domain, teacher training had been retrogressing in regard to the number of candidates and the standard of preparation given them. To improve the latter, the assembly decided in 1958 to create an *école normale* to supersede the 1-year *cours normal* which for many years had been given at Papeete's Ecole Centrale. Since the proposed Ecole Normale was to award the B.E. and to have the same standing as analogous Metropolitan institutions, applicants for admission to it were required to hold the bachelor's degree—but no candidates presented themselves when the competitive entrance examinations were to be held. In the meantime the *cours normal* had been abolished, with the result that for a 2-year period no teachers at all were trained in the territory. By September 1960, the shortage had become so acute that the authorities decided to revive the *cours normal* at Papeete and start another at Uturoa, although they realized that candidates so trained would be poorly prepared and would be awarded only an inferior B.E.P.C. diploma. In 1960, only 12 candidates entered the resuscitated *cours normal,* and three years later their number had increased to merely 20.[9] The inevitable result was that almost half the teaching staff in the state primary schools was composed of temporary teachers, whose poor preparation was matched by their lack of perseverance. Of the 537 auxiliary teachers recruited by the education service between 1961 and 1964, barely 200 were still at their posts in 1965.

This situation placed the assemblymen once again on the horns of their old dilemma. Because of the expense involved, they still refused to import more teachers from France, and because they also balked at paying the salaries—though not the travel expenses—of Metropolitan functionaries' wives who were already serving as teachers in the state system, they would not give the latter tenure in their posts. Even supposing that the territory could find the funds necessary to raise the pay and therefore the appeal of teaching for local-born candidates, as well as the money required to create a 4-year Ecole Normale, there was no certainty that such measures would lead to a rise in the number of teachers willing to serve in the outer islands.

In the early 1960s, however, an alternative was offered in the form

[9] Minutes of the territorial assembly, Jan. 7, 1965.

of conscripts of the French armed forces who were then offered the possibility of performing their military service by teaching in the overseas territories. Generally speaking, the conscripts who opted for such teaching were far better educated than most of the locally trained teachers. Furthermore, their pay cost the territory only 26,500 C.F.P. francs a month apiece, their transport to the islands was furnished free of charge by the French navy, and they had to serve wherever they were assigned by the military authorities. After considerable hesitation, the assembly decided to accept about 20 of the conscripts on condition that they be posted to the outer islands, and by 1966 the experiment was considered successful enough for the territory to assume the cost of their transport, as requested by the French government. Although the posting of the French conscripts to the outer-island schools meant the displacement of some of the local-born teachers then serving there, most of the latter were almost equally transient and could now be given further training with a view to being better qualified eventually when they were reassigned to their posts. In the meantime, even the assemblymen most dubious about the value of the experiment had to admit that the conscripts had already appreciably raised the level of teaching in the outer islands.[10]

THE POLYNESIAN ATTITUDE
TOWARD FORMAL EDUCATION

The generally poor quality of the outer-island schools has never been the sole reason why so many rural Polynesian parents have been reluctant to send their children to school. Some conservative islanders feared the radical and anticlerical views professed by certain state-school teachers and preferred to send their children to mission schools.[11] Strongly Protestant parents were unwilling to send their children to Catholic schools, and vice versa, and in some islands the choice was limited to one or the other. A few families, dissatisfied with the quality of all the teaching in outer-island schools, made considerable sacrifices to make it possible for their children to attend school in Tahiti, where they could enter boarding schools or stay with relatives. The basic difficulty, however, was that few rural Polynesians were convinced of the utility of a Western-type education, especially

---

[10] *Ibid.*, Nov. 21, 1966.
[11] Minutes of the representative assembly, March 12, 1954.

as, more often than not, such schooling as their children received in the outer islands left no permanent imprint and was unrelated to life in that milieu.

Primary-school children were taught in French by teachers who could barely speak the language themselves, and followed a curriculum similar to that of schools in France. The subjects they studied were based on an alien culture and abstract concepts which they had difficulty in understanding. Since the vernacular was the language used in Polynesian homes and churches, the children soon forgot whatever French they had learned at school, along with the fables of La Fontaine which they had had to commit to memory. Although the textbooks used in the schools during the postwar period were modified to include more local history and geography, this did not fundamentally alter the tendency to make the islands' educational system and curricula replicas of those in France.

Inasmuch as the Polynesian way of life was highly practical and as only a minority of Polynesians sought employment with the government or European firms where they could utilize their school training, the majority of rural islanders saw little of value to them in Western schooling. Moreover, outer-island parents were reluctant to permit their children to go to school before the age of 8 or to cooperate with the teachers who tried to impose discipline on them. Outer-island teachers often complained that parents connived with their truant children by excusing those who absented themselves from school, either because the parents were incorrigibly permissive toward their young offspring or because they feared to lose the family allowances that would be withheld if their children failed to attend school regularly.[12]

In the mid-1960s, a change began to be noticeable in the attitudes of both parents and children toward schooling. Because the Centre d'Expérimentation du Pacifique was then offering more well-paid jobs than there were qualified candidates to fill them, the usefulness of a formal education became more apparent than in the past. On the other hand, wherever the C.E.P. was installed, the opportunities for diversion and money-earning even for the unskilled had greatly increased. By 1966, absenteeism had become such a problem for both the mission and state schools in Tahiti that the assembly voted to impose heavy penalties on parents who failed to put a stop to their children's truancy.

[12] Minutes of the territorial assembly, Dec. 28, 1964.

In the opinion of many Western observers, such measures are unlikely to be effective, for the root of the problem seems to lie in the
Polynesians' lack of ambition and of competitive spirit. Family tradition discourages initiative on the part of the young, and in any case
the communal structure of Polynesian society offers little opportunity
for youth to acquire power and prestige. Until about the age of 8,
children are indulged by their doting parents, but thereafter they are
forced into the mold of the adult community. Even in the few primary schools now experimenting with "progressive" education, their
teachers complain that the Polynesian students are content with an
average school record and aspire only to mediocre jobs that require
little work and almost no curtailment of their personal freedom. These
attitudes have proved to be the most serious stumbling block to the
development of the islanders' education above the primary level.

SECONDARY EDUCATION

A basic tenet of French policy after World War II was the encouragement of secondary and technical instruction in the overseas dependencies. The E.F.O. benefited by the application of this policy, even
though the local service continued to stress the development of primary schooling. Indeed, the latter objective was so vigorously pursued that by the early 1960s almost all the school-age children were
attending some kind of primary school, despite the rapid growth in
their numbers. An embryonic elite having thus been created, the need
arose to provide facilities for the primary-school graduates who
wanted to continue their education. The number of scholarships for
advanced studies in France as well as in the territory was increased
appreciably, and Polynesians were encouraged to compete with the
Metropolitan, *demi,* and Chinese candidates who had theretofore
virtually monopolized such opportunities as were available. Some
slight progress in this respect was made, but generally speaking, most
Polynesian students remained uninterested in pursuing their schooling beyond the age required by law.

In the territory's secondary schools, proportionately more of the
scholarships than before were given to Polynesians, because in granting them the authorities gave more weight to the parents' financial
situation than to their children's academic record. The first secondary
schools established in the late 1940s in the E.F.O. were enlargements
of the existing state and mission schools in Tahiti; not until a decade

later was an intermediate *cours complémentaire* created in Uturoa, and it became the nucleus for developing education above the primary level in the outer islands. Local leaders were naturally gratified by such progress, but they balked in 1953 at transforming the Ecole Centrale of Papeete into the Collège Gauguin,[13] because raising its scholastic status would mean bringing professors from France.[14] The administration finally persuaded them to do so, and at about the same time they also granted subsidies to the outstanding mission schools of Papeete so that they, too, could raise their standards to approximately the same level.

By 1960, the capital had six secondary and technical schools, the majority of which were under mission control, but only a few of them prepared students for the first baccalaureate examinations.[15] Their rise in the academic scale was gradual, but this evolution nevertheless enhanced the preeminence of Papeete as the territory's educational center and strengthened the missions' domination of the school system there. The Collèges La Mennais, Javouhey, Viénot, and Notre Dame des Anges, all mission institutions, were situated in Papeete or its environs, and offered secondary education to 893 students, compared with the 477 attending the two state secondary schools. Of the latter, the Collège Gauguin was outstanding for the exceptionally high caliber of its teaching staff and the large number (309) of students in its boarding departments for boys and girls.

As a result of the burgeoning of both state and mission schools, the territory, by 1961, was allocating 25 percent of its budget to education, and this proportion seemed likely to continue rising. At the time, it could not be foreseen that within a few years the C.E.P. would be responsible for exceptionally large budget revenues, hence the assemblymen decided to ask France to bear the cost of the secondary-school system. By this step, of course, the local authorities relinquished all control over education policy above the primary level, but at the same time the territory was enabled to devote all its allocations for education to improving the primary-school system. The latter move, however, lost some of its cogency when, by 1965, the ever-larger requests for funds by the mission primary schools threatened

[13] It is ironic that this institution should be named for the great painter, who believed that the Polynesians should be left in their natural state and not be deformed by Western culture.

[14] Minutes of the representative assembly, Dec. 8, 1953.

[15] Partial plan on education (typescript dated July 29, 1960), Bureau du Plan, Polynésie Française.

to cancel out the economies realized in the secondary sector. Subsidies granted from the territorial budget to mission education had increased threefold during the preceding decade and were disproportionately large in relation to the total allocations for education, especially considering that the missions taught less than one-third of the students in the islands.[16]

In order to curb the proliferation of mission schools, the administration, as long ago as 1956, had decreed that official permission must be obtained before any new mission school might be opened. Seven years later, the government refused to approve a proposed enlargement of the mission school at Uturoa. This interdiction coincided with an unusually long delay in granting school subsidies to the Catholic mission, and it produced a strong reaction. The Catholic community was up in arms, the 3,000-member Association of the Parents of Catholic Students in Raiatea and Tahiti held a mass meeting of protest, and the ecclesiastical authorities closed all the Catholic schools for forty-eight hours to demonstrate their displeasure.[17]

The territorial Association of Lay Teachers did not hide its satisfaction at the mission's discomfiture, for its members had long been jealous of the greater success of mission students in the examinations for the *certificat d'études primaires.* Nor were the Protestant assemblymen displeased by the Catholic mission's setback, for they had always resented the smaller grants-in-aid allotted to Protestant mission schools. Catholic assemblymen reacted by accusing their R.D.P.T. colleagues of voting unduly large subsidies to the Protestant schools in the Leeward Islands because their main constituents lived there. It was evident that anticlericalism and Catholic-Protestant antagonisms remained latent forces in the territory, but on the whole they did not strongly influence the attitude of local leaders on educational questions.

TERRITORIAL-GOVERNMENT POLICY

By and large, cost was the determining factor in the Parliament's policy regarding education, and in Polynesia it played a more important role than in the French African territories. Metropolitan French diplomas had less prestige in the islands because of the Polynesians' general indifference to Western education and also because those

[16] In 1965, there were 17,194 pupils in state schools and 8,173 in mission schools. See minutes of the territorial assembly, Nov. 15, 1965.

[17] Gauze, R., "Panorama Politique de l'Après-Guerre (1945–1965)," p. 33.

diplomas were not such effective passports to political power as they were in Africa. There was never any question of founding a university in Papeete and Nouméa, and to go to distant France for a university diploma required too prolonged an absence from home for a people always disinclined to emigrate. The territorial leaders did want a well-educated, locally trained indigenous elite, but not at the price of bringing in an adequate number of Metropolitan professors.

Matters came to a head in 1965 when France's assumption of responsibility for the territory's secondary schools did not produce the financial ease expected, and when, at the same time, demands for aid from the missions grew in amount and in nature. To be sure, the F.I.D.E.S.' contribution for school-building and equipment had recently been dwindling and mission schools were becoming more crowded than ever before. Parents of scholarship holders could choose between state and mission schools, and almost invariably they chose the latter because the strongly Christianized islanders wanted their children to receive a "moral" education rather than "godless" instruction. The Chinese, too, in great majority Catholics, gave their preference to the mission schools, which were attended by four times as many of their children as were in the state schools.

Almost without exception, the assemblymen sympathized with the plight of the mission schools, but when they were asked to meet the expenditures for new buildings, more school canteens,[18] and increases in the pay of mission primary-school teachers, they felt that it was time to call a halt. Although they objected to the proposal to provide funds for buildings that would remain the property of the missions, they did accede to the plea of the church authorities in this matter. They were careful, however, to stress the "exceptional" nature of this grant, and this time to allot equal sums to Catholic and to Protestant missions. As to the requested salary increases for mission primary teachers, they stated that the territory simply could not afford to pay them on a par with their colleagues in the state schools.[19] The assemblymen felt that the ecclesiastical authorities must be made to realize that the territory could not indefinitely underwrite the cost of mission education, and that it was high time to reach a formal overall agreement with them that would clearly specify the respective obligations of church and state in this domain.

Inasmuch as it seemed impossible to reach such an agreement or

[18] Free lunches had been instituted in the rural state primary schools during the 1950s, in the hope that this would reduce truancy among pupils.

[19] Minutes of the territorial assembly, Sept. 29, 1965; Nov. 28, 1966.

to find a way out of the financial impasse, the territory as usual turned to France for aid. Those who urged making this request of the French government argued that it was incumbent on the Metropolitan power to finance all types of schools in the islands so as to develop them into "a center for radiating French culture in the Pacific"—a view that had been often expressed by the French delegate to South Pacific Commission meetings on education.[20] The more realistic members of the assembly, however, noted that it had taken 4 years for the French government to come around to paying the cost of the territory's secondary schools and that, in any case, a great deal more time would elapse before any decision in regard to primary education could be reached. In the unlikely event that France should agree to accept this additional burden, amounting to about 200 million C.F.P. francs a year, the territory would lose all of its ability to determine what kind of education its population would receive. Already France's control over the secondary-school system had led to friction between the head of the education service and the local teaching personnel, and more trouble of that kind would certainly occur.[21]

Of even greater importance in the long run was the question of finding jobs for the growing number of islanders now receiving an education above the primary level. Between 1962 and 1967, the number of students attending secondary (and technical) schools in the territory rose from 1,155 to 1,591, and that of government-scholarship holders in France from 32 to 53. In addition, several hundred Polynesian and Chinese students from the islands who were supported by private means were attending French universities and technical institutions. At first glance, so small a number of comparatively well-educated islanders would not seem to pose a major problem as to their future employment, and indeed some of them have already found jobs in France. In a few years, however, the question may become acute if the number of university graduates continues to rise at the same rate and if there is not some spectacular development of the islands' economy. As is already the case with Polynesia's surplus laborers, emigration to countries with greater economic prospects and without sufficient trained personnel may be the only course open to highly educated islanders.

20 *Ibid.*, Nov. 15, 1965.

21 Because of personality conflicts between Raymond Lunel, the *inspecteur d'académie* who headed the education service, and the faculty of the Lycée Gauguin, 4 of its 26 teachers announced in 1965 that they would not return to their posts the following year. See minutes of the territorial assembly, April 22, 1965.

CULTURAL ACTIVITIES

The islands of French Polynesia have exerted an attraction not only upon distinguished artists and writers but also upon scholars, either as individuals or as members of international organizations. Furthermore, some of the high-ranking officials and the clergymen stationed there have produced scholarly works in the course of their tenure in the territory, and under their leadership local residents have formed organizations with the aim of preserving the indigenous culture and publishing the results of study in that field.

Before World War II, the most original scholarship was devoted to philology, and the outstanding organization for the preservation of the islands' cultural heritage was the Société des Etudes Océaniennes (S.E.O.). Linguistics was the area in which the Protestant missionaries were preeminent. The first missionaries who came to the islands naturally being concerned primarily with converting the Polynesians, their most urgent self-assigned task was to translate the Bible into the indigenous language, which then had no written form. In traditional Polynesian society, language was regarded as sacred and words were believed to have magical power. Priests were the guardians of the language, and they recited from memory the legends and genealogies of local heroes and gods. Even though these have now been mostly forgotten, the power of the spoken word is still considerable, and Pouvanaa's popularity stemmed mainly from his oratorical ability. He easily moved his audience by his eloquence in the Tahitian tongue, interlarded with Biblical quotations.

In 1835, Henry Nott, a L.M.S. missionary of humble origin, translated all of the Bible into Tahitian, with the aid of King Pomaré II.[22] By his translation, Nott, besides giving written form to the Tahitian language, also "established it as the classic tongue of central Polynesia.[23] Although Nott's work had an enormous influence, it did not stabilize the language, and many of the words he used have now become obsolete. In fact, Tahitian has evolved so rapidly that the inhabitants of the Society Islands have difficulty in understanding the language spoken by Tuamotuans and Marquesans, and young children find incomprehensible some of the words used by their grand-

[22] During the building of an army barracks in 1964, a C.E.P. bulldozer inadvertently profaned Nott's tomb, and this was deeply resented by the Protestant community.

[23] *Pacific Islands Monthly*, February 1965.

parents.[24] The linguistic work done by the English missionaries was continued by their French Protestant successors. In 1935, Pastor Charles Vernier, with the collaboration of an interpreter, Alexandre Drollet, published a *Grammaire de la Langue Tahitienne,* of which a revised and enlarged edition was printed in 1959. After Vernier's term as the E.F.O.'s first deputy in the Paris National Assembly expired in October 1946, he was offered a newly created chair in the Tahitian language at the Ecole Nationale des Langues Orientales Vivantes in Paris, where he taught until his return to the islands in 1948.

That school had already been closely associated with two scholarly governors of the E.F.O. who did much to promote the study and development of Tahitian. M. L. Montagné, governor from 1933 to 1935, was one of its graduates, and Gustave Julien had taught there before serving as governor from 1915 to 1919. The S.E.O. was created under Julien's auspices, but it was L.-J. Bouge, his *chef de cabinet,* who played a more active role in that society. Not only did Bouge help to found the S.E.O., but he contributed anthropological articles to its bulletin and later, during his governorship of the colony (1928–1931), was named its honorary vice-president.[25]

The ambitious program envisaged for the S.E.O. at its formation in January 1917 was the study of all questions related to the anthropology, ethnography, philology, history, and institutions of eastern Polynesia. So rapidly did it acquire a collection of books and indigenous art objects that the post of curator for this collection was created in 1918, and the government gave it the use of a building to house its holdings. The S.E.O. also promptly began, in March 1917, to issue a bulletin whose publication has continued, although irregularly, to this day. The society's first important contribution was an inventory of the islands' known historical monuments, which was printed in the August 1927 bulletin. From its inception, the S.E.O. has also published scholarly articles on the legends, traditions, and literature of the Polynesians, some of them written by individual *amateurs.*

Between 1917 and 1939, the number of its members rose from 62 to 200-odd, including about 50 who did not live in the islands.[26] On the eve of World War II, the S.E.O.'s library contained 958 volumes, the

[24] Mazellier, P., *Tahiti,* p. 18.

[25] While *chef de cabinet,* Bouge also launched a Tahitian-language newspaper, *Te Vea Maohi,* and began work on a grammar of the Tahitian language, which he completed in 1952 after retiring from the colonial service.

[26] *L'Océanie Française,* March–April 1939.

nucleus being the collection of a monk of the Picpus order, which he gave to the society. Although the books and the museum were moved to a larger building in 1935, it also soon became too crowded to contain the ever-increasing store of art objects given to the S.E.O. Most of these were donated by E.F.O. residents who were dismayed by the rapidity with which the evidences of traditional Polynesian culture were everywhere disappearing. As early as 1888, Stevenson had noted this phenomenon in the Marquesas, and he attributed it there to the French government's zeal in banning all the songs, dances, and even tattoos which bore traces of cannibal elements.[27] The net result, he sadly wrote, was that the Marquesans "now face empty-handed the tedium of their uneventful days." Yet cannibalism could not be held responsible for the past's disappearance in the other archipelagoes, where this was due, rather, to the Polynesians' preference for novelties.

To preserve what still could be salvaged, the administration passed laws severely penalizing those who exported traditional *objets d'art,* but it failed to provide the funds needed to protect and house the S.E.O.'s collections. So pitiable had their condition become that the director of the archeological museum of Brussels, who saw them in the mid-1930s, wrote a series of articles strongly urging their transfer to some institution in France.[28]

After World War II, the representative assembly showed a greater awareness of the need to preserve Polynesia's historical relics. It created a commission for the preservation of the islands' known monuments, and voted subsidies not only to the Société des Océanistes but also to various other organizations with similar cultural objectives.[29] Even though the 100,000 C.F.P. franc annual subsidy to the S.O. provided that society with the greater part of its funds, it could not meet even its operating expenses. In 1953 the S.O.'s president successfully pleaded with the assemblymen for a 50 percent increase in its subsidy. Even with the increased subsidy, however, the S.O. could not make urgently needed repairs, much less expand its activities. In the mid-1950s, the museum building was in such an advanced stage of decay that visitors were not allowed to tour the upper gallery lest they fall

[27] Stevenson, *In the South Seas,* p. 105.

[28] *Le Petit Parisien,* May 8–13, 1935.

[29] In 1945, the S.E.O. became affiliated with the Société des Océanistes (S.O.), which in turn was closely connected with the Musée de l'Homme in Paris. See pp. 508–509.

through the floor.[30] More recently, the need to provide additional attractions for the growing influx of tourists has given rise to plans for enlarging and refurbishing Papeete's museum.

Of perhaps greater worth than such half-hearted efforts to preserve the evidences of the islands' artistic past has been the increased emphasis on scholarly research into both the origins and the contemporary cultural development of the Polynesians. The French islands have drawn scholars from such world-renowned institutions as the Bishop Museum of Honolulu, the Kontiki Museum of Stockholm, and various Western universities. Thanks to the large sums made available by the internationally staffed scientific institutions, scholars have been able to pursue research on an unprecedented scale. Archeologists and anthropologists in particular have been able to throw light on the moot question of the Polynesians' original habitats, and the area of their research has spread from Tahiti to the outer islands.

Foreign scholars doing field work in the islands have collaborated with the French scientific organizations also operating there, whose staff, generally speaking, is more oriented to the contemporary scene. In the 1950s, the Institut Géographique National took over from the French navy the task of completing its charts of the coastal area, and since then has expanded its topographic work to include the interior of some islands. The program of the Organisation Scientifique des Territoires d'Outre-Mer (O.R.S.T.O.M.), operating from its Pacific base at Nouméa, has included studies of Papeete's urban population and land-tenure problems, although its main interest has been in the field of oceanography.[31]

Naturally the leaders of French Polynesia have been gratified by the greater knowledge of the islands' past which has resulted in large part from the research undertaken by foreign scholars, but they were more keenly interested in the socioeconomic studies made by the O.R.S.T.O.M. In particular they hoped that its oceanographic work would result in recommendations for ways of increasing the food productivity of the territory's marine resources. In this they have been disappointed, for, as regards French Polynesia, the O.R.S.T.O.M. has concentrated on pure research and produced only "beautiful reports." [32]

[30] Villaret, B., *Archipels Polynésiens*, p. 269.
[31] *Industries et Travaux d'Outre-Mer*, November 1964. See also pp. 509–510.
[32] Minutes of the territorial assembly, Nov. 15, 1965.

17

Public Health and Social Welfare

The steady decline of French Polynesia's population during the late nineteenth and early twentieth centuries had both physical and psychological causes. Among the latter, the islanders' indifference to their own survival was traceable not only to their seeming inability to adjust to the socioeconomic and political changes for which the missionaries and colonial administration were responsible, but also to their failure to profit by the few efforts made by their new masters to improve their well-being and health. For many years, it is true, those efforts were far from commensurate with the need, and, too, they were largely offset by the concurrent spread among the Polynesians of alcoholism and of diseases for which foreign contacts were chiefly responsible. The Westernization of their clothing, housing, and food habits—partly imposed and partly voluntary—is believed to have made them more susceptible to maladies introduced from abroad. Smallpox, measles, and, above all, influenza decimated a people who had built up no immunity against them and for whom no adequate medical facilities had been made available.

For many years before and after World War I, resident doctors, officials, and local businessmen, as well as foreign visitors, were shocked by the misery and degradation caused by the islanders' increasing consumption of alcoholic beverages, especially in Tahiti and the Marquesas.[1] Although the first legislative attempt to counter the inroads of alcoholism dated from 1904, it was not until Gustave Julien became governor during World War I that a real effort was made to combat it, and not until 1927 that the brewing of local palm toddy (*kava*) was forbidden. All proposals to limit the importation of liquor into the islands, however, have been effectively opposed by the winegrowers and exporters of France, and no means has been devised in the territory itself to enforce the ban on *kava*-manufacture, especially

[1] *L'Océanie Française,* March–April 1927, July–August 1928, July–August 1930.

in the less accessible islands. The administration could not be considered blameless in this matter, for it was never willing to forego the revenues derived from selling licenses to local liquor dealers, and the legislative steps it took were punitive rather than preventive in regard to suppressing alcoholism. Furthermore, such regulations—even after they were codified in 1930—were not uniform throughout the territory, and the more "evolved" residents of Tahiti were placed under a regime more "liberal" than that of the other islands.

During World War II and for some years thereafter, alcoholism became even more prevalent than before. Because the hostilities had prevented the export of the colony's sugar, 80 percent of the cane grown in the islands was processed into rum, which was sold locally.[2] Between 1939 and 1947, the number of shops selling liquor increased from 57 to 95,[3] and in Tahiti the four or five clubs initially opened for members of the armed services were soon transformed into public drinking places. These developments alarmed some public-spirited residents, who set about organizing sports competitions to lure young people away from the "beer parlors," and a temperance society was formed at Papeete, which had 194 pledged members when the war ended.

Alcohol was spreading at such a rate throughout the French Union in the early postwar years that the Paris government finally was moved to take some repressive action. (Ironically enough, in Papeete it was the local liquor merchants who pressed for restrictive measures because of the competition they were encountering from the tax-free so-called clubs.) In France, the opposition came not only from the local liquor lobby, as might be expected, but also from the communist party, which protested that any ban on the sale of liquor in the E.F.O. that did not include Europeans constituted discrimination against the Polynesians.[4] Later some local restrictions were placed on the sale of strong liquor to the native population, partly as a result of pressure from the territorial health service, which has stressed the relationship between the spread of alcoholism and the growing incidence of tuberculosis. In recent years, however, such measures have been offset by the opening of more cafes and bars, to which the assemblymen have reluctantly assented with a view to encouraging tourism. Those who have argued that improved living standards would automatically lessen

---

[2] *Pacific Islands Monthly*, June 1947.
[3] Poirier, J., "Evolution Récente des Sociétés Polynésiennes."
[4] Minutes of the French Union Assembly, June 6, 1950, July 1, 1952.

the temptations of alcohol for the Polynesians have been disconcerted by the proportion of their earnings that the outer-islanders employed by the C.E.P. spend on drink. No valid statistics are available
as to how widespread alcoholism has become in the territory, but all
the evidence suggests that it is increasing.

As to the other main causes of the islands' progressive depopulation
throughout the first half-century of colonial rule, the data are more
reliable and explicit. Among them were the lack of sufficient water
resources, changing dietary habits, and the Polynesians' indifference
to Western concepts of hygiene and medical care. On the high islands,
surface water normally is plentiful, but on the atolls the population
must depend on coconut milk and the rainfall. Nowhere have the
Polynesians made any effort to keep their water supply free of pollu-
tion by periodically scouring and sealing the tanks in which it is
stored.[5]

Since World War II, the territory and the F.I.D.E.S. have spent
nearly a million Metro. francs on developing the islands' water resources, especially in the Tuamotus, where all but 37 of the atolls now
have tanks.[6] In the early 1960s, the rapid increase in Tahiti's population made it imperative to find more water, especially on the western
side of the island, and for the first time systematic prospecting and
well-digging were undertaken. When the Papeete municipality tried to
raise a loan from the C.C.C.E. in 1962 to augment the water supply
for its growing urban population, the loan was granted only on condition that the townspeople pay for the water.[7] Polynesians find it
difficult to conform to such a requirement, for they feel that water, a
natural element, should be provided free. Nevertheless, in one way or
another, more water resources must be found in order to meet the
needs of the increasing number of islanders and tourists. To this end,
the F.I.D.E.S. agreed in 1967 to finance a well-digging program in
Tahiti and Bora Bora. For this project, French Polynesia has been
aided by an American mission, which, by using the same techniques
as in Hawaii, struck subterranean water on Bora Bora in 1966.[8]

The transformation in the Polynesians' food habits has been directly
related to the rapid Westernization of their whole way of life and to
the decline of local agricultural production. On the whole, the island-

[5] *South Pacific Bulletin,* January 1962, January 1963.
[6] Minutes of the territorial assembly, Jan. 27, 1966.
[7] *Ibid.,* Jan. 24, 1966.
[8] *Ibid.,* Nov. 28, 1966.

ers cannot be said to suffer from undernourishment, but their traditional diet is monotonous and poorly balanced, consisting of starches (taro, bananas, breadfruit), fish (boiled, grilled, fried), and various citrus fruits, besides coconut pulp and milk. Red meat is rarely eaten, and the protein delicacy most enjoyed everywhere is roast pig.

Tinned food is increasingly consumed by all Polynesians, and especially by those who have given up farming and fishing in favor of wage-earning. The tonnage of canned food imported from widely varying sources has grown by leaps and bounds in recent years.[9] As one Western observer has commented:

The native Tahitian eats a meal of rice from Madagascar, French bread with butter from Australia, Ceylonese tea sweetened with sugar from Martinique, and if he is affluent a can of bully beef from New Zealand or salmon from Canada—the whole meal washed down with generous servings of red Algerian wine.[10]

The changes in the origin of the Polynesians' food supply, however, have not led to any improvement in its nutritional content. On the contrary, their diet has been directly responsible for the marked increase in tooth decay noted throughout the islands in recent years. Two surveys by experts in selected islands, in 1953 and 1960, indicated that the condition of Polynesian children's teeth was "catastrophic."[11] Their reports alarmed the territorial assemblymen into deciding to finance more school canteens and free dental care for all the islands' primary schoolchildren.[12]

The causes of malnutrition and tooth decay are the more difficult to attack because they derive from custom and traditional social attitudes. The Polynesians see no point in observing even the most elementary rules of hygiene, and they are extremely conservative about their basic diet. When they replace locally grown food by an imported item, they simply substitute one type of starch for another —for example, rice in place of taro—and if they acquire a taste for canned corned beef they always want the same brand.[13] Apathy and

---

[9] See p. 135.

[10] Cunningham, G., "Food for Tahiti."

[11] In 1953, Drs. Malcolm and Massal carried out such research in two high islands and two atolls, and in 1960 Dr. Ferro-Luzzi examined the teeth of 2,000 schoolchildren in Tahiti.

[12] Minutes of the territorial assembly, Feb. 25, 1963.

[13] The islanders have a marked preference for New Zealand corned beef rather than the Australian product, and a governor who tried to impose a French substitute suddenly found himself very unpopular. See Mazellier, P., *Tahiti*, p. 29.

resistance to change also characterize the Polynesians' attitude toward modern medical care and dentistry, especially if regular treatment is involved.

The territory is fortunate in being, on the whole, singularly free of many of the diseases often found in other tropical countries. There is no malaria, plague, yellow fever, cholera, or typhus in French Polynesia, nor do venomous snakes exist there. Although venereal diseases are still rife, tuberculosis is increasing, and infant mortality remains high, these are related to socioeconomic conditions with which purely medical care cannot cope. On the positive side, two of the worst maladies that formerly afflicted many islanders—leprosy and elephantiasis—have been almost eliminated.

Since World War II, the old policy of rounding up lepers and segregating them in isolated villages has been replaced by a medical treatment that has reduced their number to well under 1 percent of the total population.[14] Of the three prewar leper colonies—at Hivao in the Marquesas, Reao in the Tuamotus, and Orofara in Tahiti—only the last-mentioned exists today. Its 60 or so inmates are either contagious cases or patients so deformed by their disease that they fear to return to their families and, in any case, are incapable of earning their living.[15] Filariasis—of which elephantiasis is the disfiguring and debilitating final phase—formerly afflicted 7 percent of all the islanders, but it, too, has yielded to treatment by new drugs. A campaign to combat that disease, including mosquito-control measures, was launched in the 1950s, and was so immediately successful that no new cases have been reported since 1957.[16] These spectacular results can be ascribed to the care provided by the territorial health service and to the research carried on by the Institut de Recherches Médicales de l'Océanie at Papeete.

From the earliest days of French rule, the islands' health service has been staffed by military personnel. Indeed, it was the only element of the French armed forces that remained in the colony's employment after civilian administrators replaced naval officers there in 1903. The personnel of the health service, however, was not adequate to the islanders' needs,[17] and on the eve of World War II it comprised

[14] As of 1965, there were only 340 known lepers in the whole territory.

[15] Minutes of the territorial assembly, Jan. 7, 1965, Jan. 27, 1966; *La Polynésie Française* (La Documentation Française), p. 39.

[16] *New York Times*, July 3, 1962.

[17] *L'Océanie Française*, January–February 1935.

only 6 doctors, 1 pharmacist, and 19 nurses. This service underwent successive reorganizations in 1912, 1934, 1938, and 1944, accompanied by fluctuations but no marked change in the number of its personnel. As was the case with the education service, its efforts were hampered by the islands' dispersal over a huge area, by the reluctance of its personnel to live in isolated discomfort on the most inaccessible ones, and by the resident doctor's absorption in his administrative duties. Moreover, the public health service's few physicians, dentists, and pharmacists were for the most part stationed in Tahiti.

In the flush of postwar liberalism and generosity toward its overseas possessions, France provided the E.F.O. with more funds for social development than it had ever before received. To improve the equipment of the health service, the F.I.D.E.S. allocated substantial sums for building small hospital-dispensaries in the outer islands, and to meet their operating expenses the territorial budget devoted annually about 18 percent of its revenues. During the 1950s, an average of 1,000 C.F.P. francs per capita were being spent on the islanders' health.[18] In regard to qualified medical personnel in the territory, however, the shortage persisted, for the war in Indochina from 1946 to 1954 absorbed many of France's military doctors. Consequently, a greater effort was made to utilize local personnel, but few qualified Polynesians were available.

As of 1948, for the whole of the E.F.O., there were 9 doctors (of whom 3 were civilians), 2 dentists, 1 pharmacist, 36 nurses, and 13 midwives to care for a rapidly growing population then estimated at about 50,000.[19] Clearly, some means had to be found to cope with the increasing need for medical care, and that year the administration proposed both to send more Polynesians to France for training and, in the meantime, to recruit more civilian doctors in France. However, the civilian doctors turned out to be more costly to the budget than their military colleagues and generally less satisfactory, for after the termination of their contracts they either left the islands or took up private practice in Papeete. When the Indochina war ended in 1954, the assemblymen were once more able to recruit French military doctors, but they specified that those sent to the E.F.O. must hold no rank higher than that of lieutenant and be assigned to the outer islands.

At the request of the local authorities, a plan had been drawn up

[18] Massal, E., "Réalisations Médicales et Perspectives en Polynésie Française."
[19] Speech of Dr. F. Borrey to the French Union Assembly, June 24, 1948.

in 1958–1959 by Dr. Ferrand, a French expert on hospital construction, who recommended several important changes in the territory's medical institutions. He urged that a wholly new hospital be built at Papeete to replace the existing one which, albeit enlarged and modernized, dated back to 1844. The new hospital would serve the entire territory, particularly for the treatment of serious cases, but he also stressed the need to decentralize the whole public-health service by improving the secondary hospitals located at Taravao, Taiohae, and Uturoa.[20] For more than a decade, various practical obstacles prevented implementation of Dr. Ferrand's recommendations; notably, construction of the Papeete hospital was blocked by disagreements over the financing of its building and maintenance, and even over its site. The assemblymen's feelings of frustration over these interminable delays were intensified by the speed with which the C.E.P., only 18 months after its installation in the islands, had built, equipped, and staffed an ultramodern hospital for its own personnel. Furthermore, the C.E.P.'s absorption of a very large proportion of the labor supply made completion of the new Papeete hospital impossible until well into the 1970s.

Since World War II, the brightest spot in the territory's medical picture has been the remarkable achievements of the Institut de Recherches Médicales de l'Océanie. Inaugurated on September 9, 1949, through collaboration between the local health service, the University of California, and the South Pacific Commission, and through the generosity of some foreign residents, this institute has become the first permanent center for the study of tropical diseases in the Pacific islands. Its budget has increased six-fold since 1959, and a growing share of its funds is being provided by the territorial revenues and the F.I.D.E.S.

SOCIAL WELFARE

Until very recent years, the communal traditions of Polynesian society remained strong enough, especially in rural areas, to obviate many of the problems which in Western countries have given rise to

[20] Largely thanks to the F.I.D.E.S., the number of public institutions providing medical care in French Polynesia had been increased by 1960 to 28, including 12 dispensaries and 11 infirmaries in the outer islands. There the capacity of the secondary hospitals had been enlarged to 58 beds at Taravao, 60 at Uturoa, and 15 at Taiohae. See *La Polynésie Française* (La Documentation Française), p. 38.

social-welfare work. Generally speaking, outer-island families continued to take care of their aged and infirm members, except for lepers, who were forcibly removed and segregated. Before World War II, only in Tahiti did there exist institutions for the insane and for the indigent aged, and neither of them ever had many inmates. On holidays they received small gifts from the French Red Cross, which set up a branch in Tahiti in 1933. That organization also financed the building of a meeting hall for the Orofara lepers, and raised money by organizing charity fairs and fêtes to supply food and clothing to the needy of Papeete. Official contributions for such welfare activities came mainly from the *droit des pauvres,* a tax instituted in 1918, which was levied on the owners of movie houses and night clubs and the proceeds of which were distributed by the municipal council of Papeete.

The French government's decision, 3 years after the end of World War II, to create social-welfare services in its overseas dependencies was viewed by the E.F.O.'s representative assemblymen as quite unnecessary for that territory. Their opposition to the creation of an *Assistance Sociale* service, however, ceased when they learned that it would have a small staff of four workers headed by a local girl who had been trained in France.[21] In principle, that service was to embrace the whole territory, but in practice its work was restricted to Papeete. During the first few years of their work in the E.F.O., the *assistantes sociales* simply acted as advisors to the Papeete municipal council, which continued to be the main agency for distributing funds to that town's needy.[22] Insofar as the youth were concerned, Chinese young people, who formed the largest fraction of Papeete's youthful population, were docile and orderly, and the assemblymen felt no need to alter their ostrich-like attitude toward the whole problem.[23] They could justify their inaction to some degree by the fact that only 200 cases of juvenile delinquency were handled by the police between 1950 and 1960.[24]

The rapid growth of Papeete's population and the arrival of the

[21] Minutes of the representative assembly, May 11, 1950.

[22] *Ibid.,* Dec. 6, 1954.

[23] This was illustrated by their decision in 1954 not to grant a monthly stipend of 25 C.F.P. francs to each of the 34 inmates of the old-people's home, but to send them instead a few packages of cigarettes. See minutes of the representative assembly, Dec. 7, 1954.

[24] Molet, L., "Esquisse de la Jeunesse Polynésienne et ses Problèmes," pp. 46–59.

C.E.P. personnel in the early 1960s forced the local authorities to adopt a more realistic attitude toward social-welfare problems. Many immigrant families from the outer islands had so much difficulty in making ends meet that often both parents had to absent themselves from home to earn money. Their children, freed from parental supervision and the constraints imposed by traditional communal life, tended increasingly to play hookey from school and to practise petty theft. The boys did not steal systematically nor did they operate in organized gangs. They simply "borrowed" the objects they coveted, such as scooters and clothes, and when caught, promptly confessed and promised to return them forthwith.[25] Many of the girls who engaged in prostitution never became true professionals, for soon they were *fiu* (fed up) and returned to their home islands with their accumulated earnings, there to become respectable *mères de famille.* Nevertheless, such problems as they created became serious enough that the assemblymen tried for the first time to deal with them constructively. In 1965, they voted funds totaling 25 million C.F.P. francs for two centers of "reeducation" for erring boys and girls, vacation colonies for needy schoolchildren, and even pocket money for the inmates of the old-people's home. As a rule, they entrusted the management of such funds to the Catholic and Protestant missions and various private charitable institutions.

On the whole, the territorial leaders seem now to have accepted the necessity of financing institutions and organizations to deal with juvenile delinquency. They realized that although the withdrawal of C.E.P. personnel will eliminate the factor that has most contributed to the growth of delinquency, the encouragement being given to the development of tourism will simply replace that element by another. An important hopeful development has been the recent efforts to develop more youth organizations on the part of the missions, and the organizing of sports events by the Service de la Jeunesse, created in 1966. One of the territory's conspicuous shortcomings has been the lack of inexpensive and harmless diversions, especially in Papeete, where there are no reading rooms, public gardens, swimming pools, or other facilities to occupy the leisure time of the youth. This need is especially acute for a population in which 54 percent are under 20 years of age.

[25] Mazellier, *Tahiti,* p. 70.

URBANIZATION

The history of urbanization and housing in French Polynesia resembles that of many other social-welfare projects there. The postwar French government initiated planning in this field in all its overseas dependencies, where virtually none had been done before, and it provided experts and public funds for drafting and implementing such plans. However, too many reports, amendments, and debates—as was the case with Papeete's hospital—led to exasperating delays, caused partly by the conflicting views of local leaders on the subjects and partly by changing conditions in the territory, which were beyond their control. Although urbanization and housing projects were extended in 1966 to include a few settlements in the outer islands, the crux of the problem has always been the future development of Papeete and its suburbs.

The site chosen long ago for the colony's capital was swampy land which had not been properly drained when the naval government built the first public structure there. In the early years, such activity as existed was concentrated along the waterfront, Papeete's streets were little more than footpaths, and the few sidewalks were built by individual houseowners. So long as the capital remained a small administrative center, these drawbacks were considered rather picturesque, and its occasional visitors found in Papeete much of the casual charm of frontier villages in the American Far West. But when Papeete developed as a commercial port inhabited by a heterogeneous and largely foreign population, the overcrowding and the lack of sanitation and circulation facilities became crucial rather than merely inconvenient.

Since it was created in 1890, Papeete's municipal council had never had at its disposal the resources needed to make improvements that would keep pace with the population's growth. The colonial administration, for its part, was too unstable in its top echelons to undertake any long-term planning for the town. After World War II, the results of this combination of administrative negligence and lack of funds became strikingly apparent. During the decade 1935–1945, Papeete's population had risen from 8,400 to well over 12,000, and the number of motor vehicles moving through its narrow streets had risen from 53 to more than 2,000. No new construction had been undertaken during the war, no improvements had been made in sanitation facilities, and no traffic regulations were in force.

It was this situation that confronted Robert Auzelle, a French expert sent by the Paris government in 1950 to prepare a plan for Papeete's "urban renewal." [26] His principal proposal, which involved replacing Papeete's slums with modern housing, could not be carried out because neither the land nor the funds required were available.[27] In 1949, the F.I.D.E.S. had financed the construction of a small *cité ouvrière*, but this was far from solving the problem of housing for the great majority of the urban population. A new five-year plan for urban development, submitted in 1959, was rejected by the authorities because of its estimated expense.[28] Still another project, drawn up two years later, suffered a similar fate. Plans and estimates were revised several times, and in 1963, the advent of the C.E.P. precipitated another housing crisis. Consequently, the possibility of extending the capital into the surrounding hills, rather than along the littoral, was given consideration.

As finally authorized in 1965, the frequently revised master plan included the construction of 3,600 low-cost dwellings during the ensuing 3 years, and the formation of a Service de l'Urbanisme et de l'Habitat, whose operations would include the main outer-island settlements. Of the cost of these projects, estimated then at 2,407 million C.F.P. francs, private investments were expected to provide 1,510 million, the remainder to come from loans by public agencies and, to a small extent, from territorial revenues.

[26] See bibliography.
[27] *L'Echo de Tahiti,* Jan. 31, 1952.
[28] *Les Débats,* Oct. 2, 1959.

18

Communications Media

Government control over the media of communication in French Polynesia has been exercised both directly and indirectly. Only for films shown in the islands is there an official censorship board, but inasmuch as the radio and television stations are directly responsible to the governor, their programs are equally, though less obviously, subject to the administration's control. Furthermore, by omitting or abridging the treatment of controversial subjects and by allocating broadcast time generously to proadministration leaders and giving short shrift to opposition spokesmen, a form of censorship is exercised.

Insofar as the press is concerned, the decree of December 11, 1932, which empowered the governor to forbid the importation or circulation of any publication is still in force, and as recently as February 1967 it was invoked to prevent John Teariki from issuing a Tahitian-language edition of his party organ.[1] More obliquely, the French government uses leaks to the press as a device to cushion the shock which an official announcement of unpopular measures might cause. This was notably the procedure in the case of its decisions to carry out nuclear-weapons tests in the islands, recognize the government of Peking, and not permit the United States consulate to reopen.[2]

Local leaders are not, in principle, opposed to censorship of the communications media, provided they have a voice in its application. What they object to is the bias allegedly shown by the administration in imposing it. On occasion, the assemblymen have even favored stricter control over the importation of films and books that might have a "harmful effect on the morality and respect for law of our local youth."[3] Members of the assembly are extremely sensitive about reports of political matters in general and of their own debates in particular. The government is accused not so much of disseminating false information as of distorting the news by abridging and slanting

---

[1] Minutes of the permanent commission, April 25, 1967.
[2] *Pacific Islands Monthly*, May 1965.
[3] Minutes of the permanent commission, July 5, 1950.

it in a way that shows "contemptuous indifference" to the local scene.[4]

The administration, for its part, points to the increasing efforts it has made to disseminate information. For many years, because of the dearth of newspapers, their ephemeral existence, and their concentration in Papeete, radio broadcasting was especially important to the outer islanders. In 1949 the French government decided to replace at its own expense the 1-kilowatt radio station of Tahiti by an installation four times as powerful, and the F.I.D.E.S. financed the distribution of several hundred receiving sets to the outer islands, as well as loud-speaker systems for the main villages there. Five years later, the cost of operating the new station, to which the territorial budget had been contributing 200,000 C.F.P. francs annually, was entirely taken over by France—in other words, by French taxpayers—and Radio Tahiti was placed under the management of the Société de Radiodiffusion de la France d'Outre-Mer (SORAFOM). As was the case when France shouldered the expenditures for the islands' secondary-education system,[5] the assemblymen were content to be relieved of the financial burden but resentful of the consequent loss of control. They became increasingly critical of Radio Tahiti's programs, but more of its sins of omission than those of commission.

Local criticism of France's policy in this domain reached a new pitch of intensity with the announcement in 1965 that the Paris authorities intended to increase greatly the range of Radio Tahiti's operations and to install a television station in the territory, so as to make Papeete the center for "radiating" French cultural influence throughout the Pacific. Radio Tahiti was then operating 40 hours a week, one-third of the time in Tahitian and two-thirds in French, and its programs included news, music, cultural talks, interviews with local personalities, and official communiqués, Sundays being reserved for broadcasting religious services.[6] It was the jocular tone of Radio Tahiti's reporting of assembly meetings to which its members primarily objected. So long as they were "treated like ignoramuses" and not given any control over the content of the programs, they would not contribute a *centime* to the functioning of the television station that was inaugurated at Papeete on October 15, 1965.[7]

As to other forms of mass communications media, French Polynesia

[4] *Ibid.*, March 23, 1967.

[5] See pp. 203, 206.

[6] Covit, B., ed., *Official Directory and Guide Book for Tahiti*, p. 177.

[7] Minutes of the territorial assembly, Nov. 15, 1965; minutes of the permanent commission, April 1, 1966.

had to wait until 1957 to have its own French-language daily news-paper, although an astonishing number of short-lived journals and periodicals had been published there in the course of the preceding half-century. Perusal of their history, however, discloses that most of them were simply reincarnations under new titles of publications that had been banned because their contents had aroused official ire. Nevertheless, such censorship was not the sole cause of their brief existence. Other factors that contributed to their demise were their insufficient capital, the small extent of the local reading public, and, most of all, the abusive and highly personal nature of their writing.

Most admirers of the famous painter, Paul Gauguin, are surprised to learn that he was one of the earliest and most vituperative of the colony's journalists. His chronic complaints against local officials and, to a lesser extent, the Christian missionaries were frequently expressed in written form. Indeed, in the last years of the nineteenth century, he gave up painting for 18 months to launch a series of newspapers— *Les Guêpes, Le Sourire,* and *Le Monde pour Tous*—in which to at-tack his enemies.[8] His journalism succeeded neither in reforming the administration nor in winning a wide public, and, moreover, was a financial failure. Eventually he was prosecuted by the government, and the heavy fines imposed on him compounded his disappointment at the ineffectiveness of his journalistic efforts.

Gauguin's misadventures did not deter other equally inexperienced and irascible French residents from starting similar publications. Eu-gène Brunschwig, a semiliterate cabinetmaker, founded successive newspapers in which he gave vent to his hostility to the local admini-stration. In the columns of *Le Vrai* (founded in 1902), *Le Libéral* (1906), and *L'Equité* (1919), anyone with a grievance against the authorities—and their number was legion in the small world that was the Papeete of that epoch—could manage to have his diatribe printed under cover of Brunschwig's name. During World War I, however, when he published attacks on the French government, he could no longer find any local printer who was willing to work for him. He therefore had his *Le Libéral* printed in San Francisco until 1918, when Governor Julien forbade its circulation in the colony. Discour-aged finally by his successive failures, Brunschwig retired from active journalism, although he continued to express his views in letters to various world figures, including the Pope.[9]

[8] *Pacific Islands Monthly,* June 1960.

[9] O'Reilly, P., and R. Teissier, *Tahitiens: Répertoire Bio-bibliographique de la Polynésie Française,* pp. 64–65.

Another such journalist was Paul Nakety (the *nom de plume* of Jean Anselme), who was equally hostile to the local administration. Nakety's *Le Tahitien,* founded in 1916, was suspended by the government within 10 months of its birth, but was almost immediately reincarnated as *Le Journal de Papeete.* That newspaper ceased publication in 1918, and Nakety himself did not long survive its demise. C. Deflesselle and M. Pecastaing, respectively founders of *Le Fei* and *L'Echo de Tahiti* in the early 1920s, followed in the footsteps of Brunschwig and Nakety, both in their antiadministration bias and in the fate of their journalistic enterprises.[10]

These ill-starred journalistic ventures were, without exception, launched by Metropolitan Frenchmen who had no professional training and no reticence in the expression of their choleric opinions. The fact that all of them fell afoul of government censorship probably discouraged potential successors, for during the rest of the interwar period no newspapers were founded specifically for the French residents of the E.F.O. It is noteworthy that during this same period, two Chinese-language newspapers were regularly issued at Papeete, the Catholic and Protestant missions produced publications for their respective church members, the Seventh Day Adventists and both Mormon sects had their own propaganda organs, and there was even an English-language bulletin for tourists, financed by an enterprising local trader.[11] The Paris government somewhat fitfully subsidized a magazine, *Tahiti-France,* to publicize the colony in the home country, but French residents in the E.F.O. had to be content with the *Journal Officiel.* On the eve of World War II, that arid publication brought out an edition in Tahitian, *Vea Maohi,* which supplemented reports of local regulations with news of Papeete and articles about Polynesia's past history and legends.[12]

During the 4 years that followed V-J Day, the government subsidized several weeklies—successively the *Bulletin de Presse des E.F.O., Le Courrier des E.F.O.,* and *L'Echo de Tahiti.* These found little favor with the public, however, because they provided no channel for the expression of local opinion and the news they contained had already been heard over the radio, and all were short-lived. The development of political parties gave a new zest to local news, and the expansion of schooling to the secondary level created in the fast-

[10] Coppenrath, G., "Evolution Politique de la Polynésie Française depuis la Première Guerre Mondiale."

[11] *L'Océanie Française,* July–August 1927.

[12] *Ibid.,* January–February 1939.

growing population an ever-larger audience. The most solidly established periodicals were those sponsored by the various religious organizations. Among these were the Protestant mission's weekly, *Te Vea Porotetani* (circulation 2,300 in 1955), and its monthly, *Notre Lien* (300); the two monthlies of the Catholic mission, *Te Vea Katorika* (1,170) and *Le Semeur* (300); and that of the Seventh Day Adventists, *Te Vea Adivenite Mahana Hitu* (250). Of the secular publications, those with the largest circulation were the weekly *Te Aratai* (2,000), the R.D.P.T. organ, and *Les Petites Annonces* (also 2,000), which was exclusively an advertising medium. Some of these were published in French and some in Tahitian, but to appeal to the widest possible readership most of them contained articles in both languages.

The year 1957 marked a milestone in the history of journalism in the territory with the appearance of its first French-language daily, *Les Nouvelles*. (A few years later, its founder and staff brought out a glossy quarterly called *Tahiti Magazine*.) The late 1950s also saw the appearance—as well as often the disappearance—of a number of irregularly published and usually mimeographed journals of opinion, founded by individual politicians who were territorial assemblymen. These included Walter Grand's *Te Ara O Oteania*, Edwin Atger's *Te Mau Opuarau,* and Frantz Vanisette's *Les Vrais Débats*. At the same time, *Te Aratai* ceased to be the party organ for the whole R.D.P.T. and became that of the faction led by Céran-Jérusalemy.

In the mid-1960s, the arrival in French Polynesia of thousands of employes of the C.E.P. was probably responsible for a rash of new local publications. By the end of 1964, *Les Nouvelles* had been joined by two other dailies, and, in addition, there were three new weeklies and one monthly, some of which were published by the same sponsors and staff. One of the earlier of these newcomers was *Le Journal de Tahiti*, founded in 1963 by the Bambridge family, which subsequently published a lively and informative weekly, *Ici Tahiti*, devoted to local events. Their chief editor was a Parisian journalist, and the international news printed in *Le Journal* was supplied largely by United Press International, whose local correspondent was Bernard Covit, editor of the *Official Directory and Guide Book for Tahiti*. The second daily launched in the decade was *La Dépêche*, probably the most impartial of all the local publications. It was founded in mid-1964 by a group of French and Tahitian businessmen, and it, too, was edited by a professional newspaper man, Philippe Mazellier, who had formerly worked for *Le Journal.* The same group also published *La Presse de Tahiti* until August 1964, when they sold it to a newborn weekly, *Les Echos de Polynésie,* in which Alfred Poroi and other businessmen-politicians of Papeete had a controlling interest.

Although the great majority of the foregoing publications were founded by groups or individuals with specific axes to grind, they resembled the press in Western countries far more than did their predecessors in their format, contents, and the space given to photographs and sport news. To be sure, some journals of the old type, also established in the 1960s—such as Teariki's *Te Here Aia* and Vanisette's *Le Canard Tahitien*—were openly partisan and highly personal in the views they expressed. Nevertheless, the prevailing trend was toward straight news reporting by trained newspapermen, who subordinated the political opinions of the founder-owners of their papers to a lively and attractive presentation of international and local events. As to their future, however, it is doubtful whether many of them can survive the circulation decline that must follow the withdrawal of the C.E.P.'s personnel.

Part II
NEW CALEDONIA

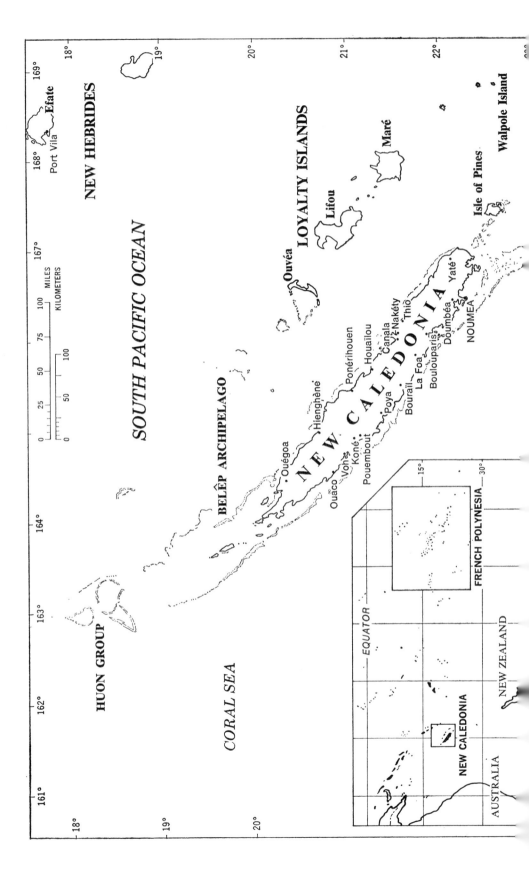

19

Land and History

New Caledonia and its dependencies, lying at the crossroads of the Melanesian and Polynesian worlds, are not only 20,000 kilometers distant from France but are also relatively isolated in the southwest Pacific Ocean. They are situated 1,500 kilometers east of Australia, 1,700 kilometers north of New Zealand, and 7,000 kilometers southeast of Japan. Groups of islands fringe the Grande Terre,[1] the most important of them, by far, being the Loyaltys (Ouvéa, Lifou, and Maré), which parallel its eastern flank at a distance of 150 kilometers. The other satellites of the Grande Terre are the Isle of Pines and Walpole and Hunter Islands to the southeast; the four Huon islands and the Belêp archipelago to the north; and the eleven coral atolls known collectively as the Chesterfields to the northwest.[2]

Two other island groups, the New Hebrides and the Wallis and Futuna Islands, are administrative but not geographical appendages of the Grande Terre. The governor of New Caledonia and the British High Commissioner of the Western Pacific are jointly responsible for the condominium of the New Hebrides, and both are represented at Port Vila by Residents. New Caledonia's governor is also the administrative link between France and the Wallis and Futuna archipelagoes, which are separated from each other by 200 kilometers of ocean and lie 2,000 kilometers from the east coast of the Grande Terre. Although those islands are ethnically part of the Polynesian world, they are even more remote (3,000 kilometers) from Tahiti than from New Caledonia, with which they have historical as well as present-day ties. Until 1959, when Wallis and Futuna became an over-

[1] This name is used by Caledonians in referring to the main island, to distinguish it from its smaller adjacent dependencies.

[2] The name of Guano Islands is sometimes given to the Chesterfields, Walpole, and Huon group, which do not form a geographical entity but have acquired this name because they are predominantly guano producers.

seas territory, they were a French protectorate, in the charge of a Resident-Doctor. (The predominant influence in those islands, however, has long been that of the Catholic missionaries.) Their population of 8,600 persons, known collectively as Wallisians, live on a total land area of 88 square kilometers and formerly earned their livelihood from copra. Copra exports have now almost entirely ceased, and the islanders' main sources of income are subsidies from the French government and the remittances sent by emigrants working in New Caledonia and the New Hebrides.

All of New Caledonia's dependencies lack the economic resources needed to assure their independent development, and their isolation, dispersal, and rapid demographic growth make them increasingly dependent on Nouméa. In relation to them, therefore, the Grande Terre has come to play the role of a metropolis, and in return benefits by the labor their emigrants supply for its economic enterprises.

The Grande Terre itself, lying in a southeast-to-northwest position, is some 400 kilometers long by 30 wide, and covers an area of 16,750 square kilometers. Its coasts, as well as the Isle of Pines, are surrounded by a great coral reef which forms what amounts to a vast lagoon varying in width from 10 to 20 kilometers. This barrier, which lies nearer to the western than to the eastern shore, is cut by deep passes opposite the mouths of the main rivers, and these permit communication with the open sea. The east coast is more deeply indented and mountainous than that of the west, where the valleys broaden out into plains covered in places by tropical vegetation and mangrove swamps. The interior is crisscrossed by irregular mountain ranges, whose highest peaks (Mt. Panié and Mt. Humboldt) reach heights of some 1,600 meters. This confused mountain mass terminates in the plain of Diahot in the north and that of the Lakes in the south. The summits of the mountains are bare but their slopes are thickly wooded, and they are transversed by rivers that form deep and often fertile valleys. In the north, only the Diahot River—90 kilometers long and navigable in part—and the Néhoué flow in the longitudinal direction of the island. In the south, the Yaté, Dumbéa, Tontouta, and Tchamba Rivers are generally transversal, much shorter, and more torrential. The tropical climate of the Grande Terre is so tempered by the trade winds as to make it suited to Westerners. Rainfall is irregular and generally inadequate, but the east coast usually receives twice as much as does the west. Droughts are not infrequent, and occasionally cyclones devastate portions of the island.

For many years after the existence of New Caledonia and its dependent islands had become known to the Western world in the late 18th century, the history and social organization of their inhabitants remained cloaked in mystery. Partly because of the lack of any permanent evidences of their past culture, and partly in consequence of the widespread assumption that the progressive decline in their numbers would soon culminate in their extinction, the islanders long failed to evoke the interest of scholars. Only the Christian missionaries, who lived in the native milieu, troubled to study the local languages and the customs of the tribesmen whom they hoped to convert. Even today, the problems posed by the mosaic of tribes, the multiplicity of their dialects, and the successive waves of immigrants and of internal migrations are of such complexity that their history is still imperfectly known.

As yet, archeologists have found no evidence that New Caledonia was inhabited before the Christian era,[3] nor do they know when or by what means the earliest inhabitants reached the Grande Terre. Now, however, it is fairly well established that in the mid-18th century large numbers of Polynesians migrated from Wallis Island to Ouvéa, in the Loyalty group, and from there some went to the east coast of the Grande Terre. This brought to New Caledonia men of physical characteristics and a hierarchized social order markedly different from those of the Melanesians among whom they settled. Generally speaking, these migrations were oriented southward and westward, across the central mountain range, and they continued over a long period of time. Probably the conflicts and changes to which their presence gave rise were responsible for the conflicting views of the first Western navigators in regard to the islanders' character. In 1774, James Cook found the natives of the northeastern area friendly and hospitable, whereas 18 years later, Bruni d'Entrecasteaux reported that those of the west coast were cannibalistic and fierce. At all events, both in the early years and since World War II the chieftaincies on the two coasts have reacted in sharply divergent ways to the French administration's policies.

MELANESIAN SOCIETY

Traditional Melanesian society was classless but was divided into a hierarchy of families, clans, and tribes. Of these, the clan was the basic unit and the tribe the most weakly structured. Yet the Mela-

[3] See E. W. Clifford, in *Journal de la Société des Océanistes*, vol. 9, December 1953.

nesian tribes were far from being anarchic groups, for they were meticulously organized into tiny independent states, each with its own language and government. Tribes lived in relative isolation in the 24 more or less transversal valleys into which the mountains divided the Grande Terre. Those in the hinterland were hemmed in by steep slopes on all sides, but the minority who lived on the coasts had a limited frontier along the sea. The term "tribe" gives Westerners an erroneous impression of great size, for in New Caledonia the largest tribe comprised no more than a few hundred persons living in small villages, whose inhabitants had—theoretically—the same ethnic origin. In reality, however, some of these villagers were sub-tribesmen, whose forebears either had been conquered by the dominant tribe or had sought an alliance with it and settled nearby for protection.

In contrast to the amorphous nature of this tribal organization, far greater homogeneity marked the clans which composed the tribe. Members of a clan claimed descent from a common ancestor, whose name, exploits, and dwelling place were kept alive in legends and traditions, and who was revered in religious ceremonies. The totem chosen by the ancestor, usually an animal or a plant, was that of the clan and was the secret symbol of its solidarity and strength. When the terrain occupied by the clan became too restricted, or for other reasons, some of its members emigrated to another area, but they maintained close contacts with those who remained. The extent to which such contacts were maintained between areas sometimes far apart was shown after World War II, when wartime restrictions on the inhabitants' mobility were ended and fellow clansmen began again to visit each other freely.[4]

The families that composed the clan followed a hierarchical order, in which the place of honor was occupied by the senior male member of its oldest branch. The paterfamilias, however, was no family patriarch, as was the case in most countries of tropical Africa, and the closest relationships were those between relatives of the same generation. This horizontal rather than vertical stratification of Melanesian society created virtual "fraternities" among relatives, and it was the oldest generation whose members acted as family counselors and arbiters. Members of the same age group—fathers and uncles, children and their cousins—all called each other indiscriminately "brothers".

[4] Deschamps, H., and J. Guiart, *Tahiti—Nouvelle-Calédonie—Nouvelles-Hébrides*, pp. 116 ff.

Polygamy existed but was not universally practiced, and men might not marry women of the same clan. No bride-price was paid in terms of money and services, as in Black African societies, but to compensate the bride's family for her loss the groom offered his sister in exchange. Although lineage was traced through the distaff side, women had no authority of their own. They had their assigned tasks, such as the rearing of children, cultivating small crops, and gathering wood and wild produce. Their social status, however, was inferior to that of men, who were the tribe's warriors, fishermen, and farmers.[5]

The adoption of children was not rare, but its practice was far less frequent and casual than in Polynesian society. Curiously enough, a man's role as father was considered insignificant, for it was the ancestor (*totel*) who was believed to be the child's progenitor. The father, although he supported and educated his children, was a far less important person in the family than his wife's brothers. The chief purpose of the great clan gatherings and periodic ceremonials known as *pilou-pilou* was to reinforce the vital bonds of the families, clans, and tribes created by matrilinear relationships.[6]

Each clan and tribe was headed by a chief, whose role reflected the paternalistic and religious character of Melanesian society. In his person, the chief combined the elements of an elder statesman, oldest "brother," and priest. His authority, far from being autocratic or coercive, derived from his people's freely given assent and respect, because he incarnated the group's unity and was its indispensable intermediary with the common ancestor and the gods. At the apex of the government and religious hierarchy stood the tribal chief, but he was not a head of state in the Western sense of that term. He could impose and lift taboos, declare war, requisition men and services, prescribe penalties, and organize *pilous*, but all such prerogatives were regulated by custom and in most cases their exercise required the approval of the council of elders.

As its name suggests, this council was composed of the oldest and most respected members of the tribe, and because the chieftaincy was not automatically hereditary it was the elders who chose the successor to a deceased chief from among his clan relatives. The council also acted as a court of appeal from the chief's judgments, and in many other ways restrained his powers. Because the elders' decisions always had to be unanimous, they required long and often secret

[5] Brou, B., "La Société Traditionelle Mélanésienne en Nouvelle-Calédonie."

[6] Faivre, J.-P., J. Poirier, and P. Routhier, *Géographie de la Nouvelle-Calédonie*, Paris, 1953, pp. 250–252.

palavers, and this enabled the elders—if they so desired—to postpone almost indefinitely taking a stand on controversial matters. Furthermore, if the tribe became involved in warfare and the chief was not an outstanding military leader, the elders could choose from among the tribesmen anyone whom they considered to be a competent war chief.

Another tribal group with which the chief shared his power, though in this instance on a permanent basis, were the Masters of the Land. These were the descendants of the first occupants of the area, who as such were entitled to tribute from the tribesmen who farmed it.[7] Their role was especially important in regions where the tribe cultivated and lived on land that it did not own, and under those circumstances the tribe's former home and sacred places, as well as its ties with related clans, took on a special importance.

The status of the chieftaincy on the adjacent Loyalty Islands was in sharp contrast with that on the Grande Terre. On the former, the predominance of Polynesian traditions, the far denser population, and the wholly different basis of the economy enabled the Loyalty chiefs to wield a much more autocratic authority. They surrounded themselves with courtiers, who resembled those of eighteenth-century Western Europe much more than did the Melanesian councils of elders, but the chiefs themselves were not immune to assassination, and the whole system in the Loyalty group was more feudalistic and marked by violence.[8] Melanesian society, on the other hand, partook more of the nature of an agrarian democracy in which the exercise of power was subject to a system of checks and balances, and its primary goal was to attain social harmony and equilibrium.[9] Authority was vested in those to whom age was believed to have brought wisdom, and their decisions were reached ponderously after long discussions that perforce terminated in unanimity. The social order was indeed hierarchized and the individual's conduct minutely regulated, but it was not rigid or inflexible. Gods were vaguely believed to possess certain powers, but they were not worshipped as supernatural beings, and in any case were far less important than were the ancestors and totems. Hostile forces could be propitiated by sorcerers, whose magical formulas could be invoked to ward off diseases and disasters. All phenomena partook of the same essence, man merged with nature,

---

[7] See p. 234.
[8] Brou, "La Société Traditionelle," p. 9.
[9] *Ibid.*, p. 13.

and there was no clearcut demarcation between the visible and invisible worlds, or between life and death.[10]

The credit for discovering New Caledonia and its adjacent islands has been disputed between partisans of the French navigator, Count Louis-Antoine de Bougainville, and those of the English Captain James Cook. However, it was the latter who, in 1774, was the first to land on the Grande Terre, which he found so resembled his native Scotland that he gave it the name of New Caledonia. Cook only visited the site of what is now Balade and sailed down the east coast as far as the Isle of Pines, but the narrative of his voyage was the first valid account of the area brought to the Western world. He reported so favorably on the Grande Terre that in 1785 Louis XVI ordered Jean-François de Galaup, Count de La Pérouse, to explore the island and assess its economic potential, but that explorer was lost at sea and it is not known whether he ever reached New Caledonia.[11] So enthusiastic did the French public become over such exploits that not even the revolution in 1789 caused it to lose interest in the fate of La Pérouse's expedition, and in 1791 the constituent assembly sent Antoine de Bruni d'Entrecasteaux to search for him. In 1792–1793, d'Entrecasteaux explored the west coast of the Grande Terre and discovered the Belêp archipelago and the two islands he named Huon and Surprise. Like Cook, he landed at Balade, where his impression of the natives was far less favorable than that of his famous predecessor. As D'Entrecasteaux was unable to shed any light on the fate of La Pérouse, still another French navigator, Dumont d'Urville, set out in 1826 at the head of a second search party. D'Urville's party found traces of La Pérouse's wrecked ship, and also reconnoitered the Loyalty Islands.

In the meantime, English explorers were not idle in that part of the Pacific, especially after Port Jackson (Sydney) was founded in 1788. Starting from bases in Australia in the late eighteenth and early nineteenth centuries, British sea captains led a series of missions in the region of New Caledonia, not only to discover and chart the land areas but also to assess their commercial possibilities. It was not until 1841, however, that sandalwood was found growing in New Caledonia

[10] Faivre, Poirier, and Routhier, pp. 250–252.
[11] Guerchy, J. de, "La Découverte et l'Histoire de la Nouvelle-Calédonie."

and on the Isle of Pines, and at about the same time, the abundance of *bêches de mer* (sea cucumbers) in nearby waters aroused the interest of Chinese traders. Increasingly, the Grande Terre and its islands became the object of intense international competition, and permanent fishing and trading posts were established along the coasts despite the resistance of the native inhabitants in some areas.

By the mid-nineteenth century, the merchants, adventurers, and crews of whaling ships frequenting the islands of the southwest Pacific were joined by more permanent groups of Westerners—the Christian missionaries. Protestants of the London Missionary Society (L.M.S.), operating out of Tahiti, gradually established themselves in the more westerly islands. By 1840 they had reached the New Caledonia area, bringing with them some of the catechists they had trained in Samoa and Rarotonga to aid them in their task of evangelization. After some early failures, they managed to gain a foothold on Lifou, the largest of the Loyalty Islands. As elsewhere in the Pacific, the French Catholic missionaries lagged behind the L.M.S., but in the region of New Caledonia they arrived only three years later. Characteristically, too, the first five Marist Fathers were brought to the Grande Terre in a French warship, whose captain profited by this opportunity to make treaties with some local chiefs whereby they recognized the sovereignty of France.

Although the Catholic missionaries did not encounter Protestant competition on the Grande Terre, the government of Louis-Philippe yielded in 1845 to pressure from London and withdrew France's claim to that island. Nevertheless, the French missionaries remained at Balade and installed a second station at Pouébo, but in both places they suffered from isolation and even more from attacks by the Kanakas,[12] who eventually murdered one of them. Then 250 shipwrecked sailors, washed up on the shores of the Grande Terre, not only worsened relations with the Kanakas, but brought with them maladies that wiped out about one-third of the local population. The Marist Fathers were blamed for this disaster and in 1847 they had to abandon the Grande Terre and move to the Isle of Pines, all of whose inhabitants they soon Christianized. It was not until 6 years later that a mission station was reestablished at Balade.

1853 was also the year in which France, through a remarkable combination of motives, annexed both the Grande Terre and the Isle

[12] At that time, the name Kanaka was applied indiscriminately by Westerners to all the dark-skinned islanders of the western Pacific.

of Pines. Rivalry with Great Britain in empire-building in the Pacific islands, as in Asia and Africa, undoubtedly prompted the French seizure. The annexation of the Grande Terre was the more gratifying to France in that it was accomplished almost within eyeshot of the captain of a British warship, who was so chagrined that he later committed suicide.[13] A minor aim of the annexation was to restore French prestige by punishing the Kanakas who, in 1850, had murdered and eaten a number of French sailors. A more cogent reason for taking possession of the Grande Terre was the example provided by Britain's action in setting up a penal colony in Australia. New Caledonia's isolation and its climate, which was far better than that of Guyane, were thought to be highly suitable for an analogous experiment there, and on September 24, 1853, the French flag was raised at Balade and five days later on the Isle of Pines. The chiefs of both places were persuaded to sign new treaties with France, which they probably did not understand and which greatly reduced their powers. In 1854, Captain Louis Tardy de Montravel was assigned to take charge of the territory, but he was placed under the authority of the French naval governor at Papeete. This arrangement, however, lasted only until 1860, when New Caledonia and its dependencies became a separate French colony. In the interval, De Montravel moved his capital from Balade to a more protected harbor in the extreme southwest, which he called Port-de-France. Its name was so easily confused with that of Martinique's capital, Fort-de-France, that within 2 years it reverted to the original one of Nouméa, derived from nearby Nou Island, which provided it with a sheltered anchorage.

THE NAVAL GOVERNMENT AND
THE PENITENTIARY REGIME

All of the French dependencies in the Pacific area were governed by naval officers during the latter half of the nineteenth century, and for New Caledonia a military regime was considered highly suitable because it was scheduled to become a penal colony. One of the outstanding naval governors was Rear Admiral Charles Guillain (1862–1870), during whose incumbency the first convicts arrived in New Caledonia, the Loyalty Islands were annexed, the judicial and administrative framework of the colony was created, the town of Nouméa took shape, and white settlers were encouraged to come to the Grande

[13] Oliver, D. L., *The Pacific Islands*, p. 325.

Terre, where they were granted land concessions. Attracted first by New Caledonia's climate and verdure and then by the discovery of gold there in 1863, European and British immigrants came to the Grande Terre from many parts of the Pacific area to farm, rear animals, and mine. (Even a utopian communal colony was organized at Yaté in 1864, but it failed within two years despite the governor's support.)

From the colony's earliest years, the Kanakas were extremely hostile to both the administration and the settlers. Guillain had to repress revolts in such widely dispersed places as Wagap, Pouébo, Bourail, and Lifou, and in order to assure the security of settlers isolated in the bush he established military posts in the interior. The most serious uprisings occurred on the west coast, but there were also rebels in the Loyalty Islands and at Hienghène, whose actions were blamed, at the time, on English machinations. A notable exception to this widespread hostility was the docile attitude of the Canala tribes, which not only accepted without protest the installing of a military post but later became invaluable allies of the French. Catholic missions not being immune to the Kanakas' attacks, Christian converts were moved away from the most vulnerable places and concentrated at Conception, in the immediate vicinity of Nouméa, where they were relatively safe. As the number of agricultural settlements expanded, so did the penitentiary regime, and the missionaries following in their wake established stations at La Foa, Bourail, and Thio.[14]

In May 1864, the first convoy of 248 convicts disembarked on Nou Island.[15] Under the control of military officers, the convicts reclaimed land on which to build Nouméa and later strung telegraph wires, constructed roads, and worked in forestry and mining enterprises. In 1866, Governor Guillain decided to permit well-behaved convicts to work under contract for individual settlers, and later he granted the most exemplary of them 5 hectares of land to farm. The progressive liberalization of their harsh penal regime, including the abolition of corporal punishment, proved to be generally disappointing. The wide dispersal of convicts among the civilian population led to such an

[14] Deschamps and Guiart, *Tahiti—Nouvelle-Calédonie—Nouvelles-Hébrides*, p. 126.

[15] A few years earlier, that island's owner, an enterprising and highly successful English trader named James Paddon, had been persuaded to exchange it for a 4,000-hectare concession at Païta, on condition that he could bring there settlers of his choice, See O'Reilly, P., *Calédoniens: Répertoire Bio-bibliographique de la Nouvelle-Calédonie*, pp. 199–201.

increase in crime throughout the island that their use as domestic servants was soon forbidden. Curbs were placed on their freedom of movement, and in 1885, they were formally denied all hope of eventual repatriation to France.

Of quite different caliber were the political deportees who began arriving in the colony in 1872. Although they included a small contingent of Arab rebels from Algeria, the great majority were French supporters of the Paris Commune of 1871. Concentrated on the Isle of Pines and at Duclos peninsula, the *communards* were not required to perform forced labor but could hire out their services for pay. Because many of them were skilled workers, they were much in demand, and they were responsible for the remarkable development of the Isle of Pines.[16] Among those who left a permanent imprint on the Grande Terre was the left-wing patriot and schoolteacher, Louise Michel, whose active interest in native culture and compassion for the Kanakas became legendary. When she reluctantly left New Caledonia in 1881, after all the political deportees except the Algerians were amnestied, she was escorted to the ship by hundreds of weeping Kanakas whom she had taught and cared for.[17]

Some 20,000 convicts were sent to New Caledonia during its 30 years as a penal colony, and to them the islands owe many useful public works. Yet the penitentiary regime's attempts to develop the Grande Terre's economy through agriculture and animal husbandry were failures, especially in the light of the vast sums expended. Much money was wasted on abortive efforts to grow silkworms, cultivate sugarcane, and manufacture rum. Its experiments in allotting small agricultural concessions to paroled convicts produced only mediocre results, for they did not try to grow crops for export but only those, such as corn and beans, for their own use.[18] Probably the only element in New Caledonia to whom the convicts' enforced presence was of immediate benefit were the settlers, whom they provided with abundant and cheap labor. Yet, in the long run, this had unfortunate psychological effects on the island's white population, for the settlers thereby acquired a disdain for manual labor and came to think of themselves as landed gentry rather than as peasants. After the last group of convicts reached New Caledonia in 1897, the supply of cheap labor soon came to an end, with the result that the settlers' liv-

[16] Kling, G., "Aperçu Historique," pp. 24–25.
[17] O'Reilly, *Calédoniens*, p. 181.
[18] *L'Océanie Française*, July 1911.

ing standards deteriorated. The prisoners still under detention gradually died off, and the great majority, who were freed and who became small farmers, settled permanently on the island and married local girls. Within a few generations their children became indistinguishable from the rest of the white population.

Aside from the millions of francs which the convicts' transportation, administration, and surveillance cost the French government, their presence gave New Caledonia an evil reputation that discouraged potential colonists from coming to the colony. It was the discovery there of gold and, in 1875, of nickel that caused an influx of Europeans and Asian laborers, whose mining activities did much to develop the economy. At the same time, the arrival of more alien intruders aggravated the unrest long evident among the Kanakas, especially after the administration began resettling the tribes in restricted areas in order to give their land to newcomers.

THE KANAKA REVOLT OF 1878–1879

The immediate cause of the Kanaka revolt, which broke out in mid-1878, was the famine that followed an exceptionally long drought, but obviously its underlying causes were of far greater significance. Among these were the expropriation of tribal land both for the settlers and for the agricultural colonies created by the penitentiary regime, the compulsory labor repeatedly required of the tribesmen living near large villages, the removal of sacred objects from the Kanaka burial grounds, the administration's neglect of the tribes' needs and welfare as well as the abuses committed by its functionaries, and the wanton destruction of native crops and irrigation works by the settlers' free-roaming cattle.[19]

On June 19, 1878, word reached Nouméa that a freed convict living on a farm 80 kilometers from the capital, along with his native wife and two children, had been killed, but as his death was ascribed to motives of personal revenge on the part of a local chief, it aroused little concern. This attitude, however, changed abruptly when it was learned a week later that 17 settlers and the entire garrison of La Foa had been massacred, as well as 84 other whites at various places on the west coast and in the villages of the southeast. Military posts were the first to be attacked, then isolated settlers and their families were

---

[19] *La Nouvelle-Calédonie*, Oct. 23, 1879, cited by W. G. Burchett in his detailed account of the revolt, *Pacific Treasure Island*, p. 129.

killed, either by clubbing or with stolen firearms, and in most cases their bodies were mutilated. Telegraphic communications with the interior were cut, but the refugees who began flocking into Nouméa brought tales of atrocities that spread near-panic among the residents of the capital.

The governor, Admiral Jean Olry, quickly organized the town's defense and sent punitive expeditions against the rebels. To supplement the 2,600 troops then stationed in the colony, he called for reinforcements from Indochina and armed not only the settlers but also some of the freed convicts, a few of the Arab deportees, and the friendly tribes of Canala and Houaïlou.[20] Nevertheless, the revolt continued to spread in every direction—to the north as far as Poya and southward to within 12 kilometers of Nouméa itself. On September 1, however, the tide turned after the mastermind of the rebellion, Ataï, chief of the Uaraï tribe near Fonwhary, was ambushed and killed, along with his son and sorcerer. Without his leadership the revolt degenerated into guerrilla warfare, but it was not until April 1879 that the settlers dared to return to their homes, and not until June 3 that the rebellion was officially declared to have ended.

The casualties of the revolt, so far as the white element of the population was concerned, came to 200 dead and 19 wounded, not to mention the destruction of buildings, machinery, and crops that represented the labor of many years. Losses on the Kanaka side have never been accurately counted (and indeed the official inquiry into the revolt was pigeonholed in Paris), but there is no doubt that the repression was as brutal as the revolt itself. That the Kanakas were capable of systematically organizing a large-scale uprising, and that white men—whether they were settlers or former convicts—could make common cause in an emergency, were perhaps the most salutary lessons learned from this disastrous rebellion. Unfortunately, it did not deflect the administration from its policy of confining the Kanakas to inadequate land reservations and of granting large concessions to settlers without respect for the natives' most elementary rights. The revolt unquestionably retarded New Caledonia's economic development by many years, not only as a result of the material damage done but also because it reinforced the undesirable reputation that the island had acquired from its years as a penal colony.

[20] Guerchy, "La Découverte"; Burchett, *Pacific Treasure Island*, p. 127.

THE NICKEL RUSH

Although the existence of deposits of gold, cobalt, chromite, copper, and nickel had been known throughout the preceding decade, it was not until the mid-1870s that they began to arouse widespread interest. The mining rush to New Caledonia started in 1873, when rich veins of copper ore were discovered in the Balade region by John Higginson, who had come to Nouméa from Australia fourteen years before. Like his compatriot, James Paddon, for whom he worked briefly, Higginson began his spectacular career modestly. In succession, and successfully, he tried his hand at trading, shipping, agriculture, and mining, profiting in all these ventures by the availability of cheap penal labor.[21] His strongest claim to renown, however, was his early recognition of the potential industrial value of the island's nickel resources, and his fortune came from his promotion of the use of the metal in Europe.[22] In 1876, shortly after he had become a naturalized French citizen, he founded the Société Le Nickel, and four years later he enlisted support for it from the Rothschild Bank, which laid the foundation of the company's present prosperity. Very few others were as fortunate or as farsighted as this "king of nickel," and the mining fever that swept over New Caledonia in the last years of the nineteenth century left bankruptcies and unemployment in its wake. The discovery of nickel in Canada, in 1892, was largely responsible for this crisis, and by 1900 only about one-third of the many mines that had been opened during the boom years were still operating. Among the companies that survived, however, French interests had largely replaced those of the British and Australians, who had theretofore dominated the island's mining industry.[23]

THE GOVERNORSHIP OF PAUL FEILLET, 1894–1902

Although the nickel boom had somewhat offset the undesirable reputation that New Caledonia had gained as a penal colony and the scene of violent native unrest, the island was still grossly underpopulated, for many of the miners and all the military personnel were only transients there. Moreover, beginning in 1901, the budget was sadly in

21 *Pacific Islands Monthly*, November 1949.
22 O'Reilly, *Calédoniens*, pp. 120–121.
23 Kling, "Aperçu Historique," p. 25.

arrears, largely because of the deficits incurred by the penitentiary regime and the cost of suppressing the Kanaka revolt. After peace was restored, and to effect economies, the Paris authorities decided to install civilian administrators in place of the naval officers who had been governing the colony. In 1894, Paul Feillet became the first civil governor of New Caledonia and its dependencies.

Feillet's academic training was in the field of law, and his previous colonial service had been in Guadeloupe and St. Pierre-et-Miquelon. During his nine years as governor of New Caledonia, he pursued a policy that is still the subject of controversy but one that left an indelible imprint on the colony's history. His first step was to persuade the Paris government to "turn off the spigot of dirty water that had been flowing into the colony," by ceasing to send convicts there.[24] He then sought to bring in, as permanent colonists, French peasants possessing a capital of 5,000 francs or more and willing to settle in the island as farmers. By an active propaganda campaign in France and by offering potential settlers 25 hectares of freehold land, he induced 525 French families to emigrate to New Caledonia between 1895 and 1902. Of these, 300 stayed on, and they multiplied so rapidly that the free colonists soon outnumbered the convict element. It is largely to them that New Caledonia owes its agricultural development, notably of coffee, and many of today's flourishing villages and towns were founded by them as farming settlements.[25]

Not all of Feillet's policies were beneficial, and indeed some of them proved to be positively harmful. To encourage his colonists, increasingly deprived of convict labor, Feillet promoted the immigration of Asians as indentured workers for them and for the mining companies,[26] and to provide them with land, Feillet continued his predecessor's policy of resettling the Kanakas on reservations—a process that was completed by 1900. In so doing, he aroused the opposition of the Catholic missions, which protested against dispossessing the Kanakas of many of their tribal lands, and also of the penitentiary authorities and large concessionaires whose domains he likewise pared down.

To further his policy of promoting "rural democracy" and to provide a counterpoise for the municipal government installed in Nou-

---

[24] O'Reilly, *Calédoniens*, p. 88.

[25] *L'Océanie Française*, March–April 1928.

[26] During his governorship, 300 Indians, 400 Javanese, and 550 Tonkinese were brought to the colony.

méa in 1879, Feillet created a general council in 1885. Its members were to be elected by all the island's male French citizens, and that same year, he established 9 rural or "mixed" communes, with councils similarly elected.[27] Ironically enough it was in the general council, which owed its existence to Feillet, that the governor was most severely criticized. His opponents used it as a forum in which to denounce his policies, and their views were echoed and even embellished in the Nouméa press of that period. Feillet's "obstinate, authoritarian, and sardonic" character did not contribute to his popularity, for the governor did not hesitate to dissolve the elected bodies he had created or to transfer functionaries whom he regarded as obstructionists.[28] By and large, however, he was supported by the government in France and by the rural community in New Caledonia, whose interests he favored vis-à-vis those of Nouméa and big business.

THE EARLY TWENTIETH CENTURY AND WORLD WAR I

The period that followed Feillet's long proconsulship and ended with the outbreak of World War I was marked by instability in the top administrative echelons, mounting antagonism between the general council and the governor, a revival of the nickel industry, the disintegration of Kanaka society, and the implantation of Protestantism in New Caledonia. The basis of the Grande Terre's economy was still small-scale farming, increasingly supplemented by large-scale animal husbandry, and although the nickel industry surmounted its boom-and-bust cycle after it began using new techniques in 1911, mining was not yet the colony's predominant occupation.

Between 1902 and 1914, New Caledonia had no fewer than 10 governors, and their rapid turnover enabled the general councilors, already restive under Feillet's dictatorial rule, to gain more independence than before. They used to the limit their control over the budget's optional expenditures, and in 1911 refused to approve the budget submitted by the governor because he had included in it an item for which they had not given formal approval.[29] All French colonial governors of that period held very wide powers, but in New Caledonia they were dealing not with native subjects but with French citizens determined to assert their rights. In his relations with their

[27] See pp. 255, 330–331.
[28] O'Reilly, *Calédoniens*, p. 88.
[29] *L'Océanie Française*, March 1913.

French poster protesting nuclear-arms testing in Polynesia

Chinese school, Papeete

J.-B. Céran-Jérusalémy

The tomb of King Pomare V,
near Papeete

Alfred Poroi, long-time mayor
of Papeete

Public transport in Papeete

Copra-drying platform,
island of Moorea

Waterfront buildings, Papeete

A church, under repair, on the Isle
of Pines, New Caledonia; the trees
behind it are *pins colonnaires*

One of the many ferries used to cross
New Caledonia's east-coast rivers

Headquarters of the South Pacific
Commission, Nouméa

Village chief,
east coast of New Caledonia

Michel Kauma — an outstanding
Melanesian politician — and his wife

Coffee-drying platform,
New Caledonia

DOCUMENTATION FRANÇAISE

Processing of nacre,
Tahiti

Cook's Bay, Moorea

elected representatives in the general council, the governor had various weapons at his disposal. He succeeded in persuading Paris to reduce the number of councilors, refused to convene that body for a long period, and then downgraded its importance by sending a civil servant in his place to open its session.[30]

In the course of such petty trials of strength, the councilors sometimes made constructive proposals. Most of these derived from the program of the Comité Républicain, the one organized party at that time, whose platform had not varied since the party was founded at the turn of the century. Among the most important of its desiderata were the development of public works, especially means of communication, more doctors and schools for French children, the encouragement of white immigration, and the transfer to settlers of the land held by the penitentiary regime.[31] Metropolitan civil servants were a main target of the councilors' attacks, and the charge was made that they either stayed in their offices at Nouméa or inspected only the coastal settlements which were easily accessible by boat.[32] As for the Kanakas, the general council evinced interest in their health and welfare only insofar as their usefulness as laborers was affected.

In its relations with the Kanakas, the administration was concerned primarily with maintaining order, collecting the head tax, and requisitioning laborers for public works. On the assumption that the Kanakas were a dying people, it left them largely to their own devices in the reservations. Charles Brunet, New Caledonia's last governor before World War I, publicly acknowledged that the government had no native policy, and because of this neglect the authority of the chiefs was shrinking, the influence of sorcerers was increasing, and the traditional tribal society was generally disintegrating.[33] The only Europeans actively concerned with the Kanakas' welfare at that time were the Christian missionaries.

For many years, because of the French administration's suspicion of English Protestant missionary activity in the Loyalty Islands, the Grande Terre remained an almost impenetrable preserve for the Catholic mission. By the end of the nineteenth century, the Marist Fathers had established a network of stations along the coasts, each surrounded by a village inhabited by their converts, but in the in-

[30] *Ibid.*, October 1911.
[31] *Ibid.*, April 1912.
[32] Froment-Guieysse, G., "La Nouvelle-Calédonie."
[33] Speech to the general council, quoted in *L'Océanie Française*, February 1913.

terior, paganism continued to be virtually untouched.[34] For various reasons—including a widespread belief that some Catholic Kanakas were among the rebels in 1878, the settlers' conviction that converts were less docile laborers than the pagans, and the prevailing anti-clerical attitude of many officials—the Marist missionaries did not enlarge the radius of their influence. They could not protect the tribal lands of their congregations from expropriation, and thus were unable to offer practical advantages that might have led to additional conversions. In any case, the administration's immobility in regard to the Kanakas was almost matched by that of the Catholic missionaries, so that a void was created which exposed a large portion of the native population to Protestant evangelism.

Despite the pledge of Napoleon III in 1868 that Protestants would have the same religious freedom in New Caledonia as in France, the local administration succeeded in restricting the L.M.S. missionaries to the Loyalty Islands. To be sure, the age-old contacts between those islands and the Grande Terre enabled some of their Protestant converts to slip over to New Caledonia from their beachhead in Maré. Of these Loyalty Island evangelists (called *natas* in New Caledonia), the most effective was Malthias, or Mathaia, who traveled along the east coast by dugout and on foot, preaching the gospel. Although he was expelled several times by the administration, Malthias kept returning to the Grande Terre and even succeeded in bringing with him other *natas* as aides. Their success among the Kanakas was immediate, not only because they were harassed by a repressive administration and opposed by the settlers, but also because they conferred positive benefits on their converts. Among their accomplishments, the *natas* taught the Kanakas reading and writing and the keeping of accounts, and forbade them to drink alcoholic beverages, with which they were being liberally supplied by unscrupulous traders. Not only did the *natas* help to arrest the tribes' physical degeneration, but they were the first to give a frustrated, isolated, and hopeless people some reason for living. In time, the authorities came to regard their efforts with favor, for the *natas* made the Kanakas healthier, easier to police, and more receptive to European ideas.[35] At long last, therefore, the French Protestant missionaries were permitted to install themselves on the Grande Terre, and in 1902 the Paris Société des Missions

[34] Guiart, J., in "Hommage à Maurice Leenhardt," p. 53.
[35] *Ibid.*, p. 59.

Evangéliques sent Maurice Leenhardt to the colony—a man who was destined to become New Caledonia's greatest scholar, preacher, and teacher.

Leenhardt could hardly have been greeted with less warmth and encouragement by the local white community. In "welcoming" him to Nouméa, its mayor asked him what he thought he could do there, "for in 10 years there will be no more Kanakas." Leenhardt took up the challenge and made his headquarters at Do Neva, near Houaïlou, which during his 24 years in the island became the center of Protestant influence throughout the Grande Terre. He immersed himself in the study of Kanaka languages and society, to which he applied modern techniques of scholarship, and organized the Protestant church around the nucleus formed by the *natas*, training native preachers to carry out their work of regenerating the tribes. Through his own research and writings, Leenhardt contributed to an understanding of Kanaka society, and he strove to persuade the administration and the settlers that their interests and those of the tribesmen coincided, for all could aid in the island's development. Perhaps the highest tribute paid to Leenhardt was that his work led to a revival of Catholic missionary activities and the emulation of his methods. In his erudition and humanism, Leenhardt resembled Charles Vernier, his contemporary Protestant colleague in Tahiti, and like him he eventually became a widely respected professor in Paris. Also like another learned and famous Protestant missionary of Alsatian origin, Albert Schweitzer, Leenhardt was persecuted during World War I for alleged pro-German sympathies.

The charge brought against both men and the demand for their expulsion were not solely the result of wartime hysteria. They derived also from a belief widely held in French colonial milieux of the time that Protestantism was fundamentally unpatriotic, in that it was associated with "Anglo-Saxon" influences and encouraged the natives' resistance to legally constituted authority. Although some anticlerical suspicion also was directed against the Catholic missionaries, it was Protestantism in general and Leenhardt in particular that were the main targets attacked in New Caledonia, chiefly because he was so generally regarded by the Kanakas as their principal protector.

The tribal revolt of 1917, which broke out in the north and northwest of the Grande Terre, was smaller and less bloody than that of 1878. According to the official record, there were 11 white victims and no more than 200 rebels killed, and it ended after its main ring-leader, Chief Noël of Koné, was murdered.[36] This revolt was pro-voked mainly by the widespread damage done to native crops by the ever-larger cattle herds of the ranchers, and to a lesser extent by the "imprudence" of military recruiters among the Kanakas,[37] to whom the authorities' preoccupation with the war in Europe seemed to offer a propitious moment to rebel. As it evolved, this uprising developed socioreligious overtones that led to a recrudescence of paganism, for which some held Maurice Leenhardt responsible. His defenders con-tended that he had in fact warned Governor Jules Repiquet several weeks before the rebellion began that the tribes were becoming agi-tated, and later he and his disciples toured the mountainous northern area trying to persuade the rebels to lay down their arms.[38] Further-more, in 1915, Leenhardt himself had urged the Kanakas to volunteer for military service, and it was at his instigation that some influential chiefs convinced their people that the war concerned them and was not exclusively a distant conflict between white men. Leenhardt has left a vivid account of the way in which the hesitations and reluctance of one tribe were overcome:

The old chief Mindia gathered his people together, stood on a tree stump and harangued them in the old style, using the traditional language. He called out the names of the clans and recalled their warlike deeds. His words struck a responsive chord in the Melanesian heart . . . and it was at that moment that the Pacific Battalion—which until then had existed in name only—was born.[39]

Later, Leenhardt's patriotic work during the war was recognized and he was indirectly exonerated from any responsibility for the re-volt. His continuing efforts to see that justice was done to the Kanaka rebels undoubtedly mitigated the severity of their punishment. Of the 75 Kanakas accused of participation in the revolt, 5 were sentenced to death, 45 to forced labor, 5 to varying prison terms, and the rest were acquitted.[40] That the uprising was relatively brief was ascribed by most observers to Governor Repiquet's energetic leadership and his

[36] The chief was reportedly ambushed by an Arab, who claimed the large re-ward offered by the government, and his head was displayed on a main highway as a warning to his followers. See *L'Océanie Française,* August–October 1917; *Pacific Islands Monthly,* August 1953.

[37] *L'Océanie Française,* September–December 1919.

[38] Guiart in "Hommage à Maurice Leenhardt," p. 26.

[39] "Les Chefferies Océaniennes," Académie des Sciences Coloniales, *Comptes Rendus des Séances,* Dec. 5, 1941.

[40] *L'Océanie Française,* September–December 1919.

effective use of the few troops at his disposal. The end of the revolt coincided with that of hostilities in Europe.

Although New Caledonia was spared bombardment, unlike Papeete, the possibility that it might have to withstand a German assault created tension among the French population. No such assault occurred, but World War I did entail isolation and some hardships for the colony, including a heavy loss of manpower. Of New Caledonia's population, estimated at about 50,000 at that time, a total of 2,170 men (1,036 Europeans and 1,134 Kanakas) were sent to the Western front between 1915 and 1918. One-fourth of them (162 Europeans and 374 Kanakas) died during the hostilities, a majority of the Kanaka casualties (207) being attributable to disease rather than to death on the battlefield.[41] The Caledonian French, too, suffered from the cold climate of France, and also from the chilly reception they initially received there. They found most of the Metropolitan French so ignorant of geography in general and of their colonies in particular that the Caledonians were regarded not as patriotic citizens volunteering for the defense of their fatherland but as "creole" conscripts.[42] Relations gradually improved as their identity became better established, and they adjusted far more readily than did the Kanakas to the difficult conditions of life in wartime France. Both ethnic groups served in all branches of the French armed forces, but mainly in the Pacific Battalion, in which the contingents sent from New Caledonia and the E.F.O. were combined and which was cited for bravery under fire in 1918.

[41] *Ibid.*, July–September 1921.
[42] *Ibid.*, August 1916.

20

The Interwar Period

On May 2, 1924, Governor Henri d'Arboussier, recently arrived from an African post,[1] opened the general council's spring session with a speech remarkable for its candor and for its freedom from the usual official banalities. For the past 2 years, he said, New Caledonia had been in the throes of increasing financial difficulties: in the near future it could not count on the payment for war damages to help balance its budget, and the year would probably end with a deficit of more than a million francs. To pay for "indispensable" increases in the salaries of civil servants and to avoid "imminent bankruptcy," he proposed new taxation and an increase in the rates of existing taxes. The tax burden in the colony—only 250 francs per capita annually— he went on to say, was light compared with that of France. He scolded the general councilors for failing to comprehend the gravity of the situation and for insisting that the deficit could be met simply by compressing administrative expenditures. In ending his speech, he reminded them that France had repeatedly warned that it would neither grant a subsidy nor authorize a loan to meet chronic deficits in the colony's operating budget, and that to qualify for French financial aid, New Caledonia must discharge its past indebtedness.

Without even discussing d'Arboussier's strongly worded appeal, the general council, two weeks later, almost unanimously passed a resolution which it asked the governor to transmit to the Minister of Colonies. The resolution concerned exclusively the Metropolitan functionaries serving in New Caledonia, and proposed ways to cut down their cost to the local budget. The councilors added that they were asking no subsidy from the Metropole but only that France not impose on New Caledonia civil servants it neither wanted nor needed, as well as other expenditures about which they had not been con-

[1] Gabriel d'Arboussier, the governor's son by a Soudanese wife, attended school and did his military service in New Caledonia, and later became an outstanding politician in French-speaking Black Africa.

sulted. They would take no action regarding the governor's tax proposal until they had learned the minister's reaction to their resolution. In due course they received from the Minister of Colonies a reply couched in conciliatory but evasive terms. He regretted the stand taken by the general council, with which the French government wanted to "work harmoniously," and hoped that its members would reconsider their position. The general councilors, meeting again in extraordinary session, found the minister's reply "unsatisfactory" and maintained their refusal to vote the tax increases requested. The French government, this time, proved equally intransigent, and on August 10 issued a decree drastically reorganizing the general council by reducing the powers and number of its members and revising the mode of electing them.

On the same day that this decree was published, a strong letter of protest was sent to the Minister of Colonies by Louis Archimbaud, New Caledonia's representative on the Conseil Supérieur des Colonies, chairman of the Chamber of Deputies' finance committee, and owner-manager of *La Dépêche Coloniale*. He reminded the minister that the government itself had made unfulfilled promises to New Caledonia and at times had deliberately undermined the general council's legitimate powers. He also pled for greater autonomy for the colony, not only out of justice to its French citizens but to obviate criticism of France by the "Anglo-Saxons, who prize self-government highly" for colonial peoples.[2]

The issues involved in the foregoing episode merit detailed study, for it was a textbook case illustrating the most significant aspects of the relations between France and New Caledonia throughout the interwar period.

CIVIL SERVANTS AND GOVERNORS

In 1877 there were more military than civilian administrators in New Caledonia, but that situation was reversed after Governor Feillet's appointment in 1884. The increase in the number of Metropolitan civil servants there during the economic depression of the early 1920s weighed heavily on the colony's budget. In their resolution of May 5, 1924, the general councilors asked that France suppress "useless" administrative posts, require its civil servants to remain in New Caledonia for a minimum of five years without taking home leave, and

[2] *L'Océanie Française,* August–September 1924.

pressure the Messageries Maritimes into reducing the price of their transport between France and the colony. The Paris authorities heeded none of these pleas, and no change was made in the government's policy until the depression of the early 1930s forced a reduction in the number and emoluments of its functionaries serving overseas.

Instability characterized the whole colonial service, including its top echelons. In New Caledonia, according to one critic,[3] the "waltz of the governors" was accelerated because "the general council so often made life intolerable for all of them." Throughout the interwar period, New Caledonia had about a dozen governors, each of whom, with two exceptions, remained there for a year or so at most. The first of these exceptions was Governor Joseph Guyon (1925–1932), who ranked with Guillain and Feillet as an outstanding governor. Guyon took up his post at an exceptionally difficult moment, but soon won widespread popularity and respect. His tact and genuine concern for the welfare of both the settlers and the Kanakas contrasted sharply with the attitude of his predecessor, d'Arboussier. During his incumbency the first public-works program for the colony was undertaken, the labor force increased considerably and became more stabilized, and the foundations of a native policy were laid. It was Guyon who induced France to restore the powers of the general council in 1927, and even before that he treated its members with such deference and consideration that he won their consent even to a pay rise for civil servants. To be sure, Guyon's governorship coincided with a period of unprecedented prosperity for the colony, and he also had the good fortune to leave it just when the lean depression years were beginning.

Guyon's successor, Governor Siadous (1933–1936), had to cope with the shrinkage of New Caledonia's revenues and also with renewed complaints from the general council concerning the number of Metropolitan functionaries serving in the colony. As of 1933, there were 443 civil servants, of whom 68 were Metropolitan Frenchmen. Together with those locally recruited, they absorbed nearly half of the budget expenditures. The councilors complained that this meant an average of one functionary per 110 residents, for in such calculations they counted only the white population and never took into consideration the existence and needs of the colony's 30,000 or so Kanakas.[4] Late in 1932, when France somewhat grudgingly granted

---

[3] See M. Noroit, *Niaouli, la Plaie Calédonienne*, p. 38.
[4] *L'Océanie Française*, January–February 1933.

a subsidy to balance the colony's budget, the councilors expressed the fear that it might be used solely to maintain Metropolitan officials in their posts.[5] In view of New Caledonia's financial plight in 1933, as well as Siadous' pleas, the French government first reduced the special privileges of those functionaries and then their number and pay, and eventually promised that when replacements became indispensable, priority would be given to local-born candidates. Nevertheless, even after the colony's financial problems became less acute in the middle and late years of the decade, the councilors (supported by the Nouméa press) continued to complain of "gross administrative irresponsibility" and to charge that its officials ignored the public interests that they were supposed to serve.[6] On the eve of World War II, the general council even refused to raise the pay of the lowest category of locally recruited civil servants.[7]

THE MUNICIPALITIES AND THE GENERAL COUNCIL

Because of New Caledonia's sizeable French population, elective local-government institutions were established there much earlier than in most of France's other colonies. In chronological order, Nouméa's municipality was the first such body to be created in the island, and it owed its birth on October 3, 1874 to an increase in the capital's citizenry. On March 8, 1879, Nouméa became a full commune, with a mayor and municipal commissioners elected by universal male suffrage but with its police force still under the governor's control. That same year, nine rural communes were also created, with elected commissioners but with mayors appointed by the colonial administration. This experiment was considered so successful that on April 7, 1888, fifteen more rural communes were formed in different parts of the Grande Terre.

Municipal elections were usually quite lively, chiefly because they became popularity contests between men personally well known to their constituents. In Nouméa, they sometimes degenerated into sharp conflicts between the governor and candidates for the post of mayor, who had divergent views as to what public works should be undertaken in the capital and what revenues the municipality should be allotted from the colony's budget. The latter issue was primordial,

---

[5] *Ibid.*, July–August 1932.
[6] *La France Australe*, Nov. 30, 1936.
[7] *L'Océanie Française*, January–February 1938.

for it was a commune's financial situation that determined its ability to raise loans, and it had little taxing authority of its own. When budget deficits occurred, as they did in all of the communes during the depression years of the early 1930s, the influence of the municipalities declined sharply. On the other hand, when their revenues prospered, as happened on the eve of World War II, the number of municipal commissioners was increased, as were their powers and responsibilities. In 1938, the membership of Nouméa's commission was increased from 15 to 27, and at the same time it was required to assume financial responsibility for the capital's police force and for a fourth of its expenditures on primary education. Nouméa held nearly half of New Caledonia's total electorate, and its candidates for public office included more business and professional men than did those of all the other municipalities combined.

Eleven years after Nouméa acquired a municipal commission, the general council was installed on an experimental basis, but within a few years it, too, was given a permanent statute. Initially, its 16 members were elected by universal male suffrage from the circumscriptions into which the Grande Terre was divided. Their term of office was six years, and half their number were to be replaced by elections held every 3 years. New Caledonia's general council was modeled on similar departmental bodies in France, and in terms of the French empire, its powers resembled those of Senegal's colonial council. It had control over property belonging to the territory, and it could legislate on the rates, assessment, and method of collecting local taxes, subject to approval by the Council of State in Paris. By far the most important power it exercised was that over the optional—as opposed to the obligatory—expenditures included in the colonial budget, and it used to the utmost the leverage afforded by such authority to assert its independence vis-à-vis the administration. Conflicts between them became a standard feature of every budgetary session, and in order to circumvent the general council's opposition, New Caledonia's governors sometimes tried to disguise optional as mandatory expenditures.

To support the governors in their perennial struggle with the general council, successive French governments periodically considered replacing that body by an appointive administrative council. But because New Caledonia's general council was elected exclusively by white French citizens, nothing more drastic was done than occasionally to punish it by reducing the size of its membership. During the first 39 years of its existence, the number of councilors fluctuated between 19 and 10, but no change was made in their powers until 1924, when the Paris authorities clamped down hard.[8] For 3 years after the decree of August 10, 1924, the general council underwent an eclipse, through a reduction in its membership to 10 and in the number of circumscriptions to one for the whole island, and through losing its control over any part of the budget.

New Caledonia's citizens did not take this lying down, and in the elections of February 8, 1925, returned to the general council nine of its former members. At its opening session, these members demanded the annulment of the 1924 decree, claiming that their election had shown overwhelming popular support for the stand they had taken. Moreover, they added, their refusal to accept increased taxation was justified by the surplus of revenues with which the year 1924 had ended, contrary to Governor d'Arboussier's dire predictions of a deficit. His successor, Governor Guyon, sympathized with their attitude, and in 1927, he finally persuaded the Paris government to restore to the council its former powers and to increase its membership to 15. The six electoral circumscriptions were not revived, however, on the ground that such divisions had encouraged a parochial spirit among the councilors and that a single circumscription for the Grande Terre would provide better representation of the whole colony's interests.

At regular intervals throughout the rest of the interwar period, elections were duly held, in which about two-thirds of the registered electorate usually voted. The only organized group functioning at that time which might be termed a political party was the Union Economique, centered at Nouméa. The general council's membership remained remarkably stable, being made up almost entirely of Nouméa's successful businessmen and prosperous settlers from the interior. Most of the members of both these groups had been born in the island and were veterans of World War I, and all were staunch French patriots, but they nevertheless wanted more autonomy for the colony. With few exceptions, they were conservatives, but they also included a few radicals.

Among those regularly reelected were five councilors who were to play an outstanding part in the Resistance during World War II, and who continued for some years thereafter to be politically prominent. The council's perennial president was Henry-Louis Milliard, Nouméa's leading businessman and head of its most important trading firm, the Etablissements Ballande. Two of the most prosperous representatives

[8] See p. 253.

of the planter-rancher electorate were James Daly of the Bourail-La Foa area (who was also associated with the Société Le Nickel and the Maison Barrau of Nouméa) and Pierre Bergès, likewise from La Foa, of which he was mayor for many years. This hard-core group of councilors also included two nonconformists, Fernand Colardeau and Florindo Paladini, both born in New Caledonia, educated in France, and later members of the French communist party. During World War II, Colardeau became a magistrate in Réunion Island, where he was elected in 1947 to the Council of the Republic. Although he returned to the island of his birth only for a visit in 1950–1951, Colardeau retained an active interest in its political evolution. Paladini, on the other hand, remained in the Grande Terre, where he became an early organizer of trade unions and cooperative societies. Through this activity he made bitter enemies, and in 1925 an attempt to assassinate him cost him the loss of an arm.[9] In 1940 he was prominent in rallying New Caledonia to the Gaullist cause, and soon after the war he founded a local branch of the communist party. At that time, his wife became one of two women candidates for election to the general council. All the men mentioned were highly individualistic and had strong personalities, but they also represented a cross section of the resident French community, which alone participated in the colony's political life and economic development.

In Paris, New Caledonia had some influential supporters, particularly among the persons or groups associated with its mining and trading companies. Officially, however, it was represented only by a delegate whom the Caledonia citizens elected to the advisory Conseil Supérieur des Colonies. Usually this delegate was a politician or civil servant who had become involved with colonial questions in the course of his professional career but had never lived in or even visited the island. This was true of Louis Archimbaud, who was elected and reelected to that post throughout the 1920s, and it was he who not only had protested against the 1924 decree but also tried to obtain a seat for the colony in the Chamber of Deputies. Archimbaud argued that because New Caledonia's white citizens were nearly twice as numerous as were those of Cochinchina, which had elected a deputy since 1882, they were entitled to make their voice heard in Parliament. Only through the governor could the general council communicate with the Minister of Colonies, and the latter felt safe in ignoring its

[9] O'Reilly, P., *Calédoniens: Répertoire Bio-bibliographique de la Nouvelle-Calédonie*, pp. 201–202.

pleas because he never had to fear a parliamentary debate on New Caledonia's problems. Moreover, under the Third Republic, the post of Minister of Colonies was not a major one, and its incumbent was frequently replaced. Lacking any adequate channel for expressing their views, the Caledonian French, still smarting under their island's notoriety as a penal colony, felt frustrated and aggrieved.

These sentiments became sharper after the Caledonians' elected council was downgraded in 1924, and were further intensified when the depression of the early 1930s brought new hardships to the colony. France's refusal of a subsidy to New Caledonia, after granting one to the E.F.O., inspired the council president, Milliard, to write a letter to the Minister of Colonies which was a veritable catalogue of the islanders' grievances:

We are French just like the French of the Metropole. We pay very heavy taxes and we get very little in return. Settlers living in the bush are without roads, doctors, and schools; their children are losing touch with France, and in time will cease to be French. During World War I we proved our patriotism . . . and it is high time that we got something in exchange . . . We produce excellent rum, but our competitors in the Antilles supply all of France's needs of that commodity. We grow good coffee, but it is no longer protected in the French market as it was before the war, and the same is true of our copra. Yet we buy French products, even though their cost is greatly increased by transport charges . . .

Many other colonies are represented in the Parliament, but this has been refused us, a white population . . . We have many lepers and cannot care for them properly . . . Our public buildings are in a shocking condition and our wharf needs repairs . . . It would take only a few million francs to make this island an earthly paradise, for nature has done much for it. In France the state bears the cost of many of the burdens we shoulder, and we must pay for our schools, roads, and lawcourts . . . France should give us help.[10]

Caledonians might think of themselves as 100-percent French and of their country as a distant province of France, but this view was not shared by the Paris authorities, although they would have found it difficult to place New Caledonia into any convenient category. Because of its large French population, it could not be properly classified as a colony; because more than half of the island's inhabitants were Kanakas, neither could it be called a *colonie de peuplement;* and because three-fourths of its white residents had never had any direct contact with France and had had almost none with French culture, they could not be regarded as nationals on a par with Metro-

[10] *L'Oceanie Française,* November–December 1933.

politan citizens. Periodically, throughout the interwar period, the question of giving New Caledonia more effective representation in Paris was raised, either in the form of resolutions passed by the general council or by its supporters in France, but to no avail. Finally, in 1938, a Metropolitan deputy tabled a motion in the Chamber asking that New Caledonia be given "access to the Parliament without hesitation or debate," and it was accepted by that body with no dissenting vote. Nevertheless, the motion had not reached the floor of the Senate by the time World War II was declared, so once again the Caledonians' hopes were dashed.

"NATIVE POLICY"

During the years when relations between the administration and the general council, and the question of New Caledonia's representation in the Parliament, occupied the forefront of the local political scene, little consideration was given to the rights of the Kanakas or to the role they might play in the colony's evolution. Because French citizens paid most of the taxes and were responsible for such economic development as the island experienced, they felt strongly that New Caledonia should be run by and for them. Assuming that the Kanakas would die out within the near future, the settlers demanded more and more of their tribal lands and, after the island ceased to be a penal colony, they also wanted the Kanakas' services as laborers.

Initially, the administration concurred, going so far as to legalize the settlers' encroachments on the native reservations and to recruit Kanaka workers for them. Against these dual pressures, the missionaries were for many years the sole defenders of the Kanakas' rights. As time went on, however, and the decline of the Kanaka population was arrested, the attitude of the French government toward them gradually changed. Although the local administration continued to be primarily concerned with maintaining law and order among the tribes, it leaned to the missionary rather than to the settler viewpoint. In the late 1920s, Governor Guyon, although his main solicitude was for the settlers, took steps to prevent them from exploiting the Kanakas, and he also tried to promote native welfare by providing the tribes with more schools and medical care.

With the aim of strengthening Kanaka society, government officials and Christian missionaries combined to urge the tribesmen to remain on their reservations and to increase their agricultural output. This policy met with settler opposition which expressed itself in the local press and in a resolution passed by the general council in 1932, in which the authorities were asked to encourage Kanaka agriculture only insofar as it did not interfere with the settlers' needs for seasonal labor.[11] By that time, however, the administration and most of the white community had come to realize that the Kanakas could never be counted upon to provide an adequate and reliable labor force, and that the colony would be well-advised to bring in more Asian workers under contract.

If the administration tried more and more to hold the balance between the settlers' demands for requisitioned labor and land on the one hand, and the promotion of Kanaka welfare on the other, it could not be said to have devised a constructive native policy either before or during the interwar period. French colonial rule everywhere was then marked by a centralized form of arbitrary government, and in New Caledonia this predilection for direct rule was reinforced by the revolts of 1878 and 1917. Long before they occurred, however, a regulation of June 16, 1859, forbade the Kanakas to own or carry firearms, and the following year the governor was given almost unlimited powers over the native inhabitants.[12] By a simple order, he could remove chiefs, dissolve the organization of any tribe, expropriate its land, and exile or imprison the natives at will. These powers were confirmed by a French government decree of May 16, 1867, but at the same time they were slightly mitigated by the requirement that before taking any drastic step the governor must obtain the colonial minister's approval. This same decree stipulated that traditional chiefs —even though they ceased to exercise their functions—were forbidden to become teachers or ordained ministers, for it was feared that they might retain too much influence over their erstwhile subjects. The only constructive aspect of this otherwise repressive legislation was its formal recognition of the tribe as a "legal and autonomous unit." The last-mentioned concession became especially important ten years later, when rural communes were created, for without such a guaranty the tribes might have been absorbed by neighboring communes and have ceased to exist as entities.

The 1878 revolt was responsible for a decree of July 18, 1887, which initiated or intensified two policies that were to have most deleterious

[11] *Ibid.*, November–December 1932.
[12] Lenormand, M., "L'Evolution Politique des Autochtones de la Nouvelle-Calédonie."

effects on the Kanakas' evolution. The first of these policies imposed on them a regime of disciplinary penalties called the *indigénat*—common to French colonies before World War II—which deprived the Kanakas of the protection of the law and placed them under the arbitrary authority of administrators who might sentence offenders to imprisonment, fines, or the confiscation of their property. The second policy accelerated the segregation of the tribes in restricted areas, later called native reservations. More often than not, these reservations comprised regions that by tradition did not belong to the tribes to which they were assigned, and inevitably this led to innumerable disputes between the newcomers and the clans already living there.[13] Furthermore, as the number of settlers grew, so did their need for more land, and they particularly coveted the banks of watercourses and the mouths of rivers included in the reservations.

Step by step, the administration yielded to the settlers' demands and progressively whittled down the reservations, despite a guaranty verbally given by Governor Feillet in 1897 that their existing boundaries would be respected. An acceleration of the long decline of the Kanakas, noted in the early years of the twentieth century, created— in the words of Governor Charles Brunet—"a striking disparity between the size of the tribes and the extent of their reservations, much of which are not cultivated." [14] Using this argument as its justification, the administration several times "revised" downward the area covered by the reservations. By the time World War II began, each Kanaka was left with only 3 hectares of land, whether arable or not, whereas under their traditional system of crop rotation, which included a seven-year fallow period, at least 21 hectares of farmland per capita were needed simply for survival.

The expropriation of tribal land and the resettling of tribes on the reservations had a traumatic effect on the Kanakas, hastened the disintegration of native society, and undermined the system of traditional authority. Inside the reservation, ownership of the land was granted not to individual families but to the collectivity as a whole, and the tribal chief was authorized by the administration to distribute it, whereas Kanaka tradition gave him no such power. To the Kanakas, land was inalienable and belonged to the Masters of the Land, the descendants of its first occupants, who alone had the right to allocate it among the families composing the clan or tribe. The French policy

13 See p. 236.
14 Speech to the general council, Dec. 4, 1913.

was based on the erroneous assumption that the tribal chief was a small-scale replica of European absolute monarchs, whose power-base was a precise geographical area. They were too ignorant of native society to realize that the chief was obeyed and respected solely because he was the spiritual head of his ethnic group, and that his authority was restricted by custom and shared with the elders.

It was Governor Feillet who, in the last years of the nineteenth century, was the architect of a reorganization of the native administration which forced Kanaka society into a rigid framework and inadvertently precipitated the decline of the chieftaincy. To his mind, the existence of many chiefs with varying and vaguely defined powers caused unnecessary confusion, into which he tried to introduce order by the regulations of October 27, 1897, and August 9, 1898. Consequently, the Kanakas, who had been living in small communities scattered throughout the valleys and along the coast, were resettled in more concentrated groups so as to facilitate their administration. The new villages, laid out in the form of a gridiron in areas of easy access, were placed in charge of minor chiefs, appointed by the governor, and they were thenceforth called tribes. What had formerly been the tribe became a district (*arrondissement*), headed by a Great Chief who was also named by the governor but, theoretically, was still chosen according to tradition. In this way there came into existence a total of 50 districts (of which 13 were in the Loyalty Islands and 37 on the Grande Terre), made up of 150 villages or "tribes."

All the districts and tribes were placed under the overall authority of officials called *syndics des affaires indigènes*. They were not only responsible for maintaining order in the reservations but also served as intermediaries between the Kanakas, the administration, and the settlers. The *syndics'* specific powers were defined in a series of regulations issued toward the close of the nineteenth century, and their essential task was described as one of "paternalistic guidance." Because the convict population was steadily declining at that period, New Caledonia was left with an unnecessarily large police force, so it was only natural that the posts of *syndics* should be filled by gendarmes, who were former noncommissioned officers in the French army.

Soon the Great Chiefs became little more than the *syndics'* auxiliaries, helping in the tasks of maintaining order, collecting the head tax, and recruiting laborers for the public-works service and the settlers. For such services the Great Chiefs were paid a salary consisting of 5 percent of the taxes they collected and 5 percent of the wages of the laborers they recruited. Inevitably this tempted the chiefs to abuse their power so as to increase their incomes, especially in the recruiting of laborers. Not only did the chief receive a percentage of their pay, but the more young men he rounded up for work outside the reservation, the larger the share of land available for the tribesmen still living there. In a circular of September 14, 1925, the governor ordered the *syndics* thereafter to include, in their reports on a Great Chief's behavior, a statement as to whether or not he had helped to increase crop production and had facilitated the operations of the public-works and health services.

The rewards for becoming minor civil servants were a regular cash income and also support and favors from the *syndic,* but many of the Great Chiefs felt unable to adjust themselves to the new order. When they proved to be balky, incompetent, or merely passive, the *syndic* simply replaced them by more amenable and useful men. When such a "straw chief" was set up, the tribesmen often ignored his orders and continued secretly to obey the chief chosen according to tradition. Moreover, the traditional chief who accepted the role of auxiliary to a *syndic* lost much of the respect he had previously enjoyed, and other concurrent developments further undermined his position. He could no longer lead his people in warfare nor convene the great *pilous,* which had reinforced his authority as well as his people's cohesion, and the mass conversion of the Kanakas to Christianity automatically eliminated the religious aspect of his role. The village chiefs and the councils of elders survived this reorganization of Kanaka society far better than did the Great Chiefs, because the French administration had not troubled to tamper with traditional institutions at their level and had left them largely alone.

Their numerical decline and social disintegration did not pass unnoticed by the Kanakas themselves, who sought an explanation and, if possible, a scapegoat for their decadence. Many of the tribes found one in a new divinity brought to New Caledonia from the New Hebrides and the Loyalty Islands after the repression of the 1878 revolt. This was a red god or *toki,* a malevolent deity who assumed the form of magical packets containing gruesome remnants of a corpse.[15] The packets' whereabouts was a closely guarded secret, and

[15] For the substance of this paragraph, the writers are indebted to J. Guiart's preface to J. Barrau, *L'Agriculture Vivrière Autochtone de la Nouvelle-Calédonie;* and to P. Metais, "Quelques Aspects de l'Evolution Culturelle Néo-Calédonienne."

their power had to be used against individuals or groups, for otherwise it would bring harm to their owners. Because they had the money to buy such packets, the owners were often young Kanaka wage-earners who used them in some cases against chiefs or elders to express their resentment of traditional authority. The existence of such supposed power in the hands of unidentifiable individuals cast Kanaka society into disarray, and various forms of sorcery were practiced to discover who were the owners of the packets and to destroy these sinister talismans.

The *toki* cult, which started in the south, spread to the northern region of the Grande Terre, and doubtless contributed to the upsurge of paganism that characterized the 1917 revolt. Its role in the uprising caught officials and, to a lesser extent, the missionaries by surprise, and made them realize how little communication they had with native society and hence how little understanding of Kanaka psychology. Most of the French residents, however, blamed the revolt on the administration's weakness in general and that of the *syndics* in particular. Yet even the settlers were beginning to grasp the fact that the complex task of administering 30,000 Kanakas should no longer be left in the hands of gendarmes, who were too few and too unqualified by their training to perform the many tasks assigned to them. Besides having to do considerable paper work, the *syndics* were required to be simultaneously policemen, court clerks, and registrars of vital statistics. Yet nothing was done to alter this obsolete system beyond increasing the size of the gendarmerie.

In some other respects, however, the administration was somewhat more farsighted, and it eased some of the constraints that had been placed on native society. During the interwar period, the tide of Kanaka depopulation was reversed, and the arrival of some hundreds of new settlers needing more laborers led to a liberalization of the *indigénat* regime. Three decrees—in 1928, 1932, and 1937—progressively lightened the penalties and reduced the range of offenses for which the Kanakas had to answer, and all native women and minor children were exempted from the *indigénat* regime. Furthermore, the power to deal with serious offenses was taken from the governor and entrusted to the Minister of Colonies.[16] Another forward step taken in this period concerned the acquisition of French citizenship by the Kanakas, for which the qualifications were widened to include marriage with a Frenchwoman, the proven ability to speak and read French, or distinguished service rendered to the administration or

16 *L'Océanie Française,* March–May 1937.

the armed forces.[17] As each case was to be considered on an individual basis and as few Kanakas fulfilled any of these requirements, only a handful of them sought or acquired French citizenship before World War II. The two communities, French and Kanaka, lived juxtaposed, but without intermingling and indeed virtually incommunicado.

[17] *Ibid.*, September–October 1932.

21

World War II and the Early Postwar Years

A month after war was declared in Europe, New Caledonia's recently arrived governor, Georges Pélissier, reached Nouméa from Martinique, where he had been secretary-general.[1] Before that, he had had a distinguished career in the army, and in Nouméa he frequented his fellow-officers and remained generally aloof from the civilian population. His popularity was not enhanced by the fact that censorship of the news was so stringent that it was only through foreign radio broadcasts that Caledonians learned in June 1940 of the fall of France, the forming of Marshal Pétain's government at Vichy, and General de Gaulle's famous call for resistance.

On June 20, the general council unanimously passed a resolution in favor of seeking autonomy for New Caledonia, at least for the war's duration, but Governor Pélissier refused to transmit this to the Vichy authorities. Four days later, however, he told the councilors that he approved of continuing the war alongside Great Britain, and the general council enthusiastically endorsed his stand. On June 29, the governor's newfound popularity suddenly evaporated when it was learned that he had had arrested three prominent Noumeans who had drafted a petition asking self-government for the colony. Although they were soon released and the governor, on July 22, repeated his earlier statement about the war, his attitude became increasingly equivocal. A week later, publication in the *Journal Officiel* of Pétain's new constitution, which automatically imposed on New Caledonia the same totalitarian regime as in France, aroused public indignation, and the governor was charged with double-dealing. It also increased public support for those who advocated either autonomy for the colony or the establishing of direct contact with General de Gaulle.

During the month of August, the vacillations, uncertainty, and con-

---

[1] Much of the account of the years 1940–1942 in this chapter is based upon the memoirs of General de Gaulle and Henri Sautot, and the eyewitness accounts of two Australian journalists, Wilfred Burchett and H. E. L. Priday.

fusion that prevailed in the island were reflected in the contradictory reactions of its French residents to the successive visits of a French naval vessel, commanded by pro-Vichy officers, and of the British High Commissioner for the Pacific. Nevertheless, the pro-Gaullist forces were gathering strength, and they secretly got in touch with Henri Sautot, the French Resident of the Franco-British condominium of the New Hebrides, who had declared for Free France late in July. They began organizing resistance to the governor and his Pétainist aides, who were also preparing for a showdown.

The demand for Pélissier's resignation, accompanied by threats of violence, became so insistent that the governor discreetly left the colony on September 4. He departed just two weeks before Sautot arrived at Nouméa on board an Australian cruiser, with authority from De Gaulle to govern New Caledonia in the name of Free France. He was deliriously welcomed by most of the urban population, headed by the Comité de Gaulle and reinforced by the presence of some 700 broussards [2] who had come to the capital the night before, armed with shotguns and pitchforks to drive out the Pétainists. The latter, however, preferred capitulation to opposition, and they were quickly taken into custody. In all, about 250 French officers and officials, with their families, were sent out of the colony to Indochina, where many of them remained for the duration of the war.[3]

Sautot succeeded in healing the dissensions that had developed inside the Comité de Gaulle and in staffing the administration with Free French personnel. Because it was generally realized that meaningful elections could not be held under existing circumstances, and because the broussards—not the general councilors—were credited with the Gaullists' "victory," the public accepted with some grumbling the dissolution of the general council on December 29 and its replacement by an appointive assembly whose chairman was Pierre Bergès. Since the new assembly's powers and most of its members were the same as those of its predecessor, it reflected the majority opinion among the French residents and maintained much the same independent attitude vis-à-vis the administration.[4] Sautot then proceeded to recruit volunteers for the Pacific Battalion, the first contingent of which left the

[2] Broussard is the term commonly applied to French settlers living in the interior, or brousse.

[3] A court-martial by the Vichy authorities at Saigon in February 1942 sentenced 142 Caledonians to death in absentia, and 13 others to hard labor for 20 years. These sentences were not annulled until October 1949.

[4] Minutes of the French Union Assembly, Jan. 20, 1950.

colony on May 4, 1941, to join the Free French forces and fought successively in the Middle East, Africa, Italy, and southern France. In the spring of that year, also, he initiated negotiations with Australia, to which he offered bases in New Caledonia in return for arms and matériel to be used in the island's defense, as well as other forms of aid to shore up its fast-deteriorating economic situation.

New Caledonia's geographical isolation, which was accentuated by France's traditional policy of reserving its colonial markets for French products, had long hampered trade with nearby countries, and now, because of shipping shortages and the war, the island was deprived of the manufactured goods that it had theretofore received from the Metropole and other industrial nations. Essential foodstuffs still came from Australia, but transport costs and high customs duties made them very expensive. The Asian laborers, however, underwent greater hardships, for rice could no longer be brought in from Indochina. Another difficulty was the shortage of foreign exchange, which was aggravated by the freezing of the Banque de l'Indochine's holdings in the United States. Had the colony not been able to sell its nickel matte to the Americans and its crude ore to the Japanese (until late 1941), it would have suffered even more from its inability to obtain provisions from abroad. The Free French authorities could not come to its aid, and in any case did not wish to see New Caledonia become dependent on foreign countries, lest this eventually lead to a permanent loss of France's market in the colony.

For nearly a year after the French Pacific islands broke with the Pétain regime, De Gaulle was powerless to give more than moral support to the local Free French officials. He backed Sautot's policies in general, and approved in particular his agreement with Australia, on condition that his own authority over New Caledonia be formally recognized by the Canberra government and that a limited number of Australian troops be sent to the island, to serve under the command of French officers there.[5] Nevertheless, he was uneasy about any increase of British influence in the colony and even more about the Caledonians' autonomist tendencies. Although the islanders had unequivocally opted for Free France in September 1940, some local leaders were reported to be still receptive to Australia's offers of aid, in the hope of gaining more freedom from French control.[6] As the

[5] De Gaulle, *Mémoires de Guerre: L'Appel, 1940–1942*, p. 361.

[6] Minutes of the French Union Assembly, Jan. 20, 1950; "G. F. R.," "New Caledonia and the War."

general saw the situation, even Sautot was not above suspicion.

In the spring of 1941, De Gaulle sent Inspector-general Brunot to the E.F.O., where he soon encountered what the general himself described as "hostility, sometimes violent, on the part of functionaries who thought, and apparently not without reason, that he had come to install himself and his friends in their place." [7] Sautot also being openly antagonistic to Brunot, "exceptional measures were necessary" when the latter appeared in Nouméa:

In July 1941, I named Captain—later Admiral—Thierry d'Argenlieu high commissioner in the Pacific, with full civil and military powers and the mission "to restore definitively and without half measures the authority of Free France, to make use for the war of all the resources to be found there, [and] to assure there, against all possible and perhaps imminent dangers, the defense of the French territories in concert with our allies."

Many British and American commentators have expressed amazement at De Gaulle's choice of emissaries for the Pacific islands at that time. The Australian periodical, *Pacific Islands Monthly,* of September 1948, described Brunot as an "undistinguished windbag," and De Gaulle himself obliquely admitted that his appointment had been unwise. As for d'Argenlieu, the naval-officer-turned-Carmelite-monk, who had escaped from German captivity to join De Gaulle in London, he had been wounded during the abortive Anglo-Free French attack on Dakar in September 1940, and still bore the physical and psychological marks of that injury. Neither he nor Brunot had had any previous experience in the Pacific, and they aroused so much local antagonism that their action brought the French colonies there to the verge of revolt. The explanation for these appointments seems to lie in the dearth of able men around De Gaulle at the time, and in the general's primary requirement of ardent patriotism and undeviating personal loyalty on the part of his followers. In his memoirs, De Gaulle observed:

I had confidence in d'Argenlieu. His abilities as a leader reassured me that our means would be used vigorously but wisely. His diplomatic talents would be much called upon . . . he conceived of the action of Free France as a sort of crusade.[8]

In their almost mystical idealization of France, chronic suspicion of foreign intrigue, and personal integrity combined with arrogance, De Gaulle and d'Argenlieu resembled each other, although the latter

[7] De Gaulle, *Mémoires de Guerre,* p. 188.
[8] *Ibid.*

proved even more inflexible than the former and also fanatically anti-communist. Cables exchanged between them during the first six months of 1942 clearly indicate the similarities and differences in their characters.[9]

D'Argenlieu, having rapidly settled the affairs of Tahiti, sailed for Nouméa, where he arrived on November 5, 1941, and received a warm welcome. Within a short time, however, he alienated the local population by his aloof and arbitrary behavior, his requisitioning of the best houses and automobiles for himself and his large entourage, his imposition of a strict censorship, and his dissolution of the administrative assembly. It was even more his attitude toward Sautot and the American expeditionary force that led to a head-on collision with the Caledonians.

In extenuation of d'Argenlieu's behavior, it should be noted that Japan's attack on Pearl Harbor, which had taken place just a month after he reached Nouméa, seemed to put New Caledonia high on the list of probable targets of Japanese aggression because of its location near Australia and its wealth in strategic minerals. Naturally, New Caledonia's exposed position also worried the Allied high command, but d'Argenlieu was not kept informed of the negotiations on this subject between Washington and De Gaulle that led to the agreement of January 15, 1942. Five days thereafter, d'Argenlieu cabled De Gaulle in London that his pressing requests for arms and planes from the United States and Australia had not been granted:

America seems determined to obtain everything it wants from us without any compensation. I have already asked you to grant [the Americans] nothing unless they furnish us in return with means of defense . . . Unless formally ordered otherwise, I shall have the loading of ore for the United States suspended if I am not assured that the needed arms will be delivered.

I suspect, though I am not certain, that a secret arrangement exists between America and Australia to land American troops here without prior consultation with us. You have forbidden me to accept that move, and I shall use all the means at my disposal to carry out your orders.[10]

His cable ended with the statement that, if necessary, he would let himself "be killed on the spot, honorably, and for the liberation of France."

D'Argenlieu's suspicions of American machinations were not assuaged when he was informed 3 days later about the Franco-Ameri-

[9] *Ibid.*, pp. 515–517, 534–541.
[10] *Ibid.*, p. 516.

can agreement, whose terms De Gaulle himself pronounced to be "satisfactory." Nor did he change his attitude after March 1, when Washington issued a public declaration to the effect that American troops would be stationed in New Caledonia but that the United States recognized the sovereignty of France over that island and the authority of the local French administration. A week later, General Alexander Patch, commander of the American land forces in the Pacific, arrived in Nouméa, where he was cordially welcomed—not by d'Argenlieu, but by Sautot. On February 25, De Gaulle had informed the high commissioner of Patch's imminent arrival, and had ordered him to "reach a friendly understanding with him as soon as possible" and provide him with the maximum assistance. De Gaulle had no objection to d'Argenlieu's accepting a subordinate role in the overall military operations in the Pacific, but, as he ordered the high commissioner, "in your arrangements with General Patch, you should do your best to assure your command of the direct defense of our colonies."

This question was destined never to be raised, because the presence of thousands of American troops, who began arriving in New Caledonia on March 13, 1942, obviated the danger of a Japanese invasion and thus deprived d'Argenlieu of any role in the island's defense. For a man of his temperament, this enforced inactivity was galling, and he took out his frustrations on Sautot, whom he regarded as overly cooperative with the Americans and thus partly responsible for his own eclipse.[11] D'Argenlieu had no choice but to stand idly by while the United States transformed New Caledonia into a huge military and naval staging area for its major battles in the Pacific. As Professor D. L. Oliver later described this period: "The American troops dominated the island's life like an army of occupation. French officials held office, but American admirals and generals decided policy in critical spheres of public order, production and trade."[12]

Sautot's popularity with the French Caledonians was not diminished by his cordial relations with the American and Australian troops, and it soared even higher as d'Argenlieu's hostility toward him became ever more apparent. The high commissioner's frequent com-

---

[11] By Sautot's account, d'Argenlieu carried his chauvinism to such a point that he saw in the installing of traffic signs in English, for the guidance of army-truck drivers, evidence of American imperialistic designs on New Caledonia. See Sautot, H., *Grandeur et Décadence du Gaullisme dans le Pacifique*, p. 126.

[12] Oliver, D. L., *The Pacific Islands*, p. 378.

plaints to De Gaulle, however, bore fruit, and by early April the general had become convinced that

the presence of the troops, the dollars, and the American secret services, in the midst of a population troubled by an obsessive fever, soon aggravated the latent causes of agitation. Part of the [local] militia . . . defied the authority of the high commissioner and placed itself under that of Patch, who made the mistake of condoning this insubordination. Furthermore, Governor Sautot, displeased by being placed under d'Argenlieu, sought to assure for himself a personal popularity which he could utilize . . . after being patient for some time, I recalled Sautot to London to give him another assignment commensurate with the services he had rendered.[13]

At first Sautot, albeit reluctantly, accepted reassignment, but on May 2 he was persuaded by some local supporters to urge the general to reconsider his decision. A delegation of leading Gaullists [14] called first on d'Argenlieu and then on Patch, warning them that if Sautot left the colony under a cloud there would be grave trouble in Nouméa. Patch was nonplussed at being drawn into what was obviously an inter-French dispute, but at the time, when the Americans had recently been defeated in the Philippines and preparations for the Battle of the Coral Sea were under way, the last thing he wanted was an outbreak in Nouméa, so he reluctantly intervened in Sautot's behalf.

Needless to say, these developments hardened d'Argenlieu's determination to eliminate Sautot, and in this he was supported by De Gaulle. The general's chronically suspicious attitude toward his allies was substantiated at this time, in his eyes, by the British invasion of Madagascar, which had been carried out without any prior notification of the Free French authorities. Consequently, after a public display of friendship with Sautot on the afternoon of May 5, d'Argenlieu, under cover of darkness, had him forcibly placed on board a French warship, which immediately sailed for London via Australia. He also seized and deported to a nearby island, as "hostages," four of Sautot's leading supporters. To forestall the strong public reaction these moves would produce, d'Argenlieu made a speech over the radio that same evening in which he stated that Sautot had left the colony of his own free will, and that certain persons, whom he described as fifth columnists working against the interests of Free France, had been arrested.

[13] De Gaulle, *Mémoires de Guerre,* p. 191.
[14] It included Captain DuBois, who had organized the Pacific Battalion; Bergès, Mouledous, and Pognon, leading members of the assembly; and Rapadzi, local manager of Le Nickel.

D'Argenlieu's double-dealing and his high-handed actions aroused the Noumeans to anger, and the next day there was a general strike in the city, accompanied by mass demonstrations against the high commissioner that continued for a week. A committee was formed to demand the hostages' return, the *broussards* once again moved on the capital to swell the ranks of the opposition, and a protest march to the governor's palace was organized. The marchers went first to the American military headquarters, where Patch addressed them briefly. D'Argenlieu called out the police and the French troops, who, however, did not fire on the crowd, and the *broussards* seized several of the officers who, they said, would not be released until the hostages were returned to Nouméa. D'Argenlieu, feeling himself unsafe in the capital, went to La Foa, which he euphemistically described to De Gaulle as his mountain headquarters, but where, in reality, he was held prisoner by the local inhabitants. Finally, on May 15, the deadlock was broken when he capitulated and sent orders to bring back the hostages to Nouméa. Two days later they returned to the city, where the townspeople gave them a big welcome and sent a cable to De Gaulle demanding the recall of d'Argenlieu and his entourage.

During this period, De Gaulle complained that he received only fragmentary reports of what was transpiring in New Caledonia, but from London he sent a stream of messages to Nouméa and Washington. He reminded the American government of its pledge to respect French sovereignty in New Caledonia, but to Patch he sent a cable expressing confidence in his military leadership in the crucial battle that was about to begin. Turning to the inter-French conflict in Nouméa, De Gaulle tried to pour oil on the troubled waters. On May 16 he cabled reassurances of his support to d'Argenlieu, but at the same time urged him to seek a reconciliation with the Americans and also with the local citizens:

I share your feelings about American interference and its unfortunate consequences. Nevertheless, it is indispensable and vital for our national interests that you draw closer to the Americans, and especially to General Patch, despite their misdeeds . . . Now that you have sent Sautot away and the population is quieting down, I ask you to do whatever is necessary to promote a lessening of tension, though naturally without making any vital concessions. Be assured of my gratitude, my friendship, and my resolve to support you personally and your authority.[15]

[15] De Gaulle, *Mémoires de Guerre,* p. 540.

By that time, however, it had become clear that d'Argenlieu's position at Nouméa was no longer tenable, and at the end of May he definitively left the colony. His departure restored calm to the capital and good relations between the American military and local civilians except for one minor incident during the governorship of Christian Laigret (September 1943 to February 1944). At a press conference, that governor criticized the American troops in the colony for their lack of discipline, contrasting it with the exemplary conduct of the Australian and New Zealand soldiers.[16] The American authorities denied this charge, but two of the officers most unpopular with the French were soon replaced, and thereafter there was no recurrence of strained relations. After d'Argenlieu's departure, the islanders happily devoted themselves to the profitable occupation of catering to the growing number of American troops, of whom several hundred thousand came to New Caledonia for varying periods of time throughout the remaining years of the Pacific war.

New Caledonia's American-inspired economic boom, which lasted nearly four years, brought to the island a prosperity such as it had never before known. Its mineral exports soared, as did all its imports, but it was the producers and traders who dealt in local goods who benefited most from the windfall. All the meat and vegetables the settlers could produce were sold at high prices to the troops, and the American soldiers spent their money freely in the new shops and bars that were opened in Nouméa to cater to their needs.[17] Moreover, the Kanaka laborers received decent wages for the first time, and thus all levels of the population shared—to varying degrees—in the prevailing prosperity. As the money poured in, real-estate values rose, and, despite the shortages in matériel and labor, more building went on during the war years than in all of the preceding decade.[18] Bank deposits increased rapidly, as did the money in circulation, but much of the newly acquired wealth was held in dollars and either hoarded or smuggled abroad in defiance of the local foreign-currency regulations.

Even after the financial floodgates closed, when the troops left in 1946 and the Caledonians were again subjected to shortages and controls, the island was never again the same as before the war. Although the "return to realities" was hard, the inhabitants realized how

16 *Pacific Islands Monthly*, September 1946.
17 Oliver, *The Pacific Islands*, p. 378.
18 "G. F. R.," "New Caledonia and the War."

fortunate they had been, in comparison with those of France and almost all the other French colonies, to whom the war had caused great hardships. Moreover, the colony was left permanently enriched by the roads and airfields that had been built by American engineers and by the equipment, worth $3 million, which the United States government donated to New Caledonia. Perhaps, however, the psychological legacy was even more important, for the Caledonians had learned to value higher living standards, local industrialists had observed what modern machinery and efficient management could accomplish, and traders had been taught the commercial worth of presenting their wares attractively.[19] Above all, the islanders would never accept a return to the status quo ante bellum—politically, economically, or socially. First by rejecting the Vichy regime and rallying to Free France, and then by forcing the recall of an autocratic high commissioner, the Caledonians had both proved their intense patriotism and asserted their independence.

In view of the climate of rising expectations that existed in New Caledonia during the latter part of World War II, it was fortunate for the islanders' relations with France that the end of hostilities coincided with the adoption of a more liberal colonial policy by the Free French government. Nevertheless, the latter did not move swiftly enough to satisfy the Caledonians, whose appetite for reforms had already been whetted by the decree of July 5, 1944, which reconstituted the general and privy councils that had been suppressed in December 1940. At the time the decree was issued, Governor Jacques Tallec (February 1944–December 1946) had also announced—prematurely, as it turned out—that after the liberation of France, New Caledonia would be given a new statute granting it greater autonomy and assuring voting rights to all the islanders, including native subjects and Frenchwomen. Events in France and in New Caledonia so long delayed the fulfilment of these promises that disillusionment became widespread in the territory. The local delays were due to the fact that considerable time was needed to update the list of eligible voters for a new general council and for New Caledonia's delegates to the two constituent assemblies in Paris. And when the constitution of the Fourth Republic was finally adopted in October 1946, it failed to give New Caledonia a new statute that would satisfy the territory's aspiration for more autonomy.

In anticipation of the first postwar elections to be held in the

19 *Ibid.*

colony, political parties began forming in 1944. First in the field were the communists, whose leaders had long been active in organizing the indentured Asian laborers. The latter had many causes for discontent, since their living and working conditions, never good, worsened during the war, and their repatriation was long overdue. In 1941 the union organizer and stormy petrel of the general council, Florindo Paladini, had created an Association des Amis de l'U.R.S.S., and after it, a local branch of the communist party, called Progrès Social. In spreading the communist gospel among the laborers, among troops stationed in the island, and among Melanesian tribes,[20] he was aided by a Franco-Spanish couple named Tunica y Casas. Tunica was a Spanish mechanic who, after fighting on the loyalist side during the Spanish civil war, had fled to France and acquired French citizenship. He married Jeanne Bernard, a French Protestant and member of the communist party, and in the late 1930s they emigrated to New Caledonia, where her father was practicing medicine.[21] Jeanne Tunica was an able organizer and propagandist, and the party organ, *Le Calédonien,* and other tracts were widely disseminated among the tribes. This propaganda contained a clear call to revolt, and told the Melanesians that the "racists have taken away the heritage of your ancestors" and "you should enjoy the same privileges as the whites: if this doesn't please them, they can return to the country of their fathers." [22]

A less radical but still liberal party, also founded in 1944, was the Comité Calédonien, headed by Pierre Bergès. Although it mainly championed autonomy for New Caledonia, it collaborated with the Progrès Social in the electoral campaign for the general council. Together the two parties called for the imposition of income tax; the nationalization of mines, the nickel plant, and public utilities; and the breaking up of the big cattle ranches. Such a platform was naturally anathema to the conservative elements among Nouméa's big traders and industrialists. They proceeded to form the Union party, which wanted to preserve the local economic status quo but also to wrest greater autonomy from France. The conservatives' strength at the polls suffered from the fact that Frenchwomen and the military

[20] After the war, the term "Melanesian" replaced "Kanaka" because the latter was considered derogatory.

[21] O'Reilly, P., *Calédoniens: Répertoire Bio-bibliographique de la Nouvelle-Calédonie,* p. 256.

[22] From a communist tract, quoted by Abbé Paul Catrice in the French Union Assembly, Feb. 21, 1950.

personnel stationed in the island were not permitted to vote in the elections for the general council, on January 7 and 21, 1945, and the Union party was badly defeated.[23]

In all, there were about 50 candidates for the 15 council seats at stake. Consequently, the votes (cast by only about half the registered electorate) were so dispersed that only one candidate was elected on the first round. The run-off, two weeks later, resulted in an overwhelming victory for the left-wing parties, which between them captured all but two of the seats. The Comité Calédonien, whose strength lay in the interior, won eight, while the Progrès Social, which had a larger following in Nouméa, won five, but again not more than half the electorate voted. Of the two successful Union party candidates, only Henri Bonneaud, director of the Etablissements Ballande, was a bona fide conservative. The other, Father Louis Bussy, qualified as a conservative only insofar as he represented the Catholic mission's hostility to communism, for he was a liberal when it came to defending the Melanesians' rights. The triumph of the liberals reflected not only the deep divisions among the French community in New Caledonia, but also the poor whites' insistence on having a greater share of the profits derived from the exploitation of local resources. Yet the whole white population was united in its desire for more self-government and for holding its own vis-à-vis the French immigrants, who had begun coming to the island in large numbers. The political slogan of the autonomists, to which all the local-born Caledonians might be said to subscribe at that time, was "Il faut que ça change," although they were far from agreed as to how and in what respect the changes should take place.

This consensus was clearly shown in the next election held in New Caledonia—that of a delegate to the first constituent assembly in Paris—in which autonomy was virtually the only local issue involved. During the preceding 10 months, the conservatives had made notable headway by inducing the Comité Calédonien to divorce itself from the Progrès Social and support the Union party's program. They were further strengthened during that interval by the enfranchisement of Frenchwomen, among whom the qualified electors (4,401) were not much fewer than the male electorate (4,789). By the time the election was held on October 21, 1945, there were nearly twice as

---

[23] Two women—Madame Paladini and Madame Tunica—were allowed to offer themselves as candidates, but neither was elected.

many registered voters as before in New Caledonia, and all of them were white French citizens.

The candidate who had the conservatives' support in this election was Roger Gervolino, a member of the Comité Calédonien and a staunch autonomist. He had the further assets of a distinguished military record in the Resistance and experience as New Caledonia's representative in the provisional Free French assembly at Algiers. On October 21, he won more votes (3,249) than his two main opponents together.[24] At the first constituent assembly in Paris, Gervolino presented the Comité Calédonien's proposals for New Caledonia in the form of a draft law which that body adopted on April 10, 1946. It provided for the creation of a 19-member general council, in which Nouméa would have nine seats and the rest of the territory ten, and whose powers were to be far more extensive than those of its prewar counterpart. The general council would be authorized to initiate financial measures and would have virtual control over the territorial budget through the elimination of obligatory expenditures. Even more important, there was to be no more government by decrees from Paris, and this meant, too, that the governor of New Caledonia could no longer suspend or dissolve the general council and that the territory was not obliged to accept the civil servants that France might choose to send there. Henceforth only the governor, the secretary-general, the head of the judiciary, and the commander of the armed forces would be appointed by Paris, and their salaries would be paid by the French treasury.

In all basic respects, this law satisfied the islanders' demands for self-government, but it was short-lived. It was automatically annulled by the dissolution of the constituent assembly after the defeat on May 5, 1946, of the constitution which that body had drafted. Ironically enough, Gervolino had contributed to this outcome by advocating a negative vote in the constitutional referendum, and New Caledonia had so voted. Nevertheless, Gervolino was not held personally responsible for this side effect of the constitution's rejection, and he was reelected early in June to the second constituent assembly by an even larger percentage of the votes cast than in the preceding October. On this occasion, all his opponents were, like himself, local-born Caledonians with impeccable Gaullist records, but his most

---

[24] Paladini received 537 votes and Maître Michel Vergès, 1,961. See *Pacific Islands Monthly*, February 1946.

serious competitor, Pierre Mariotti, the left-wing candidate, received only 1,789 votes as against 3,428 for Gervolino.[25]

The second constitution was more pleasing than the first to the conservatives, in that it lessened the powers of the legislature and enhanced those of the executive branch of the French government. Nevertheless, Gervolino again recommended that it be rejected in the referendum of October 13, 1946, for it was less liberal as to the powers of elected bodies in France's overseas territories. Once more his advice was taken by the Caledonian voters, and this constitution was rejected by an even larger majority than before (2,300 negative to 415 affirmative votes), but it was accepted by the French electorate as a whole.

Under the newly constituted Fourth Republic, New Caledonia was again subjected to government by decree and to a budget in which obligatory expenditures were restored. In certain respects, however, the territory did make some progress over its prewar status. It could now elect representatives to the National Assembly, the Council of the Republic (Senate), and the French Union Assembly, and the circumscriptions and the electoral procedures provided for in the abortive law of April 10, 1946, were retained. Nine seats in the general council were allocated to the first circumscription, which embraced Nouméa and its immediate environs (4,916 registered voters); five to the second circumscription, the west coast (3,035); and five to the third circumscription, the east coast, the Loyalty Islands, and the Isle of Pines (1,610). Thus the domination of the general council by the conservative voters in the capital was virtually assured. This was confirmed by the composition of the new general council elected under the terms laid down by a "decree of application" on October 21, 1946.

Before that occurred, however, the Caledonians were called upon to designate their first deputy on November 10, 1946. Although they were profoundly dissatisfied with the regime imposed on them by the October 21 decree, they remembered that Gervolino had opposed the second constitution as well as the first, so he was an obvious candidate for the post. This time, however, he had a new set of left-wing opponents, for Paladini did not run again and the Tunicas had left the island for Australia in August after an attempt was made to assassinate them. The outstanding liberal candidate in this election was Antoine Griscelli, a member of the French socialist party and a

25 *La France Australe,* June 3, 1946.

supporter of the May 1946 constitution. Griscelli advocated a number of local reforms, including greater powers for the municipal councils, more independence for the judiciary from administrative control, the application in New Caledonia of France's new labor laws, a higher status for local-born civil servants, and—most far-reaching of all— the gradual emancipation of the Melanesians through obligatory primary education.[26] Griscelli also attacked Gervolino's record as a do-nothing member of the two constituent assemblies, charging him with claiming undeserved credit for maintaining the value of the C.F.P. franc and a high price for Caledonian coffee. In neither assembly had Gervolino ever made a public speech, and his name appeared in the official minutes only when he presented excuses for his repeated absences from the assembly sessions. Gervolino was stoutly defended in the Nouméa press, notably in *La France Australe*, which was controlled by his fellow-members of the Comité Calédonien. He was once again elected, receiving 2,392 votes to only 1,673 for Griscelli, but the elections to the general council the following month showed that the latter's campaign had not been in vain.

The decree of October 21, 1946, required that a new general council be elected even though the councilors chosen on January 21, 1945, had served less than 2 of the 4 years of their terms. The election of December 22, 1946, was noteworthy in that it was the first in which Melanesians participated, although only about 1,000 of them were qualified to vote, either by holding posts in the administration as chiefs or by service in the First or Second World War. They were so few in number that they could do little to strengthen the liberal forces, which had been gravely weakened by the loss of their experienced leaders and the withdrawal of the Progrès Social members from the general council the preceding spring. Nevertheless, the remnants of the left wing, led by Griscelli, rallied to urge the electorate to abstain from voting, in order to show their opposition to the "trusts" as represented by the Union party. Nearly 80 percent of the registered voters did abstain—for various reasons. One was apathy, for this was the seventh time in less than two years that they had been called upon to go to the polls; another was the desire to register a protest against the regime instituted by the Fourth Republic; and still another may have been the absence of candidates with popular appeal.

The degree to which the Progrès Social's call for massive abstention influenced the outcome should not be exaggerated, because the con-

[26] *Ibid.*, Oct. 29, 1946.

servatives scored another impressive victory in the election of January 5, 1947, for the general council—an election in which the Progrès Social put up candidates. (Griscelli was not among its candidates, nor was Mariotti, who was elected as the veterans' representative.) This election showed that the innovations resulting from the October 21, 1946, decree had not arrested the spread of indifference among the electorate to the exercise of its franchise nor the steady decline in the popularity of the Progrès Social. That party's platform was much the same as the one proposed by Griscelli in the November legislative election, but the Progrès Social did not succeed in creating an image of itself as the "little people's" defender. Neither was it successful in picturing its rivals as the stooges of big business by derisively calling the Union party the Parti Ballande. In the election of January 5, 1947, all but one of the Union party's candidates were elected to the general council, and subsequently that body chose from among its members New Caledonia's senator and French Union Assemblyman.

One important reason for the Union party's easy successes in that period was that its members controlled virtually all the credit facilities available in the territory. Another was that they had so much influence in Paris that the French government could be swayed to the point of recalling even a governor who showed himself less than docile to the local vested interests.[27] Still another reason was the progressive loss by the Progrès Social of its dynamism and earlier radicalism. Although it still urged the "emancipation" of the Melanesians and the application of France's labor laws in New Caledonia, there was now, in fact, little difference between its objectives and those of the Union party. Both wanted mainly the abrogation of the October 21, 1946, decree and a return to the law of April 10, 1946, greater economic development and freedom to trade, a strengthening of the judiciary, and better health and education services for the territory. The outcome of the general-council election showed above all that autonomy was the issue on which all Caledonians had become united, and so the focus of their political interest shifted from the local scene to Paris, where it was hoped that the National Assembly would soon grant New Caledonia a new and more liberal statute.

At their first session—the first after the elections—on January 21, 1947, the general councilors voted to send a cable of protest against the decree of October 1946 to the French Overseas Minister. He soothingly replied that that decree was effective only until a per-

27 *Pacific Islands Monthly,* March 1950.

manent statute would be voted by the Parliament before July 1 of the same year. The council then proceeded to elect the territory's senator, and they chose Henri Lafleur, a highly successful and competent local-born businessman with important mining and ranching properties. In the Conseil de la République, Lafleur became a member of its overseas commission, and there he defended the Caledonian conservatives' program against Fernand Colardeau, spokesman in the Senate for the communist party.[28] Early in 1947, Colardeau drafted a new statute for New Caledonia, which would not only give wider powers to its general council but also enlarge the electorate to include all adult Melanesians. He further proposed a dual electoral system for the territory and a bicameral legislature, in which the native population would have numerically equal representation with the white French citizens and their elected representatives would vote together as a single body. Inasmuch as the communist party was insisting at that time on a single electoral college for the French Black African territories, Colardeau tried to explain this inconsistency in terms of New Caledonia's unique ethnic situation. Because the Melanesians and white Frenchmen there were roughly equal in numbers, but very unlike in regard to education, political sophistication, and economic power, Colardeau maintained that a single electoral college would lead to racial friction and the domination, if not the intimidation, of the Melanesian councilors by their white colleagues.

No action was taken on Colardeau's proposals, and the agenda of the National Assembly was so full that July 1, 1947, came and went with no change in the "temporary" regime set up under the decree of October 21, 1946. Indeed, several more years elapsed before Colardeau's statute was even debated by any of the three French parliamentary bodies. By the time it reached the floor of the French Union Assembly, to which all overseas matters had to be submitted, the Caledonian conservatives were prepared with a statute of their own devising. It was presented and defended by Colonel Maurice Bichon, a Caledonia-born professional army officer who had been elected to the French Union Assembly on October 11, 1947, by the general council. In refuting the basis of the Colardeau statute, Bichon cited certain relevant developments in New Caledonia during the three preceding years, which, he claimed, had profoundly modified the situation of the Melanesians in the territory and proved that they wanted no share in the political power there. No one could deny that the atti-

[28] See p. 258.

tude of the Melanesians had changed markedly since the war, but such changes were diversely interpreted.

Such progress as the Melanesians had made was due partly to the wartime prosperity, in which they had a meager share, but far more to the policy of the postwar French government. The few privileges granted by France to the Melanesians after the war were wholly voluntary—they were not solicited by the native population and were strongly opposed by the general councilors. In 1946, the French government had abolished forced labor, the *indigénat,* and the requirement that the Melanesians remain on their reservations unless specifically authorized by the *syndics* to work for the administration or the settlers. Throughout 1947, all the debates by the general councilors concerning the "native problem" centered around one theme—the weakened authority of both the administration and the traditional chieftaincy over the tribes. The *syndics,* deprived of their powers to control the movement and activities of the tribesmen, could no longer bolster the position of the chief, whose orders, therefore, were no longer invariably obeyed. Many of the villages created by the administration were rapidly deserted, and by early 1947 it was calculated that about one-third of the tribesmen had taken to the road, either to visit fellow-clansmen or to return to their ancestral lands.[29] Some 1,000 to 1,500 of them had drifted to Nouméa, where few found work and all lived under such deplorable conditions that they were spreading disease among the white population.[30] The general council being powerless to abrogate the new laws, which it deplored as "premature," all it could do was to protest to Paris and ask that they be applied gradually. Apparently it never occurred to them that the Melanesians' mass emigration might have been caused by the lack of sufficient land in the reservations to support their increasing numbers. Therefore, the councilors proposed only a few repressive local measures, such as an obligatory medical examination for all Melanesians carrying identity cards, and a possible reorganization of the Service of Native Affairs.

The Christian missionaries, because they were far more closely in touch with the native population than were the councilors, showed greater perceptiveness in analyzing the causes of the evolution in

---

[29] Deschamps, H., and J. Guiart, *Tahiti—Nouvelle-Calédonie—Nouvelles-Hébrides,* p. 116; Guiart, preface to J. Barrau, *L'Agriculture Vivrière Autochtone de la Nouvelle-Calédonie.*

[30] *Pacific Islands Monthly,* March 1947.

Melanesian society, and more imagination in confronting the problems posed by its future development. They realized that the very presence of so many American troops during the war had opened new horizons to the Melanesians. The high wages paid by the Americans and their openhandedness in providing free cigarettes, movies, and band concerts had created a new sense of money and the possibility of acquiring it.[31] For the first time, the Melanesians had comparatively easy and casual contacts with men whose way of life was totally different from anything they had previously known, and almost by contagion this gave them a new outlook. Their attitude and material condition were further modified by the French government's sudden removal of constraints on their freedom of action. Naturally the Melanesians' first reaction was one of bewilderment, and this was followed by a rapid breakdown of tribal discipline and an increase of idleness, alcoholism, and prostitution. The only effort to provide them with guidance and new aspirations during this period was being made by the communists, both through their propaganda in the territory and by their political proposals in the French Parliament. The missionaries, acutely aware of developments, realized that it was high time for them to counter the communists' activities by offering the Melanesians an alternative framework in which they could be oriented toward wholly different goals.

Among the Catholics, it was Father François Luneau, a missionary with 24 years of experience in New Caledonia, who took the initiative in training a Melanesian political elite. With the blessing of Monsignor Edouard Bresson, he published a pamphlet on May 25, 1946, bearing the cumbersome title, "Revendications de l'Union des Indigènes Calédoniens, Amis de la Liberté et de l'Ordre" (later abbreviated to U.I.C.A.L.O.) and the signatures of 15 Melanesian Catholics. In actuality, the pamphlet was an appeal for union addressed to "all native brothers of the Grande Terre and its islands," and it listed their "legitimate grievances." [32] Among these, by implication, were demands for respecting the inviolability of the reservations and for the restitution of family properties inside them, limitation of the head tax, more schools for Melanesian children, strict control over the sale of alcoholic beverages, a legal statute for the native population, and the election by Melanesians of fellow-tribesmen to defend their rights and interests vis-à-vis the administration and the settlers.

[31] O'Reilly, P., *Pèlerin du Ciel: François Luneau*, p. 175.
[32] *Ibid.*, p. 183.

After the U.I.C.A.L.O. was duly registered as an association and the authorities had recognized its legal existence, Father Luneau organized study groups on the east coast, which he placed in the charge of 72 catechists. At their meetings, such questions as the future of the chieftaincy and its powers, the land regime, wage-earning, and the like were debated. Resolutions embodying the conclusions reached in these discussions were presented for approval to a conference held at Païta from March 12 to 19, 1947, and attended by 41 delegates said to represent 4,000 tribesmen of the Grande Terre and its dependent islands. Officially, Father Luneau was simply the U.I.C.A.L.O.'s adviser, but it was he who organized the conference, prepared its agenda, and instructed the delegates in the parliamentary procedures for electing their officers and conducting a debate. Because it promoted the political education of the Melanesians and enabled them to make fruitful contacts with each other, the Catholic mission regarded this conference as a great success.

Obviously the Protestants could not afford to lag behind their Catholic competitors. Soon they set up an analogous Association des Indigènes Calédoniens et Loyaltiens Français (A.I.C.L.F.), the members of which were former pupils of their mission schools.[33] Leadership for this group was provided by the dynamic Pastor Raymond Charlemagne, a recently arrived missionary who was later to exert considerable influence on Melanesian education and politics. On August 12, 1947, the presidents of the two fledgling associations— Henri Naisseline, Great Chief of Maré Island, and Rock Pidjot, chief of La Conception—met to discuss a possible merger into one group that would give more effective representation to New Caledonia's nearly 30,000 tribesmen. For reasons vaguely termed "external influences,"[34] this never materialized. Probably the proposed merger foundered on the long-standing Protestant-Catholic rivalry, although responsible missionaries of both faiths insisted that their respective associations were not primarily religious groups and were wholly free of mission control.

Certainly the formation of both the U.I.C.A.L.O. and the A.I.C.L.F. was encouraged by the local administration, and with good reason. Among the resolutions adopted by both groups was one asking for the creation of an assembly made up of "competent natives" who

[33] Leenhardt, M., "La Nouvelle-Calédonie."
[34] O'Reilly, *Pèlerin du Ciel*, p. 185.

would be elected by the Melanesians.[35] This assembly was to be a purely advisory body, albeit obligatorily consulted on all proposed measures affecting tribal affairs. The resolution ended with the statement that the Melanesians were not seeking seats in the general council, for they realized that they were not yet ready to take part in its discussions. Father Bussy lost no time in circulating copies of this resolution among his fellow general councilors. Their president, Henri Bonneaud, expressed pleasure at learning that these good natives were in complete agreement with the motion embodying an identical proposal that had been voted by the council on February 4, 1947, and said that he would so notify the French Overseas Minister and New Caledonia's parliamentarians.[36]

Such an improbable concurrence of views between the general council and the two Melanesian associations, whose organization and resolutions were frankly mission-inspired, was sure to raise the suspicions of the French government and the National Assembly. In order, therefore, to substantiate the authenticity of the resolution, the conservatives realized that they must have it confirmed by some more apparently objective body. According to Colonel Bichon, it was he who suggested to the administration that a meeting of native Notables be called, at which they would be asked to discuss their people's needs and aspirations, in the hope that the Notables would express views confirming the resolution. Consequently, in November 1948, 29 Melanesians, mainly chiefs selected by the Service of Native Affairs, met under the chairmanship of Vincent Bouquet, the venerable Great Chief of Bourail.[37]

No minutes of that meeting being available, just what was said there is not accurately known, and reports of its discussions are contradictory.[38] Colonel Bichon claimed that the Notables supported the desiderata expressed by the A.I.C.L.F. and the U.I.C.A.L.O. and wanted for their people no political power but simply more schools and greater economic opportunities. A contrary view was voiced by

[35] Although they agreed on basic issues, the two associations differed as to the methods proposed for electing the chiefs and their representatives to the advisory assembly. See Lenormand, M., "L'Evolution Politique des Autochtones de la Nouvelle-Calédonie."

[36] Minutes of the general council, April 29, 1947.

[37] He had been one of the two Melanesians who unsuccessfully sought election to the general council on Jan. 5, 1947.

[38] Minutes of the French Union assembly, Feb. 2, 1950.

Marcel Egretaud, the communist French Union Assemblyman who specialized in overseas affairs and who had toured New Caledonia for several weeks soon after the Notables met. His informants, he said, had told him that neither of the two mission-sponsored associations represented Melanesian opinion and that their resolutions had been adopted under missionary pressure. He claimed that the tribesmen regarded all such sponsored gatherings as artificial and unsatisfactory, and that the Notables had declined Bichon's proposal to meet again. In fact, they never did.[39]

The conflicting statements described above were made by Bichon and Egretaud 14 months after the Notables' conference, in the French Union Assembly, during discussion of the two draft statutes that had finally been placed on its agenda. Four sessions of the political affairs committee and five meetings of the plenary assembly were devoted to debating all the issues involved, and even then they ended inconclusively, although Bichon's proposals were rejected. The inability of even that body specialized in overseas affairs to reach a clear-cut stand on a statute for New Caledonia may have discouraged the National Assembly and Senate from taking up the whole question. In any case, it was shelved in the Parliament for 20 months longer. Nor were the general councilors any more eager to debate the basic "native problem," apparently hoping that it would simply go away if they continued to ignore it. Periodically they did discuss such related matters as the pay of the Great Chiefs and the reorganization of the Service of Native Affairs, but nothing more fundamental.[40] Initially they opposed increasing the chiefs' income because the latter were no longer useful agents in recruiting native laborers, but later they had to do so after they abolished the head tax on which the salaries of the chiefs were based.[41] It was clear that the authority of the chieftaincy was steadily waning, and the only hope of arresting its decline lay in encouraging the chiefs to become spokesmen for the councils of elders, which had better withstood the erosion of time and events.

It was to the task of stabilizing Melanesian society at its current

[39] In May 1950, the general council asked the administration to reconvene the Notables' conference, but the government spokesman replied evasively, claiming that the authorities had not yet found time to study the "delicate" problems that had been raised by the November 1948 meeting. See minutes of the general council, Nov. 29, 1950.

[40] *Le Calédonien,* Oct. 17, 1950.

[41] Minutes of the general council, Jan. 29, Nov. 29, 1947.

stage of evolution that the reorganized Service of Native Affairs devoted its energies. After the arrival of a civilian administrator in August 1948 to take charge of that service, the general council authorized him to experiment "prudently" in the Loyalty Islands, where the chieftaincy had remained stronger than on the Grande Terre. His first report showed that he had fully accepted the mission of crystallizing the status quo. He said that the Melanesians were most appreciative of all that the general council was doing for them, and optimistically implied that they would not embarrass the authorities by making demands for further changes in their status.[42] His efforts were directed toward reviving the Melanesians' taste for tribal life on the reservations, so that they could fulfil their manifest destiny as a peasantry. This policy was more pleasing to the administration than to the general councilors, who still hoped that the Melanesians might be induced to leave the reservations and replace the repatriated Asians as agricultural and mining laborers. Nevertheless the general council supported it, for it promised to maintain the Melanesians in their current state of passivity. By early 1951, it was evident that no further steps would be taken by the administration, the general councilors, or the missions to anticipate or promote the further evolution of Melanesian society, and that only some external pressure could bring about any radical change in the existing situation.

[42] *La France Australe,* Nov. 27, Dec. 6, 1948.

22

The Territorial Statute

Not unexpectedly, the external pressure that precipitated drastic changes in New Caledonia's political scene came from Paris, but in this instance it was exerted inadvertently rather than deliberately. As usual, the Parliament had been slow in making vital decisions concerning the French Union, and in the spring of 1951 the imminence of the elections of overseas deputies seemed to catch its members by surprise.

Despite frequent promises to replace the supposedly temporary decrees of October 1946, under which the overseas territories were still being governed, no further action had been taken to give them a permanent statute. Now there was no longer enough time to undertake such complicated legislation, and all that could be done was to repair the omission insofar as enlarging the electorate was concerned. On May 23, 1951, the assembly passed hastily and with almost no discussion a law that vastly increased the number of native electors qualified to vote for the territorial deputies. No protest against it was voiced in the Parliament by New Caledonia's representatives, all of whom were unaccountably absent from the crucial session. This law had a particular significance for New Caledonia because of the almost equal numerical division of its inhabitants along ethnic lines. It marked a turning point in that territory's history by enfranchising nearly 9,000 Melanesian men and women, close to half the total of almost 20,000 eligible voters. Perhaps because this law was adopted only five weeks before the legislative election of July 1, its full implications seem not to have been grasped by the European community. The campaign and the election itself took place in complete calm.

For the post of New Caledonia's deputy there were four candidates, of whom only Gervolino and Paladini were familiar political figures. Paul Metadier was a relatively unknown commercial agent of Nouméa, and the fourth candidate, a pharmacist named Maurice Lenormand, presented himself as an independent. Gervolino campaigned on his parliamentary record, and in view of his past successes it was widely assumed that he would be reelected. Paladini, naturally, campaigned for the enactment of more liberal labor laws, and Metadier echoed the conservative platform of the R.P.F., of which he was a member. Lenormand was the dark horse in the campaign, for, unlike his competitors, he was a Metropolitan Frenchman without an impressive Resistance record. Moreover, he had married a Melanesian and his background, educationally and professionally, was highly orthodox. In 1933, at the age of twenty, he had graduated from the Institut Agricole of Algeria, then performed his military service in New Caledonia, after which he worked there as a chemist for the nickel-mining industry. In 1936 he married the granddaughter of the Great Chief Boula of Lifou Island, and two years later they went to France, where he engaged in business, became interested in trade-union organization, and earned a degree in anthropology on the side. During the early months of World War II, he served with the colonial infantry, and after the Franco-German armistice in 1940 he returned to Paris to study pharmacy and oriental languages. In 1945 he was back again in Nouméa, where he practiced pharmacy and became involved in various business and plantation enterprises.[1]

In campaigning for election to the National Assembly, Lenormand stressed the defense of the C.F.P. franc and the native question as the two most important issues facing the electorate. He asserted that Gervolino, by his persistent absenteeism from the National Assembly meetings and his ignorance of financial matters, was unqualified to defend New Caledonia's currency. As to the Melanesians, the outgoing deputy had simply ignored them. In support of his own candidacy, Lenormand wrote in *La France Australe* for June 16, 1951:

I have been reproached with not being a Caledonian, but I am one at heart, for my family and interests are here . . . Our neglect of the native question risks permitting the Melanesians to fall prey to unscrupulous politicians . . . Should not our role be one of guiding and reasoning with them?

On July 1, 1951, 13,667 persons—of a registered electorate then numbering 19,981—went to the polls, a larger percentage than had ever before voted. This increased participation on the part of qualified voters and, even more, the outcome of the election certainly resulted from the enfranchisement of the territory's Melanesian citizens. In the registered electorate there were still 2,150 more Europeans than

[1] O'Reilly, P., *Calédoniens: Répertoire Bio-bibliographique de la Nouvelle-Calédonie*, p. 157.

Melanesians, but many of the former simply failed to vote. That they did not take seriously the candidacy of Lenormand was shown not only by so many abstentions but also by the splitting of the conservative vote between Gervolino and Metadier. Lenormand won by 5,064 votes to 4,207 for Gervolino, 2,252 for Metadier, and 2,144 for Paladini, and the geographical distribution of these ballots indicated clearly where the candidates' respective strengths lay.[2] The Nouméa electorate cast 1,897 votes for Gervolino, 1,177 for Metadier, 646 for Paladini, and only 530 for Lenormand. The last-named obviously owed his victory, which shook and bewildered the European conservatives, to the Melanesians.

Adding to their consternation throughout the ensuing three months was the lack of any titular governor at the head of the local administration. Cournarie had left the territory on the eve of the election, and his most likely successor, Governor Louveau of Soudan, reportedly refused the post because he was not willing to contend with so troublesome a body as the general council.[3] It was not until October that Raoul Angamarre, who had served in New Caledonia and the New Hebrides during the late 1920s, arrived to become the territory's forty-third governor. During this long interregnum, the acting governor, secretary-general Bordarier, provided no strong leadership, but listened amiably and noncommittally to successive delegations of indignant councilors, *broussards*, and Melanesians.

The conservatives were infuriated by Lenormand's election, but instead of closing ranks, they split into several groups. One wanted New Caledonia to secede from France and ally itself with Australia or the United States. Another, led by Bonneaud, urged the continuance of the general council's old stand in favor of prolonging the status quo, somewhat modified, however, by the creation of an advisory assembly to be elected by the Melanesians. Still another group was headed by James Daly, who, with three other general councilors, drafted an "open letter of protest" that was printed in the July 10, 1951, issue of *La France Australe*. In it, they advocated that New Caledonia be assigned two seats in the National Assembly, which would enable both Europeans and Melanesians, voting as separate colleges, to have their own deputies. Furthermore, they proposed that each group elect its own local assembly for the discussion of their respective affairs, but the Europeans would control all matters involving the interests of the territory as a whole.

[2] *Marchés Coloniaux*, July 7, 1951, p. 1850; *La France Australe*, July 2, 1951.
[3] *Pacific Islands Monthly*, September 1951.

This letter was circulated in the form of a petition wihch, by the end of August, had gathered 2,030 signatures.[4] The Melanesians reacted strongly against it, thus disproving the conservatives' longstanding contention that the natives wanted no voice in public affairs. Their opposition to the petitioners' proposals was expressed in another open letter of "counter-protest," written by Vincent Bouquet, the Great Chief of Bourail, who had presided over the Notables' conference of November 1948. He rejected the proposed replacement of a single electoral college by a dual college as "highly injurious" to the native population of the territory and as evidence of the Europeans' unjustified lack of confidence in the Melanesians:

Our obedience, our fidelity to France, and the sacrifices of our veterans have at long last given us the rights of citizens, and we maintain that no one should take from us the rights that the French government has finally recognized.[5]

A week later, *Le Calédonien,* the left-wing newspaper which had printed Bouquet's letter, editorially supported his stand, adding that if Melanesians were unqualified to be voters it was because Europeans had kept them in a state of ignorance:

We who pride ourselves on France's civilizing mission have been unable in a century to educate the native population, and it is high time that we begin to cultivate a civic consciousness in the Melanesians.[6]

Inasmuch as *Le Calédonien* was the organ of the territory's few European radicals, the conservatives could dismiss such a statement as communistic, but it did show that the French community was not monolithic in its outlook. Even the conservatives were disunited, except in their opposition to the electoral law of May 23, 1951. To form a common front and make their protests more effective in Paris, Bonneaud called an extraordinary session of the general council on August 7, and organized its members into study groups, which met during the autumn months to work out their strategy.

At these meetings, all the councilors bewailed the malaise they attributed to the election, claiming that it had disrupted the "harmonious relationship" that had theretofore existed between Europeans and Melanesians. They denied that they were racists, describing themselves simply as realists in that they recognized the existence of "fundamental differences" in the cultural and juridical status of the

[4] *La France Australe,* Aug. 30, 1951.
[5] *Le Calédonien,* Aug. 14, 1951.
[6] *Ibid.,* Aug. 21, 1951.

two ethnic groups. Since 1947, they claimed, the general council had promoted Melanesian welfare by revamping the Service of Native Affairs, reorganizing the school for monitors, increasing the pay of the Great Chiefs, and financing public works that had benefited the tribes. In general, they favored making some further concessions, such as surveying the tribal lands, registering family property rights, drafting a code of customary law, and giving the council of elders a legal status, but that was as far as they were prepared to go. What they must work for, it was decided, were drastic changes in the electoral law of May 23, 1951, if not its abrogation. If this were not done, the Melanesians were likely to control the next general council, as well as the municipal commissions, and then grave injustice would be done to the white community, which alone had developed the country and borne the brunt of its taxation. As for the Melanesians, they "enjoyed the best of two worlds," living protected lives in their traditional society on the reservations and being educated and cared for at the whites' expense, and it was unreasonable of them to ask for more.

Despite such a wide area of agreement, the breach between the Bonneaud and Daly factions among the general councilors was not mended. The conservatives had become so accustomed to wielding unchallenged power in the territory through their wealth and their control of the general council that they were psychologically unprepared to adjust to any changes in their status or to unite behind a program of common action. They certainly could expect no help from the local administration, whose officials they had consistently harassed. Nor could they count on any real support from the rank and file of the settlers, who had tolerated their domination simply because nothing could be undertaken in the territory without the sponsorship of its financial oligarchy.[7] Isolated, individualistic, jealous of their landed property, and accustomed to having cheap labor at their disposal, the *broussards* lacked the pioneer spirit required to develop a new country. There was no prospect of their initiating any moves that would involve their assuming responsibility or participating in any policy that would require collective action. The sense of fatalistic resignation that pervaded the disunited and largely passive French community in New Caledonia also obsessed the general councilors late in 1951. They realized that their terms would soon expire and that at long last the French government was about to submit a draft statute

[7] Bastian, G., "La Nouvelle-Calédonie," *Cahiers d'Outre-Mer*, July–September 1954.

for New Caledonia to the Parliament, but not even the sense of imminent danger could awaken them from their lethargy.

Late in November 1951, the deputies debated the bill as amended by the French Union Assembly,[8] and in the National Assembly it was attacked by Lenormand and by liberal party members of many political persuasions.[9] Lenormand repeated many of the criticisms in regard to changes in the electoral circumscriptions and voting methods that had been made by the French Union Assemblymen, adding that the dual college had already been rejected by the Melanesians as well as by a majority of the French Caledonians. By allotting one seat in the general council to every 1,000 white islanders, compared with one for every 4,000 Melanesians, the government bill, he claimed, would further enhance the already privileged position of the European voters. Moreover, by no means all of the Melanesians qualified to vote under the 1951 law had received ballots in the last election, because of the deficiencies in the register of vital statistics. The electoral rolls on which they were based were not only incomplete but also out of date.

Dr. Louis Aujoulat, secretary of state for overseas France, admitted that the government bill had been drafted with a view to reinforcing the Europeans' control of the general council. This had been done, he said, because the Melanesians had not yet attained political maturity or made any contribution to the territory's development comparable with that of its white citizens. During this debate, the liberal deputies managed to increase the number of Melanesian councilors by one and to obtain a formal pledge by the government to bring the electoral rolls up to date within 4 years. The bill was accepted by the National Assembly on its first reading (by 415 votes to 198) and sent to the Senate. There it was so amended as to institute a virtual dual-college system by reinforcing the racial division between the electoral circumscriptions. This proved to be unacceptable to the deputies, who rejected the whole bill (356 to 226) on its second reading on January 25, 1952.

In early 1952, therefore, New Caledonia was still without a statute and, furthermore, with no general council, for the latter's term expired on January 19. A void was thus created which enabled the governor to rule the territory by decree—a situation denounced by Henri Bonneaud as a "scandalous violation of our rights to self-government"

[8] Minutes of the French Union Assembly, Nov. 15–16, 1951.
[9] Minutes of the National Assembly, Nov. 30, 1951.

and an "obvious penalization" of the general council because its members had frequently dared to oppose the administration.[10] Bonneaud's proposal to go to Paris at his own expense to see what could be done there was enthusiastically endorsed by his colleagues. As matters turned out, he could hardly have chosen a more unpropitious moment, for his arrival in France coincided with the fall of the Faure government, and it was not until April 11 that the question of New Caledonia's statute was again taken up in the National Assembly. By then, the situation had been further complicated by the tabling in the Parliament of two more bills, by Lafleur and Lenormand.

As might be expected, Senator Lafleur's proposal included instituting a dual electoral college, and it was revised and presented to the National Assembly by Roger Duveau.[11] Lenormand's bill rejected any "political segregation" of the Melanesians and proposed a new division of the electoral circumscriptions along geographical, not racial, lines. Because the newly invested U.D.S.R. government was not ready to present any statute of its own, and the National Assembly still could not reach any decision regarding the three bills before it, the deputies accepted a compromise proposed by the M.R.P. and supported by Lenormand, the S.F.I.O., the I.O.M., and the communist party. This compromise extended the life of the general council until June 15, by which time the government promised to present its own statute for New Caledonia.

Bonneaud returned to Nouméa on May 8, empty-handed and furious with Lenormand, whom he accused of double-dealing and of sabotaging any chance of the territory's being given the statute it needed. In a strong speech to the general council on May 31, he denounced Lenormand as no "true" Caledonian and as responsible for creating racial tension in the territory. According to Bonneaud, Lenormand had agreed to withdraw his draft bill, but at the last moment had broken his word and tabled it in the National Assembly. The president of the council wound up his diatribe by saying:

I feel ill at ease sitting in the presidential chair, for it is intolerable that the general council should owe its present authority to a law voted with the help of the communist party.

He then offered his own resignation and urged his fellow-councilors to follow his lead. Not all of them, however, agreed with his stand,

[10] Bonneaud's speech to the general council, Jan. 15, 1952.
[11] Duveau was a French lawyer who also favored a dual college for Madagascar, of which he was a U.D.S.R. deputy.

notably Senator Lafleur, who, while corroborating Bonneaud's account of Lenormand's behavior, urged the councilors not to act hastily, for "we have no assurance that the government will really take action before June 15." Nevertheless, on May 19 the general councilors resigned in a body, with the exception of Father Bussy. Doubtless he acted on instructions from his ecclesiastical superiors, who were mindful of Lenormand's vote in the National Assembly in favor of financial aid to Catholic schools. During this tumultuous session, Governor Angamarre maintained strict neutrality, and in his speech to the general council he made no reference to the political situation and dealt only with financial matters.

The French government, true to its word, did submit a bill for New Caledonia to the National Assembly on June 13, but it concerned only the general council and did not embody the expected statute for the territory as a whole. Although it slightly altered the division of the electoral circumscriptions and the distribution of the seats assigned to each, it differed little from the one sponsored by the preceding government, so that it satisfied neither the advocates of the dual-college system nor those of the single college. Consequently, the National Assembly again failed to act decisively, and instead voted to send to New Caledonia a mission of inquiry to work out some agreement on the spot. Initially this was to have been a 7-man mission representing the main Metropolitan parties, but in the end it was composed of only three deputies, all of them conservatives.[12] Considering the disunity of public opinion in New Caledonia and the brevity of their stay there—from September 13 to 18—it is remarkable that the members of the mission worked out a generally acceptable compromise. In part, this acquiescence was due to the Caledonians' weariness and to their overriding desire for some permanent statute and a new general council, but even more to the conciliatory attitude assumed by both Lenormand and Lafleur. On the eve of the mission's return to France, Lenormand offered a reception to its members, which was attended not only by conservative Europeans but also by 300 Melanesians.[13]

The compromise agreement reached by the mission was presented to the National Assembly on November 19. There was to be no increase in the powers of the general councilors and no change in the

---

[12] Brusset of the R.P.F.; Bettancourt, Independent Republican; and Laforest, Radical Socialist.

[13] *Marchés Coloniaux*, Oct. 11, 1952, pp. 2619–2620.

duration of their terms of office. The number of electoral circumscriptions remained five, and nine seats were assigned to the south, seven to the west, two to the east, four to the tribes and the Isle of Pines, and three to the Loyalty Islands. The principle of a single electoral college was maintained, although in fact, if not in law, a dual college was created in the south and west circumscriptions. Candidates were required to have lived in New Caledonia for a year, but they need not have resided in the circumscription in which they competed. Voters could now either write on the ballot the names of any candidates they might propose or select them from various party lists. Although the existing rolls would be used in the next election for the general council, scheduled to take place 2 months after the bill became law (on December 10), the government promised to revise them as soon as possible so as to include all the territory's inhabitants aged 21 years or over. This meant a radical change within the foreseeable future, when there would be nearly 18,000 Melanesian voters, or twice their present number, whereas the European electorate would remain at approximately 11,000. Even with the relatively restricted native electorate eligible to vote on February 6, 1953, for a new general council, the Melanesians proved to be the decisive element in its outcome.

For all five circumscriptions there were 60 candidates competing for the 25 seats at stake, and none of them could be called a youthful firebrand. Half the candidates were more than 50 years of age; fifteen more than 60; sixteen between 40 and 50; and only one as young as 28.[14] The only left-wing party of any importance was the Union Calédonienne (U.C.), led by Lenormand and Bergès, and its sole serious competitor was the Liste d'Union, headed by Bonneaud and Bichon.

Bonneaud's party campaigned for a "severe compression of administrative expenditures and no new taxes," for the promotion of mining and also of agricultural production (because prices for nickel and chromium might fall), and for an increase in the number of immigrant laborers and in the means of communication. Its views concerning the Melanesians were summed up in these terms:

We have the sincere desire to collaborate with the natives and want to help them enter political, economic, and social life. If we have drawn up no precise program in this respect, it is because we want first to consult with the natives as to their own wishes. We regret that our offer of union

14 *La France Australe,* Feb. 5, 1953.

with the two existing native political organizations [the A.I.C.L.F. and the U.I.C.A.L.O.] was not accepted because of their prior commitments.[15]

This tone of Olympian detachment changed rapidly when the Liste d'Union leaders learned that the "prior commitments" included a pledge of support for the U.C.'s program, which the conservatives fully believed would include the imposition of an income tax that "would ruin the territory." Even though the U.C.'s published program was noncommittal on that burning question,[16] it was in other respects so openly antagonistic to the interests of the Establishment, as represented by members of the Liste d'Union, that their fears were increased rather than assuaged.

In certain spheres, the U.C. and the Liste d'Union advocated similar policies, as in their common desire for a permanent statute and for more schools, hospitals, housing, and public works, as well as improved agricultural training. They also saw eye to eye in wanting a higher status for local-born functionaries and more powers for the general council and municipal commissions vis-à-vis the local administration. The U.C., however, went farther than the Liste d'Union, for it proposed that the French government be left with control only over the territory's foreign contacts, defense, and financial policies. It was above all in the fields of economic and native policies that they were in direct conflict. As to the local economy, the U.C. advocated breaking up the big estates and distributing their land to small holders, who would thus be able to increase their agricultural output. To finance that expansion and help the peasants obtain better sales prices, the U.C. proposed that the government terminate the monopoly enjoyed by the big firms, which controlled exports as well as—in conjunction with the Banque de l'Indochine—all the locally available credit facilities. For the Melanesians, the U.C. wanted a new legal status that would permit the "progressive adaptation" of the chieftaincy and the councils of elders to current conditions, as well as a codification and modernization of customary law, an enlargement in and more guarantees for tribal reservations and family property, obligatory primary education and more scholarships in state and mission schools, and Melanesian representation in the Chambers of Agriculture and Commerce and on the Land Commission.

---

[15] *Ibid.*, Jan. 21, 1953.

[16] *Ibid.*, Jan. 29–30, 1953; Lenormand, M., "L'Evolution Politique des Autochtones de la Nouvelle-Calédonie."

The reforms outlined in the U.C.'s platform were so comprehensive that it could not fail to appeal to the poor whites (*petits blancs*) and some of the missionaries, as well as the Melanesians. For the first time, the have-nots and the underprivileged were offered a dynamic leadership which shook them out of their habitual torpor. The outcome of the February 6, 1953, election was a landslide victory for Lenormand's party, which won 14 seats in the new council and also the support of Dr. Marc Tivoilier, the only candidate of his group (Action Républicaine et Sociale) to be elected. In Nouméa, despite the abstention of half of the electorate and a split in the conservative vote, the Liste d'Union captured all seven of that circumscription's seats, while only the leader of the "petitioners"—James Daly—was elected from the west circumscription. Among the nine new Melanesian councilors there was a majority of chiefs. As to their geographical distribution, three were from the Loyalty Islands (James Haeweng of Lifou, Michel Kauma from Ouvéa, and Luther Enoka of Maré); two were from the east coast (Matheo Aripoindi of the U.I.C.A.L.O. and Doui Matayo of the A.I.C.L.F.); and four from the west (Rock Pidjot, president of the U.I.C.A.L.O., Pastor Elia Tidjine, Kowi Bouillant, president of the A.I.C.L.F., and Raphael Bouanoué, a nurse from the Belêp archipelago).

Given the composition of the new council, it was obvious from the outset that it would become the focal point for a confrontation between the conservative minority and the left-wing majority. At its first session, on February 26, 1953, Pierre Bergès was elected president, and he soon outdid other members of the U.C. in the vehemence of his attacks on the conservatives. For the Melanesian councilors, Rock Pidjot and Kowi Bouillant became the outstanding spokesmen, and all the Melanesian councilors solidly backed the U.C. in its increasingly acrimonious conflict with members of the Liste d'Union.[17]

Actually no basic disagreement separated the two opposing parties in their common desire for greater autonomy, control over the Metropolitan civil servants in the territory, and an extension of the general council's powers. They did, however, clash over the U.C.'s financial policy, Lenormand's high-handed dismissal of functionaries and elimination of political opponents he regarded as obstructionist, his introduction of bills in the National Assembly without clearing them first with the councilors, and his proposal to reorganize the municipal

[17] *Marchés Coloniaux*, July 4, 1953, p. 1956.

commissions and the Chamber of Commerce so as to give greater representation to small businessmen and Melanesians.

The mounting criticism of Lenormand's dictatorial behavior did cause him to backtrack to the extent of promising prior consultation of the general council on any bills presented to the National Assembly, but this concession failed to placate the opposition. The parties were fundamentally divided on two issues: the passing of political power into Melanesian hands, and the U.C.'s determination to free New Caledonia from the "grip of the trusts." The conservatives repeatedly complained that the natives, who paid no taxes and performed no military service (until 1962) in return for the protection, schooling, and care they received, should not be in a position to control the territory's destiny. Because the natives were still largely unorganized and passive, they might have accepted "guidance" from the conservatives if they had not already come to trust their U.C. mentor. It was clear that the U.C. was determined to impose fiscal measures that would end the long-standing domination of the economy by Nouméa's big business firms, notably those of the mining industry. Unable to agree on a common strategy in the council, the conservatives concentrated on causing the French government to intervene, even though this would mean sacrificing some of the territory's autonomy, which they had long been at pains to increase.

Aside from the profound changes consequent to the U.C.'s acquisition of power in the territory, 1953 was also a landmark in Franco-Caledonian relations, for in September of that year the centenary of the island's annexation by France was celebrated in Nouméa. Six months before that event, the first member of the French cabinet ever to visit the territory came to New Caledonia. This was Jean Letourneau, Minister for the Associated States, who stopped for 2 days in mid-March at Nouméa on his way home from an official visit to Australia. His visit offered an unusual opportunity for the general council to make its wishes known directly to the French government, and the U.C. prepared a *cahier de doléances*. Letourneau accepted it noncommittally, merely saying that he would transmit it to the Overseas Minister, Louis Jacquinot.

The *cahier* opened with the statement that "New Caledonia intends to remain French by the permanent and irrevocable wish of its inhabitants," but as a distant province or overseas territory and not as a department of France. Among the desiderata mentioned in this document were the councilors' requests for control over local affairs, including the choice of Metropolitan functionaries to serve in the island, consultation on all measures affecting the territory before their introduction in the Parliament, and suppression of the privy council.[18]

No immediate reply was made by the government, but when Jacquinot came to Nouméa in September for the centenary celebrations, he discussed its contents in a speech to the general council. He said that his government, in principle, favored decentralization for the overseas territories and recognized the "necessity for granting you a large delegation of powers, which your distance from France and the special nature of your problems justify.[19] Agreeable as were such words to Caledonian ears, they were no more than the usual official promises-and-projects, and, therefore, gave them no real satisfaction. Because the concurrent centenary celebrations were the occasion for manifesting the Caledonians' deep attachment to France, the local demand for greater autonomy and partisan quarrels were submerged in the prevalent euphoric atmosphere—but not for long.

Because the U.C.'s control of the general council could not be challenged on legal grounds, the conservatives chose Lenormand as the most vulnerable target. Through an undercover campaign, they sought to convince the French government and public opinion that he was a fellow-traveler of the communists, and that, with communist aid, he was seeking to make New Caledonia independent of France. The conservatives' propaganda seemed to have some effect, for in 1954, two deputies visited New Caledonia to investigate their allegations. Despite the brevity of their stay on the island, they submitted a 104-page report in which they stressed New Caledonia's "unfortunate subordination" to Australia and implied that it might be advisable to curtail the general council's "excessive powers" by empowering the governor to veto its decisions.[20] Subsequently, a clause was inserted in the overseas budget which divested the council of control over certain taxes—reportedly at the instigation of the Société Le Nickel.[21]

The only other overt result of the conservatives' smear campaign at that time was the public dissociation from the U.C. of the local branch

[18] That council comprised the governor, the secretary-general, the commander-in-chief, heads of the main administrative services, and two appointed leading citizens.

[19] Quoted in *Marchés Coloniaux*, Oct. 24, 1953, p. 2894.

[20] *Pacific Islands Monthly*, May 1955.

[21] Leenhardt, M., "Unité Française et Unité d'Action."

of the S.F.I.O., whose members apparently had become convinced that Lenormand was trying to wrest the territorial trade unions from the socialists' control.[22] In all other respects, however, the U.C. was able to consolidate its authority, and it soon matched the conservatives' previous record by gaining control over the territory's three parliamentary posts. In January 1955, a U.C. member, Louis Eschenbrenner, took the seat in the French Union Assembly that had been vacated by the death of Bergès in November 1954. In June 1955, another U.C. candidate, Armand Ohlen, defeated Henri Lafleur, who was seeking reelection to the Senate, and in January 1956, Lenormand was reelected deputy by a far larger majority than before. In that election, he received 12,823 of the 20,966 votes cast by a registered electorate then numbering 27,549.[23]

The socialist government that came to power in France as the result of the January 1956 election at once began drafting a liberal statute, in the form of a *loi-cadre*, for all the French overseas territories.[24] Although Lenormand and other Caledonians were reassured thereby of the territory's long-delayed acquisition of a permanent statute, the introduction of universal suffrage, and a government council that would share executive power with the governor, the *loi-cadre* fell short of granting the degree of autonomy desired by all elements of the population. Above all, they complained, it failed to guarantee the general council full control over the budget and the civil service. Despite Lenormand's (and Pouvanaa's) opposition, the bill became law on June 23, 1956.

The struggle now centered on the decrees that were to spell out the application of the new law to the territory. The Caledonians' attention became so riveted on the relevant parliamentary debates that they failed to appreciate the significance of the visit paid to the territory by General de Gaulle in September 1956. As hero of the Resistance, he was warmly welcomed by all the islanders, but as head of the R.P.F., only by the conservatives. Vincent Bouquet, Great Chief of Bourail, used this occasion not only to thank France publicly for promoting the "bloodless revolution" of his people, but also indirectly to let the French government know that the Melanesians expected further reforms.[25] Although the chief knew that De Gaulle had come

---

[22] *La France Australe,* March 4, 1955.
[23] *Marchés Coloniaux,* Jan. 14, 1956, p. 65.
[24] See pp. 41–42.
[25] *Pacific Islands Monthly,* October 1956.

only as a private citizen and could not then influence the course of current events, his words had almost a prophetic ring, for it was during this visit that the general conceived a policy for the French Pacific islands that he later put into effect. By the time he returned to power in 1958, changing world conditions had modified the roles that he had earlier envisaged for the E.F.O. and New Caledonia, but this did not lessen the importance he attached to both territories.

If these islands were to fulfil the role he had assigned to them in his overall scheme, there must be no question of their loosening their ties with France. The well-informed journalist, Georges Chaffard, has pointed out [26] that the emissary chosen to lay the groundwork for execution of the general's policy was André Rives-Henry—a close collaborator of Jacques Chaban-Delmas—who in 1957 and 1958 made many trips between Paris and the islands. Armed with letters of introduction from Roger Frey, a prominent Gaullist who had been born in New Caledonia, Rives-Henry established fruitful contacts with conservatives in Nouméa and Papeete. Thus the local opponents of the two main autonomist leaders, Lenormand and Pouvanaa, benefited by invaluable support from unexpected quarters in France.

The strategy they worked out to undermine the two deputies was not immediately evident or operative. In the interval, the decree applying the *loi-cadre* to New Caledonia resulted in important changes in the number, election, and powers of the general councilors. So strong and widespread was the opposition aroused locally by the first reading of the decree in the National Assembly that both conservatives and liberals called a political truce. They also agreed to be represented jointly in the delegation that was invited to discuss the decree in Paris by Gaston Defferre, French overseas minister and co-author of the *loi-cadre*.[27] The changes in the decree that were proposed by the French Union Assembly [28] were further modified by the territorial delegates, and finally embodied in twenty-two amendments which Lenormand tenaciously defended during the National Assembly's second reading on April 10 and 20.

Lenormand was unsuccessful in his efforts to obtain complete control for the territory over the budget, the civil service, and important administrative services, such as those of telecommunications and

[26] "Les Rebelles du Pacifique," *L'Express*, Oct. 20, 1968.

[27] Henri Bonneaud, a member of the delegation, died in Paris suddenly on March 2, 1957, at the age of 49.

[28] Minutes of March 12, April 4, 1957.

mining, as well as to make the new government council fully responsible to the legislature, now called the territorial assembly. He was also unable to prevent the Parliament's acceptance of a new system of proportional voting in which electors could mark their whole ballot in the order of their preference. Nevertheless, the territory made substantial progress and won important concessions. Among these was the election by the assembly of an embryonic cabinet—the government council—whose 8 members would be called ministers and given charge of one or more administrative departments. Equally important was an increase in the number of assemblymen from 25 to 30 and a reduction in that of the circumscriptions from 5 to 4, as well as a revision of their boundaries so that there was now a single electoral college in fact as well as in theory.[29] The introduction of universal suffrage swelled the electorate by about 20 percent, this increase mainly affecting the Melanesians, who would be able to dominate the third and fourth circumscriptions.

The first elections for the assembly under the new law took place calmly on October 6, 1957, and were preceded by a campaign in which the personal insults exchanged were unusually few. The 30 assembly seats at stake were contested by 123 candidates, belonging to 8 parties, all but one of which—the U.C.—were new and short-lived. The conservatives were divided into three groups of widely varying importance. First came the Républicains Socialistes, headed by Georges Chatenay, a local-born lawyer who was relatively unknown except for his support of the dual electoral college and of close relations with France. The second was the Action Economique et Social, led by Henri Lafleur, and the third was a small rural party, the Paysans Indépendants, one of whose candidates was elected. The Républicains Socialistes sponsored candidates in all the circumscriptions and won 7 seats in the assembly, while Lafleur's party contested only in Nouméa, where 3 of its members were elected. Altogether there were 11 conservatives and 19 liberals in the new assembly. Of the latter group, all but one—Gabriel Moussot, the candidate of a small labor party called the Rassemblement Ouvrier—belonged to the U.C. Although there were many abstentions in Nouméa and the Loyalty Islands, 68 percent of the electorate, now totaling more than

[29] The first circumscription comprised not only Nouméa and its environs but also Yaté and the Isle of Pines, and it was allotted 10 seats; the second, on the west coast, had 8; the third, on the east coast, enlarged to include Ouégoa and the Belêp Islands, had 7; and the fourth, made up of the Loyalty Islands, had 5.

33,600, actually voted.[30] In its ethnic composition, the new assembly included 17 Europeans and 13 Melanesians, of whom only 6 former councilors—among them Lenormand and Michel Kauma—were re-elected. Of the 8 government councilors elected by the assembly, all were members of the U.C. and 2 of them were Melanesians. Michel Kauma, in January 1958, became the first Melanesian to preside over a session of the assembly, of which he had been elected a vice-president.

[30] *Marchés Tropicaux,* Oct. 12, 1957, p. 2422.

23

The Decline and Fall of Lenormand

During the first 4 months of 1958, the position of Lenormand and the U.C. seemed unassailable. With its slogan of "Deux couleurs mais un seul peuple," and a program designed to raise the living standards of all the underprivileged inhabitants of the territory, the U.C. had begun attracting to its ranks increasing numbers of *petits blancs*, particularly the European wage-earners. The party was still comfortably in the majority in the assembly, even though not all of its former councilors had been reelected, and it also had a monopoly of the posts in the new government council. In the National Assembly, Lenormand belonged to the I.O.M., and could count on the support there of a wide range of Metropolitan parties, including those that controlled the last governments of the Fourth Republic. The Caledonian conservatives might well have remained a passive if frustrated minority had it not been for two simultaneous developments in the spring of 1958. The first of these was a depression in the local mining industry, and the second, the coup of May 13 at Algiers, which inspired a similar event in Nouméa.

In New Caledonia the ringleader of the activists was Major Henri Loustau, the military *chef de cabinet* of the territory's governor, Aimé Grimald (January 1956–November 1958). Loustau had previously served in Algeria, and among the disgruntled Europeans of Nouméa he organized patriotic associations similar to those that had precipitated the Algiers coup.[1] To the Caledonian conservatives who despaired of ousting Lenormand and the U.C. by legal means, the example offered by the French officers in Algiers was a catalyst. An opportunity to execute a similar coup at Nouméa seemed to be offered by the traditional celebration there of General de Gaulle's appeal of June 18, 1940. The *broussards* who had driven the Pétainists out of the capital at that time returned annually to Nouméa to com-

[1] For a detailed account of this episode, see G. Chaffard, "Les Rebelles du Pacifique."

memorate the event, and among them were many opponents of the U.C. Since Loustau could guarantee the backing of the army, the prospects for forcing the resignation of Lenormand and his colleagues appeared good.

Just how far the plotters were prepared to go is not precisely known. A police report indicated that they planned to shoot Lenormand at the moment he placed a wreath on the monument to the war dead, but no such attempt was made. After the ceremony, however, a procession—variously estimated at 500 and 1,000 persons—marched to the governor's palace, where they demanded that Lenormand and his government council resign. To gain time, Governor Grimald said he must first talk with the deputy and councilors, but they were nowhere to be found in Nouméa. Bands of armed youths roaming the streets had made them fear for their lives, and it was not until the governor promised Lenormand a safe-conduct that the latter agreed to go to his residence. When they met, Grimald said he would refer the matter for decision to the Minister of Overseas France, but to avoid bloodshed in the meantime he would have to suspend the government council and assume full powers himself.

The Gaullist government having been so recently installed in Paris, the new Overseas Minister, Cornut-Gentille, was too preoccupied with other problems to deal immediately with those of New Caledonia. Within a few days, however, he invited both the U.C. and its opponents to send delegates to Paris to discuss the situation with him. Lenormand decided to remain in Nouméa, where he began secretly organizing his Melanesian supporters to stage a counterdemonstration. Rumors of this plan reached the ears of the European conservatives, some of whom formed a *comité de vigilance*, armed themselves, dug trenches, and erected barriers in the town in anticipation of a seemingly inevitable clash. Feeling ran so high that the vigilantes manhandled Rock Pidjot and arrested about ten U.C. assemblymen, including Senator Ohlen, whom they took to Bourail and imprisoned there. Nevertheless, Governor Grimald managed to avoid a showdown by broadcasting appeals for calm and promising to use the local naval force—not the army or gendarmes—to prevent further disorders. His call for a political truce was heeded, pending arbitration of the dispute in Paris.

On June 24, Cornut-Gentille began his talks with Griscelli and Kauma, who formed the U.C. delegation and who hotly denied that their party had any secessionist designs.[2] He also conferred with Senator Lafleur, the top man among the minority delegates, all of whom were Europeans except the conservative Melanesian chief, Henri Naisseline. Lafleur's group was somewhat disillusioned by its reception in Paris, where they had expected a warmer welcome. Cornut-Gentille said that he would not dissolve a government council that had been legally constituted, but he did agree to send to New Caledonia a "mission of inquiry and mediation," headed by former Governor Angamarre. Meanwhile, Lenormand remained discreetly in Nouméa, where Governor Grimald had headed off further clashes by forbidding Europeans to carry firearms and by stationing troops around the public buildings. Time seemed to be on Lenormand's side, and in addition he received support indirectly from Mgr. Martin, head of the Catholic mission, who chided the militant Europeans for their use of force.

The Angamarre mission reached Nouméa on July 2, and at once began trying to conciliate the opposing forces. An agreement was drafted whereby Lenormand consented to proportional representation of the minority members in the assembly committees and to their being offered the two portfolios of mines and finance in a reconstituted government council.[3] It was reported that most of the conservatives under Lafleur's leadership were inclined to accept this compromise, but the militant hard-core group, led by Thomas Hagen, a former general councilor and a supporter of the dual electoral college, would agree to nothing short of the resignation of Lenormand and all the U.C. councilors. At the urging of this group, 6 of the 11 conservative assemblymen resigned, and the Angamarre mission had to return to Paris empty-handed.

To find a way out of the impasse, both Lenormand and Lafleur were invited to France in late July for further talks, and were received by General de Gaulle. They learned of the general's plan for a new constitution for the Fifth Republic, regarding which all French citizens would be asked to vote affirmatively or negatively. In the overseas dependencies, a negative vote would result in immediate independence but also an end to all French aid. The only leader in

---

[2] The negotiations initiated at Hanoi in April 1958 by the U.C.'s Minister of Finance for the repatriation of Tonkinese laborers from New Caledonia were cited by the conservatives as proof that the majority party was arrogating to itself the rights of sovereignty. See *L'Avenir Calédonien*, May 13, 1963.

[3] *Le Monde*, Aug. 5, 1958; *Marchés Tropicaux*, Aug. 9, 1958, p. 1918.

New Caledonia to advocate a negative vote was Pierre Jeanson, the editor of *Le Calédonien* and a trade-union organizer, who attacked the Gaullist government for its subservience to the capitalists.[4] According to the official tally, 27,028 persons (of a registered electorate numbering 35,163) went to the polls on September 28, and of these, 26,085 cast affirmative votes. The assembly then chose for New Caledonia the status of an overseas territory. Thus Caledonian opinion, for once, was almost solidly united, and the conservative minority ceased charging the U.C. with promoting secessionism—but only for a short time. Although Lenormand, by his stand in favor of the constitution, was spared the fate that soon overtook Pouvanaa, who had campaigned for a negative vote, his enemies were not appeased and soon resumed the offensive against him.

Now that the Gaullists were in power in France, the local conservatives could openly join forces with them to carry out their joint policy of eliminating the autonomist leaders in France's Pacific islands. In the case of New Caledonia, they had to proceed more slowly than in French Polynesia, because Lenormand's supporters included a growing number of Europeans as well as the Christian missions. On October 30, 1958, Jacques Soustelle, France's new Minister of Information, announced that because tension still prevailed in New Caledonia its territorial assembly would be dissolved and new elections would be held on December 8. A few weeks later, the appointment of Laurent Pechoux to succeed Aimé Grimald as governor was another straw in the wind, for Pechoux brought to his new post a record of harsh—if unsuccessful—repressive measures against the African nationalists in Togo and Ivory Coast.

Pechoux could not immediately carry out his assigned task of "breaking" Lenormand,[5] because the elections of December 8 confirmed the ascendancy of the U.C., which received even more votes than in October 1957. In the new assembly, 18 seats went to that party and 1 to its ally, the Rassemblement Ouvrier. (This labor party, under the leadership of Gabriel Moussot, soon took the name of Union Républicaine.) Lenormand was reelected vice-president of the government council, of which the governor was ex-officio president, and as a conciliatory gesture he offered two portfolios to the opposition. The latter, however, refused to participate so long as New Cale-

---

[4] *Pacific Islands Monthly*, October 1958.

[5] This governor was reported to have boasted on several occasions, "Je torderai le cou du petit Lenormand," and on others, "J'aurai sa peau."

donia was governed under the provisions of the *loi-cadre*, although that law had not been fully applied to the territory since the pseudo-putsch of the preceding June.

The issue now being clearly joined over the *loi-cadre*, one of the first acts of the new assembly was to vote in favor of its full application in New Caledonia, even though the U.C., only two years before, had pronounced that law to be unsatisfactory. Governor Pechoux, far from heeding this vote, began systematically to whittle away the powers of the government council. To protest against his policy, Lenormand, accompanied by three Melanesian assemblymen, went in March to Paris, where he voiced his grievances against the local administration at a press conference.[6] He then said that Pechoux had taken away from the government council the control it had formerly exercised over the civil service, the police, and radio-broadcasting, and that the governor had sent members of his cabinet throughout the Grande Terre to spread propaganda against the U.C. ministers. By an "unacceptable trick," Pechoux had succeeded in excluding all Melanesians from participation as candidates in the senatorial election due to take place on April 26, and with the same end in view he had vetoed the holding of elections for new municipal commissions except that of Nouméa, where the conservatives had always won out. Lenormand's bitter denunciation of Pechoux' tactics elicited no support in Paris, where the government upheld its gubernatorial appointee. Consequently, on March 22 Lenormand resigned as vice-president of the government council, saying he could no longer accept responsibility for an administration over which he had no control.

Lenormand's resignation and Henri Lafleur's subsequent reelection to the Senate delighted the conservatives, but their rejoicing was short-lived. On May 24, Lenormand was returned to the National Assembly by 16,163 votes to 7,247 for his conservative opponent, and for the first time he received a majority of the votes cast by the Nouméa electorate.[7] In June, the new government council elected by the assembly was again solidly composed of U.C. members, and the post of vice-president went to Michel Kauma, one of Lenormand's foremost collaborators.[8] The year ended with still another U.C. vic-

[6] *Le Monde*, April 4, 1959.

[7] *Marchés Tropicaux*, June 6, 1959, p. 1401.

[8] The annoyance felt by the European Caledonians because of these developments was intensified by a series of articles that appeared at about that time in the mass-circulation Metropolitan newspaper, *France-Soir*. Their author, Lucien Bodart, depicted the Europeans of New Caledonia as austere, unenterprising,

tory, when ex-Senator Ohlen was reelected president of the territorial assembly.

During the 1960–1961 period, relations between the Gaullist government, the adminstration, and local conservatives on the one hand, and the U.C. on the other, unobtrusively came to a turning point. The responsibility for an attempt in April 1960 to blow up the house of Georges Chatenay, head of the local branch of the U.N.R., was never legally established, but in Nouméa it was widely laid at the doorstep of the U.C.[9] Throughout the rest of that year, Lenormand's leadership was subtly eroded. In part this was caused by his increasingly autocratic behavior toward members of his party and in part by his loss of influence in the National Assembly, where his sole support now came from the extreme left-wing parties. In the late autumn, Michel Kauma, vice-president of the government council, and Doui Matayo, Minister of the Interior, dissociated themselves from the U.C. by voting against the reelection of Ohlen as assembly president, and within a month they were expelled from the party.[10] At the same time, the defection of Gabriel Moussot, leader of the Union Républicaine and former ally of Lenormand, reduced the U.C. majority in the assembly, making the two opposing groups there roughly equal in strength.[11]

It should not be concluded, however, that these changes, significant as they were, led to an immediate breakdown in the operations of the assembly, for on many local issues, such as increasing the pay of territorial civil servants, its members were in agreement. Moreover, Lenormand's duties as deputy prevented him from attending some crucial assembly sessions when his influence might have proved decisive, and during one such absence, in January 1961, the conservative coalition, which now included the Union Républicaine, managed to gain control of the permanent commission. On the credit side of the U.C. ledger, however, the municipal elections of May 1961 showed that a majority of the territory's electorate was still faithful to Lenormand's leadership. By and large, 1960–1961 was a prosperous

and dull, and in need of collective psychiatric treatment because they could never forget their convict heritage. See *Pacific Islands Monthly*, April 1959.

[9] *Le Monde*, July 24, 1963.

[10] In May 1965, Kauma told the writers that he had originally joined the U.C. because it advocated integration of the European and Melanesian communities, and that he had left it when he realized that it was in fact sowing discord between the two ethnic groups.

[11] *Marchés Tropicaux*, Dec. 10, 1960, p. 2614.

era for New Caledonia, and the decline in the U.C.'s strength did not become apparent until the spring of 1962, when the territory experienced an economic recession.

The storm that broke over the assembly in March 1962 had been gathering during the preceding budgetary session, when an old controversy was revived there in new form. It was precipitated by a request from the Société Le Nickel that its exports be exempted from customs duties, on the ground that the company was having difficulty in selling its nickel to many of its old customers. For many years and by various maneuvers, Le Nickel had been trying to wring financial aid from the territory's budget, and now it coupled its request with the threat of closing down its refinery if the exemption it asked for were refused. Some "realists" among the assemblymen preferred granting a subsidy to coping with the large-scale unemployment that would ensue if Le Nickel actually carried out its threat. The majority, however, recalled that when Le Nickel had been receiving grants from the government it had continued to pay dividends to shareholders abroad, and they refused on principle to be blackmailed again into bailing the company out of its current difficulties.

Governor Pechoux intervened in the dispute and, terming the company's request "reasonable," asked the assembly to reconsider its decision at an extraordinary session he called on March 6. The assemblymen, however, stood their ground in a vote that cut across party lines. Two days later, a bomb exploded in the assembly hall, and although no one was hurt, this incident was certainly a factor in the French government's decision on March 9 to dissolve the assembly and to hold new elections on April 15. At the same time, it demonstrated its approval of Pechoux's stand by promoting him to a higher rank in the overseas administrative service.

If the government's dissolution of the assembly was indeed motivated, as it stated, by New Caledonia's need to have a legislature more widely representative of public opinion, Paris was again doomed to disappointment. The elections of April 15, 1962, like those of December 8, 1958, once again gave the U.C. 18 seats in the assembly. That party won a majority of the votes in all four circumscriptions, although there were changes in their geographical distribution. The U.C. lost two seats on the east coast and one in the Loyaltys to the conservatives, but it picked up three more in the circumscription of Nouméa. The opposition, too, retained the same total of twelve seats as before, but it might have been more successful if the U.N.R., the

Rassemblement Calédonien, and the Union Républicaine had backed the same list of candidates, as they had done in 1958, and if more than 45 percent of Nouméa's electorate had voted. In this election, the Union Républicaine lost its single seat, the U.N.R. improved its position with the election of 9 of its candidates, and the Rassemblement Calédonien's representation in the assembly was reduced to three.[12]

The most important change that marked this election occurred in Nouméa, which had long been an electoral fief of the conservatives. There the U.C. won 6 of the 10 seats at stake, and thus claimed an imposing victory over the forces supporting the Société Le Nickel. The U.N.R. candidates in the capital, led by Maître Chatenay, promptly appealed for the annulment of the election in that circumscription, ascribing their defeat to fraud in counting the ballots. One of the first acts of the U.C.-dominated Assembly was to pass a resolution asking for the recall of Governor Pechoux. It then elected as head of the new government council Rock Pidjot, the only one of Lenormand's early Melanesian collaborators to remain faithful to his leadership. Rock Pidjot announced that he would soon go to Paris, where he hoped to work out with the French government a new statute for the territory that would open a way out of its existing political impasse.

Before Rock Pidjot left Nouméa on May 7, there took place in the capital a series of dramatic events reminiscent of those that had occurred on June 18, 1958. Late in April, Lenormand had received anonymous letters containing dire personal threats, and he told his friends that he expected that the militant conservatives would try very soon to assassinate him.[13] At 1:30 in the morning of April 27, an explosion occurred at the party headquarters of the U.C. A few hours later, the governor ordered the army and gendarmerie to patrol the streets of Nouméa, check all cars entering the town, and set up machine guns around his own residence, where a small but angry crowd had gathered and were shouting insults against him.

Whether or not the governor really believed that the U.C. was preparing a putsch or was simply taking precautions to prevent further disorders is not known, but his tactics were much the same as those he had used before, in Africa. In any case, he banned all public meetings in Nouméa and ordered the imprisonment of three suspects—all

[12] Minutes of the Conseil de la République, June 28, 1962.
[13] *Le Monde,* May 16, 1962; Chaffard, "Les Rebelles du Pacifique."

members of the U.C.—whom the gendarmes had found at the scene of the explosion. Of the men arrested, only Michel Bernast was a Caledonian and had a certain political prominence as secretary of the U.C. party.[14] The other two men detained were Paul Ciavaldini, a Eurasian who had recently emigrated from Indochina, where he was said to have worked for the French secret police, and Maurice Galoncki, of Polish origin, who at one time had been a member of a terrorist organization in Israel. On May 26, these two men "confessed" that they had planted the bomb in the U.C. headquarters, but they claimed to have done so with the consent of Lenormand because the deputy had hoped that the blame for the damage would fall on his Gaullist opponents.

Even before Lenormand was directly incriminated by the testimony of Ciavaldini and Galoncki, it was obvious that his opponents were going to make the fullest possible use of the bombing incident to discredit him politically. He therefore lost no time in flying to Paris, both to defend himself there and to support Rock Pidjot's pleas for a liberal and full application to New Caledonia of the *loi-cadre*. In the Paris press and in the National Assembly, Lenormand attacked Pechoux's record and defended the policy of the U.C. In an interview published in *Le Monde* on May 16, 1962, Lenormand denied that the Caledonian crisis stemmed from a personal quarrel between himself and the autocratic governor or that it could be ascribed to the population's justified hostility to Le Nickel or to the Melanesians' resentment against an oppressive European minority. The cause of the territory's malaise, he asserted, was the same as that which had led to disaster in North Africa and Indochina—the French government's failure to understand and satisfy the overseas populations' aspirations by "decolonizing" its administration. He claimed that Governor Pechoux, by his illegal actions and use of force, had forfeited the confidence of both the Melanesians and a majority of the Europeans, who, as evidenced by that party's repeated successes at the polls, stood firmly behind the U.C. To sum up, he argued that Pechoux and his Metropolitan entourage should be recalled to Paris and that New Caledonia should be given a statute that would maintain its close ties with France and at the same time accord it more autonomy.

Despite Lenormand's long and eloquent speeches in the National

[14] Bernast had been arrested once before, in November 1961, on the charge of trying to prevent the military recruitment of Caledonians. See *L'Avenir Calédonien*, Nov. 19, 1963.

Assembly to that effect,[15] the tide was now clearly running against him in Paris as well as in Nouméa. Both De Gaulle and Premier Pompidou refused his request for interviews. He made no headway against the government's firm opposition in the National Assembly, where, moreover, a request had been made by the conservatives that his parliamentary immunity to arrest be lifted. In July 1962, the Conseil du Contentieux Administratif[16] annulled the April 15 elections in the circumscription of Nouméa, where the U.C. had won six seats. On October 24, the Nouméa Court of Assizes sentenced Bernast to two years' imprisonment, and Ciavaldini and Galoncki to five years. Rumors were rife in the capital that Lenormand himself was about to be arrested, but in November he recovered some of the ground that he had lost. Laurent Pechoux, at long last, was recalled and replaced by a more moderate governor, Casimir-Marc Biros. On the 13th of November, Ciavaldini retracted that part of his confession that had most seriously implicated Lenormand, and five days later the deputy was reelected to the National Assembly. Nevertheless, the waning of his popular support was reflected in that election, when he received only 15,562 of the 28,802 votes cast,[17] and the concurrent lifting of his parliamentary immunity boded ill for his future.

The year 1963 opened with still another of the spectacular happenings that marked Lenormand's whole Caledonian career, and especially the months preceding his political eclipse. On January 13, Galoncki failed in an attempt to commit suicide because of remorse at having given false testimony against the deputy. Much of the ground was cut from under the prosecution's case by the collapse of its two star witnesses, but the charge against Lenormand of having "voluntarily failed to prevent the execution of a crime" remained. Lenormand had admitted to the examining magistrate that on the eve of the bombing he had received a visit from Ciavaldini and Galoncki, but he claimed that at that time he was so overworked and harassed by his adversaries' attacks that he had paid no attention to what they were saying. Nevertheless, he was deprived by the court of his civic rights for five years and given a suspended sentence of one year in prison, and his appeal against this verdict was denied the following August. The final scene in Lenormand's personal drama took place

[15] Minutes of June 21 and July 20, 1962.

[16] This council consisted of two officials and one magistrate. It judged cases of litigation between individuals and the administration concerning the functioning of the public services, as well as those involving electoral fraud.

[17] *Marchés Tropicaux,* Nov. 24, 1962, p. 2420.

on January 31, 1964, when he was formally removed from his post as deputy. At almost the same time, the struggle that he had carried on for more than 12 years against the combined forces of his conservative opponents, the local administration, and the Société Le Nickel ended in a crushing defeat for the more liberal statute which he had sought for New Caledonia.

After the deputy's elimination from politics, Rock Pidjot tried to replace him as best he could, and the U.C. rank and file supported him in successive elections as an indirect way of voting for Lenormand. A minor crisis in January 1963 led to the resignation of the government council, but Rock Pidjot was reelected its vice-president, and he made only a few changes in the distribution of portfolios. Generally speaking, the sentence meted out to Lenormand calmed political agitation in Nouméa, and in March 1963 the long warfare he had waged against Le Nickel over the latter's fiscal liability ended in a compromise. A concurrent slump in the mining industry adversely affected all elements in the population and centered their attention on the economic recession. When Louis Jacquinot came to New Caledonia in September, he received a warm welcome only from Nouméa's business community and officialdom, for not a single member of the U.C. attended the banquet given in his honor by the territorial assembly. Rock Pidjot addressed a memorandum to the overseas minister, relating his party's boycott directly to the French government's harassment of Lenormand and reiterating the U.C.'s plea for more territorial self-government.[18]

Jacquinot, in his press conference at Nouméa and his speech to the assembly, strongly hinted that his government intended to make fundamental changes in the territory's administrative regime. His denunciation of the *loi-cadre* as "unsuited to a territory that is an integral part of the French Republic," and his announcement of a 62-million-franc subsidy for New Caledonia's budget, pointed to a tightening rather than a liberalization of French controls. To just what lengths the government intended to go was not clear, however, until it introduced a bill in the National Assembly the following December.[19] In euphemistic terms, Jacquinot characterized this bill as a "way of regulating the impartial authority of the representative of the republic in harmony with the traditional and happy participation of the population in the management of their own affairs, through

[18] *Le Monde*, Sept. 29, 1963.
[19] Minutes of the National Assembly, Dec. 10, 1963.

the medium of an assembly elected by universal suffrage and exercising very wide powers." In reality, the government had no intention of making any change in the method of electing assemblymen, and even increased their powers by enabling them to overthrow the government council by a no-confidence vote. The crux of the bill, however, was its sharp reduction of the size and powers of the government council. The post of vice-president was to be abolished and the number of councilors other than officials reduced to five. They would no longer have the title of "minister" and were to be elected by proportional representation from among the assembly membership. Their authority would be restricted to control over territorial properties and to offering "advice" to the administration. The post of secretary-general of the territory, which had been abolished under the *loi-cadre*, was to be revived, and the governor would be empowered to suspend any councilor whose activities he regarded as detrimental to the public interest.

To justify the proposed demotion of the government council, Jacquinot cited its "deplorable" record of mismanagement of public affairs over the preceding 6 years. In particular, the territory's financial, education, public-works, and health services were in such a state of confusion, and their personnel so incompetent, that the councilors had been unable to draw up the long-awaited plan for the territory's economic and social development. He had to admit that the Caledonians would not relish this decline in their autonomy, but, said he, "We must at all costs modify the administrative structure of New Caledonia."

Needless to say, Lenormand in his swan-song as deputy heatedly denounced the bill as a retrogressive step that would revive New Caledonia's prewar colonial status. In a moment of pique, he attributed the measure to Jacquinot's personal vendetta against him. Some M.R.P. and socialist deputies supported Lenormand's more basic protests: they vainly proposed returning the bill to committee for further study and, in the meantime, sending another mission of inquiry to the territory. The Parliament, however, was about to adjourn for the Christmas holidays and was in no mood to procrastinate. When at 3 A.M. it became clear that the deputies would accept the bill, Lenormand and some of his supporters walked out of the chamber, leaving the communists as the only deputies on hand to vote against it. The bill easily passed the Senate, where it was ably defended by Lafleur, and on December 21, 1963, it became law.

24

Neither Autonomy nor Independence

From 1964 through 1967, the attention of Caledonians was focused on economic affairs, and political quarrels receded into the background. The French government's emasculation of the *loi-cadre* in late 1963 and its elimination of the seat in the government council which had given the U.C. a majority there were followed by the relegating of Lenormand to political obscurity early in 1964. These developments prevented his party from being as effective politically as before, and indeed brought a lull in the activities of all the parties. Deprived of Lenormand's dynamic leadership, the U.C. for some years was but the shadow of its former self, although its members' persevering loyalty was shown by their consistent electoral support for the former leader's alter ego, Rock Pidjot.

The latter's victory on June 7, 1964, over a conservative (Edouard Pentecost) and a radical (Pierre Jeanson) opposition was the more telling in that it occurred despite the fact that the voting regulations were modified on the eve of that election. Introduced ostensibly to combat electoral fraud, this measure was in fact designed to prevent many U.C. supporters in Nouméa from voting. It required voters not registered on the electoral rolls where they resided to return to their home circumscriptions to cast their ballots, and this entailed an expenditure of time and money which few of the poorer inhabitants of the capital could afford.[1] A noteworthy feature of this election was the marked decline of the extreme left wing as a political force, as was the nonparticipation of any Metropolitan candidate. Gabriel Moussot, head of the remnants of New Caledonia's communist party, did not enter the race, and Pierre Jeanson, another union organizer and the editor of the radical paper, *Le Calédonien*, received only 514 votes.[2] Edouard Pentecost, a wealthy self-made businessman of mixed blood, born on Maré Island, was nominally an independent.

[1] *Pacific Islands Monthly*, July 1964.
[2] *Marchés Tropicaux*, July 11, 1964, p. 1761.

In reality he was the U.N.R.'s candidate, and he received 11,518 votes compared with the 14,407 cast for Rock Pidjot.

The results of the election attested to the U.C.'s continuing strength, despite the government's stacking of the cards in favor of the conservative candidate, and this seemed to intensify France's determination to bring New Caledonia even more closely under the control of the Metropole. A revealing statement by Jacquinot in the National Assembly on October 22, 1964—in answer to one of Rock Pidjot's periodic demands that the *loi-cadre* be reapplied to New Caledonia— indicated that the territory had become of vital importance to overall French policy in the Pacific. The minister admitted that the reform of December 21, 1963, had been motivated by reasons "more imperative than that of assuring a better-functioning administration for the territory." Significantly, he added to this statement the "hope that one day I may be able to explain myself clearly and firmly." In July 1964, he made another visit to Nouméa, this time in the entourage of Georges Pompidou, the first French premier ever to set foot in the territory. Although Pompidou's stopover in Nouméa was incidental to his inspection of the C.E.P. base in Polynesia, it confirmed the belief that New Caledonia had come to hold a prominent place in General de Gaulle's plan for reinforcing the French presence in the Pacific.

Although the pace of political change in the territory decelerated during 1965–1966, France made several indirect moves to tighten its grip on the territory. On September 26, 1965, the defeat of Armand Ohlen by Henri Lafleur for reelection to the Senate heartened the conservatives, but the presidential elections held the following December showed that the Gaullists had achieved no more than a political stalemate. The U.C. opted to vote for François Mitterand against De Gaulle, and though the latter won more than 60 percent of the ballot in the run-off election, it was evident that the U.C. had not yet been reduced to political impotence. Obviously, the only way to undermine the U.C.'s majority in the territorial assembly was to revise the electoral circumscriptions in such a way as to diminish its geographical base.

On the ground that Nouméa's fast-growing population should have a larger representation in the assembly, the government increased the number of seats allotted to the first circumscription and reduced that of the east coast, which had always been the U.C.'s stronghold. Nevertheless, in the elections for 35 assembly seats on July 7, 1967, the U.C. strengthened its majority by capturing 22, whereas its conservative opponents lost 3 of those that they had previously held. This miscarriage of the Paris government's plan was due to the French politicians' chronic inability to follow developments in the territory closely and to interpret their meaning correctly. They had simply assumed that Nouméa was still the bastion of local conservatism, and did not grasp the fact that the huge increase in the number of the city's European wage-earners was responsible for providing the U.C. with the bulk of its supporters. This shift in the geographical base of that party's strength should have been apparent to General de Gaulle and his advisers when he visited Nouméa in September 1966. He received a cordial welcome in the territorial capital, but one far less warm and enthusiastic than had been accorded him on his visit as a private citizen nine years earlier.

Although Rock Pidjot did not prove to be a dynamic leader for the U.C., he kept its demand for autonomy alive in the National Assembly and remained completely loyal to the person and policy of his erstwhile chief. Furthermore, Lenormand provided him with discreet but effective guidance from the pharmacy which he owned in the Nouméa suburb of Magenta. In any event, the clock could not be turned back, for it was no longer possible to efface the legacy that he had bequeathed to the U.C. Even under such an attenuated form of political democracy as had come to prevail in New Caledonia, Lenormand's policy reflected the desires of a majority of its population.

Until Lenormand had founded the U.C., local affairs had been concentrated in the hands of big business and of the more prosperous settlers, and what passed for political life in the territory was simply the electoral rivalries between the individual spokesmen for those groups. His greatest contribution was to have created the first truly Caledonian party, and through it to have drawn the Melanesians into the mainstream of local political and, to a much lesser extent, economic life. Furthermore, he had broken down the racial barriers that separated them from the poorer stratum of Europeans, by being the first politician to appeal to those two categories of voters and to offer them a means of expressing their aspirations as well as their opposition to the conservatives' self-interested management of territorial affairs. With their support and that of the local missions and liberals in the National Assembly, Lenormand won his fight to maintain the single electoral college and to institute universal suffrage in the territory. The fact that he was able to hold together in one party the urban *petits blancs* (normally the most racist of Europeans) and native peasants, separated from each other not only geographically but also by profound social, economic, and ethnic differences, was proof of his qualities of leadership.

Lenormand's weaknesses were his Metropolitan origin—not completely forgotten or forgiven even though he married an upper-class Melanesian—and his authoritarian temperament. Had he shown more flexibility in handling party affairs, he might not have alienated some of his early and ablest Melanesian supporters, such as Michel Kauma and Doui Matayo, who were won over by his opponents. Other mistakes he made were more errors of omission than those of commission, and he might have remedied these seeming oversights if he had had a longer tenure of power or had been less harassed by his European adversaries. In any case, he failed to deal with the two questions that most concerned his Melanesian followers—those concerning the land reservations and the decline of the customary chieftaincy. As regards the Europeans, he did not try to capitalize on the residual *communard* tradition by providing political leadership for the radical elements. To be sure, any moves he might have made in those directions would also have swelled the ranks and the wrath of his enemies. As it was, the issue on which they brought about his downfall was the charge that he intended to make New Caledonia independent of France under guise of pleading for greater autonomy.

The conservatives, for their part, proved incapable of profiting politically by their elimination of Lenormand, for they were united only by their opposition to him and to his alleged secessionist tendencies. They formed and re-formed parties and coalitions that foundered on personal rivalries or on ambivalent attitudes toward General de Gaulle and his policies. The smallest conservative group was that of the ultras, organized into the Rassemblement Calédonien under the leadership of Senator Lafleur. Most of its members were wealthy local-born businessmen and mine-owners, misleadingly called *petits mineurs*, who opposed Le Nickel's domination of the mining industry and also De Gaulle's policy in Algeria and Black Africa. Consequently, on some issues the Rassemblement Calédonien cooperated with the U.C. and dissociated itself from the far-larger U.N.R., which was a local branch of the Metropolitan party of that name.

A majority of the Caledonian Gaullists were members of the U.N.R., but they were divided by personal rivalries and by the varying degrees to which they supported General de Gaulle. Many of the U.N.R.

members had a sentimental attachment to him as leader of Free France, but were lukewarm in their support for his policy as it affected New Caledonia after he became the powerful president of the French state. After the legislative elections of June 1964, one element of the Gaullist forces broke away from the U.N.R. to form a splinter party, the Action Calédonienne, whose program gave priority to purely Caledonian affairs. Under the leadership of a local-born physician, Dr. Edmond Caillard, the Action Calédonienne made a surprisingly strong showing in the Nouméa municipal elections of May 1965 despite the small size of its membership. To this party gravitated some Melanesian Protestants, such as Doui Matayo, who had followed Pastor Charlemagne in his break with the Paris Société des Missions Evangéliques.[3] The fact that even the conservatives felt that they must keep a Melanesian politician active in their stable was an oblique testimonial to the effectiveness of Lenormand's policies. If the U.C. had Rock Pidjot as its nominal head, the U.N.R. had now enlisted Michel Kauma, and the Action Calédonienne, Doui Matayo.

Numerically, the Melanesians have been an important factor in local elections since 1951, but their elite is still too small and too divided in its party allegiances to be a decisive element in the Caledonian political scene. As the school system for the tribes has improved, education has been the best channel for the Melanesians' upward mobility, but as of 1965 there were only five who held the bachelor of arts degree. Consequently, there is a dearth of Melanesian leaders in the social and business domains. Although the entire population is Christian, there is only a handful of Melanesian priests and a slightly larger number of native pastors. No Melanesian is a member of the Chambers of Agriculture and Industry, and none is to be found in the higher echelons of the commercial and industrial communities.

In the late 1960s, it was estimated that some 87 percent of the Melanesians still lived in comparative isolation on their reservations, although the rapid rise in their numbers was forcing an increasing proportion of them to seek a livelihood outside such limited areas.[4] For some years, the tribesmen have been making a modest contribution to the territory's exports, and perhaps one-third of them have occupations supplementary to subsistence farming. Most of the Melanesians are peasants with almost no social contacts with the white community, and the small number of Franco-Melanesian half-castes

[3] See pp. 512–514.
[4] Sordet, M., "La Nouvelle-Calédonie: Rhodésie de Demain?"

are in striking contrast with the predominance of the *demis* in French Polynesia. Nevertheless, profound changes are taking place in the younger generation, whose growing disaffection for their traditional institutions is partly due to their rapid acculturation to the Europeans. The growing demand for more local cadres and the concurrent improvement in local training facilities may enable the Melanesians in the not-distant future to gain access to higher posts than they now occupy. At present, however, their participation in public life and economic affairs is largely restricted to the rural level, and control of the territory's development in all major fields is still disputed between rival European groups and individuals.

Into New Caledonia's crucible have been poured many divergent ethnic elements, including Australians and various West Europeans, as well as Melanesians, Polynesians, Tonkinese, and Indonesians, not to mention a sprinkling of Arabs and Indians. Except at the lowest economic levels, these groups have lived in stringently separate communities, with little intercommunication. Among the local-born Frenchmen, there has long existed a sense of particularism combined with a profound attachment to France, but their diverse and often conflicting economic interests, as well as their physical apartness and cultural differences, have precluded their developing into a cohesive and distinctive Caledonian community. Nevertheless, all of them share to varying degrees the feeling that their territory is unique and that their special economic and ethnic situation, as well as their distance from the mother country, entitles them to an administrative regime tailored to their particular needs.

From this pervasive, albeit latent, sentiment of being first and foremost *Caledonian* Frenchmen derives their resentment of being held in tutelage by the local administration and of being treated by the Paris authorities as simply another overseas dependency, basically no different from Black Africa or the Antilles. Until very recently, the main targets of their animosity were the aloof and transient Metropolitan officials empowered to administer the territory at the Caledonians' expense and without their express consent. In the postwar period, however, successive waves of white immigrants from France, Indochina, and Algeria have widened the range of their antipathies. The local-born Caledonians find many of the newcomers overbearing, troublesome, and dubiously assimilable because they lack a sympathetic understanding of the territory's special problems. Theoretically, additions to the French community that bolster its numerical strength vis-à-vis the faster-growing Melanesian population are welcomed, but in practice the advent of the newcomers has further complicated the cleavages that already plagued the European community.

Economically, as well as in the large size of the local-born European component of its population, New Caledonia has been in a much more favorable position than has French Polynesia to assert and maintain an independent attitude in its relations with the Metropole. Thanks to its richer natural resources, New Caledonia has been able, for example, to refuse France's offer to assume the cost of secondary education and thus has kept control over key administrative services, which have passed out of the hands of the elected Polynesian assemblymen. At the same time these very resources have boomeranged against New Caledonia's acquisition of greater administrative autonomy, for its mineral deposits have become so important in the eyes of the Paris authorities that they are tightening their control over all phases of the territory's development. The net results, therefore, have been similar in the two groups of Pacific islands.

International events as well as local circumstances account for the divergencies in the Gaullist policy toward New Caledonia on the one hand and French Polynesia on the other, although those divergencies spring from the same basic motivation—that of enhancing France's role in world affairs. In the case of French Polynesia, it was these islands' isolation and their dispersal over a vast area that made them seem an ideal locale for carrying out the nuclear tests that could no longer be conducted in the Algerian Sahara. As for New Caledonia, its great deposits of nickel, chromium, and cobalt have acquired such strategic and financial value that they must at all costs be preserved from covetous foreigners. This has meant that the autonomist movements in both territories must be nipped in the bud, even if this involved eliminating their leaders on obviously trumped-up charges, and that the powers of their elected assemblies must be reduced to controllable proportions. In view of the small size and disunity of the local populations, as well as their loyalty to France, the Paris government probably assumed that no effective opposition would develop in either territory. It certainly did not anticipate any concerted action on their part in favor of autonomy, for the inhabitants of French Polynesia and New Caledonia had long been mutually indifferent to each other's evolution and their leaders had only rarely cooperated in the Parliament.

For New Caledonia, the autonomy issue was revived early in November 1967 by the introduction of three bills in the National Assembly by General Pierre Billotte, Minister for the Overseas Departments and Territories. The aim of all three was to assure greater control by the French government over the territory's economy and its elected representatives, although they were ostensibly designed to promote the evolution of both. The first of these bills proposed an administrative decentralization of New Caledonia's municipal commissions, and the second provided for French aid in making investments "beyond the territory's financial means." The third and most important of the bills was presented as the means of preserving New Caledonia's valuable minerals from being exposed to the "dangerous" influences of private financiers, by requiring French government authorization for the prospecting and extracting of such deposits. Before debating these bills, the Parliament submitted them to the territorial assembly *pour avis.*

As might be expected, they were the subject of a heated debate in the assembly's budgetary session. All three were rejected by 23 votes to 8, with 1 abstention, on the ground that they would give the French cabinet unrestricted control not only of the territorial civil service but also of that sector of the economy which provided more than 90 percent of the territory's revenues. Indeed, the Paris government's very action in drafting these bills stiffened the attitude of the U.C. assemblymen so that they no longer demanded a return to the *loi-cadre* but now insisted on full autonomy. The territorial assembly passed a resolution to that effect on January 26, 1968, and at the same time voted to send a delegation to Paris—in which the opposition parties refused to be represented—to negotiate a new statute for the territory, in conjunction with a similar delegation from French Polynesia. In a strongly worded memorandum attached to the resolution and written by Rock Pidjot, he stated that

the demand for internal autonomy by the Polynesians and ourselves is due to our disgust with the ill-will and stupidity of a colonial administration attached to a mandarinate which dates from the age of sailing ships and kerosene lamps. The Polynesians, like the Melanesians, feel immensely frustrated. . . . Neither of us wants independence, which is too often illusory . . . but a new contractual relationship [with France] that will give us full internal autonomy.[5]

Not only did the French government turn a deaf ear to the two assemblies' pleas, but General Billotte refused even to receive the

[5] *Le Monde,* April 5, 1968.

delegates when they reached Paris in March. An impasse had apparently been reached when the student-and-worker outbreaks of April and May 1968 injected a new element into the situation, in the territory as well as in France. Some of the ultraconservative Algerian *pieds noirs* (settlers) living in New Caledonia formed a Comité d'Action Civique, which through tracts and demonstrations declared its members' determination to "carry on the struggle against the local autonomists."[6] To forestall public disturbances as a result of their threats, the government sent a battalion of paratroopers from France to Nouméa, but their presence provoked more unrest.

Although the crisis in France was temporarily resolved by the elections of June 1968, which gave the Gaullists an overwhelming Parliamentary majority (and incidentally returned Rock Pidjot to the National Assembly, where he was a member of the centrist P.D.M.), the stalemate continued. On July 3, the territorial assembly's president, Ohlen, hopefully invited the new overseas secretary of state, Michel Inchauspé, to visit New Caledonia, and offered, if the invitation were declined, to send another delegation to "reopen the dialogue with Paris."[7] In the face of such persistence on the part of the U.C.-dominated assembly, a new coalition of conservatives was formed in Nouméa to combat local autonomist tendencies. This party called itself the Union Démocratique de la Nouvelle-Calédonie et des Nouvelles-Hébrides, and its leaders were Roger Laroque, Henri Lafleur, and Georges Chatenay. Strengthened by their support, the Gaullist National Assembly, with little debate, passed the three controversial bills on December 9, and the Senate followed suit a week later.

The Caledonians could surely have prevented or, at any rate, mitigated this assault on their territory's authority had they banded together in a united front. The unusual prosperity then prevailing in the island certainly was a factor in weakening the opposition offered by the local autonomists. Again and again the European community, especially in Nouméa, has demonstrated its indifference to exercising its franchise by failing to vote in elections on issues crucial for the territory's evolution. More than a third of the registered voters abstained in the referendum and presidential election held, respectively, in April and June 1969. Although in both cases a majority of them supported first General de Gaulle and then former premier Georges

---

[6] Chaffard, G., "Les Rebelles du Pacifique."
[7] *Le Monde,* July 16, 1968.

Pompidou, they were little concerned with the basic issues of French domestic and foreign policies that were involved. Their attitude was determined by their opinion as to whether the Gaullists would try to diminish the powers of the territorial assembly and revive the old project of imposing a single administration for all of the French Pacific islands.[8]

How the new French government elected on June 15, 1969, will affect New Caledonia cannot as yet be foreseen, and in any case the two principal candidates were both conservatives. Among France's outstanding politicians, only Mitterand and Defferre have come out in favor of the islands' autonomy, and the poor showing made by the noncommunist left is not a hopeful augury for the U.C.'s program. In New Caledonia and the New Hebrides, Pompidou received 14,572 votes and Poher (whom both Rock Pidjot and Senator Lafleur supported), 12,089, but more than 36 percent of the registered electorate abstained.[9] Perhaps a straw in the wind is the new president's link with the Rothschild Bank and, by extension, with the Société Le Nickel. The only hint of a more flexible attitude than his predecessor's is the law of June 27, 1969, under the terms of which both Lenormand and Pouvanaa were amnestied.

The prospect of any imminent liberalization of the territorial statute by the French government has been made even more remote in New Caledonia than in French Polynesia by the economic expansion that will come from the rapid development of the former's nickel industry. As a sequel to this expansion, the fears of the Caledonian conservatives have been allayed and at the same time those of the ideological radicals have been reawakened. An evidence of the latter phenomenon occurred on September 2, 1969, when some 300 persons in Nouméa were involved in a riot in which several individuals were injured and considerable property was damaged. The immediate cause of the disorders was the arrest of the son of a Maré Island chief, who had recently returned from his studies in Paris and who was accused of writing and distributing in his home island a leaflet inciting the population to organize a coup d'état later that month. Despite the open appeal it made to anti-European sentiments, the resultant riot was not a clear-cut racial outbreak, for its participants included not only Melanesians but some white youths, a few of whom belonged to wealthy local families. Eventually all the rioters arrested were re-

[8] *The Observer*, London, May 1, 1969; see also pp. 340–341.
[9] *Marchés Tropicaux*, June 21, 1969, p. 1808.

leased, and those who were students were allowed to return to their universities in France.

Little publicity was given to this episode, which in any case was complex and confused in its motivation. It resembled the contemporary student unrest of Western countries in that it was a demonstration of protest, being a mixture of anticolonialism and support for Black Power and the revolutionary concepts of the New Left.[10] It was also locally oriented in that it reflected an indigenous hostility to the growing economic inequalities of Caledonian society, in which the extremes of wealth and poverty happened to coincide with its ethnic divisions. Above all, the incident was typically Caledonian in demonstrating the community of objectives shared by the handful of politically aware Melanesians with those Europeans who were heirs to the *communard* traditions of 1870 and those who had initially joined with the Melanesian elite in the Union Calédonienne to combat the entrenched local financial interests.

The September 1969 riot indubitably evidenced a certain malaise in the Caledonian population, as Rock Pidjot told the National Assembly 2 months later, but it could hardly be described as a threat to the government's stability. The economic inequities against which the rioters were protesting cannot but become more glaring in the near future, but it is unlikely that this will give rise to further violence. Probably the prosperity resulting from the territory's imminent economic expansion will be sufficiently widespread to offset the dissatisfaction caused by the inequality in its distribution.

[10] Griffin, J., "New Caledonia: French Forever?"

25

Local-Government Institutions and the Administration

The three categories of municipal government created in New Caledonia in the late nineteenth century were based, in theory, on existing differences in the ethnic composition, political maturity, and economic interests of its various areas. Thus Nouméa, with its concentration of European citizens and trading firms, was the first to be accorded a municipal government analogous to that of a French commune, with an elected mayor and commissioners. Next in chronological order, as well as in rank, came the *communes de moyen exercice* (mixed communes), whose commissioners were elected but whose mayors or presidents were appointed by the administration. This was the type of government established for the main villages along the east and west coasts.

Although the populations of these mixed communes had a certain homogeneity insofar as their economic interests were concerned, these being either agricultural or mining, their political backgrounds diverged sharply and their ethnic composition was not clear cut. The inhabitants of the west coast were predominantly European and those of the east coast very largely Melanesian, especially where the communes included the tribal reservations, but their racial distribution was confused because in many areas the two communities lived interspersed. Below the mixed communes came the three regional commissions of Mt. Dore, Yaté, and the Isle of Pines, which were almost wholly rural and which lacked any population concentrations even as large as those of the coastal villages.

In principle, this classification was to be transitional, the plan being to transform, eventually, the regional commissions into mixed communes and the latter into full communes as their population and revenues increased. By and large, their evolution followed this course, although nearly a century passed before it was completed, and meanwhile two unexpected developments modified their situation. The population of the rural communes did not grow as fast as anticipated because many of their inhabitants emigrated to Nouméa, and the enfranchisement of the Melanesians altered the composition of the commissions administering all of the communes. The number of commissioners varied with the size of the commune's population, ranging between 6 and 20 members.

Communal revenues were derived mainly from the dock dues (*octroi de mer*) collected at Nouméa and divided on the basis of 45 percent for that town, 45 percent for all the other communes, and 10 percent for the territorial budget. Although Nouméa had a limited degree of financial autonomy and as much revenue as all the other communes combined, its income was never enough to meet the town's essential expenditures, for which loans had to be raised. The rural communes were even worse off, for, aside from their allotted portion of the dock dues, they were dependent on meager local taxes to pay for the maintenance of roads, public buildings, and the like. In 1938, the governor saddled them with additional expenditures—the pay of personnel in the village primary schools and the health service—without providing them with any more revenues. Consequently their indebtedness became chronic and their finances so disordered that the administration, which kept a tight rein on their expenditures, not infrequently dissolved the rural commissions. Yet the new commissioners elected to replace the former ones could effect no basic improvements, for they, too, were given responsibilities without the means to carry them out, and therefore gained no real experience in the managing of public affairs.

After World War II, all the communes were faced with a backlog of overdue public works, which they were unable to undertake because of shortages of matériel and funds. These lacks were the more acutely felt because the communes could no longer count on the forced labor that had formerly been at their disposal. In 1947 the general council began to grant them annual subsidies from the territorial budget, and the following year reluctantly increased the rates for dock dues.[1] Yet these supplementary revenues were still insufficient, especially for Nouméa, where no urban improvements had been undertaken since the departure of the American troops. Nevertheless, as the territorial capital had the most advanced form of municipal

[1] Minutes of the general council, May 18, 1948.

government, its citizens could express their dissatisfaction at the polls. They did so in the first postwar municipal elections, in May 1947, by replacing the incumbent commissioners with the candidates sponsored by the Liste d'Union, which at that time also controlled the general council.[2]

Nouméa's new mayor was Henri Sautot, the popular Free French governor of the early war years, who had returned to the territory to live after retiring from the overseas service in 1946. His runner-up, also a member of the Liste d'Union, was Roger Laroque, a local-born Caledonian whose family has long been associated with the Etablissements Ballande. From 1947 to the present, the conservatives, under various party labels, have kept control of the municipality of Nouméa, and since 1953 Laroque has been its perennial mayor. During his incumbency the number of municipal commissioners increased from 15 to 17, and Nouméa's budget grew from 38.7 million C.F.P. francs to more than 183 million, rising most rapidly between 1960 and 1967.[3] Under Laroque's management, Nouméa has made spectacular improvements in its appearance and facilities, although its port needs enlargement and its housing is still deficient. Partly because of the progress effected and partly because the administration has so organized municipal elections as to favor the conservative voters, Nouméa long remained their impregnable stronghold.

When the U.C. gained control of the general council in February 1953, Lenormand seemed to recognize the hopelessness of trying to win over Nouméa's apathetic and hidebound electorate,[4] and he concentrated on reforming the rural communes. Even his political opponents agreed that changes in their organization were long overdue, for the mixed communes were still governed by only slightly modified Metropolitan laws that dated back to 1888. In fact, between 1949 and 1951, the conservative general councilors had organized four conferences to recommend communal reforms. They were held in various towns of the Grande Terre and were attended by almost all of the rural mayors, the presidents of the Chambers of Agriculture and

---

[2] *La France Australe,* May 8, 1947.

[3] Its main revenues, amounting annually to some 100 million C.F.P. francs in 1966, still came from dock dues, its public debt was 15.3 millions, and personnel absorbed more than 90 millions of its expenditures. See *Bulletin du Commerce de la Nouvelle-Calédonie et des Nouvelles-Hébrides,* Dec. 31, 1966.

[4] Abstentions in its municipal elections still average more than 50 percent, despite the increase in its registered electorate from 5,498 in 1947 to 13,283 in 1963.

Commerce, and high government officials. The consensus of these meetings was that Paris must be prodded into transforming the mixed communes into full communes, and that the territorial budget should shoulder more responsibility for their expenditures.[5] The administration apparently did not concur in these views and, indeed, refused to permit any more such conferences to be held, but it did draft its own recommendations, which were presented to the newly elected general council in March 1953. Their most important innovation was the institution of a dual electoral college for the rural commissions, in which one-third of all the seats would be reserved to Melanesians. The U.C.-dominated general council promptly rejected these proposals and voted to prolong the terms of the incumbent commissioners until Lenormand could draft his own bill. This he did in November 1953, and, surprisingly, it differed from that of the administration only in rejecting the dual-college system and raising the number of seats reserved for the Melanesians to parity with those to be occupied by Europeans. The measure was duly approved by the U.C.-majority council, and in mid-1954, elections for 23 municipal commissions were held under its provisions.

That such meager improvements in their status were unsatisfactory to the Melanesians was shown by the resolutions passed at the A.I.C.L.F. congress held in late 1959. What this enterprising organization of Melanesian Protestants wanted was proportional voting in the rural communal elections, the transformation of the regional commissions into mixed communes, and control over all communal decisions that affected their daily lives. Specifically, they sought more responsibility for the building of schools, dispensaries, and roads, "which must no longer stop at the edge of a tribal plantation or end at a European farmhouse."[6] Lenormand was not prepared to go so far or so fast, but in 1960 he proposed and the assembly accepted somewhat bolder reforms than before. These would free rural communes from budgetary supervision by the administration, upgrade the regional commissions, and have mayors as well as commissioners elected by universal suffrage and the secret ballot.[7] Curiously enough, Lenormand did not suggest increasing the commissioners' powers, and the assembly even rejected his proposal to institute proportional

---

[5] *La France Australe,* Oct. 14, 1950; minutes of the general council, April 17, 1951, Nov. 4, 1953.

[6] *Le Monde non Chrétien,* Nos. 53–54, 1960.

[7] Agence France Presse dispatch from Nouméa, Jan. 5, 1961.

voting and a committee system within each commission that would have brought the rural communes more into line with the status of a full commune.

Perhaps the assemblymen realized better than did their chief that the rural electorate which actually went to the polls still largely consisted of conservative settlers, who only gradually could be induced to accept radical changes. In the elections of May 7, 1961, the U.C. candidates won 53 percent of the votes cast and gained control of only 15 of the 30 rural communes.[8] This step-by-step approach, however, paid off six years later, when, after the introduction of proportional voting, the U.C. bettered its position by defeating the candidates of two conservative parties to win control of nineteen rural communes.

This success, which proved that U.C. strength was growing in the rural areas, may well have induced the French government at long last to present to the Parliament its bill reorganizing New Caledonia's municipalities, which had been under study for nearly a decade. This bill was one of a trio submitted to the National Assembly in November 1967,[9] and its objective, like that of the two accompanying bills, was to impose closer Metropolitan controls over the territory's development, under guise of promoting its evolution. The government proposed that all of the existing municipal organizations be transformed into full communes and that Metropolitan laws be applied to them. This would entail an increase in the number of commissioners and in their powers, and also amplify their financial resources by allotting them additional revenues. At the same time, it took back with one hand what it had given with the other. The apparent increase in the communes' autonomy was canceled out by the Metropole's assuming responsibility for the creation of new communes and for the territorial civil servants who would supervise the communal management of local affairs. Over the objections of the territorial assembly and of Rock Pidjot in the National Assembly, the bill became law in December 1968, at which time the government simply promised to raise the existing municipalities to the status of full communes within their present boundaries "as soon as possible."[10]

[8] *L'Avenir Calédonien*, May 17, 1961.
[9] See pp. 325–327.
[10] *Marchés Tropicaux*, Dec. 14, 1968, p. 3091.

THE CIVIL SERVICE

The passage of time has not lessened the antipathy felt by New Caledonia's elected representatives toward the Metropolitan civil servants sent to the territory—an antipathy that dates back to the establishment of the general council.[11] It is as strong among members of the U.C.-dominated territorial assembly as it was among their predecessors, although the focus of resentment has shifted since 1953.

When the conservatives controlled the general council, their objections were aimed mainly at the burden placed on Caledonian taxpayers by the salaries, transport, and other privileges enjoyed by Metropolitan functionaries. To a lesser degree, they objected to being forced to accept any and all officials sent by the Paris government without their approval and sometimes against their expressed wishes. Furthermore, every pay increase granted to French civil servants automatically applied to locally stationed *administrateurs de la France d'Outre-Mer,* who belonged to what was called the Metropolitan general cadre. Three successive salary increases during the early postwar years seemed likely to create a budgetary deficit for New Caledonia, and the local administration proposed to meet this additional expense by raising taxes. Any rise in taxation was resisted by the representatives of local business firms, who controlled the general council at that time, hence they sought ways of avoiding such a dire contingency.

In 1947 they appointed a committee under Bonneaud's chairmanship to recommend a reorganization of the administration that would effect drastic economies. Needless to say, this committee proposed a reduction in the "plethoric" personnel, who were absorbing half the territorial revenues and whose number was "more appropriate for the administration of a population of 150,000 than one of 60,000." [12] Then they asked the Paris authorities to permit New Caledonia's parliamentarians to study the *dossier* of every functionary scheduled for appointment to the territory. In the event that any candidate was rejected by them and the Metropole persisted in confirming his appointment, the general council would simply refuse to pay either his salary or the cost of his transportation. The first test of their resolution came in 1949 when there arrived at Nouméa an official whose candidacy

[11] See pp. 245–247.
[12] Minutes of the general council, Nov. 19, 1947.

they had rejected the previous year.[13] The councilors had to face the fact that they could do little about the situation except to protest, for the pay of general-cadre administrators fell into the category of obligatory budget expenditures, over which they had no control. The only way they found to surmount this obstacle was to hire an increasing number of agents under contract to fill permanent posts. This had the disadvantage of increasing the already marked instability of the administrative personnel, but the councilors felt that it was more than offset by their being able to hire and fire candidates of their own choice. Because the penurious councilors were unwilling to vote the funds needed to staff all the services, many of them existed merely on paper, and the only ones that had an adequate personnel were those of public works, animal husbandry, and telecommunications.

The French government, for its part, did make two gestures during that period to appease the general councilors. By a law of March 21, 1948, it assumed the cost of paying some of its highest-ranking officials serving in New Caledonia, and this meant a saving of some 10 million C.F.P. francs to the territorial budget.[14] In 1950, it acceded to the request by New Caledonia's parliamentarians and sent an inspector-general of the colonies to study the situation and propose measures to make the territory's administration less top-heavy and costly. The gratitude inspired by these concessions was soon offset, however, by still another overall pay increase for Metropolitan officials and by the reduction of their terms of duty in the territory from five years to three.

The long struggle between the council and the Paris government had reached another stalemate when the U.C. came to dominate the former body in 1953. Its members were equally resentful of the "snobbish and overpaid" Metropolitan officials who staffed the local administration, but they chose to attack the problem from another angle. Their strategy consisted of raising the status of the territorial civil servants to that of their Metropolitan colleagues, which entailed an increase in taxes. To be sure, this policy made the administration even more costly to the Caledonians than before, but the U.C. leaders were far from averse to imposing higher taxes on the more affluent citizens. This policy, they felt, had the dual advantage of enhancing the party's popularity and membership among local-born civil servants

---

[13] *Pacific Islands Monthly,* March 1949.
[14] Speech of Governor Parisot to the general council, April 30, 1948.

and of tapping sources of revenue that theretofore had largely escaped taxation. One of Lenormand's main objections to the *loi-cadre* of June 23, 1956, was that, by divorcing state from territorial civil services, it would jeopardize the improvements in the status of the latter which he had been at pains to effect. He correctly foresaw that it would lead to an increase in the number of Metropolitan officials in New Caledonia, largely through the transfer there of civil servants from the recently independent countries of Africa and Indochina. Indeed, in one 12-month period during the late 1950s, the number of transferred administrators belonging to the general cadre rose from 5 to 27, and they were assigned to various points throughout New Caledonia and its dependencies.[15]

In itself, the application of the *loi-cadre* resulted in no diminution of the gains recently made by the territorial civil servants, who now could transfer to the Metropolitan cadre if they were willing to accept posts outside New Caledonia so as further to improve their professional status. Nor did it impose a greater burden on Caledonian taxpayers, for the state service was now financed by the French treasury. It did, however, involve certain other drawbacks. Lenormand shared the Caledonians' prejudice against all Metropolitan officials on the grounds of their aloofness, transiency, and unassimilability, but he had other more cogent objections to their growing presence. He believed that they were working covertly against his party during election campaigns and, more objectionably, that they were occupying posts that should be held by "sons of the soil." Traditionally, Caledonian parents have made sacrifices to keep their children in school as long as possible so that they could enter government service, which they regarded as the most desirable field of employment.

On the issue of improving the status of local-born civil servants, as on that of opposing the proliferation of Metropolitan officialdom, members of the U.C. were in accord with their political opponents. Even the conservative general councils during the early postwar years had voted small increases in their pay and emoluments, although these slight concessions were wrung from them only as a result of two strikes by the *syndicat des fonctionnaires* in 1947. After long negotiations between the administration, the general council, and the union, agreement was reached on such matters as basic pay, bonuses to meet the rising cost of living, and official control of certain commodity prices, as well as a pledge to reorganize the local cadre so as to

[15] Speech by Lenormand in the National Assembly, Oct. 24, 1961.

eliminate "shocking inequities." [16] A few years later, however, the general council balked at applying fully in New Caledonia the Lamine-Gueye law of June 1950 which embodied the principle of complete parity between the Metropolitan and local cadres in regard to recruitment, salaries, pensions, paid vacations, and family allowances.

Less than a month after the U.C. won control of the general council in February 1953, the local-born civil servants struck over this issue. It was soon settled in their favor, and they never again went on strike, because the territorial assembly has consistently voted them whatever funds have been needed to match every improvement in the status of Metropolitan functionaries.[17] This policy has cut the ground from under the conservatives' contention that the Metropolitan leaders of the U.C. were deliberately penalizing Caledonian officials, and it has also checked the resignations of local-born civil servants, which became numerous in 1952 because their salaries were then insufficient to meet the rising cost of living.[18] It has not, of course, been within the assembly's power to dislodge the Metropolitan officials who are blocking the promotion of members of the local cadre, and the inevitable result has been a growing disinclination on the part of educated young Caledonians to enter government service.

[16] Minutes of the general council, Nov. 19, Dec. 15, 1947.
[17] *Marchés Tropicaux,* Dec. 5, 1964, p. 2978.
[18] Minutes of the general council, Feb. 26, 1953.

26

Regional Contacts in the South Pacific

AUSTRALIA

Of all the countries in the South Pacific, Australia has had the longest and most telling influence on the development of New Caledonia. Because of its comparative nearness and its complementary economy, Australia has been able to supply New Caledonia readily with essential commodities, notably foodstuffs and certain manufactured goods. It was the use of Australia as a penal colony for Great Britain that prompted France to send its convicts to New Caledonia in the late nineteenth century. In another sphere, Australia's success in stock raising served as a model for New Caledonia's far smaller and less efficient ranching activities. Even taking into account the vast differences in the size of the two countries and of their respective populations, there exist striking similarities between them. In particular, each has a settled white population which enjoys a high living standard and feels a strong sentimental attachment to the distant country of its ancestral origin.

French policy in the Pacific has most often been marked by a pervasive suspicion of all alien influences, combined with a parsimoniousness in providing the funds needed to develop the islands' economic resources. Had the mother country been more generous in its attitude toward the Caledonians and less bent on isolating them in an ocean dominated by "Anglo-Saxon" powers, it would not have needed to fear the allurement of more affluent and technically advanced countries such as the United States and Australia. Instead, to ease the burden imposed on French taxpayers by the islands' financial needs, Paris advanced various proposals that undermined the Caledonians' confidence in France's concern for their well-being and that wounded their pride as French citizens.

Whenever France has undergone periods of financial stringency, as it did after the two world wars and during the depression of the early

1930s, highly placed Metropolitan politicians have proposed changes in the administrative regimes of the French Far Eastern dependencies so as to make them less costly to the French treasury. In the early 1920s, Sarraut's *mise-en-valeur* program [1] included the proposal that rich Indochina should make a loan to "its little sisters of the Pacific" that would help those islands balance their budgets and also undertake public works that eventually would make them economically more self-sufficient. Louis Archimbaud [2] proposed the creation of a Dominion of the French Pacific that would give unity to French policy in that area. He and Sarraut concurred in seeking to utilize Indochina's wealth in money and manpower for the benefit of the long-neglected and underdeveloped islands.

Neither of these proposals won substantial support from any of the elements involved. Caledonians were not pleased by the prospect of being administered by another colony, whose white population was not only transient but smaller than theirs. Moreover, without such an administrative subordination to Indochina, they could engage Tonkinese under contract to work in their island. The Ministers of Colonies and of Foreign Affairs submitted competitive claims for control over the proposed dominion, and the Parliament refused to cede its authority in the Pacific islands to the government at Hanoi.[3] Finally, French officials in Indochina opposed a dominion because they feared that it would deplete their colony's funds and manpower. The project was revived briefly during the depression of the early 1930s, when it was presented as an economy measure, but once again it died still-born.[4]

On the eve of World War II, Georges Mandel, Minister of Colonies at that time, sponsored an amplified version of the Archimbaud proposal that would have made a single high commissariat of the Pacific responsible for the defense of the French possessions in the Far East and also a center for the spread of French culture. By that time, the French administrators in Indochina had come to recognize the usefulness of the Pacific islands as an outlet for Tonkin's surplus population, and to appreciate the need for joint defense against imminent Japanese aggression, and they no longer opposed an administrative

[1] See pp. 80–81.
[2] See p. 253.
[3] *L'Océanie Française*, January–February 1922, May 1924; minutes of the Chamber of Deputies, Dec. 24, 1924.
[4] *La Dépêche Coloniale*, Jan. 22, 1930.

merger with the E.F.O. and New Caledonia, but the war broke out before Mandel could carry out his plan.

New Caledonia's strategic location made its defense vital to Australia during the Pacific war, which also reinforced its dependence on that continent as a source of essential supplies and a market for its mineral exports. Caledonians have always felt the attraction of the thriving metropolis of Sydney, and those who could afford to do so sent their children to Australian schools for higher education, especially in technical fields. Australian and New Zealand soldiers serving in the island during the war were popular with the Caledonians, and some of them said that they wanted to settle there after the defeat of Japan.[5]

To be sure, some Australians had emigrated to New Caledonia during the late nineteenth century, but many of them had left after it ceased to offer an abundant supply of cheap penal labor. Among those who stayed on were James Paddon and John Higginson, and they greatly aided the island's development.[6] In a quite different sphere, other Australian immigrants fulfilled an important social function. The shortage of women in Nouméa during the 1870s was partly remedied by the recruitment of what were euphemistically called "barmaids." This traffic apparently took on such proportions that a Sydney newspaper of the era issued this warning to such potential emigrants: "Young women, you go to Nouméa at your peril. . . . Those of you who accept Nouméa's offers [of high wages] are of the type that Australia can well do without." [7] To this a Nouméa journal replied acidly: "These are indeed fine words coming from an Australian city where a man cannot walk 100 yards without being accosted by the raucous voices of the 'sisterhood.'" For many years, Nouméa continued to be in the eyes of Australians not only "the Pacific haven of vice" but also the source of escaped convicts who, if detected after their arrival in Queensland, were sent back to New Caledonia at Australia's expense.

The display of righteous indignation by Australians, who preferred to forget their penal-colony past and ignore their own current problems of delinquency, became less evident in the early years of the twentieth century. After France ceased sending convicts to New Caledonia, and after the Anglo-French condominium of the New Hebrides was created and the Entente Cordiale had been signed,

[5] *Pacific Islands Monthly*, September 1944.
[6] See pp. 240, 244.
[7] *Pacific Islands Monthly*, December 1948.

Australia's attitude became less critical. However, the arrival of several thousand Japanese laborers in New Caledonia during the years preceding World War I evoked the hostility of "White Australia's" defenders, who resented the presence of so many Asians on a nearby island.[8] During the interwar period, the importation of far larger numbers of Tonkinese and Javanese to work in New Caledonia's mines and plantations added fuel to this flame.

After World War II, New Caledonia's long delay in repatriating the Asian laborers and its efforts to recruit more of them continued to worry the "White Australians," whom the war had made more conscious of New Caledonia's importance to their own defense. France's decision in 1951 to permit Indonesia to open a consulate at Nouméa and, even more, its enlargement of the Caledonian electorate to include Melanesians heightened such fears. To some Australians, as to many Caledonians, Lenormand was a radical determined to open the floodgates to communism and to the "rising tide of color" that would submerge the white populations in the Pacific. On the ground that what was happening in New Caledonia was of "legitimate concern" to Australia, some members of the Australian Parliament asked the Minister of External Affairs what steps he proposed to take in the matter.[9] The situation in New Caledonia, he replied, merited close observation, but obviously Australia could not intervene in the affairs of France, another sovereign nation. Nevertheless, Australia made such vehement protests to Paris that year concerning France's efforts to recruit 2,000 Japanese workers for New Caledonia that the French government broke off its negotiations with Tokyo.

The presence and political influence of a sizeable nonwhite population in nearby New Caledonia were not the sole causes of Australian animosity toward French policy in the south Pacific. Some imperialistically minded Australians had long coveted New Caledonia's mineral deposits, and they generally regarded France's presence in the area as an obstacle to transforming the south Pacific into a "mare nostrum." Although this attitude became more pronounced after the South Pacific Commission headquarters were set up at Nouméa,[10] and especially after De Gaulle tightened his control over French Polynesia and New Caledonia, it had existed in latent form even before World War I.

[8] May, A. K. D., *New Caledonia: A Menace to White Australia,* Sydney, 1911.
[9] *Pacific Islands Monthly,* November 1952.
[10] See pp. 349–350.

Wishful thinking and ignorance of Caledonian affairs have naturally inclined the Australians to misinterpret in a way favorable to their aspirations the vacillations in French policy and the insubmission of the general council to the local administration. As long ago as 1914, Australia reportedly believed that France's declining birth rate had caused the Paris authorities to lose interest in retaining New Caledonia as a *colonie de peuplement*,[11] and that their later project to create a Dominion of the French Pacific indicated that they were eager to be rid of all their responsibilities in that region. Not surprisingly, the Australians, like some Paris politicians, mistook the Caledonians' periodic outbursts against the indifference, dilatoriness, and egocentric policies of the French government as the expression of either secessionism or a desire to be aligned with the "Anglo-Saxon" powers in the Pacific. The era of good feeling between Caledonians and Australians reached its peak during the Pacific war, but it soon gave way to mutual recriminations, for much of which the Australian press and radio have been responsible.

A broadcast from Melbourne in May 1950 stated that the question of attaching New Caledonia, among other islands, to Australia or New Zealand had been discussed at the recent south Pacific conference in Suva. This elicited what was doubtless a French-inspired rebuttal over Radio Nouméa by the Melanesian delegate to that conference, Maou Djoel, who denied that such a question had been raised at Suva either in public session or privately:

Had such proposals been made there, we would have protested vehemently. For 100 years we have proved our loyalty to France . . . It is not at the time when France is increasing our rights and placing us on the same footing with all her other children that we would dream of transferring our allegiance to another nation.[12]

Later that year, the S.P.C. again served as the springboard for a series of articles published in the Sydney *Herald* that harped on the same sensitive theme. Their author asserted that it was only to assuage French pride that France had been admitted to the S.P.C. and that its headquarters had been located at Nouméa.[13] He further asserted that the natives disliked the French colonial system and that France exploited its dependencies. The fat was put into the fire, however, by an editorial in the February 1951 issue of the *Pacific Islands Monthly*,

[11] *L'Océanie Française*, April 1914.
[12] *Pacific Islands Monthly*, June 1950.
[13] *Ibid.*, August 1950.

from the lively pen of R. W. Robson, its well-informed but tendentious publisher.

Robson attributed much of what he described as the growing friction between Paris and Nouméa to the "over-friendly" relations which some Caledonians, notably Sautot, had established with Australia during the war. This jealousy, he thought, had been kept alive by the politically biased and incompetent officials whom Paris had been so stupid as to send to New Caledonia. Robson seemed to believe that the French government, which was actually conservative at the time, was oriented toward "extreme socialism and Red domination." After asserting that the English-speaking countries had no territorial ambitions in the area, he added that

it would not surprise this writer if, within a decade or two, French Oceania weakened its ties with France and sought closer relations with its Anglo-American neighbors.

This comment was quickly picked up by the Paris press, which reprinted it as evidence of Australia's expansionist ambitions, and it was sharply criticized by Henri Bonneaud, president of the general council, in a speech to that body on April 17, 1951:

If New Caledonia finds that Paris does not always understand its problems and sends us officials who are not as competent as we would like, this is a question that concerns us alone . . . Australians should have no illusions about this, for we are firmly French and our disagreements are family quarrels.

Late in 1952, Robson, after completing a tour of the Pacific territories, did not add to his popularity among the Caledonians by describing their islands as "the most cheerless and disunited place" he had visited.[14] Similarly disparaging comments by another Sydney journalist—Irvine Douglas, writing in *Truth*, May 3, 1953—to the effect that isolated New Caledonia was 50 years behind the times, a land fertile for the propagation of communism, and a country of "almost organized decadence," were regarded as so insulting by the general councilors that they lodged a formal protest with the Australian consul in Nouméa.[15]

By the mid-1950s, the authorities in both Canberra and Nouméa seemed to realize that steps should be taken to prevent a further deterioration in the relations between their two countries. In May 1953,

[14] *Ibid.*, November 1952.
[15] Minutes of the general council, May 16, 1953.

the general council invited some Australian schoolchildren to spend a 3-week holiday in New Caledonia, and the following September the Australian government sent the president of the supreme court to attend the centenary celebrations in Nouméa. Two years later, Australian candidates were offered several scholarships at the College La Pérouse, and soon afterward, vacation courses in that institution were organized annually for Australian teachers of French. Australian tourists began increasingly to visit New Caledonia, and in 1964 Monash University began publishing a journal of French studies. Thus, at the cultural and human levels, relations improved markedly between the two areas, and New Caledonia began to fulfil the role of center for the "spread of French civilization in the Pacific" that had formerly devolved upon Indochina. (In other respects, however, the Caledonians were disappointed that France did not regard their island as the heir to its former Southeast Asian colony, for after the Dienbienphu debacle, New Caledonia received almost none of the equipment removed from Indochina, which it had expected to inherit.[16]

Political relations between Australia and New Caledonia shared only briefly in the improvement noted in less controversial domains. The policy of expanding New Caledonia's activities in the Pacific region, initiated by René Hoffherr (August 1954 to January 1965), the first governor of New Caledonia to cooperate cordially with the S.P.C., was nipped in the bud. General de Gaulle's cryptic utterances when he visited Nouméa in the autumn of 1956 were correctly interpreted in Australia as a warning to Caledonians against their predatory neighbors.[17] The policy pursued by the general after his return to power in 1958 showed that he believed that the Caledonian autonomists were lending a willing ear to Australian blandishments. Although Lenormand asserted that he had never been a "party to any extension of Australian influence in New Caledonia" and would make every effort to combat it,[18] the Gaullists were skeptical of his sincerity. Lenormand's attempts to use Australia's attraction for the Caledonians as leverage to win political concessions from France did lay him open to suspicion, and they were certainly a main cause of his prosecution. For the eleven years that De Gaulle was in power, his regime made every effort to isolate New Caledonia from its English-speaking neighbors. Better than any single episode or succession of incidents, the

[16] Mousset, P., "En Nouvelle-Calédonie."
[17] *Pacific Islands Monthly,* October 1956.
[18] *Ibid.,* January 1960.

history of the S.P.C. illustrates France's policy in shaping New Caledonia's relations with its Pacific neighbors.

THE SOUTH PACIFIC COMMISSION [19]

Inevitably the Pacific war caused the governments of Australia and New Zealand to be concerned for the security of their countries, and on January 21, 1944, they signed an agreement for mutual military and political aid.[20] The Japanese offensive had made them aware for the first time of the strategic importance of the Pacific islands for their own defense, and of the need to plan a common program in regard to their future development. They therefore attached to their 1944 pact, as an annex, a project to create a regional advisory commission of international membership that would study the economic and social problems of the nonautonomous territories in the south Pacific and would recommend common solutions. It was not, however, until more than a year after the war had ended that Great Britain, the Netherlands, France, and the United States agreed to join the commission. A constituent meeting, called the Conference of the South Seas, was held at Canberra in January and February 1947, and was attended by delegates from the six governments that had island dependencies in that part of the Pacific. Except for one Indonesian member of the Dutch delegation, all of the government representatives were Western politicians, officials, and technicians. The commission being the brainchild of the Australian Minister of External Affairs, Dr. Evatt, he was naturally the prime mover at that meeting. Australia's offer to pay 30 percent of the commission's annual expenditures not only evidenced Dr. Evatt's great interest in its future but also was perhaps not unrelated to his hope that Port Moresby would be chosen as its permanent headquarters.[21]

From the outset, there were marked differences in the attitude of the six member governments toward the organization of the South Pacific Commission (S.P.C.) and the nature of its future operations. The Australian, New Zealand, and American delegates were enthusiastic about its creation, the English generally indifferent, and the French and

---

[19] The following account of the S.P.C. does not attempt to offer a comprehensive analysis of that organization's evolution or activities, but tries simply to study its relationship to French policy in the Pacific, with special reference to New Caledonia.

[20] *Pacific Islands Monthly,* September 1947.

[21] *Ibid.,* March 1947.

Dutch cautious and reserved. The heads of the two last-mentioned delegations insisted successfully that the S.P.C. should deal exclusively with economic and social subjects, whereas the Australian and American delegates would have preferred to leave the door open to a possible extension of its activities into the political sphere. The French also succeeded in making the S.P.C. a strictly intergovernmental body, independent of any organic connection with the United Nations, although cooperation with the world body's specialized agencies was to be permitted. The S.P.C.'s overall objective was defined as the encouragement and strengthening of international cooperation in promoting the economic and social welfare of the non-self-governing islands of the south Pacific under their authority.[22] Its activities were to be purely advisory and supplementary to those undertaken by the various territorial administrations, particularly for projects that concerned two or more territories.

A charter embodying the foregoing principles was drafted and was accepted by all of the delegates present at Canberra, including Pierre Augé, French Minister to Australia, who initialed the document on behalf of his government. The agreement signed on February 6, 1947, was to run for five years, after which any member government might withdraw after serving notice of its intention 12 months in advance. The area defined as lying within the S.P.C.'s competence comprised the fifteen nonautonomous island territories south of the equator and east of, but including, Dutch New Guinea. It covered 35 million square kilometers and had a total population roughly estimated at 2.5 million. The annual dues to be paid by each member government (see table 6) were based on the size of their respective native populations and of their territories' yearly revenues. English and French were to be the S.P.C.'s official linguistic vehicles, and most of its publications were to be issued in both languages. Each member state was to name two commissioners and as many alternates and advisers as it cared to appoint. The commissioners were to meet twice a year, they alone had the right to vote, and chairmanship of the session was to rotate among them. General-policy questions could be decided by a simple majority of the two-thirds of the commissioners needed to make up a quorum, but on issues involving any increase in the member governments' financial contributions to the S.P.C., unanimity was required.

[22] Skinner, C., "Self-government in the South Pacific."

TABLE 6

DATA CONCERNING AREAS WITHIN THE COMPETENCE OF THE SOUTH
PACIFIC COMMISSION, AS OF FEBRUARY 1947

Area	Population (thousands)	Administering authority	Annual dues (share of S.P.C. budget, percent)
Fiji	250 ⎫		
Solomon Islands	100 ⎬	Great Britain	12.5
Gilbert and Ellice Islands	30 ⎭		
Papua	275		
Norfolk Island	1		
New Guinea (protectorate)	1,000	Australia	30
Nauru (protectorate)	1		
Cook Island	14 ⎫	New Zealand	15
Western Samoa (trust territory)	50 ⎭		
Dutch New Guinea	300	Netherlands	15
Eastern Samoa	10	United States	12.5
New Caledonia	60 ⎫	France	12.5
E.F.O.	60 ⎭		
New Hebrides	40	Anglo-French condominium	2.5 [a]

[a] Contribution divided between Great Britain and France.
Source: *Pacific Islands Monthly*, May 1948.

The Canberra charter also provided for the establishment of a general secretariat and two permanent advisory bodies, the research council and the south Pacific conference. The secretary-general, to be named by the commissioners for a five-year term, was given no executive authority or voice in policy decisions. He was to be in charge of the S.P.C.'s permanent staff, whose personnel was to be recruited, so far as possible, in the island territories. His essential role was that of administration and coordination, particularly of the work done by the research council. This council was to be formed by experts in the various fields of research with which the S.P.C. was concerned, and its tasks were to draft and carry out annual programs that had been approved by the commissioners. Its three executive officers headed the departments of health, economic development, and social welfare, and they operated under the supervision of a deputy chairman who was himself responsible to the secretary-general.

The south Pacific conference, the second advisory body formed under the 1947 charter, was to meet every 3 years in one of the island territories. It was charged with making recommendations to the commissioners on matters of common interest, as laid down in the charter. Each group of territories could send two delegates to the triennial conferences, but differences arose among the member governments in regard to the method of selecting them. As before, it was the Australians, New Zealanders, and Americans who wanted the delegates to be elected by their fellow-islanders, and it was the French—to some extent supported by the Dutch and English—who preferred to have them selected by the territorial administrations from among the "most representative and articulate" members of the native communities. Once again the more conservative view prevailed, and all the member governments finally agreed that the resolutions passed by the conferences should in no way aim to alter the existing relationship between the islanders and their respective administrations or to derogate from the latter's prerogatives.[23]

For nearly two years after the charter was signed, the S.P.C. marked time until it could be ratified by all the legislatures of the signatory governments. France was the last to ratify, and the S.P.C. was able to hold its initial meeting at Sydney on May 11, 1948. At that session, W. D. Forsyth, an Australian civil servant with experience in Pacific administration, was chosen as its first secretary-general, and an ambitious work program was drawn up. Five months later, the S.P.C. met again at Sydney to choose a site for the organization's permanent headquarters. Inasmuch as the charter required that it be located within the S.P.C.'s area of geographical competence, all Australian and New Zealand cities were automatically ruled out, and the choice was narrowed down to Suva, Port Moresby, and Nouméa.

In the end, Nouméa was selected, largely because it was the only one of the three that could offer accommodations for the commission and housing for its staff. Many of the buildings which the Americans had constructed there for their wartime needs were available, and the French government and Caledonian general council promised to finance the needed repairs and renovations. Later, when the choice of Nouméa came increasingly under attack, it was erroneously claimed that it had been selected as an inducement to France to join the commission. Actually, the French Parliament had ratified the Canberra charter five months before Nouméa was chosen—mainly for practical

[23] Gaignard, H. G., "La France Doit Jouer un Rôle Important à la Commission du Pacifique-Sud."

reasons—on October 29, 1948. In the spring of 1949 the S.P.C. moved into its new headquarters, and its third session was held at Nouméa in May of that year.[24]

Eleven months later, the first south Pacific conference met at Suva, and was attended by 24 delegates from the island territories, accompanied by their Western advisers. Political topics were taboo, and it was the Western advisers who did most of the talking, drew up the reports, and formulated the recommendations to be submitted to the commissioners at their next meeting. Obviously many of the island delegates barely grasped what was going on, and only a handful of them took any part in the debates. Some observers, consequently, were inclined to write off this conference as an expensive and useless farce, for it was an unwieldy body whose delegates were too inexperienced and uninformed to discuss the main items on the agenda. Nevertheless, the Suva conference was a landmark in the annals of the Pacific, for it gave the islanders their first opportunity to make contacts with each other. That they had learned much more than was thought at the time from this "apprenticeship" session was shown at the second south Pacific conference, held in 1953 at Nouméa. There the more active part taken by the islanders in the proceedings gave evidence of their greater self-confidence and understanding of the S.P.C.'s functions.

This development enabled the most evolved islanders to appreciate better the value of the S.P.C., and it also confirmed the views of those Westerners who desired more effective utilization of that organization's potential. Although all concerned expressed approval of the S.P.C.'s achievements, there was growing criticism during the mid-1950s of its stagnation and apparent inability to bring about a tangible improvement of the islanders' welfare. Not surprisingly, it was again R. W. Robson who, through the medium of his periodical, was the main propagandist for reforms.[25] He praised the S.P.C. as a "unique, bold and wise experiment," whose machinery had functioned smoothly and whose research council had amassed useful data. Its weaknesses he attributed to the S.P.C.'s incapacity to implement the recommendations of its experts and to pursue a policy of continuity. To remedy the latter defect, he proposed that a permanent secretary-general with executive power replace the short-term civil servants who had only

---

[24] In 1954, the semiannual sessions were abandoned in favor of one meeting to be held in the autumn of each year.

[25] *Pacific Islands Monthly*, January 1952; May, September 1954; October 1955.

limited authority and were usually so advanced in age as to be on the verge of retirement. As to the research council, he felt that its technicians should stop devoting themselves to basic research and voluminous reports, and should concentrate instead on practical problems directly related to the islanders' needs. Their recommendations, Robson believed, should be submitted to the territorial administrations, thus bypassing the member governments, which usually ignored them and pigeonholed their reports. To implement the experts' proposals, the funds at the S.P.C.'s disposal should be substantially increased so that more qualified men could be employed and their services retained for a long period. In conclusion, he gave his support to those advocating that the S.P.C.'s headquarters be transferred from Nouméa to Sydney, which was more accessible and provided far better library and other facilities for the organization's operations.

Robson certainly voiced the frustrations and wishes of many of the English-speaking islanders, commissioners, and officials, particularly W. D. Forsyth, who served two terms as the S.P.C.'s secretary-general.[26] Of all the men who served in that post, Forsyth certainly gave it the most single-minded devotion and vigorous leadership, but he also saddled it with a top-heavy administration, was not easy to work with, and was jealous of any encroachment on its competence by the U.N.'s specialized agencies.[27] The reform movement which he and Robson spearheaded was supported by the British commissioners, and beginning in 1956 they campaigned to effect significant changes in the Canberra charter. Although not all the member governments were agreed as to the need to make drastic reforms in the S.P.C., they did consent to meet at Canberra in June 1957 to review and appraise the work which that organization had accomplished during its decade of existence.

At the June 1957 meeting, some progress was made in streamlining the research council's organization and activities. Its members were instructed to cut down on the "avalanche of publications" and to orient their studies to practical problems whose solution was desired by the territorial administrations. The S.P.C.'s function as a clearing house for miscellaneous information about the islands was to become subordinate to its role of providing more technical assistance in the

[26] The secretaries-general have been W. D. Forsyth, 1948–1951 and 1962–1966; Sir Brian Freeston, 1950–1953; Dr. Ralph Bedell, 1954–1957; Traffer Smith, 1957–1962; Sir Gawain Bell, 1967–1969; Harry Moors, 1969 to date.

[27] Those with which the S.P.C. has worked most closely are the F.A.O., W.H.O. and UNESCO.

form of training for specific economic and social enterprises. Nevertheless, agreement could be reached at the 1957 meeting only in regard to changes made within the framework of the existing charter, and none at all in respect to the appointment or powers of the secretary-general. It was not until 1962 that somewhat more fundamental reforms were undertaken. These were forced upon the S.P.C. by two developments in the Pacific area, which were the main topics of discussion at the second review conference held at London in July 1963. One was the decision of New Zealand to grant independence to its trust territory of Western Samoa, and the other was the transfer of administrative authority over Dutch New Guinea (West Irian) to Indonesia.

The withdrawal of the Netherlands from the S.P.C. caused a deficit in its budget that entailed an increase in the dues paid by the other five member governments, and also necessitated a decision as to whether or not Indonesia should be admitted to the commission.[28] Little difficulty was encountered in resolving the financial aspect of this problem, for it had long been realized that the S.P.C. could not continue to operate on a shoestring budget if it was to carry out its program. The remaining member governments therefore accepted an overall increase in their contributions, with the expectation that the balance needed would be met by grants from the F.A.O., W.H.O., and UNESCO for specific projects within the fields of their respective competence. The admission of Western Samoa, however, posed a wholly new problem, for the expansion of the S.P.C.'s area to include Guam and the American Pacific trust territories in November 1951 had not required an amendment to the Canberra charter. Western Samoa fell into a category for which no provision had been made, since it was not a sovereign Occidental nation with dependencies in the south Pacific. It took 18 months for the S.P.C. to find an acceptable formula, and not until July 1965 did Western Samoa become a member of the commission, entitled to a single vote and responsible for providing 1 percent of the organization's expenditures. At the same time, care was taken to prevent Indonesia's joining the commission by redrawing the geographical limits of the S.P.C. to exclude West Irian. Aside from the foregoing adjustments, the members made no further changes. A majority of them rejected a New Zealand proposal made in 1961 to replace the research council and south Pacific conference by a regional council which would meet annually and in which the is-

[28] *Pacific Islands Monthly,* December 1962.

landers would be given more responsibility for determining S.P.C. policies.

Coincidentally with the admission of Western Samoa, the sixth south Pacific conference was held at Lae, New Guinea. There for the first time the island delegates took the initiative in pleading for a drastic reform in the charter that would enable them to utilize the S.P.C. as an instrument for their own political advancement.[29] They took pains to express approval of the work being done by the S.P.C. and of the Western powers' continued membership in the commission. Their goal, however, was the eventual relegation of the colonial governments to the role of advisers and financiers of the organization, and the gradual assumption by the islanders of responsibility for the formulation and execution of policy.

The British islanders, specifically the delegates from Fiji and Tonga, were the most outspoken and aggressive in their proposals at Lae. Earlier, at the first south Pacific conference at Suva in 1950, Prince Tugi of Tonga had annoyed the French delegation by proposing that the teaching of English be made compulsory throughout the islands, and had also shocked the Roman Catholics present by advocating birth control to obviate the problems of overpopulation.[30] At Lae, in 1965, it was Ratu Mara of Fiji who described the S.P.C. as an obsolete, exclusive club, and who alienated the other delegates by his "arrogant" assumption that the Fijians were the most politically advanced people in the south Pacific. Not far behind the Fijians in their demand for radical reforms were the Western Samoans, who, at the first session of the S.P.C. which they attended in October 1965, warned their fellow-commissioners that the organization would be superseded by other international bodies unless they increased native participation in it and augmented their financial contributions.[31]

Most of the resolutions passed at the Lae conference were subsequently implemented. Small increases were made in the S.P.C. budget which brought it up to a total of $983,893 for 1969, but this is still an extremely small amount compared with the expenditures made by the member governments in their own island dependencies.[32] Then, too, although the operations of the S.P.C. have been of more practical benefit to the islanders, the latter have not yet been granted any ap-

[29] *New York Times,* July 15, 1965.
[30] *Pacific Islands Monthly,* May 1950.
[31] *Ibid.,* December 1965.
[32] *Le Monde Diplomatique,* November 1968.

preciable responsibility in the management of the organization. That they remained unsatisfied in this respect was shown by the strong resolution adopted at the seventh south Pacific conference in October 1968. At the 31st session of the commission, which met at the same time, it was decided to associate the conference delegates more closely with the preparation of the S.P.C.'s budget and work program, thus enlarging their role, and also to hold annual instead of triennial meetings of the conference. It is clear, however, that the Western member governments want the S.P.C. to remain a technological organization largely under their control. The islanders are so dispersed and so divided by ethnic, linguistic, and cultural differences that they are unable to accelerate appreciably the pace of change. Probably any drastic relaxation of the Western powers' control must be a voluntary decision on their part and may result from events outside the Pacific world.

Among the member governments least disposed to make fundamental changes in the S.P.C., France is regarded as the most adamant. Since the inception of the organization, France has been suspicious of the intentions of the "Anglo-Saxon" majority, believing that the latter intend to utilize the S.P.C. to promote self-government throughout the region and the spread of their language and influence.[33] The French authorities have resented the aspersions openly cast on their native policy in French Polynesia and New Caledonia, as well as the characterization of their attitude in the S.P.C. as obstructionist. With some justification, they have argued that the large white and half-caste populations in their islands, as well as the establishment there of elected representative institutions in the late nineteenth century, have given those territories a unique and politically more advanced status than exists in any others of the area. What amounted virtually to an open break between France and the critics of its policy in the Pacific occurred at a meeting of the south Pacific conference in September 1970, when the French delegation walked out, after a denunciation of its nuclear-weapons testing in Polynesia by some of the islanders.

Until that episode occurred, it had been principally in minor matters —such as their insistence on the use of the French language in S.P.C. meetings and on the accuracy of translations from documents prepared in English—that the French commissioners irritated their usually unilingual British colleagues. The sustained agitation for the transfer of S.P.C. headquarters away from Nouméa has been motivated in

33 "Aspects de l'Evolution Récente des Sociétés Océaniennes."

part by its staff's feeling of linguistic as well as geographic isolation, and also by their resentment of New Caledonia's high cost of living. Furthermore, neither the territorial administration nor the French residents have been notably cordial to the commissioners or personnel, although it must also be said that the latter seem to have made little effort to ingratiate themselves with the local community.

In fact, France takes a genuine if largely negative interest in the S.P.C.'s work, pays its dues promptly and in full, and sends large delegations, including many islanders, to south Pacific conferences and seminars. Moreover, French Polynesia and New Caledonia have profited by many S.P.C. operations.[34] In the economic sphere, they have benefited by the S.P.C.'s introduction of useful plants and edible fish, the propagation of modern agricultural techniques and control of plant diseases, and by the study of cooperative societies. As regards social welfare and health, the S.P.C.'s contributions to the analysis of urbanization, labor, and land-tenure problems, and the improvement of rural hygiene and of water-distribution systems, have been greatly appreciated. Special mention should be made of three S.P.C. projects that have been carried out in the French islands: the coconut-palm research station at Rangiroa; the campaigns against tuberculosis, filariasis, and dental decay in French Polynesia and against leprosy in New Caledonia; and finally, the training in boat-building techniques at Nouméa.

As the usefulness of such work has become increasingly apparent to the French authorities, they have progressively adopted a less negative attitude. Moreover, in recent years, the British commissioners, for their part, have made greater efforts to elicit French cooperation. The French islands have been frequently chosen as the site for S.P.C. technical meetings and study groups, bonuses have been granted to bilingual personnel, and a French edition of the *South Pacific Bulletin* was started in July 1960. Although no French secretary-general has yet been named—all the incumbents thus far have been either British or American—Frenchmen have filled two of the three executive posts in the research council.[35]

Relations among the S.P.C. member governments have improved with a growing realization on the part of all the Occidental powers

[34] Gounelle, H., "Les Positions Culturelles de la France dans le Pacifique-sud."
[35] Dr. Jacques Barrau was placed in charge of economic development in 1959, and Dr. Guy Loison succeeded Dr. Emile Massal in 1964 as head of the health department.

involved that unity among them is essential if the Pacific islands are to be maintained within the Western orbit. They also recognize that the S.P.C. is a unique and thrifty organization which performs services in the Pacific area that none of the U.N. agencies can match as regards cost, experience, or expertise. There is no doubt that the work accomplished by the S.P.C. has given satisfaction to the member governments and islanders alike. Undoubtedly there also exists a desire for change in the organization, scope, and powers of the commission, more on the part of the islanders than of the governments. Under the leadership of Sir Ramisesi Ratu, the chief minister of Fiji, the more evolved conference delegates are increasingly challenging the domination of the commission by the Western governments. Specifically, they are demanding an equal voice in, if not control of, the commission's financing and other powers, and the appointment of an islander as secretary-general. The last-mentioned desideratum has now been satisfied by the choice of an islander, Harry Moors, as secretary-general.

27

The Inhabitants[1]

Since the French arrived, the population of New Caledonia has been characterized by great diversity in the origin of both its European and nonwhite elements, sharp fluctuations in their numbers, and low density. Despite the lack of accurate statistics, especially for the early period, it is clear that the marked decline in its Melanesian component during the late nineteenth and early twentieth centuries was first arrested and then reversed during the interwar period. Since World War II, and notably since 1956, both the nonwhite and European populations have been increasing at an overall rate of 3 percent per annum. Nevertheless, the Grande Terre still has only 4.5 inhabitants to the square kilometer, Maré and Lifou 5, and Ouvéa 15.[2]

Two other phenomena characterize both main ethnic groups in recent years. One is a better-balanced sex ratio and greater youthfulness, especially marked among the Melanesians, and the other is the increase of Nouméa's population at the expense of the rural districts, notably among the Europeans. (See table 7.) According to the 1963 census, 48 percent of the total population is under twenty years of age and only 6 percent over sixty. Numerically, the Melanesians and Europeans form the most stable elements among New Caledonia's heterogeneous inhabitants, and their numbers have been increased both by immigration and by high birth rates. (See table 8.) Although the repatriation of thousands of Javanese and Vietnamese has greatly reduced the Asian component, the recent influx of immigrants from neighboring islands has added to the Oceanian element. To what degree these immigrants will be transients or permanent residents cannot as yet be foreseen.

[1] The chapter on labor deals with the Asian inhabitants.
[2] *La Nouvelle-Calédonie et Dépendances* (La Documentation Française), p. 6.

TABLE 7

New Caledonia: Population centers, 1956 and 1963

Locality	Population 1956	1963	Locality	Population 1956	1963
West coast:			*East coast:*		
Nouméa	22,235	34,990	Canala	2,544	3,097
Boulouparis	429	635	Hienghène	1,581	2,109
Bourail	2,076	2,312	Houaïlou	1,918	2,808
Dumbéa	143	463	Poindimié	2,200	2,519
Farino	(a)	172	Ponérihouen	1,853	1,900
Kala-Gomen	994	1,228	Pouébo	1,287	1,388
Koné	2,437	2,340	Thio	1,517	2,253
Koumac-Poum	2,646	2,059	Touho	1,381	1,375
La Foa	1,310	1,407	Yaté	730	925
Moindou	338	392			
Mont-Dore and					
Ile Ouen	852	2,640	*Islands:* a		
Ouégoa	1,197	1,363	Belêp archipelago	—	573
Païta	959	1,903	Isle of Pines	—	930
Pouembout	(a)	577	Lifou	—	6,082
Sarraméa	(a)	307	Maré	—	3,240
Voh	1,317	1,475	Ouvéa	—	2,087

a Data for 1956 not available.
Source: *La Nouvelle-Calédonie et Dépendances* (La Documentation Française).

TABLE 8

New Caledonia: Population, by ethnic groups, 1963

Ethnic group	Number	Percent of total population
Europeans and *assimilés*	33,355	38.6
Melanesians (including Loyalty Islanders)	41,190	47.6
French Polynesians	2,542	2.9
Wallisians and New-Hebridesians	3,016	3.5
Vietnamese	2,811	3.3
Indonesians	3,563	4.1
Miscellaneous	41	—

Source: Based on census of 1963; see *La Nouvelle-Calédonie et Dépendances* (La Documentation Française).

THE MELANESIANS

The Marist Fathers, like the early European navigators, were long confined to the coastal areas, notably the northeast coast and the Isle of Pines, and they believed that the Melanesians totaled some 90,000.[3] In 1887, the first official French census reduced that figure by about half, to 41,874, and the more methodical count made in 1911 further reduced it radically, to 28,835.

During the 24-year interval between the two last-mentioned censuses, certain physical and psychological developments accounted for the enormous population decline, regardless of the accuracy of their respective totals. The Melanesians, like the Polynesians in the E.F.O., were losing their zest for living under the combined impact of an alien government and of a religion that undermined their traditions and social order, and they had seemingly resigned themselves to imminent extinction. In the case of New Caledonia, however, there were other more tangible explanations for the Melanesians' sharp numerical decrease, which was not arrested by the ending of tribal warfare and cannibalism. One was the great losses they suffered during the revolt of 1887 and its repression, another was the policy of restricting the tribes to inadequate reservations, and still another was the growth of alcoholism and the spread of diseases. For these developments, the convicts, the settlers, and a negligent administration were all responsible.

During the first quarter of the twentieth century, all those factors except the first-mentioned were still operative, but at that period the continued decline in the birthrate also had other causes. These were the prevalence of monogamy as a result of the Melanesians' mass conversion to Christianity, the inbreeding induced by enforced village segregation, and the casualties incident to military service during World War I and the influenza epidemic of 1918. Nevertheless, during that period the pace of depopulation was slowed down by the introduction in 1907 of a medical service for the tribes and by the enactment of laws forbidding the sale of alcohol to the Melanesians. Their relatively small loss of 1,989 persons between 1911 and 1926 was followed by a stabilization of their number at about 27,000 in the late 1920s.

Paradoxically, the world depression of the early 1930s, which caused

[3] *L'Océanie Française,* July–August 1930.

a massive exodus of Europeans and Asians from New Caledonia, witnessed the beginning of a rise in the Melanesian population, albeit at the very low rate of 0.5 percent per annum. The last prewar census, in 1936, was the most accurate up to that time because an *état civil* (the obligatory registration of vital statistics) for the tribes had been instituted in the preceding year. This census gave the total number of Melanesians as 29,055, of whom 17,091 lived on the Grande Terre and 12,097 on the Loyalty Islands. Moreover, it showed a marked improvement in the sex ratio and the percentage of young people, especially in the Loyaltys.[4]

Although credit should be given to the efforts of doctors and missionaries to rehabilitate the tribes, the causes of the improvement in the demographic situation—as also for its earlier decline—were probably as much psychological as physical. The income earned by the Melanesians from the sale of export crops during the 1920s had been assumed to be the reason for the general improvement in their health and life span, yet the depression of the early 1930s, which greatly reduced their earnings, coincided with the first net increase in their numbers. Maurice Leenhardt believed that the Melanesians' resurgence was due to the adjustment which they had been able, at long last, to make to the new conditions imposed by European colonization through the adaptation and modernization of their traditions and beliefs.[5] His conviction that the Melanesians had psychologically turned the corner was later substantiated by their continued numerical increase, despite an epidemic of grippe and measles in 1938 and the toll taken by combat service during World War II. During the Pacific war their number rose from 30,201 in 1942 to 30,763 in 1946.[6] Their increase during the 20-year period of 1930–1950 was slower than that of the European community, but it was gathering greater momentum. The 1956 census listed 34,969 Melanesians, and that of 1963, 41,199. In the latter year they constituted 47.6 percent of the total population of New Caledonia, and the Europeans (33,355) accounted for only 38.6 percent.[7]

The overall rise in New Caledonia's total population has been accompanied by its geographical redistribution, notably reflected in the rapid growth of Nouméa. This change has been less radical in the

[4] As of 1936, there were 9,136 women, 9,456 men, and 10,181 children. See *L'Océanie Française,* November–December 1937.

[5] Leenhardt, M., *Gens de la Grande Terre.*

[6] *La France Australe,* Feb. 5, 1947.

[7] *La Nouvelle-Calédonie et Dépendances* (La Documentation Française), p. 6.

case of the Europeans, who have always formed a large majority in the territorial capital, but for the Melanesians it has been a postwar phenomenon. As of 1936, only 732 Melanesians had been granted permission to live and work in Nouméa, and 522 of these were men.[8] After the 1946 law gave the Melanesians freedom of movement, more and more of them drifted to the capital, where, ten years later, they numbered 2,594. Many of these, however, were Loyalty Islanders, and probably at least three-fourths of the natives of the Grande Terre still lived on their reservations. Furthermore, they had become more numerous on the east coast than before the war, both comparatively and in absolute terms. Whereas in 1936 the Koné district of the west coast had the greatest single concentration of Melanesians (1,182), its population fifteen years later (1,318) was smaller than that of the east-coast areas of Canala (2,089), Houaïlou (1,895), Poindimié (1,797), and Ponérihouen (1,496).[9] Today, most of the Melanesians still live in the north and center of the east coast, between Pouébo and Canala, and very few of them have moved to the mining centers in the southeast. Melanesians form almost the entire population of the Isle of Pines, the Belêp archipelago, and the Loyalty Islands.

IMMIGRANT ISLANDERS

The rapid postwar rise in the Grande Terre's population has resulted not only from higher birth and lower death rates among the native Melanesians, but also from immigration from other parts of Oceania. Many of the newcomers are Polynesians from Tahiti and from Wallis and Futuna, but there is also a sprinkling of New-Hebridesians. The last-mentioned are of mixed Melanesian and Polynesian blood, and they were among the first island immigrants used as laborers in New Caledonia. As of 1891 they numbered nearly 2,000 in the Grande Terre, but they dwindled rapidly as labor needs in their home islands grew apace, and by 1936 only 157 were left. Today they are such a negligible quantity that they are grouped with the far more numerous Wallisians in census reports.

Although the Loyalty Islanders are Melanesians and cannot properly be classed with the Polynesian immigrants, they are an important

[8] McTaggart, W. D., "Présentes Migrations des Autochtones, au Sein de l'Archipel Néo-Calédonien."

[9] Faivre, J.-P., J. Poirier, and P. Routhier, *Géographie de la Nouvelle-Calédonie*, p. 221.

migrant element in the Grande Terre's population which merits special mention. They never underwent so rapid and drastic a decline in numbers as did the natives of the Grande Terre, and they maintained a greater social cohesiveness and independence vis-à-vis the Nouméa administration.[10] Moreover, as the result of the "wars of religion and of empire" in their home islands between the English Protestant and French Catholic missionaries, they gained a maturity and cultural development that has made them the most industrious, literate, and disciplined of the islanders living in New Caledonia, and consequently very popular with European employers.[11] They were, in fact, so much in demand that in 1893 the governor decreed that a *laisser-passer* should be issued to any Loyalty Islanders willing to work in the Grande Terre, and for many years thereafter adolescent boys came to harvest the settlers' coffee crops. This arrangement ended in 1927 when Loyalty Island parents refused to permit their sons to migrate any longer, alleging that they were ill-treated by the Caledonian settlers and also that they were needed to increase food production at home.[12]

After World War II, migration between the Loyaltys and the Grande Terre was revived, but only for adults. It took mainly the form of seasonal commuting, especially after an airplane service was established in 1955, which is increasingly used by whole families of Loyalty Islanders. Just how many have settled in the Grande Terre is hard to estimate, since such a large proportion regularly return home for the yam-planting season between June and October, but 4,000 of them were listed by the 1963 census as residing there. About three-fourths of the Loyalty Islanders are to be found in Nouméa, where they live in groups according to their occupations and their island of origin. For example, those working in the building industry come mainly from Ouvéa, *plantons* (messengers) in the administration from Lifou, and employees of the communications service from Maré.[13]

Because the Loyalty Islanders are Melanesians and mostly transients in the Grande Terre, their presence there is more acceptable to the natives than is that of the more recent Polynesian immigrants. In 1947, the Wallisians began emigrating to New Caledonia as the result of a catastrophic decline in the productivity of their islands' coconut

[10] See also pp. 236, 443.

[11] Leenhardt, M., "Iles Loyalty," *Encylopédie Mensuelle d'Outre-Mer,* March 1955.

[12] *L'Océanie Française,* September–October 1928.

[13] Doumenge, F., "L'Economie de la Grande Terre Calédonienne."

palms throughout the preceding decade. Until 1952, the Wallisians were almost wholly transients in the Grande Terre, where fewer than 200 were permanently installed.[14] During the mid-1950s, however, the Grande Terre's prosperity attracted increasing numbers of Wallisians, more and more of whom began bringing their wives and children with them. In New Caledonia they benefited from a more liberal system of family allowances than at home and, moreover, enjoyed being free there from the restrictions imposed in Wallis and Futuna by the Catholic missionaries and feudal chiefs. New Caledonia is the territory to which three-fourths of the Wallisian emigrants have gravitated, and because they are a young and prolific group, the permanent Wallisian colony in the Grande Terre has grown rapidly.

During the 1960s, this colony averaged about 3,000 persons, of whom the majority lived in Nouméa and only about one-third were wage-earners. As of 1966, there were among them 876 men and 125 women gainfully employed as manual laborers in the mining industry, of whom 90 percent were unskilled and 64 percent illiterate.[15] In Nouméa they live under wretched conditions and in a compact group, aloof from other elements of the urban population and adhering strictly to their own traditions. They maintain close contacts with their relatives at home and regularly send them money. In the Grande Terre they are unpopular with the Melanesians, who consider them culturally inferior, clannish, and quarrelsome.[16] On several occasions, the Nouméa police have had to intervene either to keep order in the community or to prevent fighting between them and the Melanesians. Although the Wallisians are neither docile nor skilled workers, the Grande Terre's economy has become increasingly dependent on their labor. As the population of their home islands continues to increase without any corresponding economic improvement, the influx of Wallisians will probably grow, and with it the size of their permanent colony.

Tahitians form the second group of Polynesian immigrants whom conditions of overpopulation and economic stringency at home have periodically forced to seek employment abroad.[17] Nearly a decade later than the Wallisians, they began coming to New Caledonia, where the building of the Yaté dam assured them of well-paid jobs. As this coincided with an economic recession in French Polynesia, the number of

[14] Videau, D., and C. Cotter, "Les Wallisiens en Calédonie."

[15] *Bulletin du Commerce de la Nouvelle-Calédonie et des Nouvelles-Hébrides*, Oct. 4, 1967.

[16] *Pacific Islands Monthly*, October 1955, January 1959.

[17] See p. 174.

Tahitian immigrant workers increased rapidly, rising from 169 in 1955 to 1,084 in 1957.[18] Early in 1960, after the completion of New Caledonia's big public-works program, some of them returned to Tahiti but many remained in the Grande Terre and were joined by their families. A few Tahitian women opened shops in Nouméa, and the men showed a remarkable adaptability to the employment opportunities available in the Grande Terre. Their superior education and skills enabled them to fill a greater variety of well-paid jobs than was the case for the Wallisians, and although the majority worked in the mining and transport industries, some were employed in hotels, restaurants, and night clubs. A mission sent in 1964 by the territorial assembly of French Polynesia to investigate the situation of the Tahitian immigrants in the Grande Terre reported that they were doing well there and that their employers were well satisfied with their services. Nevertheless, the Tahitians are, in general, disinclined to settle permanently in New Caledonia, except for a few Chinese who brought with them enough capital to set themselves up as merchants there. Those Polynesian Tahitians who have amassed sufficient earnings or who have reached the retirement age usually return home. Indeed, whenever well-paid employment is available in French Polynesia, as it was during the C.E.P.'s period of greatest activity, the flow of Tahitian workers to New Caledonia has decreased. If nuclear testing at Mururoa should cease in the late 1970s, there may well be another sizeable exodus.

For many of the same reasons, neither group of Polynesian immigrants is cordially welcomed by the natives of the Grande Terre. This attitude, however, is not true of local European employers, who have come to regard them as the best available replacements for the Asian manual laborers. The employers' opinion may change if the Polynesians progressively desert manual occupations to take up trade. As for the Polynesian immigrants' relations with the Melanesians, it is not competition in the labor market that lies at the roots of the latter's resentment, but rather the Polynesians' assumption of their own ethnic superiority and their refusal to be culturally integrated into the Melanesian milieu.

WHITE SETTLERS AND TRANSIENTS

Although the census reports of the twentieth century for New Caledonia are far more accurate than those of the preceding half-

[18] Doumenge, "L'Economie de la Grande Terre Calédonienne."

century, they can only reflect the situation as it existed at the time they were taken. Consequently, for a society so constantly in a state of flux as that of the territory's white community, the picture they present is of only comparative value. A large proportion of New Caledonia's white population is made up of the transients who are its officials, members of the armed forces, missionaries, and businessmen. In addition, there are others who emigrated to New Caledonia with the intention of settling there but who, for various reasons, decided to leave.

Aside from the Catholic missionaries, the first Europeans who arrived in the mid-nineteenth century were a mixture of British, German, and French adventurers and traders. Most of them came in hopes of making a fortune by collecting sandalwood or by mining, and perhaps the only ones who, from the outset, intended to remain were the score of idealists who founded the ill-fated utopian colony at Yaté.[19] Not until the penitentiary regime was established in 1864 did New Caledonia receive a substantial number of permanent—if involuntary —residents. Convicts were the first colonists who founded settlements at Bourail, La Foa, Pouembout, and elsewhere, and who cultivated the land and reared animals in haphazard fashion.

The penal period, which lasted until 1897, was disastrous for New Caledonia both economically and psychologically. Huge tracts of land, allocated to the penitentiary regime, were used solely to provide food for the convicts and their guardians, as well as for the colony's few officials and members of the armed forces. The crops cultivated purely for subsistence purposes quickly exhausted the limited amounts of arable soil, and the rearing of cattle on the vast ranches to supply cheap meat ruined the Grande Terre's pastureland and twice drove the Melanesians to revolt. This waste of natural resources deformed the agricultural basis of the island's economy and retarded its later development. To be sure, the convicts undertook some useful public works, but such short-term benefits were more than offset by the permanent harm which they did to the native inhabitants and to the free white settlers.

Psychologically, the abundance of cheap penal labor was responsible for the disdain with which the Caledonian whites have looked upon all manual occupations and for their perennial efforts to bring in immigrants who would perform such tasks for them. At the same time, the settlers refused to offer such inducements as would encourage the Asian and Oceanian immigrants to remain as permanent residents and

[19] See p. 240.

to become an integral part of the community. This attitude accounts, in part, for New Caledonia's failure to become a melting pot, and almost impenetrable barriers have been raised not only between the Caledonians of European and colored origin but also between members of its white society. Another unfortunate psychological legacy of the penal period has been the Caledonians' tendency to oversell the attractions of the territory for free white settlers, in an attempt to obliterate its reputation as a colony for jailbirds.

The local administration was instrumental in bringing only the first wave of white immigrants. In inducing colonists to come to New Caledonia, Governor Feillet tried to select them carefully from among French farmers who possessed a modicum of capital. Moreover, he prepared for their arrival and aided them to install themselves as well as he could under the conditions prevailing at the end of the nineteenth century. At that time too little was known about the island's economic potential and the Melanesians' social structure for him to foresee the consequences of many of his policies. It was such ignorance that was mainly responsible for his unfortunate encouragement of cotton and sugarcane cultivation and of large-scale ranching, and for his segregating of the tribes on inadequate reservations. Yet despite these errors, it was the Feillet colonists who were the most successful and enduring of all the groups of white immigrants. Largely through natural increase, his free white settlers became so numerous that within a few years they outnumbered the convict element, which gradually disappeared during the first quarter of the twentieth century. By 1920 the number of convicts had dwindled to 2,310, and this accounted for the diminution of the white population as a whole from its peak of 23,419 in the former year to 16,482 at the end of that 20-year period.[20] By 1921, however, not only was the free white element almost seven times larger than that of the convicts, but the number of those born in the colony accounted for more than three-fourths of the total. The 1936 census reported only 17,384 white residents in New Caledonia, and though the birthrate among them was extremely high there was still a dearth of European women and very few recent immigrants.

In the mid-1920s, there arrived in the Grande Terre 236 French colonists, collectively called the Nordists because they had come from France's *département du Nord*. They had been recruited there by an enthusiastic former mayor of Nouméa, Marx Lang. On his own initi-

20 *L'Océanie Française,* January–February 1922.

ative and without the knowledge of either the French government or the local administration, Lang had conducted a one-man propaganda campaign with the aim of increasing New Caledonia's white population. Because no care was taken to select suitable human material and no preparations were made to receive them in New Caledonia, this second attempt at agricultural colonization—this time on a cooperative basis—was a failure. Half the Nordist immigrants were active men, but they lacked both capital and farming experience. Although the administration allotted them a large area of arable land near Nouméa, they not only complained of the lack of facilities and the presence of deer and mosquitoes, but also quarreled among themselves. Soon 23 of the families demanded repatriation and were sent back to France, 13 others went to the New Hebrides, 48 took up trade in Nouméa, and only 34 remained on the land.[21] This small residue received aid from the administration and were generally welcomed by other settlers, who by that time had come to fear that the white population might soon be submerged by the Asians and, to a lesser degree, by the Melanesians.

Because of the Nordist fiasco following the partial failure of Feillet's efforts to promote white colonization, the local officials became much more cautious about encouraging further immigration from France. They took pains to correct the erroneous notion in the mother country that New Caledonia's soil was rich and its land abundant. To provide arable and ranching land for the comparatively few white colonists who had, either perforce or voluntarily, settled in the colony, first the penitentiary regime and later the civilian government had initiated the disastrous policy of encroaching on tribal property. Furthermore, the ensuing inequities in the land regime had already divided the white community into two conspicuously unequal groups. One consisted of a handful of wealthy ranchers and mineowners, and the other of a far larger number of subsistence farmers barely able to eke out a living from the small-scale cultivation of a few crops. On the eve of World War II, the territorial authorities had a more accurate knowledge of the Grande Terre's capacity for absorbing newcomers, notably as regards the areas suitable and still available for agricultural colonization and the job opportunities open to white men. To discourage all impecunious and unqualified white immigrants, the administration decreed on July 13, 1938, that upon arriving in Nouméa, Frenchmen as

[21] *Ibid.*, September–October 1926, September–October 1927, November–December 1927.

well as all other foreigners must post a bond against their possible later repatriation.

New Caledonia's economic boom during the Second World War, caused by the presence of great numbers of American troops, was misinterpreted in France as a permanent state of affairs. Some of the 15,000 or so Frenchmen who emigrated after the liberation of France went to New Caledonia, but by the time they arrived, its wartime prosperity had ended. In 1946 there were 1,979 arrivals and 1,443 departures of Frenchmen, although it should be noted that by no means all the members of either group were settlers, either past or future. Those who came with the intention of remaining found that the cost of living was high, housing was short, there were no jobs for such skills as they possessed, no need for their services in an overstaffed administration, and no welcome or help from the Caledonians.[22]

In theory, the Caledonians wanted more French immigrants so as to enlarge the white population, but in practice they were either indifferent or actually hostile to the newcomers, whom they called by the disparaging terms of "zoreilles" or "zozos." [23] The local-born population was growing rapidly, and felt, not unnaturally, that it deserved the best posts available in the territory. Actually, they wanted only those immigrants who would become and remain manual laborers, and the postwar immigrants from France were not capable or willing to perform such tasks. Moreover, they were disconcerted to find the rural areas of New Caledonia lacking in such amenities as electricity, roads, schools, and hospitals to which they were accustomed. About four hundred of these immigrants stayed on, but the others were disillusioned and left the territory, some having to be repatriated at New Caledonia's expense.[24]

Although this wave of white immigration was smaller and more spontaneous than the two previous ones, it was so obviously a failure that it marked a turning point in the attitude of the Caledonians toward would-be white settlers. The general councilors, who in 1947 had asked that the law of 1938 be rescinded and that Frenchmen be allowed to enter the territory freely, reversed themselves in 1950 and

[22] *Marchés Coloniaux*, July 17, 1948, p. 1282.

[23] The origin of these terms is obscure. It is thought that they derived from pidgin French and to have been applied to men from a cold climate who have to cover their ears to keep them warm. By way of contrast, the Caledonians call themselves "niaoulis," which is the name of a dwarf eucalyptus that grows abundantly in the Grande Terre in regions where there is no tropical forest.

[24] *Marchés Coloniaux*, May 12, 1951, p. 1404.

voted to have the former restrictions restored.[25] The local administration and Nouméa businessmen went further and made a determined effort to discourage unqualified potential settlers. The governor urged the Paris government by cable to screen applicants more rigorously, and told a Metropolitan journalist that there were job openings at that time in New Caledonia for only a dozen French technicians at most.[26] The Nouméa Chamber of Commerce, for its part, published in Paris newspapers what was perhaps the first frank semiofficial statement describing current conditions in the territory. It stated that there was still room there for industrious and intelligent young Frenchmen but that they must be willing to work hard and to accept "modest" positions. New Caledonia was not a romantic island that could support indolent youths who wanted to lie on the beach under the shade of coconut palms, nor did it offer opportunities to those expecting to amass a fortune rapidly.

So that such warnings should not wholly discourage French emigration to New Caledonia but simply keep it within realistic bounds, the Economic and Social Council in Paris accepted a report on April 21, 1953, written by one of its members, which contained the following statement:

At the same time as guaranteeing to the Kanakas an extension of their crops and reserving to the European youth of New Caledonia facilities that would enable them to return to the land, expert local opinion holds that there are still at least 100,000 hectares of unoccupied land suited to the cultivation of coffee and cereals. . . . In the near future, New Caledonia could receive from 500 to 1,000 French farmers.[27]

By that time, however, most Caledonians no longer shared this view. They felt that in the future the territory should receive no more immigrants, of whatever origin, who might insist on seeking nonmanual occupations, assimilation to the European population, and even French citizenship. Consequently, the general council rejected a Dutch proposal in 1953 to open New Caledonia's doors to Eurasian immigrants from Indonesia, as well as a similar suggestion from the French government in 1955 in regard to Eurasians from Vietnam.[28] Even French applicants from Réunion Island were turned down on the ground that they might introduce communist propaganda or, con-

[25] *La France Australe*, May 20, 1948, Nov. 30, 1950.
[26] *Pacific Islands Monthly*, March 1950.
[27] *Marchés Coloniaux*, Oct. 24, 1953, p. 2904.
[28] Minutes of the general council, May 20, 1953, April 4, 1955.

versely, that they might display the same racist tendencies that had made them unwelcome in Madagascar. In 1962, when some senators led by Henri Lafleur advocated the admission of several thousand *pieds noirs* (French colonists who had left Algeria after it became independent), the territorial assemblymen refused their consent, and in this they were supported by the Caledonian union leaders, who feared that so many newcomers might result in unemployment among the local-born.[29]

Although some of the Algerian French did come to settle in New Caledonia, the whole question of white immigration has now become less acute for several reasons. One is the satisfactory rate of growth in the white Caledonian community, which in 1963 reached the record total of 33,355 persons. Indeed, the birthrate among the Caledonians of European origin is said to be one of the highest in the world, and nearly half of them are under 20 years of age.[30] Although the Europeans still account for only 38.6 percent of the total population, compared with 47.6 percent for the Melanesians, the former are increasing at a more rapid rate. A second and more cogent reason is the widespread realization that New Caledonia can never become a territory with large-scale agricultural production, and that its future economic development depends almost wholly on the continued expansion of the mining industry. The negative aspect of this view is confirmed by the progressive desertion of the farming areas by young Caledonians, who have increasingly been moving to Nouméa. There they are forming an embryonic urban proletariat, among whom the Union Calédonienne has found its largest group of urban supporters. Aside from the political implications of this development, their movement to the capital has been responsible for a significant redistribution of the territory's population.

Because the mountains made the interior of New Caledonia difficult of access—the region in any case being inhospitable to human habitation—the first villages founded by the convicts and early settlers were all located along the two coasts and could easily be reached by sea. After the 1887 revolt, almost all of the Melanesians were driven away from the west coast and resettled mainly on the eastern flank of the Grande Terre. Into the areas which they had evacuated moved the

[29] *Communautés et Continents,* July–September 1962; *L'Avenir Calédonien,* July 16, 1963.

[30] In 1953 it was reported that 66 percent of the married men had 5 children or more. See *Marchés Coloniaux,* Oct. 24, 1953, p. 2911.

Europeans, and the west coast is still the region with the greatest concentration of white settlers living outside Nouméa and its suburbs. Although the western plains have a low overall density of 1.8 persons to the square kilometer, their three main towns—Koumac, Bourail, and Koné—contain some 6,600 persons, most of whom are white settlers. The slightly higher population density of 2.7 inhabitants to the square kilometer on the east coast is due almost wholly to the presence there of two-thirds of the total Melanesian population. On that coast the only place where Europeans live in any number is the mining center of Thio.

Although the Melanesians are still predominantly rural, they, too, are becoming more urbanized. According to the New Zealand scholar, P. H. Curson, who in 1962 studied the composition of the territory's thirty-six villages (with populations ranging from 25 to more than 2,600), 68 percent of all the inhabitants of the Grande Terre then lived in such settlements.[31] In eighteen of them, Europeans accounted for more than 60 percent of the total, and in seven others, more than 70 percent. The Asian and Oceanian immigrants have naturally gravitated to the places where jobs are available, and these are the settlements dominated by Europeans. Curson found Asians scattered along both coasts, but in large numbers only in thirteen settlements. The nonindigenous elements of the population were certainly the most urbanized of all; 95 percent of the Vietnamese, 97 percent of the Wallisians and New-Hebridesians, and 98 percent of the Tahitians lived in the population centers. Only 12.5 percent of the Europeans still lived in truly rural areas.

Despite some recent improvements in the means of transportation, including an internal airplane service and several transversal roads, the northern region of the Grande Terre has little overland communication with the south. New Caledonia's grandiose and somber interior is almost uninhabited except for some small, dispersed farm homesteads, many of them located far from the main coastal settlements. Considering their isolation and their lack of comfort and diversions, not to mention the meager revenue derived from small-scale farming, it is no wonder that more and more young rural Caledonians are leaving the countryside and moving to the capital.

Over the years, Nouméa's population has grown by fits and starts, and generally in a haphazard fashion. The town began as a military port built by penal labor, and two years after its founding in 1854

[31] *South Pacific Bulletin*, April 1965.

Nouméa had a population consisting of a garrison of 100 men and 25 civilians. It developed as a trading center with Australia, but even more as the port through which thousands of convicts were funneled into the interior. At the turn of the century, it was losing its vitality, and its population declined from a peak of 8,100 in 1897 to 7,437 in 1902.[32] During the next twenty-odd years, the number of Noumeans increased slowly, its inhabitants totaling only 10,226 in 1926, but between then and 1956—when the first detailed census of the population was made—it more than doubled. The city's growth accelerated between 1961 and 1968, and in the latter year it was estimated to have about 45,000 inhabitants.[33]

Nouméa is a city of civil servants and traders, its only important industry being the Doniambo smelter on the outskirts. The upper crust of Nouméa society is composed very largely of transients—officials, businessmen, and military officers—who rarely mingle with its permanent residents. The clear-cut divisions among the white Noumeans are usually attributed to the transients' aloofness and snobbery, and the unpleasant atmosphere thus generated is said to be the main reason why so many Metropolitan immigrants decide to leave the territory. Visitors from France, especially during the interwar period, often complained that Nouméa was also a dull town, lacking in any artistic or intellectual life and even in such diversions as outdoor cafes and night clubs.

Considerable improvements in the town's sanitation, roads, and lighting were made by the American troops stationed there during World War II, and their presence was also responsible for the mushrooming of shops and bars. Although such amenities remained after the Americans left, the town lost much of its liveliness and lapsed into its prewar provincial lethargy. Since then the Asians and Oceanians living there in increasing numbers have contributed a modicum of exotic charm and a cosmopolitan flavor. Their presence, but even more the agreeable climate of Nouméa and its "French atmosphere" and cuisine, attract an ever-larger influx of Australian tourists each year. And to the rural Caledonian youths, who have never known anything but the monotony and isolation of the farm, Nouméa seems a thriving metropolis with an irresistible magnetic allure.

[32] Laroque, R., "Nouméa."
[33] *Marchés Tropicaux*, April 5, 1969, p. 1056.

28

The Rural Economy

For many years, and especially since World War II, New Caledonians have been concerned about the decline in the local agricultural production. Indeed, agriculture now occupies such a minor position in the Grande Terre's economy that it is often forgotten that farming was the basis for European colonization there. From the days of the penitentiary regime to those of the Nordist immigrants, certain crops have successively aroused the enthusiasm of Caledonian settlers, but each time hope has given way to disillusionment. In 1968, the territory's sole agricultural exports were copra and coffee, and together they accounted for no more than 1.5 percent of total exports, by value. A general pall of discouragement with agriculture has settled over the territory since the depression of the early 1930s, and has deepened with the passage of the years. Yet the early illusion that white men, working with their hands, could make New Caledonia into a small-scale Australia dies hard, and even today has not been wholly abandoned.

Many explanations for the progressive abandonment of agriculture in New Caledonia have been offered, some attributing it to natural causes and others to man. Natural handicaps include the lack of permanent watercourses and the dearth of extensive areas of arable land, as well as frequently adverse climatic conditions. The man-made causes are more complex, ranging from the introduction of large-scale ranching and certain export crops to the land-tenure system, the evolution of the labor situation, the long neglect of scientific research, and the stubborn individualism of the European planters. In recent years, the decline of agriculture has been ascribed chiefly to the growing importance of the mining industry, which has drained manpower from the rural areas. Agriculture has never been a remunerative occupation in the Grande Terre, and it is becoming less so, despite a rise in the number of consumers and improvement in the means of communication.

Because of the lack of agronomic and other scientific data, it is hard to estimate just how much of the Grande Terre is arable. The secretary of the Chamber of Agriculture, in a study made in 1936, admitted that the current classification of the island's land surface, covering 1,612,000 hectares, according to the type of occupancy indicated only approximately its basic economic character.[1] The native reservations, for example, were supposed to comprise almost exclusively farming land, but much of their area was not arable. Similarly, many of the vast ranches contained considerable stretches of land that could be, but were not, cultivated. Furthermore, even those areas he described as of "prime quality" were exposed to periodic cyclones and floods that destroyed crops. Even today, when scientific studies of the soil are much further advanced, experts hazard only tentative figures. The arable land is now generally estimated to cover between 80,000 and 100,000 hectares, of which 14,000 at most are cultivated, while much of the area described as suited to stock-raising contains heavily wooded stretches. Most of the rest of the island is vaguely classified as mining land.

Primarily it is the small size and wide dispersion of the arable areas that make difficult not only an accurate survey but also their cultivation. They are studded with mountain ranges, forests, and swamps, and many of them have been overwhelmed by vast growths of lantana.[2] Their vegetation has also been damaged by herds of wild deer. On the whole, tropical crops have fared better in the Grande Terre than have those of the temperate zone.

About 46 percent of the cultivated land is now planted to coconut palms, 32 percent to coffee, 13 percent to tubers, and the remainder to miscellaneous crops such as wheat, rice, vegetables, and fruit trees.[3] Without exception, cultivation of those crops today is either stagnant or declining. The lack of labor, the distance from markets, and the predominance of the mining industry are together largely responsible for the decline of agriculture. There is no doubt that, from a technical standpoint, New Caledonia's agricultural potential is far from being realized, and that even in economic terms it could be further developed

[1] *L'Océanie Française*, January–February 1936.

[2] This plant, introduced into New Caledonia about 1860 by the missionaries for their gardens, moved from the littoral to the hinterland, where it has spread up the mountain slopes, stifling trees even on their summits.

[3] *Europe-France-Outremer*, no. 421, 1965.

within realistic bounds. Yet this has not been done, because it would entail drastic changes that New Caledonia's individualistic and conservative European farmers are still unwilling to make. They have preferred either to take up ranching as easier and less risky than farming or have supplemented the meager earnings they derive from cultivating various crops by engaging in paid jobs, craft work, or trade.

Land tenure

The striking inequities of New Caledonia's land-tenure system can be ascribed to the greed of its white settlers, the ignorance and insouciance of the administration, and the incapacity of the Melanesians to defend themselves. Consequently, the Melanesians—who today form 47.6 percent of the total population—possess recognized property rights to only about 8 percent of the Grande Terre,[4] whereas individuals and companies mainly of European origin own or rent 38 percent of its total surface, barely one-tenth of which has been cultivated. The unequal distribution of land between the two main ethnic groups is matched by an analogous maldistribution among members of the white community: 41 percent of the land ceded or rented to non-Melanesians is in the hands of only 10 persons or business firms.

It seems curious that a situation of such glaring inequity should have persisted for nearly a century without any fundamental change. From time to time, piecemeal improvements in the system have been made, but despite the rapid growth of the territory's population and its recent redistribution, there has never been an overriding demand for agrarian reform. The main causes of this immobilism have been the fast-declining importance of agriculture in New Caledonia's economy and the shrinkage in its rural labor force.[5]

Virtually all the laws that still determine New Caledonia's land-tenure system date from the late nineteenth century.[6] After France acquired sovereignty over New Caledonia in 1853, all the Grande Terre automatically became state property, and the new colony's naval governors lost little time in regulating the land question. By what was known as the concordat of January 29, 1855, France recognized the Melanesians' collective and individual property rights to all of the area that they occupied. Their chiefs and tribesmen were forbidden to dispose of such

[4] In New Caledonia's island dependencies, on the contrary, all the land is in native hands.

[5] See pp. 384, 462–463.

[6] Lenormand, M., "L'Evolution Politique des Autochtones de la Nouvelle-Calédonie."

land to other tribes or to foreigners, and only the French government could purchase it to add to the public domain, either for sale or concession. A supplementary regulation of October 5, 1862, declared all "vacant and ownerless land" to be state property, and because the French authorities at that time were ignorant of the Melanesians' traditional agricultural cycle they believed that all uncultivated lands fell into that category.

The decision in 1864 to create a penal colony inevitably altered the government's land policy in New Caledonia. Its expectation that the Grande Terre could produce enough meat and vegetables to feed thousands of convicts and their keepers was confirmed by the unduly optimistic report made in 1863 by Jules Garnier, a geologist sent by the Minister of Colonies to survey the island's agricultural potential.[7] Vast tracts of land, therefore, were allocated to the colony's few white settlers and, above all, to the penitentiary regime, with a view to their development by penal labor. From this period date most of the huge properties that still cover much of the island.

Since a large proportion of this ceded land was suited only to ranching, the government took steps to extend its control over the more limited arable areas. A regulation of January 21, 1868, contravened the 1855 concordat by making the tribe collectively owner of all the land it occupied, which had formerly been held by its members on a family or individual basis, and the Great Chief was made responsible for dividing it among them. Although a regulation of December 24, 1867, had given legal recognition to the tribe's autonomy, a law adopted March 6, 1876, resulted in a drastic curtailment of the area collectively owned by the tribes. The governor was empowered to delimit the area held by each tribe, and thus the Melanesians were no longer guaranteed ownership or even the use of the land that they had traditionally occupied. Furthermore, the government arrogated to itself the right to determine just how much land each tribe required and to allocate it accordingly. This flagrant violation of the 1855 concordat, as well as of the Melanesians' customary property rights, created a widespread fear among them of total dispossession, and it was a major cause of the 1887 revolt.

Some foreign observers contend that the successive Melanesian revolts were engineered by the colonial administration so as to increase

---

[7] Garnier was better qualified as a mining engineer than as an agronomist, for he was the first to discover New Caledonia's nickel deposits.

the land area under its control.[8] Because the cost of such rebellions in terms of human life and material damage was so great, it seems unlikely that such was the deliberate official policy. The net result, however, was the same, for the state simply annexed to its domain the land abandoned by the fleeing rebels and did not restore it even to those who later were amnestied or acquitted. Feillet's policy of encouraging white colonization, as shown in his regulation of November 13, 1897, increased the pressure to acquire more land for the new settlers' use. In this way the administration simply proclaimed its right to expropriate any form of landed property in the public interest and to transfer the tribes at will from one place to another. To be sure, the law now required that the tribal chief be consulted prior to any such population transfers, but this was largely a device to induce a readier acceptance of such a move on the part of his tribesmen. Since the population transfers were compensated by a small money indemnity paid to the chief, he was willing to cooperate insofar as sharing the onus of responsibility was concerned.

The new basis on which tribal lands were thenceforth delimited was that of 3 hectares of arable land for each Melanesian. This 3-hectare limitation had been arbitrarily decided without any understanding of the rotation system for native tuber crops or scientific study of the island's soils. It was based on the prevailing assumption that because their number was sharply declining, the Melanesians were doomed to imminent extinction. The process of spoliation continued throughout the interwar period, even after it had become clear that the Melanesians, far from dying out, were becoming more numerous.

The years during which New Caledonia served as a penal colony roughly coincided with the period when the government handed out land concessions most lavishly. By a decree of 1884, the Grande Terre's best lands were granted to the penitentiary regime, but a decade later Governor Feillet succeeded in so modifying that law that he was able to recuperate nearly 63,000 hectares of such land.[9] Moreover, the land taken from the tribes under the November 13, 1897, regulation was also distributed to the Feillet settlers, and the Melanesians were thus forced to move away from the coast and higher up

[8] Burchett, W. G., *Pacific Treasure Island*, p. 34; Oliver, D. L., *The Pacific Islands*, p. 324.
[9] *L'Océanie Française*, August 1912.

on the mountain slopes. The white colonists moved into the coastal plains, where they founded permanent settlements. As their numbers steadily increased, the settlers wanted still more tribal lands, and in 1911 they gained support for their demands from the influential Comité de l'Océanie Française in Paris. One of its directors, Georges Froment-Guiyesse, wrote a series of articles, which appeared in that committee's periodical,[10] strongly endorsing their pleas. He argued that because the Melanesians had failed to cultivate all the reservations and were moreover a dying race, it was only reasonable that some of their unused land should be given to settlers who would develop it. Far from being hemmed in by the colonists, he added, it was the Melanesian reservations that were holding the settlers in a vise, impeding their expansion, and denying them access to the sea.

The backing which the settlers managed to obtain in Paris did result in a further paring down of the reservations, although not so fast or on such a scale as before. Under the Feillet regime, the number of agricultural concessions granted had grown from 130 to 434,[11] but the tempo slowed down for some years after 1903. It picked up speed gradually after World War I so that in 1924, land grants totaled 202— twice the number granted in 1913—and in the single year 1928, 286 were ceded. The need to provide land for the Nordist immigrants [12] accounted for the high 1928 figure, for during the preceding decade the administration's attitude toward the settlers' insatiable demands for Melanesian land and labor had been undergoing a marked change. Officials now realized that the Melanesian population was becoming stabilized, and they began to encourage the cultivation of food and export crops on the tribal reservations. To obtain more accurate information as to the extent of existing land holdings and of the arable areas still available for colonization, Governor Guyon in January 1926 appointed an advisory land committee composed of officials and representatives of the settlers. This committee worked at a snail's pace, and by the time it had selected 10,800 hectares deemed suitable for future colonists, the plan to grant plots to World War I veterans had fallen through, few of the Nordists remained in New Caledonia, and the world depression had made many of the island's export crops unsalable.

This new economic situation forced the French administration to

[10] *Ibid.*, July–November 1912.

[11] Robequain, C., *Madagascar et les Bases Dispersées de l'Union Française,* p. 464.

[12] See pp. 366–367.

revise certain aspects of its land-concessions policy, which derived mainly from a regulation of July 10, 1895. According to its provisions, areas of 10 to 25 hectares could be given or sold under specified conditions only to French farmer-immigrants, military personnel, or civil servants who had retired in the Grande Terre after serving in the colony, and to Caledonians under twenty-one years of age who had performed their military service and who were not employed by the administration. All concessionaires were required to develop their land, and either live on it or have it managed by an officially authorized agent. Only after fulfilling these conditions for a minimum period of five years would they be granted permanent titles. As to land belonging to public domain, it could not be sold or conceded but only rented for the number of years specified in each lease.

The depression of the early 1930s exposed the uneconomic character of New Caledonia's land regime. The state's revenues from rented land were absurdly small. In 1935, for example, the rich Tiébaghi mine paid a rental amounting to only eight francs per hectare a year. Furthermore, many of the big concessionaires simply ignored the conditions under which they had acquired title to their property, developing the land only when it was profitable for them to do so. The far more numerous smallholders, on the other hand, had so little land that they were unable to practice mixed farming—the only way of gaining a livelihood under existing conditions. At the same time as they demanded more land, they also insisted that they needed more immigrant labor to work it, and this was the period when large numbers of indentured Asians were being repatriated. Since the white Caledonians could not be induced to cultivate the soil themselves, and since most of the big concessionaires—including the Catholic mission —held permanent titles to their land, the local administration had only one recourse. This was to place a tax on undeveloped properties that would bring in more revenue to the state or, if unpaid, would enable the government to take them over and thus increase the public domain. Nothing came of this proposal because of determined opposition from the big ranchers and because the improvement in New Caledonia's economy during the late 1930s made such a "drastic" step seem no longer necessary. On the eve of World War II, native reservations stood at about 126,000 hectares, whereas the area either rented or conceded to the white community comprised 560,000 hectares.[13]

[13] *L'Océanie Française,* November–December 1939.

After that war ended, the situation was greatly altered by a radical change in the labor supply,[14] the growth of both the European and Melanesian populations, and an expansion of the mining industry. The smaller number of laborers available and their increased cost meant that less land was cultivated, and the great ranches, too, became less productive than before. By 1952, so many of the tribes had outgrown their reservations that the government at long last was compelled to allot them more land. There was still no general policy, however, in this respect, and each such request by a tribe was considered on an individual basis by the advisory land committee. Because this procedure entailed long delays and because many of the younger tribesmen had emigrated to the towns, the overall enlargement of the tribal reservations was negligible. By 1960 the reservations totaled no more than 141,000 hectares (only about 15,000 more than before World War II), of which more than half were situated on the east coast.[15] Furthermore, no attempt was made by the authorities to regulate the question of land ownership inside the reservations, which was giving rise to ever more disputes among the tribesmen. The development of export crops had made the limited amount of arable land far more valuable for coffee-growing than for cultivating food crops, and contention over its allocation was undermining the authority of the Masters of the Land. There still existed no generally recognized authority, either customary or juridical, which could settle such land disputes. Both the administration and the territorial assemblymen took the position that this was purely an intertribal affair, in which they could not and would not intervene.

Only two noteworthy changes have been made in the land-tenure system since World War II. One, largely negative, was the government's decision to grant no more big concessions, for ranching on an extensive basis had definitely ended. The second and more positive change stems from the increased income the state has derived from land taxes, and its use of such revenues to buy back undeveloped properties. When the general council voted in 1953 to raise the average annual rental for state land from six C.F.P. francs per hectare to amounts varying with the size of the area leased, the large landholders were furious. They claimed that the U.C. was deliberately taxing the

---

[14] See pp. 284–285, 441–442.
[15] *La Nouvelle-Calédonie et Dépendances* (La Documentation Française), p. 4.

Caledonians so as to get their land for redistribution to their Metropolitan supporters.[16]

Although some of the undeveloped land regained for the public domain either through taxation or purchase has been redistributed in accordance with criteria which probably reflected political favoritism, there was no rapid change in the overall situation that had existed in 1950, and which is indicated in the following tabulation: [17]

Number of Landowners	Area Owned by Each (*hectares*)	Share of Total Area Ceded (*percent*)
6	5,000 or more	29
89	500 to 5,000	43
1,738	Less than 500	28
1,833	TOTAL: 318,500	100

Number of Tenants	Area Rented by Each (*hectares*)	Share of Total Area Leased (*percent*)
4	5,000 or more	12
80	500 to 5,000	48
1,186	Less than 500	40
1,271	TOTAL: 233,500	100

As to the geographical distribution of European-held properties, they were still more extensive on the west than on the east coast. Only about 20 percent of all the land owned or rented from the public domain was developed, mainly for herding, and the farmers, properly speaking, disposed of only 3 percent of the total area.[18] Ten years later this situation had not been greatly modified. There had been a small increase in the area held under permanent title, from 318,500 hectares to 332,800, and a more marked shrinkage in that rented, from 233,500 to 157,400.[19] Furthermore, as regards the landowning component, the number of those holding less than 500 hectares had in-

[16] See article entitled (in translation) "Settlers and Herders, Lenormand, Bergès & Co. have signed the Edict for your Eviction," *La France Australe,* Dec. 22, 1953.

[17] Data from speech of Governor Cournarie to the general council, Nov. 14, 1950.

[18] Faivre, J.-P., J. Poirier, and P. Routhier, *Géographie de la Nouvelle-Calédonie,* p. 171.

[19] *La Nouvelle-Calédonie et Dépendances* (La Documentation Française), p. 11.

creased from 1,738 to 2,190 (accounting for 33.2 percent of the total area), 103 controlled areas of 500 to 10,000 hectares (52.5 percent), and 2 held more than 10,000 hectares each (14.3 percent).

Although the settlers and officials with whom the writers talked in 1965 were agreed that a profound agrarian reform was long overdue and must be undertaken they differed as to the urgency of the land-tenure question. The head of the Catholic mission described it as "the great drama" of New Caledonia, whereas a prominent member of the U.C. accorded it a relatively low priority. All seemed to realize that the revision of the land-tenure system must be attempted, but the general consensus was that it would occur later rather than sooner.

The European colonist farmers

Between 1860 and 1866, the first white colonists arrived from the island of La Réunion, bringing with them to New Caledonia some Indian coolies, plants, seeds, and the farming methods of their native island.[20] The advent of the penitentiary regime gave a big stimulus to farming, for the settlers were assured not only of a supply of cheap labor but also of a large local market for their crop output. By 1885, the total area cultivated by Europeans had grown to 2,300 hectares, but many of the individual farms had only a few coffee bushes and even smaller patches of corn and beans. After the penal colony began to diminish, it became clear that coffee was the only local crop with an export potential. Feillet therefore forcibly oriented his settlers to the cultivation of arabica coffee, in the hope that it would become, as he expressed it, New Caledonia's "state religion."

In his ignorance of the Grande Terre's climatic and pedological conditions, Feillet overzealously pushed coffee-growing in unsuitable areas. Consequently, many of the areas so planted were soon abandoned, and those of his settlers who remained on the land—without abandoning coffee—added other crops, such as corn, beans, cotton, wheat, potatoes, and rice. Gradually and on a smaller scale the Melanesians began to emulate them, although they continued to devote most of their attention to the traditional tuber crops. In the early interwar period, the advent of the Nordist colonists and, above all, the influx of Asian immigrants should have led to an appreciable expansion of farming and crop output. Yet on the eve of World War II, a population totaling some 55,000 persons produced only a few thousand tons of coffee and copra for export and such small food crops that the

[20] *L'Océanie Française*, January–February 1936.

colony was importing annually many millions of francs worth of flour, sugar, potatoes, rice, tobacco, and dairy products—all of which could have been produced locally.

To save shipping space and to provision its troops in the Pacific with fresh vegetables during World War II, the American government developed agricultural production in Fiji, Samoa, the New Hebrides, and New Caledonia. In the Grande Terre, a total of 571 acres was farmed either directly by American military personnel and the Foreign Economic Administration, or indirectly by subsidizing local farmers, and in 1944 they produced altogether 750 tons of foodstuffs.[21] This experience proved that New Caledonia could become self-sufficient in vegetable production if cost were a negligible factor and modern machinery and expert technical advice were used. In 1946 the New Caledonia administration bought most of the American farm equipment in the hope of maintaining the level of agricultural production reached during the war. However, it lacked the necessary technical expertise, and an even more serious handicap was the ever-increasing cost and scarcity of labor, which made production on such a scale prohibitively expensive. As a result, European agriculture tended to relapse into its prewar state of stagnation.

The freeing of Asians and Melanesians from the constraints imposed by the indentured-labor and forced-labor systems rapidly reduced the number of farm workers and caused a huge increase in the wages of those still available. At the same time, because of the repatriation of the American troops and of many Asian immigrants, the scope and purchasing power of the domestic market appreciably declined. World War II was the halcyon period for New Caledonian agriculture, and the European settlers proved incapable of adjusting themselves to the far less favorable conditions that prevailed in the postwar years. All the efforts made by the authorities during the 1950s and 1960s to provide additional funds, technical research and training, guaranteed prices to the planters, and more generous credit facilities, as well as to organize producers' cooperative societies and to modify the land-tenure system, were to little avail.

The confidence of Caledonians in their country's agricultural future has not been restored, and they are increasingly turning to more remunerative work in the mining industry. To be sure, there has been some improvement in the Grande Terre's crop output, but there have

[21] Coulter, J. W., and Bowman, R. G., articles in *Geographical Review*, July 1946.

been far greater increases in the tonnage of imported food products, which are cheaper in the Nouméa market than those locally grown. By the early 1960s, only about 7,800 hectares were under cultivation by white settlers, and no more than 1,000 Europeans were engaged primarily in farming. Furthermore, even those who persevered as small-scale cultivators had to make ends meet by taking on supplementary money-earning occupations, for their average cash income per family amounted to only about 10,000 C.F.P. francs a year.[22]

Any hope for an improvement of New Caledonia's agriculture seems to depend on the Melanesian element of the population. About 9,000 of the 12,000-odd active Melanesian males cultivate the soil as virtually their sole occupation, despite the fact that their earnings from agriculture amount to only about one-tenth of those of a white farming family of the same number. There are indications, however, that the younger generation of Melanesians will not long remain content with a standard of living that is now notably lower than even that of the poorest white Caledonian farmer. If the Melanesians' income can be increased, even to a small extent, many of them may well stay on the land, for they are essentially a peasant people.

Melanesian agriculture

Yams and taros have long been the traditional crops grown by Melanesians, and their staple diet consists of these tubers, together with bananas. Yams, "the noblest food of all," were planted in pre-colonial times on the alluvial plains, and their culture required 9 months of the year. Magical rites were performed to assure the proper amounts and timing of sunshine and rainfall. Taro culture demanded even more time and elaborate techniques, for terraces had to be carved out of the mountain slopes and irrigation works had to be built to bring and hold the water at a constant high level. The ancient Melanesians' farming equipment and methods were primitive, but they undoubtedly were able to feed a far larger population than that of today. The extent of their taro fields and the ingenuity of their farming methods evoked the admiration of the early European explorers. Unfortunately, the traditional Melanesian agricultural cycle resulted in such widespread erosion that in many places the primary forest was destroyed and was replaced by the fire-resistant niaouli trees.[23]

With the colonial period there came fundamental changes in the

[22] "Aspects de l'Evolution Récente des Sociétés Océaniennes."
[23] Faivre, Poirier, and Routhier, *Géographie de la Nouvelle-Calédonie*, p. 247; *Marchés Coloniaux*, Oct. 24, 1953, p. 2916.

Melanesians' crops and farming techniques. Forced labor, for both the government and the settlers, often took able-bodied men away from their own fields, thus leaving many of the hard farming tasks to be done by the women. Incidentally, however, the Melanesian laborers learned from their employers (and the missionaries) how to use metal implements and cultivate new crops, notably manioc for their own consumption and coffee for export, the latter bringing them in a cash income. By 1938 the Melanesian production of coffee came to 510 tons, of copra to 1,837 tons, and of corn to 424 tons.[24]

The Melanesians were also taught by the settlers to rear domestic animals and to utilize them for food and transportation. Unhappily, they never learned to associate animal husbandry with agriculture and, in particular, to utilize manure as fertilizer. This proved to be a grave drawback after they were removed from their traditional tribal lands and had to grow food on the more restricted reservations. Whether or not those large-scale transfers were a cause or a consequence of the shrinkage in their numbers, there were progressively fewer Melanesian mouths to feed until the 1920s. It was no longer possible to engage in extensive cultivation, and the Melanesians farmed the same fields every year without ever putting back in the form of fertilizers what they took away from the soil. The results were smaller harvests and lower yields, and irrigated taro culture was the principal agricultural casualty of that period. On the whole, however, the influence of European agricultural policy and techniques on Melanesian farming was more positive than negative. The Melanesians learned to grow more widely varied crops, of which some improved their health by enriching their diet and others raised their standards of living by bringing in a cash income. Although the area allotted to the reservations has become inadequate for their needs, it is nevertheless a shield for them because it is inalienable.

To maintain Melanesian agricultural production even at its present level and to prevent the tribal villages from being progressively deserted, farming must be made more remunerative. This could be done by improving cultivation techniques and by enlarging the area of the reservations. The government is indeed steadily acquiring undeveloped land for redistribution to farmers,[25] and the settlers are renting larger areas of their land than before to the Melanesians, but both developments are occurring on a small scale and at a slow pace. One reason for the official reluctance to enlarge rapidly the amount of land

[24] *L'Océanie Française,* November–December 1938.
[25] See pp. 380–382.

at the Melanesians' disposal is the fear lest this aggravate their tendency to expand the planted area rather than to obtain higher yields by the use of improved cultivation methods.[26]

Export crops

Despite the small quantities produced and the progressive replacement of the valuable arabica variety by the less remunerative robusta, New Caledonia's coffee is of good quality and remains its chief agricultural export. It has survived two serious plant pests—*Hemileia vastatrix* at the turn of the century and *scolyte* in the postwar years—as well as the exodus of almost all the immigrant laborers who formerly harvested the crop. Between 1930 and 1950, production was stabilized at around 1,500 to 1,800 tons a year, of which Europeans produced about two-thirds and Melanesians the rest. Plantations are small, averaging no more than 10 hectares, because the territory has very few large areas suited to this crop.

Although both the arabica and robusta varieties grow in the humid valleys of both coasts, the former is predominantly the crop of European west-coast farmers (with 1,643 hectares, producing 240 tons a year). Most of the robusta is grown by Melanesians on the east coast (1,876 hectares, yielding 684 tons). Since 1960, the proportion of the total crop for which Europeans are responsible has been declining, particularly with regard to the arabica type. Indeed, on the east coast the European settlers are turning over more and more of their coffee lands to Javanese sharecroppers, who are entitled to two-thirds of the harvest. This development accounts in part for the decline in the quality of New Caledonia's coffee, but it is also true of the output from wholly European plantations. Despite the creation of a price-support fund in 1956 and improved technical advice from the Agricultural Service, the white planters are not replacing their overage arabica bushes nor giving them the proper care. Robusta production is forging ahead of that of arabica because the former variety is hardier, requires less upkeep, and gives larger yields (600 kilograms to the hectare as against 300 for arabica). As of 1966, about two-thirds of the 1,000-odd tons of coffee exported that year from New Caledonia consisted of the robusta variety.[27]

---

[26] See J. Barrau, *L'Agriculture Vivrière Autochtone de la Nouvelle-Calédonie*, p. 143.

[27] *La Nouvelle-Calédonie et Dépendances* (La Documentation Française), p. 11.

Copra, New Caledonia's second-ranking agricultural export, is unlike coffee in being a bulky and "poor" product, for which the market price has been consistently low except when wartime conditions have caused a world shortage of fats and oils. Furthermore, it is almost wholly a Melanesian crop. Yields are extremely small, because the Melanesians do not give any care to the natural groves of palms that exist along the littoral of the Grande Terre and, especially, on Lifou and Ouvéa, nor do they cultivate those which they themselves have planted. Their processing of the nuts being almost equally negligent, the quality of New Caledonia's copra is mediocre. Because copra production is largely a native family industry, it is far less dependent on seasonal wage-earners than is coffee. When the price of copra falls very low, as it did in the early 1930s, the Melanesians simply stop gathering the nuts and concentrate on food production, with no marked change in their living standards. Another characteristic that has made the government less solicitous about aiding New Caledonia's copra producers is that each time the market price has risen, the Melanesians have planted larger areas to palms without making any greater effort to improve the quality of their output. It has, therefore, usually been only in conjunction with the measures taken to aid producers in all of the French dependencies, such as the law of August 6, 1933, that Caledonian copra exports have received subsidies and protection in the Metropolitan market. In more recent years, however, the local administration and the general council have added premiums for quality exports, and in January 1957 a price-support fund was established to encourage Melanesian copra producers.

Because the volume of New Caledonia's copra exports—which are almost tantamount to production—has been determined by their monetary returns to the producers, they have fluctuated widely over the years. Coconut palms cover a total of some 7,000 hectares, of which more than half are in the Loyalty Islands. On the eve of World War II, they yielded 2,569 tons of copra, and in 1952 the output fell to 1,984 tons, but two years later it reached the record total of 3,348 tons.[28]

Because copra production was declining in the Loyalty Islands, where it has long been the main source of income, an official mission was sent there in 1962 with the aim of improving the yields and quality of their output. In the Grande Terre, however, no such effort

[28] *Marchés Coloniaux*, Oct. 24, 1953, p. 2915; *Marchés Tropicaux*, July 14, 1962, p. 1520.

was made and production is likely to remain stationary. The limits of the zone of coconut culture there have almost been reached, and the financial inducements offered to copra growers are not enough to persuade them to replace their aging palms with selected trees or to increase their yields by the use of fertilizers. The most that can be hoped for this product is an improvement in its quality, and it is to that end that the Agricultural Service has been providing growers with technical advice and modern drying equipment for their copra.

Cotton was the third export crop to which many of New Caledonia's early settlers devoted their energies. Climatic conditions seemed favorable, and experience proved that good-quality long-staple cotton could be grown in certain areas of the Grande Terre. Furthermore, it enjoyed a great advantage over New Caledonia's other export crops in that, from the outset, it was assured of a ready and protected market in France. In the mid-1920s, the bright prospects for New Caledonia's cotton were mainly responsible for the immigration of the Nordist colonists. During the first years of that decade, cotton plantations in the Grande Terre multiplied rapidly, especially in the Koné-Pouembout region. Ginned-cotton exports to France rose from 110 tons in 1923 to 318 tons three years later, largely as the result of official encouragement. That they had overexpanded was shown in 1926, when there occurred a sharp fall in the world market price because of surplus American production, and at about the same time, New Caledonia's cotton plants were attacked by parasites. All but one of the Nordists' cotton-cooperative ventures failed and most of their members left the island.

After considerable effort, Governor Guyon managed to get help from the Association Cotonnière in France, which in 1930 granted New Caledonia's cotton planters a subsidy of 159,000 francs. It was raised to 200,000 francs the next year, but was entirely eliminated between 1933 and 1936, and during that period the local cotton industry barely survived. World War II gave New Caledonia's cotton its *coup de grace*. Despite a half-hearted attempt to revive its culture in 1947, cotton is no longer exported, and it is now grown by European farmers only in very small amounts and along with other minor crops.

Secondary crops

All of New Caledonia's secondary agricultural output except cotton and tobacco consists of food crops whose culture dates back to the penitentiary period. There is a large local demand for rice, corn, potatoes, manioc, wheat, and fruit grown in the Grande Terre, but only three of those crops have attained any importance. Manioc has joined yams and taro as a basic element in the Melanesian diet, rice finds a ready market among the Asian population, and corn is used as the main feed for some of the island's animals, but none of them is produced on a scale that comes anywhere near satisfying the domestic demand. Uncertainties in the climatic conditions and labor supply make production irregular, and they cost more in Nouméa than do analogous imported items. Because the market is so small and easily saturated, the Agricultural Service has been discouraging farmers from increasing such crops.

Official policy and governmental services

The oldest agricultural institution in New Caledonia is the Chamber of Agriculture, a semiofficial body whose role is mainly advisory but whose activities cover a wide range of operations. It was founded before World War I, largely to promote the interests of small and medium European planters and herders. Later it developed as a governmental agency for the introduction of new crops and the improvement of existing ones, through the distribution of selected seed and technical advice, as well as of premiums to cotton, coffee, and copra producers and exporters. It also collected data on the extent of planted areas, the damage done by plant pests, and the yields of certain crops, and for such services it received a subsidy from the local budget.

Because the Chamber's activities were largely uncoordinated and far from comprehensive, it was not immune to criticism. Yet its operations were sufficiently effective for the general councilors, throughout the interwar period, to reject the administration's pleas to create an agricultural service.[29] In 1936, however, the administration did succeed in having an agricultural section instituted as part of the Animal Husbandry Service.

The only other official accomplishments before World War II were the creation of a Commission des Etudes Biologiques (1932), an agricultural-credit fund, the Crédit Mutuel Agricole (1934), and a bureau of agricultural statistics (1937). As regards agricultural training, the councilors would accept only in principle the setting up of a territorial farm school and experimental station, but they failed to provide the funds needed to bring them into being. Of these meager achievements, the only one of any value to the colony was the Crédit

[29] Minutes of the general council, April 11, 1929, June 27, 1934, Oct. 25, 1935.

Mutuel Agricole. Until it was established, the only sources of loans to individual farmers were the Banque de l'Indochine and some of Nouméa's trading firms. None of them had a primary interest in increasing agriculture, and after the depression struck the colony, all of them claimed that they had no more funds available for loans to the planting community. To put the Crédit Mutuel Agricole on its feet, the government arranged for a loan of 1 million francs to it by the Banque de l'Indochine, but this sum was so small that it could not meet more than a small fraction of the local need. By the time World War II began, the Crédit had received unfulfilled requests for loans aggregating 800,000 francs, and was already deeply in debt.[30]

For a few years immediately after World War II, the Paris government produced a wide array of projects aimed at improving the agricultural production of overseas France. Among those that related to New Caledonia were proposals to create cooperative societies, grant more credit to farmers, and improve crop yields and quality by scientific research—all of which were to be carried out within the framework of a development plan.[31] Some of these proposals were actually incorporated in the territorial plan, although the engineer sent from Paris to study them on the spot stated frankly that only New Caledonia's mineral resources seemed to be worth developing. In 1947, the Institut Français de l'Océanie (I.F.O.), a research organization and laboratory for the study of local agricultural problems and especially soil analyses, was created at Nouméa and staffed by technicians employed by the O.R.S.T.O.M.[32] In that same year, the Agricultural Service was formed as an autonomous unit and was given charge of a new experimental station near Païta, more funds were allocated to the Crédit Mutuel Agricole, and the ceiling was raised on the amount of individual loans that it was authorized to grant. Three years later, the general council created a special fund to aid farmers hard hit by natural catastrophes, such as cyclones and floods, and also financed a farm school which was built at Port Laguerre and to which the Païta experimental station was attached.

Although these moves were financed largely from funds provided by the French government, the general councilors showed in various ways their determination to promote local agriculture, even if the food crops so produced should prove costlier to the Caledonian taxpayer

[30] L'Océanie Française, November–December 1938.
[31] See pp. 480–481.
[32] See pp. 509–510.

and consumer than the increasingly plentiful imported equivalents. During the early postwar years, this attitude led them to sponsor an unfortunate experiment in mechanized agriculture which somewhat discredited both the new Agricultural Service and the cooperative societies associated with it. Neither mechanized agriculture nor cooperative societies were innovations in New Caledonia, but the history of both had not been encouraging. The mechanization of farming had been unsuccessfully attempted on a small scale in 1928, and the cooperative societies formed by the Nordist colonists were an even more dismal failure.

Nevertheless, the general councilors decided to buy the farm equipment used very effectively by the American armed forces in New Caledonia during the war. Experience showed, however, that few Caledonians knew how to operate such machinery, and that neither sufficient funds nor technicians were locally available to maintain and repair it, and in 1948, the administration decided to sell it to the Coopérative Centrale Agricole, which was able to purchase it, thanks to a loan from the Crédit Agricole.[33] That cooperative society had been founded in 1941 for the transportation of food crops from the interior to the Nouméa market, and it had turned only recently to promoting agricultural production. The cooperative soon encountered the same difficulties as had the Agricultural Service, and furthermore, few of its members owned farms large enough to make the equipment worth renting. Consequently, the cooperative was unable to repay its loan to the Crédit Agricole, and most of its costly unused equipment deteriorated.

Although the history of successive farm schools in New Caledonia is as discouraging as that of almost all of the territory's other agricultural enterprises, that of Port Laguerre, which began functioning in 1953, shows more promise. It covers an area of some 1,600 hectares, part of which is cultivated with both new and traditional crops, the rest being improved grazing land. The station maintains a herd of pigs and about 50 cattle, including 20 dairy cows whose milk is used to make butter and cheese.[34] The school itself can accommodate 50 boarding pupils, who are trained in a three-year course in which practical demonstrations take precedence over theoretical instruction. It is attended by Europeans and Melanesians in about equal numbers, and in recent years has also attracted a few Tahitian students. Obviously

[33] *La France Australe,* Dec. 14, 1953.
[34] S.P.C. *Bulletin,* January 1965.

a long time must pass before the training given at Port Laguerre can result in visible improvements in the territory's agricultural production, and this will also require sustained and sufficient support of the school for many years. Whether this will be accorded is doubtful, for Caledonians in general and the assemblymen in particular tend to demand quick and spectacular results.

Certainly the successive crop failures that have marked New Caledonia's economic history are enough to discourage all but the stoutest defenders of its agricultural vocation. All of the experts who have studied the territory's potential are pessimistic as to its agricultural future, and the younger generation of Caledonians obviously shares this view. Technically, there is no doubt but that New Caledonia could become self-sufficient in foodstuffs and could greatly increase its coffee exports, but for economic reasons this is most improbable. It is possible, however, that many of the Melanesians might be induced to remain on the land if technical improvements enabled them to earn more from farming. As for the white Caledonians, it is unlikely that enough drastic changes could be made in existing conditions for agriculture ever to become competitive with mining in terms of financial returns.

Nevertheless, there has survived in New Caledonia a strong tradition of rugged *colon* individualism and enterprise—so much so that the territorial assemblymen have voted, year after year, large subsidies for the support of coffee, copra, rice, wheat, and potato crops. The French government has gone along with this trend to the extent of providing funds for developing New Caledonia's rural economy, expert advice, and a preferential market for some of its exports. Far more than on local subsidies, the future of New Caledonia's agriculture rests on the continuation of France's benevolence in financing such supports. In the immediate future, it seems probable that the present level of crop output will be maintained but not appreciably increased.

ANIMAL HUSBANDRY

Animal husbandry is the most important activity of New Caledonia's rural economy, and it owes its genesis and rapid development to the penitentiary regime. To provide cheap meat for the convicts and their keepers, nearly one-third of the entire surface of the Grande Terre was ceded for stockraising. Because the Grande Terre's white colonists were too few in number, its labor force too unskilled and indifferent, and its pasturelands too meager, the vast areas earmarked for cattle husbandry were not utilized efficiently. In fact, the vegetation cover on the ranches was soon destroyed by overgrazing and erosion, and the pastures were taken over by the all-pervasive lantana and by niaouli trees.

For more than a decade before New Caledonia ceased to be a penal colony, it was evident that its climate and vegetation were unsuitable for stockraising on a grand scale. Even the huge ranches could not provide enough grass and water for their animals,[35] and their owners were almost wholly ignorant of the care and rearing of cattle. Throughout the penal-regime period, however, the basic weaknesses of this branch of the economy did not cause concern either to officials or to the herders themselves. So long as the convicts supplied not only plentiful and cheap labor but also a steady market for meat, stockraising was a lucrative occupation. Not until after the number of convict laborers and consumers had sharply declined and Feillet was trying to develop New Caledonia as a colony for free white farmers was it realized how little arable land was still available, and to what extent animal husbandry had been overextended. By that time, however, the damage could not be undone. The bases for New Caledonia's inequitable land-tenure system had been laid, the Melanesians were segregated on their reservations, and the differences in occupation and income had hardened into clear-cut divisions in the white community. The "policy of cheap meat" had been promoted by the government without consideration for its socioeconomic consequences, or even for an eventual market outside the Grande Terre.

Herds

Almost none of the domestic animals found in New Caledonia today are indigenous to the Grande Terre. Captain Cook introduced a few pigs into the island, and the governor of Manila presented Mme. Guillain with some pet deer, and both of these animals have multiplied in New Caledonia. Goats, too, have done well there, but sheep are reared in limited numbers and only for their meat, because the lantana ruins their fleece. The basis of New Caledonia's animal husbandry is beef cattle, imported mainly from Australia and to a lesser degree from France.

The influence of Australia on New Caledonia's animal husbandry is obvious not only in its orientation toward meat production but also

[35] It has been estimated that from 3 to 6 hectares per head of cattle are required.

in its extent, methods, and terminology. Concessions were granted to herders as though New Caledonia disposed of land on the same continental scale, and ranches were called "stations" and cowboys "stockmen." New Caledonia's first cattle were imported from Australia, but unfortunately the cost of replenishing the stock from that source and of fencing ranches was so high that the island's herds were allowed to deteriorate. Only a few of the wealthier ranchers have ever tried to develop purebred strains and to hire enough Melanesian cowboys to round up their cattle regularly for castration and branding. Most of New Caledonia's animal herds exist without care and are free to multiply, roaming widely over vast areas in search of pasture and water.

The location and ownership of the Grande Terre's various animal species follow an economically logical pattern, for they are dictated more by economic than by natural considerations. Because cattle husbandry has been practiced in New Caledonia on an extensive scale, it requires great areas of land and therefore is in the hands of the Europeans, who alone possess large concessions and who live for the most part on the west coast. Although that is the area receiving the least rainfall, four-fifths of the cattle herds and 95 percent of their owners live there, mainly around the four centers of La Foa, Bourail, Poya, and Koné.[36]

On the better-watered east coast, the Melanesians own only 6,000 to 7,000 head, because they have neither enough money to buy many cattle nor the grazing land needed to maintain them. For many of the same reasons, 85 percent of the Grande Terre's sheep are European-owned. Sheep, however, are of comparatively slight commercial importance, and much the same could be said of the island's untended pigs, poultry, and horses, although in other respects they are invaluable assets to their predominantly Melanesian owners.[37] Pigs and poultry are fed on food scraps and coconuts, and they provide protein in the Melanesian diet but bring in no cash income. Horses are indispensable for transporting humans and crops, yet they are never stabled and are left to forage for their food as best they can.

Over the years, as shown in table 9, there has been little variation in the number of horses but a marked increase in that of goats, pigs,

---

[36] As of 1963, there were about 68,000 cattle on the west coast and 14,000-odd on the east coast. See *Marchés Tropicaux,* Jan. 12, 1963, p. 87.

[37] 72 percent of the pigs, 60 percent of the horses, and almost all the goats are in the hands of Melanesians.

TABLE 9

NEW CALEDONIA: SIZE OF HERDS, IN SELECTED YEARS
1929–1966 (THOUSANDS OF HEAD)

Year	Cattle	Horses	Sheep	Goats	Pigs
1929	82.0	10.1	3.1	5.5	10.2
1938	102.7	11.1	5.0	13.4	10.5
1945	95.4	10.8	6.6	11.4	14.0
1952	96.0	10.8	3.5	18.8	13.2
1966	105.0	10.0	5.0	21.0	18.0

Source: *Marchés Coloniaux*, Oct. 24, 1953; *La Nouvelle-Calédonie et Dépendances* (La Documentation Française), p. 12.

and poultry. Cattle herds have fluctuated considerably, for several reasons. Among the natural phenomena responsible are the periodic floods and droughts to which the Grande Terre is subject, and which in 1951 so decimated the herds that beef had to be rationed in the Nouméa market. Animal diseases have never been more than a negligible factor, for rinderpest is unknown in New Caledonia and the health of its cattle was generally good until World War II. At that time, the importation of mules and horses from Australia for the American army introduced a tick pest that caused heavy mortality among the island's cattle and great expense to the territory to combat it.[38]

The chief determinant of the size of the territory's cattle herds is the market for their beef. For New Caledonia's ranchers, the period of greatest prosperity coincided with the years when the colony had its largest number of Asian immigrants, for under the terms of their contracts, each indentured laborer was entitled to 250 grams of meat a day. When thousands of the Asians were repatriated during the depression, this reduced the annual sale of cattle by 9,300 head and led to such a rapid increase in the herds that by 1935 they numbered 118,000 head.[39] When the ranchers found that they could not dispose of their surplus animals even at public auction, they resorted to wholesale castration and slaughtering so as to offset the natural increase by

---

[38] Between 1944 and 1953, the tick-control campaign of the veterinary service cost nearly 11.5 million C.F.P. francs. See Faivre, Poirier, and Routhier, *Géographie de la Nouvelle-Calédonie*, p. 181.

[39] *L'Océanie Française*, March–April 1934, January–February 1936.

10,000 to 12,000 head a year and to prevent the overgrazing of New Caledonia's dwindling pastureland. By the eve of the Second World War, such measures did succeed in reducing the cattle herds to about 100,000, which was considered the maximum number that the island could support under the prevailing system of extensive husbandry.

During World War II, excessive slaughtering to meet the needs of the American troops, and later the herds' decimation by tick fever, further appreciably reduced the number of New Caledonia's cattle, but to exactly what extent was not known. Animal censuses were taken annually by the gendarmerie, but they were based on the voluntary declarations of the cattle-owners, who consistently understated the size of their herds so as to avoid taxation. Governor Cournarie called the general councilors' attention on November 16, 1948, to the discrepancy, amounting to 20,000 to 30,000 head, between the figures cited by official reports and what he described as "the reality." Because of the dispersal of animals over large and often inaccessible areas, the "reality" has never been accurately known, but there is little doubt that during the first 20 postwar years the herds were gradually reconstituted. This means, however, that there is now locally available about the same amount of meat as there was in 1918, when New Caledonia's population was only about half its present size.

FORESTRY

The government's generally laisser-faire attitude, already noted in the case of animal husbandry, has been even more pronounced in regard to New Caledonia's forest resources. The consequences of its neglect, however, have been less harmful because forests play a comparatively unimportant role in the territory's economy. They are neither extensive nor valuable, for the few commercially exploitable species are dispersed. Although the wooded area covers nearly a third of the Grande Terre's surface (250,000 to 300,000 hectares), it is largely composed of secondary growth. In many places the primary forest has been destroyed, and for this, man is far more to blame than is nature. The progressive deforestation of the Grande Terre has been due to erosion and abusive exploitation, and no attempts were made by the government to control either until after World War II.

Violent rains alternating with drought have eroded some areas of New Caledonia. The spread of erosion, however, has been the result of the bush fires set by farmers and herders as a quick and cheap way of fertilizing the ground, and of the wanton cutting down of trees either for export or to clear regions for mineral prospecting. Cattle and deer have also played a part in eliminating the vegetation that formerly protected the soil and covered much more of the island's surface than it now does. Its disappearance has permitted lantana bushes and niaouli trees to proliferate in the denuded areas. The spread of lantana has been harmful to man and beast, but the niaouli tree (which accounts for perhaps one-third of the entire wooded area) has some redeeming features. It is fire-resistant, its wood can be used as lumber, and it contains an essence having certain pharmaceutical properties.[40] The only two species of trees of commercial value, both locally and for export, are the kauri and the araucaria, whose wood has been fairly regularly exported to Australia.

It seems strange that the cessation of exports of niaouli essence because of competition from eucalyptus oil, and of sandalwood, a victim of overexploitation, failed to spur the administration to take action. Furthermore, for many years during the interwar period, the warnings by both experts and settlers as to the dangers of unchecked erosion went unheeded by the French government.[41] The law of March 18, 1910, which provided a basis for New Caledonia's forest regulations, was never put into effect, and a local "forestry service" existed only on paper. Landowners, mining prospectors, and Australian lumber companies were allowed to fell trees without control or supervision and also without any obligation to replant.

New Caledonia's first development plan, in 1947, initiated the official measures aimed at arresting the destruction of the territory's forests. Subsequently, steps were taken to curtail wood exports and to create an effective forestry service. That service was charged with classifying New Caledonia's wooded areas and with protecting them by limiting the number of cutting permits and by replanting with saplings grown in newly created tree nurseries.[42] For lack of real support in the form of sufficient funds and technicians, the Forestry Service was not very effective until the 1960s. Then a Fonds Forestier was created to provide money for the conservation and better utilization of local forest products (1960), a reforestation program was

[40] Niaouli essence is marketed under the name of *gomenol,* derived from that of the village of Gomen, where it was first distilled.

[41] *L'Océanie Française,* July–August 1929, January–February 1932, January–February 1939.

[42] Minutes of the general council, Jan. 31, April 23, 1947.

devised for the replanting of 500 hectares a year (1962), and a Conseil de la Recherche Forestière was appointed to associate representatives of the timber trade and forest industries with technicians of the I.F.O., the Forestry Service, and relevant government officials (1967).

The measures described above were so belatedly undertaken that they can do little more than arrest erosion and conserve what is left of New Caledonia's forest heritage by limiting the amounts of timber legally available for exportation and local use.

FISHERIES

The abundance of New Caledonia's natural resources in shell (nacre) and fish is in sharp contrast with the slight importance of fishing in the territory's economy. As was the case with sandalwood, the *bêches-de-mer* (sea slugs), which were the other main attraction of New Caledonia for the first foreign traders, were so abusively exploited that they disappeared long ago from its external trade. Shell still has its place in the territory's foreign trade, albeit a steadily declining one, and in general its production and export has followed the same trend as in French Polynesia.[43] To replace what is obviously a moribund occupation, the local authorities, with the cooperation of the I.F.O. and the S.P.C., are trying to develop other types of fishing.

The Grande Terre's rivers and coastal waters contain many varieties of edible fish yet they can be bought in the Nouméa market only in small quantity and at excessive prices. Partly for that reason and partly because of the competition from meat, fish hold only a small place in the Caledonian diet, although from 300 to 400 tons of tinned and frozen fish are imported into the territory each year. The size of the local catch is not even approximately known. Fishing has become a popular weekend sport for many Europeans, who consume what they catch, and most of the coastal tribesmen fish—for their own consumption—simply as an occupation subsidiary to the gathering of shell. In all, there are perhaps 400 fishing boats and 2,000 part- or full-time fishermen in the Grande Terre, but fewer than 100 of the latter are professionals.[44] It is they who provision the Nouméa market, but they have not sought to increase the supply lest they bring down the pre-

[43] See pp. 124–125; Faivre, Poirier, and Routhier, *Géographie de la Nouvelle-Calédonie*, p. 181.
[44] Report of the Senate mission, minutes of the Conseil de la République, June 28, 1962.

vailing high prices for their catch.[45] Furthermore, the rivers and lagoon have been largely depleted of their edible species by the use of dynamite and poisons, and along the coast even the professional fishermen do not venture farther than 60 kilometers to the north or south of Nouméa.[46]

It is obvious that fish sales in the domestic market could be greatly increased if the virtually untouched resources of the open sea were exploited, and the official agencies have been working to that end. For some years, the I.F.O. has been studying the migratory habits of the coastal species, and the S.P.C. has been teaching Caledonians how to build bigger and better boats that will enable them to fish in deep waters. The administration itself has taken several steps. It has forbidden the use of explosives in fishing and has organized Nouméa's fishermen into a cooperative society whose members can now borrow the sums needed to buy improved equipment and can market their output more profitably. In addition, it negotiated an agreement with a Japanese company which would fish for tuna and build a refrigerated plant at Nouméa to store and process its catch.[47] However, the agreement was not carried out, because prospective operating costs were excessive.

Although the local administration has been dilatory about conserving and developing New Caledonia's fish resources, the outlook for a fishing industry is more promising than that for any other sector of the territory's rural economy.

[45] *Marchés Coloniaux,* Nov. 24, 1956, p. 3110.
[46] Devambez, L., "L'Exploitation des Ressources de la Mer en Nouvelle-Calédonie."
[47] See *Marchés Tropicaux,* Aug. 17, 1963, p. 2807.

29

Industry

Because of the Grande Terre's huge mineral resources, its inhabitants often refer to the island as "le Caillou" (the Pebble), and some foreigners of a romantic turn of mind have called it the "Pacific Treasure Island." Although even now New Caledonia has not been thoroughly or systematically prospected, deposits of gold, iron, coal, gypsum, lead, zinc, copper, manganese, cobalt, chromite, and nickel are known to exist. At one time or another, all of these deposits have been worked, but only three ores—those of chromite, nickel, and iron—have been mined on an extensive and commercial scale. Since World War II, small tonnages of iron were irregularly exported, but the chromite mines have closed down. Only nickel-mining has survived, and in recent years the industry has grown at a rapidly increasing rate.

New Caledonia's mining industry has been developed largely by private enterprise, with only occasional help from the public powers in the form of subsidies, loans, and preferential tariffs during periods of crisis. In the nineteenth century, prospecting and mining were initiated mainly by British and American individuals and companies, and the companies were financed, for the most part, by nonresident shareholders. Gradually, French private interests took over the Grande Terre's mining industry, notably its nickel sector.

New Caledonia being so far removed from markets and having such high production costs, the early wide range of its mining activities has shrunk to the point where, in recent years, mining and metallurgy have been almost wholly confined to nickel and to one producing company, the Société Le Nickel. Nickel is the only one of New Caledonia's array of minerals of which there is a virtually inexhaustible supply and for which world demand is rising. Although earlier there were some individual producers of varying importance, known collectively as the *petits mineurs*, they have been relegated to the background. Le Nickel, as owner of two-thirds of the island's richest concessions and of its sole smelter, has been able to control New Caledonia's nickel production and prices, as well as most of its sales. This company's preeminent position cannot be ascribed to a pioneering spirit, brilliance in developing new techniques, or good will locally generated by its activities. It is due, rather, to the company's ample financial resources and influential connections, its shrewdness in cornering production, the lack of alternative remunerative occupations for the Caledonians, and, above all, the world shortage of nickel. Although Le Nickel is responsible for New Caledonia's exceptionally high living standards, both through the revenues that its exports and imports bring to the territorial budget and the employment that it provides to some thousands of Caledonians, their very dependence on a "soulless monopoly" has been galling to the local population. Since World War II, and especially during the 1960s, New Caledonia has become increasingly dependent on Le Nickel, but the territory has now learned from hard experience that the only way to extricate itself from that company's grip is to exchange it for tighter controls by the French state.

New Caledonia's "nickel rush" began ten years after that mineral was discovered in 1863. Between 1873 and 1900, some 600,000 tons of ore were mined, and by 1923 the total had risen to 3 million tons. Production was irregular because it was dictated by fluctuating world demand, but even in the most prosperous years before World War II it never exceeded 350,000 tons annually.[1] In 1940, 478,000 tons were mined, but in the years 1947 to 1949 output fell less than 100,000 tons annually. The Korean war naturally stimulated metals production, and although thereafter the demand for nickel was not steady, production increased rapidly on the whole, averaging some 3 million tons a year during the middle 1960s. If the Caledonian nickel industry's present projects for expansion materialize, that figure will be doubled in the 1970s without any danger of exhausting New Caledonia's ore reserves.

Each year the discovery of new nickel deposits in the Grande Terre is reported, and they seem to exist in all parts of the island, but as yet

[1] Rapadzi, J., "L'Industrie Minière."

their full extent is not known.[2] Probably the best-quality ores have already been taken out of the ground, but it is believed that some hundreds of millions of tons of 2 to 3 percent metal content still exist. Thus far, the east coast has been the most productive area, accounting for more than half the total produced, and the Thio mine has contributed about 40 percent of that amount. The west coast, however, does not lag far behind, and there the Koniambo *massif* has supplied 30 percent of that area's total and the region of Népoui 5 percent.[3] The mining and industrial center now being completed at Poro, near Houaïlou, is expected to out-produce even Thio. The mountainous interior has been neglected by prospectors because the coastal deposits were naturally the first to be worked. Their proximity to the sea has facilitated the loading of ores onto boats and barges that carry them to the processing plant at Doniambo, which has a port in close proximity to Nouméa.

Between 1873 and 1916, mining was largely in the hands of the *petits mineurs,* and their ore was transported in its crude state to Europe in large sailing ships. However, the new process used at the Doniambo plant by Le Nickel beginning in 1910, and the mounting demand for refined nickel, rapidly altered that situation. By the end of World War I, the *petits mineurs,* faced with rapidly shrinking markets for their crude ore, had to sell most of their output to Le Nickel. Between 1911 and 1931, such exports averaged annually only 150,000 tons, but in the mid-1930s two new markets came into the picture—Japan and Germany.

During World War II, those markets naturally were closed, and the *petits mineurs* ceased their activities. In 1952, however, the Japanese resumed buying, and that year Lenormand won his first battle with Le Nickel by getting official permission for the *petits mineurs* to export shipments of 50,000 tons of ore, or more, direct to foreign markets.[4] Nevertheless, such sales to Japan fluctuated widely until 1964, when a long-term agreement was negotiated with five Japanese companies, which agreed to buy a million tons annually for each of the ensuing five years. This market is the sole foreign outlet for the *petits mineurs'* ore exports, because the Japanese metallurgists have been the only ones willing and even eager to refine New Caledonia's low-grade ores. Despite the Japanese outlet, probably at least two-thirds of the ore

[2] *Marchés Tropicaux,* Aug. 23, 1969, p. 2346.
[3] Callot, F., "Les Richesses Minières."
[4] *Marchés Coloniaux,* Mar. 1, 1952, p. 651.

mined in the Grande Terre finds its way into the hands of Le Nickel, either through purchases from the *petits mineurs* or through its own concessions. (There are still some 110 *petits mineurs* in New Caledonia, but only a handful of them are important producers, notably Senator Lafleur and Edouard Pentecost, whose wealth makes the term *petits mineurs* extremely inapposite.)

The Société Le Nickel was founded in 1880 to mine not only nickel but also chromite and cobalt. Five years later, it built a plant at Doniambo to smelt nickel ore and another at La Havre to refine the matte of Doniambo into pure metal. In its early years, Le Nickel was the world's foremost nickel producer, but it soon lost its predominant position to a much-faster-growing rival, the International Nickel Company (INCO). That Canadian concern mined ores that were easier to process and closer to markets than were those of New Caledonia. Furthermore, before World War I, Le Nickel's main local rival, the Société Caledonia, built its own processing plant at Thio, where it was able to produce matte of higher metal content than Doniambo's by developing a new hydroelectric process.[5] During World War I, however, Le Nickel partially recouped its position by buying the German mines located between Thio and Boulouparis, which had been seized by the French government, and in 1918 it raised the nickel content of the matte processed at Doniambo from 45 percent to between 75 and 77 percent. The economic recession of the early 1920s caused Le Nickel's matte sales to fall slightly below their wartime annual level of 5,500 tons, but by 1930 they had risen to the record figure of 6,743 tons.

In contrast to its unfortunate effects on Caledonian exporters of products other than minerals, the world depression of the early 1930s paradoxically improved Le Nickel's overall position. In 1931 the Société Caledonia merged with Le Nickel, which thus acquired control of mining concessions covering a total of 150,000 hectares. Then Le Nickel closed down the Thio processing plant as well as all but three of its most productive mines, thus concentrating all its smelting operations at Doniambo and reducing the company's operating costs. The following year, a gentlemen's agreement was negotiated with INCO, through the agency of the French government, whereby Le Nickel appreciably enlarged its market in Europe. In fact, during the middle 1930s INCO permitted Le Nickel to increase its share in the world market from 10 percent to 17 percent and to peg the price of

[5] *L'Océanie Française,* March–April 1932.

nickel in Europe at a level 50 percent higher than its own price in North America.[6] Consequently, during the pre-World War II decade Le Nickel was able not only to increase its exports to a total of 14,000 tons annually but also to finance improvements in its Doniambo plant. No analogous modernization of its mining techniques, however, was made, for Le Nickel, like all other Caledonia producers at that time, had an abundant and inexpensive supply of indentured Asian laborers. Thus by 1939 the only breach in the local monopoly which Le Nickel had by then established was the *petits mineurs'* ore exports to Germany and Japan, and even that gap was closed during World War II.

During the months between the Franco-German armistice of June 1940 and the end of that year, Le Nickel's financial position became very precarious, because it was deprived of the funds normally supplied by its Paris headquarters. Late in 1940, however, it reached agreements with Australia, the United States, and INCO whereby its Doniambo plant was kept operating at the prewar level despite the closing of some of its mines. Although the price for Doniambo's matte was slightly raised, Le Nickel was somewhat in the red by the time the war ended, and it also was holding unsold stocks amounting to some 104,000 tons. In 1946 the shortage and higher cost of labor, as well as of Australian coal, created a crisis for the company that dragged on for 6 years. It had to close its Doniambo plant for 10 months in 1947, and its matte exports that year fell to 1,200 tons. Its directors realized that Le Nickel could survive only by reducing production costs, and for the first time in its history the company used some of its profits to mechanize its operations. As a reward for these investments, which totaled more than 2 billion Metro. francs between 1949 and 1951, the general council reduced the export duty on matte and eliminated the duties on imported equipment for an eighteen-month period.

Despite the improvements in its plant and its fiscal position, Le Nickel found itself unable to cope with the sudden demand for nickel created by the Korean War. It was still hampered by labor shortages and strikes, as well as by the need to import expensive fuel. In 1951 it processed 390,000 tons of ore and exported 6,354 tons of nickel matte to Le Havre for further refining, but this output fell far short of the rising demand. In 1953, Le Nickel obtained the French government's

---

[6] L. S. Feuer asserted that this extraordinary concession on the part of INCO was motivated by the fact that it preferred to await a revival in world trade rather than lower its own sales price in the United States. See *Far Eastern Survey,* Jan. 19, 1946.

approval for an expansion program that included construction of a second hydroelectric dam at Yaté, and at the same time it asked the general council for further fiscal concessions. In anticipation of the doubling of its matte production, Le Nickel began to develop new mines, although the general councilors were proving obstinate about acceding to its requests. Production and exports both rose steadily until 1962, when the industry underwent a recession, but the upward surge was soon resumed and swiftly gathered momentum.

Between 1954 and 1964, the number of Le Nickel's employes doubled to reach a total of more than 3,000, its output of matte more than quadrupled, from about 6,000 tons to 26,000, and its share in the free world's nickel production rose from 10 percent to 18 percent. By 1964, Le Nickel was selling its output in twenty-five countries, including Communist China and Cuba, but its main markets were still in Europe and especially in France, where it was supplying 72 percent of that country's nickel requirements.[7] As the world demand for nickel continued to grow at a rapid rate, largely because of technical advances that created new uses for that metal, Le Nickel prepared to increase its production still further. It was at that time that the company decided to build a 32,000-kw. generating plant and to enlarge the capacity of its Doniambo smelter to 50,000 tons. Soon, however, the company raised its sights higher, to double that figure, but claimed that to reach such a goal it must have the "cooperation" of the public powers.

By the mid-1960s, Le Nickel's unprecedented prosperity and its even rosier prospects had intensified the Caledonians' long-standing hostility to the company. Although they realized that the territory owed its high living standards to Le Nickel, this very dependence generated antagonism. In particular, they resented the fact that Le Nickel was responsible for one-third of the territorial revenues and for the employment of one-fifth of all wage-earners who were not in the civil service, and that it owned 170,000 hectares, more than half the total area covered by the mining concessions. During the 1962 recession it had dismissed 800 of its employes, and it used the threat of another serious unemployment crisis as a form of blackmail to wrest concessions from the territorial assembly that would further its new expansion program. In soliciting such concessions, Le Nickel's spokesmen argued that the existing fiscal system favored the *petits mineurs,* who during the nickel boom then under way were enriching

[7] Sordet, M., "La Nouvelle-Calédonie: Rhodésie de Demain?"

themselves without contributing to the islands' development, that INCO's earnings were ten times those of Le Nickel and that its tax burden in Canada was lower, and that it was only logical for the territory to sacrifice some of its current revenues for the expansion of an industry whose prosperity would eventually bring it greater benefits. All of these arguments were eminently reasonable, but they failed to take account of local psychological factors that dated back many years.

Although Le Nickel had experienced losses because of adverse market conditions in 1884, 1902, 1922 to 1924, 1947 to 1949, and again in 1962, its operations as a whole had been highly profitable to its largely absentee owners. Of its two main stockholders, the Rothschild Bank and the Banque de l'Indochine, the latter was already very unpopular with Caledonians because of its long monopoly of local credit facilities and its failure to invest more in the territory. The latter charge was also made against Le Nickel, which, until after World War II, had repatriated its profits rather than invested them locally. Moreover, the company was always seeking financial favors from the French government and Caledonian elected representatives without, in turn, making contributions to promote the territory's welfare. Indeed, the impressive success of the leftist parties in the local elections of January 1945 was due in part to their demands for the nationalization of New Caledonia's major mining enterprises.[8] The combined strength of conservative elements in Paris and Nouméa, however, was sufficient not only to block execution of that demand but to lighten Le Nickel's fiscal burdens in 1949. It was not until Lenormand became deputy in 1951 and the U.C. gained control of the general council 2 years later that Le Nickel began to encounter effective opposition.

The issue was joined in 1953 over a request by Le Nickel for exemption from export duties for a six-year period, during which time it pledged to carry out an expansion program that would be highly beneficial to the territory. To substantiate its plea, Le Nickel stressed that it had financed the 1949–1951 improvements largely from its own resources, paid an annual wage bill amounting to 1,345 million Metro. francs, and was contributing to New Caledonia's budget 617 millions

[8] See p. 277. During that campaign, the Progrès Social had given wide publicity to extracts from Le Nickel's report for 1938–1939 showing that its profits were more than three times as large as the entire revenues of the colony at that time.

more in the form of taxes and duties.[9] In Paris, the company found an audience far more responsive than the general council, partly because several geological missions sent to New Caledonia during the early postwar years by the French government had failed to find commercially exploitable minerals other than nickel. Furthermore, a Senate mission which in 1954 examined Le Nickel's expansion program reported on it favorably because "a healthy metallurgical industry in New Caledonia is better than no industry at all." The French government therefore agreed to finance much of the construction of the second Yaté dam, but made no further concessions. Two years later it refused to continue paying higher-than-world prices for Le Nickel's output, on the ground that the company no longer needed such aid. Its exports were soaring and the territorial assembly had relented in 1956 to the point of granting Le Nickel a special fiscal regime for the duration of its equipment program. In 1960 it added a premium for a certain percentage of the company's matte exports.

In 1961, Le Nickel returned to the charge, claiming that it was unable to finance all of its program and asking for supplementary tax exemptions, but this time the territorial assembly was deaf to its plea. Le Nickel, it said, should never have embarked on a program for which it had not asked the assembly's approval and for which the available funds were insufficient, and they were not prepared to sacrifice 100 million C.F.P. francs in revenues so that it could be carried out.[10] By the end of 1962, however, Le Nickel obviously was in real trouble because of an abrupt decline in the world demand for its products, and might soon dump more of its workers onto the labor market. Consequently, in its session of February 26, 1963, the territorial assembly proposed a compromise to end its two-year dispute with the company. In return for Le Nickel's pledge to maintain production at a certain level regardless of market conditions, they agreed to exempt the company's equipment imports from further duties.

At that time and later, the assemblymen refused to accede to Le Nickel's reiterated requests for a fifteen-year exemption from export duties, dock dues, and license fees. In fact, the opposition to Le Nickel has hardened with the growth of its operations, and on this issue the ultraconservatives, as represented by Senator Lafleur and other *petits mineurs,* have joined forces with the U.C. More than one assemblyman has frankly expressed skepticism as to the accuracy of the figures

[9] Minutes of the National Assembly, Aug. 27, 1954.
[10] *Marchés Tropicaux,* Aug. 12, 1961, p. 2058.

presented by Le Nickel's defenders. They point to the annual reports to the company's stockholders, which have shown a phenomenal rise in its net profits from 11.2 million Metro. francs in 1965 to 30.3 millions in 1968.[11] Le Nickel having thus publicly acknowledged such a scale of earnings, it was obviously in a position to contribute generously to the territory's development rather than to ask Caledonian taxpayers to make further sacrifices. Gradually the assemblymen became convinced that the only way to loosen the growing grip of Le Nickel's tentacles on the territory's economy was not simply to resist its demands but to encourage the installation of a powerful rival company capable of breaking its monopoly. The logical candidate for such a role was Le Nickel's great rival, INCO, which had long wanted to operate in New Caledonia and which, moreover, was believed to have developed a secret technique whereby it could refine low-grade nickel ores.

To enable INCO to create a subsidiary in the territory, a change had to be made in the French mining law of January 28, 1913 (amended by the decrees of January 16, 1916, and February 27, 1924). That legislation had been inspired by France's desire to curtail the granting of concessions to foreigners, whose enterprise and capital had been responsible for developing northern New Caledonia as a mining area in the nineteenth century. Foreigners did gradually withdraw from mining operations in the colony, but for reasons other than the legistative restrictions put upon them. As the Japanese learned in the 1930s, it was easy enough for a foreign-owned concern to form a dummy company with headquarters at Nouméa and then find obliging French nationals willing to serve as its nominal directors for a good salary. It was rather such economic factors as high production and transport costs, as well as the lack of local fuel and of sufficient deposits of valuable ores, that effectually discouraged not only foreign but also French enterprises.

The attitude of the French government toward Le Nickel has always been somewhat equivocal. Because it is a wholly French company and has made New Caledonia the only industrialized territory in the south Pacific, successive governments in France have granted it direct and indirect subsidies and aided it in negotiating international agreements. On the other hand, the Paris authorities have been aware of the imbalance that Le Nickel has created in New Caledonia's economy

[11] *Le Monde,* July 18, 1967, June 22, 1969.

and of the resentment of many Caledonians toward its monopoly. Yet to permit another nickel company to establish itself in the territory would mean opening that industry to foreigners, specifically to British and American mining interests, which alone had the capital and techniques required to compete with Le Nickel. The situation was further complicated under the Gaullist administration by its leaders' conviction that "Anglo-Saxon" infiltration was being used by the U.C. as leverage to acquire greater local autonomy. As world demand for nickel grew, so also did the requests from foreign companies for concessions in New Caledonia, the Caledonians' insistence that they be granted, and the French government's determination to control the output of a metal that placed France in the forefront of the world's nickel producers.

Early in 1966, INCO notified the French government of an agreement it had reached with the outstanding French mining firm, Pechiney, to study New Caledonia's nickel potential with a view to their developing it jointly. On July 7 of that year, the territorial assembly voted its support for that initiative and also stated that any interpretation of such support as disloyalty to France was wholly unjustified. When General de Gaulle visited Nouméa the following September, the Caledonians' hopes that he would announce his decision in accord with the assembly's wishes were disappointed. Although in his oracular speeches at Nouméa the general did not name INCO or even mention nickel, he made it clear that he intended to keep New Caledonia's vast mineral resources firmly in French hands. This, however, did not preclude granting production rights to a second French company, and the following December this possibility was confirmed by the Minister of Overseas Territories. At the same time, the Minister indicated that foreign interests might be associated with the French company, albeit in a minority position.[12]

As no developments along this line were apparent for some months, the Caledonians became increasingly impatient. Time was of the essence, they believed, for Australia had just announced the discovery of extensive new nickel deposits, and foreign capitalists might decide either to exploit low-grade ores in other countries or find a substitute for nickel. Throughout the spring of 1967, propaganda for a second nickel-mining company was intensified by the Nouméa press, but the French government still failed to commit itself. The world demand for

12 *Ibid.*, Dec. 10, 1966.

nickel was growing rather than declining, and with it the applications from foreign companies for mining rights in New Caledonia. Outstanding on the list of applicants were the Patino, Hanna Mining, Dennison Mines, and American Metal Climax companies, and, of course, INCO.

The French government's announcement at long last, in July 1967, that it had opened negotiations to form a second French company in New Caledonia "in association with an important foreign group" seemed to galvanize Le Nickel into unwonted activity. First it attempted, though in vain, to improve its deplorably bad public relations with the local population, and then in September it announced that, in conjunction with the American Kaiser Aluminum Corporation, it would create two companies to produce nickel and to market it in North America. This move was followed in November by another agreement, this time with the Nippon Yakin Kogyo Company, to set up a joint subsidiary in Japan to process Caledonian ores. Negotiations with a view to creating a French-controlled competitor to Le Nickel proved to be difficult, dragging on throughout 1968 and not culminating until February 1969. The new company was to be called COFIMPAC (Compagnie Financière, Industrielle, et Minière du Pacifique), for which INCO would provide 40 percent of the capital and a group of French mining and banking firms 60 percent.[13] Six months later, a third nickel company was formed at Nouméa by Pennaroya (a subsidiary of Le Nickel) and the American Metal Climax Company. That company may be joined by a third industrial giant, the important French mining firm of Pechiney.

After years devoid of any change in the status quo, this avalanche of new companies so long desired by the Caledonians has nevertheless failed to satisfy their aspirations. At the same time that it was negotiating with INCO, the French government pushed through the Parliament mining laws which gave the state not only control over the production and sale of New Caledonia's nickel, chromium, and cobalt, but also over its fiscal regime.[14] These developments cannot but lead to the elimination of the *petits mineurs* both as producers and as exporters, for their concessions are being rapidly bought up by the new companies. The future of the Caledonian mining industry now lies with the technically advanced and internationally financed organizations,

[13] The French consortium included the Bureau Minier, Mokta, Ugine-Kuhlmann, the Banque de l'Indochine, and the Banque Nationale de Paris. For details, see *Marchés Tropicaux,* March 22, 1969, p. 842, and *Le Monde,* Feb. 18, 1969.

[14] See pp. 325–327.

whose large-scale investments and activities will surely make the territory's economy more lopsided than before. Le Nickel's monopoly has indeed been broken, but its grasp—far from being destroyed—has now simply become more complex.

In 1969, Le Nickel increased its production over that of the previous year by 6.6 percent and began to enlarge its Doniambo operation. Then, in the spring of 1970, its directors decided to form a new firm with the Patino Company of Quebec to build a second processing plant, and a mining village near Poum, with a view to producing a total of 200,000 tons of ferro-nickel a year by 1976. Furthermore, in cooperation with two other companies, Le Nickel began prospecting for nickel deposits in Australia and Canada. This sudden and vast increase in Le Nickel's operations was spurred by the large-scale competition it probably will soon encounter if COFIMPAC's present projects are carried out. In December 1969, the president of the latter company announced plans to invest between 1.5 and 2 billion Metro. francs in the production of 50,000 tons of nickel a year, by what he described as a "revolutionary process" that would for the first time utilize New Caledonia's low-grade lateritic-ore deposits.[15]

To provide the labor needed to carry out the foregoing projects, New Caledonia will require by 1975 the services of 13,500 additional workers and technicians, who will perhaps be recruited in Indonesia, Fiji, and France. Moreover, the Grande Terre cannot cope physically with such developments unless its infrastructure is enormously improved and enlarged, and the French government has already approved the inclusion in its sixth Plan of a big program of port, road, and urban construction in that island. In their introduction to that Plan, its authors wrote that "Never since the end of World War II, have the prospects for New Caledonia's expansion in almost every domain seemed so favorable." [16] Such optimism, of course, is based on the assumption that the present demand and price for nickel not only will be maintained but will markedly increase over the next decade.

All these new developments may well bring greater prosperity to New Caledonia, but how equitably the benefits will be shared among the local inhabitants remains to be seen. In the immediate future, New Caledonia, in return for a radical expansion of its economy, is involuntarily being deprived of its chance to gain greater autonomy, and in political terms, the price it is called upon to pay seems very high.

[15] *Marchés Tropicaux*, Dec. 20, 1969, p. 3456.
[16] *Le Monde*, July 8, 1970.

Some aspects of the world situation at the end of 1969 in regard to nickel are indicated in the following tabulation: [17]

Principal Producing Companies and Their Yearly Output (tons)		Main Consuming Countries and Yearly Consumption (tons)	
INCO	218,000	United States	145,000
Le Nickel	37,319	European Economic	
Falconbridge	32,000	Community	143,000
Sheritt-Gordon	7,000	Japan	53,000

Anticipated New Caledonian Yearly Output (tons), 1975–1980	
Le Nickel-Kaiser	110–115,000
COFIMPAC	50,000
Pennaroya-Amax	40–50,000
Le Nickel-Patino	40,000

CHROMITE

New Caledonia's chromite deposits, unlike those of its other minerals (except nickel), were mined continuously and profitably during the eighty-four years from 1880 to 1964.[18] The Grande Terre still has important, although widely scattered, deposits of chromite (the ore of chromium), by far the most considerable being those of the Tiébaghi *massif* in the Néhoué region of the northwest. From that area has come 80 percent of New Caledonia's chromite production, and 60 percent of this was supplied by the mine called "Le Tiébaghi," which has long been considered the richest of its kind in the world. The second-most-productive area, from which 14 percent of the total output has been derived, lies east of Nouméa.

Between 1900 and 1912, New Caledonia was the source of about 25 percent of the world's chromite, its annual production being some 50,000 tons. With the exhaustion of the surface deposits, which were mined in the early days from open pits, the territory's small mine-owners were superseded by more heavily financed companies. Out-

---

[17] *Jeune Afrique*, Dec. 23, 1969.

[18] For details concerning chromite production, see *L'Océanie Française*, March–April 1928, March–April 1932, January–April 1939; *Pacific Islands Monthly*, April 1945, August 1954, February 1955, October 1964; *Marchés Coloniaux*, Feb. 11, 1956, p. 422; *Marchés Tropicaux*, July 27, 1963, p. 1945, Aug. 29, 1964, p. 2096; Feuer, L. S., "Cartel Controls in New Caledonia," *Far Eastern Survey*, Jan. 19, 1946.

standing among these was the Société Le Tiébaghi, formed by London chromium interests after they bought the French Société Le Chrome in 1910. Two years later, after the discovery of new chromite deposits in Turkey, New Caledonia's share in the world market fell to 12 percent. Despite fluctuations in production ranging from 40,000 to 70,000 tons, the Grande Terre maintained its position as the second-ranking producer and even bettered its output during the depression. In the mid-1930s, however, a rising demand for chromium alloys led to an expansion of chromite mining in competing countries, and by 1937, New Caledonia's share in the world market had dropped to 4 percent. In the last year before World War II, the colony exported nearly 40,000 tons, of which the United States took 18,892 and Germany 13,513.

Large stocks accumulated in New Caledonia during the Second World War despite a critical shortage of the metal. This was due to the refusal of the Société Le Tiébaghi, until the summer of 1945, to agree to the conditions laid down by the Free French government. These included the conversion into francs of its dollar and sterling earnings, a higher export duty, and a lower price for its output. After the war, that company pushed its output above prewar levels by mechanizing its operations, and in 1948, New Caledonia exported more than 75,000 tons of chromite. In 1949, all but two of the producing companies merged to form the Société Calédonienne du Chrome, whose sales accounted for one-fourth of all the territory's exports in terms of value. Like all other strategic minerals, chromite enjoyed a boom during the Korean war, and in 1952, New Caledonia exported record shipments totaling 107,708 tons. Beginning in 1953, however, their decline was equally spectacular, and the following year the territory had stocks amounting to 30,000 tons, with no buyers in prospect. By then, the American market was closed to New Caledonia's chromite, and France could not be persuaded to buy more than a third of its chromite requirements from the territory. French industrialists complained that the composition of New Caledonia's ores made them difficult to concentrate and that they cost more than the easier-to-process ores of its competitors.

Twice the general council tried to aid the local chromite miners, first in 1955 by reducing the export duty on ores, and then in 1962 by offering a premium for any shipment totaling 30,000 tons sold in a country other than one of the traditional markets. These measures were to no avail, and exports dwindled rapidly from the record figure of 122,000 tons in 1953 to 22,000 tons in 1961. The following year, the Société Le Tiébaghi reduced its force of more than 300 employes to 30, and in August 1964 finally went out of business. That company, in its 59 years of existence, had produced a total of 2,100,000 tons of ore, and the village which it built for its employes is now a ghost town. In 1967, the Tiébaghi mine reopened, only to close down again within a few months. It is unlikely that it can be profitably operated until some way has been found to solve its technical problems and high production costs. One consequence of the cessation of chromite mining has been to enhance the importance of nickel in New Caledonia's economy.

MINOR MINERALS [19]

Gold was the mineral that first drew prospectors to New Caledonia, but gold mining there has been marked by successive disappointments. It got off to an unpropitious start in the mid-nineteenth century when all but one of a group of seven prospectors in the interior were killed and eaten by the Melanesians. Since then, other courageous individuals and government geologists have found some gold, but not in paying quantities, and in the years immediately after World War II the search for it was abandoned. Similarly but even earlier, the hopes aroused by traces of zinc and lead in the north were dissipated. The small deposits of copper also discovered in the northern region were studied thoroughly before and after World War II, first by geologists

[19] For details concerning the mining of—
   gold: see *L'Océanie Française*, November–December 1935, January–February 1939; *Marchés Coloniaux*, Dec. 27, 1947, p. 1925, April 2, 1949, p. 617.
   iron: see *L'Océanie Française*, November–December 1935, March–May 1938, January–February 1939; *Marchés Coloniaux*, Sept. 16, 1950, p. 2241; *Pacific Islands Monthly*, April, October 1955, October 1956; *Marchés Tropicaux*, Oct. 24, 1953, p. 2951, Sept. 9, 1961, p. 2247, June 10, 1967, p. 1630.
   cobalt: see *L'Océanie Française*, March–April 1939; Robequain, *Madagascar et les Bases Dispersées de l'Union Française*, p. 467; *Pacific Islands Monthly*, December 1954, April 1955; *Marchés Coloniaux*, Oct. 24, 1953, p. 2951.
   asbestos: see *Pacific Islands Monthly*, May, August 1947; *Marchés Coloniaux*, April 2, 1949, p. 617.
   manganese: see *Marchés Coloniaux*, Sept. 17, 1949, p. 1993, Sept. 16, 1950, p. 2241, Oct. 24, 1953, p. 2948; *Pacific Islands Monthly*, June 1950.
   coal: see *L'Océanie Française*, September–October 1927, January–February 1928; *Pacific Islands Monthly*, October 1948, August 1949.

employed by the Banque de l'Indochine and then by the French official Bureau Minier, but they failed to fulfil their early promise. Much the same could be said of the asbestos prospected in 1947 near the Diahot River. Two missions sent from New Zealand later that year to examine the deposits reported that they were not worth developing. Iron, manganese, and coal are three other mineral resources whose future looks more promising, for after their production had been abandoned for some years, interest in them has recently revived.

In the mid-1930s, Japan's rearmament program was responsible for that country's development of rich iron deposits found at Goro in the south of the Grande Terre. A Franco-Japanese company, the Société Le Fer, was formed, was granted three concessions, and began mining the ore. It planned to export to Japan some 500,000 tons a year, but had shipped out only 300,000 tons by the time World War II began. The long delay in concluding a Franco-Japanese peace treaty immobilized the Japanese mining properties in New Caledonia for some years after the war ended, but in 1955 the Broken Hill Proprietary Company agreed to take a trial shipment of 10,000 tons of ore for smelting in Australia. Between 1955 and 1966, the Australians bought from 160,000 to 310,000 tons a year, but in 1967, with the discovery of new iron deposits in their home country, their purchases of Caledonian ore declined by 20 percent, and in 1969 they ceased altogether. The Plaine des Lacs region, notably at Goro and Prony, has reserves estimated at more than 100 million tons, of 52 to 58 percent metal content, but in association with so much chromite and nickel as to make the ore difficult to process. To resolve that problem, a company of mixed economy called the Société des Mines du Goro was formed in the late 1960s, but thus far no progress has been reported.

The Grande Terre's production of nickel, like that of its chromite, has been hampered by high labor costs since World War II, but its other main handicap, which is of even longer standing, has been the territory's lack of fuel resources. Of the two substances other than ore and fuel required to make nickel matte,[20] limestone is abundant in the Nouméa region, but New Caledonia's gypsum deposits are insufficient and must be supplemented by imports. Prospecting for coal began after World War I, and a promising deposit of anthracite was discovered in the Moindou area in 1921. The Ballande company and the

[20] The Doniambo smelter required 25 tons of Australian coal to produce 1 ton of nickel matte. Doniambo's output also includes ferro-nickel, but it is usually included in export data under the heading of matte.

Société des Hauts Fourneaux invested many millions of francs to develop that deposit, in the hope of eliminating the expensive Australian coke then being imported to fuel the Doniambo nickel smelter. Mining installations were built with great speed, a labor force of 265 was hired, and a village was constructed at Moindou to house them. By 1928, production of coal was progressing at the rate of 1,500 tons a month, but soon it was found to be of too poor quality, too difficult to mine, and the deposits too small and scattered to meet Doniambo's needs. Perforce, the Société Le Nickel had to revert to Australian imports, and in 1938, some 162,000 tons of coal were shipped to Doniambo from New South Wales.

To enable New Caledonia to keep producing the nickel matte needed for the Allies during World War II, Australia continued to supply Le Nickel with coal in return for a specified tonnage of its exports. After the war, however, New Caledonia was short of the currency then needed to pay for such coal imports, which, moreover, were frequently interrupted because of strikes called by the Australian colliers. In 1947 such strikes were mainly to blame for a breakdown in the barter agreement that had been negotiated between the two governments to exchange Caledonian timber for Australian coal, and the Doniambo smelter was able to operate only because shipments of American coal were allocated to it under the Marshall Plan.

As this was no more than a temporary solution of the fuel problem, the French government sent several geological missions to search for new coal deposits and also for petroleum in New Caledonia, but none was found. So the small hydroelectric plant at Yaté, which had ceased operating during the depression, was reactivated, but it failed to reduce appreciably the Doniambo smelter's dependence on imported coal. By the mid-1950s, such imports were amounting annually to between 25,000 and 30,000 tons and accounting for about a fourth of Doniambo's operating expenses, hence it was decided to build a second hydroelectric dam at Yaté.

The new dam was inaugurated with considerable fanfare in September 1959 by the Minister of Overseas Territories. He stated on that occasion that it would revolutionize New Caledonia's economy by enabling Doniambo to increase its output and lower its production costs. Time was to show that the dam did not live up to such high expectations. One reason was the dependency of the amount and continuity of the current generated at Yaté on rainfall in that area, which was irregular and usually inadequate. Another was the decision in the mid-

1960s by Le Nickel's directorate to expand greatly its production of matte. In 1967, therefore, Le Nickel built a thermal generating plant to "provide Doniambo with unlimited power and make it independent of climatic vagaries."

At the time when the Yaté dam provided electrical current for Doniambo, as well as for the city of Nouméa, it was operated by ENERCAL. This was a company of mixed economy in which the territory, the Société Le Nickel, and a local firm, UNELCO, were shareholders. UNELCO was a private company long established in Nouméa, where it had been supplying current to that town under a contract negotiated in 1928 with the colonial administration. In 1932, the concessionary company had built a thermal generator and, with an exclusive franchise, had begun distributing current in Nouméa and its suburbs at rates fixed by the general council. Since almost none of New Caledonia's waterfalls could be used to produce hydroelectric power, the few settlements of the interior which had electric current were supplied by small, privately owned thermal plants. Before World War II, electric-power consumption even in Nouméa was very low, but the arrival of American troops in 1942 more than doubled demand. After that war, because of the wider use of electrical appliances, the demand for electricity continued at about the same rate. Nevertheless, aside from the power requirements of the Doniambo smelter, industrial demand for electricity in New Caledonia was small because of the minimal development of secondary industries.

Tanneries have never been developed on a commercial scale in New Caledonia, and dairy cattle form only a small proportion of the total herds. Rawhides and skins are shipped abroad, normally to Australia, and are returned to the territory in the form of leather goods. No dairy industry has long survived in the island, despite periodic attempts to manufacture cheese and butter locally.[21] From the colony's earliest years, visitors from the Metropole were astonished to learn that even on the great ranches, their owners and personnel used canned milk and dairy products imported from Australia.[22] Today, thanks to high import duties, locally produced milk supplies about 30

[21] The record for longevity in this industry is held by the Fromagérie de la Néra at Bourail, founded in 1950, which failed 11 years later.
[22] Robequain, *Madagascar et les Bases Dispersées*, p. 465.

percent of the local demand, but Caledonian consumers continue to prefer the taste and lower price of Australian cheese and butter, whose sales in Nouméa steadily increase.

Meat-tinning is the only animal-products industry in New Caledonia worthy of the name, but it has by no means always flourished. Although overproduction rather than shortage of meat has characterized local animal husbandry, all of the island's canneries either have gone bankrupt or have had to suspend operations. The most important of these is Senator Lafleur's Société de Ouaco, which has vast ranches in the north and at one time owned a herd of 20,000 cattle. Minor handicaps have been a shortage of tins (after World War II) or a high duty on their importation (as in 1924), but its main and most persistent difficulty has been that of finding a steady and remunerative external market. In the early 1920s, the Ouaco company was awarded a contract by the French army, but after the first shipment, the agreement was canceled. Later in that decade, the company entered into another contract, this time with the local administration and on onerous terms. Their stipulations included the improving and fencing of the company's pastures and a large increase in the cultivating and canning of vegetables for the local market.[23] The Ouaco company, however, continued to supply about one-tenth of the 10,800 cattle slaughtered each year for domestic consumption (and also to export rawhides and skins) until the depression sharply reduced the number of consumers and their purchasing power. Mutton and venison began to replace beef on the Caledonians' tables, and two of New Caledonia's three meat-packing plants had to close down.[24]

By 1933, the decline in the sale of beef to the canneries, along with that of purchases by consumers of fresh meat, caused a crisis for New Caledonia's ranchers, whose herds of unsalable cattle were multiplying inordinately. As always during such recessions, the breeders formed an association, besought the administration for aid, and disbanded after they had received it. This time, Governor Siadous responded by forming a committee to study their problems, and also by urging the French Ministry of War to give the Ouaco company another chance to supply the army with tinned meat. His request was granted on condition that the company modernize its plant, and to finance this he persuaded the general councilors to guarantee a loan and also to give a premium to exporters. The indefatigable governor also garnered

23 *L'Océanie Française*, January–February 1928.
24 *Ibid.*, March–April 1933.

orders for a few hundred tons of tinned meat from Guyane and the French Antilles. There is no doubt but that Governor Siadous saved New Caledonia's cattle owners and meat packers from disaster, and by 1938 they were considered to be out of danger.[25] Not long after came the windfall of American army orders during World War II, and the whole industry enjoyed another period of outstanding prosperity.

During the years since the war, New Caledonia several times has repeated the familiar cycle of feast and famine, the depressed periods generally exceeding the prosperous ones. The Ouaco company failed to win permanent markets abroad but, thanks to the imposition of a high duty on tinned meat from Australia, was able to sell to local consumers until 1960, when it was again compelled to cease operations. Just after the war ended, the herders were once more on the verge of bankruptcy. They claimed that the sudden rise in labor costs prevented them from paying their stockmen, repairing fences, and keeping the lantana from invading their pastures. As they had done in 1911 and 1933 under similar circumstances, they formed a *syndicat des éléveurs* and sought financial help from the territory. This time a permanent price-support fund was established for them, but it failed to satisfy their demands and they asked permission to charge local consumers more for their beef. They argued that since Caledonians were eating more meat than ever before, they could afford a price rise, but they chose to overlook the fact that the high cost of their beef had already resulted in widespread clandestine slaughtering and the increased consumption of venison, mutton, and pork. By the early 1960s, at all events, the population's growth and, above all, the upturn in the mining industry increased the number of their customers who were willing to pay remunerative prices, and the Ouaco company seriously considered reopening its plant.

Despite this revival, the government decided that it was necessary to reorganize animal husbandry in New Caledonia if it were ever to be put on a sound basis and cease to be dependent on fluctuating market conditions and official subsidies. It was patently absurd for a territory in which a majority of the rural inhabitants were engaged in stock raising, and a third of whose surface was ceded as ranches, to import virtually all of its dairy products and even some of its meat. To reduce the mortality caused by recurring droughts, the herds had to be assured of an adequate water supply, hence a program of hydraulic prospecting and well-digging was drawn up and a start was made on

25 *Ibid.*, March–April 1939.

putting it into effect. More facilities were provided for long- and medium-term bank loans to ranch owners for the improvement of their pastures, and experiments in developing new types of fodder grass were undertaken at the Port Laguerre station. A refrigerated plant for storing meat (and also vegetables) was built at Nouméa in 1963, as the first in a *chaine de froid* that is to be constructed in the main settlements for the regular provisioning of their markets with perishable foodstuffs.

This official program, certainly long overdue, is as yet at too early a stage in its evolution to be evaluated. It seems well conceived in that it aims to promote the interests of stock owners, meat packers, and consumers in about equal proportions. Since New Caledonia cannot hope to compete in the Pacific with the far larger, cheaper, and better-quality exports from Australia, its animal husbandry must be oriented toward the domestic market. In this, as in so many other domains, the imponderable element is the future status of the mining industry, by which local purchasing power is determined.

Most of New Caledonia's minor industries have suffered a decline and fall, as have the territory's minerals other than nickel. At one time the Grande Terre produced such export commodities as sugar and rum, ginned cotton, niaouli essence, shell buttons, and tinned meat. Today, however, such few small industries as exist cater solely to domestic consumers and none of them fully meets the local demand. They include food and beverage enterprises (beer, soft drinks, Italian-style pasta), two soap factories (one of which has an oilmill), a plant producing compressed gas and oxygen, about a dozen sawmills, and a few building concerns. Moreover, they have been able to survive only thanks to tariff protection. The small size of the internal market, which in fact is confined chiefly to Nouméa, the proximity of Australia's highly developed industries, and the heavy cost of labor, transportation, and electric current account for the failure of former industries, as well as for the general discouragement about launching new ones.

30

External Trade

For a territory with such obviously high living standards as those of New Caledonia today, it is surprising to note how many years of economic depression it has experienced. Indeed, the sharp fluctuations in its foreign trade have given it longer periods of unfavorable than of favorable trade balances. New Caledonia produces a very small quantity and range of consumer commodities and almost no manufactured goods, hence it is dependent on imports to fill about 80 percent of its needs. Local purchasing power is increasingly linked with nickel exports, and these have been determined by the highly unstable conditions characteristic of the world metals market.

In the early 1890s, the sudden appearance in that market of Canadian nickel created such a competitor for New Caledonia that the colony's economy was virtually paralyzed for the following two years.[1] Its recovery, which began in 1896 and was maintained until 1900, was due to the development of alternative agricultural exports, notably coffee, by the Feillet colonists. At about the same time, mineral exports nearly doubled in value, rising from 6 million to 10 million francs, and imports increased by 57 percent during those years. This prosperous period was followed by another depression between 1902 and 1909, when New Caledonia's exports underwent an overall decline of about 30 percent.

Although, from the latter year until the outbreak of World War I, New Caledonia's foreign commerce generally improved, the cumulative trade deficit for the 1906–1914 period amounted to 12.5 million francs.[2] Nevertheless, it was before World War I that the colony's exports were more varied than at any other time in their history. They comprised cotton, vanilla, rubber, and rum, as well as the hardy perennials—copra, coffee, shell and mineral ores. Thanks to what was euphemistically called New Caledonia's "tariff assimilation" to France,

[1] *L'Océanie Française,* August 1911.
[2] *Ibid.,* January–February 1931.

approximately half of its foreign commerce was with the Metropole, despite the geographic absurdity of trading so extensively with a country 24,000 kilometers away.

The First World War isolated New Caledonia from its major market, and its commercial exchanges were perforce intensified with Australia, the United States, and Japan. As a result of the reduction that this reorientation effected in transport costs, and also of the higher wartime prices paid for its exports, New Caledonia enjoyed one of its rare periods of favorable trade balances, and by 1918 it had accumulated a surplus of 13.5 million francs. Then, owing to the poor sales of its minerals in markets that had become overstocked, there followed a recession that was not offset by a slight concurrent growth in its agricultural exports. Between 1914 and 1919, coffee shipments rose from 468,000 kilograms to 598,000 and those of copra from 3,103 tons to 3,238, and cotton exports for the first time exceeded 900 tons.[3] Tinned-meat production had increased so rapidly during the war—from 737 to 1,396 tons—that in 1917–1918 two new meat-packing plants were built. For some years after the war, imports continued to come principally from Australia and Japan but those from the United States tapered off because of their higher prices. By the mid-1920s, however, France had resumed its former place as New Caledonia's principal supplier, thanks to an improvement in the shipping situation and the reimposition of tariff barriers against foreign competition.

The period from 1925 through 1928 saw an appreciable improvement in New Caledonia's foreign commerce, but by the end of the latter year the trade deficit had reached the large total of 385 million francs. Although exports had risen steadily, imports had grown even faster, less in tonnage than in terms of price (largely because of the franc's depreciation). In 1928, the peak year of that period, exports totaled 84,450 tons, valued at 75.5 million francs, but imports, which aggregated only 19,453 tons, cost 183.2 million francs.[4]

New Caledonia began to feel the world economic depression late in 1929, and during the ensuing three years its foreign trade declined abruptly. Between 1931 and 1932, imports dwindled by more than 32 percent and exports by some 50 percent, and both touched bottom in the latter year, when their total value came to only 91 million francs. Nickel-matte exports had decreased, those of chromite were suffering from Soviet competition, and France had stopped buying the colony's

3 *Ibid.*, March–April 1921.
4 *Ibid.*, March–April 1929.

tinned meat, rum, and shell. Governor Guyon, however, saved Caledonian coffee and cotton planters from ruin by persuading France to grant bonuses for their export, but he failed to do as much for copra growers. Although imports declined with the shrinking earnings from exports and the repatriation of thousands of Asian laborers, the deficit in New Caledonia's trade balance persisted.

In 1933, the revival of mineral exports marked a general upturn in the colony's commercial situation, and the improvement continued throughout the following year. By 1935 New Caledonia had its first trade surplus since 1918, for imports continued to be at a low level whereas the prices for mineral exports—and consequently their volume—had increased. Chromite and nickel accounted for 75 percent of all shipments in terms of value, coffee and copra for 15.5 percent, meat and hides for 2.2 percent, and shell also for 2.2 percent.[5] A further rise in world prices for minerals and, even more, the franc's devaluation in 1936 doubled the nominal value of New Caledonia's foreign commerce. The colony continued to experience a trade deficit, for while devaluation had naturally stimulated export sales it had also made imported goods more expensive. Between 1936 and 1938, the imports of foodstuffs and manufactured goods doubled in volume but tripled in price. Consequently, the cost of living rose so rapidly that some Nouméa firms granted special allowances to their employees and the administration formed a committee to control the prices for essential goods.

The fluctuations of New Caledonia's foreign trade between 1914 and 1938, in terms of value, are indicated in the following tabulation, based on data in *L'Océanie Française* for March–April 1929, May–June 1930, and January–April 1939:

	Value (millions of francs)		
Year	*Imports*	*Exports*	*Total*
1914	16.6	15.4	32.0
1920	47.4	43.0	90.4
1928	159.9	98.8	258.7
1932	50.8	43.1	93.9
1936	59.0	54.9	113.9
1938	158.5	146.4	304.9

The 1930s, as a whole, confirmed the preeminence of mineral exports and the decline or stagnation of those from the rural sector, at the

[5] *Ibid.,* March–April 1936.

same time that France strengthened its role as the colony's main client and provisioner. By the eve of World War II, France and its empire were buying 70 percent of New Caledonia's exports, mainly nickel matte, coffee, shell, and copra, and were supplying between 40 and 45 percent of the colony's imports. Nevertheless, food and, even more, coal imports from Australia still accounted for 30 to 35 percent of New Caledonia's purchases from foreign sources, although Australia was taking only 10 percent of the French colony's exports. Similarly, Japan was selling more textiles, machinery, and manufactured goods to New Caledonia than it was buying of the colony's iron and nickel ores.

Because New Caledonia had by then become more dependent on trade with France than ever before, its economy was more affected by the reorientation of its commerce during the Second World War than during the First. Beginning in September 1939, shipping shortages and higher maritime insurance rates deflected Caledonian trading to the Pacific area, as had happened in 1914. This trend was intensified after the colony aligned itself with Free France in September 1940. The period from then until the Pacific war broke out was a time of increasing privation for the Caledonians. Fortunately for them, this situation improved markedly thereafter, especially after American troops were stationed in the island.

To be sure, some Nouméa importers (and some American exporters) complained that private traders were being frozen out because the Free French purchasing mission in Washington insisted that all commerce between the United States and New Caledonia be conducted on a government-to-government basis. Nevertheless, from March 1942 through 1946, Caledonian businessmen and producers alike were making unprecedented profits. Money flowed freely, even the long-dormant building industry boomed, and the living standards of the poorer classes rose markedly.[6]

The departure of the American troops coincided with two steps taken by the French government, and together they caused local business to relapse into its prewar trading habits and general torpor. To reorient New Caledonia's external commerce away from the Pacific area and back to France, the Paris authorities revived the old tariff barriers and instituted new controls. All of the island's copra and coffee exports thenceforth had to be sent to France, although French

---

[6] By the end of war, the colony had received through Lend-Lease operations 39 million francs worth of civilian goods, not to mention military equipment worth another 43 millions, in return for local services valued at 67 millions. See "G. F. R.", "New Caledonia and the War."

industry had not yet recovered to the point where it could supply Caledonians with the manufactured goods they needed. Moreover, to increase France's small reserves of hard currency, New Caledonia was required to hand over to the French treasury its earnings in dollars and sterling from mineral exports. In return it received only scanty allocations of those currencies with which to buy minimal imports from Australia and the United States. Caledonians regarded this treatment as a poor reward for their early support of Free France and protested vigorously.[7]

The combined pressures exerted by the administrators, politicians, and businessmen of all the French Pacific islands induced France to relax its draconian regulations, and by mid-1947 the Caledonians were again able to buy more than three-fourths of their imports in Australia and the United States.[8] The French government, however, was not so obliging in regard to the concurrent pleas by Caledonian industrialists and planters that the Metropole waive application to the territory of France's new social laws, which had not only raised local wages but enabled Asian laborers to leave their manual occupations and take up trade.[9]

Higher production costs and the shortage of consumer goods, combined with the considerable amounts of money left over from the wartime boom, greatly stimulated the inflationary trend and led to a sharp rise in prices. The general councilors roundly reproached the local administration with failing to protect consumers by strictly enforcing price controls, while permitting "certain merchants to make scandalous profits." [10] Yet it was these very councilors who were the defenders and spokesmen for local big business, as represented by the Etablissements Ballande, Maison Barrau, Banque de l'Indochine, and Le Nickel, many of which shared the same directors. Their trading philosophy remained that of the Colonial Pact,[11] and their goal that of making profits to be repatriated to the parent companies in Bordeaux, Mar-

[7] Minutes of the general council, Feb. 29, 1947.

[8] *L'Economie*, Oct. 2, 1947.

[9] As of 1948, there were in New Caledonia 2,472 licensed merchants (as compared with 2,259 in 1947), of whom 1,697 were Frenchmen, 474 Melanesians, 224 Vietnamese, 43 Javanese, and 34 miscellaneous foreigners. By January 1957 their number had grown to 3,880, of whom 2,339 were Frenchmen, 967 Melanesians, 396 Vietnamese, 117 Javanese, and 61 "other foreigners." See *Marchés Coloniaux*, April 2, 1949, p. 617, and April 6, 1957, p. 895.

[10] Minutes of the general council, Dec. 23, 1947, and June 3, 1948.

[11] A misleading term applied to France's traditional policy of utilizing its colonies as sources of raw materials and as a reserved market for French manufactured goods.

seille, and Paris. It was by opposing their grip on New Caledonia's economy and by insisting that they reinvest their earnings locally that Lenormand won electoral victories for his party in the early 1950s, as well as the implacable hostility of local big business. Actually, it was less the Union Calédonienne's policy of favoring high wages and the interests of small local traders than the labor shortage, the Korean war, and the expansion of the mining industry that were responsible for the territory's soaring cost of living.

Despite the Caledonians' frequent complaints about rising prices, labor shortages and expense, and the growing imbalance of New Caledonia's economy, the Korean war ushered in a long period of profitable trading which has continued, with only two short interruptions, to this day. Indeed, the growth in the territory's foreign trade since 1952 has been remarkable, and since 1963 nothing less than spectacular, with each successive year establishing a new record. Between 1948 and 1952, the volume and value of exports were highly irregular, owing to fluctuations in world prices, and the same was true of imports, though to a lesser degree. The stimulus provided by the Korean war boom to the price of metals naturally accounted for the upsurge of the territory's ore and nickel-matte exports, and further strengthened their already preponderant position in New Caledonia's foreign trade. What was surprising was the continuation and even the growth of demand for nickel after the war ended. Thanks to this rise, the proportion of minerals in the value of New Caledonia's total exports grew from 88 percent in 1953 to 92.4 percent in 1959, then to 96.5 percent in 1960, and climbed steadily throughout the ensuing decade until it reached 98.6 in 1968.[12]

In 1950, New Caledonia's foreign trade amounted to only 215,000 tons (1,272 million C.F.P. francs), and by 1968 the respective figures were 3,687,629 tons and 18,514 million francs, the biggest increases occurring between 1966 and 1968. The trade balance was consistently adverse during the first decade after World War II and irregularly so between 1953 and 1959. In 1954, for the first time in 20 years, New Caledonia enjoyed a trade surplus (141 million C.F.P. francs) and in 1955 a much larger one (300 millions), but in 1956 and 1957 the balance of trade was again unfavorable and in 1958 seriously so (408 millions). The year 1959, however, brought an improvement, with a surplus of 138 millions, and spectacularly larger ones occurred in 1960 (1,162 millions) and 1961 (668 millions). Then in 1962, a sizable

12 *Marchés Tropicaux*, Aug. 23, 1969, p. 2346.

TABLE 10

New Caledonia: Volume and value of external trade, 1955–1968 (in millions of tons and millions of C.F.P. francs)

Year	Imports		Exports		
	Volume	Value	Volume	Value	Value of minerals (Percent of total value)
1955	401.0	1,640	458	1,940	86.0
1956	404.0	2,105	873	1,982	92.4
1957	530.6	3,209	1,386	3,196	92.0
1958	441.0	3,438	567	2,030	92.0
1959	493.8	2,519	1,145	2,657	92.0
1960	472.7	3,441	1,340	4,603	96.5
1961	525.0	4,284	1,370	4,952	96.1
1962	341.0	3,682	963	3,087	96.0
1963	420.0	3,452	970	3,999	96.1
1964	617.8	4,888	1,472	5,596	96.2
1965	675.6	6,837	1,247	5,848	95.5
1966	779.0	6,037	1,405	6,268	97.1
1967	728.9	7,068	1,806	7,099	97.7
1968	921.5	8,352	2,766	10,164	98.6

Source: *La Nouvelle Calédonie et Dépendances* (La Documentation Française); *Marchés Tropicaux*, Aug. 23, 1969.

deficit of 595 millions occurred after Japan abruptly ceased buying nickel ores. New Caledonia's foreign trade, however, made a rapid recovery, and its trade surplus, which amounted to 547 million C.F.P. francs in 1963, trebled by 1968, when it reached 1,812 millions.

The upsurge in the volume and value of mineral exports demonstrates the decline in New Caledonia's sales abroad of its output from the rural sector. Shell shipments have fallen almost to the vanishing point since the peak year of 1946, when they amounted to 1,221 tons, and in 1965–1968 they averaged between 35 and 40 tons, earning less than half a million C.F.P. francs. Coffee and copra are the only two nonmineral exports of any importance. Though they have generally held their own during the last decade, they aggregate only a little more than 2,000 tons, worth about 75 million C.F.P. francs annually. Of the two, coffee is by far the more valuable, for it brings in nearly two-thirds of that total.

Local purchasing power having become almost wholly dependent on the mining industry, New Caledonia's imports generally, though not wholly, have reflected fluctuations in the sale of nickel. However, the large unfavorable balance in 1958 was due to massive imports for construction of the Yaté dam, and in 1965 the big increase in imports of building materials was related to the Pacific Olympic games which were to be held at Nouméa the following year. Although, since 1953, imports have grown fairly steadily in both volume and value— except in 1959, 1962, and 1963, when they receded slightly—the years in which they rose most sharply were those in which Le Nickel was carrying out its expansion program. The importation of equipment materials has been consistently followed by a growth in the earnings from mineral exports, and these in turn were directly related to increases in consumer-goods imports. As such earnings reached ever-higher levels in the middle and late 1960s, so did the tonnages of imported foodstuffs, alcoholic beverages, automobiles, fuel, textiles, and the like. Between 1957 and 1967, the cost of living climbed by 50 percent, but so did wages, which were pegged to the former by an automatic sliding scale. During that decade, living standards rose even faster than during World War II, and it was calculated that as of mid-1966 there was one automobile for every 4.4 inhabitants of the territory.[13]

France is by far the most important market for New Caledonia's exports, taking most of its nickel matte and almost all of its coffee, copra, and shell. In terms of value, the Metropole's share of the trade in these commodities attained a high point of 76 percent in 1956, and although subsequently it has varied from year to year, the percentage has never fallen below the level of 44.4 percent reached in 1966. France's position in the territory's import trade has never been so outstanding, ranging from 37 percent in 1954 to 62.5 percent in 1965, but it has always headed the list of New Caledonia's provisioners and it supplies the territory with the widest range of merchandise. For many years Australia ranked second after France as New Caledonia's main source of imports, particularly of foodstuffs and fuel, but since 1953, when it supplied 30 percent of the total, its share fell to about 18 percent in 1967 and 1968. Australia has never bought much from New Caledonia, taking only limited amounts of timber and iron ore, but even those purchases have steadily declined, and as of 1968 they accounted for less than 1 percent of the territory's total exports.

New Caledonia's commercial exchanges with Japan were almost

13 *Ibid.*, Sept. 10, 1966, p. 2351.

equally unbalanced for many years, though that country's position was exactly the reverse of Australia's. It was not until the mid-1950s that Japan resumed its prewar place as an important market for New Caledonia's ores. Its share in the territory's export trade rose rapidly, however, from 13 percent in 1955 to 20.1 percent in 1960 and to 38.9 percent in 1968, and in the last-mentioned year Japan and France together accounted for 86 percent of New Caledonia's total foreign sales. Furthermore, the Japanese have recently been correcting the imbalance of their trade with the territory, and are supplying it with ever-larger amounts of textiles and cement.

The other countries with which New Caledonia trades vary only as to the degree of their insignificance. The United States, formerly a good customer for the territory's chromite, now buys only 4 percent of its exports, and the American share in the import trade fell from 20 percent in 1952 to 6.7 percent in 1968. Three new trading partners, however, made their appearance in the 1960s. These are Indonesia, which sells to New Caledonia small tonnages of petroleum products; West Germany, which has become an important source of coke; and Canada, which, surprisingly enough, began to purchase nickel matte in 1966 so extensively that it ranked third among the territory's clients that year.

New Caledonia's foreign trade has an extremely precarious base, for its exports—and consequently its imports—are clearly at the mercy of world market conditions beyond its control. While this is also true of many one-crop countries, it is more serious for a remote island which has increasingly neglected food production, the exportation of agricultural products, and even local processing industries in its concentration on promoting nickel mining and smelting. In the event of a sudden fall in the world's demand or price for its nickel, New Caledonia would probably be bailed out by France, but in the process its present high living standards would be sacrificed. Such a contingency may well figure among the considerations that have made some Caledonians unwilling to press for greater autonomy from the French government. For the majority, however, this probably seems only a remote and unlikely possibility, despite the frequency with which the territory has undergone economic recessions. The speculative character of the mining industry has created an attractively exciting atmosphere in Nouméa, with the result that most Caledonians are simply basking unreservedly in the euphoria of the territory's present remarkable prosperity.

31

Transportation

New Caledonia and French Polynesia have similar communications problems except in regard to roads and interisland shipping. Both territories have suffered from their isolation, both internally and in relation to the outside world, and because of their distance from France, with which they have maintained close political and economic ties. Their trade and populations are too small to make any means of communication a paying proposition, and providing them with regular transportation services has necessitated heavy subsidies from France as well as from their territorial budgets. Internal trade is insignificant because of the small size of the domestic market, and their only exports of any value—mineral products—have been transported by the producing companies. Since both territories are made up of islands, and since all their settlements are concentrated in the coastal areas, communication by sea was the first to be developed. French Polynesia's dispersal over many small islands, however, has made it more dependent on interisland shipping than is New Caledonia, whose land mass is far larger and more concentrated.

LAND COMMUNICATIONS

The natives of New Caledonia and its adjacent dependencies, unlike the Polynesians, are not a seafaring people but are farmers attached by religion and traditions to their ancestral lands. When the Europeans came to the Grande Terre they found the Melanesians living in the deep valleys and around the mouths of rivers, isolated from each other by mountain ranges, mutually incomprehensible languages, and tribal hostilities. Progressively the Melanesians were brought closer together and segregated on reservations, mainly in the northern and eastern parts of the Grande Terre, while the Europeans founded scattered settlements in the coastal areas that had been perforce abandoned by the tribes.

As these settlers began to develop the island's economy, they spread over all but the most inaccessible regions of the Grande Terre, and consequently became more widely dispersed than the Melanesians. With the help of penal labor, large areas were cleared for farming, mineral prospecting, and above all ranching, with the result that many of the whites lived in isolation. The harsh conditions of their life at that time brought forth a special breed of rough diamonds known as the *broussards*, whose independence and self-reliance were matched by their conservatism and parochialism. To get provisions, they had to ride on horseback, often for great distances, over mountain trails to the nearest coastal settlement.[1] Their only other outside contacts were occasional trips to Nouméa, either to sell their cattle or on personal business. Their contempt for town-dwellers was proverbial, as was their hospitality. So eager were they for social contacts that the occasional traveler who ventured into the interior risked beng kept for days on end by his *broussard* hosts.

Strangely enough, it was a navy captain, Pallu de la Barrière, who between 1882 and 1884 created a network of muletracks in the interior. His work was continued by Feillet to provide better communications for his settlers, but the governor's main energies in this domain were devoted to building a railroad, which he hoped would eventually encircle the Grande Terre. This was the period when rail construction was being undertaken on a grand scale in most of the French colonies, and Feillet's initial proposal for a 152-kilometer line between Nouméa and Bourail was modest for that era. In 1898 he asked Paris for a 10-million-franc loan, of which half was to be used to build the tracks as far as Tontouta, a distance of 53 kilometers. The loan that was granted in 1901, however, totaled only 5 million francs, and as the actual cost exceeded the estimates it got no farther than Dumbéa. In 1909 a second loan carried it to Païta, 39 kilometers from Nouméa, but it never went beyond that point.

Under the management of the local administration, this railroad incurred heavy annual deficits, for it failed to attract either passengers or merchandise traffic in sufficient quantity. The Colonial Inspectors sent out from France reported unfavorably on its operations, and urged the development of coastal shipping as preferable to an extension of the railroad. Most of the Caledonian settlers, however, opted for the railroad, on the ground that the lagoon surrounding the Grande Terre was often rough and also was full of dangerous uncharted

[1] Mariotti, J., "Quelques Aspects de l'Evolution de la Nouvelle-Calédonie."

reefs, and that the frequent transshipments at coastal ports made this an uneconomic means of communication.[2] Nevertheless, the Paris government did not share this view, and Sarraut's *mise-en-valeur* program of 1921 gave priority to the port of Nouméa and a road network as New Caledonia's most urgent needs in respect to infrastructure. By 1933 the local administration had become convinced that the cost of running New Caledonia's minuscule railroad was wholly disproportionate to the service it rendered, and the general council reluctantly agreed to reduce the number of weekly trains in service.[3] Finally, in 1940, the line was abandoned, despite the protests of Caledonian foresters who had been providing its locomotives with wood fuel.

In the mid-1920s, Governor Guyon drew up the colony's first comprehensive road program, and partially carried it out. When he arrived in New Caledonia the only real road outside of Nouméa was the one that connected the capital with Bourail, but of its 170 kilometers only 20 were worthy of the name. Elsewhere cart tracks covered 359 kilometers and mule paths another 1,179 kilometers, but floods sometimes made them impassable. In 1913, Governor Brunet had appointed a committee to coordinate the existing system, such as it was, but World War I broke out shortly afterwards.[4]

Guyon was the first governor to recognize that roadbuilding was the *sine qua non* for any lasting development of the Grande Terre's economy, and with the cooperation of the municipalities and the public-works service he succeeded in providing the colony with the semblance of a road network. By the end of his incumbency, the Grande Terre had 876 kilometers of "colonial highways," 1,000 kilometers of secondary roads, and 700 kilometers of communal paths.[5] The Nouméa-Bourail highway was open to traffic throughout the year, and although the secondary roads had only a few stretches that were passable in the rainy season, Guyon succeeded in orienting the Grande Terre's means of communication away from the sea and toward the land.

This trend was furthered by the construction work done by American troops during the Pacific war. By their use of modern machinery and techniques in building roads and airfields, they showed what could be done to improve transportation even in such difficult ter-

[2] *L'Océanie Française*, November 1912, March 1913.
[3] *Ibid.*, January–February 1934.
[4] *Ibid.*, February 1913.
[5] Mariotti, "Quelques Aspects."

rain as that of New Caledonia. They provided the Grande Terre with 136 kilometers of paved road 6 meters wide, built a few bridges, and also improved other portions of the west-coast roads.[6] Their operations unfortunately did not extend to other parts of the island, which remained isolated from each other and also from the southern and western regions. Primarily in the hope of remedying that deficiency, New Caledonia's first postwar plan gave priority to the infrastructure in general and to road-building in particular, but it offered no solution to the problems of maintenance. As regards the technical aspect of the communications situation, the general councilors obstinately refused to authorize the recruitment of Metropolitan engineers, charging that the public-works service was already overstaffed with inefficient expatriates.

Since the time it was established, the public-works service had been a target of sharp criticism from the general councilors and the public. It came to be regarded as a voracious and nonproductive consumer of a huge portion of the territorial revenues. It was alleged to be incapable even of maintaining the roads built by the Americans, much less of undertaking new construction.[7] An impasse seemed to have been reached when the technician sent to New Caledonia in 1947 to study the first plan asserted that the territory was suffering from "road inflation," and that only such road work as had been begun should be continued with F.I.D.E.S. funds. He was, however, overridden by the general councilors, who insisted on going ahead with new construction, notably in the northern and eastern regions, and so such work was included in the second plan.

In the 1950s, the increase in the territory's revenues, and consequently in the number of its motor vehicles, both aided and encouraged further road-building and improvement. Between 1947 and 1957, the number of passenger cars rose from 1,634 to 4,232, trucks from 1,168 to 2,357, and motorcycles from 192 to 1,063.[8] Most of these vehicles could circulate only in Nouméa and its environs, or as far as Bourail on the west coast, because elsewhere roads were either nonexistent or in bad condition. In 1957, therefore, the general council agreed to the creation of a Fonds Routier, to be financed by a tax on gasoline, and New Caledonia thus acquired for the first time a

[6] *Pacific Islands Monthly*, June 1945.

[7] Minutes of the general council, Jan. 31, 1947, Dec. 9, 1948.

[8] *Marchés Coloniaux*, July 17, 1948, p. 1282; *Marchés Tropicaux*, April 6, 1957, p. 895.

steady source of income exclusively for the improvement of its road system. As territorial revenues grew rapidly in the 1960s, a 20-year road-building program that would require the expenditure of more than one billion C.F.P. francs was drafted. In this program, priority was still given to the west-coast system, but five bridges were to be built across east-coast rivers to replace the obsolete and often hazardous ferries.

As of 1965, New Caledonia's road network consisted of three sectors totaling 4,500 kilometers, of which 2,000 kilometers were described as "acceptably motorable." [9] The trans-island roads in particular need considerable improvements in the way of surface, itinerary, and bridge construction so as to facilitate the circulation of the 20,000-odd motor vehicles now in use.

SHIPPING

France's earliest trade with the Pacific area was for many years handled almost exclusively by the Atlantic ports of Nantes and Bordeaux. After the Suez Canal was opened, however, Marseille became the nearest port for France's Far Eastern colonies. The European center of such trade, therefore, shifted to the Mediterranean port, although Le Havre soon became the site of the Société Le Nickel's refinery and Bordeaux continues to maintain close ties with Nouméa, where the outstanding trading firm, the Etablissements Ballande, was of Bordelais origin. Similarly, the Maison Barrau, founded by an emigrant Marseillais, was the main link between Nouméa and his native city, whose many soap factories were increasingly important purchasers of the Pacific islands' copra.[10] It was thus only logical that the Marseille-based navigation company, the Messageries Maritimes, should become the principal carrier of passengers and merchandise between France, New Caledonia, and the E.F.O.

In 1882 the Messageries Maritimes initiated its service between Marseille, Sydney, and Nouméa with new ships that were so fast and comfortable for that era that they were often used by Australians traveling to and from Europe.[11] As time went on, however, the company lost interest in that sector of its itinerary because of the lack of

[9] *La Nouvelle-Calédonie et Dépendances* (La Documentation Française), p. 16.

[10] *Marchés Coloniaux,* March 7, 1953, p. 761.

[11] *L'Océanie Française,* December 1927.

freight revenues between Sydney and Marseille, and it took its best ships off that run even before the outbreak of World War I. During the war a large part of its fleet was sunk or damaged, and it was only gradually reconstituted in the 1920s, thanks to a government subsidy and to German reparations. Even after its Far Eastern service was revived and it began using the Panama Canal route as well as that of Suez, the Messageries Maritimes concentrated on the Marseille-Saigon run, sending only its oldest and slowest ships to the Pacific islands even less frequently than before.

Caledonians vainly complained that the voyage which had taken 36 days between Nouméa and Marseille in the 1880s required 45 in the 1920s, and that the Messageries' former clientele was shifting its patronage to the more modern ships of foreign companies. Nouméa's merchants also complained that the cost of living there was rising because the Messageries' ships demanded too high freight rates, stayed too short a time in New Caledonia, and provided insufficient space to carry the cargo.[12] The company, for its part, claimed that the subsidy received from the government (50,000 francs a year) was inadequate even to make ends meet, and the more frequent its service to the Pacific islands the greater its deficit became. This line simply did not pay, and the French government maintained it solely out of considerations of national prestige. In brief, the Messageries Maritimes was bound by its contract to serve Nouméa and Papeete but did so as little and as poorly as possible, while the Caledonians had no choice but to use its inadequate services.

Poor as was New Caledonia's shipping situation in the 1930s, it became even worse after World War II. Once again a world war had depleted France's merchant marine, and this time there were no German reparations or government funds to repair the damage. The Messageries Maritimes' service between Marseille and Nouméa became even less frequent, slower, and more uncomfortable than before, and for one 5-month period not a single ship of the line called at the Pacific islands. To add insult to injury, the company raised its freight rates between Sydney and Nouméa by 25 percent in 1951, and the territory was saved from total maritime isolation only by foreign ships.[13] In 1952, however the Messageries Maritimes added two new ships to the three old-timers on its islands service and stepped up the

[12] *Ibid.*, September–October 1931, January–February 1932.
[13] Minutes of the French Union Assembly, Oct. 24, 1950; *Marchés Coloniaux,* July 7, 1951, p. 1850.

schedule of its round trips from six to nine a year. In 1955, it began a new monthly service between Nouméa and Brisbane, and in the 1960s small freighters owned by two new local companies began competing with it on the Nouméa-Sydney run.

The increase in sea traffic impelled the authorities to revive the long-dormant plan to modernize and enlarge Nouméa's port and give it an autonomous administration. To judge by the frequent complaints published in the local press, such improvements were long overdue. These criticisms centered on the lack of dredging for the past 25 years, the failure to provide a tug service, the inadequacy of the warehouses and customs shed, and the inability of the quay to berth more than one large ship there at a time. In 1968, a 20-year loan of 90 million C.F.P. francs was granted by the Common Market fund and the F.I.D.E.S. to build a deep-water quay and a causeway to link Nouméa to Nou Island. That same year, the port of Nouméa handled 2,900,000 tons of freight, and the proposal to give it financial autonomy (which dated back to 1910) was finally approved. The port's budget for 1969, about equally divided between operational and investment expenditures, totaled 79,190,000 C.F.P. francs.[14] The prospect of such improvements, however, did not prevent the American Matson Line, whose cruise ships had been calling regularly at Nouméa since August 1962, from eliminating that stop from its schedule early in 1969 on the ground that Nouméa's port was "ugly, dirty and expensive."[15]

If New Caledonia's maritime links with France and its Pacific neighbors improved in the 1960s, the same could not be said for the territory's coastal shipping. During the early years of the French occupation, large sailing ships and, later, schooners provided the only means of communication between Nouméa, the smaller settlements, and the nearby islands. Most of them belonged to Nouméa merchants, whose boats delivered imported merchandise and picked up coffee and copra for their return voyage. As in French Polynesia, the itinerary and schedules of these boats were determined wholly by the traders' and not by the producers' interests. To provide a more regular service for passengers and freight, the government subsidized a small private company, the Tour de Côtes, at an annual cost to the colony's budget of about 1.5 million francs during the interwar period. Although, by the terms of its contract, this company was required to follow a monthly itinerary that included the main settlements of the Grande

---

[14] *Journal de la Marine Marchande*, Sept. 25, 1969.
[15] *Pacific Islands Monthly*, March 1969.

Terre and its dependent islands, there were many complaints in the local press about the irregularity of its sailings and its excessive freight rates. The northern settlements of the Grande Terre and the Bélep archipelago, in particular, were neglected, and that inaccessible and underpopulated area would have been completely isolated had it not been for the recently developed interisland airline service.[16]

AIR TRANSPORT

On April 5, 1932, the first plane flown from France to New Caledonia arrived at the small airfield of Tontouta almost exactly a month after it had left Paris. Seven years later, a Nouméa pharmacist made the same trip in the opposite direction in 150 hours. These were isolated achievements without commercial significance, but they did have the psychological effect of making Caledonians feel closer to France than ever before.[17] It is to the American troops who were stationed in New Caledonia during the Pacific war that the territory owes its airfield infrastructure. Army engineers improved the Tontouta airfield and built four smaller ones in the southern and western parts of the island. Of these, the one with the greatest potential importance was that of Magenta, 5 kilometers south of Nouméa.

During the years following World War II, New Caledonia's air communications with the outside world burgeoned, but they were soon curtailed by a decrease in the services provided by Air France and Qantas and the cessation of all flights there by Pan American Airways. This retrogression was caused mainly by the inadequacy of the territory's airfields, which in turn was due to the authorities' failure to make improvements in them to keep abreast of the rapidly growing demands of international aviation. As early as 1948, New Caledonia's parliamentarians in Paris had been urging prompt action, but the French government could not reach a decision as to which of the Caledonian airfields—Tontouta or Magenta—should be developed. Opinion on the subject, both locally and in Paris, remained divided until 1955, when a decision in favor of Tontouta was finally made.[18] In the meantime, the number of planes using that airfield had fallen in a single year from 250 to 28, and New Caledonia virtually lost its external air communications. The only local activity in aviation

[16] See *Bulletin du Commerce de la Nouvelle-Calédonie,* April 3, 1967.
[17] *L'Océanie Française,* May–July 1939.
[18] Minutes of the French Union Assembly, March 3, 1956.

was that of the Aero Club of Nouméa, which possessed a single plane and whose members made up in enthusiasm what they lacked in funds. To encourage them in their efforts to train pilots and mechanics, the general council granted the club a small subsidy.

The years 1955–1956 marked a turning point in the history of New Caledonia's aviation. In September, a local company, TRANSPAC, began a regular service between Nouméa, the main settlements of the Grande Terre, and the Loyalty Islands. It had only one pilot and a single plane, but was able to make a contract with the territory whereby it received considerable financial support in return for its service in carrying passengers and mail. Then, in October 1956, the privately owned French company, Transports Aériens Intercontinentaux (T.A.I.), started a fortnightly service between Paris, New Caledonia, and the E.F.O., and later extended it to include the New Hebrides and Wallis Island. At the end of 1955, work on the Tontouta airfield had been begun, and the authorities foresightedly anticipated its utilization by jet planes of commercial airlines services. Similarly, in mid-1969, they lengthened the Tontouta runway so that it can now receive "jumbo jets."

During the 1960s, New Caledonia continued to make rapid progress in both internal and international flights. When TRANSPAC (soon to be renamed Air Calédonie) celebrated its tenth anniversary in 1964, its record was unblemished by a single accident. During the preceding decade it had carried 32,000 passengers and 640 tons of freight on regular flights—some daily and some twice weekly—between Nouméa, the Isle of Pines, Lifou, Maré, Ouvéa, Houaïlou, Poindimié, Koné, and Koumac.[19] It announced plans to buy additional planes and was already improving the east-coast airstrips.

Internationally, New Caledonia is now served by four companies, three foreign and one French. Air New Zealand maintains weekly flights between Nouméa and Auckland, and the Caledonian capital is linked with Sydney, also weekly, by jet service provided alternately by Qantas and the Union des Transports Aériens (U.T.A.). The latter company was born in 1963 of the union between T.A.I. and the Union Aéromaritime des Transports (U.A.T.), which, in agreement with Air France, then divided between them the air services between France and the former French colonies. In 1967, Pan American re-

[19] *La Nouvelle-Calédonie et Dépendances* (La Documentation Française), p. 17.

sumed its service to New Caledonia by scheduling stops there on its weekly flights between San Francisco and Australia. The Tontouta airfield now handles traffic amounting annually to about 50,000 passengers and a thousand tons of freight and mail.

32

Labor

The history of labor in New Caledonia has been marked by several distinct phases. The first was that of the penitentiary regime, when there was an abundance of cheap penal labor in the colony. Then, in 1897, the advent of a civilian governor, who encouraged white agricultural colonization, gave rise to the institution of forced labor by the Melanesians. In addition, Asian coolies were imported under contract in numbers which assumed massive proportions during the interwar period. Between 1924 and 1929, the number of Asian laborers in New Caledonia tripled, and in the latter year they totaled more than the entire European population. To finance their immigration, many settlers and mine owners became heavily indebted, and when the depression struck New Caledonia in the early 1930s the Banque de l'Indochine refused them further credit. Consequently, between 1930 and 1932, more than 3,000 Asians were repatriated as their contracts expired, entailing a heavy loss to the colony of producers and consumers. When prosperity returned to New Caledonia during the middle years of that decade, the recruiting of Asian coolies was resumed. On the eve of World War II, the immigrant Asian population numbered 9,996—an appreciable increase over the depression years but still far below its 1929 peak of 14,535.

In 1927, Governor Guyon persuaded the general councilors to accept his "bold and radical" proposal to permit some of the indentured laborers to remain in the colony as free residents. Conservative councilors feared that a free Asian community would cause a difficult problem of control and also occupy too much of New Caledonia's limited arable land. Guyon convincingly argued that such a liberal measure would disprove current criticism that Caledonians maltreated their Asian laborers and, even more cogently, he pointed out that the free Asians would form a stable labor reserve. As a matter of fact, few Asian immigrants took advantage of this offer, and as of 1937 they totaled only 972, of whom 639 were Javanese and 333 Annamites.[1] The only other noteworthy development of that period was the application to New Caledonia in the late 1930s of some of the Popular Front government's liberal labor legislation, but it had almost no effect on the status of New Caledonia's immigrant workers.

The outbreak of World War II prevented further Asian immigration as well as the repatriation of those laborers whose contracts expired during the war years. The need to provision the Allied forces in the Pacific forced the pace of New Caledonia's mineral production, and this not only canceled out the small improvements made in the Asians' living and working conditions during the preceding years but intensified the coercive aspect of their labor. With the ending of the Pacific war, however, their status, as well as in that of the Melanesians, was profoundly transformed. The negative aspects of this transformation were perhaps more significant than the positive. The abolition of the indenture system and of forced labor was followed by the creation of new institutions to apply some of France's liberal postwar labor legislation to New Caledonia. Of the greatest immediate impact was the freedom newly given to Asian and Melanesian workers to move about the Grande Terre and choose the type of employment—if any— which they cared to accept. The next development, and one even more far-reaching in its effects, was the departure of the great majority of Asian immigrants, drawn back to their home countries by nostalgia and a new-found patriotism.

Those Javanese and Vietnamese who chose to remain in New Caledonia have been progressively leaving their jobs in mining and public works for employment in other occupations. All subsequent efforts by private employers and the French government to revive the current of Asian immigration failed. Gradually, replacements for the Asians were found among the Oceanians, but to attract the latter to the Grande Terre it was necessary to improve greatly the wages and working conditions there.

These improvements, together with the mechanization of the mining industry, have brought new elements into the labor market, mainly young Melanesians and white Caledonians from the hinterland areas, who have gravitated to the mining camps and to the Doniambo smelter at Nouméa. The overall effects of this marked change in the labor picture are a decline in agricultural production, both for domestic consumption and for export, and a weakening of the structures of rural

[1] *L'Océanie Française*, March–April 1939.

society, European as well as Melanesian. At the same time, the remarkable progress of nickel exports and that of labor legislation has
given New Caledonia's wage-earners such high living standards that
they no longer welcome immigrants whose competition might jeopardize the gains they have made. (The composition of New Caledonia's
nonindigenous working force, as of January 1967, is shown in table
11.) Their current prosperity, however, as well as that of the whole
territory, depends upon a steady expansion of the mining industry.

TABLE 11

New Caledonia: Nonindigenous wage earners,
as of January 1, 1967

Nationality or ethnic group	Men	Women	Total
Indonesians	876	173	1,049
Vietnamese	399	61	460
Italians	111	5	116
Spaniards	20	3	23
Portuguese	3	2	5
Others	162	29	191
	1,571	273	1,834

Source: *Bulletin du Commerce de la Nouvelle-
Calédonie,* Oct. 4, 1967.

Today the economy of New Caledonia still suffers from a lack of
trained workers, as well as from the instability and heterogeneous
composition of its labor force, but it is no longer handicapped by an
inadequate supply of unskilled wage-earners. Furthermore, from
being technically and socially one of the most backward European
colonies, New Caledonia now ranks among the most advanced territories in the Pacific as regards its equipment and labor legislation.
It is noteworthy that in effecting this rapid transformation, politics and
trade unions have played a role secondary to that of economic forces.

THE INDIGENOUS MELANESIANS

The numerical decline in the Melanesian population and the administration's recognition of its responsibility for the disintegration of
tribal society gradually led to a mitigation of its earlier demands on

native labor. No longer were Melanesian men required to harvest the settlers' coffee crops and labor on public works far from their homes and for an indefinite period, to the detriment of their own crops and their families' well-being. In 1927, some categories of Melanesian society—chiefs, veterans of World War I, permanent employes of the administration and private firms, and fathers of three or more minor children—were wholly exempted. Furthermore, those still subject to prestation could not be required to work for more than two weeks a year or farther than 6 kilometers away from their homes, and they must invariably be provided with food and a minimum wage by their employers.[2]

As the administration progressively became less amenable to the settlers' demands, encouraged native agricultural production, and enacted measures to promote Melanesian welfare, friction developed between the officials and the white planters and herders. Some of the latter, to be sure, recognized that the demands made on the Melanesians had often been abusive, but the majority reproached the administration with neglecting, even with working against, the settlers' legitimate interests.[3] In general, however, private employers had long since become convinced that their best hope of assuring an adequate labor supply lay not with the Melanesians but with the indentured Asian immigrants.

After World War II, the abolition of both the indenture system and forced native labor intensified the settlers' discontent with the government's policy, but for some years they continued to believe that their economic security depended on the administration's providing them with an abundant supply of cheap immigrant laborers. Although they still regarded the Melanesians as an inadequate and unreliable working force, the mining companies were the first to tap this little-utilized source of wage-earners, and in 1938, 30 Loyalty Islanders were employed to work at the Tiébaghi mine. The experiment was so successful that by 1952 there were 540 Melanesians employed in the mining camps, and four years later they constituted one-fifth of New Caledonia's wage-earners.[4] Melanesian workers joined the existing trade unions, and when a strike was called they supported the demands made by laborers of other ethnic groups.

[2] *Ibid.*, November–December 1927.

[3] See the exchange of letters written by *colons, L'Océanie Française,* July–August 1932.

[4] Minutes of the general council, Dec. 1, 1950; *Marchés Coloniaux,* Oct. 24, 1953, p. 2903; Governor Grimald's speech to the general council, May 5, 1956.

Nevertheless, the Melanesians were not so avid for personal gain as were the immigrant Asians, and they continued to prefer farming to wage-earning. In recent years, however, the attitude of the young tribesmen has been changing under the pressures brought to bear by their traditional chiefs. Custom required any Melanesian holding a remunerative position, especially in the administration, to use his earnings for the benefit of his family and clan. The chiefs insisted that the young men who got employment outside the reservations should send back to them for distribution not only their wages but their family allowances as well. Because the young emigrant bachelors preferred to buy consumer goods for their own use, and as they did not qualify for family allowances, the chiefs decided in 1963 to permit only fathers of large families to leave the tribal reservations and become wage-earners.[5]

Although, as of 1965, 11 percent of the wage-earners at Doniambo and 35 percent of the total personnel employed by the Société Le Nickel were Melanesians, the chiefs' decision still further reduced the small number of young and active Melanesians who were contributing to the territory's productivity as wage-earners. The indigenous tribesmen offered the advantage of being geographically the most stable element in New Caledonia's labor force, but had the drawbacks of being less efficient and more prone to drinking and absenteeism than the Loyalty Islanders.

IMMIGRANT WORKERS

Among the deportees in the late nineteenth century, the only group that did not eventually merge with the local population was the Arabs. Most of them live in or near the old penitentiary center of Bourail, where they cling to their Muslim religion and customs and dabble in various occupations. Some Arabs have acquired wealth and an unsavory reputation as unscrupulous speculators in land, keepers of clandestine brothels, and vendors of alcoholic beverages to the Melanesians. Probably they now number no more than a few hundred individuals at most.

The introduction of Asian and Oceanian immigrant workers into New Caledonia was due both to private initiative and governmental action. During Governor Feillet's proconsulship, the first Indians,

[5] Mace, A., "Nouvelle-Calédonie: Ce Paradis du Contribuable est Pourtant un Territoire Français."

Javanese, Tonkinese, and Hebridesians were brought in to provide the farmer-colonists with the labor no longer available from the shrinking ranks of convicts. The 500-odd Indians imported to cultivate sugarcane proved disappointing as laborers, and in any case the sugar planters soon went bankrupt and the British government stopped Indian emigration to the French colonies. The 1911 census included a total of only 112 Indians, and by the eve of World War II their number was further reduced to 85, some of whom were French citizens from the old *comptoirs* of the Coromandel coast. In 1954, a delegation from Fiji came to New Caledonia to see if the territory might offer employment to Fiji's surplus Indian population. The project fell through because the Fijian authorities did not want the Indians to work in the mines, and because the local administration feared it might not be able to stem the influx of Indians once the barriers were let down.[6]

The Japanese

In the last decade of the nineteeenth century, the development of mining in New Caledonia made it imperative to hire more manual laborers. To fill this need, mine-owners at first turned to the Far Eastern countries, such as Japan, whose governments were not so concerned as were the British about the treatment accorded to their nationals in a French colony. In 1892, the Société Le Nickel imported the first group of Japanese laborers under contract. Industrious, sober, and polite, these Japanese immigrants were an immediate success and more were recruited in 1900 and 1902.[7] That they also found New Caledonia congenial was shown by the large number of them who chose to stay on as free residents at the end of their contractual period of service. Many, however, did not long remain laborers but took up trade, and their legal status locally was improved by the Franco-Japanese treaty of 1911, under whose terms the Japanese in New Caledonia were classified as Europeans.

By 1918 the Japanese residents in New Caledonia numbered 2,458, of whom 353 lived in Nouméa and 2,105 in the interior. This numerical and geographical expansion, as well as the competition they were beginning to offer to French merchants, led the government to prohibit further immigration the following year. Their number steadily declined thereafter, and they totaled only 1,126 when the Pacific war broke out. Since unmarried Japanese women were not allowed to

[6] *Pacific Islands Monthly*, January 1954.
[7] *L'Océanie Française*, May–June 1934.

emigrate, and since the local administration refused to recognize the validity of marriages by proxy, the pureblooded Japanese community in New Caledonia remained small.[8] In 1934, 584 of the resident Japanese were still laborers, but 265 farmed the land, 237 were traders and artisans, and 22 were clerks. This widening in the range of their competitive economic activities caused the administration, in 1936, to forbid them to engage in certain occupations and to import unlimited quantities of Japanese goods. However, it was mainly their acquisition of real property, especially mining concessions, that most alarmed the French authorities and local businessmen.

With the rise of Japanese militarism during the 1930s, the Tokyo government began to take a more active interest generally in its overseas nationals and particularly in their mineral production in New Caledonia. In 1932, all the Japanese living there, except the 24 who had become French citizens, were required by their government to join an association that was placed under the control of the Japanese consulate in Australia. The Société Minière de l'Océanie and the Société Le Fer, formed respectively in 1934 and 1938, were Japanese-owned although, in conformity with the local regulations, a majority of their boards of directors were French nationals.[9]

On the eve of World War II, the sharp increase in those companies' exports of iron and nickel ore to Japan, the establishing of a Japanese consulate at Nouméa, the increasing number of Japanese fishermen in Caledonian waters, and the good relations which the ubiquitous Japanese traders were cultivating with the Melanesians—all were related to Japan's growing aggressiveness in the Pacific. Caledonian opinion became so concerned that, late in 1941, the local administration banned further sales of local ores to Japan. After the Pacific war broke out, all the Japanese citizens in New Caledonia were arrested and deported to Australia, their property was seized, and the whole "Japanese problem" was liquidated.

The Javanese

Even before Japanese immigration began to taper off, the New Caledonian authorities were importing Tonkinese and Javanese coolies through agreements made respectively with the French administration in Indochina and the Dutch in the Netherlands Indies. Of all the Asian immigrants, the Javanese have long been regarded as the most

---

[8] As of 1940, of the more than 200 children born in the colony to Japanese fathers, 145 were the offspring of Annamite, Melanesian, and white mothers.

[9] Burchett, W. G., *Pacific Treasure Island*, p. 144.

satisfactory except for tasks requiring great physical stamina. They were the most docile, orderly, and adaptable, and were utilized in such diverse occupations as mining, domestic service, and, above all, farming. Furthermore, they also adapted themselves better to conditions of life in New Caledonia than any other Asian group. Consequently they were and still are the most numerous Asian element and also the most widely distributed throughout the Grande Terre. It was principally the Javanese indentured laborers who accepted Guyon's offer to become free residents, and they founded small farming colonies along the west coast. It was again mainly the Javanese who, after World War II, elected to remain in New Caledonia rather than return to their own country after it became independent.

Only reluctantly did the N.E.I. government agree in 1903 to the recruitment of 300 Javanese for work in New Caledonia. Then and later, the arrangements concerning them were made between the Caledonian immigration bureau and the Batavia administration. The Dutch laid down stringent conditions regarding their transportation at the employer's expense, working hours, and pay, but they empowered the New Caledonia authorities to penalize any Javanese charged with infractions of their contractual obligations. By and large, the working and living conditions for Javanese employed as domestic servants were better—or less bad—than those for mining and agricultural laborers. Periodically, a Dutch official was sent to check on the situation of Javanese laborers in New Caledonia, but his inspection tours were usually superficial. Indeed, according to Governor Guyon, the main criticism offered by the Dutch inspector concerned the French employers whose "familiarity" with their Javanese employes, he claimed, harmed the white man's prestige.[10]

The number of Javanese working in New Caledonia reached a peak of 7,602 in 1929, but by the end of 1933 repatriations and death had reduced their number to 3,541. An upturn in New Caledonia's economy in 1934–1935 led to negotiations for a renewal of Javanese immigration. This time the Dutch authorities eliminated the French administration's right to punish delinquent Javanese laborers, but they did not succeed in reducing the duration of contracts from five to three years or in increasing the pay. New Caledonian employers, for their part, managed to lower the Dutch charges for the recruitment and transport of Javanese coolies, but in economic terms the latter were still too costly for the services they rendered.

At the end of World War II, there were in New Caledonia 3,602

[10] *L'Océanie Française*, July–August, September–October 1928.

Javanese engaged in mining, 2,170 in agriculture, 312 in public works, 280 in trade, and 685 in private employment.[11] Even before the Pacific war ended, the Dutch showed that they were going to be far less permissive than before if Javanese emigration to New Caledonia were to be resumed at all. In the spring of 1945, the Dutch inspector who visited New Caledonia succeeded in getting the Société Le Nickel to build better housing for its workers and no longer to employ Javanese women in its mines and smelter. In the early postwar years, however, the position of both the Dutch and the Javanese in the Pacific was changing drastically. New French laws now permitted the Javanese in New Caledonia to live in Nouméa, and also to choose jobs in the interior that offered the most advantageous conditions. Many of them left the island for home, and by mid-1948 some 2,000 Javanese had been repatriated. Their departure was not offset the following year by the immigration of 600 Javanese for a three-year period, and at greatly improved wages.

The second Dutch "police action" in 1949 marked the beginning of the end of the Netherlands' control over the East Indies. Thereafter the government of independent Indonesia refused to authorize any further emigration, despite the numerous missions sent there by New Caledonian employers. Concurrently, there was a marked change in the occupations of those who remained in the territory. By 1955, the total number of Javanese in New Caledonia had fallen to 2,900, of whom only 800 were manual laborers.[12] Although by then about half of them lived in Nouméa, they remained a more rural community than any of the other Asian immigrant groups. As conditions in Indonesia worsened, more Javanese voluntarily emigrated to New Caledonia, but the growth in their community there was largely due to natural increase. The 1963 census showed that the Javanese then numbered 3,563, of whom at least one-third were women and children, and 1,900 of the total lived in Nouméa.

A study of the Noumean Javanese made by an American anthropologist, Professor Alice Dewey, in 1963–1964 discloses interesting features of the urban component of that group. Professor Dewey found them to be a well-defined cultural community, with no extremes of wealth or poverty, proudly maintaining their distinctive customs.[13]

[11] Faivre, J.-P., J. Poirier, and P. Routhier, *Géographie de la Nouvelle-Calédonie*, p. 228.
[12] Doumenge, F., "L'Economie de la Grande Terre Calédonienne."
[13] *South Pacific Bulletin*, October 1964.

The great majority were Muslims from Central Java, who often met together socially, especially on religious and national holidays. They had no mosque in Nouméa and no formal structure of community authority, although there was a resident Indonesian consul. Probably because they were only discreetly nationalistic and took no part in local politics, they maintained good if distant relations with other ethnic groups. The sole reproach made against the Javanese by the French Caledonians was the slowness with which the older generation among them accepted French culture. The young Javanese, on the other hand, who had attended local schools, were more inclined to adopt a European way of living and to use French rather than Javanese as their means of intercommunication. In all respects other than their delayed assimilability, the Javanese of New Caledonia were generally regarded as a model community.

The Vietnamese [14]

In every respect, the immigration of the Tonkinese presented New Caledonia with thornier problems than did that of the Javanese, although the local administration was dealing with other French officials and not with a foreign government. Almost all of the first 768 brought to the Grande Terre in 1891 were taken from among the prisoners held on Poulo Condore island off the coast of Cochin-China. Reportedly they proved unsatisfactory to the settler responsible for their importation, so it is not surprising that the last census before World War I found only 366 Tonkinese in New Caledonia.

The Grande Terre's economic expansion of the 1920s required a vast increase in its labor force, and the most logical source of such manpower was the overcrowded Tonkin delta in northern Indochina. The main opposition to their emigration came from the French planters of Cochin-China, who wanted to keep in that colony an abundant supply of cheap Tonkinese labor. Nevertheless, sufficient pressure in the name of "imperial solidarity" was brought to bear on the French officials at Hanoi to permit the New Caledonian authorities to recruit under contract a large number of Tonkinese coolies. Although they were engaged under terms generally analogous to those for the Javanese, the Tonkinese were less costly to their employers and physically better suited to working in New Caledonia's mines. Despite

[14] Before World War II, the term "Tonkinese" was used for all the Annamite laborers in New Caledonia, although some of them came from Annam and Cochin-China. After 1945, they were called Vietnamese.

these advantages, fewer Tonkinese were imported into the Grande Terre, and even in 1929—the peak year for all Asian immigrants— only 6,230 Tonkinese were employed there, as against 7,690 Javanese. Employers' preference for the latter was due to the Tonkinese laborers' greater resistance to discipline and to the support given in Indochina to their complaints of maltreatment in the Pacific islands.

In 1925, the French government sent a colonial inspector, Delamarre, to investigate these complaints. His report, said to be more favorable to Caledonian than to Hebridesian employers, was never published. Its only visible effect was to permit Tonkinese women to accompany their emigrant husbands, and the recruitment of coolies from the Tonkin delta region continued unabated. Then, on February 3, 1927, the Tonkinese working at the Moindou mines and at Doniambo went on strike. In Nouméa this was attributed to communist propaganda,[15] but it also served to revive the opposition in Indochina to Tonkinese emigration. This time the "crusade" there was led by the Marquis de Monpezat, a member of both the Conseil Supérieur des Colonies and the Indo-China government council, whose important investments in Tonkin were jeopardized by the exodus of local laborers to the Pacific islands.

In a series of articles published in August 1927 in *La Volonté Indochinoise*, which he owned, Monpezat described in gruesome detail the conditions under which this "yellow-slave trade" was being conducted. He alleged that, on the ships transporting the Tonkinese coolies and in the islands' mines and plantations, they lacked medical care, proper food, and any respect for their most elementary rights, and that in New Caledonia they were brutally treated by their Kanaka foremen. The New Caledonia administration promptly denied these charges, claiming that it had always taken steps to remedy any abuses called to its attention. Furthermore, the officials in Indochina who examined the repatriated Tonkinese reported them to be healthier than when they had left, and in any case they were better off in New Caledonia than they had been in Tonkin.[16] If there were any complaints, it was further said in rebuttal, they should come from Caledonian employers, who found their Tonkinese laborers given to gambling, violent quarrels, and feigned illness when they should be working at their jobs.[17]

In 1930, the whole question became largely academic because of the

15 *L'Océanie Française,* July–October 1928.
16 *Ibid.,* January–February 1930.
17 *Ibid.,* March–April 1929.

world depression. Not only did it put an end to the recruitment of Tonkinese, but 1,975 of them were repatriated during the following year. Unlike the Javanese, the Tonkinese showed little inclination to remain in New Caledonia, and by the end of 1930, 94 of the 184 free residents had left the Grande Terre permanently. The Tonkinese had come to New Caledonia simply to earn money and to return home with their savings. They had never established cordial relations with either the Melanesians or the Javanese, whom they regarded as inferiors and who, in turn, disliked and feared them as aggressive competitors.[18] Even after more Tonkinese were recruited in the mid-1930s —at an even lower pay scale than before—their number in New Caledonia on the eve of World War II (3,471 indentured laborers and 285 free residents) was not much more than half of what it had been a decade before.

Between June 1940 and January 1946, there was no coolie traffic in either direction between New Caledonia and Indochina, but during that interval the Tonkinese colony in the Grande Terre grew through natural increase by more than 1,000 persons. Their repatriation being impossible and their contracts having expired during the war, the indentured Tonkinese laborers tried to leave their jobs and obtain employment with the American forces, which offered them ten times as much pay.[19] This they were forcibly prevented from doing, and the result was a series of strikes in the mining industry, which employed 36 percent of all the Tonkinese laborers at the time.

Much of this labor agitation was locally attributed to the Tunicas,[20] who diligently propagandized communism among the indentured workers during the war. It was probably they who initiated the two attempts by New Caledonia's Tonkinese community to enlist the sympathies of the American military command in their behalf. The excellent French style of the second letter, sent on March 14, 1944, to the general commanding the American forces in Nouméa—which contained a reference to Abraham Lincoln—could hardly have originated with the illiterate coolies whose names were appended to it.[21] Because they had no way, the letter stated, of making their voices heard by the French government, they asked the American general to follow Lincoln's example of freeing the slaves and to intervene on their behalf with General de Gaulle.

[18] Doumenge, F., "Vietnamiens et Indiens en Mélanésie."
[19] Oliver, D. L., *The Pacific Islands*, p. 378.
[20] See p. 277.
[21] Excerpts were published in the *Pacific Islands Monthly*, September 1945.

By failing to comply with the Tonkinese pleas, the local Americans found themselves in the awkward position of seeming to support forced labor. Because New Caledonia's mineral output was considered vital to the war effort, they cooperated with the mining companies and the French administration to suppress a strike at Doniambo on April 1, 1945. A few months later, however, the imminent end of the Pacific war obviated any further need for such coercion, and indeed by July 5, 1945, all the indentured laborers were freed to seek work when and where they pleased. Most of the Tonkinese workers quickly deserted the mines and the plantations and moved to the towns, especially to Nouméa, where they eventually became merchants or artisans. Consequently mineral production fell rapidly and crops went unharvested because the mine-owners and planters claimed that they could not pay the "exorbitant" wages now demanded by the free laborers. The angry and alarmed general councilors vainly pleaded with the administration to compel the Tonkinese and Javanese to return to their former jobs, but all they could obtain was an official promise in January 1947 to grant no more trading licenses to competitive Asians.[22]

On the whole, the Tonkinese and Javanese were less interested in earning a living in New Caledonia than in returning home, and this was more true of the former than of the latter. Despite the shipping shortage in late 1945 and early 1946, some 1,800 Tonkinese were repatriated, but after the outbreak of hostilities in Indochina in December of the latter year, the French refused to send any more back to an area controlled by the Viet Minh. The declaration of independence by the Democratic Republic of North Vietnam simply intensified the demand for repatriation by the local Vietnamese, as they were now called, and that regime's appeal was further enhanced by the propaganda clandestinely circulated in such Viet Minh newspapers as *Phuoc Quoc* and *Vietnam Hon.*[23] In reply to a questionnaire sent out by the immigration bureau in 1947, all but 13 of the Vietnamese opted for repatriation. However, when the last convoy of repatriates to depart for some years left Nouméa at the end of 1950, the Vietnamese community in New Caledonia numbered 2,935, of whom 847 were children, but it did not long remain stabilized geographically, numerically, or occupationally.

The marked orientation of the Vietnamese to trade, their concen-

[22] Minutes of the general council, Jan. 27, 1947.
[23] Doumenge, "Vietnamiens et Indiens en Mélanésie," and Furnas, J. C., *Anatomy of Paradise*, p. 368.

tration in Nouméa, and their crystallization as a foreign cultural community strongly impregnated with communism gradually transformed what had been the Caledonians' fears of the Vietnamese economic competition into outright hostility. As the war in Indochina dragged on and the local Vietnamese lost hope of early repatriation, they invested their capital in urban real estate, trade, and industry. When they celebrated the tenth anniversary of the outbreak of the Indochina war in 1956, their community included 391 licensed merchants compared with 97 in 1947, and totaled some 5,000 persons, of whom nearly half were children. The Caledonians' pervasive resentment of this community as a whole was heightened by the presence of so many Vietnamese children in Nouméa's schools, especially as their academic record was usually better than that of other pupils.

All the foregoing factors contributed to making the repatriation of the Vietnamese increasingly a political issue in New Caledonia, and a local Comité de la Défense des Interêts Calédoniens was formed specifically to put pressure on the authorities into hastening their departure.[24] Another evidence of the widespread anti-Vietnamese local feeling was the unanimous vote by the territorial assembly in November 1956 of a heavy annual tax of 2,400 C.F.P. francs on foreign residents. Inasmuch as its main target was obviously the Vietnamese community in New Caledonia, and as the Saigon government wanted no more of them sent back to the Viet Minh-controlled area, President Ngo Dinh Diem threatened retaliatory measures against French interests in South Vietnam. He would agree to the repatriation only of those emigrants who chose to return to Saigon, but a poll taken by the Nouméa administration in 1957 showed that the great majority of the Caledonian Vietnamese still wanted to return to the north.[25]

On Lenormand's initiative, the government council decided in April 1958 to break the deadlock by sending a three-man delegation to Hanoi to negotiate directly the repatriation of Caledonian Vietnamese to North Vietnam. This independent action angered the Paris government, which promptly disavowed the U.C. mission and forced the resignation of the minister of finance, who had headed the delegation.[26] The ensuing stalemate created by the attitude of the Paris government, the Diem regime, and the Caledonian Vietnamese lasted for 2 more years. By 1960 the local Vietnamese community had grown to

[24] *Pacific Islands Monthly,* January 1957.
[25] *Ibid.,* April 1958.
[26] Brou, R., "La Société Moderne en Nouvelle-Calédonie en 1966," p. 9.

some 6,000 persons, of whom 74 percent lived in Nouméa, where more than half of its active male members were engaged in trade and the balance in industry and transport.[27] Finally, in that year, arrangements were made for the departure of three convoys which carried 1,637 Vietnamese back to Indochina. Because the great majority of them had chosen to go to North Vietnam, where they were given a hero's welcome, the Saigon government in April 1961 once more put a stop to the repatriation operations. This decision dealt a heavy blow to those forced to remain in New Caledonia, for in anticipation of their imminent departure they had liquidated most of their possessions there.

After another 2-year interruption, negotiations for their repatriation were resumed, this time with added pressure from the Caledonian administration and mining companies. In 1962 the nickel industry was undergoing such a serious recession that employers, who had previously offered every inducement to Vietnamese laborers to remain, were now anxious to speed them on their way.[28] As before, however, the Saigon government moved with the utmost deliberation, and it was not until March 1963 that it sent a representative to New Caledonia to study the situation anew and to open an office in Nouméa. As this step seemed to foreshadow the establishment of a consulate in the Caledonian capital, the territorial assembly hastily voted its opposition to the appointment of any Vietnamese consul to Nouméa, whether by the Saigon or the Hanoi government. Diem's assassination in November 1963 removed the last stumbling block to the repatriation of all the local Vietnamese who still wanted to return to North Vietnam. However, by that time, some unfavorable reports they had received from relatives living in the Hanoi area about conditions there caused some of them to change their minds. Finally, in February 1964, all those who persevered in their initial decision left Nouméa, carrying with them an astonishing array of consumer goods that included automobiles, bicycles, clothing, medicines, and even food.[29]

The departure of the Vietnamese who had been mining laborers and market gardeners somewhat adversely affected New Caledonia's productivity, but it also lightened the territory's commercial structure and the overcrowding of Nouméa's schools. Of the 972 who chose to remain in New Caledonia, 837 lived in the capital, 288 were men, 197 women, and 457 children.[30] Most of them were Catholics, and 435 of

27 Doumenge, "Vietnamiens et Indiens en Mélanésie."
28 *Marchés Tropicaux*, May 19, 1962, p. 1102.
29 *Ibid.*, Feb. 29, 1964, p. 424.
30 *Pacific Islands Monthly*, September 1964.

those born in New Caledonia promptly applied for French nationality. As of 1967, 399 men and 61 women were wage-earners, but many will probably take up commerce and crafts when they have amassed enough capital. Given the now almost equal sex ratio and their tendency to proliferate, the Vietnamese community in New Caledonia is expected to grow rapidly. Since most of their children will be French citizens and are being educated in local schools, it is hoped that they will become a more stable and assimilable element, culturally and politically, than their parents. Should this prove to be the case, they could make a valuable contribution to the territory, which sorely needs their dynamism, industry, and skills.

LEGISLATION AND OFFICIAL CONTROLS

During the years when first convicts and later indentured Asians constituted almost all of New Caledonia's labor force, it was regulated by laws that bore little relation to fluctuating economic conditions. As for the immigrant Asian laborers, the regulations applied to them were embodied in the agreements made by the French government with the administrations of the Netherlands Indies and Indochina. For the far smaller free-labor market in New Caledonia, the local administration and general council determined most of the rules.

This intricate mass of legislation was aimed chiefly at providing the colony with the maximum number of manual laborers at the lowest possible cost to the colonial administration and to their employers. Moreover, the efficacy of such laws as regulated the working and living conditions of contract laborers and also of requisitioned Melanesians depended on their application. Because the Dutch and French officials sent to inspect New Caledonia's mines and plantations made only rare and largely perfunctory tours, they exercised no real control over the laborers' situation. Furthermore, because disciplinary authority over non-free workers had been vested in the local administration— which in turn entrusted it to employers in the case of contract laborers and to the *syndics* in that of the Melanesians—officials intervened only on the rare occasions when extreme abuses had been called to their attention. As for the labor unions which might have defended the workers' interests, only white salaried employes were permitted to organize them. Thus, in practice, the vast majority of manual workers in New Caledonia were subjected to an arbitrary regime against which they had no recourse.

When defending this system against its critics, the New Caledonian administration and employers usually pointed to the number of immigrant laborers who voluntarily renewed their contracts. Indeed, more than half the Javanese and Tonkinese usually did sign up for another 5-year engagement, but this hardly proved that they were satisfied with the indenture system. Some of them undoubtedly had become so indebted to their employers, either at the company store or through the penalties imposed on them for alleged breaches of contract, that they had no choice but to remain and work off their obligations. Probably the main motive behind such renewals of contracts was their realization that conditions in their home colonies were even worse, and that eventually they would carry back with them that portion of their pay which had been withheld until their repatriation. Except during World War II, they were duly repatriated at the expense of their employers when their contracts expired. The law required that employers pay a fixed amount per year for each coolie in their service to the immigration bureau, which handled the transport operations. The only other relevant official organization in New Caledonia until the eve of the Pacific war was the Office du Travail, which had been created in 1934 as a labor exchange for the few hundred free Asian residents who sought employment.

If wage-earners in the colony were almost totally unorganized, their employers, on the contrary, had strong organizations, in the form either of mining companies with large funds and influence or of the Syndicat Agricole for planters and ranchers. The latter organization in particular aroused the ire of those officials who tried to see that employers carried out their contractual obligations. In general, it was the big employers of labor who complied with the regulations and the small, dispersed planters and mine-owners whose abuses of their authority escaped official detection.

The socialist government of the Popular Front in the mid-1930s introduced liberal labor legislation in France, of which some measures were made applicable to New Caledonia. Among these were the laws of June 20 and 21, 1936, which instituted family allowances, the 40-hour working week, and paid vacations. This decision caused widespread consternation among Caledonian employers, who claimed that they were already sufficiently generous to their employes, and among the general councilors, who asked that the new laws be applied only gradually and "liberally" to the colony.[31] Shortly afterwards, the

[31] L'Océanie Française, November–December 1936.

franc's devaluation caused such a sharp rise in local living costs that business firms in Nouméa were forced to increase salaries, and the administration briefly toyed with a project to freeze the prices of necessities.

Although comparatively few of the Popular Front laws were introduced into New Caledonia, their addition to the already confused mass of decrees, regulations, and administrative orders made it necessary to devise some new mechanism to simplify the labor legislation and supervise its application. In 1937 the general council accepted the administration's proposal to establish a labor bureau, whose officials were to analyze the colony's labor needs for the next 5 years and to study projects to improve vocational training in the colony. The new bureau was to include a labor inspector, who was to replace the head of the mines service, until then responsible for the application of all labor laws in the colony.

World War II prevented this bureau from materializing, and indeed canceled out such progressive labor measures as existed at the time by restoring, for example, the 60-hour working week. It was the abolition of the indenture system, forced labor, and the *indigénat* in 1946—albeit a negative move—which had a revolutionary effect on New Caledonia's economy. As regards more positive Metropolitan legislation favoring New Caledonia's wage-earners, they had to wait 6 more years, until the Overseas Labor Code of December 1952 was finally enacted.

Meanwhile, the growing need to attract more laborers to the territory induced the local administration and general council to initiate some progressive measures. These included the establishment of a labor inspectorate, limited family allowances, and a labor court to arbitrate disputes between employers and employes. This progressive trend gathered momentum throughout the 1950s and 1960s. Family allowances were granted to all wage-earners regardless of ethnic origin (1954); facilities were set up for the rapid training of unskilled workers (1955); and wage-earners in the private as well as the public sector benefited by a provident fund, pensions for aged workers, work-accident and health insurance (1961), and a fourth week of paid vacations (1963).

Concurrently, New Caledonia acquired new organizations through which wage-earners could participate in proposing welfare legislation and in maintaining satisfactory industrial relations. For the purpose of consultation on all matters affecting the health and safety of workers in a given industry, an advisory labor committee, made up of an equal number of employers and employes and headed by the labor inspector, was formed, as well as a technical committee of similar composition (with the addition of government officials). From lists submitted by the most representative trade unions, workers chose their representatives to share in the management of the funds related to family allowances and work accidents, and also in the operation of the labor bureau. Wage levels were pegged to a periodically revised cost-of-living index, which included such "luxury" items as tobacco, gasoline, and theatre tickets, as well as basic necessities. Thus, by the middle 1960s, New Caledonia had moved within the relatively short span of 20 years from being one of the most backward European colonies as regards labor to the position of one of the most advanced territories in the Pacific, offering wage-earners a standard of living comparable with that prevailing in Australia and New Zealand.[32]

LABOR ORGANIZATIONS

The spectacular progress made since World War II by New Caledonia's wage-earners in respect to working and living conditions has been based almost wholly upon liberal legislation, inspired for the most part by the shortage of local labor and very little by trade-union activity. Even before the war, unions—because they were few in number, poorly organized, and composed wholly of white members— played a very minor role in the Grande Terre. Not only were the indentured laborers forbidden by law to organize, but on the few occasions when strikes were called by the white unions they were used as scabs. The contempt in which the white Caledonians held manual labor, and the type of education they received in the colony's schools, fitted them only for white-collar occupations. Some of them held jobs in the administration and others in commercial and industrial firms, and despite their small number they suffered from unemployment during the depression. Japanese artisans supplied the colony's needs for craftsmen, Metropolitan French officials denied them access to the top posts in the civil service and even in the ranks of the gendarmerie, and half-caste Tonkinese, Japanese, and Javanese clerks were preferred by European employers because they would accept lower wages. In the mid-1920s, Florino Paladini organized a Fédération des Syndicats Calédoniens among them, but it was never an effective organization.

[32] Mace, A., "Nouvelle-Calédonie."

Most of New Caledonia's few prewar strikes were initiated by Tonkinese laborers who, through their concentration in the mining industry and their ethnic solidarity, were able to take action even though they could not form a trade union. During World War II, the Tunicas helped them to organize and gave them a radical political orientation that became obvious during the strikes at the Tiébaghi mine and the Doniambo smelter in 1944–1945. France's postwar legislation included the right of all overseas workers to organize unions and to strike, and this enabled Paladini in 1946 to revive his union and place it under the auspices of the Confédération Générale du Travail (C.G.T.). Consequently, for the first time, organized labor was a party that year to the wage negotiations carried on between the mining companies and the free Asian workers. The French communist party, however, did not consider New Caledonia a sufficiently fertile field to send its emissaries there to organize unions as it did in the French African territories and Madagascar. This was also the view of the other major French labor federations, which never established branches in the territory. Later, when Gabriel Moussot came from France and tried to organize labor in the nickel industry according to the French model, he made no headway because such a pattern was unsuited to the situation in New Caledonia and because Caledonians were always suspicious of Metropolitan influences. Some local unions have agreed to affiliate with analogous organizations in France, but they have never accepted directives from them and remain purely Caledonian groupings in their form and objectives.

In the first years following World War II, New Caledonian unions did play some part in effecting improvements in the minimum wage ("SMIG," or *salaire minimum interprofessionelle garanti*) and in calling strikes when employers proved unamenable to negotiation. The longest such strike was the three-month work stoppage by Vietnamese workers at the Tiébaghi mine, and it ended with partial satisfaction of the laborers' demands for higher wages and longer paid vacations. In 1955 and 1956, strikes occurred at the Thio mines, the Doniambo smelter, and the Yaté dam, and in 1964, 1966, and 1967 at Nouméa and Doniambo. It is noteworthy that comparatively few of these strikes concerned wage increases, the great majority of them simultaneously affected the mines and the smelters, and beginning in 1955 they were supported by wage-earners belonging to all the ethnic groups. Caledonian employers were both surprised and alarmed that dispersed European, Melanesian, Vietnamese and Javanese workers could display such solidarity in the defense of their common occupational interests.[33] The strikes of 1955 and 1956 were the result of the workers' insistence on better working and living conditions, mainly in the mining industry, but those of 1961 and 1967 had other origins. When Governor Pechoux in 1961 tried to get the Conseil d'Etat to annul a law passed by the territorial assembly instituting pensions for aged workers, a strike was called by the employes of both the mining industry and mercantile firms. The 1967 strike at Thio stemmed from the fact that the laborers there took offense at disparaging remarks by a European engineer concerning a recently organized union.[34] In 1966 the Doniambo workers went on strike because Le Nickel opposed the unionization of its laborers.[35]

Generally speaking, by the mid-1960s there was no longer any need for workers to strike on behalf of higher pay and better living conditions, and in any case labor disputes more often than not were settled by arbitration. Wages, already higher than those in France for analogous occupations, rose automatically with the cost-of-living index, and family allowances (see table 12) were twice as large as in the Metropole and were a main stimulus for Tahitian and Wallisian immigration. New Caledonia's total wage bill had risen from 1,721 million C.F.P. francs in 1959 to 3,660 millions in 1966,[36] although the number of wage-earners had not even doubled during that period. To be sure, Caledonian wage-earners were not wholly devoid of grievances, but most of their complaints were minor. They claimed, for example, that wage increases lagged too far behind the cost of living and were not based on a sufficiently wide range of essential commodities. Then another strike at Doniambo in January 1969 showed their dissatisfaction with the amount of their rent allowance, as well as their insistence on effective price controls. Despite such desiderata, New Caledonia's wage-earners have enjoyed—except in 1962—full employment for more than a decade and one of the highest living standards among the so-called underdeveloped countries. In his report for 1969 to shareholders, the president of Le Nickel claimed that "generally speaking, a Caledonian worker's purchasing power is about double that of a Metropolitan worker of approximately the same capacity." [37]

[33] *Pacific Islands Monthly,* May 1955.
[34] *Peuples du Monde,* May 1967.
[35] *Le Monde,* Oct. 18, 1966.
[36] Guiart, J., "L'Emploi en Nouvelle-Calédonie."
[37] *Le Monde,* June 24, 1970.

TABLE 12

New Caledonia: Family Allowances, as of 1966

Population group	Families receiving allowances	Children per family
Europeans	3,593	2.59
Melanesians	2,438	3.29
Wallisians	581	3.52
Tahitians	391	3.08
Aliens	44	2.52

Source: Data issued by Family Allowance and Accident Insurance Fund, reproduced in Guiart, "L'Emploi en Nouvelle-Calédonie." Guiart considers the data on Wallisians and Tahitians as defective.

Since the end of World War II, progressive labor legislation, originating both in France and locally, has been responsible for such substantial benefits to New Caledonia's wage-earners that there has been no need for union agitation. Although the Fédération Calédonienne du Travail supported and was supported by the Union Calédonienne, it was not that federation but the party which was the spur for the legislative improvements. The unions of New Caledonia, unlike those of French Polynesia, have neither the backing of Metropolitan labor federations nor that of the Christian missions.[38] Actually the Caledonian labor unions are not politically oriented and have little impact on the local situation. They are fragmented by personal dissensions among their leaders, their membership is unstable, and they frequently change names and officials. Many of them have only a nominal existence, and only three—the Fédération Calédonienne du Travail, the Union des Syndicats Autonomes, and perhaps the Syndicat des Travailleurs d'Outre-Mer—carry any real weight. Indeed, only a fraction of New Caledonia's wage-earners belong to any union at all, for organized labor there cannot lay claim to achievements that would attract large numbers of members. The sole activity in which unions have been effective independently of any political group is their long and successful opposition to the immigration of European competitors, specifically Italians and *pieds noirs*.

[38] In May 1965, Mgr. Martin told the writers that the Catholic mission had organized no Christian workers' union in New Caledonia because it had become disillusioned with the evolution of the so-called Christian labor federation in Tahiti, over which it had no control.

The generally enviable situation of New Caledonia's wage-earners today has momentarily disguised but has not eliminated the territory's perennial labor problems. These have been created by the small size, lack of skills, and instability of its labor force. Although the forms assumed by these problems are undergoing rapid change, their physical and psychological causes are still much the same as they have been during the past half-century. Most of New Caledonia's current labor difficulties are highlighted by the ever-more-dominant position of the mining industry, and because the outlook for that industry is now so favorable, the problems created by its already overwhelming importance are likely to be intensified rather than attenuated.

Today there is not one source of employment in New Caledonia, with the possible exception of the civil service, that does not depend directly or indirectly on the territory's maintaining a high level of nickel exports. Because New Caledonia is still underpopulated, the mining companies must offer high wages that both attract immigrants from less-favored nearby islands and drain workers from the territory's rural regions, to the detriment of agricultural production. For some years the minimum wage in New Caledonia has been 75 percent higher than in France, and the mining companies pay even their unskilled workers considerably more than the SMIG.

Oceania, and no longer Asia, is now the main source of the territory's immigrant laborers, and though there are enough of them to meet current needs for unskilled workers, they remain unstable both geographically and occupationally. Oceanian immigrants are becoming more deeply rooted in New Caledonia, but the Polynesians in particular still return to their home islands whenever conditions there are propitious for their employment. Occupationally, too, they tend to follow the example of the earlier Asian immigrants, leaving manual work as soon as they are able to take up trade and crafts. Thus there is a constant turnover in this category of employment as fresh immigration is required to fill the ranks that they are deserting. More indigenous Melanesians than ever before are now employed by the mining industry, and this trend will doubtless be intensified, for their rapidly growing numbers are outstripping the capacity of their land reservations to support them. Nevertheless, they do not yet find wage-earning particularly congenial; hence they are unlikely to become a sizeable and stable element in the labor picture within the near future.

The economic opportunities created by the growth of the mining industry in recent years are reflected in the phenomenal increase in the number of firms and wage-earners in New Caledonia. In 1959 there were 1,504 employers and 12,093 employes, whereas in 1966 the former numbered 2,383 and the latter 20,202.[39] Even taking into account the deficiencies noted in table 13, it is clear that the number of wage-earners engaged in farming and herding declined by half during that period, and that those in the building industry, transportation, trade, and public services each far outnumbered the personnel employed in mining.

TABLE 13

NEW CALEDONIA: EMPLOYMENT, BY OCCUPATIONS, 1966

Occupation	Employers	Wage-earners
Agriculture and herding	246	811
Building	290	2,584
Trade	376	2,784
Transportation	123	984 [a]
		2,096 [b]
Office work	48	452
Liberal professions	43	226
Public services	122	2,826
Domestic service	950	1,115
Mining	38	1,940
Minor enterprises	147	3,946

[a] Permanent.   [b] Temporary.

Source: Data issued by Family Allowance and Accident Insurance Fund, reproduced in Guiart, "L'Emploi en Nouvelle-Calédonie." Guiart warns that the figures on employment in mining and agriculture were supplied only by the main mining companies and big ranchers and do not include many temporary workers or those employed by certain small enterprises. Furthermore, he believes that the figure given for the number of domestic workers is lower than was actually the case.

Nevertheless, the relative importance of the various occupational categories cannot be gauged solely on a numerical basis. This is true not only because the capacity to employ labor in so many of New Caledonia's enterprises is determined by the fluctuations in the profits made by the mining industry, but also because of the differences in their respective wage scales. Of the territory's entire wage bill in

[39] Guiart, "L'Emploi en Nouvelle-Calédonie."

1966, the Société Le Nickel paid nearly one-third. Between 1954 and 1965 the number of that company's employes rose from 1,800 to 3,500, and in the latter year it employed one-fifth of the territory's wage-earners and provided a livelihood for some 14,000 persons.[40] Inasmuch as the salaries and wages that Le Nickel must pay to attract workers are the major element in its production costs, that company inevitably seeks ways and means to reduce its dependence on human labor. Soon after World War II ended, its directors realized that the advantageous prewar conditions in regard to labor could never be restored. The obvious solution was to mechanize its operations as far and as fast as possible, and this was done in the early 1950s with surprising rapidity and efficiency.

Automation in itself has raised a host of new labor problems for the mining industry, for skilled workers are required to run and repair the machinery. To operate its machines, Le Nickel has drawn heavily on young white Caledonians from the rural communities. Because they do not regard such occupations as manual labor and therefore demeaning, and because they earn far more than from farming, they have come virtually to monopolize such tasks. This development has not only caused agricultural production to decline but has prevented many capable colored workers from moving upward from the un-skilled category. To some extent, therefore, it has canceled out the benefits they might have derived from the recent improvements in the territory's vocational-training facilities. These local facilities, however, have not yet reached the point where they provide higher technical instruction. Consequently, Le Nickel has been bringing in an increasing number of Metropolitan engineers to fill posts at the highest technical level. There is no dearth of qualified candidates for such positions, for the salaries paid by Le Nickel are twice those prevailing in France for the same category of employment, not to mention the offer of free transport to and from New Caledonia for such employes and their families.

Nevertheless, even among the expatriate engineers the turnover has not been any less marked than for unskilled laborers. Some of them came to do a specific job and return home, but others who intended to remain in New Caledonia have not always done so. Such newcomers are regarded with suspicion on two counts—that of being Metropolitan Frenchmen and of offering the local-born dangerous professional competition—and their employment on a scale commensurate with Le

[40] *Marchés Tropicaux*, Sept. 10, 1966, p. 2351.

Nickel's expansion has hardly added to that company's popularity in the territory.

If the mining industry's future development lives up to its present promise, more and more immigrant employes from the various ethnic groups and with varying degrees of skill may be expected to come to New Caledonia. Between 1967 and 1969, the number of employes registered with the Labor Office rose from 18,340 to 22,380. Of these, in the latter year, 9,452 were Europeans, 6,685 Melanesians, 1,139 Tahitians, 1,504 Wallisians, 1,215 Indonesians, 419 Vietnamese, 143 Italians, 24 Spaniards, 5 Portuguese, and 1,794 described as "miscellaneous." [41] In anticipation of an appreciably bigger demand for Metropolitan personnel after the new mining companies are installed in the territory, the restrictions on the entry of qualified European personnel for them were eased by a decree of June 13, 1969. Friction between the immigrants and the natives may well remain in abeyance so long as there are enough well-paid jobs for all, but as many of the newcomers will occupy top-ranking positions, their presence cannot but create jealousy and resentment. In any case, the fact that so many of the wage-earners are transients and can return to their homes during periods of prolonged unemployment is certainly a main advantage of the present system. On the other hand, so long as the Caledonians resist integrating socially either unskilled colored laborers or highly trained white technicians, the territory will lack a stable, trained force of wage-earners.

[41] *Ibid.*, Aug. 2, 1969, p. 2181.

33

Finances and Planning

New Caledonia's financial evolution is in many ways paradoxical, and in this respect the territory is unique among France's dependencies. Because New Caledonia was a penal colony in the late nineteenth century, France accepted responsibility for its finances to a remarkable degree, particularly after the adoption of the law of April 13, 1900, which required all the French colonies to meet their operating expenses from local revenues. As time went on, however, and the number of convict survivors dwindled, France began to treat New Caledonia more like its other dependencies. That is to say, Paris would come to New Caledonia's rescue only in times of economic crisis and lend money to it for public works of general local or imperial interest. Nevertheless, the attitude of successive French governments toward New Caledonia remained distinctive, for of all the colonies it had the largest proportion of white nationals, whose elected representatives were resistant to local administrative and even Metropolitan controls. Only occasionally and on important issues did France intervene to impose its will arbitrarily in Caledonian financial affairs.

As a rule, the Paris authorities permitted the general council to determine the territory's fiscal system, except in regard to the budget's obligatory expenditures and the tariff regulating its trade with France and foreign countries. In the latter respect, particular solicitude was shown for New Caledonia's mining industry, not only because of its long preeminence in the territory's economy, but also because of its increasing importance to French industry and France's foreign policy. As nickel exports mounted, and with them the territory's revenues and investments by private capital, France's policy began to change. Its subsidies to New Caledonia tapered off, and it moved to "safeguard national interests" by controlling the production and orientation of the mining industry. At the same time, however, it was careful not to tamper with the local fiscal system that was working so profitably for all concerned.

Each time France has tried to get a grip on New Caledonia's export earnings in hard currency, as after World War II, or to institute tariff barriers that would curtail the territory's trade with the sterling and the dollar blocs, it has had to backtrack. Successive devaluations of the franc, of which the most recent occurred in August 1969, have usually been followed by the imposition of foreign-exchange controls. Sooner or later they have had to be abandoned, however, because New Caledonia's geographical location makes circumvention easy, notably through exchange of the local currency for Australian dollars in the New Hebrides. Much the same fate has attended the largely abortive attempts by the U.C.-dominated assembly to distribute the fiscal burden more equitably and to force the mining industry to devote more of its profits to the territory's development. Neither France nor the U.C. has dared to risk killing the goose that was laying ever-larger golden eggs. Perforce, both have had to be content with half-measures that have only slightly modified the existing financial system.

The period between the end of the penitentiary regime and the outbreak of World War I was marked by France's attempts to make New Caledonia pay for more of its operating expenses and to reduce France's subsidies to the colony's budget.[1] To compensate for these losses, the general council wanted to raise the export duties on minerals, but for four years Paris delayed granting its permission, and only in 1907 did it resume the payment of subsidies to the territory's operating budget.

To be sure, France had granted a loan of 5 million francs for railroad construction in 1901, but this was only half the amount requested by the colony. In any case, the loan did nothing to ease New Caledonia's straitened budgetary situation, for the concurrent decline in its export trade had sharply reduced territorial revenues. By 1913, however, the colony's financial position could be described as more satisfactory: it had paid its back debts and had balanced its budget amounting to 4.3 million francs. In fact, by the time World War I broke out, New Caledonia's reserve fund had a total of 418,000 francs, and its trade balance was so favorable that the Parliament reduced its subsidy to the budget that year to 85,000 francs.[2]

[1] One such step, taken in 1903, was allegedly motivated by France's intention of making New Caledonia financially responsible for current expenditures in the New Hebrides. See *L'Océanie Française*, August 1911.

[2] *L'Océanie Française*, January–March 1920, October–December 1921.

Although New Caledonia received some income from the tobacco monopoly, a sales tax, and dock dues, its principal revenues came from export and import duties. Subsidies from France and the income derived from the rental of state lands were helpful adjuncts, but it was foreign trade that determined its budgetary position. Consequently, the decline in its commercial exchanges with France because of the shipping shortage during World War I resulted in a budget deficit of 337,000 francs in 1915. By the next year, however, its increased trade with foreign countries improved revenues, but not to the point where they offset the loss of France's subsidy to the budget and, more important, the cost of suppressing the 1917 revolt.

Although, when the war ended, New Caledonia's budget had grown to 5.8 million francs, it had incurred a large deficit and the reserve fund was reduced to 224,000 francs. Beginning in 1919, the colony's financial position deteriorated rapidly, largely because of the far smaller purchases of its minerals by the Allies' defense industries, and in 1921 it had to raise locally a million-franc loan simply to meet its operating expenses. A climax was reached in 1924 when the Minister of Colonies rejected New Caledonia's request for a 3-million-franc loan and the general council refused to vote the budget presented by Governor d'Arboussier.[3] Although the latter episode resulted in the general council's downgrading, it was but the most acute phase in the long struggle between the administration and all of New Caledonia's elected bodies over the inclusion of "obligatory expenditures" in the colonial budget. From the turn of the century until 1953, successive general councilors resisted all of the administration's proposals to increase taxation, proposals whose main objective was to provide higher salaries for Metropolitan civil servants.

Guyon was the only governor of the interwar period to undertake basic fiscal reforms which, moreover, had the approval of the general councilors. He even won their consent to appreciably higher taxation in return for his promise to use the proceeds to improve the rural economy and not to tamper with the land tax. It was he who instituted a stamp tax and a tax on the income from stocks and bonds, as well as an increase in the duty on imported luxury goods from 7 percent to 15 percent ad valorem. At the same time, however, he reduced the import duties on building equipment, foodstuffs, and cultural materials, and lowered the export duties on certain items shipped to foreign countries. In 1926, he divided the colony's budget into two categories,

[3] See pp. 252–254.

and to provide funds for the sector earmarked for economic equipment he imposed a 3 percent duty on exports of agricultural products, including tinned meat and shell. Emboldened by this success, Guyon created a tax in 1927 on business turnover (*chiffre d'affaires*) and doubled the head tax from 20 to 40 francs.[4]

Such measures were made acceptable not only by the tact and understanding with which Guyon handled the general councilors, but also by his allocation of almost a fourth of the territorial revenues to public works of obvious interest to most Caledonians. Moreover, his incumbency coincided with a period of unusual commercial prosperity for the colony, and from 1925 through 1928 New Caledonia enjoyed substantial annual budgetary surpluses. Furthermore, at the same time that the total volume of the budget rose from 11.2 million to nearly 40 million francs, the governor reduced general administrative expenditures from 25 percent to 15 percent of the total, and this naturally endeared him still more to the thrift-minded general councilors. Although Guyon left the colony before it felt the full weight of the world economic depression, he had anticipated its effects on New Caledonia's revenues by securing from France a 95-million-franc loan to help carry out the public-works program he had initiated.

Guyon's successor, Governor Siadous, had to bear the brunt of the local repercussions of New Caledonia's declining revenues and of renewed criticism from the councilors about the administration's "extravagance." The total volume of the budget fell from 39.9 million francs in 1929 to 32.6 millions in 1932, and in the latter year its deficit amounted to 8.5 million francs.[5] Throughout the depression years, the governor regularly presented budgets that he claimed were pared to the bone, only to have the councilors lop off 2 to 3 million francs from the administration's proposed expenditures. By such devices, the general council was able to maintain the budget at about 28.5 million francs from 1933 through 1937, even though the colony's foreign trade was obviously recovering during that period.

The only new expenditures that the councilors were willing to authorize were those for direct aid to the rural sector, such as premiums for cotton, coffee, and copra producers and a subsidy to the Crédit Agricole. Contrary to the allegations of some critics of New Cale-

---

[4] All local Europeans and Melanesians 16 years of age and over were liable to this tax except veterans of World War I, members of the armed forces on active duty, and the fathers of families with four or more minor children.

[5] *L'Océanie Française,* January–February 1932, January–February 1933.

donia's fiscal system,[6] the councilors showed no special tenderness toward the mining industry, and although they failed to increase its taxes, they refused in 1935 to accept the administration's proposal to reduce the export duty on ores and matte.[7] Their concern was for the white settlers, who, they claimed, bore an unfair share of the taxation, whereas Metropolitan officials and the Melanesians paid nothing. On occasion, too, they granted increases in the salaries paid to local civil servants, but only to a very limited extent.

The councilors' argument was that the budget could readily be balanced without recourse to new taxation if the administration would compress its expenditures, particularly those for its personnel. The sole "obligatory expenditures" they would accept without demurring were payments on the colony's public debt. In general, they believed that revenues should come almost wholly from export and import duties, even though this increased both production and living costs, and if budgetary deficits were unavoidably incurred they should be met by subsidies or loans from French public funds. Consistently they refused even to consider the administration's frequent proposals to impose an income tax. Only reluctantly did they vote increased allocations for the health and education services, and they did so only in view of the growth of the white population and its increasing insistence on such basic amenities. In response to the administration's contention that greater production was the only means of permanently increasing revenues, the councilors could only urge the government to provide more and cheaper labor for European farmers and miners, but they would not provide the funds needed to modernize their equipment.

The devaluation of the franc in 1936 had contradictory effects on New Caledonia's finances. Although it increased the cost of imported merchandise from Australia and the United States, this increase augmented the revenues from import duties. Furthermore, the devaluation automatically reduced the colony's public debt to France to 10.7 million francs and also made New Caledonia's exports more salable. The resultant rapid growth in foreign-trade revenues induced the general councilors at long last to authorize a rise in the volume of the budget, which increased to 34 million francs in 1938 and to 44.1 millions the following year.

[6] "G. F. R.," "New Caledonia and the War"; Feuer, L. S., "Cartel Control in New Caledonia."

[7] *L'Océanie Française*, November–December 1936.

This trend was accelerated during World War II, and by 1944 the budget totaled 92 million francs. During the war period, export duties were suspended and a wartime tax was imposed on the excess profits then being made by the mining industry, but no effort was made to find new permanent sources of revenues. In 1945, the victory of the leftist parties, which had campaigned on a platform that advocated the institution of an income tax, was short-lived. The conservatives, who soon gained control of the general council, promptly restored the fiscal status quo ante bellum that rested primarily on indirect taxation. The rejection of France's first postwar constitution in May 1946 dashed New Caledonia's hopes for the elimination of obligatory budget expenditures. By 1947 New Caledonia found itself with the same financial structure it had had a decade before, despite the huge increase in the volume of its budget to 223.4 million C.F.P. francs, and especially in its expenditures.

Some of the growth in those expenditures was due to far larger allocations for the local health and education services, to which the councilors could hardly object, but most of it was caused by the higher salaries for Metropolitan officials made mandatory by postwar French legislation. Inevitably this gave rise to vigorous protests from the general councilors and revived the old tug-of-war between them and the government in regard to the scale of administrative expenditures and the additional taxes proposed to defray them. In the debate on the 1948 budget, President Bonneaud told his fellow councilors that New Caledonia was on the verge of a financial abyss. "We are not dupes," he added, "and personally I see no necessity for new taxation." [8] Nevertheless, the special committee appointed by the council to examine the accounts of each government department failed to find ways of paring down such expenses, and the 1948 budget of 249.6 million C.F.P. francs even showed a slight rise over that of 1947. Although France now agreed to pay annually some 152 million francs toward the salaries of a larger number of its officials serving in New Caledonia, the territory still had to draw 15 millions from the reserve fund to balance its budget.[9]

Until the general council resigned in May 1952,[10] neither its members nor the administration budged from their respective traditional positions. Although the territory's foreign trade declined during the

[8] Minutes of the general council, Nov. 15, 1947.
[9] *Ibid.*, April 30, 1948.
[10] See pp. 296–297.

greater part of the preceding four years, the total volume of the budget continued to grow, and with it the annual deficits. Nevertheless, the councilors firmly rejected the administration's customary proposals to increase taxes, preferring to dip into the reserve fund, and the administration showed equal firmness about refusing to reduce its expenditures. Still, there were some significant changes in New Caledonia's finances during those years. In 1951, the French government wiped out New Caledonia's past indebtedness to the French treasury, amounting to 47 million francs. Between 1948 and 1950, not only did local revenues rise from 1 billion to 1.4 billion C.F.P. francs, but the proportion of revenues derived from direct taxation shrank from 20.8 percent to 18.4 percent.[11] Indeed, the budget's growing reliance upon export and import duties paid off in 1952, for the Korean war boom in strategic minerals greatly enhanced the territory's income from the duties on shipments of nickel and chromite. The year 1952 ended with a surplus of 20 million C.F.P. francs, and the outgoing councilors could boast that this justified their long-standing contention that New Caledonia could more than balance its budget without recourse to fresh taxation.

The interregnum between general councils in 1952–1953 enabled the Minister of Overseas France to draw up and enforce by decree the territory's 1953 budget without encountering the usual local opposition. This budget attained the much larger total of 428.5 million C.F.P. francs—an extraordinarily big figure for a territory which had a population of only some 65,000 at that time, and whose revenues were based on an archaic fiscal system that had changed little since before World War II. Customs duties accounted for 74 percent of New Caledonia's income in 1955, compared with 61 percent in 1938, whereas during that same period the share derived from direct taxation had shrunk from 10 percent to barely 8 percent.[12] Half the territory's income from direct taxation came from merchants' licenses, registration fees, and stamps, and revenues from taxes on land and on transferable securities amounted to only 12 million C.F.P. francs. Expenditures, on the other hand, had changed in character more than had revenues. Although operating costs had risen only from 61 percent to 62 percent of total expenditures, payments on the public debt had declined from 14 percent to 3 percent and those for maintenance operations from 25 percent to 12 percent. The principal change, how-

[11] Speech of Governor Cournarie to the general council, April 17, 1951.
[12] *Marchés Coloniaux*, Oct. 24, 1953, p. 2931.

ever, was in the proportion allocated to government services of social interest. By 1953, New Caledonia was spending a far larger share of its revenues on such services for the local population—37,000 Metro. francs per capita—than was any other French dependency at the time.

From the opening day of the November 1953 budget session, it was apparent that the new U.C.-dominated general council was determined to pursue a financial policy very different from that of its predecessor. For the first time in New Caledonia's history the administration's proposals for new taxation were not met with resistance. The whole debate lasted only two hours instead of days taken up with interminable wrangling. The new taxes proposed by Lenormand differed from those initiated by the governor in being designed not to fall on the consumer but on those who had theretofore largely escaped fiscal burdens. His main targets were large landholders, the owners of undeveloped urban property and luxury vehicles, and, above all, the mining industry. Furthermore, Lenormand divided the surplus resulting from the big expansion in mineral exports during 1953—21.3 million C.F.P. francs—between the reserve fund, then virtually depleted, and a special budget he set up to finance social development, especially public housing. Besides increasing the allocations for the education and health services, Lenormand included, in the 1954 budget, grants to raise the pay of local functionaries, pensions for the indigent, and family allowances for farmer-settlers, and he also increased the subsidies to municipalities for improving their roads and water-distribution systems.[13]

As might be expected, the U.C. budget elicited cries of pain and indignation from the opposition parties, which continued to insist that the new taxes were unnecessary. Antagonism to the budget even temporarily united their warring factions. *La France Australe*, Nouméa's conservative daily newspaper, ran a banner headline in its November 17, 1953 issue ("Une Bagatelle, 29.2 Millions de Francs en Nouveaux Impôts,") over an article which denounced the budget as "the first fruit of Lenormand's spendthrift policy." Its author asserted that it was unjust and improper for those who paid no taxes—that is, the white proletariat and Melanesians—to wreak vengeance on more fortunate Caledonians. He further argued that the minority opposition, from experience, had proved that no higher taxes were necessary. Naturally, Lenormand was not moved by this thesis, and during his

[13] *Ibid.*, Feb. 20, 1954, p. 558; minutes of the general council, Nov. 27, 1953.

years of political power he persevered in the policy initiated in 1954. Not only did he steadily increase the volume of the budget, which grew from 589 million C.F.P. francs that year to 1,564 millions in 1963, but he also raised the proportion of expenditures on social and cultural projects to 40 percent of the total.[14]

In 1954, 1956, and 1959, the assembly, which he dominated, voted successive tax increases but, insofar as possible, on items that did not figure in the living costs of the poorer classes of the population. As a sequel to this policy, the share of direct taxes in the budget revenues rose from 8 percent to 18 percent. It should be noted, however, that the volume of New Caledonia's extraordinary budget did not keep pace with the rise in its operational budget. It grew from 98 million C.F.P. francs in 1954 to a maximum of 153 millions in 1962, only to decline sharply to 76.8 millions the next year as the result of a trading depression.[15] Undoubtedly Lenormand regarded such contributions as New Caledonia could make from revenues to the territory's economic and social equipment as merely supplementary to the far larger grants from the F.I.D.E.S. and, to a lesser extent, the European Common Market fund under the successive Plans.

After Lenormand's downfall in 1963, the U.C. simply pursued the financial policy he had formulated without introducing any radical innovations. The volume of successive budgets grew, along with the revenues earned from New Caledonia's foreign trade, reaching in 1970 the record total of 4,915 million C.F.P. francs, of which indirect taxes accounted for 3,253 millions. Except in 1962, the only recession year of the whole decade—when the territory had to solicit a 62-million-franc subsidy from France and to take 70 millions from the reserve fund—there were ever-larger annual budgetary surpluses. The foundation for enduring financial prosperity of this scope, however, remains highly precarious, for even more than in the past it depends on maintaining the volume and value of New Caledonia's exports and imports.

CURRENCY AND BANKING

In traditional Melanesian society there was neither poverty nor wealth, for the tribes lived virtually without what are now called consumer goods and did not practice even barter trading.[16] Currency in the

[14] *Marchés Tropicaux*, May 18, 1963, p. 1127.
[15] See pp. 426–427.
[16] Brou, B., "La Société Traditionelle Mélanésienne en Nouvelle-Calédonie."

modern sense of the term was unknown, and the sole form of indigenous "money" that existed was small shells that had merely a symbolic and almost religious value. Strung like beads, these shells were offered as gifts or as tribute, but so rarely that they are now sought by collectors. On solemn occasions, such as the signing of a treaty of peace or alliance, small packets containing bones and hair and shaped like a human being were exchanged, possibly to indicate the donor's total commitment to an obligation.

After New Caledonia acquired a civilian administration, the Banque de l'Indochine (B.I.C.) was granted the same note-issue privilege as it held in the E.F.O., and until the postwar period it was the sole source of banking credit in the territory. On occasion, some trading firms in Nouméa also acted as bankers, but they, too, were generally dependent on loans from the B.I.C. During the prosperous 1920s, importers and exporters in the colony found it easy to obtain short-term loans from either of those sources at annual interest rates averaging 8 to 9 percent. Indeed, credit was made so easily available to them that a large proportion of the colony's businessmen became heavily indebted.[17] This situation changed radically after New Caledonia began to feel the effects of the world depression in the early 1930s. Not only did all loan sources rapidly dry up, but the main activity of both the trader-bankers and the B.I.C. was then devoted to collecting delinquent debts and safeguarding their funds and position.

When the B.I.C.'s note-issue privilege was renewed on March 31, 1931, the French government laid down as a condition that that bank must share some of its profits with the colony. Yet 4 years later all it had done was to hand over the ludicrous sum of 20,408 francs to the newly created agricultural-credit fund and to lend it a million francs. Even so conservative a periodical as *L'Océanie Française,* in its January-February 1935 issue, contained the incisive comment that "in no respect can the B.I.C. be counted upon to contribute to the economic development of New Caledonia." The B.I.C. had no reason to change its policy, for its position both in France and in the colony was impregnable. It operated extensively and profitably throughout the Far East, and as the second-largest shareholder in the Société Le Nickel it both strengthened and was fortified by that company's outstanding position in New Caledonia.

For many years, therefore, no competitive credit institutions were created there, despite frequent pleas for such establishments by the

[17] Noroit, M., *Niaouli, la Plaie Calédonienne,* p. 13.

general council and individual Caledonians. To be sure, a local savings bank had been created by the decree of October 5, 1923, but a limit of 5,000 francs was placed on the amount that any single person could deposit therein. Later that ceiling was slightly raised, and by 1939 the savings bank had 12,753 depositors, including 4,742 Europeans with accounts aggregating 20 million francs, and 8,008 Asians with some 3.2 millions, but there were no Melanesian depositors. Although in 1934 a Caisse de Crédit Agricole Mutuel had been created, it had so little capital that it could not appreciably aid the farming community.[18] New Caledonia had to wait for 10 years after the end of World War II before being provided with an institution that granted long- and medium-term loans at reasonable interest rates.

During the Second World War, because of New Caledonia's mineral exports to the United States and Australia and, above all, the presence in the colony of the American and Australian armed forces, the territory was flooded with dollars and sterling. Banknote circulation rose from 44 million francs in December 1940 to 308 millions in August 1945. This monetary influx was also reflected in bank deposits, which between 1942 and 1945 grew by 147 million francs, while the savings-bank accounts increased to 45 millions. The restrictions that had been placed on foreign-currency holdings in September 1939 were generally disregarded by the prosperous Caledonians, who either hoarded their dollars and pounds or smuggled them out of the colony by way of Australia. At the end of the war it was calculated that about 6 to 7 million dollars had in this way escaped all official control.[19]

After the war, the French government made two moves that had important repercussions on New Caledonia's monetary situation. On December 25, 1945, it created the C.F.P. (Colonies Françaises du Pacifique) franc for New Caledonia and the E.F.O., and instituted more stringent controls over both territories' holdings of hard currency. The dissociation of the Pacific from the Metro. franc, which destroyed the prewar unity of the French empire's monetary system, was motivated by the need to take into account the existing divergencies between the economy of liberated France and those of its overseas dependencies. It did not, however, alter the value of the Caledonian franc in relation to other currencies as fixed in April 1944 at 50 C.F.P. francs to one American dollar and 200 to the pound sterling. Nevertheless, the conversion rate of the Pacific and the Metro. franc under-

---

[18] See pp. 389–391.
[19] "G. F. R.," "New Caledonia and the War."

went successive and frequent changes.[20] These fluctuations in the relationship of the two currencies caused confusion and anxiety in New Caledonia, and gave rise to recurrent rumors of further devaluations. Such devaluations occurred in September 1957, when the C.F.P. franc was assigned a value of 0.055 Metro. franc, and in August 1969 when the value of both francs was reduced by 12.5 percent. They naturally affected the territory's export trade and, to a lesser but still important degree, they had repercussions on its imports, especially those from the dollar and sterling areas.

France's grave shortage of hard currency in the early postwar years made the French government eager to get its hands on New Caledonia's wartime earnings, and also to monopolize the proceeds from its future sales of mineral products outside the franc bloc. Through a branch of the Metropolitan Office des Changes which was installed at Nouméa, France allocated only minimal amounts of the dollar and sterling credits it had received from the resale of New Caledonia's output. This parsimony caused considerable hardship and indignation in the territory, where consumer goods were scarce and the cost of living was soaring. Protests from the local administration, general council, and traders were unavailing until Senator Lafleur in 1947 went to Paris to plead the Caledonian cause.

Citing New Caledonia's early alignment with Free France and its geographical location in an Anglo-American-dominated area, Lafleur succeeded in negotiating a new currency agreement, by whose terms the territory was accorded free disposal of the hard currency it had earned during the war. Furthermore, France agreed to regulate on a quarterly basis its trade balance with New Caledonia in francs that were convertible into dollars and sterling. This greatly improved the territory's monetary position, and since France's own currency situation had also improved in the interval, the Lafleur agreement was extended beyond its expiration date on June 30 of that year. Minimal currency controls, however, were maintained by the local Office des Changes, but they were easily circumvented.[21]

Although New Caledonia's hard-currency reserves steadily grew, thanks to its increasing mineral exports during the Korean war, it still had no adequate local-credit institutions until September 1955. At that time there was created the Crédit de la Nouvelle-Calédonie (C.N.C.), a state company whose initial capital of 20 million C.F.P.

[20] See pp. 145–146, 291.
[21] *Pacific Islands Monthly*, May 1954.

francs was supplied in equal parts by the territorial budget and the Caisse Centrale de la France d'Outre-Mer. It was legally authorized to grant medium- and long-term loans to groups and individuals, with a view to encouraging the productivity of fishermen and craftsmen and the activities of traders, members of the liberal professions, and the tourist industry. Its interest rates varied with the borrower concerned, ranging between 3.5 and 6 percent. The C.N.C.'s capital was progressively increased to 140 million C.F.P. francs, and its record of repayment is considered to be good. Nevertheless, as time went on it was criticized on two counts. The U.C. leaders charged that its conservative management showed political favoritism in the granting of loans,[22] and other Caledonians criticized it for failing to encourage sufficiently production in the rural sector. As the C.N.C. conceived of its role, it was not one of replacing normal banking operations but of supplementing them by promoting promising small-scale enterprises that required longer-term loans and involved some risk.

As of 1962, the loans granted by the C.N.C. since its creation to agricultural projects represented only 11.7 percent of its total activities, to traders and members of the liberal professions 10.4 percent, to craftsmen and small industrialists 4.4 percent, and to the tourist industry 2.7 percent.[23] Its main operations were oriented mostly to the field of building and housing, particularly in Nouméa. Loans for construction were granted chiefly to landowners who could offer little or no security but who wanted to replace derelict dwellings that existed on their properties. The rapid increase in Nouméa's population was causing an acute shortage in low-cost housing, which the C.N.C. was trying to remedy.[24]

Since its inception, the C.N.C. has granted loans totaling annually about 240 million C.F.P. francs to some 3,000 individuals or groups, and it has received requests for additional loans aggregating several hundred millions more. The recent evolution in New Caledonia's banking situation suggests a significant increase in its credit facilities and important changes in the role of the B.I.C. In 1967, the B.I.C. lost its note-issuing monopoly for the south Pacific and, that same year, opened additional agencies throughout the area. That move was forced on the B.I.C. by the prospective installation at Nouméa in

[22] See Lenormand's speech to the National Assembly, April 27, 1961.

[23] Report submitted by Y. Attali to the S.P.C. technical conference on economic development, March 14, 1962.

[24] See pp. 493–494.

March 1969 of the Banque Nationale de Paris, which for the first time is offering serious competition to the B.I.C. The new mining companies soon to be installed in New Caledonia will certainly stimulate further expansion of banking operations, already growing rapidly as a result of the territory's current prosperity. Between 1967 and 1968, the note circulation rose from 1,482 million C.F.P. francs to 1,634 million, and during that period bank deposits and savings accounts increased by more than 1,573 million C.F.P. francs.[25]

New Caledonia, unlike the great majority of French colonies before World War II, had a long-term plan for economic development that was in part actually carried out. This was the twenty-year program drawn up in 1925 by a committee of the general council and a Metropolitan expert under the guidance of Governor Guyon, who was a pioneer in this field. To Guyon, the Grande Terre's future development depended first of all on improving the means of communication, and consequently his plan concentrated on its infrastructure. It also embraced lesser projects for providing the settlements with electricity and a better water supply, as well as for increasing native agricultural production. Guyon's main concern, however, was to diminish the isolation of the white settlers so as to augment their productivity, and to raise their living standards by giving them more social amenities. Nevertheless, when the Guyon plan was submitted to the general council in December 1928, he ran into trouble, not over its technical aspects but in regard to its financing.

When the councilors realized that the plan's execution would entail higher taxation, they postponed reaching a decision, on various pretexts.[26] Stronger objections were voiced by the Chamber of Commerce, whose members flatly refused to approve any plan that could not be financed from existing revenues. Finally, a compromise was reached whereby France was to be asked for a 95-million-franc loan, and the balance needed, 30 million francs, was to be derived from German reparations.

The Parliament was slow about granting the loan, and by the time it was authorized, New Caledonia's share in the German reparations had been reduced to 15 million francs. By then, too, the world economic depression had greatly reduced local revenues.[27] In the mean-

25 *Marchés Tropicaux,* Aug. 23, 1969, p. 2315.
26 *L'Océanie Française,* May–June 1929.
27 *Ibid.,* July–August 1932.

time, however, Guyon had utilized such funds as were still available from the prosperous trading years in the 1920s to launch his program of road-building. After he left New Caledonia, only the projects he had already begun were completed, and there was no question of undertaking the rest of his program even after the colony's revenues increased in the late 1930s. The whole concept of planning was abandoned, not to be revived until after World War II.

Even before France was liberated, the Free French authorities devoted much attention to development plans for all parts of the empire, and after the war they set up the legal and financial structure required for their fulfilment. By the law of April 30, 1946, the Fonds d'Investissement pour le Développement Economique et Social (F.I.D.E.S.) was created and the Caisse Centrale d'Outre-Mer (C.C.O.M.) was made its agent for the financing of each territory's plan. According to the general principles laid down in that law, the F.I.D.E.S., operating through the C.C.O.M., would grant either subsidies or long-term, low-interest loans for specific construction projects to promote economic and social development, but the overseas territory concerned had to provide the funds for their maintenance.

In 1946, the F.I.D.E.S. directorate sent an engineer, M. Dorche, to Nouméa to draft New Caledonia's first four-year plan. Its cost was estimated at 409.5 million C.F.P. francs, of which 191 millions would be used for economic improvements and 218.5 millions for social equipment. In the economic sector, 36 percent was earmarked for transportation and communications and 15 percent for rural production; in that of social development, expenditures for the health and education services accounted for 19 percent of the total, the balance to be devoted to urbanization and to water-distribution systems.[28] Dorche's plan took a dim view of New Caledonia's agricultural potential and proposed concentrating on the development of the mining industry as its most promising resource. He believed that mining and metallurgy should remain the province of private enterprise, and that the F.I.D.E.S. should be restricted to financing a systematic prospecting and mapping of the territory's mineral deposits. As to agriculture, the lack of available arable land and the frequency of cyclones inclined him to rule out all export crops except coffee and possibly cotton, but he thought that New Caledonia could and should be made self-sufficient in food production. He held much the same view of

[28] Speech of Governor Parisot to the general council, April 25, 1946.

stock-raising, advocating intensive herding and the production of meat and dairy products wholly for domestic consumption because their export could never compete with Australia's output. Similarly, local industries should concentrate on processing the production of the rural sector for the internal market so as to reduce the territory's dependence on imported foodstuffs, building materials, soap, and leather. In the field of transportation, he agreed that New Caledonia should have a first-class airport but disapproved of further road-building. In the social domain, Dorche was in favor of building more schools, hospitals, and dispensaries, especially in the interior.

Eventually, Dorche's general policy was accepted, and its guidelines greatly influenced New Caledonia's three subsequent plans. At the time, however, his views were sufficiently controversial to cause a delay of several years in even an initial move to carry out the first plan. In fact, this program was not fully completed by 1953, when it was superseded by the territory's second plan. In the meantime, the F.I.D.E.S. itself had undergone considerable changes of organization, financing, and orientation. In the interests of greater efficiency, its operations were divided into two parts. The general sector was concerned with scientific research and the promotion of companies financed fully or partly by public funds for all the French dependencies. In New Caledonia, the general sector operated mainly through the Organisation de la Recherche Scientifique et Technique d'Outre-Mer (O.R.S.T.O.M.) with which the Institut Français de l'Océanie was integrated.[29] In each territory, the local section of the F.I.D.E.S. dealt with that territory's plan, and the procedures were cumbersome and time-consuming. The annual segments of each territorial plan were drawn up and approved by the local administration and elected assembly; next they were studied by the technical services of the French Overseas Ministry, and then submitted to the Paris directorate of the F.I.D.E.S. After modifications or rejections at each stage in this process, they were returned to the territory for final approval or amendment.

New Caledonia's general council went over each annual plan with a fine-tooth comb, in order to see how its cost to the territory might be reduced and in what areas local technicians and services could be given preference over Metropolitan experts and enterprises.[30] As re-

[29] See pp. 509–510.
[30] See *La France Australe*, May 21, 1947, June 1, 1948.

gards certain projects, such as the encouragement of local processing industries, Nouméa's traders were opposed to any increase in production that might curtail the profits they were making on imported merchandise. In practice, the councilors generally begrudged the expenditures required for the upkeep of schools and dispensaries built by F.I.D.E.S. funds, although in principle they readily admitted the need for them, especially in the rural areas.[31] While they were still engaged in debating the first plan, they learned that there would be an appreciable reduction in the F.I.D.E.S.' original allocation of funds to New Caledonia, and this required adjustments that further delayed the plan's execution. To force the general council to reach final decisions, the F.I.D.E.S. directors had to threaten to cancel New Caledonia's allocations if they were not utilized within a specific time limit.

While the second plan was being drafted in 1953, new elements entered into the picture. One was the general reorientation of all the overseas plans to increase the productivity of the individual territories. In New Caledonia, a greater effort was to be made to improve the output of agriculture, livestock, and forests, but the main objective of the second plan was to aid the mining industry, largely by constructing the Yaté dam. Only what then remained of the territory's allocations were to be spent on raising the living standards of the least-favored elements of the local population. This policy was in contradiction to the platform on which the U.C. had just won control of the general council in 1953, but its victory came too late to effect any radical change in the second plan. It was not until the third plan (for 1961–1966) was being drafted that the U.C. had any opportunity to exert an influence that should logically have reflected its views and the altered balance of local political power.

In his campaign for reelection to the National Assembly in 1959, Lenormand stressed the need for better geographical distribution of the F.I.D.E.S. funds and their use for a greater diversification of New Caledonia's economy. To obtain the funds needed, he called on local private capital, with the plea that the 2 billion or so C.F.P. francs then being hoarded or deposited in bank accounts should be invested in enterprises that would promote the territory's economic and social development.[32] Unfortunately for the success of Lenormand's program, it was announced at the time of Governor Pechoux's arrival in Nouméa. In the ensuing trial of strength between the two men,

---

[31] Minutes of the general council, Nov. 14, 1950.
[32] Speech to the National Assembly, April 27, 1961.

Pechoux succeeded in shelving Lenormand's plan and replacing it with one of his own devising.

In Gaullist circles in Paris, Pechoux created the impression that Lenormand was incapable of drawing up a rational plan for New Caledonia's development and of presenting it properly to the authorities. Lenormand, for his part, charged that the governor's own plan was "unbalanced and irrational," including the expenditure of F.I.D.E.S. funds on such items as the construction of a morgue, "in which presumably he intends to bury the law." [33] He wound up his attack in the National Assembly by asking how a territory with 7 billion C.F.P. francs in revenues could consider itself to be other than underdeveloped when many of its white settlers could hardly make ends meet and the tribesmen were paupers.

Even if Lenormand had not been forced out of power 2 years later, there is no certainty that he would have succeeded either in increasing the F.I.D.E.S. allocations to New Caledonia or in utilizing them to alter appreciably its evolution. In proportion as the territory's revenues swelled throughout the 1960s, the funds granted it by the F.I.D.E.S. shrank. During the period 1961–1968, the F.I.D.E.S. contributions aggregated only 39.5 million Metro. francs, of which 45.5 percent went to the infrastructure, 37 percent to production, and 17.5 percent to social equipment.[34] The total was only about 2 million Metro. francs more than the funds supplied by the Common Market's Fonds Européen de Développement,[35] most of which were spent on building schools and dispensaries. A supplementary source for financing development investments was the territory's extraordinary budget, the amount of which varies annually, depending upon the budget surplus. To attract private capital investments on the scale required by New Caledonia's fast-developing mining industry, a new investment code was promulgated in September 1970 which offers tax inducements to enterprises creating new activities or expanding those already in existence.

In terms of local revenues, contributions from outside sources, and private investments, New Caledonia's population of less than 100,000 is certainly in a privileged position. As of 1967, the gross national

[33] *Ibid.*

[34] *Europe-France-Outremer*, no. 473, June 1969.

[35] On June 1, 1964, the French Pacific territories became associate members of the European Economic Community. Even before this occurred, New Caledonia had received from that source $2.2 million between 1958 and 1963, and it was granted $4.2 million in the 1964–1969 period.

product came to 16,229 million C.F.P. francs, and it has increased since then.[36] The foregoing figures indicate that New Caledonia should not be classified as an underdeveloped country of the Third World, but they do not show how unevenly its wealth is distributed and how unbalanced is its economy. Had public and private funds been invested otherwise, the imbalance of the territory's economy might to some degree have been corrected. There is no conclusive evidence, however, that New Caledonia's development would have been revolutionized, because of certain physical and psychological factors.

On the material side, the territory's geographical isolation and geological formation are the immutable elements in its history. Psychologically, the determining influences have been the Caledonians' distaste for hard work, especially manual labor, and their anarchic individualism combined with an intense loyalty to France. Any plan aimed at developing all of the island's resources would probably have failed because of the small number of its producers and consumers. Its chronic underpopulation can be remedied only slowly by natural growth, because of the Caledonians' refusal to accept and assimilate other than transient manual laborers. In any case, the abundance of New Caledonia's mineral resources has predestined it for industrial development. Furthermore, the very meagerness of its nonmineral production and the small scope of its domestic market have been conducive to the growth—and acceptance—of trading and banking monopolies.

So long as the mining industry brings in large revenues to the budget and provides full employment at high wages, the Caledonians seem little concerned about the fast-rising cost of living, the progressive neglect of their other resources, and the widespread and growing imbalance of their territory's economy. They resent France's increasing assertions of control, but expect the Metropole to come to their rescue during recessions in their foreign trade.[37] When nickel sales are booming, as they have done for the past decade, the Caledonians enjoy the feverish atmosphere engendered by sudden prosperity and more and more of the material comforts of life. Given the prevailing physical and psychological conditions, it is not surprising that none of the plans

[36] *Marchés Tropicaux*, Aug. 30, 1969, p. 2371.

[37] Even under the territory's present prosperous conditions, France supplies it with funds amounting annually to about 1,200 million Metro. francs, not counting financial aid to the mining industry.

drawn up for New Caledonia has succeeded in its objectives. Indeed, it is doubtful whether such plans could have accomplished any marked change in the territory's evolution, even had more money been made available for their execution, for the Caledonians are antipathetic to the very concept of planning for their country's future development.

34

Health and Housing

Considering its situation in the south Pacific, New Caledonia is remarkably free of many of the diseases normally associated with the tropics. That the climate of the Grande Terre is generally healthful for Europeans is shown by the large size of most settler families who have lived there for several generations. New Caledonia has no malaria, and the outbreaks of plague that periodically occurred during its early years as a colony were soon brought under control, thanks to the serum produced by the Institut Bourret at Nouméa. Two-thirds of the maladies from which Westerners suffer are respiratory, digestive, and cardiovascular. Among the Melanesians, the worst ravages have been caused by leprosy, tuberculosis, and alcoholism, and the government's efforts to combat them have varied widely in their effectiveness.

As in most other French colonies, the health service in New Caledonia, from its beginning, was in the charge of military personnel. Under the penitentiary regime, its medical officers were euphemistically called *médecins de colonisation,* and as the number of convicts declined, its doctors transferred their ministrations to the growing free European population. Their care, however, did not extend to the native tribesmen until 1911, when an Assistance Médicale Indigène (A.M.I.) was established in the hope of saving what remained of the fast-shrinking Melanesian population. To encourage the Melanesian birthrate, a *prime de natalité* was granted to large Melanesian families in an effort to counteract practices encouraged by sorcerers, who were held responsible for the growing frequency of abortions among the tribal women. Subsequently it was noted that during the periods when European doctors were scarcest, as was the case after the two world wars, there was invariably a resurgence of the sorcerers' influence, with deleterious effects on the health of the tribes.

In addition to the influenza, venereal diseases, and measles brought in by European sailors, merchants, and settlers, which decimated all the islanders of the south Pacific, there were two other maladies to which the Melanesians were highly susceptible—leprosy in the rural areas and, later, tuberculosis in Nouméa. It was against leprosy that the colonial administration took the first steps, particularly after 1911, when it had become apparent that some Europeans had contracted the disease. Leprosy had been introduced into New Caledonia by Chinese traders in 1875,[1] and it spread rapidly, especially in the Loyalty Islands. Although the Melanesians soon recognized that it was contagious, they were so reluctant to have lepers separated from their families that to detect them was difficult.

To determine the incidence of the disease and propose remedial measures, the French government sent to New Caledonia Dr. Leboeuf, whose report, submitted in 1911, laid the basis for its antileprosy policy. These proposals included maintaining an asylum on Ducos peninsula for European (and later Asian) lepers, and six semi-segregated colonies for Melanesian lepers, of which four were installed in the Loyaltys and two on the east coast of the Grande Terre. The Loyalty Islands leper villages were staffed by Protestant deaconnesses and those at Hienghène and Houaïlou by Catholic nuns. The administration, which granted subsidies for such mission activities, itself ran the Ducos asylum. According to the 1936 census, there were then in New Caledonia 109 European and Asian lepers and 614 known cases of the disease among the Melanesians.[2]

During the interwar period, New Caledonia was divided into medical districts, but this was largely a paper organization, as there were few qualified personnel. The number of doctors fell from seven before World War I to three during the early 1920s, with the result that many settlements, not to mention the reservations, were without medical care.[3] Under Governor Guyon, some improvements were made in medical personnel and equipment, owing to the prosperity of the colony's budget during his incumbency. Specifically, the colony was able to match the higher salaries paid to French doctors serving in Indochina by raising the pay of physicians practising in New Caledonia. By the time Guyon left Nouméa, there were then in the colony nine military doctors and four private practitioners, and this number sufficed for the capital's two public hospitals and its civilian popula-

[1] *L'Océanie Française,* November 1911.

[2] *Ibid.,* September–October 1937.

[3] *Ibid.,* January–February 1922.

tion, as well as for the small state-run hospital-dispensaries at Bourail, Canala, and Ponérihouen. The Société Le Nickel provided a hospital at Thio for its mine laborers, and the Christian missions two others, at Ouaco and Lifou.

The colony's main medical establishment was the old military hospital at Nouméa, headed by the military doctor who was also in charge of the colony's health service. Annexed to it was the laboratory of the Institut Bourret, and at Nou Island an asylum for the insane. In 1939, Nouméa's municipality financed the construction of an Institut d'Hygiène Social. Treatment was provided free of charge at all the state-run institutions only to civil servants, the military, and Europeans and Melanesians who could produce an official certificate of indigency. As regards general health regulations, immigrants were subjected to a medical examination before disembarking in the colony. All the planters and mining companies employing indentured Asian laborers were required by law to provide medical facilities for them. As to the Melanesians, none of them could leave the reservations without a medical certificate signed by the *syndic* and a doctor of the A.M.I.

Until World War II, the administration seems to have felt that the health situation in general, and leprosy in particular, were under control. In 1946, however, the general councilors were faced with a new situation—how to deal with the current increase in communicable diseases. This became the subject of several heated debates which reflected the European community's growing fear of contagion resulting from the new mobility of the Asians and Melanesians. In increasing numbers the last-mentioned were gravitating to the towns, where they lived under deplorable conditions, and control over their movements became so lax that even the lepers from the Ducos asylum were roaming the streets of Nouméa.[4] The local administration no longer had the legal authority to enforce segregation and, in any case, the territory lacked the facilities to do so. Nevertheless, the general council, recently empowered to initiate budgetary expenditures, for the first time began to assume more responsibility for the territory's public-health service. With great reluctance, the councilors voted to increase appreciably the grants to that service, which rose to 32 million C.F.P. francs in 1948 compared with 7 millions in 1942. At the same time, however, they required the Nouméa hospital to raise the rates for its paying clientele.[5]

[4] Minutes of the general council, Feb. 5, 1947.
[5] *Ibid.*, Jan. 28, Feb. 8, May 1, 1947.

After World War II, the F.I.D.E.S. provided substantial funds for the enlargement and equipment of the existing medical institutions and for the construction of new buildings. This windfall, however, did not solve the problem of recruiting and paying additional medical personnel, which was deficient in the rural areas and especially on the reservations. In the main settlements, the resident doctor was required to tour his district once a month to care for the settlers' families, whereas the A.M.I. doctors visited the tribes in their areas only every 3 months. In the interior the means of communication were so inadequate and difficult that even the most conscientious doctor would be taxed beyond his capacity if he were to carry out his assigned tasks. Nouméa offered the best facilities of what was generally a poor and inadequate medical organization.

Gradually New Caledonia's budgetary resources, swelled by the rapidly growing prosperity of the mining industry, enabled the territory to employ more doctors and dentists under contract. For some time this policy was opposed by Nouméa's private practitioners, who were themselves unwilling to serve in the interior but who were reluctant to accept any competition for the territory's small paying clientele. Nevertheless, by 1955 a mobile health unit had been created to track down and treat diseases of the population living in the most remote rural areas, the medical examination of primary school children had become obligatory, the Bourret laboratory had been transformed into a branch of the Pasteur Institute, and a sanatorium for tubercular patients had been built at the Col de la Pirogue. A beginning had also been made in providing a safe and abundant water supply in the main settlements, though much still remains to be done in this domain.

At present, the interior comprises 16 medical districts, each staffed by a qualified resident doctor and one or more nurses. Some 650 patients can be hospitalized in the dispensaries, and only the most serious cases are sent to Nouméa for treatment. The capital's main hospital, and three clinics operated by the missions, provide hospital beds for 509 persons. In addition, the Nouville asylum can accommodate 150 mental patients, and the Col de la Pirogue's sanatorium 130. The territory is served by more than 50 physicians, of whom 20 are private practitioners in Nouméa, as well as 10 pharmacists and 30 medical assistants.[6] In recent years, the territory has been spending between 12 and 16 percent of its revenues on public health, and the

---

[6] *La Nouvelle-Calédonie et Dépendances* (La Documentation Française), pp. 26–27.

execution of its third plan should bring further improvements and enlargements in the existing institutions as well as the construction of new buildings.

SOCIAL WELFARE

New Caledonia's rapid population growth, which derives far more from natural increase than from immigration, is a testimonial to the effectiveness of its modern medical services. The health organization, however, has not attacked the fundamental causes of two of the main afflictions of the Melanesian community—alcoholism and tuberculosis —although it provides some care and treatment for advanced cases of both. Tuberculosis did not give cause for concern until the postwar rural exodus had created slum conditions in the main towns and particularly in Nouméa. Alcoholism, on the other hand, was long regarded as a "social disease" whose cure was the province of the Christian missions. Under pressure from the French wine industry, and to increase revenues from import duties, the administration indirectly encouraged the consumption of alcoholic beverages, and its only direct intervention took the form of a few sporadic repressive measures.

Traditionally, the Melanesians of New Caledonia are among the most temperate islanders of the south Pacific, and not even *kava* was as widely consumed there as in other archipelagoes.[7] According to mission sources, the Melanesians at first rejected whiskey as the "water that burns," but soon, because its sale was promoted by European traders and paroled convicts, they developed a craving for it. Among the outstanding addicts in the early twentieth century was the Great Chief Mindia, who became such an inveterate drunkard that the administration was on the point of deposing him.[8] This threat, combined with the exhortations of Protestant missionaries, induced him to reform so wholeheartedly that he petitioned the government to forbid the sale of alcoholic beverages to his fellow tribesmen.

Governor Liotard, arguing that wine was harmless and "our national beverage," refused to accede to Mindia's request, but the latter persisted in his campaign to enforce Melanesian sobriety. A few years later, in 1905, Governor Picanon became concerned by the spread of

---

[7] *Kava* is a fermented drink, with symbolic value, made from the roots of an indigenous plant. The root yields a more intoxicating drink if used in the dried state rather than green.

[8] Leenhardt, M., "La Nouvelle-Calédonie."

alcoholism among the tribes and supported Mindia's plea, but this time the general council, fearing the loss of budgetary revenues, refused its approval, as did the Minister of Colonies. It took the native revolt of 1917—when the sale of firearms to the rebels followed what was then called the *route du vin*—to convince Governor Repiquet that access to alcohol must be forbidden to the Melanesians. He persuaded the French government to decree that alcohol could be sold to Melanesians only by licensed European dealers, but this did not end its clandestine sale by unscrupulous traders.

During World War II, the presence of American troops led to the opening of many public bars, where it was difficult to screen the customers. This, together with the postwar laws granting greater freedom of movement to the Melanesians and Asians, was responsible for a resurgence of alcoholism, which became apparent in 1946. At the instigation of the missions, both the U.I.C.A.L.O. and the A.I.C.L.F., at their constituent congresses that year, passed resolutions asking the government to impose total prohibition, and early in 1947 the general council voted severer penalties for infractions of the law with respect to alcoholic-beverage sales.[9] It proved impossible, however, to enforce the law because the Melanesians were loath to testify against illicit traders, and the importation of alcoholic beverages, especially beer, continued to increase. In 1951, Lenormand urged the National Assembly to authorize the governor to impose quotas on such imports, and a campaign publicizing the evils of alcohol was conducted by the local radio and press. It was sponsored by the head of the public-health service, who was also president of the newly formed Comité Calédonien de Défense contre l'Alcoolisme.[10] These moves were followed by new regulations which severely penalized public drinking by the Melanesians. Since certain categories of the native population were exempted from application of these measures, they were ineffectual and, indeed, the sale of alcohol became more lucrative than before. In 1956 twice as much beer was imported into New Caledonia as in the previous year, and the local brewery, which was working to capacity, planned to enlarge its plant.

The long controversy between the pro-temperance elements, on the one hand, and the importers and local dealers on the other, continued inconclusively for some years. By 1963, however, the subject had become so politically controversial that the latter group won a signal

[9] Minutes of the general council, Jan. 24, 1947.
[10] *La Tribune du Pacifique,* Feb. 26, 1952.

victory by portraying as a measure of racial discrimination any law forbidding the sale of alcoholic beverages to Melanesians. Consequently, in July of that year, the territorial assembly lifted the embargo on such sales except in the tribal reservations.[11] Although it is still too early to evaluate the long-term effects of this move, no marked change in the drinking habits of the Melanesian community has so far been reported.

HOUSING

The effort to eradicate tuberculosis, second only to alcoholism among New Caledonia's health and social problems, has encountered fewer difficulties, both economically and politically. Although its incidence is linked with profiteering—to the degree that tuberculosis is caused by housing conditions for which some of Nouméa's landlords are responsible—no lobby has existed either in the territory or in France to oppose measures designed to combat it. Tuberculosis has spread largely through negligence and the failure of the authorities to anticipate the rural exodus to the towns after World War II.

In the early twentieth century, Nouméa, like many other colonial capitals, grew like Topsy, and it lacked such urban amenities as sewage, an adequate water supply, and electricity. Nevertheless, it had a distinct business district and a residential area for well-to-do Europeans, while on its outskirts the working-class population lived in jerry-built houses. The site of Nouméa had been chosen for its potential as a port, and gradually the town spread out to cover loosely some 10 square kilometers along the waterfront and up the slopes of the adjoining hills. Nouméa's roads, like its buildings, had been constructed in haphazard fashion, and very few of them were paved.

Although, by the interwar period, nearly half of New Caledonia's Europeans lived in the capital, they still numbered only some 11,000 persons. Many of them had been established there for years and were used to its comparatively primitive conditions and lack of distractions. To be sure, they enjoyed maritime sports, horse-racing, and gossip, and there were a few social clubs, but Nouméa was almost unique among French towns in lacking theatres and outdoor cafés, and women did not frequent the public bars. As for the main settlements in the interior, they were merely villages and even more isolated, provincial, and lacking in amenities.

[11] *Marchés Tropicaux*, Aug. 17, 1963, p. 2087.

World War II brought to Nouméa many new buildings and other improvements, as well as temporary traffic jams and overcrowding by troops, but it was not until the postwar years that its population began to expand rapidly. As a result of the wartime prosperity, the Noumeans aspired to better living conditions, and the arrival of many newcomers made such improvements, especially housing, indispensable. The postwar French government, for its part, encouraged town planning in New Caledonia by sending an expert on urbanization to Nouméa and authorizing the F.I.D.E.S. to finance the plan he drew up. Paved streets and electric lighting were welcomed by the Noumeans, but their major concern—and that of the authorities—was with more housing. To promote such building, the administration and the general council considered and experimented with various projects.

While the general councilors were inconclusively debating different proposals, Nouméa's population was growing by leaps and bounds. It was not until 1956, however, that a generally satisfactory formula was found with the creation of the Crédit de la Nouvelle-Calédonie (C.N.C.).[12] Although the C.N.C. was a multiple-purpose institution, it became increasingly involved in trying to solve the housing crisis. In this respect, Nouméa differed from many other overcrowded capitals, for its basic problem was not the poverty of its inhabitants—wages were good and jobs were plentiful—but the physical shortage of rental housing. The costs of land and construction were so high that few landholders could afford to build houses on their own property, and private companies could earn larger profits from investments in other enterprises.

To deal with this complex situation, it was intended that the C.N.C. should act as both a real-estate and a building agency and should provide flexible credit facilities for house-building. Its most important venture was the construction of two housing estates near Nouméa for different categories of the capital's wage-earners. The Sainte-Marie Estate, financed by state funds, was built for white workers holding steady jobs who wanted to own the houses they occupied, hence they were given facilities to acquire title to them on a hire-purchase basis. At the Montravel Estate, which had been financed by territorial funds, only rental housing was available. There most of the tenants were Melanesians, of whom only the upper stratum was permanently employed in the civil service or by trading firms, whereas the majority intended eventually to return to their native villages. For still other

12 See pp. 477–478.

workers, who did not live in either of the estate developments and who wanted to own their own homes, the C.N.C. in 1962 started a savings system to help them amass sufficient capital to make a down payment. By the end of 1967, the C.N.C. had granted 2,708 loans for housing of one kind or another, totaling 1,210 million C.F.P. francs.[13]

During the 1960s, hundreds of dwellings were built in Nouméa and especially in its suburbs, thanks to the operations of the C.N.C. They have attenuated but not solved the town's acute housing shortage, especially as its population continues to grow. Many tenements, inhabited mainly by immigrants, remain a health and fire hazard, and they cannot be demolished until alternative housing is provided. To compel private firms to build lodgings for their employes, the general council in 1965 levied a tax of 2 percent on a certain proportion of the wages they paid their labor force. There remained, however, the problem of acquiring suitable land for house-building, because it was being held for exorbitant prices by speculative owners. To a small extent this situation was eased in 1967 by a donation from Nouméa's municipal council of 200 hectares of its holdings for public housing, and by a similar cession on the part of the Société Le Nickel to provide land on which some of its poorly housed employes could build.

By such piecemeal progress, Nouméa may be on the way to providing adequate dwellings for its residents, though in this domain, as elsewhere, improvements depend on the continuing prosperity of the mining industry. An analogous development may occur in the interior settlements, especially in the areas where that industry will mine nickel and build metallurgical plants. As to the reservations, there has been little improvement in tribal housing since the failure of the attempt in that respect by the C.N.C. in 1957.[14] Very few of the loans then granted on an experimental basis to 17 Melanesian families were used for the purpose for which they had been intended. Some of the borrowers built houses in the traditional style, while others, who had constructed modern dwellings, defaulted because so many relatives moved in with them. In any case, the collective ownership of tribal land makes it virtually impossible for the great majority of Melanesians who live in the reservations to offer the guarantees required to raise loans. Only if public funds on a generous scale are made available for that purpose can any real improvement in tribal housing be expected.

[13] *Bulletin du Commerce de la Nouvelle-Calédonie,* Nov. 18, 1967.
[14] *Ibid.*

35

Education, Cultural Activities, and the Christian Missions

EDUCATION

Since the mid-1950s, New Caledonia has claimed that all of the territory's school-age children were receiving a primary education which was both obligatory and free of charge. This achievement is the more remarkable in view of the inadequacy, both quantitatively and qualitatively, of its primary schools until the post-World War II years, as well as of the confusion that still characterizes the whole educational system. The diversity in the ethnic origin of the territory's students is matched by variations in the curricula and in the qualifications of its teaching staff. Both the state and the Christian missions provide instruction at the primary, secondary, and technical levels to European, Melanesian, Polynesian, and Asian youth, but its quality varies markedly. Recently, however, the trend has been toward greater uniformity and the alignment of educational standards at all levels with those in equivalent French institutions. Today, it is only at the university level that there are no educational facilities available in New Caledonia.

New Caledonia is distinguished from many other French dependencies by the harmonious relations that have consistently prevailed between the mission and the state educational authorities. As elsewhere throughout the former French empire, the Christian missionaries were pioneers in the educational field, but in contrast to the situation in French Black Africa, their schools now maintain parity numerically with those of the state. Since World War II, the number of pupils attending mission and public primary and secondary schools has been roughly equal, but the quality of the instruction provided in the state secondary and technical schools is somewhat better, mainly because of the latter's larger financial resources. Although the territory has been increasingly generous in subsidizing the mission schools such grants amount to only one-fourth of the total funds allocated to education, which now come to some 500 million C.F.P. francs a year. At present, New Caledonia is spending about 25 percent of the territory's income on education, compared with 16 percent in the early 1950s.

The superiority of the public secondary and technical schools will soon become even more marked as the result of France's assumption of responsibility in 1967 for their total cost. (At those levels the missions have always found it difficult to compete with the state schools even though—and perhaps because—they have charged small fees for attendance.) This decision by Paris was reluctantly accepted by the general councilors so as to enable New Caledonia to concentrate its own financial resources on improving its primary schools. The poorest of all the schools at that level have been those in the tribal villages, which are run mainly by the missions, and an improvement in their quality would eliminate a major handicap to the evolution of Melanesian youth. Because for many years the Melanesians did not aspire to posts in the civil service or in the liberal professions, and because the authorities preferred that they remain as farmers on their reservations, there was no question of applying the Metropolitan curriculum in the tribal schools. Indeed, both the secular and mission educators concurred in orienting the instruction given Melanesians to the practical needs of their rural milieu.

In determining the respective zones of influence for the mission and state schools, chronology was a decisive factor. The Marist Fathers, the first in the field, built schools for Melanesians at their mission stations and gradually extended such facilities to the coastal tribes as they became converted to Catholicism. Initially, they gave priority to religious instruction and taught Melanesians in the vernacular, but by the end of the nineteenth century they had begun to include secular subjects and to use French as the sole linguistic vehicle. It was at about this time that the Protestant missionaries gained a foothold on the east coast of the Grande Terre, and they followed the Catholics' example both in concentrating their schools in their stronghold at Houaïlou and in using French as the medium of instruction. Although the Catholics and the Protestants also opened schools in Nouméa, their expansion was limited by a perennial shortage of funds and personnel. Consequently, large areas of the island had no schools at all, and it was the children of settlers in the interior who suffered most from this neglect.

Mainly to fill the void left by mission education, the government created a public-school system at the turn of the century, but the administration was careful not to trespass on the areas staked out by the missions. Its principal effort was directed to providing a French-type education for European children, and only much later did it widen its operations to include the Melanesians. At first the government built schools in the main settlements, particularly at Nouméa and on the west coast, where most of the Europeans lived. In 1899 the Collège La Pérouse was constructed in the capital, and a short-lived normal school for Melanesian monitors at Wé on Lifou Island also dated from that year.

Despite the combined efforts of the government and the two missions, comparatively few Melanesian and European children attended any school at all in the early twentieth century, and those who did received a very inferior education. Like the missions, the government lacked the funds needed to equip and staff its schools, for a law of 1902 had made the municipalities financially responsible for operating them. As a result, there was little money to pay teachers, whose salaries, moreover, varied with the revenues of the municipality concerned. In almost none of the public or mission schools except those in Nouméa was instruction given by trained teachers. Indeed, in many of the municipal schools, local officials and even noncommissioned officers were pressed into service, and in the mission schools the teaching was almost wholly in the hands of priests and nuns. Many of the settlers lived too far apart and too remote from the settlements to send their children there to school, and the isolated tribal villages had no schools at all.

Governor Brunet, during his tour of the Grande Terre in 1912, was shocked by the "growing proportion of illiterates" among the rural French children, and he learned that the demand for schools topped the list of the settlers' desiderata.[1] As for the Melanesians, the Protestants provided their converts with highly practical instruction, whereas the Catholics were more zealous in spreading their doctrine than in offering a more general education. Probably the most durable contributions made by the mission schools of this period were a wider diffusion of the French language and some instruction in farming techniques, and they should also be credited with initiating the training of Melanesian girls in household tasks. Before World War I, the best of New Caledonia's inadequate schools were undoubtedly those of Nouméa, whose comparatively prosperous municipal resources per-

[1] *L'Océanie Française,* August 1912.

mitted it to provide an embryonic form of secondary and technical education. Yet the school situation even there was deplorable. Its primary schools were so overcrowded that some classes had as many as 80 pupils.[2] The secondary course at the Collège La Pérouse had only 29 students because applicants were required to have a *certificat d'études primaires* (C.E.P.), which was awarded only to graduates of the very few Metropolitan-type primary schools. Annexed to that college was a vocational section, which taught ironworking and carpentry to almost as many students (20) because it had no such stringent academic requirements for admission.

To remedy this unsatisfactory state of educational affairs, Governor Brunet proposed that the colony's budget take over from the municipalities the cost of operating the public schools.[3] World War I began before his reforms could be carried out, and it also deprived the colony of many of its few teachers. By the time the war ended, there were altogether only 2,500 European children attending the primary public and mission schools, 100 in the Collège La Pérouse, and 2,300 Melanesians in the tribal village schools.[4] In the early 1920s, limited progress was made in the construction of new schools and in the teaching personnel. Graduates of a new school for Melanesian monitors at Montravel were assigned to the tribal villages, a handful of trained Metropolitan teachers were hired for the few schools which had the same curriculum as that of France, and boarding schools for rural European children were built at Nouméa and Bourail. Later in the decade, Governor Guyon listed among his achievements the construction of more primary schools in the interior and of a boarding school for girls at Nouméa, as well as an increase in the number of scholarships available for Caledonians both in local schools and in Metropolitan institutions.[5]

Despite the world depression in the early 1930s, the school network did expand during the pre-World War II decade, although not in proportion to the overall increase of the population. By 1938, of the 2,395 European children living in Nouméa 1,580 were attending school, and of the 3,025 such children in the interior only 1,316 were actually receiving a primary education. (The largest proportionate increase had occurred at the Collège La Pérouse, which had 289 stu-

[2] *Ibid.*, November 1912.
[3] Speech to the general council, June 19, 1912.
[4] *L'Océanie Française*, May–June 1921.
[5] Speech to the general council, April 11, 1929.

dents, but 64 of these were in its primary classes, 57 in its vocational section, and 168 in its secondary course.) The educational facilities available to Melanesian children were even more deficient, for fewer than 4,000 out of a school-age population nearly twice as large as that of the European community were attending the inferior tribal schools. Nevertheless, this represented an improvement over the past, and it was largely due to the efforts made by the gendarmes of the Native Affairs Service. Although those *syndics* knew next to nothing about pedagogy, they were zealous in touring the village schools, where they gave more encouragement to the monitors than did the primary-education inspector on his infrequent and rapid official visits.[6]

Table 14 indicates the predominance at that period of state schools in the education of European children, and of the missions in the schooling of young Melanesians. Other notable differences concerned the ratio of boys to girls in the public and mission schools, as well as in the Catholic and Protestant schools. The only noteworthy innovations in the whole educational system have been those introduced by the unorthodox Protestant missionary, Raymond Charlemagne.[7]

TABLE 14

New Caledonia: Schools and enrolment, in selected
years 1928–1937

	Schools for Europeans			Schools for Melanesians		
Year	Mission	State	Total	Mission	State	Total
1928	596	1,726	2,317	2,169	580	2,749
1932	603	1,954	2,557	2,348	832	3,180
1937	740	2,156	2,896	2,694	1,058	3,752

Source: *L'Océanie Française*, March–May 1938.

After World War II, the French government as well as the local authorities assumed far more responsibility than before for New Caledonia's educational system. Through the F.I.D.E.S., French public funds were provided for improving the equipment of existing schools and for building new ones. Then the general council voted much larger allocations to state schools and granted ever-more-substantial subsidies to their mission counterparts. The distribution of such grants to

[6] Guiart, J., "Sociologie et Administration (Nouvelle-Calédonie 1959)."
[7] See pp. 286; 512–514.

Catholic and Protestant schools was based on the number of their registered students and the success of those students in passing the official
examinations. Inasmuch as the Catholic mission educated about 40
percent of the school-age population and consequently awarded more
C.E.P.'s to their graduates, it received subsidies nearly three times
greater than those for the Protestants, who educated only 5 percent.
During the 1950s, the grants to mission schools rose from 7 million
C.F.P. francs annually to nearly 40 millions, and by the mid-1960s
they exceeded 100 millions. Of these funds the bulk was earmarked
for teachers' salaries and comparatively little for equipment and textbooks, so that the missions were able to recruit more and better-
qualified teachers. Furthermore, the training of Melanesian monitors
had greatly improved, for after their school was transferred from Montravel to Nouville in 1950, its standards were raised so that it could
award the *brevet élémentaire* to its graduates.

As for the public schools, World War II had depleted their teaching
staff by more than half. In 1946 such schools employed only 22 instructors, compared with 57 before the war. In 1939 the colony's teaching
personnel had been divided into two cadres, whose salaries were determined by the diplomas they held and not by the work they performed.
In practice, this meant that the Caledonian teachers were paid less
than their Metropolitan colleagues, who alone possessed the higher
degrees. This differentiation was deeply resented by the local-born
instructors, and after the war they formed a *syndicat des instituteurs
de la Nouvelle-Calédonie* and campaigned for "equal pay for equal
work" and the return to a single cadre for all the territory's teachers.
Even after the standards of the new normal school annexed to the
Collège La Pérouse were raised, its graduates still could not qualify
for admission to the higher cadre. Few of the Caledonians who went
to France for a university education entered the teaching profession on
their return. The number of Caledonian instructors in the public
schools, therefore, has steadily declined, particularly after the mining
industry was able to offer posts with salaries far larger than could be
earned by teaching.

Fortunately for the tribal schools, the situation there was reversed.
Since World War II, both the number of Melanesians entering the
teaching profession and their training have greatly improved. As
teaching offered the best means of upward mobility open to the
Melanesians, the number of native candidates increased, and with
their improved qualifications the level of instruction given in the tribal

schools rose. Furthermore, this enabled increasing numbers of Melanesians to qualify for admission to the schools whose curriculum was modeled after that of France, and in growing numbers they pursued their studies beyond the primary level. In 1962 the first Melanesian received a B.A. degree, and by 1965, Melanesians accounted for 7 percent of the student body in the Nouméa *lycée* and 12 percent of those studying in its higher technical school. There were then six Melanesian scholarship-holders studying in France.[8]

For various reasons vocational training has attracted more Melanesians than European Caledonians. One reason is that entrance requirements are less stringent than those for other secondary studies, and another is the relative facility with which technicians can find well-paid jobs in the private sector. Although this holds true also for the Caledonians, the latter's aversion to manual labor generally leads them to seek what they consider to be more prestigious employment in the civil service. In consequence, the number of qualified local-born applicants for technical positions is far below the current demand, despite efforts by the authorities since World War II to make vocational training and employment more attractive to all Caledonians.

The vastly increased postwar financial allocations to education have been largely devoted to improving secondary and especially technical instruction. This conforms to France's overall policy in its dependencies, the needs of local business firms, and the desire of all of New Caledonia's political leaders to replace Metropolitan employes and officials by the local-born. General secondary education is now available in three state, four Catholic, and two Protestant institutions, and two more *lycées* are being built at Nouméa and Poindimié. In the early 1960s, the Collège La Pérouse (which had 768 students in 1967) was raised to the rank of a *lycée* and it now offers the complete Metropolitan curriculum for the baccalaureate. In the two other public secondary schools at Koumac and Poindimié, in the Catholic institutions at Nouméa, Païta, Bourail, and Thio, and in the two Protestant colleges near Houaïlou, there are altogether some 800 students attending courses leading to the *examen probatoire* (formerly called the first part of the baccalaureate).

A number of courses in the field of vocational and professional instruction are available in the capital and in the interior. In the top rank stands the Lycée Technique of Nouméa, which has been enlarged, reequipped, and reorganized to accord with Metropolitan

[8] Interview with the head of the education service at Nouméa, May 25, 1965.

standards. At a lower level, another state school in Nouméa awards the C.A.P., and there is also a rapid-training center nearby which turns out mechanics, electricians, and masons. Commercial courses are offered at several places in the capital for white-collar workers. At the five mission technical schools in the interior, in 1967, 237 students were preparing for the examination that leads to the C.A.P.[9] Mention should also be made of the Agricultural School built in 1952 at Port Laguerre, which trains Europeans and Melanesians in modern farming and animal-husbandry techniques.[10]

From time to time, the French government has considered establishing at Nouméa an institution of higher learning that would be open to all the inhabitants of its Pacific islands. This has not come into being, however, because the cost would be excessive in view of the small number of its potential students. Caledonians wanting instruction at the university level continue to go mainly to France, although a few attend Australian and American institutions. At present, about 127 of them are studying in France, approximately half of these having been awarded scholarships either by the territorial or French government. In 1961, the territory bought a building in Paris to serve as a hostel for its students there, and it also contributed financially to the construction at the Cité Universitaire of the Maison de la France d'Outre-Mer.

With the improvement in the territory's secondary-school facilities, there is no longer any question of granting scholarships for study abroad below the highest academic and technical levels. Indeed, for various reasons, there is little likelihood that there will be any marked increase in the number of scholarships for Caledonians wishing to study in foreign countries or even in France. For long there has been much criticism in the general council as to the lavish scale on which scholarships have been granted.[11] Recipients have included the children of families able to finance their studies abroad and of influential local politicians, and moreover, some of them have been unwilling to return to work in the territory at whose expense they obtained their degrees. More recently, political considerations have become a factor in the scholarship situation. Allegedly, some nationalistic members of the Association des Jeunes Calédoniens in Paris were involved in the

---

[9] *La Nouvelle-Calédonie et Dépendances* (La Documentation Française), p. 26.

[10] See pp. 391–392.

[11] Minutes of the general council, May 16, 18, 1953.

violent outbreak that occurred at Nouméa on September 2–3, 1969.[12]

Since World War II, New Caledonia has benefited by building funds from the F.I.D.E.S. and, more recently, from similar grants from the European Common Market fund. Most of the money for improvement of its educational system, however, has come from the territory's own resources. Probably because all the general councilors were cognizant of the educational needs of New Caledonia and willing to vote the funds necessary to meet them, the authorities did not draw up any overall plan for school development until 1961, when they asked for external aid in building a second *lycée*. Soon the planners ran into unexpected difficulties, both technical and political. Collection of relevant data began in 1962, and they were incorporated into the *plan de scolarisation* submitted by the head of the educational service in June 1964. Before that document could even be approved by the authorities, France offered to assume responsibility for the cost of New Caledonia's secondary and technical schools, and this injected a new element into the situation which necessitated a drastic revision of the plan.

France's proposal aroused the old specter of "departmentization" and the assemblymen's fears lest they lose control over the education of young Caledonians.[13] Furthermore, because of the territory's mounting revenues, the financial need for French aid was not pressing, and so the U.C. majority turned down the offer. The conservative minority, however, which had wanted to accept the French proposal and was supported by the Nouméa press, joined forces with the administration to reverse the vote. Indirect pressure was exerted by the governor a few months later when he submitted to the assembly a budget that included new taxes totaling 300 million C.F.P. francs. He claimed that they were indispensable if the territory was to meet from its own resources the larger expenditures required for its secondary and technical schools.

Because of the sizeable growth in the budget and a realization that the mining industry might once again undergo one of its recurrent depressions, the U.C. assemblymen had second thoughts, and reluctantly they agreed to accept the French offer. When the change-over goes fully into effect, New Caledonia's educational system will be a replica of the French one up to the university level. A first step was taken in 1967, when the age-span of compulsory schooling for children was

[12] *Le Monde*, Oct. 7, 1969.
[13] *L'Avenir Calédonien*, April 12, 1966.

raised to 6 to 16, instead of 6 to 14. This development will undoubtedly improve the training provided in New Caledonia's schools, but whether it is the type of education best suited to the territory's needs is another issue and one that has never been publicly discussed there.

MASS COMMUNICATIONS MEDIA

The slight amount and mediocre quality of the information available to New Caledonia through the local mass media are both symptoms and causes of the Caledonians' generally low cultural level and limited horizon. As regards the press, the territory has far less choice in the number and variety of its newspapers than has French Polynesia. This is the more surprising in view of the equally high literacy rate among the Caledonians and the larger proportion of Europeans in a population of roughly equal size. Nor can the territory's backwardness in this respect be attributed to a late start, for *Le Moniteur Impérial* was published as early as 1859, and the first issues of the daily *La France Australe* and the semi-weekly *Bulletin du Commerce de la Nouvelle-Calédonie* date from 1899.[14]

Nevertheless, it should be noted that the two last-mentioned publications have survived for seventy years, and today they are the only ones in the territory that can boast of a circulation of over 3,000 copies. The *Bulletin du Commerce,* as its name suggests, concentrates on news of interest to the business community, but it also prints thoughtful articles on related subjects. *La France Australe,* which prides itself on being the oldest French-language newspaper in the Pacific, remains the outstanding journal of general information. It publishes international, Metropolitan, and local news, including abridged reports of the territorial assembly debates and accounts of S.P.C. meetings. From the beginning, it has accurately described itself as the "organ of French interests in the Pacific."

Caledonians who want a wider coverage of the news, both domestic and foreign, subscribe to Metropolitan and English-language newspapers and periodicals, limited quantities of which are also available in a few Nouméa bookstores. A number of specialized magazines, such as *Marchés Tropicaux,* the *South Pacific Bulletin,* the *Revue du Pacifique,* those of the local Catholic and Protestant missions, and the

---

[14] For a concise history of the press in New Caledonia, see P. O'Reilly, *Bibliographie Méthodique, Analytique et Critique de la Nouvelle-Calédonie,* pp. 297–320.

Pacific Islands Monthly, as well as Paris newspapers like *Le Monde, Le Figaro,* and *L'Express,* contain reports and articles about New Caledonia that are often more informative than is the local press. The inadequacy of Nouméa's publications cannot be ascribed to direct censorship on the part of the authorities, for Caledonian journalists have always expressed themselves with as much freedom as those in France, and this is particularly true of the writers for the U.C. organ, *L'Avenir Calédonien.* Only as regards prohibiting the importation and circulation of publications from abroad, or those in a foreign or Oceanian language, was the governor empowered to act, by a decree of December 29, 1922. It seems paradoxical that Caledonians at present offer a smaller market for interesting journalism than before World War II, when they were far less numerous but read newspapers that were much more lively and colorful.

One might conclude from the current caliber of Nouméa's press that the territory's radio broadcasting provided more substantial and interesting fare, but such has not been the case. Until 1967, little effort was made financially or technically to promote broadcasting. In part this was doubtless due to the territory's mountainous configuration and adverse atmospheric conditions, which made reception, especially in the interior, so poor that it was said Nouméa's broadcasts could be more readily heard in Australia than in La Foa. In any case, "La Voix de la France dans le Pacifique," as the local station was pretentiously called, was frequently criticized for its failure to attract listeners. As of 1950, there were estimated to be no more than 1,425 receiving sets in Nouméa and 511 elsewhere in the territory.[15] The Nouméa station had only 8 employes, and for their salaries as well as its operating costs the French government granted an annual subsidy ranging between 650,000 and 1 million C.F.P. francs.

The Nouméa station was managed by the Information Service, which meant that its broadcasts consisted of dry official communiqués and such commentaries and other news as the authorities chose to transmit. Its failure to report fully the general council debates annoyed the conservative members of that body, and its alleged slanting of local political news to the detriment of the U.C. angered Lenormand.[16] Radio Nouméa has become even more vulnerable to such criticism since the French government in 1958 decided unilaterally to take it over completely. Then, in 1967, it installed a new and more powerful

[15] Minutes of the general council, Jan. 28, 1950.
[16] See his speech to the National Assembly, Oct. 24, 1961.

radio station near Nouméa, as well as the second television station in the south Pacific islands. (The first such station was built in American Samoa.) These moves are a further indication of the importance that New Caledonia has recently assumed in the eyes of the Gaullist authorities.

CULTURAL ACTIVITIES

Perhaps because the Melanesians have never had the reputation for glamor and beauty that has drawn outsiders to the Polynesians, they have failed to attract writers and artists to anything like the same degree. New Caledonia has produced a few poets and novelists, among whom Francis Carco is outstanding, but their writing is better known in France than in their native land. Nor has New Caledonia been as fortunate as French Polynesia in having governors and officials who filled their leisure hours with scholarly pursuits. Among the territory's politicians, Maurice Lenormand is exceptional in having contributed articles on the island's anthropology and languages to learned journals, but he was not born or educated in New Caledonia. Indeed, it is to two other Metropolitan Frenchmen, the missionaries Maurice Leenhardt and Patrick O'Reilly, that the West owes most of its knowledge about New Caledonia's history and inhabitants.

It would be hard to exaggerate the importance of Leenhardt's scholarly contributions. Through his books on Melanesian languages, anthropology, and sociology, and his organization of art exhibits and of Oceanic studies, he was the first to inform the Western world about the antiquity, originality, and complexity of Kanaka society. To Father O'Reilly, students of modern New Caledonia are indebted for the first complete bibliography of written materials on the territory, and for detailed biographical data on its leading personalities, both European and Melanesian. Some of his work was published in 1953 in connection with the celebration of the centenary of France's occupation of New Caledonia. That occasion gave rise to a considerable amount of scholarly research on the island, and the publication of books by Mariotti, Person, Faivre, Poirier, Routhier, and others.[17]

That the impetus for the preservation and study of New Caledonia's cultural heritage has come not from Caledonians but from France and Metropolitan Frenchmen is probably due to the character and composition of the local population. Not surprisingly, the descendants of

[17] See bibliography.

convicts and peasant farmers have little education and a narrow outlook, and even Nouméa's "aristocracy" of well-to-do businessmen and
industrialists exhibit few intellectual or artistic interests. A survey
of local European society made in the early 1950s showed that among
its active population only 7 percent of the men and 5 percent of the
women had had even a secondary schooling, and that the percentages
of those with any higher academic or professional training were, respectively, 4 percent and 3 percent.[18] New Caledonia's isolation, together with the overwhelming importance of the mining industry,
has created a materialistic atmosphere in which intellectual stimulation
is lacking.

Some leaven was provided in the late nineteenth century by such
communards as Louise Michel and, more recently, by an occasional
official who has had a university background, but the great majority
of the Caledonians are insular in their views and preoccupied with
earning a living. For many years, the general councilors, who represented local business interests, reflected this attitude, and only
rarely and parsimoniously did they allocate funds for promoting
cultural activities. The European community as a whole regarded
the Melanesians as primitive tribesmen without any culture of their
own and, moreover, incapable of acquiring that of the West. By and
large, the colony's administrators were equally unperceptive, and, for
example, no official voice was raised in protest when some overzealous
gendarmes in the 1930s forced the Kanakas to destroy their orna-
mented huts and replace them with so-called European-style dwellings.[19] Only recently have the European Caledonians come to recognize any relationship between economic profits and scientific research
to the point where they are willing to subsidize the latter.

The first attempt to create a local museum had its origins in a committee formed at Nouméa to collect Caledonian art objects for a Paris
colonial exposition. The harvest proved to be so abundant that in
1889 the government allocated 3,000 francs to house the surplus in a
permanent building.[20] In 1901 this museum was attached to the library
that had been given the colony by a local mining magnate, Lucien
Bernheim, who also provided an endowment of 100,000 francs for its
upkeep. The library grew to the detriment of the museum, whose

[18] Faivre, J.-P., J. Poirier, and P. Routhier, *Géographie de la Nouvelle-Calédonie*, p. 262.
[19] Leenhardt, M., "La Société des Océanistes."
[20] Chevalier, L., "Le Musée Néo-Calédonien."

collections deteriorated and eventually disappeared without a trace. After World War I, the endowment fund no longer sufficed to provide proper care of the library, whose books were becoming moldy and whose building was being damaged by termites.

Partly in order to salvage what remained of the Bernheim library, and partly to promote local scholarship, a Société d'Etudes Néo-Calédoniennes et Néo-Hébridésiennes was founded in 1929.[21] This society, however, did not survive the world depression, and it was not until the eve of World War II that Maurice Leenhardt was able to reawaken interest in its aims. On July 20, 1938, at a lecture given in Nouméa's town hall, he spoke so convincingly of the need to create a local scholarly organization for the study of the Grande Terre and its inhabitants that the Société des Etudes Mélanésiennes (S.E.M.) was founded with 23 members, the following October.[22]

The S.E.M.'s objectives were to publish scholarly articles on New Caledonia and to take inventories of Oceanic art objects owned by museums and private collectors throughout the world, and also of such indigenous cultural vestiges as still existed in the Grande Terre and its dependent islands. Before World War II caused the S.E.M. to suspend its activities, its leaders succeeded in persuading the government to ban any further exportation of art objects from the colony, and it was able to publish two issues of its bulletin. In France, during the war, research on New Caledonia received a fresh impetus, thanks to the enterprise of Leenhardt and O'Reilly. The former, who had already set up a department of Oceania at the Musée de l'Homme in Paris, took the initiative in founding a Société des Océanistes there in 1945. From then until his death in 1954, Leenhardt was president of that society and editor of its *Journal des Océanistes,* which is still published, albeit irregularly. Father O'Reilly, who had earlier organized a Centre d'Etudes Océaniennes, merged it with the Société des Océanistes, and for many years thereafter worked closely with Maurice Leenhardt. Their collaboration in the interests of Oceanic scholarship provided a rare example of Protestant-Catholic *entente cordiale.*

At Nouméa, Leenhardt revived the S.E.M. in March 1947. The S.E.M., like its older counterpart at Papeete, became an integral part of the Société des Océanistes in Paris, though it maintained a separate existence and in January 1948 began publishing its own periodical, *Etudes Mélanésiennes.* About 750 copies of each issue of this publica-

[21] *L'Océanie Française,* July–August 1929.
[22] Barrau, J., "Un Quart-Siècle d'Etudes Mélanésiennes."

tion are sent to scholarly groups throughout the world, and the S.E.M.'s membership has grown to some 300. It has worked closely with foreign scholars, specifically in aiding a research mission to the Isle of Pines headed by the Australian anthropologist, J. Colson, and in publishing the linguistic studies of New Caledonia written by the New Zealand professor, K. J. Hollyman.

Another postwar scholarly organization, the Institut Français de l'Océanie (I.F.O.)—with more funds and institutional backing than those of the S.E.M.—was established at Nouméa in August 1946. It is the Oceanic branch of the Office de la Recherche Scientifique des Territoires d'Outre-Mer (O.R.S.T.O.M.), which was created and financed by the French government to pursue scientific research in its overseas dependencies. In 1949 Leenhardt became the I.F.O.'s first director, and it was he who drew up its initial work program. Before he was appointed, however, the Paris headquarters of the O.R.S.T.O.M. had sent out a marine biologist, Dr. R. Catala, to choose a suitable site in Nouméa. Dr. Catala was able to get the United States government to turn over to the nascent I.F.O. a building and certain laboratories that had been part of a hospital complex for American troops during the war. Later, unhappily, Dr. Catala's ties with the I.F.O. were severed, but in 1956 he and his wife built nearby an aquarium which is a tourist attraction and also of unique value to students of marine biology.

Initially it had been planned to attach the I.F.O. to the Ecole Française d'Extrème-Orient at Hanoi, but after war broke out in Indochina this became impossible. Organizationally, the I.F.O. is modeled after the Institut Français d'Afrique Noire at Dakar, and its program of research is similar. By the end of 1947, seven scientists were working at the I.F.O. on various projects in such fields as plant pathology, hydrology, and oceanography. It was already in full operation by the time a geological mission arrived from France to assess the resources of the territory,[23] and it antedated by several years the installation of the S.P.C. at Nouméa. With both groups it quickly established good working relations.

Half of the I.F.O.'s budget of some 3 million C.F.P. francs annually is financed from French public funds and half from territorial revenues. Because the I.F.O. has stressed applied research, the practical-minded assemblymen have been willing to vote sums for its operations. It is oriented mainly to the natural sciences, although the anthropolo-

[23] See p. 407.

gist, Jean Guiart, was among its first research associates, and in 1964 it added a department of social sciences. The I.F.O. is now concentrating on marine studies, to which 15 of its 36 specialists are devoting their time.[24]

The history of educational and scholarly enterprises in the territory has not been free of the personality and political conflicts that have also plagued many other aspects of Caledonian life. In the case of such outstanding intellectual leaders as Leenhardt, Charlemagne, and Guiart, the fact that all three were Protestants had some bearing on the difficulties they encountered locally in the pursuit of their work. This was due not so much to their religious affiliation *per se* as to their identification with the role played by Protestant missionaries in the territory's political evolution.

THE CHRISTIAN MISSIONS

A major casualty of the period since 1951 has been the decline of the Christian missions' initiative in providing political leadership for the Melanesians. This has been due partly to their failure to seize all the opportunities in this domain, and partly to the loss of their most far-sighted and experienced missionaries. The Catholic mission in particular, until it was revitalized during the interwar period by Father Luneau,[25] tended to atrophy, for it felt secure in the monopoly of Christian converts and of their schooling that it had gained in the nineteenth century. To its membership also belonged a majority of the European community, although many of the latter were not always sympathetic with many of the mission's activities. Its complacency was shaken only to a slight degree in the early twentieth century by the native revolt of 1917 and, rather more, by the inroads made by Protestantism.[26]

With the arrival in New Caledonia of Maurice Leenhardt in 1903, the Protestant missionaries launched a movement to educate the Melanesians so that they could defend themselves against the settlers' and the administration's demands for their land and their labor. The Catholics trailed behind in this respect until 1930, when Father Luneau founded a seminary in which the Melanesians had their first chance to obtain an education above the primary level. The seminary's

[24] *Le Monde*, July 10, 1969.
[25] See pp. 285–286.
[26] See pp. 238, 247–249.

founding, however, did not entail any conflict with the Protestant mission, for by this time zones of Protestant and of Catholic influence had been established and were mutually respected. Although in the most remote regions of the Grande Terre there still existed pockets of a few hundred pagans, all the Melanesians could be said to be—at least nominally—Christians. To be sure, certain indigenous traditions had survived, but the influence of the sorcerers and the cult of ancestors had more of a magical than of a strictly religious character. On the part of both missions there was an evident flagging of evangelical zeal, for there was no one left to convert and no reason to attempt to win over members of the other faith. Both missions continued their work of educating the Melanesians and of improving their economic and social conditions by teaching them better farming methods, combatting alcoholism, and organizing youth groups. Generally speaking, however, they were content to rest on their laurels.

World War II and its aftermath of liberal French legislation gave the Melanesians a new outlook, freedom of movement and employment, and a few political rights, and a small group of European radicals quickly capitalized on these developments.[27] The headway made by communist propaganda among the Melanesians represented the first challenge in many years to the missions' leadership of the native population. This time it was the Catholic authorities who first perceived the danger and took action, thus reversing the situation which had existed during Leenhardt's prime, when the Protestants had been the champions of Melanesian emancipation. The Catholic missionaries, who—more than any other organized group—had precipitated the decline of traditional Melanesian institutions, now stepped into the void they had created and helped the Melanesians to utilize the rights they had recently acquired.

Early in 1946, Father Luneau organized the U.I.C.A.L.O., drafted its manifesto, and gained the administration's recognition for it.[28] The Protestants, who had lost headway even in their old strongholds of Do-Neva and the Loyalty Islands, realized that they must jump on the bandwagon. Soon they had organized their own political group, the A.I.C.L.F. The areas from which each group drew its membership were identical with those already established as zones of Catholic and Protestant influence, and the next step was to find suitable Melanesian officers to head each of them.

[27] See pp. 276–278.
[28] See pp. 285–287.

In seeking candidates for such posts, the Catholics, despite Father Luneau's efforts, were handicapped by their dearth of native cadres. It was not until nearly 6 months after the U.I.C.A.L.O. was set up that the first two Melanesian priests were ordained. In explanation of its failure to promote native leadership, the Catholic hierarchy usually cites its "disastrous" attempts in the 1890s and 1920s to train Melanesians for the priesthood. In any case, it chose from among its abundant European personnel a French priest, Father Bussy, to become the Catholic mission's spokesman in the first postwar general council. As Catholic laymen to head the U.I.C.A.L.O., it selected Rock Pidjot and Michel Kauma. In contrast, the Protestants had a far wider range of native talent at their disposal, since they had long pursued a policy of training Melanesian pastors and had instituted a more democratic form of church government. The Protestants' choice to head the A.I.C.L.F. fell on Henri Naisseline and Doui Matayo. Within five years, however, both groups were merged with the U.C.

The Christian missionaries have made no open attempt to reassert their political leadership of the Melanesians since the U.C. seized the torch from their hands. Seemingly they are resigned to working behind the scenes through their influence with individual leaders and with their flocks. By and large, both the Catholic and Protestant missions have supported the U.C. because it is the only party to give priority in its platform to native welfare and also consistently to favor large subsidies for mission schools. There are other reasons for the Catholic mission's support of the U.C.: both Lenormand and Rock Pidjot are practising Catholics who have voted for Catholic-sponsored bills in the National Assembly and who, even more cogently, head a party which has controlled the general council of New Caledonia since 1953. For the U.C., the electoral discipline imposed by the Catholic hierarchy on its church members is of crucial importance, for some 60 percent of the Melanesians are Catholics.

The position of the Protestants in relation to the U.C. has become less clear-cut and stable in recent years. The unity of the Protestant community has been fragmented by the growing success of such sects as the Seventh Day Adventists and Jehovah's Witnesses and, more profoundly, by a split in the ranks of the French Reformed Church. During the mid-1950s, one of its outstanding Metropolitan pastors, Raymond Charlemagne, who had been a founder of the A.I.C.L.F., began to advocate a more aggressive political role for the Protestant mission in New Caledonia than the mother church in France was willing to sanction. Although the mission hierarchy has maintained a discreet silence, it is known that Charlemagne was formally relieved of his pastoral duties on November 30, 1957, and recalled to France.[29] He refused to leave New Caledonia, and went about organizing his personal followers, now believed to number some 6,000.[30] In this way was founded the Eglise Evangélique Libre de la Nouvelle-Calédonie et des Iles Loyalty, which Charlemagne maintains is a branch of Protestantism but which is not recognized as such by either the Reformed Church of France or the Société des Missions Evangéliques.

Since he became separated from orthodox Protestantism, Charlemagne has wielded considerable influence, particularly in Melanesian education, and his dissidence has also acquired political overtones. Apparently he is convinced that too little has yet been done to promote the Melanesians' political and social development, and he believes that this can be accomplished by reforming the educational system so as to hasten their evolution. For this purpose he founded the Fédération Libre de l'Enseignement Protestant, which has introduced innovations in the training of Melanesian monitors and which also gives special instruction to school dropouts in its Centres Culturels. Charlemagne's contributions in the educational field have won high praise from top officials of the government, but they have been accompanied by obscure political maneuverings that brought him into conflict with the U.C.

In theory, Charlemagne and the U.C. should be natural allies, for the avowed goal of each is to further the Melanesians' evolution, but in actuality a power struggle has developed between them. It so happened that when Charlemagne's dissident movement was gathering strength, the U.C. in 1960 expelled two of its outstanding leaders, Kauma and Metayo, for failing to respect party discipline. The conservative parties were quick to seize upon the disunity in the Melanesians' ranks engendered by both Lenormand's intransigency and Charlemagne's break with the Protestant mission. The U.N.R. managed to win over the Catholic Kauma, and the Action Calédonienne the Protestant Metayo, and both those parties supported, and were supported by Charlemagne.

The ideological basis for Charlemagne's decision to throw the weight of his influence on the side of the conservatives is hard to discern. In the case of the U.N.R., he may have wanted the govern-

[29] *La Vie Protestante,* Feb. 25, 1962.
[30] Sordet, M., "La Nouvelle-Calédonie: Rhodésie de Demain?"

ment's approval, and he did receive official backing, perhaps because he opposed the U.C. In regard to the Action Calédonienne, his motivation is easier to understand, for its candidate at the polls was Edouard Pentecost, a wealthy half-caste Loyalty Islander and a Protestant. His hostility toward the U.C. may have been due to his feeling that that party had become so preoccupied with the autonomy issue and keeping control of the territorial assembly that it had lost sight of questions of greater importance to the Melanesian population.[31]

The U.C.'s vituperations against Charlemagne [32] are not so hard to explain, for he threatened not only that party's power base but also its fundamental policy of maintaining a united front between Melanesians and *petits blancs*. Not unnaturally, the U.C. leaders have accused Charlemagne of trying to create a religio-political movement for his own aggrandizement and of being so pro-Melanesian as to advocate in effect a *racisme à rebours*.

Whether or not Charlemagne's dissident sect, or at least its present orientation, will survive his eventual disappearance from the Caledonian scene, only time can tell. It is noteworthy that in all these conflicts, as well as in the policy decisions of the mission hierarchies, the Melanesians remain in the background and the Europeans are the main protagonists. Any marked change in the existing cultural pattern of New Caledonia society depends on how soon and to what degree the Melanesians can assume positions of leadership.

[31] See pp. 321–322.
[32] *L'Avenir Calédonien*, April 27, 1963, Sept. 15, 1964.

Conclusion

The comparative study of French Polynesia and New Caledonia indicates that the similarities between them today are greater than the differences. The latter are not only ethnic, historical and cultural, but also economic. In the French Pacific islands, social cohesion and the sense of a common past are stronger among the Polynesians than the Caledonian Melanesians, and the two dominant factors in the history of New Caledonia—its years as a penal colony and the importance of minerals in its economy—have had no counterparts in French Polynesia. Yet the leveling process which began in the nineteenth century, after the mass conversion of the inhabitants of both to Christianity and their subjection to a generally uniform French colonial policy, has become more pronounced in the twentieth century. Both island groups have been drawn ineluctably onto the international scene, and world events have precipitated the changes in French policy which, in turn, have accelerated the pace of their evolution and brought them more tightly under French control.

Under the initial impact of the two new forces of Christianity and French rule, the populations of both French Polynesia and New Caledonia declined rapidly and the structure of their societies almost totally disintegrated. Curiously enough, the reactions of the more venturesome seafaring Polynesians and those of the Melanesian peasant-farmers were much the same. At first each group reacted occasionally with violence against interference in its traditional ways of life, but after a few brief revolts each came to accept foreign political and cultural domination without making any concerted effort to modify its consequences for them.

During the interwar period, unexpectedly, the Polynesians and Melanesians not only survived physically but even began to proliferate. This necessitated a drastic revision of the premise on which the colonial administration and foreign settlers and businessmen had been operating for nearly a century. This was the assumption that, because the islanders were unwilling or unable to work as wage-earners for them and, in any case, were doomed to imminent extinction, the prospective void in the population, as well as current needs for economic development, could be filled only by immigration. After World War II, it became clear that these immigrants, whether Metropolitan French or Asians, would not become either producers or consumers on a scale sufficient to make the islands viable economic entities, yet they had already left a permanent imprint on the indigenous populations.

The new blood and alien cultures introduced by the immigrants revitalized the indigenous peoples ethnically, economically, and psychologically. In French Polynesia the ethnic admixture was more pronounced, for there the barriers to social integration were almost nonexistent, whereas on the Grande Terre the segregation of Melanesians on reservations sharply curtailed intermarriage. Although the immigrant Asians acquired a far larger stake in French Polynesia than in New Caledonia, in both island groups the political and most of the economic power had already come into the hands of westerners. However, these Westerners, including the *demis* of Polynesia, formed no monolithic bloc, for they were divided among themselves by political, economic, social and cultural differences. The cleavage has been and still is widest between the transient Metropolitan officials, who wield almost undiluted political power, and the local-born population. The one constant theme in the history of both French Polynesia and New Caledonia has been the pressure on the Paris government exercised by virtually all the local-born population to replace Metropolitan personnel by islanders, yet this common ground has not yet been strong enough to unite the population or to give birth to a local nationalism.

Inevitably the split in the European community created a sense of chronic tension which has not been appreciably eased by their sharing a sense of loyalty to France. Among the local-born French, patriotism is idealistic rather than realistic, for few of them have ever even seen the "mother-country." It has been intensified by their isolation in a culturally alien world, an isolation that has further accentuated the parochialism of their outlook. They tend to resent policies adopted in Paris because they have had no hand in shaping them and because those policies often clash with the islanders' strictly local interests. Both their sentimental patriotism and their feeling of grievance were heightened by World War II and, even more, by France's postwar liberal legislation, whose avowed purpose was to emancipate the indigenous colored peoples.

As time went on, the major political parties of French Polynesia and New Caledonia came to cooperate in demanding more self-government from Paris, and only on this issue did the native elements join forces with some of the conservative local-born Europeans. In the mid-1950s, spokesmen of these parties in the French Parliament, with some help from sympathetic Metropolitan politicians, succeeded in loosening the tight control of the Paris authorities over both territories. Soon, however, the limited autonomy thus gained was whittled away after General de Gaulle came to power, for in his foreign policy, designed to restore France's *grandeur*, both island territories had been assigned a role that required even more stringent French controls. This process was inadvertently aided and abetted by personal and ideological differences between island parties and between their leaders, and by the mutual suspicions or indifference that prevented French Polynesia and New Caledonia from uniting to resist the pressures from Paris.

The two main island leaders suspected of harboring proindependence sentiments under autonomist guise were gradually eliminated from the political scene on trumped-up charges, and most of the authority that had been briefly exercised by the territorial assemblies was transferred back to the Metropolitan officials who ran the local administration. To propitiate the islanders' resentment of such retrogressive measures, France offered them various sops ranging from costly public works and budget subsidies to permission for foreigners to breach the long-standing local monopolies held by Metropole-based banking, commercial, and industrial enterprises.

These concessions have weakened the autonomist movements to some degree, but have not eliminated them, especially in French Polynesia, which has had a longer and stronger tradition of indigenous opposition to the French administration. Yet there, too, the most ardent Polynesian autonomists, with few exceptions, have stopped short of demanding independence, for they are realistic enough to realize that, given their islands' meager natural resources, even a booming tourist industry could probably never replace the assurance of continuing French financial support. New Caledonia, despite its more solid economic base for self-government, has never produced leaders who believed that the territory could make its way alone, and a sub-

stantial part of the European community there has even clamored for
closer ties with France. In both cases, an economic recession due to
world developments beyond their control would certainly reduce the
appeal of a greater autonomy that would probably lead to a decline
in the islanders' current high living standards.

The major problems with which French Polynesia and New Caledonia must cope sooner or later are primarily economic, for they color
the two territories' relations with France and cause most of the local
political dissension. Outstanding among them are the dearth of skilled
labor, the land-tenure system, the rural exodus and consequent decline
in agricultural production, and the uneven distribution of wealth.
Furthermore, the growing imbalance of both territories' economy, because of the dominant position of the nickel industry in New Caledonia and of the C.E.P. in French Polynesia, has increased their dependence on external economic developments and their habit of expecting financial manna from France.

The long struggle for greater autonomy derives from no desire to
exchange the sovereignty of France for that of another nation. Nor has
it been accompanied by a willingness to pay the price of self-government in economic terms. For example, the alien Oceanians who have
now replaced the Asians as a source of manual labor have not yet been
given a sufficient stake in either territory to transform them into permanent residents. So long as the various communities remain as indifferent to each other's welfare and as compartmentalized economically as they now are, they will fail to attain enough cohesion to present a united front in support of their demands. It is widely assumed
that some *deus ex machina*—a horde of free-spending foreign tourists
or, more probably, France—will materialize to spare the islanders the
grim necessity for hard and sustained work and for carrying out pain-
ful and difficult basic reforms. For the time being, France still holds
the key to their emotional attitude and their financial viability.

The coming of age, economically and politically, of the Polynesians
and Melanesians has been long delayed, and though they have become
newly important population elements in their islands since World
War II, they are not yet a decisive factor in the development of those
islands. Only very recently have they come to realize the advantages
of active participation in the current economic and political life of
their countries. Until they produce more effective leadership, however, the power is likely to remain where it now is—in the hands of
Europeans and, to a lesser extent and in the economic sphere, of the
Asians.

Selected Bibliography

Listed below are the main sources used in preparing this book. There are many bibliographies relating to the French Pacific islands that are more comprehensive, and among these the volumes on Tahiti and New Caledonia compiled by Father Patrick O'Reilly are outstanding. The *Journal de la Société des Océanistes* lists and usually reviews relevant current publications.

GENERAL

Archimbaud, L., "Un Commissariat Général dans le Pacifique," *Revue du Pacifique,* December 1922.
"Aspects de l'Evolution Récente des Sociétés Océaniennes," *Politique Étrangère,* 1962, No. 1.
Bourgeau, J., *La France du Pacifique.* Paris, 1955 (2d ed.).
Buttet, Colonel de, "Le Bataillon du Pacifique de la Grande Guerre 1916–1918," *Revue Historique de l'Armée,* August 1965.
Centenaire des Missions Maristes en Océanie. Lyon, 1935.
Chaffard, G., "Les Rebelles du Pacifique," *L'Express,* Oct. 20, 1968.
Chazel, P., "Grandeurs et Servitudes des Missionaires en Océanie," *Le Monde non Chrétien,* October–December 1951.
"Constitutional Development in the French Pacific Territories," *Current Notes on International Affairs* (Canberra), July 1952.
Deschamps, H., and J. Guiart, *Tahiti—Nouvelle-Calédonie—Nouvelles-Hébrides.* Paris, 1957.
Doumenge, F., *L'Homme dans le Pacifique.* Paris, 1966.
Faivre, J.-P., *L'Expansion Française dans le Pacifique, 1800–1842.* Paris, 1953.
Guiart, J., *Les Religions de l'Océanie.* Paris, 1962.
Javaudin, Chef d'Escadron, "La Gendarmerie du Pacifique," *Revue Historique de l'Armée,* August 1965.
Journal de la Société des Océanistes (Paris), December 1945—.
Le Goyot, Lt.-Col. "Le Bataillon d'Infanterie de Marine et du Pacifique," *Revue Historique de l'Armée,* August 1965.
Leroi-Gourhan, A., and J. Poirier, *Ethnologie de l'Union Française.* Paris, 1953.
Loste, H., "La Situation Economique des Territoires du Pacifique," *La Nouvelle Revue Française d'Outre-Mer,* August–September, October, 1956.
Massal, E., and J. Barrau, "Pacific Subsistence Crops," *S. P. C. Quarterly Bulletin,* January, April, July 1956.

Le Monde non Chrétien, quarterly (Paris), 1931—.

L'Océanie Française, monthly, July 1911—March–April 1940.

Oliver, D. L., *The Pacific Islands.* Cambridge: Harvard University Press, 1961.

O'Reilly, P., "Mouvements Messianiques en Océanie," *La Vie Intellectuelle,* December 1956.

Pacific Islands Monthly (Sydney), 1930—.

Pacific Islands Year Book (R. W. Robson, ed.). Sydney.

Parliamentary debates:
  Conseil de la République.
  French Union Assembly.
  National Assembly.

Réalites du Pacifique, quarterly (Paris), 1963—.

Regelsperger, G., *L'Océanie Française: la Nouvelle-Calédonie, les Nouvelles-Hébrides, les Etablissements Français de l'Océanie.* Paris, 1922.

La Revue du Pacifique, monthly—irregular (Paris), 1924—March 1937.

Riu, C. "Le C. F. P.," *La France Australe,* Oct. 22, 24, 1953.

Robequain, C., *Madagascar et les Bases Dispersées de l'Union Française.* Paris, 1958.

Ryan, P. L., "The South Pacific Commission: What it is—What it does," *South Pacific Bulletin,* October 1963.

Skinner, C., "Self-government in the South Pacific," *Foreign Affairs,* October 1963.

South Pacific Bulletin, quarterly (Sydney), January 1951—.

"Territoires Français du Pacifique," *Revue Historique de l'Armée,* August 1965.

Tudor, J., *Pacific Islands Year Book and Who's Who.* Sydney, 1968.

FRENCH POLYNESIA

"L'Amélioration du Réseau Routier à Tahiti," *Industries et Travaux d'Outre-Mer,* April 1967.

Antherieu, E., "Polynésie: Atolls et Atome," *Le Figaro,* Aug. 3, 1965.

Antin de Vaillac, G. d', "Les Chinois en Polynésie Française," *L'Afrique et l'Asie,* No. 55, 1961.

Archimbaud, L., "La Population et le Commerce de l'Océanie Française," *Revue du Pacifique,* December 1927.

Atea, J.-P., *Sous le Vent de Tahiti.* Paris, 1951.

Aubert de la Rue, E., *Tahiti et Ses Archipels, Polynésie Française.* Paris, 1958.

Auzelle R., *Plan Directeur d'Aménagement de l'Agglomération de Papeete.* Paris, 1950.

Barrau, J., "L'Agriculture Polynésienne au Contact des Etrangers," *Journal de la Société des Océanistes,* vol. 15, 1959.

———, "Les Atolls Océaniens," *Etudes d'Outre-Mer,* August–September 1957.

———, "Rangiroa Coconut Research Station," *South Pacific Bulletin,* October 1960.

Bernast, R., "Water Supply in French Oceania," *South Pacific Bulletin,* April 1955.

Bouge, L.-J., *Le Code Pomaré, 1819.* Paris, 1953.

Breaud., "Les Etablissements Français de l'Océanie, *La Nouvelle Revue Française d'Outre-Mer,* October 1954, July–August 1955.

Calderon, G. ("Tittoti"), *Tahiti by Tahiti.* London, 1921.

Capet, H., "Death for Tahiti," *The Atlantic Monthly,* July 1963.

Chadourne, M., *Vasco.* New York, 1927.

Chaffard, G., "Les Bases Nucléaires du Pacifique," *L'Express,* Aug. 6, 1964.

———, "Les Essais Nucléaires Français Stimulent les Sentiments Autonomistes des Polynésiens," *Le Monde Diplomatique,* September 1968.

Chatelain, N., "De l'Eden à l'Ere Atomique," *Le Figaro,* Oct. 6, 1966.

Chauvois, P., "Les Expérimentations Nucléaires Françaises au Pacifique," *Revue de la Défense Nationale,* August–September 1964.

"Coconut Research at Rangiroa," *South Pacific Bulletin,* October 1963.

"Le Conseil d'Administration des Etablissements Français de l'Océanie," *L'Océanie Française,* July–August 1930.

Coppenrath, G., "Evolution Politique de la Polynésie Française depuis la Première Guerre Mondiale," *Journal de la Société des Océanistes,* vol. 15, 1959.

———, *Les Chinois de Tahiti,* Paris, 1967.

Covit, B., *Official Directory and Guide Book for Tahiti.* Papeete, 1965.

Cunningham, G., "Food for Tahiti," *Economic Geography,* October 1961.

Curton, E. de, *Tahiti, Terre Française Combattante.* London, 1942.

Danielsson, B., *Forgotten Islands of the South Seas.* London, 1957.

———, *Raroia, Happy Island of the South Seas.* Chicago, 1953.

Deschanel, P., *La Politique Française en Océanie.* Paris, 1884.

Devambez, L., "Fisheries Development in French Polynesia," *South Pacific Bulletin,* January 1965.

Doumenge, F., "L'Ile de Makatea et Ses Problèmes," *Cahiers du Pacifique,* September 1963.

Dourthe, J., "Agricultural Education in French Polynesia," *South Pacific Bulletin,* April 1967.

Dunoyer, J.-M., "Voyage aux Antipodes," *Le Monde,* May 29, 30, 31, June 1, 1963.

Etablissements d'Océanie (Carnets de Documentation sur L'Enseignement dans la France d'Outre-Mer, No. 20), Paris, March 15, 1946.

"Les Etablissements Français de l'Océanie," *L'Océanie Française,* January–February 1939.

"Les Etablissements Français d'Océanie," *Marchés Coloniaux,* October 24, 1953.

"Les Etapes Principales de la Mission Protestante" (typescript). Paris (?), 1957.

Faivre, J.-P., "Chronique de l'Histoire Coloniale: L'Océanie et le Pacifique, 1939–1964," *Revue Française d'Histoire d'Outre-Mer,* 1955, 1965.

Farwell, G., *Last Days in Paradise.* Adelaide, 1964.

Ferre, G., *Tahiti Toute Nue.* Paris, 1934.

Ferro-Luzzi, G., "Etude Nutritionnelle en Polynésie Française," *Journal de la Société des Océanistes,* December 1962.

Finney, B., "Anthropological Research in Tahiti," in B. Covit, ed., *Official Directory and Guide for Tahiti* (Papeete, 1965), pp. 113–125.

Froment-Guieysse, G., "Tahiti, Les Iles Sous-le-Vent, Les Iles Marquises, L'Archipel des Tuamotu" (five articles), *L'Océanie Française,* 1913–1914.

———, "Tahiti: Situation Actuelle, les Réformes," *L'Océanie Française,* January–March 1920.

Froment-Guieysse, G., "Les Etablissements Français d l'Océanie," *Revue du Pacifique*, 1924, pp. 486–500.

Furlich, J., "The Relations Between French Oceanic Possessions and French Culture" (typescript), M.A. thesis, University of Chicago, March 1952.

Furnas, J. C., *Anatomy of Paradise*. New York, 1947.

Gauze, R., "Panorama Politique de l'Après-Guerre (1945–1965)" (typescript). Papeete, 1966.

――――, "La Minorité Ethnique Chinoise en Polynésie Française" (typescript). Papeete, Feb. 1, 1964.

Gerbault, A., *Un Paradis qui Meurt*. Paris, 1949.

Griffin, J., "Tahiti: Romance and Reality" (pamphlet). New York: The Alicia Patterson Fund, Oct. 5, 1969.

Gug, M., "Breeding Cattle and Horses in French Polynesia," *South Pacific Bulletin*, January 1958.

――――, "Mother-of-Pearl Industry in French Oceania," *South Pacific Bulletin*, July 1957.

Guiart, J., "L'Emploi en Polynésie Française," *Outre-Mer Français*, 1er trimestre 1968.

Guillaume, M., "Etudes de l'Economie Rurale de l'Océanie Française— Rapport de Mission" (mimeographed). Papeete, August 1956.

Huetz de Lemps, A., *L'Oceanie Française*. Paris, 1954.

I.N.S.E.E. (Institut National de la Statistique et des Etudes Economiques), *Comptes Economiques de la Polynésie Française, 1959*. Paris, 1960.

――――, *Comptes Economiques de la Polynésie Française, 1960–1966*. Paris 1967.

Isnard, J., "Tahiti à l'Ere Atomique," *Le Monde*, July 16, 17–18, 19, 1966.

Jacobs, H. S., "Tahiti Learns about the Bomb," *New York Times*, Dec. 5, 1965.

Jag-Martin, S., "De la Noix de Coco à l'Atome," *Croissance de Jeunes Nations*, Jan. 19, 1967.

Jore, L., *L'Océan Pacifique au Temps de la Restauration, 1815–1848* (2 vols.). Paris, 1959.

Jullien, M., "Réflexions sur un Problème Tahitien," *Actualités d'Outre-Mer*, Dec. 20, 1962.

Kling, G. (ed.), *Tahiti, Moorea, Bora-Bora* (Les Guides Bleus Illustrés). Paris, 1965.

Lacroix, R., "Le Nouveau Port de Papeete," *Journal de la Société des Océanistes*, No. 21, December 1965.

Langlois, Lieut., "Jeunesse en Polynésie Française," *Tropiques*, February 1958.

Lassalle-Séré, R., "Rat Control Schemes for Tahiti Planters," *South Pacific Bulletin*, April 1955.

――――, "Tahiti aux Tahitiens," *Climats*, Jan. 19, 1950.

Lavadiery, H., "Le Musée de Papeete," *Le Petit Parisien*, May 8–13, 1935.

Lebrun, A., "Les Etablissements Français de l'Océanie," *L'Océanie Française*, March–April 1926.

Loursin, J.-M., *Tahiti*. Paris, 1963.

"Makatéa: Bilan Socio-Economique d'un Demi-siècle d'Expérience," *Journal de la Société des Océanistes*, December 1959.

Malcolm, S., and E. Massal, *Etudes sur la Nutrition et l'Alimentation dans les Etablissements Français de l'Océanie* (S. P. C. technical document No. 85). Nouméa, April 1955.

Massal, Dr. E., "Réalisations Médicales et Perspectives en Polynésia Française," *Journal de la Société des Océanistes,* December 1959.

Mazellier, P., *Tahiti.* Lausanne, 1963.

"La Mission Catholique de Tahiti" (typescript). Papeete, undated.

Moench, R., "The Chinese in Tahiti," in B. Covit, ed., *Official Directory and
Guide Book for Tahiti* (Papeete, 1965), pp. 151–154.

————, *Economic Relations of the Chinese in the Society Islands.* Cambridge: Harvard University Press, 1963.

Molet, L., "Esquisse de la Jeunesse Polynésienne et ses Problèmes," *Revue
de Psychologie des Peuples,* 1er trimestre 1963.

————, "Importance Sociale de Makatea dans la Polynésie Française,"
Journal de la Société des Océanistes, vol. 20, 1964.

————, "Notes Scientifiques sur la Polynésie Française," (C.H.E.A.M.
Mémoire No. 3773). Paris, 1962.

————, "Problèmes de Socio-économie Polynésienne," *Cahiers de l'Institut
de Science Economique Appliquée,* January 1964.

O'Reilly, P., "Le Français Parlé à Tahiti," *Journal de la Société des
Océanistes,* December 1962.

O'Reilly, P., and E. Reitman, *Bibliographie de Tahiti et de la Polynésie
Française.* Paris, 1967.

O'Reilly, P., and R. Teissier, *Tahitiens: Répertoire Bio-bibliographique de
la Polynésie Française.* Paris, 1962.

Panoff, M., *Les Structures Agraires en Polynésie Française.* Paris, 1964.

————, "Tahiti et le Mythe de l'Indépendance," *Les Temps Modernes,*
February 1965.

"Le Plan de la Polynésie Française," *Industries et Travaux d'Outre-Mer,*
August 1961.

Poirier, J., "L'Evolution Récente des Sociétés Polynésiennes," *Journal de la
Société des Océanistes,* December 1950.

La Polynésie Française (La Documentation Française, *Notes et Etudes
Documentaires,* No. 2776), May 5, 1961.

"La Polynésie Française et le Centre d'Expérimentation du Pacifique,"
Bulletin du Commissariat à l'Energie Atomique, May–June 1966.

Preiss, G., "The Church in Tahiti," *International Review of Missions,*
October 1957.

"Problèmes Economiques des Etablissements Français de l'Océanie,"
Marchés Coloniaux, Aug. 27, 1955.

Ranson, G., "Les Problèmes de l'Huitre Perlière et de la Nacre en Océanie
Française,"*Marchés Coloniaux,* Oct. 24, 1953.

————, "Rehabilitation of Pearl Oyster Beds in French Oceania," *South
Pacific Bulletin,* July 1955.

Rey-Lescure, P., "Education de Tahitiens en France," *Le Monde non
Chrétien,* July–December 1957.

Robson, N., "French Oceania Takes Stock," *Pacific Affairs,* March 1953.

Robson, R. W., "In Tahiti: Some Impressions," *Pacific Islands Monthly,*
November 1952.

Russell, S., *Tahiti and French Oceania.* Sydney, 1935.

Schmitt, R. C., "Urbanization in French Polynesia," *Land Economics,*
February 1962.

Service des Affaires Economiques et du Plan, Polynésie Française, *Situation
Economique et Perspectives d'Avenir, 1959–1960.* Papeete, 1960.

Simon, J., *La Polynésie dans l'Art et la Littérature de l'Occident.* Paris,
1939.

Spoehr, A. (ed.), *Pacific Port Towns and Cities.* Honolulu: Bishop Museum Press, 1963.

Stace, V. D., "Vanilla—A Profitable Cash Crop in French Polynesia," *South Pacific Bulletin,* January 1961.

Stevenson, R. L., *In the South Seas.* Edinburgh, 1896.

Suggs, R. C., *The Hidden Worlds of Polynesia.* New York, 1962.

——, *The Island Civilizations of Polynesia.* New York, 1960.

Tastes, L. de, "Le Rapport sur les Etablissements Français de l'Océanie," *L'Océanie Française,* November–December 1933, January–February 1934.

T'Sterstevens, A., *Tahiti et Sa Couronne* (3 vols.). Paris, 1950–1951.

Valenziani, C., *Renaissance Démographique en Océanie Française.* Rome, 1940.

Verin, P., "La Conversion des Iles Australes et Ses Conséquences," *Le Monde non Chrétien,* April–June 1966.

Vernier, C., *Tahitiens d'Autrefois, Tahitiens d'Aujourd'hui.* Paris, 1948 (2d ed.).

Villaret, B., *Archipels Polynésiens.* Paris 1956.

West, F. J., *Political Advancement in the South Pacific.* Oxford University Press, 1961.

NEW CALEDONIA

"Agricultural Training in New Caledonia," *South Pacific Bulletin,* January 1965.

Archimbaud, L., "Le Conseil Général de la Nouvelle-Calédonie," *Revue du Pacifique,* 1924, vol. 2, pp. 229–234.

——, "La Situation en Nouvelle-Calédonie," *Revue du Pacifique,* Jan. 15, 1927.

Arnette, A. "Au Sujet de la Colonisation en Nouvelle-Calédonie," *L'Océanie Française,* November–December 1939.

Attali, Y., "Le Crédit de la Nouvelle-Calédonie" (report to the South Pacific Conference on Economic Development), Mar. 10, 1962.

Barrau, J., *L'Agriculture Vivrière Autochtone de la Nouvelle-Calédonie.* Nouméa, 1956.

——, "Pasture Improvement in New Caledonia," *South Pacific Bulletin,* October 1953.

——, "Les Problèmes de l'Agriculture Neo-Calédonienne," *Marchés Coloniaux,* Oct. 24, 1953.

——, "La Situation Economique en Nouvelle-Calédonie," *Actualités d'Outre-Mer,* September 1962.

——, "Un Quart-Siècle d'Etudes Mélanésiennes," *Etudes Mélanésiennes,* Nos. 14–17, December 1959–December 1962.

Bassi, M., "Le Général de Gaulle a Ecouté les Revendications d'Autogestion," *Le Figaro,* Sept. 5, 1966.

Bastian, G., "Nouméa," *Cahiers d'Outre-Mer,* October–December 1951.

Baudoux, G., *Légendes Canaques.* Nouméa, 1953.

Belouma, G., "Problèmes Economiques et Sociaux Autochtones à Gomen," *Etudes Mélanésiennes,* Nos. 12–13, December 1958–December 1959.

Belshaw, C. S., *Island Administration in the South West Pacific.* London, 1950.

Bergé, E., *Nouvelle-Calédonie: Certaines Conditions de Colonisation et d'Exploitation Agricoles.* Paris, 1948.

Bergès, P., "Pour la Brousse," *Revue du Pacifique*, 1928, vol. 1.

Bichon, M., "Les Liaisons Maritimes et Aériennes," *Marchés Coloniaux*, Oct. 24, 1953.

Boilot, P., "Les Communications Routières," *Marchés Coloniaux*, Oct. 24, 1953.

Bourgeau, J., "La Nouvelle-Calédonie après Cent Ans de Présence Française," *Chroniques d'Outre-Mer*, September 1953.

Boutin, Pere, "Cent Dix Ans de Présence de l'Eglise Catholique," *La France Australe*, Oct. 24, 27, 29, 31, 1953.

Bowman, R. C., "Army Farms and Agricultural Development in the Southwest Pacific," *Geographical Review*, July 1946.

Brou, B., "La Société Moderne en Nouvelle-Calédonie en 1966." C.H.E.A.M. Mémoire No. 4154, 1967.

―――, "La Société Traditionelle en Nouvelle-Calédonie." C.H.E.A.M. Mémoire No. 4144, 1966.

Burchett, W. G., *Pacific Treasure Island: New Caledonia.* Melbourne, 1941.

Callot, F., "Les Richesses Minières de la Nouvelle-Calédonie," *Marchés Coloniaux*, Oct. 24, 1953.

Carbon, L. de, "Le Plan d'Equipement en Nouvelle-Calédonie," *Marchés Coloniaux*, Oct. 24, 1953.

Catala, R., "The Nouméa Aquarium," *South Pacific Bulletin*, December 1966.

Centenaire de la Présence Française en Nouvelle-Calédonie. Nouméa, 1953.

Charlemagne, R., "Le Mariage et la Communauté dans la Société Mélanésienne," *Le Monde non Chrétien*, October–December 1952.

Chevalier, L., "Le Musée Néo-Calédonien," *Etudes Mélanésiennes*, September 1952.

Condominas, G., "Maurice Leenhardt, l'Ethnologue de la Nouvelle-Calédonie," *France-Asie*, April–May 1954.

Cordier-Rossiaud, G., *Relations Economiques entre Sydney et la Nouvelle-Calédonie, 1844–1860.* Paris, 1957.

Cormary, H., "L'Enseignement en Nouvelle-Calédonie," *Marchés Coloniaux*, Oct. 24, 1953.

Courmarie, P., "Le Problème Démographique en Nouvelle-Calédonie," *Chroniques d'Outre-Mer*, January 1951.

Cousot, P. M., *La Civilisation Canaque en Nouvelle-Calédonie, 1853–1960.* Paris, 1968.

―――, *Histoire de la Nouvelle-Calédonie, 1853–1946.* Toulon, 1964.

Curson, P. H., "The Small Urban Settlement in New Caledonia," *South Pacific Bulletin*, April 1965.

Curry, L., "La Culture Irriguée du Taro en Nouvelle-Calédonie," *Etudes Mélanésiennes*, Nos. 14–17, December 1959–December 1962.

Devambez, L., "L'Exploitation des Ressources de la Mer en Nouvelle-Calédonie," *Etudes Mélanésiennes*, Nos. 14–17, December 1959–December 1962.

Dewey, A., "The Nouméa Javanese," *South Pacific Bulletin*, October 1964.

"Discours de M. Lenormand," *L'Avenir Calédonien*, Nov. 19, 26, 1963.

Dizier, J., "Au Secours d'une Race qui se Meurt," *L'Océanie Française*, July 1930.

Dollfus, R., "Enquête sur la Mission de Nouvelle-Calédonie," *Journal des Missions Evangéliques*, 1951, pp. 312–322.

Doumenge, F., "L'Economie de la Grande Terre Calédonienne," *Cahiers d'Outre-Mer*, July–September 1961.

———, "Les Iles Dépendantes de la Nouvelle-Calédonie et Leurs Problèmes," *Cahiers d'Outre-Mer*, October–December 1961.

———, "Vietnamiens et Indiens en Mélanésie," *Bulletin de l'Association de Géographes Français*, 1964.

Dousset, R., *Colonialisme et Contradictions*. Paris, 1970.

Faivre, J.-P., "L'Océanie et le Pacifique," *Revue d'Histoire d'Outre-Mer*, 1955, 1965.

———, "Vue Générale de l'Histoire Calédonienne," *Journal de la Société des Océanistes*, vol. 9, December 1953.

Faivre, J.-P., J. Poirier, and P. Routhier, *Géographie de la Nouvelle-Calédonie*. Paris, 1955.

Fallon, J., *Pacific Pantomime*. London, 1952.

Feuer, L. S., "Cartel Control in New Caledonia," *Far Eastern Survey*, Jan. 19, 1946.

Forsyth, W. D., "Les Activités de la Commission du Pacifique Sud en 1963–1964," *Bulletin du Pacifique Sud*, October 1964.

Froment-Guieysse, G., "La Nouvelle Calédonie," *L'Océanie Française*, July–November 1912.

Frouin, M., "The 'Bibliobus' and Education in New Caledonia," *South Pacific Bulletin*, October 1963.

Gaignard, H.-G., "La France Doit Jouer un Rôle Important à la Commission du Pacifique-Sud," *Marchés Coloniaux*, July 16, 1949.

Gascher, P., "Regards sur l'Administration Coloniale en Nouvelle-Calédonie (1874–1894)," *Le Monde non Chrétien*, January–June 1969.

Gaulle, Gen. Charles de, *Mémoires de Guerre: L'Appel, 1940–1942*. Paris, 1954.

"G. F. R.," "New Caledonia and the War," *Pacific Affairs*, December 1946.

Gifford, E. W., "L'Archéologie Néo-Calédonienne en 1952," *Journal de la Société des Océanistes*, vol. 9, December 1953.

Gifford, E. W., and D. Shutler, Jr., *Archeological Excavations in New Caledonia*. Berkeley: University of California Press, 1956.

Gounelle, H., "Les Positions Culturelles de la France dans le Pacifique-Sud," *Le Monde*, Aug. 25, 1965.

Griffin, J., "New Caledonia: French Forever?" (pamphlet). New York: The Alicia Patterson Fund, March 25, 1970.

Grosjean, G., "Etapes dans le Pacifique," *Nice-Matin*, July 9, 15, 16, 1964.

Guerchy, J. de, "La Découverte et l'Histoire de la Nouvelle-Calédonie," *Marchés Coloniaux*, Oct. 24, 1953.

Guiart, J., "L'Emploi en Nouvelle-Calédonie," *Outre-Mer Français*, 1er trimestre 1966.

———, "Nouvelle-Calédonie 1968: L'Inquiétude," *Le Monde non Chrétien*, January–June 1968.

———, "Organisation Coutumière en Nouvelle-Calédonie," *Le Monde non Chrétien*, April–June 1957.

———, "L'Organisation Sociale et Coutumière de la Population Autochtone de la Nouvelle-Calédonie," in J. Barrau, *L'Agriculture Vivrière Autochtone de la Nouvelle-Calédonie* (Nouméa, 1956).

———, "Les Origines de la Population d'Ouvéa (Loyalty) et la Place des

Migrations en Cause sur le Plan Général Océanien," *Etudes Mélanésiennes,* September 1952.

———, "Un Problème Foncier Exemplaire en Nouvelle-Calédonie: la Vallée de Tchamba," *Le Monde non Chrétien,* December 1960.

———, "Sociologie et Administration (Nouvelle-Calédonie 1959)," *Etudes Mélanésiennes,* December 1958–December 1959.

———, "Le Sociologue," *Le Monde non Chrétien,* January–March 1955.

Guieysse, P., "Le Problème Calédonien," *L'Océanie Française,* August 1911.

Guyon, J., "La Colonisation Calédonienne," *L'Océanie Française,* January 1925.

———, "La Condition de la Main-d'oeuvre Indochinoise dans les Etablissements Français du Pacifique Austral," *L'Océanie Française,* July–August, September–October 1928.

———, "Les Etablissements Français du Pacifique Austral," *Comptesrendus de l'Académie des Sciences Coloniales,* vol. 14, 1929–1930.

———, *Etude de la Mise en Valeur de la Nouvelle-Calédonie.* Nouméa, 1925.

Hoffherr, R., "La Prospérité de la Nouvelle-Calédonie," *Cahiers Français d'Information,* July 15, 1955.

Hollyman, K. J., "Linguistic Research in New Caledonia," *South Pacific Bulletin,* January 1964.

"Hommage à Maurice Leenhardt," *Le Monde non Chrétien,* January–March 1955.

"Les Japonais en Nouvelle-Calédonie," *L'Océanie Française,* May–June 1934.

Kling, G., "Aperçu Historique," in *Nouvelle-Calédonie, Iles Loyauté, Ile des Pins* (Les Guides Bleus Illustrés). Paris, 1964.

Lacouture, J., "Un Paradis Ambigu à l'Envers du Monde: la Nouvelle-Calédonie," *Le Monde,* Dec. 27–28, 29, 30, 1964.

Lambert, P., *Moeurs et Superstitions des Néo-Calédoniens.* Nouméa, 1900.

Lang, M., "L'Elévage en Nouvelle-Calédonie," *L'Océanie Française,* January 1925.

———, *La Nouvelle-Calédonie.* Paris, 1925.

———, "La Population Indigène de la Nouvelle-Calédonie," *L'Océanie Française,* October–November 1925.

Laroque, R., "Nouméa," *Revue Historique de l'Armée,* August 1965.

Larsen, M. and H., *The Golden Cowrie—New Caledonia: Its People and Places.* Edinburgh, 1961.

LeBorgne, J., *Géographie de la Nouvelle-Calédonie et des Iles Loyauté.* Nouméa, 1964.

Leenhardt, M., *Arts de l'Océanie.* Paris, 1948.

———, "Les Chefferies Océaniennes," *Comptes-rendus des Séances de l'Académie des Sciences Coloniales,* 1941, pp. 359–376.

———, *Do Kamo, La Personne et le Mythe dans le Monde Mélanésienne.* Paris, 1947.

———, *Gens de la Grande Terre.* Paris, 1953 (2d ed.).

———, *La Grande Terre, Mission de Nouvelle-Calédonie.* Paris, 1922.

———, "La Nouvelle-Calédonie," *Le Monde non Chrétien,* July–September 1953.

———, "La Société des Océanistes," *Journal de la Société des Océanistes,* vol. 1, no. 1, December 1945.

Leenhardt, M., "Unité Française et Unité d'Action," *Cahiers Internationaux,* May 1955.

Leenhardt, R.-H., "Un Exemple de Réflexion Politique," *Le Monde non Chrétien,* January–June 1960.

Lefort, E. J. E., "Problems of Coffee Production in New Caledonia," *South Pacific Bulletin,* October 1956, January 1957.

Le Goupils, M., *Comment on Cesse d'Etre Colon.* Paris, 1910.

———, *Dans la Brousse Calédonienne—Souvenirs d'un Ancien Planteur.* Paris, 1928.

Lenormand, M., "Communications Adressées à la Section des Sciences Sociales du VIIe Congrès Scientifique du Pacifique," *Etudes Mélanésiennes,* No. 4, 1949.

———, "L'Evolution Politique des Autochtones de la Nouvelle-Calédonie," *Journal de la Société des Océanistes,* vol. 9, 1953.

———, "Le Problème Démographique en Nouvelle-Calédonie," *Marchés Coloniaux,* Oct. 24, 1953.

———, "La Situation et l'Avenir de l'Elevage," *Marchés Coloniaux,* Oct. 24, 1953.

Loustau, Capt. "Jeunesse en Nouvelle-Calédonie," *Tropiques,* February 1958.

Macaigne, P., "Les Français au Bout du Monde," *Le Figaro,* April 6, 7, 8, 9, 1964.

Mace, A., "Nouvelle-Calédonie: Ce Paradis du Contribuable est Pourtant un Territoire Français," *Transmondia,* April 1965.

Malignac, G., *Rapport Démographique sur la Nouvelle-Calédonie.* Paris, 1957.

Mander, L. A., *Some Dependent Peoples of the South Pacific.* New York, 1954.

Mariotti, J., "Quelques Aspects de l'Evolution de la Nouvelle-Calédonie," *Encyclopédie Mensuelle d'Outre-Mer,* January 1955.

McTaggart, W. D., "Présentes Migrations des Autochtones au Sein de l'Archipel Néo-Calédonien," *Etudes Mélanésiennes,* December 1959– December 1962.

Meller, N., "Political Change in the Pacific," *Asian Survey,* April 1965.

Metais, E., "Déstructuration Sociale et Sorciers dans une Tribu Indigène," *Cahiers Internationaux de Sociologie,* July–December 1954.

Metais, P., "Démographie des Néo-Calédoniens," *Journal de la Société des Océanistes,* vol. 9, December 1953.

———, "Quelques Aspects de l'Evolution Culturelle Néo-Calédonienne," *Journal de la Société des Océanistes,* December 1953.

Morison, S. E., *History of United States Naval Operations in World War II,* vol. 5. New York, 1949.

Mousset, P., "En Nouvelle-Calédonie," *Revue des Deux Mondes,* Jan. 1, 1963.

Noroit, M., *Niaouli, la Plaie Calédonienne.* Paris, 1932.

Nouvelle-Calédonie, Service des Affaires Economiques, *L'Economie de la Nouvelle-Calédonie* (annual).

Nouvelle-Calédonie, General Council minutes (through 1956).

Nouvelle-Calédonie, Territorial Assembly minutes (1957—).

La Nouvelle-Calédonie (Carnets de Documentation sur l'Enseignement dans la France d'Outre-Mer, No. 16). Paris, Feb. 15, 1946.

"La Nouvelle-Calédonie," *Union Française et Parlementaire* (special issue), April 1957.

"La Nouvelle-Calédonie, 1853–1953," *Marchés Coloniaux* (special issue), Oct. 24, 1953.

"Nouvelle-Calédonie, 1853–1953," *Tropiques* (special issue), October 1953.

"La Nouvelle-Calédonie à l'Heure du Choix," *Communautés et Continents,* July–September 1962.

La Nouvelle-Calédonie et Dépendances (La Documentation Française, *Notes et Etudes Documentaires,* No. 3382), April 17, 1967.

"Nouvelle-Calédonie, Perspectives de Développement," *Industries et Travaux d'Outre-Mer,* February 1963.

Nouvelle-Calédonie, Iles Loyauté, Ile des Pins (Les Guides Bleus Illustres). Paris, 1964.

O'Reilly, P., *Bibliographie Méthodique, Analytique et Critique de la Nouvelle-Calédonie.* Paris, 1955.

———, *Calédoniens: Répertoire Bio-bibliographique de la Nouvelle-Calédonie.* Paris, 1953.

———, "Le Français Parlé en Nouvelle-Calédonie," *Journal de la Société des Océanistes,* December 1953.

———, "Paul Feillet, Gouverneur de la Nouvelle-Calédonie," *Revue d'Histoire des Colonies,* vol. 40, 1953.

———, *Pèlerin du Ciel—François Luneau, Soldat Nantais et Missionaire Calédonien, 1890–1950.* Paris, 1952.

Person, Y., *La Nouvelle-Calédonie et l'Europe, 1774 à 1854.* Paris, 1954.

Plan de Scolarisation 1964–1968, Nouvelle-Calédonie et Dépendances (mimeographed). Nouméa, June 1964.

Poirier, J., "Nouvelle-Calédonie et Dépendances," in A. Leroi–Gourhan and J. Poirier, eds., *Ethnologie de l'Union Française,* vol. 2 (Paris), pp. 716–777.

Poroi, A., "La Ville de Papeete," *Revue Historique de l'Armée,* August 1965.

"Rapports et Résolutions de l'Assemblée de l'A.I.C.L.F.," *Le Monde non Chrétien,* January–June 1960.

Rau, E., *Institutions et Coutumes Canaques.* Paris, 1944.

Rapadzi, J., "L'Industrie Minière," *Marchés Coloniaux,* Oct. 24, 1953.

"Les Rélations Economiques entre Sydney et la Nouvelle-Calédonie, 1844–1860," *Revue d'Histoire des Colonies Françaises,* 1956, no. 2.

Rey-Lescure, P., *Géographie de la Nouvelle-Calédonie.* Papeete, 1930.

Rivière, H., *Souvenirs de la Nouvelle-Calédonie: L'Insurrection Canaque.* Paris, 1881.

Sautot, H., *Grandeur et Décadence du Gaullisme dans le Pacifique.* Melbourne, 1949.

S.E.D.E.S. (Société d'Etudes pour le Développement Economique et Social), *Rapport sur le Développement de Nouvelle-Calédonie.* Paris, 1961.

Shepherd, J., "New Caledonia: Orphan of the South Pacific," *Pacific Affairs,* December 1940.

"Un Siècle d'Acculturation en Nouvelle-Calédonie," *Journal de la Société des Océanistes* (special issue), vol. 9, December 1953.

"La Situation Economique des Territoires du Pacifique: Nouvelle-Calédonie," *Nouvelle Revue Française d'Outre-Mer,* August–September–October 1956.

Sordet, M., "La Nouvelle-Calédonie à l'Heure du Marché Commun du Pacifique," *Le Monde Diplomatique,* June 1967.

———, "La Nouvelle-Calédonie: Rhodésie de Demain?", *Combat,* Jan. 31, Feb. 1, 2, 3, 5, 6, 1967.

Sordet, M., "Nouvelle-Calédonie, un Paradis qui Ira Loin," *Jeune Afrique,* Feb. 19, 1967.
————, "La Ruée vers le Nickel," *Jeune Afrique,* Dec. 23, 1969.
Verdalle-Cazes, Dr. C., "Mother and Child Welfare in New Caledonia," *South Pacific Bulletin,* July 1962.
Videau, D., and C. Cotter, "Les Wallisiens en Nouvelle-Calédonie," *Journal de la Société des Océanistes,* December 1963.

Index